DARWINIAN
IMPACTS

an introduction to the Darwinian Revolution

DARWINIAN IMPACTS

an introduction to the Darwinian Revolution

D.R.OLDROYD

THE OPEN UNIVERSITY PRESS
Milton Keynes

Published in Australia by the
New South Wales University Press Limited,
Box 1, PO Kensington, NSW Australia 2033

First published in this edition 1980 by
The Open University Press, a division of
Open University Educational Enterprises Limited
12 Cofferidge Close
Stony Stratford
Milton Keynes MK11 1BY
England

Printed in Australia by
Macarthur Press Pty, Ltd.,
Parramatta, NSW Australia 2150

British Library Cataloguing in Publication Data
Oldroyd, David Roger
   Darwinian impacts.
   1. Darwin, Charles — Influence
   2. Evolution — History
   3. Intellectual life — History
   I. Title
   909.8   QH31.D2

ISBN 0-335-09001-X

Contents

Foreword

A GREAT deal of ink has already been spilled about Darwin and Darwinism and one is doubtless courting criticism by adding to this extensive literature. There are books that give accounts of Darwin's life and times with enough detail to satisfy even his most devoted admirer. There are scholarly editions of his works, as well as books of readings that give selections from his major writings and learned articles on Darwinism. There are diatribes against Darwin; there are eulogies that praise him. Detailed accounts of his work appear in the standard histories of biology or in biological text-books. Several collections of essays have resulted from the various centenary and other Darwin 'festivals'. The academic journals are quite weighed down with erudite discussions of his views. He appears in travel books. Although he spent only a few weeks ashore in Australia, it has been thought appropriate to devote half a volume to a consideration of his brief visit here. In short, anyone with enough energy and patience and access to a good library can readily formulate a synthesis of all this literary activity, scholarly and otherwise. The Darwin Industry, as it has recently been called, will surely minister to his needs.

But if one wants to find a single book that deals with the Darwinian theory of evolution, the way in which it fitted into the history of Western thought, its subsequent influences, and the general consensus among contemporary scholars as to the status of the theory and the role that it plays in biology, then it is hard to know where to turn. Much of the up-to-date material does not deign to give a clear exposition of the whole topic. It is true that plenty of straightforward accounts of the theory of evolution by natural selection can be found in elementary biological texts, but one will not, I think, find it possible to locate a similar account of the Darwinian Revolution as a whole. This book is intended to help fill this gap. Its aim is chiefly expository rather than analytical, but it also attempts the wider task of providing a general elementary synthesis of recent historical investigations in this field, of offering certain personal reflections on the subject, and, by means of the references and suggestions for further reading, giving an *entrée* to further study of this aspect of the history of ideas.

It may interest readers to know that what is offered here has been taught for a number of years in lecture courses in the School of History and Philosophy of Science at the University of New South Wales. As such, it is hoped that the material will have particular interest for undergraduates concerned with studies in intellectual history. But I also hope a wider audience will be reached: students of the biological sciences with a liking for the historical and philosophical aspects of their work; secondary-school students working for public examinations in history; and, of course, the general reader. Moreover, it is hoped that such a book may do something towards showing the great interest and satisfaction to be derived from the study of intellectual history.

The fact that this book has been written in Australia provides a ready explanation for the rather large number of 'antipodean' examples that have been used in illustration of my account. It is hoped, however, that these examples will not prove unduly irksome to readers in the northern hemisphere. Indeed, they may serve to underscore the point that ideas do not allow themselves to be confined by strict geographical boundaries. Thus Darwinism and evolutionism found a ready welcome in Australia and New Zealand in the last century, as well as in northern climes. And the situation is not so very different today, particularly in relation to social and political questions.

A number of friends and colleagues have provided much welcome assistance in the preparation of this text, and it is a pleasure to acknowledge their assistance with all possible warmth here: Randall Albury, Margaret Campbell, George Daniel, Paul Foss, Guy Freeland, John Greene, Ian Langham, Bill Leatherdale, Monica MacCallum, Evelleen Richards and Jonathan Stone. However, the literary and historiographical solecisms that may remain are, of course, entirely my responsibility.

David Oldroyd
Sydney, 1980

Preface

Just three years after Charles Darwin died in 1882 his *Origin of Species* was likened to a 'bombshell' that had set off 'a revolution in every mode of thought and feeling' — the 'great Darwinian revolution'. Mrs Darwin found this interpretation 'prancing', and in the century since her pronouncement there have been similar accounts to which it might apply. This book is not one of them. David Oldroyd has written an introduction to Darwin's revolutionary impacts which is painstaking and provocative, a textbook that deserves the widest exposure among students of intellectual history and among biologists interested in the historical and philosophical aspects of their field.

Darwinian Impacts affords the best evidence to date that the antipodes are inhabited by historians and philosophers of science who are interested in Darwin. Oldroyd teaches in the School of History and Philosophy of Science at the University of New South Wales. There, for a number of years, he has offered lecture courses which form the basis of his book. This explains at once the clarity and vivacity of many passages and the several references throughout the text to Australia and its affairs. Readers will be reminded that Darwin visited Sydney in 1836 during his voyage on the *Beagle* and that, eleven years later, T. H. Huxley met his future wife there while he served as surgeon aboard H.M.S. *Rattlesnake*. Readers will also be informed, perhaps for the first time, about the role of social Darwinism in Australian politics and political theory since the end of the nineteenth century.

How *Darwinian Impacts* measures up as a textbook is of course for students to judge. But in its favour I can point out that the following pages contain a straightforward exposition and synthesis of recent scholarship in the history and philosophy of the biological and human sciences. The exposition is elementary, being undertaken from the standpoint of intellectual history; the synthesis is the most comprehensive one available in the vast Darwinian literature. Oldroyd has no illusions that his work contains the last word on its subject. On the contrary, he cautions at the outset that his chapters on the 'consequences of Darwinism' should be regarded as suggestive rather than definitive — a needful caveat in my view — and he frankly acknowledges the formidable problems confronting the historical standpoint he adopts. Such candour is refreshing, and I believe students can only benefit from the example, if not from every precept, to which it gives rise in Oldroyd's 'concluding remarks and personal reflections'. Indeed, the appendix and bibliographic essay that follow offer ample opportunity for students to make their own assessments of the book.

It remains to be seen in what degree *Darwinian Impacts* provides evidence for a 'Darwinian Revolution'. Certainly the metaphor was well established in the literature as an approbative catchword even before Thomas Kuhn gave 'revolution' a technical meaning in the history and philosophy of science. Since then historians of Darwinism have weighed the evidence for the change and continuity which Kuhn's interpretation requires, and Oldroyd might have been expected to broach the matter in the text. But, in fairness, *Darwinian Impacts* is proposed as a basic introduction to the conventional 'Darwinian Revolution', not to a Kuhnian one, and as such it has no peer. As general background for studying the transition in Western thought from theistic to secular and naturalistic interpretations of human life I can hardly recommend a single more useful book.

James R. Moore
London, 1980

Introduction

IT SEEMS to be widely accepted among students of intellectual history that the publication of Charles Darwin's *The Origin of Species* in 1859, and the events that occurred as a result of the appearance of this work, marked a major change in man's thinking about the animal and plant worlds, about himself, and indeed in his view of the cosmos as a whole. The great shift in biological theory that was brought about by Darwin, with all the associated changes such as those in theology, philosophy, political theory and literature, is usually referred to as the Darwinian Revolution. It is believed that this 'revolution' in thought was comparable in importance to such changes in world-view as the Copernican Revolution (involving the change from the view of the Earth as the static centre of the universe to a mobile planet orbiting a somewhat insignificant star), the so-called Freudian Revolution (involving the discovery of the unconscious mind), or the rise of Marxism as the dominant political philosophy in many cultures. It is unlikely, therefore, that anyone will wish to brush aside the subject of this inquiry on the grounds that it is a trivial or insignificant feature of the historical landscape. Clearly, we are dealing with a major theme – a matter of interest and concern to anyone seeking to know something of the deep-seated roots of the doctrines (or prejudices) that govern our ideas and actions. But before starting our investigation, a few preliminary remarks are in order.

Several versions of biological evolutionism were propounded in the first half of the nineteenth century, well before the publication of *The Origin*. These ideas of biological evolution could claim support from studies of the fossil record and development of embryos, but there was no accepted theory to account for the paleontological and embryological observations. (The French naturalist Lamarck did propound an important evolutionary theory, but it gained little support.) It was Darwin's great achievement to present biologists with a theory that supplied answers to many of their problems, including those that arose in paleontology and embryology. He also provided an invaluable framework for subsequent investigations. For this reason, if no other, we may choose to study Darwin's work — simply as an episode in the history of science.

But Darwin's significance goes far beyond what he achieved in the restructuring of biological theory. His ideas were taken up and applied in a whole range öf human activities. Moreover, they were used to provide support for several grand cosmic evolutionary philosophies of nature that were formulated in the nineteenth century. Some of these — such as the system of Herbert Spencer — were proposed before 1859. Others — such as the system of Henri Bergson — came well after Darwin. It cannot be said that these cosmic evolutionary philosophies all stemmed from Darwin's system alone. But many of them drew support from the success of the theory of the evolution of organisms by the Darwinian mechanism of natural selection. So in addition to considering the purely biological questions we must deal also with these grand cosmic evolutionary schemes, together with the many ramifications of Darwin's theory in such fields as social theory, politics and literature. Consequently, the Darwinian Revolution becomes a very tangled and complex affair, far transcending the confines of purely biological studies.

Certain difficulties will doubtless present themselves to the critical reader. Did the 'extra-biological effects' really flow from Darwin's theory alone, or did they have much wider and deeper causes? If so, what were those causes? Was Darwin's theory really a product of the grand cosmic evolutionism that characterised the nineteenth century, or was it a major — perhaps the chief — cause? And, if the grand cosmic evolutionism was a cause rather than an effect, to what might *it* be attributed?

Such questions are extremely difficult to answer, yet they are always likely to arise in intellectual history, or the discipline known as the 'history of ideas'. This book will not seek to answer these questions of causality in a definitive way, though it may throw some light on such matters. The main body of the work aims at clear exposition, simply drawing the reader's attention to the main features of the Darwinian Revolution, without delving into problems of historical causation in any detail. However, the reader should be aware that in a work about ideas — how they grow, spread, and interact with each other — there are always considerable historiographical problems,* and there is always the danger that these may be glossed over in an introductory text. For this reason, some general remarks about problems in historiography of science and philosophy of history are offered in the Appendix at the end of the book. But we will not try to determine the precise causes of the nineteenth-century evolutionary movement. This is too complex a problem to be dealt with in an introductory text. (Indeed, some critics maintain that such problems are not susceptible to historical analysis, and should not come within the purview of the historian.)

In Part One of the book we look at what I take to be the chief intellectual antecedents of the Darwinian theory. In Part Two there is a fairly detailed

---

* For the meaning of the term 'historiography', see page 357.

account of Darwin's life and work, with an exposition and elementary philosophical critique of his theory of evolution by natural selection. We also look at the work of A. R. Wallace (the co-discoverer of the Darwinian theory), the work of Mendel, and certain aspects of the subsequent development of evolutionary theory in the late nineteenth century and in the modern period. Part Three offers an exposition of some of the many consequences of the work of Darwin. It is in this third section that problems of historical 'influence' become especially acute, and it is here that the text should be regarded by the reader as a basis for further reading and research, rather than a definitive treatment of these problems.

Chapter 1 discusses three topics that are not closely integrated, but which provide information useful for an understanding of the subsequent argument. We consider, first, traditional accounts of man's place in nature, some of which were still widely held at the time of the publication of *The Origin*. An understanding of the nature and strength of the traditional views will enable the reader to appreciate the kind of opposition Darwin's theory had to overcome, and the measure of the change in outlook required to accept the new theory. Next we discuss some of the ancient ideas of classification — ideas which were intimately linked with traditional ideas about epistemology (theory of knowledge) and methodology (ways of proceeding in the acquisition of knowledge). This discussion should enable the reader to grasp a major feature of Darwin's achievement: his restructuring of the theory of biological classification. But more importantly it should convey an understanding of certain leading features of ancient epistemology and methodology. This understanding will help the reader comprehend later discussions of the influence of Darwinism (or evolutionism) on philosophy. Also in the first chapter we have a discussion of the so-called doctrine of the Great Chain of Being. This allows a very brief treatment of some of Plato's doctrines, as well as certain aspects of Neo-Platonism and beliefs about the 'celestial hierarchy'. Perhaps more importantly, it allows a brief consideration of one of the leading biological theories of the eighteenth century, and of one of the major 'world-views' in the period between the Renaissance and the Enlightenment.

Chapters Two, Three and Four discuss the ideas of some of the leading naturalists of the pre-Darwinian period, and in Chapter Five we look at two further important intellectual antecedents of the Darwinian doctrine — this time chiefly of a non-biological character. For convenience I have chosen here to base the account on a consideration of the writings of certain individuals. But this manner of exposition is selected for didactic reasons, not because of an adherence to the so-called 'great man' theory of history.

The method of treatment in Parts Two and Three should be self explanatory and requires no introductory remarks here. I may mention, however, that the concluding discussion does offer some tentative explanation of the causes of the rise of the evolutionary movement in the nineteenth century.

A word of caution should perhaps be injected here. The reader should recognise that the term 'Darwinism' can be used in a considerable number of ways. It can, for example, be taken to refer specifically to the biological theory of Darwin and Wallace. Sometimes, much more broadly, it is taken to mean any kind of evolutionism. Some writers use it to refer to *any* evolutionary theory that rejects the Lamarckian doctrine of inheritance of acquired characteristics, but which relies on the natural selection principle. Sometimes it is simply equated with Social Darwinism (on which see page 204). Or it may be used as a shorthand for a general evolutionary world-view, often including such ideas as a naturalistic conception of man and history and a faith in the efficacy of the methods of science. It is sometimes difficult to avoid a certain looseness in the usage of the term, and certainly in the later chapters of this book it is used in a very broad sense. Nevertheless, it is hoped that the meaning of the term that is intended on each occasion that it is used should be sufficiently clear from the context.

Part 1
Antecedents of Darwinism

1

Three Important Concepts: Animals and Man; Taxonomy; the Great Chain of Being

1 Animals and man: man's place in nature

ONE OF the most characteristic features of the arguments employed by Darwin was his constant emphasis on the existence of a close analogy between animals and man. This, of course, is a natural corollary of the Darwinian theory of evolution by natural selection. For a Darwinian evolutionist, man is envisaged as just one of the many different species of animals that live on this planet. Man shows innumerable structural features similar to those of apes and other animals, and this naturally suggests some kind of biological affinity. Moreover, some animals apparently display certain elements of rationality, or the capacity to think. They also seem to have simple systems of communication. It appears that they may have some capacity to express emotion, and perhaps also very limited aesthetic sensibilities. Darwin, at any rate, thought that this was so, and devoted a considerable amount of his life's work to investigating the 'mental powers' of animals.[1] Doubtless he would have been delighted to learn of the recent work being carried out in which, so it seems, humans are finding it possible to communicate directly with chimpanzees by sign languages.[2] All this suggests a considerable degree of continuity and analogy between men and other animals.

But this recognition of the general unity of the animal kingdom, where man is viewed as essentially the same as other animals, though marked by an exceptional intelligence, is a fairly recent feature of Western thought. And although it would be going too far to claim that Darwin was solely responsible for the general change in opinion about the position of man within the animal kingdom, his contribution was one of the major factors leading to the reappraisal of man's position and role in the scheme of things. Accordingly, we may usefully begin our discussions by giving some brief account of the earlier ideas on the relationship of men to animals. Many of these early opinions were not logically consistent one with another, though all were widely held at different times. The Darwinian theory, and the associated evolutionary world-picture that he helped to inaugurate, served to remove certain intellectual tensions, giving a more coherent and consistent view of the world.

Other problems have, of course, beset us since the nineteenth century, and — as will be demonstrated in some detail below — many of these problems may be attributed fairly directly to the Darwinian Revolution. Nevertheless, I think it may reasonably be claimed that Darwin has provided us with a more coherent and consistent, and more generally acceptable view of the relationship of man and animals, than existed in pre-evolutionary days.[3] An important aspect, therefore, of the Darwinian Revolution was the fundamental change which it brought about in understanding the relationship between men and animals. What, then, were some of the leading pre-Darwinian views on this question? To answer this it is necessary to go back to antiquity, for many of the ideas that Darwin sought to counter were of very ancient standing in Western culture.

Probably the strongest influence on Western thought about man and animals is derived from the Old Testament and the subsequent Christian tradition. In the first chapter of *Genesis* we have the famous words:

> So God created man in his own image, in the image of God created he him; male and female created he them.

> And God blessed them, and God said unto them, Be fruitful, and multiply, and replenish the earth, and subdue it: and have dominion over the fish of the sea, and over the fowl of the air, and over every living thing that moveth upon the earth.[4]

Here is a supposed divine sanction for men to *dominate* both the Earth and its living inhabitants. Later, in the second chapter of *Genesis* (and in the Bible's second account of Creation), Adam is said to have given names to all living creatures, thereby, it appears, gaining a *quasi*-magical power over them. As we know, the subsequent history of our planet can surely be seen as a story demonstrating the Earth's ever-increasing domination by man. Only in the last twenty years or so has the wisdom of this unbridled dominance and exploitation been widely questioned in Western cultures.[5]

It is wrong, however, merely on the basis of the text of the first chapter of *Genesis,* to suggest that the view of man as being utterly separate from and dominant over animals was generally characteristic of Jewish thought in the pre-Christian era. The author of *Ecclesiastes,* for example, seemingly placed men and animals on a similar level:

> For that which befalleth the sons of men befalleth beasts; even one thing befalleth them: as the one dieth, so dieth the other; yea, they have all one breath; so that a man hath no pre-eminence above a beast: for all is vanity.[6]

In fact, the rigid dichotomy between men and animals is chiefly a Christian tradition, with Stoic roots. St Augustine (354-430) believed that animals lacked rational souls, and were 'not related to us by a common nature'.[7] And according to the earlier Stoic view, animals were totally devoid of reason, and consequently lacked any form of 'rights'.[8] Animals existed purely for the interest of mankind. St Paul, drawing on Stoic traditions, implied that God had no special care for animals, but only for men.[9]

In the Middle Ages, St Thomas Aquinas (1225-1274) maintained that there was no particular reason why man should show kindness to animals, except that cruelty to animals might encourage cruelty to one's fellow men.[10] Animals, *per se*, however, deserved no special consideration. They were subordinate to and different from mankind.

These attitudes continued in the seventeenth century, despite the fact that this period saw the first rise of modern science, under the aegis of the so-called 'mechanical philosophy'. According to the new 'mechanical' view, phenomena were to be explained in terms of matter and motion (usually, in the last analysis, in terms of the motions of small hypothetical corpuscles or atoms), and the model of the machine became the favoured metaphorical means of scientific explanation. René Descartes (1596-1650), the chief exponent of the new mechanical philosophy, tried to explain the nature of the whole cosmos in terms of the motions and mechanical interactions of three kinds of hypothetical corpuscle; and he viewed men and animals as essentially different. They both functioned as if they were kinds of machines and their actions could supposedly be explained in purely mechanical terms. But there was one fundamental difference: men, possessing *rational* souls, had the capacity to speak and to think rationally. Animals, lacking these two essential traits, could be regarded as mere automata. In a famous passage in Descartes' *Discourse on Method* (1637) we read:

> What they [animals] cannot do is speak, as we speak, that is to say, by showing that their words express their thoughts . . .
> And this does not only show that animals have less reason than men; it shows that they have none at all . . . [They] have souls of an entirely different nature from ours . . . [The] fact is . . . that they have no intelligence at all . . .[11]

It was probably sentiments of this kind that permitted some eighteenth-century naturalists such as the Reverend Stephen Hales (1677-1761) to carry out experiments on live animals that would today be regarded as unconscionably cruel, and morally quite unacceptable.[12]

A great gulf separating man and animals was also perceived by Immanuel Kant (1724-1804) at the end of the eighteenth century, as when he wrote in his *Critique of Judgement* (1790):

> As the single being upon earth that possesses understanding, and, consequently, a capacity for setting before himself ends of his deliberate choice, he [man] is certainly titular lord of nature, and, supposing we regard nature as a teleological system, he is born to be its ultimate end.[13]

Here, then, we have ample evidence of the long pre-Darwinian tradition that saw man and animals as essentially distinct. By the end of the eighteenth century there were signs of change in this tradition. A well-known eighteenth-century judge, Lord Monboddo (1714-1799), suggested that language might not be innate in man and brought ridicule on his head by suggesting that there might be men with tails.[14] And there was considerable interest during this period about whether orang-outans were speechless men. But it is still true to say, I think, that it was only Darwin's work, in the latter part of the nineteenth century, that finally convinced most people of the essential genealogical affinity of men and animals, though even now opinion on this is still somewhat fluid. The doctrine of man's immortal soul is still a force to be reckoned with in some quarters.

2 Taxonomy: essences

It may well be helpful also, in this first chapter, to lay some further foundation for the subsequent argument by saying something about early views on taxonomy (classification) and also the philosophical accompaniment of these views.

First, a word about Greek ideas on geometrical axiom systems — epitomised in the work of Euclid. It was, perhaps, the 'science' of geometry that the Greeks cultivated with the greatest success, and it is clear that geometry had a considerable influence on the philosophical ideas of both Plato (428/7-348/7 BC) and Aristotle (384-322 BC).[15] In Euclid's *Geometry,* one works through chains of deductive reasoning, beginning with certain definitions, axioms, and postulates, which collectively we may call 'high-level principles'. Once these are accepted, the deductions to the host of theorems follow without difficulty. The process of working through such a chain of deductive steps the Greeks called *synthesis.* By contrast, the process whereby the high-level principles might themselves be established was termed *analysis.* Euclid and the other Greek geometers made no attempt to inform us how they arrived at their high-level principles, and Descartes suggested in a famous passage[16] that although they *did* have an analytic method they preferred to keep it secret!

Aristotle's methodology was somewhat similar to the geometrical procedure. One began with experience; with observations of the world. Supposedly, as a result of an examination of the world, one might apprehend certain general first principles (a suitable set for each branch of 'science') which would serve as the starting points for deductive syllogistic reasoning to the properties of things. Thus the aim of Aristotle's science may be seen to have been an attempt to draw up a kind of dictionary of the correct definitions of things, from which all their properties would 'flow' deductively. If found successfully, the correct defining formulae would express the *essences* of things. And, a correct *definition* was to be given in terms of *genus* and *species.*[17] For example, a triangle was to be defined as being three-sided (the *specific* characteristic), and a plane figure (the *generic* characteristic). The essence of a man was that he was rational (the *specific* characteristic), and an animal (the *generic* characteristic).

The Aristotelian methodology worked admirably in geometry, for it was, after all, based on the geometrical model. But in other fields the scheme was a failure. One *cannot*, as Aristotle claimed, logically infer the 'properties' of man (such as that he is capable of learning grammar) from the definition of his essence, that he is a rational animal.

Defining an object in terms of genus and species suggests that some kind of classificatory procedure is required. Aristotle was himself a gifted biologist[18] (as well as metaphysician, physicist, political theorist, cosmologist, logician . . .). So we may expect to find a general application of his essentialist methodology and ontology in his biological investigations. Just as a quadrilateral is *essentially* different from a triangle, so, it might seem, cats are *essentially* different from dogs. They should, therefore, have different definitions for their essences; and it might be hoped that this would become evident when they were located within a hierarchical classificatory structure of the animal kingdom. Consequently, one might hope to find a system of classification looking something like Figure 1, when Aristotle's biological works are examined.

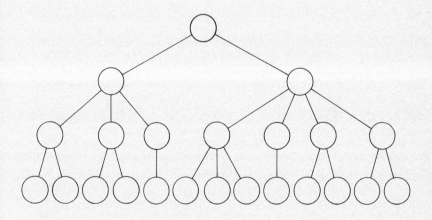

Figure 1. Representation of an 'Aristotelian' hierarchical Taxonomy

But the reader of Aristotle will be disappointed if he sets out hoping to find something just like this, and it was not until well into the Christian era that we find such a system clearly set down. This was the celebrated 'tree of Porphyry', which offered a means of defining the essence of man within a taxonomic system:[19]

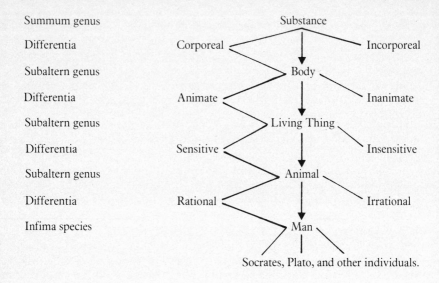

Summmum genus		Substance	
Differentia	Corporeal		Incorporeal
Subaltern genus		Body	
Differentia	Animate		Inanimate
Subaltern genus		Living Thing	
Differentia	Sensitive		Insensitive
Subaltern genus		Animal	
Differentia	Rational		Irrational
Infima species		Man	

Socrates, Plato, and other individuals.

Figure 2. The Tree of Porphyry

A man could thereby be defined as a 'rational, sensitive, animate, corporeal substance'. Or, since animals constituted the level of 'sensitive, animate, corporeal substances', man could be defined as a 'rational animal'. Jeremy Bentham (1748-1832), it may be noted, was so taken with this that he is said to have described Porphyry's tree as being of 'matchless beauty'.[20] This it may well have been, but unfortunately we find nothing comparable in Aristotle's biological texts, where one might have hoped to have found it if the doctrines of the 'theory of predicables', as set out in the *Topica,* had been consistently applied to the study of the animal kindgom.

In fact, what one finds in Aristotle's biological works is a largely *linear* classification of the animal kingdom. Even this is not apparent from a first reading of the texts, but conveniently it has been teased out from them by the historian of biology, Charles Singer, so as to yield the following table, traditionally known as the *'Scala natura':*[21]

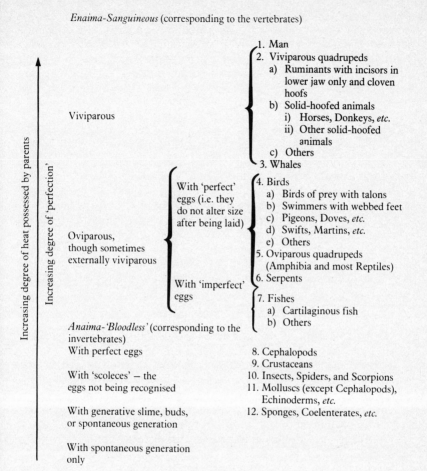

Figure 3. Aristotle's 'Scala Natura' (after Singer)

As Singer, Peck, and other commentators on Aristotle's biological work have shown, there were numerous criteria used for the development of this roughly linear taxonomy of animals. But the chief consideration seems to have been that of arranging animals in order according to their supposed degree of 'perfection', which supposedly corresponded to the relative heats of the various organisms and the character of the eggs or the embryos that they produced. Aristotle's biological writings do not, therefore, provide us with a neat dictionary of the 'essential' definitions of the species of the animal kingdom. But the idea of distinct 'natural kinds' — cats and dogs, essentially different from one another — is most certainly an important feature of Aristotle's system. Moreover, it should be noted that he includes *man* within his general system of animal taxonomy. For Aristotle, writing well before the Christian era, the biological gulf between man and other mammals was no greater than that between, say, birds and reptiles.

3 The Great Chain of Being

One other important theoretical concept must be introduced in this opening chapter. This is the doctrine of the 'Great Chain of Being', publicised by the notable book of that title by the historian of ideas, A. O. Lovejoy.[22] To give some account of the concept of the Great Chain of Being, it is necessary to make a few prefatory remarks about Plato's doctrine of 'ideas' or 'forms'.

Plato (Aristotle's mentor) rejected the doctrine of empiricism (that sense experience is the only source of knowledge), claiming that sensory experience could only yield 'opinion' rather than true 'knowledge'. He held that the objects around us are transient or impermanent, and so do not provide a stable foundation for knowledge. But by exercise of his rationality, man may discover another world, that of changeless 'forms' or 'ideas' (*essences*), transcendent with respect to the mundane world of everyday experience. These 'forms' may be apprehended through the study of mathematics and philosophy, and with the help of dialectical discourse. It is the world of 'forms' (or concepts, if you like) that contains the ultimate realities.

According to Plato's view, therefore, a triangle drawn on a geometer's slate would always be to some degree imperfect, not exactly exemplifying the concept of triangularity. But in the transcendent world of 'forms' or concepts there *is* a perfect triangle, of which our terrestrial triangles are but imperfect 'copies', or manifestations. The same might be said for all other 'natural kinds' or classes of natural objects. Each has its own 'form', or, as it is sometimes called, its own 'paradigm', 'exemplar' or 'archetype'.

This is certainly not the appropriate place to enter upon a critique of Plato's epistemology,[23] which held that knowledge was achieved when the pure concepts or 'forms' were intellectually apprehended with the help of a 'dialectical' inquiry.[24] It may be noted, however, that it has always been a source of difficulty about how one might suppose that 'forms' could be said to exist quite independently of physical objects, or even of our intellectual processes. Even Plato's own pupil, Aristotle, though utilising the doctrine of 'forms' in his theory of the four causes, maintained that 'forms' were immanent, and in no way transcendent as Plato and Platonists supposed. It should not surprise us, therefore, that for the later Neo-Platonists (followers of Plotinus, 205-270 AD) the 'forms' were construed as 'ideas' in the mind of God. I do not suggest that this modification really makes the doctrine any more intelligible to us, but it does at least get away from the problem of 'ideas' floating around, as it were, unattached, in a wholly metaphysical realm, without any thinker acting as their generator.

Following Plato, Plotinus placed the 'forms' in a hierarchy, the '... being envisaged as the 'Good' or the 'One'. And each 'form' in the hier... supposedly owed its being to the supervening 'form'. The doctrine \... clearly expressed in the following passage from the Neo-Platonis... commentator, Macrobius (born *circa* 360 AD):

> Since, from the Supreme God, Mind arises, and from Mind, Soul, and since this in turn creates all subsequent things and fills them all with life, and since this single radiance illumines all and is reflected in many mirrors placed in series, and since all things follow in continuous succession, degenerating in sequence to the very bottom of the series, the attentive observer will discover a connection of parts, from the Supreme God down to the last dregs of things, mutually linked together and without a break. And this is like Homer's golden chain, which God, he says, bade hang down from heaven to earth.[25]

This is an interesting and highly important passage in the history of Western thought. The Neo-Platonists frequently used the analogy of a source of light or heat as a means of explaining the activity of the 'One'. Just as a sun may give 'being', so to speak, to our solar system, radiating its light, warmth and energy upon us, and making our existence possible, so too was the 'One' envisaged in the Neo-Platonic tradition as the cause of all the being and activity of the hierarchy of forms.

The upper levels of this 'celestial hierarchy'[26] had the character of Platonic 'forms', but as one passed down each link in the chain, the forms became ever more corporeal, so that eventually one might reach terrestrial objects (themselves also in an ordered hierarchy), extending right down to the most mundane earth or slime – the lowest of the low. It is clear from the analogy of the multiple reflections in parallel mirrors used by Macrobius that it was intended that there should be an infinite number of links in this 'Chain of Being'.

Following this brief exposition, one may now readily envisage how the idea of the Great Chain of Being might be applied to serve as the basis of a number of interesting doctrines in cosmology, psychology, biology, and even in considerations of status or standing in society. For the mystical Neo-Platonic philosopher, the aim of existence might be taken to be the elevation of the 'soul' to higher levels in the hierarchy of 'forms'. For the purposes of biological[27] theory, one might imagine all animals arranged in a linear hierarchical fashion, from man at the top, down through an *infinity* of forms to the lowest 'zoophytes'. And any person would have his own rank or standing in society. It should be noted that the doctrine was to some degree compatible with the *Scala natura* of Aristotle's biological works. But whereas Aristotle envisaged discrete and distinct natural kinds, the Neo-Platonic view contemplated an infinity of natural kinds, so that each shaded off into its neighbour in the Chain.

Neo-Platonism has for long exerted a powerful influence on the Christian West, particularly in the Florentine period of the Renaissance. And it might be said that the doctrine of the Great Chain of Being formed part of the general mental furniture of most educated men from the Renaissance until almost the end of the eighteenth century, along with such ancient notions as the theory of the four elements and the theory of the four humours. References to the Great Chain of Being abound in Spenser,[28] Henry More,[29] and Milton.[30] One finds it in the philosophical writings of Leibniz,[31] Spinoza[32] and Locke[33] in the seventeenth century, and in the eighteenth century it was one of the standard ways of conceptualising nature, as the following table extracted from a work by the Genevan naturalist, Charles Bonnet (1720-1793), well illustrates:[34]

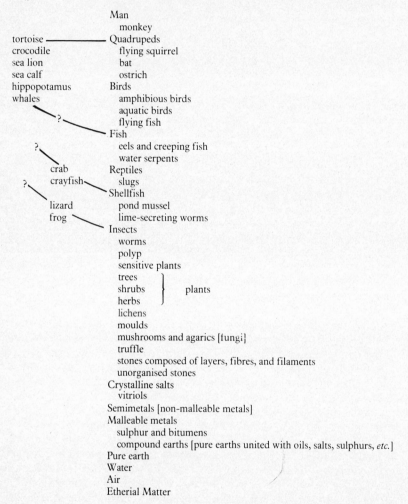

Figure 4. *The Great Chain of Being According to Bonnet (after Ritterbush)*

Above the Earth in Bonnet's Chain were conceived higher worlds and even higher universes. In these higher realms also the thread of the Chain continued, through angels, archangels, seraphim, cherubim, choirs of angels, virtues, principalities, dominations and powers. At the very summit of the hierarchy was 'the Eternal' — 'that which *is*, possessing alone [*seul*] the plenitude of its being'.[35] The parallel with the ancient Neo-Platonic hierarchy of Plotinus is quite remarkable.

The doctrine of the Great Chain of Being probably had its last resting place (at least among biologists) among the German Nature Philosophers of the nineteenth century, immediately before Darwin's time. But the Christian doctrine of a celestial hierarchy is not yet defunct.

NOTES CHAPTER 1

1   For our discussion of Darwin's investigation in psychology, see below pages 285 to 287.
2   For a popular account of investigations in this area, see E. Linden, *Apes, Men, and Language*, Penguin, New York, 1975.
3   This remark may appear unconscionably 'Whiggish', suggesting that our twentieth-century mental picture is notably 'superior' to that of earlier times, or that we have a specially privileged viewpoint from which we may judge the past. For example, it might seem that I am suggesting that the man of the past took a view of the world that was essentially incoherent, but that he lived with it, *faux de mieux*, as with a stone in his shoe. I must hasten to emphasise that nothing like this is intended. There would seem to be no reason to doubt that Plato was well satisfied with the coherence of his philosophical system. Aquinas, likewise, achieved a masterly synthesis of Aristotelian and Christian doctrine that provided him and later Thomists with a wonderfully unified and satisfying metaphysical system. Bat for various reasons, some of which will become apparent in the course of this book, such systems are no longer widely adhered to, although to some degree they continue to colour even our present outlook. They do contain features that clash with the empirical results of modern science and the metaphysical presuppositions of the modern world — and it seems to us they present certain logical difficulties which prevent their acceptance today. One such problem, that of the essentialist approach to taxonomy, is discussed further in the present chapter. (For discussions of the inadequacies of so-called 'Whig history', see H. Butterfield, *The Whig Interpretation of History*, Penguin, Harmondsworth, 1973 (1st edn, 1931) — and J. Agassi, 'Towards an historiography of science', *History and Theory*, Beiheft 2, 1963. See also the discussion of historiographical problems in the Appendix below.)
4   *The First Book of Moses called Genesis*, Chapter 1, Verses 27-28.
5   For an excellent discussion of this whole issue, see J. Passmore, *Man's Responsibility for Nature: Ecological Problems and Western Traditions*, Duckworth, London, 1974. The following section has drawn freely on this book as a source of ideas and references. See also Passmore's article 'The treatment of animals', *Journal of the History of Ideas*, Vol. 36, 1975, pp.195-218, and C. W. Hume, *The Status of Animals in the Christian Religion*, Universities Federation for Animal Welfare, London, 1956.
6   *Ecclesiastes; or, the Preacher*, Chapter 3, Verse 19.
7   St Augustine (tr. D. A. & I. J. Gallagher), *The Catholic and Manichaean Ways of Life*, Catholic University Press, Washington, 1966, p.91.
8   E. V. Arnold, *Roman Stoicism*, Cambridge, 1911, p.274 (republished Routledge, London, 1958).
9   *The First Epistle of Paul the Apostle to the Corinthians*, Chapter 9, Verse 9.
10 St Thomas Aquinas, *Summa Contra Gentiles*, Book III, Chapter 112 in A. C. Pegis (ed.), *Basic Writings of Saint Thomas Aquinas*, 2 vols, Random House, New York, 1945, Vol. 2, p.222.
11 R. Descartes, *Discourse on Method and other Writings*: translated with an introduction by Arthur Wollaston, Penguin, Harmondsworth, 1960, p.81.
12 Stephen Hales, *Statical Essays, Containing Haemastaticks, or an Account of some Hydraulick and Hydrostatical Experiments made on the Blood and Blood-vessels of animals*, Vol. II, London, 1733 (republished Hafner, New York, 1964).

13   I. Kant, *The Critique of Judgement*, translated with analytical indexes by James Creed Meredith, Clarendon Press, Oxford, 1952, p.94.

14   For a recent account of Monboddo's life and work, emphasising his contributions to the development of theories of language, see E. L. Cloyd, *James Burnett: Lord Monboddo*, Clarendon Press, Oxford, 1972.

15   It should be noted, however, that Euclid's synthesis of Greek geometry (*circa* 300 BC) was achieved a little *after* the time of Plato (428/7-348/7 BC) and Aristotle (384-322 BC).

16   R. Descartes, *Réponse aux Secondes Objections* [to the *Meditations*], Paris, 1641, § 122 in R. Descartes, *Oeuvres Philosophiques*, 2 vols, Garnier, Paris, 1967, Vol. 2, p.583.

17   Aristotle's texts in this area are obscure and confusing. But see particularly *Posterior Analytics*, 96 b 15–97 a 23 and *Topica*, 101 b 38–102 b 26 (*Aristotle Posterior Analytics* by Hugh Tredennick; *Topica* by E. S. Forster, Heinemann & Harvard University Press' London & Cambridge, Mass., 1960, pp.231-235, 281-287.

18   On Aristotle as a biologist, see, for example, W. D. Ross, *Aristotle*, Methuen, London, 1923; C. Singer, *A Short History of Anatomy from the Greeks to Harvey*, 2nd edn, Dover, New York, 1957, pp.17-28; D. M. Balme, 'Aristotle's use of differentiae in zoology', in J. Barnes, M. Schofield & R. Sorabji (eds), *Articles on Aristotle: 1. Science*, Duckworth, London, 1975, pp.183-193; G. E. R. Lloyd, 'The development of Aristotle's theory of classification of animals', *Phronesis*, Vol. 6, 1962, pp.59-81; M. Grene, *A Portrait of Aristotle*, Faber, London, 1963.

19   This is to be found in a work of the Neo-Platonist commentator Porphyry (232/3 – *circa* 304 AD), entitled *Isagoge* – an 'introduction' to Aristotle's *Categories*. Porphyry's work was in its turn the subject of a commentary by Boethius (470-525 AD), and a pictorial representation of Porphyry's 'tree' may be found in this, whereas Porphyry himself merely spelled it out in words. See Boethius, *In Porphyrium Dialogi a Victorino Translati: Dialogus Primus*, in J. P. Migne, *Patrologiae Cursus Completus, sive Bibliotheca Universalis . . . Series (Latina) prima*, 221 vols, Paris, 1844-1864, Vol. 64, columns 9-48 (cols 41-42 for diagram). For an English translation of Porphyry's text, see E. W. Warren, *Porphyry the Phoenician: Isagoge*, Pontifical Institute of Mediaeval Studies, Toronto, 1975. For an accessible pictorial representation of the 'tree', and discussion, see M. R. Cohen & E. Nagel, *An Introduction to Logic and Scientific Method*, 'Complete edition', Routledge & Kegan Paul, London, 1963, p.236. It should be noted that Porphyry's 'taxonomy' employed so-called 'logical dichotomy' (or the 'method of division') as recommended by Plato, and was therefore rather different from the method of Aristotle, where divisions were made in such a way as to try to match Nature's groupings, rather than following the requirements of strict bipartite division at each level.

20   M. R. Cohen & E. Nagel, *op. cit.* (note 19), p.236.

21   See C. Singer, *op. cit.* (note 18), p.26. (Singer's table has been slightly modified here.) A. L. Peck, an influential commentator on Aristotle's biological works, has pointed out that Aristotle did not follow the ideas on definition and classification put forward in his logical and metaphysical works very assiduously in his biological writings (Aristotle, *Historia Animalium*, in three volumes with an English translation by A. L. Peck, Heinemann & Harvard University Press, London & Cambridge, Mass., 1965, Vol. 1, pp.viii-ix).

22   A. O. Lovejoy, *The Great Chain of Being: A Study of the History of an Idea*, Harper & Row, New York, 1960 (first published Cambridge, Mass., 1936). For some discussion of Lovejoy's work as an historian of ideas, see the Appendix below.

23   For a good general exposition of Plato's doctrines, see, for example, F. Copleston, *A History of Philosophy: Volume 1 Greece and Rome*, Burns Oates, London, 1946, Chapters 19 and 20.

24   In the method of dialectic (as envisaged by Plato), the philosopher searches for suitable definitions of terms. A suggestion is put forward and its implications and adequacy are considered. The definition is then modified or a new one sought, and the discussions proceed until general agreement is reached as to the adequacy and acceptability of the proposed definition. In *The Republic*, for example, the speakers seek the meaning of the term 'justice'. In *Theaetetus* the nature of 'knowledge' is sought. In *The Sophist* it is suggested that the 'method of division' (which produces a hierarchical taxonomy of genera and species) may be employed. In *Cratylus* an analogy is drawn between the operations of weaving and the method of dialectic.

25   Macrobius, *Commentary on the Dream of Scipio*, translated with an introduction and notes by William Harris Stahl, Columbia University Press, New York, 1952, p.145.

26   The union of the Neo-Platonic hierarchy of 'ideas' and Christian doctrine was largely due to a Neo-Platonic tract which was for many years thought to have been written by one of the early Christians. See *The Celestial and Ecclesiastical Hierarchy of Dionysius the Areopagite* now first translated into English from the original Greek, by the Rev. John Parker, M.A., London, 1894.

27   The use of the term 'biological' or 'biology' in this context is undoubtedly anachronistic, for it was not introduced until the beginning of the nineteenth century by Treviranus and Lamarck. (See W. Coleman, *Biology in the Nineteenth Century: Problems of Form, Function and Transformation*, Wiley, New York, 1971, pp.1-3.) The meaning intended here for biology is 'the study of living organisms'. To

write these words on every occasion would be tedious, and to write 'naturalist' or 'natural history' would not be wholly satisfactory either, for this term has its own special meaning, implying a particular approach to the observation, classification and naming of objects.

28   E. Spenser, 'An hymne of heavenly beautie'; in J. C. Smith & E. de Selincourt (eds), *The Poetical Works of Edmund Spenser*, O.U.P., Oxford, 1912, pp.596-599 (reprinted 1952).

29   H. More 'The argument of Democritus Platonissans, or the infinitie of worlds', in: *Philosophical Poems, by Henry More*, Cambridge, 1647, pp.191-218 (§§50 and 51).

30   J. Milton, *Paradise Lost*, London, 1667, Book V, Lines 469-490 (facsimile edn, Scolar Press, Menston, 1968).

31   A very precise statement of the doctrine, according to Leibniz, is given in A. O. Lovejoy, *op. cit.* (note 22), pp.144-145.

32   B. Spinoza, *The Ethics*, Part I, Proposition 16, 1st Latin edn, Amsterdam, 1677; republished by Dent, London, 1910, p.15.

33   J. Locke, *An Essay Concerning Human Understanding*, Book III, Chapter 6, § 12, ed. A. S. Pringle-Pattison, O.U.P., Oxford, 1924, pp.247-248. (Locke used the idea of the Great Chain of Being in his arguments against the existence of discrete species, each with their own *essential* characteristics.)

34   Extracted from C. Bonnet, *Contemplation de la Nature*, 2 vols, Amsterdam, 1764, Vol. 1, pp.33-69, following P. C. Ritterbush, *Overtures to Biology: The Speculations of Eighteenth Century Naturalists*, Yale University Press, New Haven & London, 1964, p.71. (On Bonnet and the Great Chain of Being, see also L. Anderson, 'Charles Bonnet's taxonomy and chain of being', *Journal of the History of Ideas*, Vol. 37, 1976, pp.45-58.)

35   C. Bonnet, *Contemplation de la Nature*, 2nd edn, Amsterdam, 1769, p.84.

2

Some Eighteenth-Century Views: Linnaeus and Buffon

If one examines a notable instance of eighteenth-century architecture such as the Royal Crescent at Bath;[1] if one listens to a typical piece of eighteenth-century music such as Haydn's 79th Symphony;[2] if one looks at a characteristic example of eighteenth-century portraiture such as Sir Joshua Reynolds' *Lady Elizabeth Delmé and her Children*;[3] if one looks at a fine eighteenth-century garden such as that of Charles Bridgeman at Stowe[4] — in each case the regularly structured and *ordered* character of the art will probably become immediately apparent. The compositions are carefully framed by particular artistic and aesthetic conventions, chiefly those of classical antiquity. Symmetry, regularity, and order are obviously of paramount importance in these eighteenth-century creations.

I suggest that such criteria were not merely restricted to the artistic or aesthetic spheres, but may have been factors of considerable significance in shaping the science of the time, especially natural history. In this chapter we shall look at a notable eighteenth-century botanist whose work admirably exemplifies the style of investigation of animals and plants during that period. Thereby we may gain a useful insight into the scientific background to Darwin's investigation — although this is not to suggest that Darwin was directly combating eighteenth-century scientific thought. And it should not be thought that by focusing special attention on a particular figure I wish to be interpreted as an adherent of the so-called 'great man' theory of history. It is simply that for introductory purposes it is convenient to deal with a single person as an exemplar of the thought of a period. In any case, we will draw contrasts between our chosen figure and certain other eighteenth-century naturalists.

Linnaeus

Carl von Linné (1707-1778),[5] or Carolus Linnaeus as he is perhaps better known, trained in medicine, but spent the greater part of his working life teaching natural history at the University of Uppsala in Sweden. As a young man, Linnaeus made an extensive expedition into the northern parts of his country – a journey which, for its intellectual inspiration, may be compared with Darwin's later voyage on H.M.S. *Beagle,* or Huxley's travels aboard H.M.S. *Rattlesnake.* In his later years Linnaeus continued to travel through his country, although his first-hand experience of natural history was restricted to the northern part of Europe. But his students travelled assiduously in many parts of the world, trying to apply the teachings of their mentor in a variety of new situations. Daniel Solander (1733-1782), a pupil of Linnaeus, accompanied Cook on his first voyage, and, with Joseph Banks (1743-1820), made the first botanical observations in Australia in 1770.

Linnaeus's fame rests upon his work as a systematist, or taxonomist, of the animal, vegetable and mineral kingdoms, and in particular on his sexual system for the classification of plants. This taxonomic work was carried out in an endless stream of publications, beginning with the first edition of the celebrated *Systema Naturae* of 1735, published while he was still a student, and finishing with the *Systema Vegetabilium* in 1774.[6]

In all this work, Linnaeus was striving to find the order and pattern of nature, and to present it in the form of a simple, comprehensible, rational taxonomic system. Nature itself was divided into her three kingdoms, which were then treated more or less separately. Each kingdom was divided successively into classes, genera and species, all of which were then presented in the form of a table, which enabled the whole classificatory system of a particular kingdom to be taken in almost at a glance. To illustrate the results of this, Figure 5 shows a translation from the Latin of the major components of Linnaeus's classificatory table of the animal kingdom, as given in the first edition of the *Systema Naturae.*

From the twentieth-century point of view, there may seem to be a great many deficiencies in this tabular representation of the animal kingdom. The class of 'worms' (*vermes*), for example, seems to be doing duty for a great miscellany of animals. The order of 'beasts of burden' (*jumenta*) is seemingly based upon anthropocentric criteria, and according to the modern judgement fails to form a 'natural' grouping of the animal kingdom. But the work should not be judged in modern terms. As far as it is possible for us to do so, it should be viewed through eighteenth-century eyes. And what we have here is Linnaeus's youthful vision of the very plan of nature itself. Indeed, if the naturalist were able to perform his task satisfactorily, then, according to Linnaeus's way of thinking, he would be able to reveal the very design of the animal kingdom that God had employed at the time of the Creation. This was the task to which Linnaeus's life work was directed: the revelation of the *order* of God's design, and the appropriate naming of the products of His creation. The tidy tabular ordering of the taxonomic system should be emphasised for it is in this respect that one may readily see an analogy with the artistic products of the eighteenth century.

Linnaeus's taxonomy of the animal kingdom was by and large an example of what is called a 'natural' rather than an 'artificial' system of classification.

Figure 5. *Animal Kingdom, according to Linnaeus's* Systema Naturae, *1735*

I Quadrupeds		II Birds		III Amphibia	
Of human form	Man Apes, Monkeys Sloth	Birds of prey	Parrot Owl Falcon, Eagle, Vulture, *etc.*	'Serpents' (Reptiles)	Tortoise Frog, Toad Lizard (including Crocodile, Chameleon, *etc.*) Blind worm
Carnivores	Bear Lion Tiger, Panther Cat Weasel, Stoat Marsupials Otter Walrus Seal Hyena Dog Civet Mole Hedgehog Bat	Woodpecker-like birds	Bird of Paradise Raven Crow Cuckoo Woodpecker Creepers Nuthatch Hoopoe Bee-eater	*Paradoxa*	
				Hydra Fishing frog Unicorn Pelican (self-wounding) Satyr Scythian lamb Phoenix Barnacle goose Dragon Death-watch beetle	
		Long-beaked birds	Crane Stork Heron		
Rodents	Porcupine Squirrel Beaver Mouse, Rat Lemur, Marmot Rabbit, Hare Shrew	Geese-like birds	Spoonbill Pelican Swan Duck Diver Grebe Sea-gull		
Beasts of burden	Horse Hippopotamus Elephant Pig	Snipe-like birds	Oyster catcher Plover Lapwing Sandpiper Curlew Coot		
Cloven-hoofed animals	Camel Deer Goat Sheep Ox	Fowls	Ostrich Cassowary, Emu Bustard Turkey Hen Grouse		
		Passerine (sparrow-like) birds	Pigeon, Dove Thrush, Blackbird Starling Lark Wagtail Nightingale, Robin, Flycatcher, Wren Crossbill Swallow, Swift Finch		

IV Fish		V Insects		VI Worms	
Plagiuri	Walrus Sperm whale Narwhal Baleen whale Dolphin	Beetles	Cockroach Water boatman Blister beetle Earwig Longicorn beetle Tumbling flower beetle Nut weevil Long-horn beetle Stag beetle Scarab beetle Skin beetle Tortoise beetle Leaf beetle Ladybird Whirligig *Necydalis* (Longicorn beetle) Leaf-rolling weevil Leather-winged beetle Ground beetle Tiger beetle *Leptura* (Longicorn beetle) Long-horned woodborer Lamellicorn beetle	'Reptiles' (crawling animals)	Hair-worm Tape-worm Leech Slug
Cartilaginous fish	Skate Shark Sturgeon Lamprey			Shell-fish	Gasteropod Nautilus Cowrie Ear-shell Limpet Tooth-shell Conch-shell Barnacle
Fish with free gills covered with membrane (*Branchiostegi*)	Angler fish Lumpfish Trunk fish File fish			'Zoophytes'	Sponge Sea urchin Star fish Sea anemone Cuttlefish Micro-organisms
Fish with spiny dorsal fins (*Acanthopterygii*)	Stickleback John Dory Sculpin Gurnet Weever Perch Gilthead *Labrus* Mullet Mackerel Sword fish Goby	*Angioptera*	Butterfly Dragonfly May-fly Ant-lion Scorpion fly Lacewing Bee Ichneumon Fly		

Soft-finned fishes	Electric eel
	Eel
	Blenny
	Cod
	Flat fish
	Sand eel
	Lance fish
	Sucking fish
	Pike
	Salmon, Trout
	Smelt
	Whitefish
	Herring
	Carp, Roach,
	  Minnow, Dace,
	  Chub, *etc.*
	Barbel, Loach
	Pipefish
	or
	Seahorse
		Hemptera (not with modern denotation)	Grasshopper,
			  Locust
			Glow-worm
			Ant
			Bed-bug
			Boat-fly
			Water scorpion
			Scorpion		

		Aptera (wingless 'insects')	Louse Flea Cyclops Mite Spider Crab Wood-louse Centipede		

Consider, for example, his genus[7] of *Leo* (lion). Lions certainly form a definite category of the animal kingdom, the members of which are marked by distinctive characteristics of shape, size and colour, and mode of life. And this apparent taxonomic discreteness may be confirmed by the fact that animals of this taxon breed to produce fertile offspring only with each other, and not with animals of neighbouring groups. On the other hand, there are no very obvious criteria that may be specified to guarantee that the system of classification drawn up is 'correct'. For example, crows and ravens are placed in different genera, but are they 'essentially' different? And if so, is it a generic or a specific difference? Is it just a matter of convenience to separate soft-finned from spiny-finned fish, or is there some *essential* difference between fishes in these two groupings, and if so why should this difference be particularly manifest in the fins? Was the form of a fin a true *mark* of some *essential* difference in the nature of fishes?

It can, I think, be seen that despite the shift in emphasis that Linnaeus made in the eighteenth century – in that through his search for order he is seeking the divine pattern of the universe – his problems, and to some extent his attempted methods of dealing with them, are remarkably similar to those facing Aristotle in antiquity. Linnaeus is seeking to group animals in 'natural kinds', place these within a hierarchical taxonomic system, and give names (in terms of genus and species) to each natural grouping. Hopefully, there will be a readily determinable characteristic mark (such as hair) which will serve as an appropriate criterion for characterising each pigeon hole of the taxonomic hierarchy. But exactly what method should be employed in the construction of such a table is hard to say. Aristotle, it seems, supposed that the 'scientist' could perform the task by applying his intellect ('*nous*') attentively to the data. But what does this mean? The task seems to reduce itself to something like the shuffling of the pieces of a jigsaw until they fall into a 'natural' pattern. To achieve this – with no theoretical guide-line other than the earnest belief that there *is* a pattern to be discovered if one is sufficiently industrious – is indeed a daunting problem.

In dealing with the animal kingdom, Linnaeus's task was considerably lightened by the fact that his knowledge of animal kinds was fairly limited. The same was true, though to a lesser extent, in the plant kingdom, for he was chiefly familiar with the rather restricted flora of northern Europe. Nevertheless, even when dealing only with the restricted range of plants with which he was familiar, Linnaeus was forced to abandon any hope of presenting a 'natural' system, and consequently he resorted to the use of 'artificial' groupings or taxa. So in classifying plants according to the Linnaean system, the basic rule was to count the numbers of stamens and carpels in the flower. The number of stamens was used to determine the classes (*Monandria, Diandria, Triandria,* etc.) of the classification; and the orders were determined by the number of carpels (*Monogynia, Digynia, Trigynia,* etc.).[8]

This so-called 'sexual system' was Linnaeus's invention, and it provided the fundamental basis of his botanical classifications, enabling him to handle the vast mass of botanical information that was assembled year by year in the course of the eighteenth century. It made the classification and naming of the flowering plants a relatively simple process that could be employed by quite unsophisticated students; and it remained in general favour for about ninety years after the first publication of the *Systema Naturae*. Unfortunately, however, classifying plants according to this simple system utterly failed to bring together what are self-evidently 'natural kinds' according to their general appearances. For example, in the order *Monogynia* of the class *Tetrandria* we find scabious, mimosa, plantain, dogwood, bedstraw and others all lumped together. By no stretch of the imagination, therefore, may this be thought of as a 'natural' grouping which brings together plants that are essentially similar. On the other hand, for the 'finer' parts of the classification, particularly at the level of genera, Linnaeus was dealing with groupings that might reasonably be said to be 'natural'. And, if we are maintaining that the animal system was more 'natural' than that of the plants, it must not be forgotten that some of the higher groupings for the animals, such as the 'beasts of burden', were anything but 'natural'.

It should be noted that there was no question of the element of time entering into Linnaeus's taxonomy. His was an atemporal, or static, representation of the world, based purely on the observations of the external features of living objects. What was directly visible to the naked eye served as the basis for the classification. Little attempt was made to uncover internal features of either animals or plants for taxonomic purposes. In his general discussion of the theory of botany, Linnaeus stated that one should be concerned with the *number, proportion, figure* and *situation* of the parts of flowers[9] and he did not go beyond these to minuter anatomical details. We will consider in a later chapter how the criteria for the classification of organisms were modified in the period leading up to Darwin's work.

Linnaeus was a firm believer in the biblical doctrine of the Creation, though he held a somewhat idiosyncratic view of the nature of the Garden of Eden. He was aware that there was observational evidence for the slow fall of the waters of the Baltic around the Swedish coast,[10] and so he supposed that the waters of the ocean were receding on a world-wide scale, with a constant extension of the area of dry land. The original home of Adam and Eve was envisaged as an island, somewhere near the equator, on which the original pairs of all the animals and plants were created.[11] As the area of dry ground extended, the multiplying creatures grew and spread themselves, until eventually they reached the situation as it existed in the eighteenth century. So, through this supposed direct genetic linkage between primordial and contemporary conditions, Linnaeus could believe that his taxonomic investigations would truly reveal the original divine plan according to which God had created the world.

It might be objected that Linnaeus's system was extraordinarily naive, for if the first pair of lions, for example, ate the first pair of sheep, or if the first antelopes ate the first specimens of a particular kind of grass on the first day of their creation, then those particular kinds would disappear for ever. This objection was raised several times in the eighteenth century,[12] but Linnaeus never seems to have been worried by it. Nor need it delay us here.

The Linnaean world-view was the complete antithesis of an evolutionary system. Linnaeus contemplated a perfect *economy* of nature, involving a *balance*[13] between propagation and destruction, with the gradual spread of this system over the expanding dry portion of the Earth. There was a due and just proportion between propagation, geographic distribution, destruction and conservation. But this proportion was not so much a result of the interactions of these, as it was a kind of determinant of them. The economy of nature, for Linnaeus, was simultaneously the economy of the divine wisdom, for nature did nothing in vain. Each creature had its necessary role to play in the scheme of things. The naturalist was able to see beyond the apparent waste and carnage, and appreciate the manner in which the beautifully designed parts interlocked or interacted with each other. And, as befitted the outlook of an eighteenth-century man of Enlightenment, for Linnaeus the good unquestionably outweighed the bad. But the economy of nature that Linnaeus envisaged was probably modelled on the social hierarchy of the stratified society in which he lived.

The fact that Linnaeus included man within his tabular representation of the animal kingdom should be emphasised. In his day, this was a somewhat startling innovation, which linked his scheme with Aristotle's *Scala natura* of antiquity,[14] while placing it at odds with the usual schemes of his eighteenth-century contemporaries.[15] Man was an essential component of Linnaeus's system, and had a particular role to play in the polity of nature. Man's function was to see and comprehend the beauty of creation, and to sing the praises of the Creator. Man was as if a spectator to the drama of nature, which consequently could be thought of as a kind of theatre viewed by the naturalist. In fact, nature herself might be put on display in a zoological or botanical garden or in a museum. In a zoo, each cage should display an example of a single pair of animals of a natural kind, such as were first created in the Garden of Eden. Indeed, we may think metaphorically of the bars of the cages as representations of the rigid eighteenth-century taxonomic boundaries surrounding each species. Likewise, the botanic garden should exactly parallel the system of plant taxonomy.

It is particularly interesting that Linnaeus redesigned the botanical gardens at Uppsala, according to his own newly-devised system of plant taxonomy, and sowed plants of his taxa in separate beds within the garden, which thereby became a kind of actualisation of the supposed original plant creation, set out according to the taste and ordered style of a typical eighteenth-century garden. Linnaeus's gardens were restored to their eighteenth-century condition in 1909, and so visitors to Uppsala today may walk right back into the botanical plan of the world, as Linnaeus conceived it some two hundred years ago. Probably — or so it was suggested by the Swiss naturalist Albrecht von Haller (1708-1777)[16] – Linnaeus thought of himself as a kind of second Adam, giving names to animals and plants, just as Adam had once done in the Garden of Eden. And this parallel may perhaps be carried a step further, for Linnaeus's town house lay within the walls of the botanic gardens. He lived in his Garden of Eden. And the interior of his country residence a few miles outside Uppsala was as much a museum as a private dwelling house: the walls were papered with botanical illustrations,[17] with stuffed specimens of animals prominently displayed in *show*-cases.

It is important to emphasise that the system of interrelationships (propagation, destruction, etc.) that Linnaeus perceived in the economy of nature was not an eighteenth-century ecology. Ecology in the modern sense became possible only after the establishment of the Darwinian theory, and in fact the name was only introduced in 1866 by the German evolutionary biologist, Ernst Haeckel (1834-1919).[18] Linnaeus was concerned with an ever-expanding hierarchy of forms, but the relationships between those forms remained constant in time. The position of a particular species within the hierarchy could never alter. It always bore a constant relationship to other members of the hierarchy. And the whole structure was in a sense rather brittle or fragile. One could not imagine any part being added or subtracted, since the whole was known to be a perfect design, and any change would assuredly be for the worse. Consequently, there was no sense in which the system might be said be be *evolving*. The fixity of species formed the very basis of the whole scheme. Or so it seemed to Linnaeus in his younger days.

In 1741, however, an event occurred[19] which forced Linnaeus to reconsider his theoretical position. In that year, an Uppsala student, Magnus Ziöberg, discovered a specimen of unusual form, a plant now thought to have been produced by a process of gene recombination (*Peloria* from *Linaria*), and this was passed to Linnaeus for examination. Linnaeus suggested that it must be some kind of hybrid. Hybrids, however, were generally thought to be sterile, like mules, yet this one seemed perfectly fertile. The discovery presented something of a crisis for Linnaeus, for it suddenly appeared that the regular plan underlying God's work was much less stable, regular and fixed than had at first been supposed. Perhaps the economy of nature was not fixed once and for all, as had been previously believed.

In his later work, the solution to the problem that Linnaeus proposed was that God originally created the upper levels of the taxonomic hierarchy, but genera and species could be regarded as the 'offsprings of time':

> We may suppose God at the beginning to have proceeded from simple to compound, from few to many; and therefore at the beginning of vegetation to have created just so many different plants, as there are natural *orders*. That He then so intermixed the plants of these orders by their marriages with each other; that as many plants were produced as there are now distinct *genera*. That Nature then intermixed these generic plants by reciprocal marriages (which did not change the structure of the flower) and multiplied them into all possible existing *species*; excluding however from the number of species the mule plants produced from these marriages, as being barren.[20]

Possibly also climate and geographical circumstances could have played a part in the gradual proliferation of new genera and species by the mechanism of hybridisation.

A considerable number of Linnaeus's theoretical views were not published in his own works, but appeared in the dissertations of his various students. One such concept, to be found in a posthumous work edited by P. D. Giseke and published in 1792, is of particular interest and probably gives a reasonable indication of Linnaeus's views in the latter part of his life. Giseke represented the vegetable kingdom by a kind of map showing what he took to be the natural affinities of plants. Each circle represented a particular order of the vegetable kingdom, and their spatial separations were taken to be indicators of their taxonomic relationships.[21]

Figure 6. A Map-like Representation of the Vegetable Kingdom, according to P. D. Giseke.

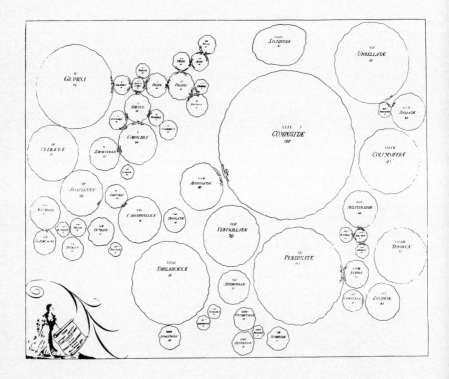

It will be noted that such a scheme is rather like what one might obtain by taking a time-slice through a Darwinian evolutionary tree, and I think it can be seen that there is in fact some limited degree of analogy between the way Darwin and Linnaeus/Giseke offer their theoretical solutions to the problem of interpreting and representing the diverse phenomena of nature. But the analogy is severely restricted. In the absence of a time dimension to the Linnaeus/Giseke system, the two schemes have very substantial differences.

The Giseke map marked a limit beyond which the Linnaean system was unable to proceed. It did not break away from the eighteenth-century tabular, static view of nature, and certainly should not be regarded as an incipient evolutionary theory. Nevertheless, the tension and theoretical shifting that occurred within the Linnaean system during the latter part of the eighteenth century are to be noted. They mark internal problems in natural history that would eventually find their resolution in Darwin's work, although this was not, of course, apparent at the end of the eighteenth century.

Buffon

Comparable in influence to Linnaeus among eighteenth-century naturalists was G. L. L. de Buffon (1707-1788),[22] keeper (or director) of the Royal Botanical Gardens (the *Jardin du Roi*) in Paris, and author of one of the most massive works of natural history of all time – the celebrated *Histoire Naturelle,* which appeared in forty-four volumes between 1749 and 1804.[23] This remarkable series of volumes dealt with most branches of the animal kingdom, besides treating minerals and giving an account of Buffon's theories of the Earth.

The literature on Buffon is considerable, and at one time a good deal of attention was given to the question of whether he was or was not an evolutionist.[24] However, we will not be particularly concerned with this question, but will attempt rather to give a general conspectus of Buffon's views, in so far as they are relevant to our theme, comparing and contrasting these views with those of his Swedish contemporary. By this means we may hope to gain a clearer picture of the general structure of thought of the eighteenth-century natural historians.

In the first volume of the *Histoire Naturelle,* Buffon reveals himself as an exponent of the doctrine of the Great Chain of Being, with man being placed at the top of the Chain.

> The first thing that emerges from this thorough examination of nature is something that is perhaps rather humbling for man; it is that he must himself be ranked among the animals . . . Thus surveying successively and in order all the various objects that make up the universe, and placing himself at the head of all created beings, he will be surprised to see that one can descend by almost insensible degrees from the most perfect creature down to the most unformed matter, from the best organised animal to purely brute mineral matter; he will recognise that these imperceptible gradations are nature's handiwork; and he will find these gradations not only in size and form, but also in manners of movement and generation, and in the successions of all species.[25]

In accordance with this view of an infinite number of forms shading into one another, Buffon believed it was foolish to build up hierarchical taxonomic systems such as Linnaeus had proposed in his *Systema Naturae*. Classes, orders, and genera, he said, exist only in the imagination. It would seem, therefore, that Buffon's position might be construed as that of a *nominalist*, the very antithesis of an Aristotelian essentialist. In describing Buffon in this way we are using a term to be found in the writings of John Locke (1632-1704) in the seventeenth century,[26] and which may be traced back further through the mediaeval period without difficulty.[27] A word or two of explanation about the doctrine of nominalism may be useful here.

Locke objected strongly to the Aristotelian view that if the correct essential definitions of kinds could be found, one could determine the properties of those kinds deductively from their definitions.[28] He pointed out that one could never find out new empirical facts, simply by ratiocination from verbal definitions. A definition, he maintained, could tell how names were to be used (by conventional agreement or customary usage), but it could never be a source of new factual information. Even the best definitions, therefore, merely gave the *nominal* essences of things, never the *real* essences. The names of things simply indicated the classes of things for which, by general usage, the names were deemed appropriate. And conventions about word usages were susceptible to change. The categories by which objects were grouped and named were in no way God-given or fixed according to certain essential criteria. In principle, it would be perfectly possible to group objects in unconventional ways and allot new names or redistribute the old names. This view of the matter is generally referred to by the term *nominalism*.

So it would appear that Buffon's attitude towards the problem of classifying and naming the members of the animal and vegetable kingdoms was indeed in accordance with the general philosophical position adopted by Locke, and diametrically opposed to Linnaeus's viewpoint. Believing in an infinity of forms grading into one another, according to the doctrine of the Great Chain of Being, it might appear that *all* divisions of a taxonomic system would be purely arbitrary. Buffon's view of 1749 could therefore seem to be that species as well as higher taxa are figments of the taxonomist's imagination. This would be the logical consequence of an unbridled nominalist premise. However, while Buffon certainly believed that the higher taxonomic groupings were purely conventional, he didn't quite commit himself on the question of species in the 'Preliminary discourse' of 1749. And in the same year he published an essay on animals[29] in which he seems to have given recognition to the existence of species as discrete entities in nature, independent of the vagaries of classificatory preferences. In this second essay of 1749, Buffon was already drawing attention to the ability of animals and plants of particular kinds to self-replicate (that is, to mate and produce fertile offspring) as the appropriate criterion of species. By 1753, in the fourth volume of the *Histoire Naturelle*, he was prepared to offer a precise definition of the concept of species, based on the phenomenon of self-replication, rather than general similarities of form:

It is not the set of similar individuals that makes up the species, it is formed by a constant succession and uninterrupted renewal of the[se] individuals.[30]

But Buffon continued to be utterly opposed to the attempt to group species in higher taxa such as the genera or orders of Linnaeus's *Systema Naturae*.

Buffon's criterion of species had much to recommend it, both then and now. It got away from a search for 'essential' definitions or speculations about descent from original divinely-created pairs of animals or plants, and placed the emphasis firmly on functional observables. Species could be defined functionally, although this was not considered to be evidence that they had any special ontological status. Species, *per se*, had no being.

Subsequently, Buffon modified his stance of 1753 to some extent. Man, he suggested, could create genera by domestication[31] — that is, by altering the environmental conditions, he could cause an initial group to split up into a set of related but distinct species. In his summary of the natural history of the quadrupeds, published in 1766, Buffon suggested that something similar could also occur in the wild state.[32] From the single stock (*souche*) of horses, for example, there might have appeared zebras and asses. The total grouping now became known as a species. This avoided a difficulty which had become apparent to Buffon during the course of his investigations, namely that hybrids such as the mule were very occasionally found to be fertile. He referred to the splitting of a group into sub-groups in the course of time as a process of 'degeneration'. This, of course, is by no means the same as evolution, though it may be suggested that Buffon was groping towards this concept. It should be noted that the position adopted was close to the view held by Linnaeus at about the same time, that species had developed in the course of time out of the higher taxa.[33] Thus both Buffon and Linnaeus, although they began as non-evolutionists, moved some way towards evolutionary views during their lifetimes. But both were thinking more in terms of retrogression than progression.

We have seen that in 1749 Buffon placed man in the first rank of the animal hierarchy of the Great Chain of Being. So, like Linnaeus, Buffon was fully prepared to treat man as a part of the animal kingdom.[34] But did he consider that man was related to apes in any way? For example, might men and the orang-utan have diverged from some common stock? Could this ape be some kind of degenerate man? It seems that Buffon would have unhesitatingly replied 'No' to both these questions. The ape's apparent total inability to speak was still, for Buffon, a mark of an unbridgeable separation from man, even though they were so similar from a morphological point of view. Thus, despite the fact that Buffon left us some hints of thinking along evolutionary lines — at least to the extent of envisaging substantial changes during the course of time — he never allowed that man might be related to or descended from apes. If anything, apes were 'degenerate' men.

From the preceding discussions it should be apparent that although Linnaeus and Buffon presented markedly different aspects of the work of the eighteenth-century natural historian — Linneaus's views being most closely related to the Aristotelian tradition, whereas Buffon's ideas seemingly had roots in the neo-Platonic doctrine of the Great Chain of Being – the two men also had a good deal in common. They both worked within the intellectual framework of the eighteenth century. Their attentions were directed to the study of the external features of organisms. They did not attempt to relate these features to internal structures and functions, and although both were prepared to concede some changes in organisms over time, this did not amount to an evolutionary concept of one species changing in time into another, and so on indefinitely. Describing, naming and classifying were the chief objects of their inquiries. Both made some limited attempt to relate the characteristics of organisms to the conditions of the environment, but this did not entail the practice of anything resembling the modern science of ecology. Indeed, much of their work was carried out with dead and preserved specimens. There was no science of comparative anatomy. And although temporal changes were envisaged, there was no *historical* inquiry into the Earth's past, and its former organisms.[35] Nevertheless, Buffon should be recognized as an important precursor of Darwin in that he tackled a number of questions – such as geographical distribution and variation under domestication – from somewhat similar points of view.

NOTES CHAPTER 2

1   See W. Ison, *The Georgian Buildings of Bath from 1700 to 1830*, Faber, London, 1948, pp.154-156, Plate 5b and *passim*.
2   J. Haydn (H. C. R. Landon ed), *Sinfonia No. 79 Score*, Haydn-Mozart Presse, Salzburg, 1965.
3   This painting (1777-1789) is held by the National Gallery, Washington. A reproduction of it is to be found in E. H. Gombrich, *Art and Illusion: A Study in the Psychology of Pictorial Representation*, Pantheon, New York, 1960, p.54
4   See C. Hussey, *English Gardens and Landscapes 1700-1750*, Country Life, London, 1967, Frontispiece and Chapter 13.
5   Perhaps the most attractive account available in English of Linnaeus's life and work is W. Blunt, *The Compleat Naturalist: A Life of Linnaeus*, Collins, London, 1971.
6   C. Linnaeus, *Systema Naturae 1735: Facsimile of the First Edition With an introduction and a first English translation of the "Observationes" by Dr M. S. J. Engel-Ledeboer and Dr H. Engel*, B. de Graaf, Nieuwkoop, 1964; *Systema Vegetabilium*, Göttingen & Gotha, 1774.
7   Today, we think of lions as forming a species, rather than a genus. But Linnaeus offered no subdivision of his genus, *Leo* and the same term was used for the species which constituted this genus.
8   This gives only a much simplified account of Linnaeus's system. For a more detailed description see: J. L. Larsen, 'The species concept in Linnaeus', *Isis*, Vol. 69, 1968, pp.291-299.
9   C. Linnaeus, *The Elements of Botany*, London, 1775, p.38.
10   See A. G. Nathorst, 'Carl von Linné as a geologist', *Annual Report of the . . . Smithsonian Institution . . . for the year ending June 30, 1908*, Washington, 1909, pp.711-743.
11   Linnaeus's views are expounded in . . . *Oratio de Telluris Habitabilis Incremento. Et Andreae Celsii . . . Oratio de Mutationibus Generalioribus quae in Superficie Corporum Coelestium Contingunt . . .*, Leyden, 1744. It should be noted that his interest in changes in sea level was probably stimulated by the work of his compatriot, Emanuel Swedenborg as a geologist', in E. Swedenborg, *Opera quaedam aut Inedita aut Obsoleta: De Rebus Naturalibus*, 3 vols, Royal Swedish Academy of Sciences, Stockholm, 1907, Vol. 1

(*Geologica et Epistolae*), pp.xix-li; see also E. Wegmann, 'Changing ideas about moving shore lines', in C. J. Schneer (ed.), *Toward a History of Geology*, M.I.T. Press, Cambridge, Mass. & London, 1969, pp.386-414. The idea of life having originated in some high mountain region emerged later in the hypothesis that the West was colonised from the mountainous regions of central Asia, thereby giving rise to the pernicious Aryan myth. (See below, page 300).

12   See P. J. Brand, *Select Dissertations from the Amoenitates Academicae . . .*, Vol. 1, London, 1781, pp.119-120.

13   For a general discussion of this aspect of Linnaeus's philosophy of nature, see the introduction by C. Limoges to C. Linnaeus, *L'Equilibre de la Nature: I Oratio de Telluris Habitabilis Incremento (1744) Oeconomia Naturae (1749) Politia Naturae (1760) II Curiositas Naturalis (1748) Cui Bono (1752) . . .*, Vrin, Paris, 1972, pp.7-22.

14   See page 7 above. It should be noted also that in a number of Linnaeus's earlier writings he showed himself to be sympathetic to the doctrine of the Great Chain of Being. (See P. C. Ritterbush, *Overtures to Biology*, Yale University Press, New Haven & London, 1964, pp.109-115.) But in his later work he preferred the analogy of a map such as that illustrated in Figure 6.

15   For a discussion of eighteenth-century views on man's place in nature, see J. C. Greene, *The Death of Adam: Evolution and its Impact on Western Thought*, Mentor, New York, 1961, Chapter 6.

16   The comment was made by von Haller when reviewing Linnaeus's *Fauna Suecica* (Stockholm, 1746). See W. Blunt, *op. cit.* (note 5), p.122.

17   The engravings by Ehret were from C. Plumier (ed. J. Burman), *Plantarum Americanarum fasciculi*, Amsterdam, 1755-1760.

18   E. H. P. A. Haeckel, *Generelle Morphologie der Organismen*, 2 vols, Berlin, 1866, Vol. 1, p.238 and Vol. 2, p.286.

19   For an account of the episode, see J. L. Larsen, *Reason and Experience: The Representation of Natural Order in the Work of Carl von Linné*, California, U.P., Berkeley, Los Angeles & London, 1971, pp.99-104.

20   C. Linnaeus, *Systema Naturae . . .*, 13th edn, Vol. 2, Part 1, Leipzig, 1788, pp.viii-ix (translation by J. L. Larsen, *op. cit.* (note 8), p.297).

21   The plate is to be found in the following volume: *Caroli a Linné . . . Praelectiones in Ordines Naturales Plantarum: e proprio et J. C. Fabricii . . . Msto. edidit P. D. Giseke, . . . Accessit uberior Palmarum et Scitaminum Expositio praeter plurium novorum Generum reductiones*, Hamburg, 1792. It should be noted that Linnaeus had earlier suggested the analogy of a map: 'Nature doesn't make [sudden] jumps. All plants show affinities on all sides, like the territories in a geographical map' (*Philosophia Botanica . . .*, Stockholm, 1751, p.27).

22   A useful elementary account of Buffon's life and work is O. E. Fellows & S. F. Milliken, *Buffon*, Twayne, New York, 1972.

23   G. L. L. de Buffon, *Histoire Naturelle, Générale et Particulière, avec la Description du Cabinet du Roi*, 44 vols plus Atlas, Paris, 1749-1804. Only 35 volumes were completed in Buffon's life-time, and for these he received considerable assistance from several co-authors. The remaining volumes were the work of the Comte de Lacépède (1756-1825).

24   See particularly J. S. Wilkie, 'The idea of evolution in the writings of Buffon', *Annals of Science*, Vol. 12, 1956-1957, pp.48-63, 212-227, 255-266. For good general discussions of Buffon's biological work, see R. Wohl, 'Buffon and his project of a new science', *Isis*, Vol. 51, 1960, pp.186-199; P. L. Farber, 'Buffon and the concept of species', *Journal of the History of Biology*, Vol. 5, 1972, pp.259-284; P. R. Sloan, 'The Buffon-Linnaeus controversy', *Isis*, Vol. 67, 1976, pp.356-375; and O. E. Fellows & S. F. Milliken, *Buffon, op. cit.* (note 22), pp.112-124.

25   G. L. L. de Buffon, *op cit.* (note 23), Vol. 1, pp.12-13.

26   J. Locke, *An Essay Concerning Human Understanding*, Book III, Chapter 6, § 2 (ed. A. S. Pringle-Pattison, O.U.P., Oxford, 1924, p.242).

27   See, for example, M. H. Carré, *Realists and Nominalists*, O.U.P., London, 1946.

28   See above, p. 4, and J. Locke, *op. cit.* (note 26), Book III, Chapter 6, §§ 49-50 (ed. A. S. Pringle-Pattison, p.252).

29   G. L. L. de Buffon, 'Histoire des animaux', *op cit.* (note 23), Vol. 2, pp.1-426. (It should be noted that the first three volumes of the *Histoire naturelle* were all published together in 1749 and represented a synthesis of the ideas developed in the preceding decade.)

30   G. L. L. de Buffon, *op. cit.* (note 23), Vol. 4, 1753, p.384.

31   *Ibid.*, Vol. 11, 1753, p.369.

32   G. L. L. de Buffon, 'De la dégénération des animaux', *Ibid.*, Vol. 14, 1766, pp.311-374.

33   See above, page 21.

34   It was Linnaeus's categorisation of sloths with man that was partially responsible for Buffon's disapproval of the Swede's groupings of species in higher taxa.

35   There is, I suggest, an important distinction to be made between what we may call 'genetic' and *historical* accounts of the past. An historian rummages in archives and libraries, collects evidence, judges it critically and attempts to build up an account of the past on the basis of the evidence that has been accumulated. A paleontologist or stratigrapher may attempt to do something rather similar on the basis of empirical investigations of strata and fossils, thereby building up an historical account of the Earth's past. But an account of the past, such as that proposed by Linnaeus, in which the original hypothetical conditions – and the laws of change – are described, does not serve as an *historical* explanation of the world; the term 'genetic' is more suitable. For further discussion of the intended distinction between 'genetic' and 'historical' explanation in science, see my paper, 'Historicism and the rise of historical geology', *History of Science*, Vol. 17, 1979, pp.191-213.

3

Lamarck, Cuvier, Lyell

In this chapter, we shall consider three more of Darwin's important scientific predecessors, each of whom, in different ways, made a major contribution towards laying the foundations for Darwin's theory of 1859.

Lamarck
Jean Baptiste Pierre Antoine de Monet (1744-1829),[1] or the Chevalier de Lamarck as he is better known, is one of the most interesting and important — yet also poignant — figures in the history of biology. Indeed, he was one of the first persons to employ the new word, *biology*,[2] and this in itself is a point of some significance, for the neologism marked a profound change from the eighteenth-century studies in natural history, with emphasis on classifying and naming, to the new nineteenth-century science which studied animals and plants as *living* organisms, functioning as unified wholes that interact with the physical environment and with each other.

Lamarck's name is generally associated with a theory of evolution thought to be quite different from that of Darwin, although Darwin's theory was in fact somewhat similar to that of Lamarck in that they both believed that the environment could be a major determinant of evolutionary change, and they both accepted the notion of the inheritance of acquired characteristics.[3] Darwin had a very low opinion of Lamarck's work, which he criticised in the strongest terms in his private correspondence.[4] Moreover, Darwin notwithstanding, the principle of inheritance of acquired characteristics is no longer favoured in biology.[5] So, with Darwin's opposition and the modern biologist's rejection of one of the basic premises of Lamarck's evolutionism, Lamarck himself has in the past been a somewhat undervalued figure in the history of science. Yet it must be recognised that his work was of considerable influence in his own day, and in fact his role in the history of biology has been profound. Some points of his system should therefore be given careful attention here.

As a young man Lamarck served as a soldier, but he was discharged from the army as an invalid and subsequently studied medicine and botany, becoming intimate with Rousseau, and working with the eminent Swiss botanist, A. P. de Candolle (1778-1841). In 1778, he published a general flora of France,[6] and in 1788 he was appointed with the support of Buffon to a position at the *Jardin du Roi* (renamed the *Jardin des Plantes* after the Revolution). It was only at the age of 50 that Lamarck turned to zoology when he obtained a professorship at the great *Muséum d'Histoire Naturelle*, established by the National Convention in 1793. Yet even there, Lamarck's position was considered to be one of inferior rank. His previous work had been primarily botanical, and it is said that he was given responsibility for the lowly invertebrates when no one else showed any interest in the appointment in this field. Moreover, Lamarck's ideas were at odds with those of the influential Georges Cuvier (1769-1832), who held a dominating position in French science and Government at the time. As secretary to the *Institut de France*, Cuvier was responsible for the presentation of Lamarck's funeral eulogy after he died, blind and poor, in 1829.[7] It is believed that Cuvier to some degree misrepresented and denigrated Lamarck's theoretical opinions in the eulogy and that this was at least part of the reason why his work was subsequently neglected to such a degree.

Although part of his career was in the nineteenth century, much of Lamarck's thinking was characteristic of the previous century, or earlier. For example, he adhered to the venerable theory of the four elements (earth, water, air, and fire) long after this doctrine had been superseded by the new chemistry of the Lavoisier school. And his biological theory was in effect a much modified version of the ancient doctrine of the Great Chain of Being, though he did not approve of the ideas of its chief exponent, Charles Bonnet. On the other hand, Lamarck's evolutionism had certain nineteenth-century characteristics, though even in this — which has at times led to his being hailed as a forerunner of Darwin — earlier ways of thinking were still prominent.

Only three of Lamarck's many writings need be noted here:

1 *Recherches sur l'Organisation des Corps Vivans*, 1802,[8] which contained a statement of the *idea* of evolution;
2 *Philosophie Zoologique*, 1809,[9] which contained a statement of how evolution might occur, given in two laws; and
3 *Histoire Naturelle des Animaux sans Vertèbres*, 1815-1822,[10] which contained four laws of evolution, instead of the two of 1809, and many examples of the application of the evolutionary doctrine to invertebrate animals.

In 1809, the two 'laws of nature, which are always verified by observation' were given as:

(a) In every animal which has not passed the limit of its development, a more frequent and continuous use of any organ gradually strengthens, develops and enlarges that organ, and gives it a power proportional to the length of time it has been so used; while the permanent disuse of any organ imperceptibly weakens and deteriorates it, and progressively diminishes its functional capacity, until it finally disappears.

(b) All the acquisitions or losses wrought by nature on individuals, through the influence of the environment in which their race has long been placed, and hence through the influence of the predominant use or permanent disuse of any organ; all these are preserved by reproduction to the new individuals which arise, provided that the acquired modifications are common to both sexes, or at least to the individuals which produce the young.[11]

In the *Histoire Naturelle des Animaux sans Vertèbres* these were expanded to:

(a) Life, by its internal forces, tends continually to increase the volume of every body that possesses it, as well as to increase the size of all the parts of the body up to a limit which it brings about.[12]

(b) The production of a new organ in an animal body results from a new need [*besoin*] which this need originates and maintains.[13]

(c) The development of organs and their force [or power] of action are always in proportion to the employment of these organs.[14] (This corresponds to the first law of 1809.)

(d) All that has been acquired, marked on [*tracé*] or altered during the organisation of individuals in the course of their life is preserved by generation, and transmitted to new individuals which proceed from those which have undergone these changes.[15] (This corresponds to the second law of 1809. It is what is usually known as the principle of the inheritance of acquired characteristics.)

On the basis of these laws (*if* they are true), it is easy to see how evolutionary development could occur. The example often given in popular expositions is that of a blacksmith, who by the exercise of his trade develops biceps of exceptional strength. If the principle of inheritance of acquired characteristics is correct, then it would follow that the sons of the blacksmith would be endowed with powerful biceps to an even greater degree, or would develop them with less effort or more quickly than is customary. And so the process might continue from generation to generation in the blacksmith's family, yielding men with ever increasing muscular development – until the requirements of the 'environment' are met.

In Chapter 7 of his *Zoological Philosophy*, entitled 'The influence of the environment on the activities and habits of animals', Lamarck gave numerous examples of this kind of argument. For example, he wrote of the giraffe, which

> is known to live in the interior of Africa in places where the soil is nearly always arid and barren, so that it is obliged to browse on the leaves of trees and to make constant efforts to reach them. From this habit long maintained in all its race, it has resulted that the animal's fore-legs have become longer than its hind legs and that its neck is lengthened to such a degree that the giraffe, without standing up on its hind legs, attains a height of six metres.[16]

Or:

> Snakes . . . have adopted the habit of crawling on the ground and hiding in the grass; so that their body, as a result of continually repeated efforts at elongation for the purpose of passing through narrow spaces, has a considerable length, quite out of proportion to its size.[17]

But the legs, little used in these circumstances, have atrophied. In general, Lamarck supposed that organisms made 'efforts' to meet the exigencies of their environment. Their bodies were modified accordingly, and the modifications were transmitted to subsequent generations, thereby producing evolutionary changes.

These illustrations provide an approximate view of the Lamarckian theory, but they do not give full justice to all the complexities of his teaching and of his system. As we have seen, Lamarck held a version of the ancient doctrine of the Great Chain of Being. Yet it was unlike the typical eighteenth-century version, for it was not conceived as a rigid, static structure. By their struggle or striving to meet the requirements of the environment, and with the help of the principle of the inheritance of acquired characteristics, organisms could supposedly work their way up the Chain — from microbe to man, so to speak. And man, as he exists today, was by no means the final limit of evolutionary possibilities. In Lamarck's view, the Chain could be extended indefinitely in the future. Moreover, new creatures were constantly appearing at the bottom of the Chain, arising from inorganic matter through spontaneous generation — a point that will be discussed further below. Ascent of the Chain involved a continuous process of complexification, due to the so-called 'power of life'.

C. C. Gillispie has suggested the attractive metaphor of an 'escalator of being' as a means of portraying Lamarck's doctrine.[18] A. O. Lovejoy, on the other hand, has spoken of the 'temporalizing' of the Great Chain of Being, meaning that the Chain supposedly grew and developed in the course of *time.*[19] Both of these are useful ways of envisaging an important aspect of Lamarck's theory. However, it should be noted that in a famous diagram in the *Zoological Philosophy,* Lamarck presented a branched Chain rather than a single line, for he had come to realise that it was quite impossible to represent the whole of the animal kingdom by means of just one linear continuum. On the other hand, the idea of 'movement' of organisms along each of the branches was the same as might be expected if the Chain were simple and linear.

In the eighteenth century, the term 'evolution' meant something rather different from what it does today. At that time, the word was normally used to refer to the gradual 'unfolding' of *immanent* qualities, as for example in the development of an embryo or a seed.[21] It was a *quasi*-Aristotelian process in which the potentialities of something were gradually actualised, rather as a Japanese paper flower unfolds in water. In certain respects, Lamarck's system was something like this. In a sense, his progression of organisms *was* analogous to an unfolding of immanent qualities. Yet there was also the idea of one kind of organism changing into another in the course of time — an important aspect of the modern understanding of the evolutionary process. Thus, in the *Zoological Philosophy* we read that:

> . . . after a long succession of generations . . . individuals, originally belonging to one species, become at length transformed into a new species distinct from the first.[22]

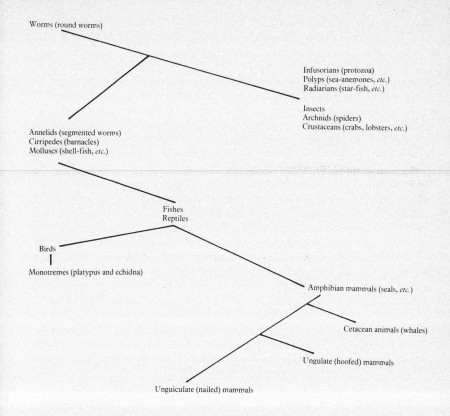

Figure 7 Table 'showing the origin of the various animals', according to Lamarck (1809).[20]

This is a clear statement of an evolutionary view, in a modern sense. But it should be noted that Lamarck, unlike Darwin, was not primarily concerned with the problem of the origin of discrete species. And although change occurred constantly, organisms did *not* become extinct in Lamarck's system.

In the previous chapter we contrasted Linnaeus's emphasis on taxonomy with Buffon's interest in species defined in terms of reproductive capacity and his repudiation of higher-order taxa. Lamarck took a view that may be regarded as intermediate between these two positions. In his *Flore Françoise* he suggested that there *was* a natural arrangement for plants and this consisted in their placement in linear array from the least to the most 'perfect'. (The criteria for perfection were obscure, but were probably influenced in part, at least, by ancient doctrines associated with Aristotle's *Scala natura.*) Then each genus would have only two natural neighbours: one above and one below on the scale. So classification of animals and plants, for Lamarck, was apparently not a purely arbitrary matter, as a hard-line nominalist might suppose. But on the other hand a *continuum* up the scale was envisaged, so that taxonomic divisions would presumably have to be arbitrary to some degree. Seemingly the theory was slightly incoherent.

Lamarck's ideas were intertwined with his chemical, physical and geological theories in a number of interesting ways. In the eighteenth century, it was usual to postulate various 'subtle fluids' to account for particular phenomena such as combustion, magnetic, electrical and thermal effects.[23] Lamarck made much use of such explanatory devices in his 'zoological philosophy', proposing, for example, that a 'subtle penetrating vapour' produced by the male might be responsible for the process of fertilisation.[24] Moreover, the process of spontaneous generation might be held to take place in a process analogous to that which occurs in fertilisation, with 'subtle surrounding fluids' acting upon mucilaginous matter suspended in water, thereby producing cellular tissue.[25] The agent for this process of spontaneous generation was believed to be distributed throughout the Earth, particularly in hot climates.

For the simplest organisms of the Lamarckian Chain of Being, it was supposed that they were actually animated 'by the influence of the subtle surrounding fluids, such as caloric[26] and electricity, which stimulate in them the movements constituting life'.[27] Thus at these low levels of being it was the external environment that was held responsible for the very phenomenon of life. But then:

> These subtle fluids moving incessantly in the interior of their bodies soon carve out special routes which they always follow till new ones are open to them . . . Hence . . . the appearance of an irresistible propensity to carry out movements which, when continued or repeated, give rise to habits.[28]

And these habits could supposedly be transmitted to subsequent generations. Gradually, the exterior force of the environment could be 'interiorised',[29] and so the evolution of organisms might proceed, with ever increasing complexification.

Such a model could supposedly account for the establishment of instinctive behaviour patterns, with the 'nervous fluid' flowing in particular nerve channels. And ultimately organisms might develop an autonomous will of their own.[30] On the basis of such a model, Lamarck sought also to develop a psychological theory of considerable interest; but the details of this need not concern us here. We should note, however, that while the environment supposedly exerted its influence with total directness for the lower organisms, the more complex creatures would only respond indirectly to the conditions presented by the environment, by the flow of fluids to appropriate parts of the body, thus producing development or degeneration of particular parts according to the organisms' needs. Also, acquired habits and organic parts could come to be fixed in subsequent generations, but Lamarck said little about the mechanism whereby this transmission of acquired characters might take place.

In geology, Lamarck was what is today often referred to as a *uniformitarian*.[31] His major geological treatise, *Hydrogéologie (1802)*,[32]

offered a 'cyclic' theory of the Earth, with an endless success.
transgressions and retrogressions, and no overall directionalist tr
various processes that have been described above, Lamarck belie
organisms might constantly adapt themselves to their environments, a
'needs' arose from the changes in geological conditions. Fossils represented ...e
remains of organisms whose descendants had been forced by changing
circumstances to undergo biological modification. But they were not *extinct*
kinds in our sense, for Lamarck never envisaged kinds dying out, but always
being modified to new forms in the course of ages. He could not conceive any
process or agent that might cause the extinction of a species.

There was, in Lamarck's system, a kind of order and economy of nature, just
as there had been in Linnaeus's 'balanced' system of nature. But it will be
appreciated that what Lamarck proposed was a dynamic condition of order,
rather than the brittle, static composition of Linnaeus. The break-up of the
eighteenth-century world of classical order and harmony was beginning to
manifest itself in Lamarck's new biology.

A few words may be included here about the origins of Lamarck's
evolutionary ideas. Lamarck himself gave some account of this at the
beginning of his *Zoological Philosophy*.[33] He tells us that he was trying to
establish certain general zoological principles when preparing material for his
teaching, and he noted the variation in complexity of animals from the least to
the most perfect. According to what Lamarck says here, this led him to the view
that 'nature had successively produced the different bodies endowed with life,
from the simplest worm upwards'.[34]

But a recent paper by R. W. Burkhardt presents a rather different view of the
matter.[35] Burkhardt maintains that Lamarck arrived at his evolutionary
hypothesis in the period 1799-1800, as a result of his particular interest in
conchology at that time. At that period there was considerable discussion in
Paris about whether fossil shells had modern counterparts which might, for
instance, be found in hitherto unexplored parts of the oceans. Lamarck, as a
professor of invertebrate zoology, was regarded as an expert on this question,
and his opinion was solicited. Still holding to aspects of the eighteenth-
century doctrine of the economy of nature, he was not prepared to entertain the
possibility of extinction. But it certainly seemed that particular forms were no
longer to be found alive. So, almost willynilly, he was driven to the conclusion
that evolution of organisms had occurred.

The later history of Lamarckism, after Lamarck's death, is one of
extraordinary interest, though by no means easy to disentangle. Lamarck's
ideas were not highly regarded by his peers, and Cuvier, giving the impression
that Lamarck believed that animals simply evolved according to their 'wants'
or 'desires', rather than their needs as laid down by the requirements of the
environment, almost completely destroyed Lamarck's reputation for many
years, although it must be confessed that by writing of the *'sentiment intérieur'*
of certain animals fairly high in the Chain (though below man)[36] Lamarck
undoubtedly laid himself open to easy criticism, and perhaps also
misrepresentation or misunderstanding. Charles Lyell, however, read

Lamarck carefully and gave a balanced account of his ideas in the *Principles of Geology* (1830-1833).[37] Darwin, as we have noted above, represented himself as being quite opposed to Lamarck's doctrines, but it was the ideas of spontaneous generation, subtle fluids, and organisms striving to fit themselves to the circumstances of the environment that Darwin and other critics found unacceptable. About the doctrine of inheritance of acquired characteristics there was no demur, and as we shall see further in Chapter 10, Darwin made much use of this concept himself, particularly in the latter part of his career. Darwin, however, did not suppose that the 'inner feelings' of organisms were in any way responsible for the acquisition of the new characteristics.

Lamarckism is understood by modern biologists largely as a synonym for the principle of the inheritance of acquired characteristics, or as a process whereby changes in the body cells produce changes in the reproductive cells. Also, the inheritance of acquired behaviour patterns is usually regarded as a variant of Lamarckism, and there has been considerable dispute about whether this process does or does not take place in animals.[38] It should be noted that the environment can in fact produce inheritable changes, as, for example, when radiation produces genetic damage. But this does not count as Lamarckian inheritance, *sensu strictu.* The body cells have not been the agents of genetic change; and certainly the organisms have not been changing according to their needs, as Lamarck's theory envisaged. When biologists have sought empirical evidence for Lamarck's theory, they have looked for such things as — to take a simplistic example — the transmission of acquired suntans from mother to infant, and it appears that positive evidence for *this* kind of change is not forthcoming.[39] However, the controversies about the role of 'nature' and 'nurture' in evolution, and particularly about matters of social concern are by no means finished. The issue of 'nature and nurture' in educational theory and policy is now being actively debated. These points will be pursued further below, especially in Chapter 13.

In later chapters I will on occasions refer to the term 'Neo-Lamarckism', in relation to the later appearance of Lamarck's doctrines, either in whole or in part, and either with or without modification. For the most part, one may say that a Neo-Lamarckian is a proponent of the doctrine that evolution may occur through the mechanism of the inheritance of acquired characteristics, the characteristics having been acquired in response to the 'stimuli' provided by the environment. I would not wish to suggest that a Neo-Lamarckian is a supporter of Lamarck's speculations about spontaneous generation or 'subtle fluids'. However, in the case of one or two of the Neo-Lamarckians we will encounter below, such as Samuel Butler and George Bernard Shaw, the conceptual (though not necessarily the historical) links are very close indeed, with the idea that organisms might evolve according to their efforts being particularly prominent in some of Shaw's writings.[40] And the Nietzchean doctrine of 'will to power' has a very strong Lamarckian ring.[41] Clearly, Lamarck, or the theory he espoused, has played a role of considerable importance in the development of Western thought, and it is really in no way surprising that his admirers maintain that he has been unjustly treated by history.[42]

Cuvier

While Lamarck held the supposedly inferior professorship of invertebrate zoology at the *Muséum d'Histoire Naturelle,* his powerful and influential peer, Georges Cuvier (1769-1832),[43] held the much more exalted position of professor of vertebrate zoology at the same institution, and greatly excited the public imagination by his reconstructions of giant extinct mammals and reptiles. Lamarck's later years were always overshadowed by his brilliant and extrovert colleague, and it was chiefly the Cuvierian system that provided the biological paradigm in the first half of the nineteenth century. It was against this paradigm and its ramifications that Darwin's arguments were principally aimed, either directly or indirectly, although as we will see below, the issue is not really so clear-cut as has sometimes been supposed.

Cuvier was a man of extraordinary intellectual powers capable of work of fundamental importance in many different fields, both as a scientist and administrator. But he is chiefly remembered today for his theoretical contributions to geology and zoology, and especially to comparative anatomy. His early work was carried out in the late eighteenth century on the bones of living and extinct animals of the elephant type, including the Siberian mammoth. A description of these bones was published in 1799,[44] and in that paper Cuvier gave his first account of the principles of the new science which he came to establish: comparative anatomy.

We have seen that in the work of Linnaeus there was an attempt to build up a systematic classification of animals and plants, based upon the examination of a limited number of external characteristics. Little attention was paid to internal features, and there was not much concern with the ways in which the different parts of organisms were related to, or interacted with, one another. For since Linnaeus's program was chiefly the classification and naming of organisms, for which complete specimens were provided, it was hardly necessary to go deeper than the readily visible external features. Besides, the eighteenth-century delight in external order, and harmony of form, would have been a disincentive to the consideration of interior characteristics, invisible without the aid of a scalpel.[45] But the methods of Linnaean natural history would not have been of much use to Cuvier when dealing with jumbled heaps of fossil bones. Consequently, Cuvier found it necessary to devise a new approach that would enable him to meet the requirements of the new problems, namely the reconstruction of vertebrate fossils, and the attempt to envisage what the total organism might have been like, using incomplete specimens as evidence.

Cuvier's basic premise was that any organism is so adapted to its environment (or 'conditions of existence') that it can *function* successfully in that environment. And for this adaptation to be successful, all the parts must cohere to form a *viable* whole, suited to the conditions of existence. If, for example, an animal is a land-living carnivore, it must have lungs for breathing, suitable limbs and muscles for running and catching its prey, teeth to tear the flesh, and a suitable stomach and intestine for the digestion of the meat. Also there must be a suitable nervous system (with appropriate sense organs) to activate all the parts of the body. In other words, all the parts must be suitably correlated so that the organism can successfully meet the requirements of the conditions of existence. This is Cuvier's well-known *principle of the correlation of parts.* In his own words:

> In the living state, organs are not merely brought together [*rapprochés*], but they act one on the other and co-operate towards a common end. Accordingly, modifications of any one of them have an effect on all the others. Such modifications as are incompatible with one another reciprocally exclude themselves, whereas others are called into being, so to speak; and this applies not only for organs that have a direct inter-relationship but also for those that at first sight seem furthest apart and most independent.[46]

Cuvier also stated a second leading anatomical postulate, known as the *principle of subordination of characters:*

> The separate parts of every being must . . . possess a mutual adaptation; there are, therefore, certain peculiarities of conformation which exclude others, and some again which necessitate the existence of others. When we know any given peculiarities to exist in a particular being, we may calculate what can and what cannot exist in conjunction with them. The most obvious, marked, and predominant of these, those which exercise the greatest influence over the totality of such a being, are denominated its *important or leading characters*; others of minor consideration are termed *subordinate.*[47]

In accordance with this principle, Cuvier supposed that certain fundamental parts show little variation from one species to another. The mammalian heart, for example, an organ of fundamental importance, shows little variation from one species to the next, except in size. On the other hand peripheral parts such as teeth, skin or feet display enormous variety. These, however, are only subordinate characters.

Cuvier's argument, then, was that the fundamental parts, which show little variability, should provide the main basis for a system of classification. The major divisions (which Cuvier termed '*embranchements*') should be based on a consideration of the fundamental unvarying anatomical parts. Lower divisions (into species, for example) could rest on subordinate characters. This was to be the basis of Cuvier's taxonomy, but it required a decision about which of the major body systems should be deemed the most fundamental. After considering the various possibilities, such as the means of locomotion or the circulatory system, he decided upon the choice of the nervous system, though in fact this was to some degree arbitrary.[48] It was, however, in good accord with the principles that have just been outlined.

So, using the nervous system as his criterion, Cuvier reckoned that the animal kingdom could be divided into four main *embranchements,* which gave him the arrangement shown in Figure 8.[49]

Figure 8 Subdivision of the Animal Kingdom into four 'Embranchements' *according to Cuvier (1812).*

First *Embranchement* (Vertebrates) (These possess a single main spinal nerve cord, and brain.)
    Class 1 Mammals
    Class 2 Birds
    Class 3 Reptiles
    Class 4 Fish
Second *Embranchement* (Molluscs) (These have many scattered nerve masses (ganglia) interconnected by 'nervous threads'.)
    Class 1 Cephalopods (Cuttle-fish, Squids, *etc.*)
    Class 2 Gasteropods (Snails, *etc.*)
    Class 3 Pteropods (Small free-swimming marine creatures, with wing-like appendages)
    Class 4 Acephala (Lamellibranchs or Pelecypods)
Third *Embranchement* (Jointed or segmented animals) (These have two ventral nerve cords, with distinct ganglia at intervals.)
    Class 1 Worms
    Class 2 Crustaceans (Lobsters, *etc.*)
    Class 3 Spiders
    Class 4 Insects
Fourth *Embranchement* (Zoophytes, *i.e.*, resembling both animals and plants, also called Radiata) (These have no special nervous system or sense organs.)
    Class 1 Sea urchins, Starfish
    Class 2 Intestinal animals (Mostly Nemotode worms)
    Class 3 Polyps (Corals, Sea anemones, Hydra, *etc.*)
    Class 4 Infusorians (*I.e.*, animals found in 'infusions', mainly Protozoa)

It must be admitted that to some degree Cuvier was arguing in a variety of logical circles. The taxonomy was supposedly based on the major postulates of the new science of comparative anatomy. But in fact, in order to arrive at the four main *embranchements*, Cuvier must have surveyed the nervous systems of the members of the animal kingdom and noted that there appeared to be four main types, which apparently correlated with other observable broad anatomical differences. The observations of nature led to the principles, and the principles led back to the description of nature. But this is not necessarily methodologically vicious. It is, rather, an exemplification of the very ancient methodological procedure of 'Analysis' and 'Synthesis'.[50] And although Cuvier was to some degree guilty of proving what he was already assuming, the overall result of his investigations was certainly fruitful.

It should be noted that in setting up his four discrete *embranchements* of the animal kingdom, Cuvier was doing away entirely with the concept of the Great Chain of Being. The old idea of a continuum of nature was swept away, though the ancient Aristotelian doctrine of differences in degree of 'perfection' was perhaps still present.

Unlike Lamarck, with his 'temporalised' version of the Great Chain of Being doctrine, Cuvier's system of four *embranchements* was wholly non-evolutionary, or fixist, in character. The only organisms that could exist were those that were viable within the constraints laid down by the conditions of existence. This was a fundamental postulate of Cuvier's zoological system.

And the four *embranchements* represented four general ways in which organisms might meet the conditions of existence on this planet. By this line of reasoning, any organism that might be created in some way outside the confines of one of the four *embranchements* would necessarily fail to be viable. Deviation from the four main patterns would supposedly yield organisms that would not have all their parts correlated satisfactorily, and consequently would fail to meet the conditions of existence. Therefore, such organisms could not survive, even if they did happen to be created as 'monsters'. Again, there is some question-begging here, but this need not concern us. The point to note is that according to the postulates of Cuvier's zoology, evolution could not in principle occur. Change could only be for the worse, so to speak, and therefore it could not and would not occur. It may readily be appreciated, therefore, how the Cuvierian system might stand in the way of Darwin's evolutionary doctrines.

Cuvier, it should be emphasised, was a geologist and vertebrate paleontologist as well as a zoologist and comparative anatomist.[51] And it was well known at the beginning of the nineteenth century that the stratigraphical column[52] shows very clear evidence for many changes in animal forms; changes which could well incline the observer to accept some kind of evolution. How, then, did Cuvier reconcile the stratigraphical column as it was known in his day with the principles of his non-evolutionary biology?

The theoretical answer that Cuvier gave to this question was provided in the Preface which he wrote to accompany his major palaeontological work, the celebrated *Recherches sur les Ossemens Fossiles*.[53] The Preface, or *Discours Preliminaire*, was later published as a separate work with the title *Discours sur les Rèvolutions du Globe*.[54] For a number of years, this became one of the major statements of theoretical geology, and the theories it espoused were widely adopted.

Cuvier proposed that the geological history of the globe was interrupted from time to time by great 'revolutions' or 'catastrophes', and these catastrophes were supposedly responsible for bringing to a close each major stratigraphical sequence, killing off all the creatures living in the parts of the globe where the catastrophes were presumed to have occurred. Then, after each catastrophe, things settled down and the stricken area was restocked with new forms, different from those which had previously been living there.[55] On this basis, the stratigraphic column looked something like that shown in Figure 9, according to Cuvier's ideas on the matter.[56]

But, one may ask, where did the new forms that were so clearly apparent after each major break in the stratigraphic column come from? How was an area restocked after a catastrophe had wiped out earlier forms? As we have seen, Cuvier did not allow the possibility of evolutionary change. He believed that there had been an original (divine?) creation of animal forms, but these were only supposed to have shown minor variations since the time of creation. So evolutionary change could not provide a solution to Cuvier's difficulty. In answer to the problem, therefore, he proposed that after each catastrophe the destroyed organisms were replaced by migrations from neighbouring

Figure 9 Geological and Paleontological Successions as Understood by Cuvier (after Coleman)

Period	Deposit	Fossils	Catastrophe
Modern	Alluvia	Contemporary species only	Certain (Noah's flood?)
	Standstones, fresh-water deposits, loose transported material	Mastodons, Mammoths, Rhinoceros- and Hippopotamus-like animals, marine and fresh-water shells and fish	
Tertiary?			Probable
	Gypsum	*Paleotherium, Anoplotherium,* marine shells and fish	
			Probable
	Rough limestone	First mammals, marine shells and fish	
			Certain
	Limestone	Maestricht' animal, marine shells and fish	
Secondary?			Probable
	Below the limestone	*Ichthyosaurus, Plesiosaurus,* Thuringian monitors	
			Probable
Primary?	Deeper deposits	No quadrupeds, only fish and shells	
			?
	Transition rocks Primitive rocks	No fossils	
Ancient			

unaffected areas.

To illustrate this hypothesis we may consider a simple example. If Australia were suddenly devastated by some major geological catastrophe it might subsequently be restocked from South-East Asia by pouchless mammals that would replace the previous pouched forms. To a paleontologist investigating the situation a million years later it might well appear that there had been a sudden and catastrophic removal of one set of creatures and a sudden creation of new forms to replace them. In fact, however, there would have been no 'special creation' of new forms.

The obvious difficulty facing Cuvier's solution to the problem was that if there were a long succession of catastrophes there would be a gradual whittling away of forms, rather than the apparent increase and complexification that could seemingly be observed in the stratigraphical column. But, to my knowledge, Cuvier did not discuss this difficulty, although it was presumably evident to his contemporaries, for the generally accepted view of geologists in the 1820s (particularly in Britain) was that there were divinely-caused *special creations* of organisms after each geological catastrophe. This meshed well with the characteristic fundamentalist natural theology that was commonly espoused in the period. The Oxford geologist, William Buckland (1784-1856), for example, explicitly identified the last of Cuvier's geological catastrophes with the Biblical flood, and he made a considerable reputation for himself by his investigations of cave deposits, which were supposedly emplaced by the deluge of Noah.[57] Buckland's interpretations were highly regarded in Darwin's younger days, by both scientists and laymen.

Before concluding our brief consideration of Cuvier's work one other point should be raised. It has been suggested above that Cuvier's anti-Lamarckism and anti-evolutionism would probably have stood in the way of Darwin's views. Cuvier's zoology and Darwin's evolutionary theory were seemingly quite antithetical. But this is not, I think, exactly the way in which the matter should be interpreted.

Referring once again to Linnaeus's early tables representing the economy of nature, such as that of the animal kingdom illustrated above on page 16, we recall their non-evolutionary characteristics. The basic framework of the system — the fundamental layout of the major taxa[58] — was supposedly established at the time of the Creation. New groups might perhaps appear within the major pigeon holes of the tables, but these holes were themselves quite fixed. And conceptually, because of the static economy of nature, and because the tables were based on a hierarchy of signs (according to the external features of the organisms), all these pigeon holes were fused together, so to speak. Change of the orders or classes with respect to each other was a theoretical impossibility in the Linnaean system.

But Cuvier's system, though at first sight somewhat similar, was really fundamentally different. For the higher groupings of Cuvier's taxonomy each represented definite organisational types. Each higher grouping (as well as each species) had its particular anatomical and physiological characteristics, appropriate to their functions within the conditions of the environment. So the incubus of nominalism was dispelled. For Cuvier, genera, orders and classes 'existed', as did species (which had long been definable in terms of reproductive capacity). But the particular anatomical and physiological structures and functions formed part of the conditions of existence of an organism, as much as the exterior conditions, for all the parts of the organism had to function together smoothly if it were to be viable. Each individual, therefore, because of the principle of subordination of characters, carried within itself, so to speak, the class, order, genus and species to which it belonged. This was not so in the Linnaean table, where a system of external marks or signs had to serve as a classificatory basis.

Cuvier, then, wrenched the Linnaean table of animals apart to produce the four *embranchements*. These were now 'freed' from each other, as it were, and although each was static in Cuvier's representation of the theory, it was open to some other person to develop an evolutionary theory by allowing the component parts of the table to develop separately with respect to one another in the course of time. For the new links were thought to lie in the interrelationships with the environment (both 'internal' and 'external'), rather than in the relationships with the other parts of the table, in the 'economy' of nature. If this argument is correct, then, it follows that *the route from Linnaeus to Darwin lay through the work of the anti-evolutionist Cuvier, as much as the evolutionist Lamarck.*[59]

Cuvier, however, was not the only theoretical stepping-stone linking Linneaus's natural history and Darwin's evolutionism. Another important link was provided by the work of the British geologist, Charles Lyell.

Lyell

Charles Lyell (1797-1875)[60] was a gifted and wealthy man who was a close friend of Darwin for many years and perhaps had the greatest intellectual influence on him. Lyell studied at Exeter College, Oxford, with the intention of becoming a lawyer, but his interest in geology was stimulated while still an undergraduate through his voluntary attendance at the lectures of William Buckland, from whom he gained an understanding of the basic principles of geological science, seen from a catastrophist standpoint. After graduating, Lyell spent some time in London practising law, but he found this work irksome, and eventually decided to give it up in favour of a career in geology. As he was of independent means, Lyell was able to do this without difficulty. He travelled widely, sought the company of eminent geologists, including Cuvier, and soon found himself elected to the position of Secretary of the Geological Society of London.

It did not take Lyell long to come to the conclusion that the catastrophist doctrines of Cuvier and Buckland, and their many followers, could not be sustained.[61] He objected to catastrophism chiefly on methodological grounds, for he considered it foolish to invoke causes in scientific explanations (such as the catastrophes of Cuvier's theory) for which there were no modern analogues that might be investigated empirically. In Lyell's view, if there was no analogy with present causes or processes, any kind of vague or wild speculation would be permissible — and the proffered explanations would simply cease to be scientific. But, in addition to this methodological argument, Lyell also reckoned that there was much empirical evidence to justify the view that geological changes occurred as a result of the slow and steady action of present-day forces, rather than occasional cataclysmic events.

Lyell's ideas were synthesised in his celebrated *Principles of Geology* (1830-1833),[62] which ran to twelve editions, the exposition being constantly revised as geological knowledge increased during the course of the nineteenth century.[63] Lyell's geological system was *open-ended* and *non-directionalist*, in contrast to the views of most of his contemporaries, who believed in an initial creation of the Earth and a subsequent directionalist history. Lyell also believed that the Earth was of extreme age (of the order of hundreds or thousands of millions of years).[64] Some of his contemporaries still believed that the Earth was created in 4004 BC, according to the seventeenth-century estimate of Bishop Ussher — though by the 1820s most scientists, including the catastrophists, believed the planet was much older than this. They were, however, reluctant to offer precise estimates.

Developing ideas published by the Scottish geologist James Hutton (1726-1797) in 1795,[65] Lyell supposed that the different parts of the Earth's crust were all slowly rising or falling quite randomly so that the configurations of the oceans and continents were constantly changing, with erosion and deposition of sediment occurring correspondingly. Changes in the level of the land might sometimes be accompanied by severe earthquakes, but these were never of the paroxysmal violence that the catastrophists envisaged. Lyell cited the evidence of the Temple of Serapis on the Mediterranean coast near Naples. This Roman temple had three columns still standing which were marked by the borings of marine shells at a height of fourteen to twenty-three feet above the present sea level. This indicated that the land had fallen and risen by at least twenty-three feet since Roman times, without the columns toppling over. This was one of Lyell's strongest empirical arguments for slow and steady geological changes, although he had many others.

Lyell agreed that there would be constant changes in climatic conditions because of the variations in the configurations of the oceans and continents. But he supposed that these changes would be of limited extent, and would be non-directional. How did he reconcile this theory with the apparent 'directed' character of the stratigraphical column?

The solution to this problem, in Lyell's view, was to propose that while the major groups of organisms had (so far as one could tell) always been present, or had been present since the original creation, individual species had appeared and disappeared from time to time as the geological environment fluctuated. We may represent this idea by means of the diagram in Figure 10, though such a figure is not to be found anywhere in Lyell's own works.

This theory was more or less compatible with observations.[66] The fact that birds, for example, were not known from the lowest members of the stratigraphical column, whereas invertebrate remains were common in the older rocks, was explained away by suggesting that vertebrate remains were not preserved as easily as invertebrates. And what appeared to be great breaks in the stratigraphical column were not seen as evidence for great geological catastrophes but simply as indications of long periods of non-deposition, when a particular area might have been dry land. The theory was not, however, wholly in accord with Lyell's own methodological maxims, for no one had actually seen a new species come into being in modern times.

Figure 10 shows that according to Lyell's theory there would be a slow turnover of species, and accordingly this could be used as a basis for the division of the Tertiary rocks, classifying them according to the percentage of still-extant fossils they contained.[67] The Secondary and Tertiary rocks had almost no fossils in common, which implied that the time interval separating these two epochs was greater than the time that had elapsed during the whole of the Tertiary — assuming, that is, that the rate of turnover of species was

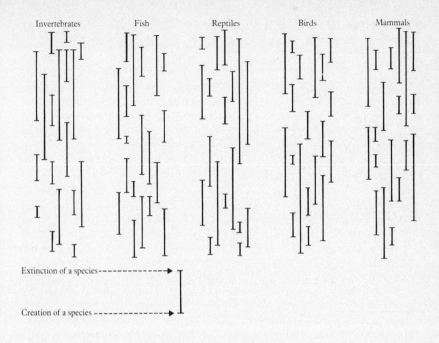

Figure 10 Diagrammatic Representation of Lyell's Theory of Creations and Extinctions of Organisms

constant. This, of course, followed from the major premise of uniformitarianism in *Principles of Geology.*

It is interesting to note that Lyell envisaged a strong degree of 'environmental determinism' in his theory, for he maintained that if the appropriate geological conditions should ever recur, one might look forward to the re-appearance on Earth of such long-extinct creatures as the iguanodon.[68] The appearance of the new species must therefore have been linked to the conditions of the environment in some manner. But Lyell was extremely reticent about the actual mechanism whereby the creation of new species might have occurred, or how the environment might determine the forms of organisms existing at different epochs.

Lyell's system was never adopted very widely in all its details, despite its very considerable influence, for it did not square sufficiently well with the fairly obvious directionalist character of the stratigraphical column.[69] On the other hand, the ideas of uniformity of process, the alterations of the levels of the land and the sea, and the great age of the Earth, became widely accepted in scientific circles in the middle years of the nineteenth century. Darwin made known his ideas on evolution to Lyell some time before their public declaration in *The Origin of Species.* And in his later life Lyell somewhat reluctantly accepted Darwin's new theory. But he was probably never entirely happy with it. Having staked his early reputation on the doctrine of non-progressionism, it is not perhaps surprising that Lyell was so reluctant to accept the progressionist evolutionism of Darwin. Eventually, however, Darwin's arguments proved too persuasive, and Lyell found that he had to defer to his friend's opinion. In this chapter, however, we are concerned with Lyell's thought as a precursor of the Darwinian evolutionary model, rather than with the way in which Lyell's opinion developed during the course of his life.

NOTES CHAPTER 3

1   A detailed monograph on Lamarck in English has only been published recently: R. W. Burkhardt, *The Spirit of System: Lamarck and Evolutionary Biology*, Harvard University Press, Cambridge, Mass. & London, 1977. For an attractive thumb-nail sketch of Lamarck's character and work, see C. C. Gillispie, *The Edge of Objectivity: An Essay in the History of Scientific Ideas*, Princeton University Press & O.U.P., Princeton & London, 1960, pp.267-276. Lamarck was honoured by being the subject of an international colloquium in 1971. See J. Schiller (ed.), *Colloque International "Lamarck" Tenu au Muséum National d'Histoire Naturelle Paris les 1-2 et 3 Juillet 1971*, Blanchard, Paris, 1971.

2   Sketches for a book entitled *Biologie, ou Considérations sur la Nature, Les Facultés, Les Développemens et l'Origine des Corps Vivants* were prepared by Lamarck about 1802 or 1803, but remained unpublished. (See P. P. Grassé, "La Biologie' Texte inédite de Lamarck', *Revue Scientifique*, Vol. 5, 1944, pp.267-276.) Lamarck referred to this projected publication in the Preface to his *Philosophie Zoologique* (see note 9 below), using there the term *'biologie'* in reference to the new science of living bodies.

3   Lamarck's theory is often identified simply with the 'inheritance of acquired characteristics'. But this does little justice to the subtleties of his system and he was not the originator of the notion of inheritance of acquired characteristics. Some other aspects of this are outlined in the following pages.

4   Darwin wrote of Lamarck's work as 'veritable rubbish', 'absurd though clever', 'extremely poor', and suggested that 'one-half of Lamarck's arguments were obsolete and the other half erroneous' (F. Darwin (ed.), *The Life and Letters of Charles Darwin*, 3 vols, John Murray, London, 1887, Vol. 2, pp.29, 39, 215 and 189).

5   For further discussion of this point, see below, pages 176 to 187.

6   J. B. P. A. de Monet de Lamarck, *Flore Françoise, ou Description Succincte de Toutes Les Plantes qui Croissent Naturellement en France, Disposée selon une Nouvelle Methode d'Analyse, et à Laquelle on a Joint la Citation de leurs Vertus . . . en Médecine, et de leur Utilité dans les Arts*, 3 vols, Paris, 1778.

7   G. Cuvier, 'Eloge de M. de Lamarck', *Mémoires de l'Académie Royale des Sciences de l'Institut de France (Histoire)*, Vol. 13, 1831, pp.i-xxxi. (Cuvier's *Eloge* was read to the *Académie* by 'M. le baron Silvestre'.)

8   J. B. P. A. de Monet de Lamarck, *Recherches sur l'Organisation des Corps Vivans et Particulièrement sur son Origine, sur la Cause de ses Développemens et des Progrès de sa Composition*, Paris, 1802.

9   J. B. P. A. de Monet de Lamarck, *Philosophie Zoologique, ou Exposition des Considérations Relatives à l'Histoire Naturelle des Animaux*, 2 vols, Paris, 1809; *Zoological Philosophy*, translated with an introduction by Hugh Elliot, London, 1914; reprinted Hafner, London & New York, 1963.

10   J. B. P. A. de Monet de Lamarck, *Histoire Naturelle des Animaux sans Vertèbres*, 7 vols, Paris, 1815-1822.

11   J. B. P. A. de Monet de Lamarck, *op. cit.* (note 9, 1963), p.113.

12   J. B. P. A. de Monet de Lamarck, *op. cit.* (note 10), Vol. 1, p.182.

13   *Ibid.*, p.185.

14   *Ibid.*, p.189.

15   *Ibid.*, p.199.

16   J. B. P. A. de Monet de Lamarck, *op. cit.* (note 9, 1963), p.122.

17   *Ibid.*, p.117.

18   C. C. Gillispie, *op. cit.* (note 1), p.272.

19   A. O. Lovejoy, *The Great Chain of Being*, Harper & Row, New York, 1960, Chapter 9.

20   J. B. P. A. de Monet de Lamarck, *op. cit.* (note 9, 1963), p.179. (The branching of the Table was ascribed by Lamarck to the environment imposing different 'needs' on the organisms. See p.176.)

21   The Latin word *evolvere* means to unroll or to unfold.

22   J. B. P. A. de Monet de Lamarck, *op. cit.* (note 9, 1963), p.39.

23   'Phlogiston', the principle of combustibility, is today the best remembered of these eighteenth-century hypothetical scientific entities.

24   J. B. P. A. de Monet de Lamarck, *op. cit.* (note 9, 1963), p.241.

25   *Ibid.*, p.242. (Note that Lamarck did not mean here the 'cell' of modern biological theory. The cell theory was not established in biology until the 1840s.)

26   'Caloric' was a hypothetical fluid formerly held to be responsible for the phenomena of heat.

27   J. B. P. A. de Monet de Lamarck, *op. cit.* (note 9, 1963), p.102.

28   *Ibid.*, p.345.

29   *Ibid.*, pp.346-347.

30   *Ibid.*, p.358.

31   It should be noted that this term was only introduced by William Whewell in 1832. See *Quarterly Review*, Vol. 47, 1832, p.126.

32   J. B. P. A. de Monet de Lamarck, *Hydrogéologie*, Paris, 1802; *Hydrogeology by J. B. Lamarck* translated by Albert V. Carozzi, Illinois University Press, Urbana, 1964.

33   J. B. P. A. de Monet de Lamarck, *op. cit.* (note 9, 1963), 'Preface', pp.1-8.

34   *Ibid.*, p.1.

35   R. W. Burkhardt, 'The inspiration of Lamarck's belief in evolution', *Journal of the History of Biology*, Vol. 5, 1972, pp.413-438.

36   J. B. P. A. de Monet de Lamarck, *op. cit.* (note 9, 1809), Vol. 2, p.281 and *passim*.

37   C. Lyell, *Principles of Geology, being an Attempt to Explain the Former Changes in the Earth's Surface, by Reference to Causes now in Operation*, 3 vols, London, 1830-1833, Vol. 2, pp.3-17. (A facsimile of the first edition of Lyell's *Principles*, with an introduction by M. J. S. Rudwick, has been published by the Johnson Reprint Corporation, New York & London, 1969.)

38   For further discussion of this, see below, pages 176 to 178.

39   For further discussion of this, see below, pages 164 to 165.

40   See below, page 327.

41   See below, page 276.

42   This is the main burden of a book by perhaps the most ardent of Lamarck's recent admirers: H. G. Cannon, *Lamarck and Modern Genetics*, Manchester University Press, Manchester, 1959.

43   The standard work on Cuvier in English is W. Coleman, *Georges Cuvier Zoologist: A Study in the History of Modern Evolution Theory*, Harvard University Press, Cambridge, Mass., 1964. For an attractive illustrated account of Cuvier, with reproductions of extracts from his published works and unpublished manuscripts, see P. Ardouin, *Georges Cuvier: Promoteur de l'Idée Evolutioniste et Créateur de la Biologie Moderne*, Expansion Scientifique Française, Paris, 1970. An interesting account of Cuvier's methodical work-habits which enabled him to maintain concurrently and with success several independent research programs was given by Charles Lyell: K. M. Lyell (ed.) *Life, Letters, and Journals of Sir Charles Lyell, Bart.*, 2 vols, London, 1888, Vol. 1, pp.249-250 (republished Gregg, Farnborough, 1970). It is also recorded that Cuvier's brain was of quite exceptional size and weight: T. H. Huxley, *Man's Place in Nature and other Essays*, London, 1906, p.72 (republished University of Michigan Press, Ann Arbor, 1959).

44   G. Cuvier, 'Mémoire sur les espèces d'elephans vivantes et fossiles', *Mémoires de l'Institut des Sciences et Arts (Mémoires de la Classe des Sciences Mathématiques et Physiques)*, Vol. 2, 1799, pp.1-22.

45   This is not to suggest, of course, that there were no investigations of the anatomical structures of organisms or dissections before the close of the eighteenth century. Certainly there were. But the results of such investigations (conducted chiefly for medical purposes) were only of subsidiary concern to natural historians and were little used in their taxonomies. Cuvier, on the other hand, was concerned with problems of taxonomy and sought to solve these problems by a new method, which probed deeper than the external characteristics that had served as a limit for the inquiries of earlier natural historians.

46   G. Cuvier, *Leçons d'Anatomie Comparée*, 5 vols, Paris, 1800-1805, Vol. 1, p.46.

47   G. Cuvier, *The Animal Kingdom Arranged in Conformity with its Organization*, 15 vols, London, 1827-1835, Vol. 1, p.9.

48   In his decision to use the nervous system as the basis for the fundamental taxonomic divisions, Cuvier drew on the work of J. J. Virey: 'Animal', *Nouveau Dictionnaire des Sciences Naturelles*, Paris, 1803, Vol. 1, pp.419-466.

49   G. Cuvier, 'Sur un nouveau rapprochement à établir entre les classes qui composent le règne animal', *Annales du Muséum d'Histoire Naturelle*, Vo. 19, 1812, pp.73-84.

50 As mentioned above (p.4), in the geometrical work of the ancients, the term 'synthesis' was used in reference to the deductive chains of reasoning from axioms (or first principles) to theorems. The process leading back from theorems to principles was called 'analysis'. But this term was also used on occasion for movement from uncertain to known theorems, so that if such deductions could be performed successfully the uncertain or unproven (from first principles) theorems could be made secure. In later writings, there was considerable confusion about the proper meaning of the terms 'analysis' and 'synthesis' in scientific methodology and they were sometimes used in exactly opposite senses.

51 His major geological work, carried out in conjunction with Alexandre Brongniart, was a stratigraphical investigation of the Tertiary rocks of the Paris Basin: G. Cuvier & A. Brongniart, *Essai sur la Géographie Minéralogique des Environs de Paris avec une Carte Géognostique et des Coupes de Terrain*, Paris, 1811.

52 Stratigraphical column: the entire succession of stratified rocks, or a composite diagram representative of this.

53 Paris, 1812.

54 Paris, 1825.

55 G. Cuvier, *Essay on the Theory of the Earth . . . with Geological Illustrations by Professor Jameson*, 5th edn, Edinburgh & London, 1827, p.113.

56 W. Coleman, *op. cit.* (note 43), pp.128 & 133.

57 W. Buckland, *Reliquiae Diluvianae; or Observations on The Organic Remains, contained in Caves, Fissures and Diluvial Gravel, and on other Geological Phenomena, Attesting the Action of the Universal Deluge*, London, 1823.

58 Singular: 'taxon', or classificatory unit.

59 This interpretation is derived from the work of Michel Foucault: 'La situation de Cuvier dans l'histoire de la biologie', *Revue d'Histoire des Sciences et de leurs Applications*, Vol. 23, 1970, pp.62-69.

60 The standard work on Charles Lyell's earlier years is L. G. Wilson, *Charles Lyell: The Years to 1841: The Revolution in Geology*, Yale University Press, New Haven & London, 1972. See also *The British Journal for the History of Science — Lyell Centenary Issue: Papers delivered at the Charles Lyell Centenary Symposium London 1975*, Vol. 9, 1976, pp.91-240.

61 Lyell did not arrive at this conclusion wholly independently. He was, for example, much influenced by the work of the English geologist G. P. Scrope. See M. J. S. Rudwick, 'Poulett Scrope on the volcanoes of the Auvergne: Lyellian time and political economy', *The British Journal for the History of Science*, Vol. 7, 1974, pp.205-242.

62 C. Lyell, *op. cit.* (note 37).

63 The twelfth edition of *Principles* was published in 1875. Lyell also published six editions of his *Elements of Geology* (1st edn, London, 1838), in some editions entitled *A Manual of Elementary Geology*. This attempted to apply the general geological principles delineated in *Principles* to yield an elucidation of the geological history of the globe.

64 In a letter to his sister, dated October 19, 1830, Lyell stated his belief that the fossil shells of the 'recent' beds underlying Etna were of the order of 100,000 years old. (See P. Tasch, 'A quantitative estimate of geological time by Lyell', *Isis*, Vol. 66, 1975, p.406; and 'Lyell's geochronological model: published year values for geological time', *Isis*, Vol. 68, 1977, pp.440-442. See also M. J. S. Rudwick, 'Lyell on Etna, and the antiquity of the Earth', in C. J. Schneer (ed.), *Toward a History of Geology*, M.I.T. Press, Cambridge, Mass. & London, 1969, pp.288-304.)

65 J. Hutton, *Theory of the Earth, with Proofs and Illustrations*, 2 vols, Edinburgh, 1795 (reprinted Cramer, Leutershausen, 1959).

66 C. Lyell, *op. cit.* (note 37), Vol. 2, pp.124 & 129; Vol. 3, pp.32-33.

67 The figures suggested (Vol. 3, pp.54-55) were

Newer Pliocene	96%	recent fossils
Older Pliocene	35-50%	,, ,,
Miocene	17%	,, ,,
Eocene	3½%	,, ,,

For further details of Lyell's scheme and a discussion of the likely sources for the theory, see M. J. S. Rudwick, 'Charles Lyell's dream of a statistical palaeontology', *Palaeontology*, Vol. 21, 1978, pp.225-244.

68 C. Lyell to G. A. Mantell, 15 February, 1830, in K. M. Lyell (ed.), *op. cit.* (note 43), Vol. 1, p. 262; and C. Lyell, *op. cit.* (note 37), Vol. 1, p.123.

69 See M. Bartholomew, 'The non-progress of non-progression: two responses to Lyell's doctrine', *The British Journal for the History of Science*, Vol. 9, 1976, pp.166-174.

4

German Nature Philosophy; Robert Chambers

German Nature Philosophy

If we were to content ourselves with tracing the essential determinants of Darwin's theory, we might now glance at the theological and social ideas of Paley and Malthus respectively and then pass immediately to a consideration of Darwin's own contributions. With Linnaeus, Lamarck, Cuvier and Lyell, and also Paley and Malthus who will be considered in Chapter 5, we do have the major intellectual (but not the empirical) influences which shaped Darwin's theory. However, if our theme were developed in this way we should be leaving out of consideration a major component of early nineteenth-century biological thought – a component, moreover, which gave rise to a particular kind of evolutionism that is of considerable interest, even though the modern evolutionary theory largely arose through the alternative route of Darwinism. The subject matter of the present chapter may seem, therefore, to be something of a digression. But this will only be the case if we blinker ourselves so that we are merely interested in the antecedents of Darwinism that were, so to speak, 'logically' necessary for the formation of the theory of evolution by natural selection. I prefer not to be constrained in this way, and I will follow a more circuitous route – one that takes cognizance of important historical antecedents of the Darwin/Wallace theory.

Towards the end of the eighteenth century, there arose in Germany a new philosophical, artistic and social movement, closely associated with the Romantic movement, known was *Naturphilosophie* or Nature Philosophy. The men of the Enlightenment[1] emphasised the importance of clear, rational thinking, wished to abolish all obscurity and obscurantism through the establishment of suitable programs of educational reform and urged the use of the methods of science for the solution of mankind's problems. Moreover, they believed that all problems were in principle soluble by the man with the 'enlightened' mind. The reaction against this optimistic world-view began first in Germany, at that time finally shaking off the ravages of the Thirty

Years War, beginning to think of itself as a national entity, and cohering around the language that was common to all the German petty dukedoms, electorates and kingdoms occupying the central part of Europe.

Unlike the French *philosophes* of the late eighteenth century, many of whom were aristocrats and often free-thinkers, the new breed of German scholars and philosophers were chiefly men of quite humble origin, frequently pastors imbued with the doctrines of the characteristically German brand of Protestantism known as Pietism.[2] This religion preached a turning inwards on oneself to achieve an interior religious harmony, rather than some outward display of religious zeal. It emphasised the inner development of each human soul.

The German scholars and philosophers emphasised the value of history as a means of comprehending the nature of man and society. And a study of history entailed achievement of a state of empathy with the man of the past, and with cultures different from one's own.[3] An historical approach to understanding of the law was deemed appropriate, rather than trying to determine what was right or wrong by legal codes based on alleged natural-law doctrines.[4] The law should be comprehended by finding out how it had grown and developed.[5]

The contrast between the man of the French Enlightenment and the German Romantic of the early nineteenth century has been admirably stated in an important book by M. H. Abrams, *The Mirror and the Lamp*.[6] For the eighteenth-century *philosophe*, the mind was thought of as a 'mirror' or 'reflector' of external objects. But for the nineteenth-century Romantic the mind could be likened to a 'lamp' that illuminated and transformed external objects. The metaphor is, I think, most suggestive. If, for example, one compares Reynolds's *Lady Elizabeth Delmé* (1777-1789),[7] with Turner's *Light and Colour* (1843),[8] the contrast is indeed very striking, admirably illustrating the kind of contrast that Abrams wishes to reveal.

Nature Philosophers, then, did not wish to produce a kind of 'photocopy' of nature when they carried out their scientific investigations. Rather, by an almost poetic process, they hoped to lift the external veil (that which is encountered directly with the senses) and reveal the hidden inner meaning of nature. By an act of imaginative creation, the Nature Philosopher might hope to construct his own universe, so to speak, in a process that was partly scientific and yet also was moulded by an aesthetic component of marked significance. And in presenting in literary form the understanding thus achieved, a deal of poetic imagery and metaphor might be employed. Needless to say, this has had the effect of making the world of Nature Philosophers extremely difficult to understand today, for we are accustomed to a fairly clear-cut division between art and science. But this should not cloud the fact that they achieved certain insights of considerable importance – insights that in many cases remained beyond the grasp of the French *philosophes* with their penchant for totally 'clear and distinct' ideas. Among such seminal notions of the Nature Philosophers was the concept of *Entwicklung* or 'development', which, though by no means the same as the doctrine of evolution by natural selection, entailed an evolutionism of a kind.

The men of the French Enlightenment characteristically saw the universe as a machine; but the Nature Philosophers saw it as an organism, returning to the use of a metaphor that had been commonplace in antiquity and the Renaissance, but which had gone out of favour with the rise of the scientific movement in the seventeenth century.[9] Also, in the writings of the Nature Philosophers, we see a resurgence of Platonism though in a new and somewhat bizarre form. Goethe (1749-1832), for example – a man who was an extraordinary amalgam of poet and scientist, a man of truly universal genius and attainments – believed that nature, despite all its diversity, was a manifestation of a single archetypal plan or 'Idea'. Consequently it was his objective, and indeed the quite general objective of the Nature Philosophers or Romantic scientists, to reveal the underlying *unity* of nature.

This approach was sometimes surprisingly helpful, as, for example, in the case of Goethe's botanical investigations. Goethe believed that all the parts of plants must be variants of a single fundamental ideal structure, or archetypal plan.[11] Consequently, he interpreted parts of the plant such as petals, sepals, cotyledons and stamens as being modifications of a single fundamental ideal structure – the leaf. As it happens, this is morphologically correct, according to modern interpretations made in the light of evolutionary theory and with the help of detailed microscopic investigations. So it seems that in plant anatomy, what may appear to us as a rather wild and speculative philosophical fancy led to an hypothesis that was quite fruitful for science. Such a situation is, however, not uncommon in the history of science.

In addition to considering a common plan for the various parts of plants, Goethe also postulated that there was a single archetypal plant for all plants – the *Urpflanze*, and a single archetypal animal for all animals – the *Urtier*.[12] A skeleton of a man, for example, is similar, though not identical, to that of a chimpanzee. If one follows Goethe's doctrine of the *Urtier*, this could be explained without difficulty by supposing that man and chimpanzee are both separate manifestations or actualisations of the archetypal *Urtier*, not – as Darwin would have us believe – two organisms which happen to have evolved in the course of time by a process of natural selection from some common ancestor. Thus can two utterly different approaches produce explanations of the same phenomenon.

Among the many metaphors, often highly poetic in character, which the Nature Philosophers employed in their attempts at apprehending and attuning themselves with nature, the one that was perhaps most frequently used was *polarity*. All nature was construed as an interplay of opposing forces, natures or processes: positive and negative, attractive and repulsive, centripetal and centrifugal, oxidative and reductive, male and female, real and ideal. By the resolution of the supposed 'tension' or 'conflict' between these opposites, progressive development or *Entwicklung* could occur (this, of course, is something like the dialectical theory of Hegel). If, then, the

'Ideal' is represented as the 'Absolute' or the 'Absolute Idea', and the 'Real' as the physical universe, then the dialectical resolution of the 'conflict' between the two might be thought to be the 'cause' of the motion, life and development of the cosmos. According to this view, the 'conflict' might finally be resolved in man's mind where 'Real' and 'Ideal' finally achieve a state of identity.[13]

No doubt this may seem a far-fetched notion, but let us see where it led in the writings of Lorenz Oken (1779-1851), the leading Romantic biologist. The following gives a highly condensed account of how he saw the dialectical unfolding or development of the cosmos.[14]

The 'Absolute' (or nothing) supposedly creates its polar opposite, matter, or rather a primary unorganised chaos of ether. By the action of the organising activity of the basic polarity of repulsion and attraction, the suns and planets are formed out of this ether. The polar tension between the suns and planets results in the production of light and heat, and then new polarities of electricity, magnetism, and chemism arise successively. These bring about the first formation of living matter. A new chaos of infusorial mucus-vescicles comes into being, a material which Oken referred to as *Urschleim* or primal slime. Organisms are formed from the *Urschleim*, and on death and decomposition they break down into this primal substance, from which new organisms are formed in their turn.

It will be seen from this outline that Oken envisaged a general process of *Entwicklung* or development. But the framework of his aprioristic speculations is hardly likely to appeal to the modern reader, and we may therefore tend to dismiss him without further ado. In fact, however, Oken's speculations were linked with certain empirical evidence which had a very considerable bearing on the development of evolutionary theory, and his ideas should not be dismissed too hastily. Let us, therefore, examine his ideas in a little more detail.

As did Lamarck, Oken offered a kind of temporalisation of the Great Chain of Being. For Oken, the Chain was a manifestation of the general cosmic *Entwicklung*. Moreover, man might be seen as the archetype for all the 'lower' animals. Oken wrote:

> The animal kingdom is only *one* animal ... The animal kingdom is only a dismemberment of the highest animal, i.e. of Man.[15]

And:

> Man is the summit, the crown of nature's development, and must comprehend everything that has preceded him, even as the fruit includes within itself all the earlier developed parts of the plant. In a word, Man must represent the whole world in miniature.[16]

This doctrine, which evidently bears some similarity to the very ancient doctrine of the macrocosm and microcosm,[17] attributed to man the archetypal role that Goethe had given to the *Urtier*. Each animal, then, according to Oken's view, was a variant on the unifying theme provided by archetypal man. By this means, the similarities of the chimpanzee and man might be rendered intelligible. Moreover, man was supposedly a 'repetition' of the whole universe, which was itself conceived as a kind of super-organism.

Man, for Oken, represented the full realisation of the 'Absolute Idea'. And animals low in the Great Chain were to be thought of as 'steps' on the way to man himself. In addition, each animal, in the course of its own development, would repeat the development (*Entwicklung*) of the whole animal kingdom, ascending the Chain until it reached the stage characteristic of that particular kind of animal. Man, therefore, being at the top of the Chain, would repeat or recapitulate the development of every kind of animal in the Chain.

Put in this way, the theory may appear as a somewhat bizarre and fanciful speculation. But Oken was able to show, by means of dissection of embryos at various stages of their development, that humans do, in fact, pass through stages that resemble different steps of the evolutionary history of the animal kingdom.[18] The human embryo, he suggested, is first like a simple infusorian, then like a coral, then an acephalous animal, a mollusc . . . a worm, a crustacean, an insect, a fish, a reptile, a bird, and finally a mammal. This was a rather unsophisticated version of the theory of recapitulation. But embryologically, some degree of recapitulation does occur. It is well known, for example, that human embryos pass through a stage where they possess structures closely analogous to the gills of a fish. Oken's speculations, therefore, were by no means entirely divorced from the results of empirical inquiries. And the 'embryological argument' has for long been a powerful weapon in the dialectical armoury of the evolutionist. Darwin himself made considerable use of it, both in *The Origin of Species* and *The Descent of Man*.

As we have seen, the Nature Philosophy movement and 'Romantic' biology were primarily expressions of German thought. But spokesmen for the movement were found in other countries — most notably the comparative anatomist Richard Owen (1804-1892) in England, and Etienne Geoffroy Saint-Hilaire (1772-1844) in Paris.

Following the German lead (or perhaps independently), Geoffroy Saint-Hilaire believed that there was a common plan for *all* animals.[19] So, carrying the argument to its logical conclusion, he tried to reveal general anatomical similarities between both vertebrates and invertebrates. This regrettably led to some very unlikely analogies being drawn, such as comparisons between the shells of snails and tortoises, or the segments of insects and the ribs of vertebrates. Also, he sought to maintain such bizarre claims as that fishes have breast bones and crustaceans have ribs. And most famously, he tried to show that there was a general similarity of plan in cephalopods (particularly cuttle-fish) and vertebrates.

It was over this point that a vigorous controversy arose between Cuvier and

Geoffroy Saint-Hilaire. It will be appreciated that the notion of a single archetypal animal plan or *Urtier* was a complete anathema to Cuvier, who believed that there were no less than four utterly distinct *embranchements* of the animal kingdom. The debate became finally focussed on the anatomical characteristics of the cuttle-fish.[20] It is generally accepted that Cuvier had the better of this particular point,[21] and in fact Geoffroy Saint-Hilaire rapidly switched away from talking about cuttle-fish to the question of homologies[22] among the vertebrates. But Saint-Hilaire was working within a general evolutionist or developmentalist theoretical framework. And in this he was the man of the future, so to speak, whereas Cuvier's thinking was generally conservative on this issue, though, as we have seen, it was also of fundamental importance to the establishment of the evolutionary picture of Darwin.

Robert Chambers

There was really only one writer in Britain before Darwin who put forward a detailed argument for biological evolutionism, though there were (as Darwin discovered to his dismay, after the publication of the first edition of *The Origin*) several men of minor reputation who put forward versions of the natural selection principle in rather obscure publications.[23] But these little-known writers had virtually no influence on public opinion. By contrast, the anonymous work of the Edinburgh publisher Robert Chambers (1802-1871), entitled *Vestiges of the Natural History of Creation*,[24] first published in 1844, caused something of a sensation. And although Chambers' work was not based upon the hypothesis of evolution by natural selection, but rather on the cosmic evolutionism of the German Nature Philosophers, and although the doctrines of *Vestiges* never achieved any degree of public acceptance, the work fulfilled a considerable role in preparing the public mind in Britain for the consideration and eventual acceptance of Darwin's doctrines.

Chambers and his brother William came from a lower-middle-class Scottish family, with little money but enormous energy and a driving enthusiasm for the benefits of education. Starting virtually from nothing, they succeeded in building up the foundations of the very successful Chambers publishing house. They were classic examples of the self-help, self-improvement ethos which so characterised Victorian social thinking.[25]

Besides being a writer, Robert Chambers was an amateur naturalist of minor reputation, and he published some research papers in geology. In his day, scientific opinion in England was for the most part vigorously opposed to evolutionism. But in Scotland, which had quite close intellectual links with the Continent,[26] there was some penetration of the ideas of German Nature Philosophy and Geoffroy Saint-Hilaire's biological theories,[27] and it appears that Chambers must have been considerably influenced by these views. Eventually, he took a year off from publishing and spent the time in extensive reading and writing, the outcome of which was the anonymous publication of the *Vestiges*.

It was immediately subjected to the most vigorous critical attacks[28] for it ran totally against the generally received doctrine of special creations, and it utterly failed to cohere with the characteristic natural theology of nineteenth-century British thought. So we find the eminent Cambridge geologist, Adam Sedgwick (1785-1873), writing the following bitter words:

> If the book be true, the labours of sober induction are in vain; religion is a lie; human law is a mass of folly, and a base injustice; morality is moonshine; our labours for the black people of Africa were works of madmen; and man and woman are only better beasts![29]

Sedgwick referred to the 'inner deformity and foulness' of the work, and its 'gross and filthy views of physiology — all going back to the opinions of Geoffroy Saint-Hilaire and his *dark school*. He suspected that the book came 'from a woman's pen', for it was 'so well dressed, and so graceful in its externals'. He attacked *Vestiges* further in his lectures at Cambridge, accusing it of unsound logic, lack of reverence, and containing false facts.

There was, it must be admitted, some truth in Sedgwick's criticisms, for *Vestiges* did indeed have some connection with German Nature Philosophy, but it is clear from his remarks that he found the book frightening largely for social rather than scientific reasons. His reaction is well worth recording here, however, as it gives us a kind of preview of some of the subsequent criticisms that were thrown at *The Origin* and its author — although no one, to my knowledge, dared to be quite so vehement in his accusations against the highly respected naturalist, Darwin, as Sedgwick was in his review of the anonymous Chambers.

Vestiges was concerned with two major themes — the evolution of the solar system according to the nebular hypothesis,[30] and the evolution of living organisms. Only the latter need be considered here, although it should be emphasised that it was to be subsumed under a more general cosmic evolutionism — a kind of universal 'gestation" such as Chambers seems to have entertained.

Unlike Darwin, Chambers thought that it might be possible to say something about the beginnings of life itself, but in doing this he was led into one of his most egregious errors, such as Sedgwick found so inexcusable. Chambers cited experiments performed by a man named Crosse, in which, so it was supposed, life had actually been created by the action of an electric discharge on solutions of potassium silicate and copper nitrate. It was subsequently shown that what Crosse had observed was a well-known organism (the mite, *Acarus horridus*) which inadvertently had been introduced into the solution. Chambers' gullibility on this question was cheerfully seized on by his critics.

Nevertheless, Chambers had two most cogent arguments in favour of his evolutionary hypothesis: (a) the recapitulation argument from embryological studies, or the general similarity of the evolutionary development of organisms (as revealed by the evidence of the stratigraphical column) to the pattern of development of embryos; (b) the obvious structural similarities (or homologies) that may be seen in most vertebrates. These Goethe and his

HYPOTHESIS OF THE DEVELOPMENT OF — THE VEGETABLE AND ANIMAL KINGDOMS.

SCALE OF ANIMAL KINGDOM. (The numbers indicate orders:)	ORDER OF ANIMALS IN	ASCENDING SERIES OF ROCKS.	FOETAL HUMAN BRAIN RESEMBLES, IN
RADIATA (1, 2, 3, 4, 5) - - - - -	Zoophyta - - - - - - Polypiaria - - - - -	1 Gneiss and Mica Slate system 2 Clay Slate and Grauwacke system	
MOLLUSCA (6, 7, 8, 9, 10, 11) - - - -	Conchifera - - - - - - Double-shelled Mollusks - -	3 Silurian system	1st month, that of an avertebrated animal ;
ARTICULATA { Annelida (12, 13, 14) - - - - Crustacea (15, 16, 17, 18, 19, 20) Arachnida & Insecta (21—31)	Crustacea - - - - - - Annelida - - - - - - Crustaceous Fishes - - -	4 Old Red Sandstone	
Pisces (32, 33, 34, 35, 36) - -	True Fishes - - - - - Piscine Saurians (ichthyosaurus, &c.)	5 Carboniferous formation	2nd month, that of a fish ;
Reptilia (37, 38, 39, 40)	Pterodactyles - - - - - Crocodiles - - - - - Tortoises - - - - - Batrachians - - - - -	6 New Red Sandstone	3rd month, that of a turtle ;
Aves (41, 42, 43, 44, 45, 46) -	Birds - - - - - - -	7 Oolite 8 Cretaceous formation	4th month, that of a bird ;
VERTEBRATA — 47 Cetacea, 48 Ruminantia, 49 Pachydermata, 50 Edentata, 51 Rodentia, 52 Marsupialia, 53 Amphibia	(Bone of a marsupial animal) - - Pachydermata (tapirs, horses, &c.) Rodentia (dormouse, squirrel, &c.) Marsupialia (racoon, opossum, &c.)	9 Lower Eocene	5th month, that of a rodent ; 6th month, that of a ruminant ;
Mammalia — 54 Digitigrada, 55 Plantigrada	Digitigrada (genette, fox, wolf, &c.) Plantigrada (bear) - - - - Cetacea (lamantins, seals, whales)	10 Miocene	7th month, that of a digitigrade animal ;
56 Insectivora	Edentata (sloths, &c.) - - - Ruminantia (oxen, deer, &c.) -	11 Pliocene	
57 Cheiroptera 58 Quadrumana - - - 59 Bimana - - -	Quadrumana (monkeys) - - - Bimana (man) - - - -	12 Superficial deposits	8th month, that of the quadrumana ; 9th month, attains full human character.

Figure 11 Comparisons of Stratigraphical Column, Foetal Development, and Animal Taxa, according to Robert Chambers.[31]

followers had ascribed to the existence of a common archetypal plan, but Chambers referred the homologies to indications of common descent.

Chambers' argument, based on the common pattern of development in embryos and in the stratigraphical column, was presented most convincingly, as shown in Figure 11. It will be evident from even a cursory consideration of this table that Chambers was putting forward evidence that could not readily be brushed aside by Sedgwick's rhetoric. The comparisons at once became intelligible when seen from an evolutionary perspective, whereas the special creationists (with whom Sedgwick was aligned) could scarcely account for the multitude of analogies that Chambers identified.

Chambers offered his own version of the doctrine of recapitulation, as is shown in Figure 12.[32]

Figure 12 Robert Chambers' Representation of his Theory of Embryonic Development

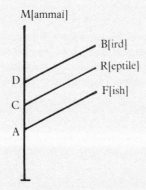

He wrote:

> The foetus of all the four classes may be supposed to advance in an identical condition to the point A. The fish there diverges and passes along a line apart, and peculiar to itself, to its mature state at F. The reptile, bird, and mammal, go on together to C, where the reptile diverges in like manner, and advances by itself to R. The bird diverges at D, and goes on to B. The mammal then goes forward in a straight line to the highest point of organization at M.[33]

In effect, this is a statement of von Baer's version of the recapitulation theory (see note 18), for the embryos of mammals pass through stages resembling the *embryonic* forms of the lower vertebrates.

Thus, to bring about the evolution of a new species according to Chambers' theory, all that would be required would be that the embryo would deviate slightly from its normal course of development. And this was by no means thought to be an impossibility. There had, in the first half of the nineteenth century, and earlier, been considerable interest in the study of 'monsters' (teratology) and Geoffroy Saint-Hilaire had been active in work of this kind. Deviations from the normal pattern of foetal development, thought Chambers, might themselves be indicators of the evolutionary history of organisms. For example, the heart of a child born with a 'hole' in it might be likened to the three-chambered heart of a reptile, and such a 'monstrosity' might be ascribed to the adverse conditions that had faced the embryo during its development. On the other hand, it might be maintained that especially favourable environmental circumstances might produce beneficial changes in the embryo. Rather fancifully, Chambers wrote:

> It is no great boldness to surmise that a super-adequacy [in the favourable circumstances] . . . would suffice in a goose to give its progeny the body of a rat, and produce the ornithorhynchus [platypus], or might give the progeny of an ornithorhynchus the mouth and feet of a true rodent, and thus complete at two stages the passage from the aves [birds] to the mammalia.[34]

This argument had certain Lamarckian overtones, except that it was applied to embryos rather than adults, but it was fairly evidently indebted principally to the ideas of Geoffroy Saint-Hilaire and his teratological investigations. It is interesting to note, incidentally, that both Robert and William Chambers were themselves 'monsters' of a kind, for both of them were perfect hexadactyls, each having six fingers on each hand. No doubt this circumstance did something towards directing Chambers's attention towards teratology, and influenced him in the formation of the explanatory hypothesis he favoured.

Chambers was not a major figure in the history of science; he did not make original contributions. Nevertheless, *Vestiges* was important from a social standpoint, and possibly drew some of the fire that might later have been directed against Darwin. And the synthesis of various items of evolutionary evidence that Chambers achieved was certainly a worthwhile contribution. But it is fairly clear that his arguments, in themselves, were insufficiently powerful to bring about a general change in scientific, social, and cultural perspective. This achievement was reserved for Darwin, who by 1844 had already written some provisional account of his new theory.

NOTES CHAPTER 4

1   This popular historiographical unit for Western intellectual history is ill-defined. It is, however, sometimes taken to be bounded by the English and French Revolutions of 1688 and 1789 respectively.

2 A branch of the Lutheran Church formed by the followers of Philipp Jakob Spener, about 1670, emphasising piety and the reform of religious education.

3 For a valuable discussion of eighteenth-century German historiography, see P. H. Reill, *The German Enlightenment and the Rise of Historicism*, California University Press, Berkeley, Los Angeles & London, 1975.

4 That is, ideas which were supposedly self-evident or known *a priori* to any right-thinking rational person.

5 The classical statement of this view is to be found in F. C. von Savigny, *Of the Vocation of our Age for Legislation and Jurisprudence*, translated from the German by A. Hayward, London, 1831.

6 M. H. Abrams, *The Mirror and the Lamp: Romantic Theory and the Critical Tradition*, O.U.P., New York, 1953.

7 See above p. 14.

8 J. W. Turner, *Light and Colour (Goethe's Theory) — the Morning after the Deluge*, in G. Reynolds, *Turner*, Thames & Hudson, London, 1969, p.189. (The original is in the Tate Gallery, London.)

9 For a succinct discussion of this change in world view, see, for example: H. Kearney, *Science and Change: 1500-1700*, Weidenfelt & Nicolson, London, 1971, Chapters 3-5.

10 The literature on Goethe is immense. See, for example, E. M. Wilkinson & L. A. Willoughby, *Goethe, Poet and Thinker*, Arnold, London, 1962; H. B. Nisbet, *Goethe and the Scientific Tradition*, Institute of Germanic Studies, London, 1972; R. Magnus, *Goethe as a Scientist*, Collier, New York, 1961.

11 See A. Arber, 'Goethe's botany . . .', *Chronica Botanica*, Vol. 10, 1946, pp.63-126. This contains a translation of Goethe's well-known *Metamorphose der Pflanzen* (Gotha, 1790).

12 See G. A. Wells, 'Goethe and evolution', *Journal of the History of Ideas*, Vol. 28, 1967, pp.537-550. Goethe stated that the *Urtier* is 'in the last analysis the idea of the animal'.

13 This paragraph and some other sections of this chapter are indebted to E. Richards, *The German Romantic Concept of Embryonic Repetition and its Role in Evolutionary Theory in England up to 1859*, Ph.D. Dissertation, University of New South Wales, 1976.

14 From L. Oken, *Elements of Physiophilosophy* (trans. A. Tulk), London, 1847. (First German edition, Stuttgart, 1839-1841.) For convenience, I have drawn on the English translation of Oken's views, but these were expressed much earlier in the nineteenth century, for example in *Lehrbuch der Naturphilosophie*, Jena, 1809-1811.

15 *Ibid.* (1847), p.494.

16 *Ibid.*, p.2.

17 That is, the view that there are significant analogies to be drawn between man (the microcosm) and the cosmos at large (the macrocosm). Man becomes the 'key' whereby the universe may be comprehended.

18 This is what is generally referred to as the doctrine of 'recapitulation'. In early statements of the doctrine, such as those of J. F. Meckel and É.-R.A. Serres, it was supposed that each animal, as it developed, passed through forms resembling the succession of lower animals. Thus a developing human would be first a worm, then a simple vertebrate, then a fish, a reptile, and so on. Later (1828), K. E. von Baer suggested as an alternative that each developing embryo passed through stages resembling the embryos of lower organisms at similar stages of development. Thus a human embryo would never resemble an adult fish, though it would be similar to a fish in its corresponding early stage of embryonic development.

19 É. Geoffroy Saint-Hilaire, *Philosophie Anatomique*, 2 vols, Paris, 1818-1822, Vol. 1, pp.xxxj-xxxij.

20 It is sometimes the case in the history of science that disputants will agree that certain crucial observations or experiments will be allowed to decide definitely between two conflicting theories. But such a situation is not nearly as common as is generally supposed. Very often the side which is faced with disconfirming evidence patches up its theory with various '*ad hoc*' hypotheses, rather than admitting defeat on the point at issue.

21 For discussions of the debate, see J. Piveteau, 'Les discussions entre Cuvier et Geoffroy Saint-Hilaire sur l'unité de composition du règne animal', *Revue d'Histoire des Sciences et de leurs Applications*, Vol. 3, 1950, pp.343-363; F. Bourdier, 'Geoffroy Saint-Hilaire versus Cuvier: the campaign for palaeontological evolution (1825-1838)', in C. J. Schneer (ed.), *Toward a History of Geology*, M.I.T. Press, Cambridge, Mass. & London, 1969, pp.36-61.

22 Structural homologies: for example, the wings of birds and the fore-limbs of mammals.

23 A list of Darwin's precursors may be found in the introductory 'Historical Sketch . . .' which he included in the fifth and sixth editions of *The Origin of Species*.

24 [R. Chambers,] *Vestiges of the Natural History of Creation*, London, 1844 (republished Leicester University Press, Leicester, 1969).

25 The classical statement of this doctrine is to be found in Samuel Smiles, *Self-Help; with Illustrations of Character and Conduct*, London, 1859 (republished John Murray, London, 1958).

26 Robert Jameson, for example, the Professor of Natural History at Edinburgh University, liked to include translations of recent Continental scientific papers of importance in his *Edinburgh New Philosophical Journal*.

27   Robert Knox and Robert Edmund Grant, in particular, acted as spokesmen for these ideas. (In his *Autobiography*, Darwin recalls that he became acquainted with Grant while he was a student at Edinburgh and was made aware by him of Lamarck's evolutionary doctrines. But, said Darwin, 'I listened in silent astonishment, and as far as I can judge, without any effect on my mind'.

28   For an extended account of these, see M. Millhauser, *Just Before Darwin: Robert Chambers and Vestiges*, Wesleyan University Press, Middletown, 1959.

29   J. W. Clarke & T. M. Hughes, *The Life and Letters of the Reverend Adam Sedgwick*, 2 vols, Cambridge University Press, Cambridge, 1890, Vol. 2, p.84.

30   This hypothesis, put forward independently by Kant and Laplace in the eighteenth century, suggested that the bodies of the solar system had a common origin and might have condensed out of the sun (with a vast surrounding 'atmosphere'), or a general 'nebular' fluid.

31   [R. Chambers,] *op. cit.* (note 24), pp.226-227.

32   *Ibid.*, p.212

33   *Ibid.*

34   *Ibid.*, p.219.

5

Further Important Antecedents of Darwin: Paley and Malthus

Deism and Paleyism

In Charles Darwin's *Autobiography*, one may read the following interesting passage:

> During the three years which I spent at Cambridge my time was wasted, as far as the academical studies were concerned, as completely as at Edinburgh and at school. I attempted mathematics, and even went during the summer of 1828 with a private tutor to Barmouth, but I got on very slowly. The work was repugnant to me, chiefly from my not being able to see any meaning in the early steps in algebra. This impatience was very foolish, and in after years I have deeply regretted that I did not proceed far enough at least to understand something of the great leading principles of mathematics, for men thus endowed seem to have an extra sense. But I do not believe that I should ever have succeeded beyond a very low grade. With respect to Classics I did nothing except attend a few compulsory college lectures, and the attendance was almost nominal. In my second year I had to work for a month or two to pass the Little-Go,[1] which I did easily. Again, in my last year I worked with some earnestness for my final degree of BA, and brushed up my Classics, together with a little Algebra and Euclid, which latter gave me much pleasure, as it did at school. In order to pass the BA examination, it was also necessary to get up Paley's *Evidences of Christianity*, and his *Moral Philosophy*. This was done in a thorough manner, and I am convinced that I could have written out the whole of the *Evidences* with perfect correctness, but not of course in the clear language of Paley. The logic of this book, and, as I may add, of his *Natural Theology*, gave me as much delight as did Euclid. The careful study of these works, without attempting to learn any part by rote, was the only part of the academical course which, as I then felt, and as I still believe, was of the least use to me in the education of my mind. I did not at that time trouble myself about Paley's premises; and taking these on trust, I was charmed and convinced by the long line of argumentation. By answering well the examination questions in Paley, by doing Euclid well, and by not failing miserably in Classics, I gained a good place among the οἱ πολλοὶ or crowd of men who do not go in for honours.[2]

This passage, besides throwing considerable light on Darwin's personality and the character of higher education among the English upper classes in the early nineteenth century, also tells us immediately that Darwin found the works of the English natural theologian, William Paley (1743-1805), of consuming interest when he was a young man. And it might be said that in fact Darwin's whole life-work ultimately came to be a battle fought against the arguments put forward so ably by Paley in his *Natural Theology*[3] — arguments that were quite central to the general mode of thinking in Britain in the early nineteenth century. It was Paley and his various expositions of the so-called 'argument from design' that provided one of the chief philosophical arguments used at that time in favour of a belief in the existence of God. This argument, it should be emphasised, was no mere theological exercise of little practical consequence, for it was held to be the very lynch-pin of the whole social system of that time.

The argument from design can be put very simply: all things that show design have designers; this universe of ours (and particularly the living organisms that are to be found on the Earth) show design; consequently, the universe has a designer — and this designer may be called God.

The argument from design is an ancient one, and it still has its admirers.[4] It may be found in Book 10 of Plato's *Laws*. The regular, ordered motion of the universe was ascribed by Aristotle to what he called the 'unmoved mover',[5] which was for Aristotle an *immanent* cause of the apparent design of the cosmos. The argument was stated by the Stoic, Sextus Empiricus (*circa* 160-210 AD), and its analogical form was emphasised.[6] It formed one of the 'five ways' discussed by St Thomas Aquinas (1225-1274) in his *Summa Theologiae* which might be used to justify belief in the existence of God.[7] However, it really only came to the fore in the seventeenth century, after the establishment of the scientific movement and the mechanical philosophy. The new science, centred on mechanics and astronomy, regarded the universe as a mechanism rather than an organism, and design was seen in the law-like motions of the parts of this mechanism. The argument was fundamental to the philosophy of Robert Boyle (1627-1691) and John Locke (1632-1714) and was given immense prestige by the authority of Newtonian physics. And it became the very basis of a new theology, deism, which claimed that one did not know the existence and character of God through revelation, that is, through some kind of personal communication such as might be attained by reading His word in the Bible. Rather, God was to be known through the application of the argument from design.[8]

It will probably be evident to the reader that such a theology would have had a considerable appeal to the men of the Enlightenment, and certainly one finds that leading members of that movement, such as Voltaire (1694-1778), explicitly embraced the deist position. Nevertheless, the argument was subject to a two-pronged attack in the eighteenth century. Orthodox theologians maintained that deism was the beginning of the steep and slippery slope leading to atheism. For Christianity, it was claimed, was a *personal* religion, not an arid intellectual exercise. And if one placed all reliance on a rational argument such as the argument from design, and if subsequently that argument were found wanting in some respect, then all religion would be lost. A just combination of the knowledge of revelation and the knowledge by rational argument was needed.[9]

From the other side, the design argument was attacked by the Scottish philosopher, David Hume (1711-1776), on the grounds that in fact it failed to achieve what it set out to achieve: it failed to meet the criteria of sound ratiocination.[10] Hume emphasised that the argument was analogical in character, and it was — so he claimed — based on a weak analogy at that, for the world shows plenty of disorder as well as order and has evil in it as well as good. For all that the argument could show to the contrary, said Hume, the world might be the work of an apprentice designer, or a worn-out, bungling designer. Or it might have had many designers; it might have been designed by a committee, so to speak. The argument certainly did not allow one to infer the monotheism of the Judaeo-Christian tradition. Moreover, the world is in *some* respects like a vegetable, rather than, say, a machine. So, by an analogical argument, it might have been produced by a seed, rather than some divine artificer. Again, it was a *logical* possibility that the world had caused itself.

Here we may note that in a sense this is just what Darwin later showed to have been the case. For he demonstrated that by a process of evolution by natural selection the apparent design could in fact be produced without invoking any external designer. The Darwinian needed no divine architect to account for the order of plant and animal forms.

The arguments of Hume, though they may seem quite persuasive to us today, carried little weight in the late eighteenth and early nineteenth centuries. Hume himself, that luminary of the Scottish school of Enlightenment philosophers, was always suspected of flirting with atheism. But more importantly, despite the cogency of Hume's arguments, the apparent design in the universe was still not explained adequately by any means other than the postulation of a divine artificer. Nevertheless, we can well imagine that further instances of design would be thought invaluable as strengthening the arguments of deism and natural theology and all the social connotations that accompanied these. Paley's writings, therefore, with the extraordinary number of instances of design in nature that he presented to his readers, were considered to be works of major significance in the theology of his day. Consequently, it is not surprising that their study formed an important component of the curriculum in Darwin's years as an undergraduate at Cambridge.[11] Moreover, they were evidently of special interest to Darwin because they used arguments drawn from natural history.

William Paley received his university education at Christ's College, Cambridge (where Darwin also was a student). He worked for a time as a schoolmaster, later obtained a College fellowship, and spent some time working in various country parishes in the north of England. His final appointment was to the position of an archdeacon at Carlisle Cathedral.

Paley did not begin the *Natural Theology* with a mass of detail in support of his thesis. Instead, with seeming artlessness, he chose to introduce his argument by inviting his readers to consider what their thoughts might be should they happen by chance one day to discover a watch on the path, while out for a walk. The introductory passage is a famous one, and worth quoting here almost as much for its style as for its content. Paley's measured prose has almost the finely-wrought structure of the slow movement of Haydn's 79th Symphony, the order and balance of the Royal Crescent at Bath, or the consummate technique of Reynolds's *Lady Delmé*! Paley wrote:

> In crossing a heath, suppose I pitched my foot against a *stone,* and were asked how the stone came to be there, I might possibly answer, that, for any thing I knew to the contrary, it had lain there for ever: nor would it perhaps be very easy to shew the absurdity of this answer. But suppose I had found a *watch* upon the ground, and it should be enquired how the watch happened to be in that place, I should hardly think of the answer which I had before given, that, for any thing I knew, the watch might have always been there. Yet why should not this answer serve for the watch, as well as for the stone? Why is it not as admissible in the second case, as in the first? For this reason, and for no other, viz., that, when we come to inspect the watch, we perceive (what we could not discover in the stone) that its several parts are framed and put together for a purpose, e.g. that they are so formed and adjusted as to produce motion, and that motion so regulated as to point out the hour of the day; . . . This mechanism being observed (it requires indeed an examination of the instrument, and perhaps some previous knowledge of the subject, to perceive and understand it; but being once, as we have said, observed and understood), the inference, we think, is inevitable; that the watch must have had a maker; that there must have existed, at some time, and at some place or other, an artificer or artificers who formed it for the purpose which we find it actually to answer; who comprehended its construction, and designed its use.[12]

In other words, Paley is saying, things that show design have designers.

The rest of the book is chiefly devoted to innumerable descriptions of the many remarkable 'contrivances' shown by living organisms whereby they are enabled to function successfully as living bodies and within the context of their particular environments. It begins with one of the best possible examples – the eye. The eye, he says, is a sure cure for atheism! And certainly even Darwin had to admit that it was difficult to believe that the mechanism of evolution by natural selection was a sufficiently powerful process to account for the production of an organ as intricate as the eye.[13]

Consider, for example, Paley's discussion of the nictitating membrane that is to be found in birds:

> The commodiousness with which it [the membrane] lies folded up in the upper corner of the eye, ready for use and action, and the quickness which which it executes its purpose, are properties known and obvious to every observer; but, what is equally admirable, though not quite so obvious, is the combination of two different kinds of substance, muscular and elastic, and of two different kinds of action, by which the motion of this membrane is performed. It is not, as in ordinary cases, by the action of two antagonist muscles, one pulling forward and the other backward, that a

reciprocal change is effected; but it is thus: The membrane itself is an elastic substance, capable of being drawn out by force, like a piece of elastic gum, and by its own elasticity returning, when the force is removed, to its former position. Such being its nature, in order to fit it up for its office it is connected by a tendon or thread with a muscle in the back part of the eye; . . . When the muscle behind the eye contracts, the membrane, by means of the communicating thread, is instantly drawn over the fore-part of it. When the muscular contraction . . . ceases to be exerted, the elasticity alone of the membrane brings it back again to its position . . . [But] in the configuration of the muscle, which, though placed behind the eye, draws the nictitating membrane over the eye, there is, what . . . [is] deservedly call[ed] a marvellous mechanism . . . The muscle is passed *through a loop formed by another muscle*; and is there inflected, as if it were round a pulley. This is a peculiarity; and observe the advantage of it. A single muscle with a straight tendon, which is the common muscular form, would have been sufficient, if it had had power to draw far enough. But the contraction, necessary to draw the membrane over the whole eye, required a longer muscle than could lie straight at the bottom of the eye. Therefore, in order to have a greater length in a less compass, the cord of the main muscle makes an angle. This, so far, answered the end; but, still further, it makes an angle, not round a fixed pivot, but round a loop formed by another muscle; which second muscle, whenever it contracts, of course twitches the first muscle at the point of inflection, and thereby assists the action designed by both.[14]

In this most persuasive passage Paley must surely have brought conviction to the mind of even the most doubting Thomas!

Paley discusses in detail the skeletal structure of the human body, the musculature, the blood vessels, the alimentary canal, the excretory organs, and so on. He then considers the functioning of the human body as a whole, before moving on to deal with adaptations of other animals, such as the modifications of birds for flight or the suitability of pigs' snouts for rooting in the ground. He discusses the humps of camels, the fangs of vipers, the swim-bladders of fish, the pouches of 'possums, the tongues of woodpeckers. All 'why' questions in natural history may seemingly be answered in terms of the teleological or design argument.[15] Why do young deer have no horns? Because if they did the horns would spike their mothers' udders. How do spiders catch flies?

The spider lives upon flies, without wings to pursue them; a case, one would have thought, of great difficulty, yet provided for; and provided for by a resource, which no stratagem, no effort of the animal, could have produced, had not both its external and internal structure been specifically adapted to the operation.[16]

Instances of design could also be found in the physical world. How fortunate, for example, that the particles of light[17] are of so little weight that they are not felt pressing on the body when the sun shines!

Paley's writing admirably sums up the naive optimism of the Enlightenment — the latter-day Leibnizian doctrine that we live in the best of all possible worlds:

It is a happy world after all. The air, the earth, the water, teem with delighted existence. In a spring noon, or a summer evening, on whichever side I turn my eyes, myriads of happy beings crowd upon my view . . . A *bee* amongst the flowers in spring, is one of the cheerfullest objects that can be looked upon . . . At this moment, in every given moment of time, how many myriads of animals are eating their food, gratifying their appetites, ruminating in their holes, accomplishing their wishes, pursuing their pleasures, taking their pastimes?[18]

Towards the end of the *Natural Theology,* Paley does consider the problem of evil. But he asserts that it is never the 'object of contrivance', and is in any case out-balanced by the good in the world. This, of course, sounds as a forerunner of the early nineteenth-century utilitarianism of Bentham and Mill, in which an attempt was made to draw up a kind of 'calculus' of pleasures and pains, the morally correct actions supposedly being those that gave a maximum of pleasure and a minimum of unhappiness. But it was also rather similar to the doctrines of the French *philosophe,* C. A. Helvétius (1715-1771).

We will consider, below, the work of the economist, T. R. Malthus, and his doctrine that mankind was always destined to live in a state of misery, since population would always tend to outrun available food resources. Paley read Malthus, but was not disheartened by the economist's pessimism. Paley simply believed that the average happiness of a population would rise as population increased.[19] He supposed that such evils as occur arise from the misuse of human free-will, rather than inadequate or inappropriate initial design.

Paley was very much a spokesman for the established social order. He believed that differences in rank and social standing were perfectly unexceptionable. And, of course, he saw no forward development or evolutionary change. In many ways, then, he perfectly summed up the popular metaphysics of his day, and it is for this reason that we have given him such attention here. As a philosopher, he is today generally regarded as being a mere second or third rater. But Paley admirably synthesised the eighteenth-century knowledge of natural history and the dominant natural theology of his day. There can be no doubt that he occupies a place of considerable importance in British intellectual history.

Malthus and the Workhouse

As in our consideration of Paley, it may be convenient to open our discussion of Malthus with an important passage from Darwin's *Autobiography:*

In October 1838, that is, fifteen months after I had begun my systematic enquiry [into the theory of evolution and the origin of species], I happened to read for amusement Malthus on *Population,* and being well prepared to appreciate the struggle for existence which everywhere goes on from long-continued observation of the habits of animals and plants, it at once struck me that under these circumstances favourable variations would tend to be preserved, and unfavourable ones to be destroyed. The result of this would be the formation of new species. Here, then, I had at last got a theory by which to work; but I was so anxious to avoid prejudice, that I determined not for some time to write even the briefest sketch of it. In June 1842, I first allowed myself the satisfaction of writing a very brief abstract of my theory in pencil in 35 pages; and this was enlarged during the summer of 1844 into one of 230 pages, which I had fairly copied out and still possess.[20]

The material of this quotation will be considered further in our discussions of the origins of Darwin's theory, but here it is sufficient to note that Darwin himself considered that the role of Malthus was of special importance. Accordingly, some exposition and evaluation of Malthus's theories will be given here.

Malthus (1766-1834)[21] was educated at Jesus College, Cambridge, and took holy orders, although he was not specially interested in ecclesiastical matters. (He has sometimes been referred to by his detractors as *parson* Malthus.[22]) He travelled extensively in Europe as a young man, and in 1805 he became professor of History and Political Economy at Haileybury College, an institution established by the East India Company for the training of young men going into its service. Malthus was elected a Fellow of the Royal Society in 1819, and the following year he became a founder member of the Political Economy Club, along with such persons as Grote, Ricardo and James Mill.

Like many men of his day, Malthus was a prolific writer, but he is now chiefly remembered for his major work, the *Essay on the Principle of Population*.[23] This was first published in 1798; the second edition of 1803 — a considerably modified version — contained the definitive statement of his views.

Malthus's ideas had two principal determinants, one broad and general and the other quite specific. In the first place he was reacting against the optimistic ideals of the Enlightenment. The *philosophe* Condorcet, for example, had believed that through the help of suitable education programs and the due exercise of rationality, men might be able to ascend to a kind of Utopian plateau, and he hoped that the French Revolution might be the instrument whereby this could be achieved.[24]

Malthus, however, argued that it would never be possible for such ideals to be realised, for they took no account of an absolutely fundamental feature of society, namely the problem of population growth. Population, he declared, always tends to increase in 'geometric ratio' (e.g., 2, 4, 8, 16 . . .) whereas the means of subsistence can only be increased in 'arithmetic ratio' (e.g., 2, 4, 6, 8 . . .),[25] by bringing new land into cultivation, for example. From this, Malthus concluded that mankind must always be subject to famine, poverty, disease and war unless some means of limiting population could be found.

This was a bleak conclusion indeed, and quite at odds with eighteenth-century optimism. However, even in the first edition of the *Essay* there was some attempt to offer grounds for hope. The imbalance between population and resources could serve as a spur to activity rather than despair. By their activity, some men at least might gain new qualities and new powers fitting them for a better place in a future life than they could occupy in the present world.

The *Essay* generated much controversy, and it is interesting to note that

Malthus changed the direction of his argument to some considerable degree in the second and later editions. Here he took the view that one should attempt to alleviate suffering in the present world, rather than being concerned with what might happen in the next. And the way to improve conditions was, he claimed, by the exercise of what he termed 'moral restraint', by which was meant the delay of the average age of matrimony, and sexual abstinence or restraint within marriage. Malthus sought to show that in fact most peoples had some means for limiting population artificially; for example, by having large priestly classes of celibates, by concubinage, late marriage, infanticide or polyandry. Man was a reasoning creature, capable therefore of moral restraint in a way that was not open to animals.

These considerations made the second edition of the *Essay* a somewhat less pessimistic work than the first edition, and it was the second and later editions that were read most widely. Nevertheless, it was the bleak conclusions of the first edition that left their mark on nineteenth-century consciousness.

It was stated above that there were two chief determinants of Malthus's thinking. We have just said something about his reaction to the eighteenth-century optimism that was epitomised in the thinking of Condorcet. In the second place, there was his response to a particular political controversy that was being debated in England in the late eighteenth century about the restructuring of the poor laws. There was, at that time, a limited number of workhouses, but they were only used by the aged and the unemployable. For the most part, money was paid in the form of 'outdoor relief' – that is, outside the doors of the workhouses. Relief was provided from the parishes in terms of doles, family allowances, and 'aid-in-wages'. This became known as the Speenhamland system, after a decision in 1795 by the Justices of the Peace of the Speenhamland district in Berkshire to provide allowances out of the poor rates for agricultural workers to supplement their wages, the allowances to be dependent on the size of their families and the current price of bread. The system was adopted in several other counties, and William Pitt proposed a bill in Parliament that would allow the system to be introduced generally. He was concerned to raise the birth rate in Britain as an aid to the prosecution of the Napoleonic wars.

Malthus's *Essay* was a statement of his objections to the proposed system. He argued that if people were given extra financial support this would merely encourage them to breed more, meaning that more relief money would be required, so that the poverty problem would simply be exacerbated. Everyone would eventually be dragged down together, and a large population of starvelings would do nothing to increase Britain's military strength. Malthus's argument proved persuasive, and Pitt withdrew his bill.

There were, of course, innumerable social and economic problems in Britain in the early nineteenth century, but it is now considered doubtful that the Speenhamland system was much to blame for the situation. The Napoleonic wars and the beginnings of the Industrial Revolution were the cause of far greater problems, and when this particular form of poor relief was withdrawn in 1834 it did not seem to produce a very significant effect. Nevertheless, Malthus has sometimes been regarded as a lackey of the manufacturing bourgeoisie or landed gentry because of his expressed objection to the old poor-law system. This does not seem to be entirely fair, however. Malthus was putting forward a case which was carefully and well argued, and he appears to have acted from concern for what he took to be the general interests of the community.

Malthus has, of course, been bitterly denounced and attacked from the time he wrote his *Essay* until the present. Marx objected that Malthus's population law applied peculiarly to capitalist societies, and could not be generalised to all social systems.[26] Cobbett stated outright that he detested Malthus.[27] Hazlitt described the *Essay* as a work 'in which the little, low, rankling malice of a parish beadle, or the overseer of a workhouse, is disguised in the garb of philosophy', and he wondered how 'such a miserable reptile performance should ever have crawled to that height of reputation which it has reached'.[28] Disraeli (a novelist as well as politician) satirised Malthus in his novels.[29] But despite such criticism, Malthus's opinions exercised a very considerable influence on the formulation of social policies in Britain during the nineteenth century. 1834, the year of Malthus's death, saw the introduction of the New Poor Law, in which the 'outdoor relief' system was replaced by that disgusting Victorian phenomenon, workhouse relief. Conditions in the workhouses were deliberately made harsh to dissuade people from coming into them, and once in them the two sexes were strictly segregated in order to discourage the production of children. Certainly, Malthus's thinking had a profound effect on the lives of many people, as well as being one of the chief factors leading to the establishment of Darwin's theory.

NOTES CHAPTER 5

1   The colloquial name given to the first examination for the Cambridge B.A.
2   *Autobiography of Charles Darwin with two Appendices, Comprising a Chapter of Reminiscences and a Statement of Charles Darwin's Religious Views, by his Son, Sir Francis Darwin*, Watts, London, 1929, pp.21-22.
3   W. Paley, *Natural Theology: or, Evidences of the Existence and Attributes of The Deity, Collected from the Appearances of Nature*, London, 1802 (reprinted Gregg, Farnborough, 1970).
4   For example, *Did Man get here by Evolution or by Creation?*, Watch Tower Bible and Tract Society of Pennsylvania, New York, 1967, p.40.
5   This doctrine is found in Book Λ of Aristotle's *Metaphysics*. See *Aristotle's Metaphysics* edited and translated by John Warrington, Dent, London, & Dutton, New York, 1956, pp.345-349.
6   *Sextus Empiricus* with an English translation by R. G. Bury, 4 vols, Heinemann & Harvard University Press, London & Cambridge, Mass., 1960-1961; Vol. 3, *Against the Physicists*, p.27.
7   St Thomas Aquinas, *Summa Theologiae*, I, 2, 3 in *St Thomas Aquinas Summa Theologiae: Latin text and English translation*, 40 vols, Blackfriars, with Eyre & Spottiswoode and McGraw-Hill, London & New York, 1964-1966, Vol. 2, p.17.

8   A theology based on the use of reasoning powers (to prove the existence of God), as opposed to knowledge of God by revelation, is called a 'natural theology'.

9   The chief British exponent of this line of argument in the eighteenth century was Bishop Joseph Butler, in his *Analogy of Religion* (1736). Butler maintained that the supposed truths of science and the rational arguments for God were by no means 'clear and distinct' (to use Descartes's phrase), and that revelation was an essential component of religious thought.

10   D. Hume, *Dialogues Concerning Natural Religion* (1779), republished in R. Wollheim (ed.), *Hume on Religion*, Fontana, London, 1963, pp.99-204.

11   A study of Paley formed an important part of the curriculum until the early years of the *twentieth* century.

12   W. Paley, *op. cit.* (note 3), pp.1-4.

13   J. W. Burrow (ed.), *The Origin of Species by means of Natural Selection or the Preservation of Favoured Races in the Struggle for Life Charles Darwin*, Penguin, Harmondsworth, 1968, p.217. And in a letter to the American botanist, Asa Gray, Darwin admitted that 'The eye to this day gives me a cold shudder'. (F. Darwin [ed.], *The Life and Letters of Charles Darwin*, 3 vols, John Murray, London, 1887, Vol. 2, p.273.)

14   W. Paley, *op. cit.* (note 3), pp.38-41.

15   That is, explanations couched in terms of purposes, 'ends' or 'final' causes. (Greek, $\tau\epsilon\lambda os$ = 'end'.)

16   W. Paley, *op. cit.* (note 3), p.302.

17   Paley was seemingly a mechanical philosopher of sorts, as well as an arch-exponent of design. His mention of particles of light suggests his adherence to the Newtonian corpuscular theory of light, itself an expression of the seventeenth-century mechanical world-view, according to which natural philosophers sought to account for phenomena in terms of hypothetical corpuscular components of matter.

18   W. Paley, *op. cit.* (note 3), pp.490 and 496.

19   *Ibid.*, p.541.

20   C. Darwin, *op. cit.* (note 2), p.57.

21   For a thorough account of Malthus and his work, see J. Bonar, *Malthus and his Work*, London, 1885 (2nd edn, Allen & Unwin, London, 1924).

22   See note 26, below.

23   [T. R. Malthus,] *An Essay on the Principle of Population, as it Affects the Future Improvement of Society; With Remarks on the Speculations of W. Godwin, M. Condorcet and Other Writers*, London, 1798 (republished Penguin, Harmondsworth, 1970).

24   M. J. A. N. Caritat [Marquis de Condorcet], *Esquisse d'un Tableau Historique des Progrès de l'Esprit Humain, Ouvrage Posthume*, [Paris,] 1795 (English tr. J. Barraclough, Weidenfeld & Nicolson, London, 1955).

25   This doctrine, which is chiefly associated with Malthus's name, certainly did not originate in his *Essay*. In his *Advancement of Learning*, for example, Francis Bacon wrote: 'Custom goes in arithmetical, Nature in geometrical progression'. (Quoted in T. Bonar, *op. cit.* (note 21), p.66.)

26   Marx wrote: 'Every particular historical mode of production has its own special laws of population, which are historically valid within that particular sphere. An abstract law of population exists only for plants and animals, and even then only in the absence of any historical intervention by man'. (K. Marx, *Capital: A Critique of Political Economy*, Volume One introduced by Ernest Mandel, translated by Ben Fowkes, Penguin, Harmondsworth, 1976, p.784.)

27   W. Cobbett, 'To Parson Malthus', *Political Register*, Vol. 34, 1819, p.1019.

28   W. Hazlitt, *A Reply to the 'Essay on Population'*, London, 1807, pp.19-20.

29   B. Disraeli, *Sybil or the Two Nations*, Peter Davies, London, 1927, p.160 (1st edn, London, 1845).

Part 2
Darwinism

6

Darwin's Life and Work

In a book such as this, chiefly concerned with intellectual history, there is no need to devote too much attention to the 'life and times' of individuals – perhaps not even to Darwin himself. However, despite the fact that there are many books and articles that deal in comprehensive fashion with Darwin's life, work, and character,[1] just a few points of importance will be touched on in this chapter, partly for the sake of general interest, and partly because they do, of course, have a definite bearing on our account of the development of the theory of evolution in general, and the Darwinian Revolution in particular.

Charles Robert Darwin (1809-1882) was a member of one of England's great intellectual families. Indeed, it is sometimes said that there is only one really notable intellectual family in Britain, for the Darwins, the Wedgwoods, the Trevelyans, the Macaulays, the Huxleys, the Arnolds and the Cornfords are all related.

Darwin himself was born in Shrewsbury, the son of a wealthy doctor, Robert, and grandson of the well-known physician, poet, philosopher and naturalist, Erasmus.[2] Darwin attended Shrewsbury School from 1818 to 1825, where the education was principally in the classics, although he also learned some elementary mathematics. It seems that he did not achieve very much at Shrewsbury; but in his teens he already displayed some interest in science, and he and his elder brother, Erasmus, liked to carry out chemical experiments in a makeshift laboratory in their garden. Charles's father, we are told, generally disapproved of his son's activities, saying: 'You care for nothing but shooting, dogs, and rat-catching, and you will be a disgrace to yourself and all your family.'[3]

After leaving Shrewsbury, Darwin went to Edinburgh University to study medicine. However, he did not enjoy his time there, being disgusted by the sight of operations performed without anaesthetics, as was necessarily the practice in the early nineteenth century. He attended the 'geognostic'[4] lectures of Robert Jameson (1774-1854), but did not regard them with much favour. He collected marine molluscs, and read one or two minor papers of his own at meetings of the Plinian Society.[5] In Edinburgh, Darwin met the zoologist, Robert Grant (1793-1874), who later occupied a chair at University College, London. As previously mentioned, it was Grant who introduced Darwin to some of Lamarck's ideas, and it is possible also that Darwin came into contact with ideas concerning evolution in other ways. As has been noted above, Scotland was more open to the ideas of continental Nature Philosophy than were intellectual circles in London, Oxford and Cambridge.

Darwin left Edinburgh without completing any medical qualification, and moved to Cambridge where he took the usual arts degree through Christ's College. We have already seen that he studied Paley and Euclid with care. His consuming interest seems to have been shooting, but he also attended the meetings of the several natural history societies in Cambridge. There must have been something rather remarkable about the young man, for he quickly formed acquaintances with several of the University staff, such as J. S. Henslow (1796-1861), the Professor of Botany; Adam Sedgwick (1785-1873), the Professor of Geology; and William Whewell (1794-1866), the Professor of Mineralogy, later to become a notable philosopher and historian of science. Darwin and Sedgwick went on a three-week field excursion together in North Wales during one of the University vacations. This was virtually the only training that Darwin received in geology, although he subsequently made a number of important contributions to this science.[6]

On completing his degree, Darwin did not pursue his original intention of entering the Church, but, at the recommendation of Henslow, was fortunate enough to obtain a post as naturalist[7] aboard the vessel, H.M.S. *Beagle*, which was then about to set out on what was to be a five-year voyage (1831-1836) surveying in South American waters and circumnavigating the globe. The captain, Robert Fitzroy (1805-1865), was a man of extremely conservative views, both on questions of theology and of politics. But he was an excellent seaman and the voyage proved highly successful.

Just before the vessel left England, Henslow advised Darwin to buy a copy of the first volume of Lyell's *Principles of Geology*. It is clear from the observations made during the voyage and from his subsequent geological work that Darwin was profoundly impressed and influenced by Lyell's doctrines and that he constantly attempted to apply the uniformitarian methodology and the concept of the continuous upward and downward movements of the Earth's crust with concomitant periods of weathering and erosion and deposition of sediment. Thus at St Jago in the Cape Verde Islands off the central West African coast, the first landfall of the voyage, Darwin immediately noticed a layer of limestone with marine shells, forty-five feet above sea level, and similar material forming today at sea level. Here, straight away, was an observation that accorded well with Lyell's uniformitarian doctrine and his ideas on Earth movements.

Beagle left Africa and sailed across to Brazil, where Darwin obtained his first sensation of being in a tropical jungle. Years later, he recorded that this was for him the most sublime experience of the whole voyage. He wrote in his diary:

> The day [29 February, 1832] has passed delightfully: delight is however a weak term for such transports of pleasure: I have been wandering by myself in a Brazilian forest: amongst the multitude it is hard to say what set of objects is most striking; the general luxuriance of the vegetation bears the victory, the elegance of the grasses, the novelty of the parasitical plants, the beauty of the flowers, the glossy green of the foliage, all tend to this end. A most paradoxical mixture of sound and silence pervades the shady parts of the wood: the noise from the insects is so loud that in the evening it can be heard even in a vessel anchored several hundred yards from the shore: yet within the recesses of the forest a universal stillness appears to reign. To a person fond of Natural History such a day as this brings with it pleasure more acute than he ever may again experience.[8]

Clearly, the young naturalist was a man with highly developed aesthetic sensibilities.

As *Beagle* sailed south, Darwin made several excursions into the interior, sometimes alone, sometimes accompanied by native or Spanish guides, or by members of the ship's company. Numerous specimens were collected and preserved. Particularly interesting were the remains of recently extinct giant fossil mammals: *Megatherium* and *Megalonyx* (giant sloths), *Scelidotherium* (a giant ant-eater), *Myledon* and *Glyptodon* (giant armadillos), *Mastodon* (a mammoth-like creature), *Toxodon* (a giant rodent), and *Macrauchenia* (an extinct camel-like animal, with claws). Darwin speculated on the possible causes of the extinction of these creatures, but was unable to suggest any very plausible explanation. The glacial theory had not become widely known or clearly expressed at that time. Later, the extinction of these creatures, so similar to extant forms, was to influence Darwin's thinking on questions of evolution.

In due course, *Beagle* got right down to Tierra del Fuego, where some of the world's most primitive people were to be found. They were practically naked, despite the intense cold. Their language seemed to be a hoarse guttural clicking. The natives also seemed to be entirely devoid of any religious sense, though this has subsequently been questioned, for they do bury their dead.

On a previous voyage, Fitzroy had taken three natives back to England: Jemmy Button, York Minster and Fuegia Basket. They were now returned to their homeland. We are told that 'the meeting [between Jemmy Button and his relations] was not so interesting as that of two horses in a field'.[9] A missionary named Matthews, intending to fulfil Fitzroy's ambition of civilizing the natives, attempted to stay on the island, together with Jemmy, York and Fuegia. But the natives were unwilling to accept this mission and Matthews had to be taken off.

By 1834, *Beagle* had surveyed the region of the Straits of Magellan, had rounded the Horn, had paid a visit to the Falkland Islands and a return visit to the East coast of South America, had passed through the Straits of Magellan again, and had gone as far north as Valparaiso in Chile. Darwin visited various mining districts and was appalled to see the conditions there. No doubt he would have been equally appalled if he had visited the British mines of the 1830s, but like many gentlemen of his age he scarcely ventured into the industrial parts of his country.

In February, 1835, the expedition experienced a severe earthquake at sea, and the effects of this were very obvious when the ship arrived at Concepción. Darwin noticed that land elevation had occurred (he had been collecting evidence for this all around South America), and also that volcanic activity in the Andes seemed to be associated with the occurrence of the earthquake. A new island appeared off the coast near Juan Fernandez, Robinson Crusoe's island. Darwin suggested that the mountains were formed by rents occurring in the Earth's crust as land was elevated, and molten rock rose from the Earth's interior to fill the cracks formed.[10]

From Santiago, Darwin made a crossing of the main divide of the Andes, to the town of Mendoza, passing over a high pass at more than fourteen thousand feet. He noted that although the climatic conditions were quite similar on the two sides of the mountain range the flora and fauna were markedly different. This was later to become a significant piece of evidence in favour of the theory of evolution, for the role of geographical isolation was of the greatest importance in accounting for the formation of species. But at the time, Darwin gave a conventional explanation in terms of the theory of special creations.

The return over the mountains was made by an easier but longer route. *Beagle* sailed north to Peru, and then out into the Pacific to the celebrated Galapagos Islands. This small archipelago of volcanic islands lies almost on the equator, about six hundred miles from the mainland. The flora and fauna have general South American affinities, but nevertheless form unique communities on each island, the forms varying from one island to another. The main types are reptiles and birds, and the only native mammal is a mouse on the island closest to the mainland. The birds are particularly interesting. Chiefly, they belong to the finch family, yet they show unusual adaptations that are not commonly found among these birds. For example, some are insectivorous, while others are seed eating, as is more often so with finches. One special kind in the Galapagos Islands even uses twigs as tools to prise small animals out of their hiding places. Moreover, the finches differ slightly from one island to the next.[11] At this stage, however, Darwin did not state that the observations provided considerable support for an evolutionary theory. In the second edition of his published *Journal* (1845), he wrote, still rather non-committally:

> Seeing this gradation and diversity of structure in one small, intimately related group of birds, one might really fancy that from an original paucity of birds in this archipelago, one species had been taken and modified for different ends.[12]

But this passage was written *after* the theory had been formulated. It does not appear in the first edition of the *Journal* (1839).

The reptiles were also remarkable, and Darwin found that the local inhabitants could tell him from which island a particular giant tortoise had come. But at this stage, he seemed unprepared to commit himself on the question of the origin of species. It is probable that the theory was only beginning to take some rather indefinite shape in his mind, and was by no means fully formulated.

From the Galapagos Islands, *Beagle* went on to Tahiti, which Darwin much admired, and various coral islands were visited in the Pacific. Some of these appeared to be sinking while others were rising, and later Darwin was able to map whole areas of the Pacific according to these movements.[13] This fitted in with the general Lyellian doctrine of continuous slow Earth movements in the vertical plane.

Beagle called at New Zealand and then at Sydney, where Darwin was much impressed by the rapid growth of the town and its apparent prosperity, though he showed his distaste for the convict settlements. He made a trip on horseback over the Blue Mountains to Bathurst in the middle of summer, and did not find the interior particularly attractive, though he was much impressed by the beautiful golden-orange cliffs and gorges of the Blue Mountains. He suggested that the valleys might have been eroded by the sea – a mistaken opinion we now think.[14] The voyage continued to Hobart, south-west Australia, Capetown, Brazil again, then the Cape Verde Islands, the Azores, and finally back home in 1836. The choice of the two archipelagos suggests that Darwin had some influence on Fitzroy on the selection of route in the later part of the voyage.

On returning to England, Darwin was at first much occupied with Henslow at Cambridge, sorting out the specimens and preparing the *Journal of Researches* for publication. In 1837, Darwin moved to London, where he stayed for two years. The zoological and geological results of the voyage were written up, and he joined the influential Geological Society, and soon became one of its secretaries. During this period he carried out some interesting geological field work in Scotland.[15] Darwin also 'went a little into society' at this period of his life.

In 1837, Darwin opened the first of his notebooks in which he collected information which had a bearing on the species question, and he went on adding to this information for many years.[16] Also at about this time he drew up a list of 'pros and cons' on the question of whether he should get married. Without much difficulty he reached the decision that the arguments in favour of matrimony outweighed the arguments against. Accordingly, he proposed to his cousin, Emma Wedgwood, and was promptly accepted.

Initially the couple lived in London. Darwin was elected a Fellow of the Royal Society, and thereby made the acquaintance of the eminent botanist, Joseph Dalton Hooker (1817-1911), who later became Director of the Botanical Gardens at Kew. Hooker later became a confidant for Darwin's ideas, and afterwards his strong public supporter. His *Flora of Tasmania*[17] was the first published botanical work to be based on evolutionary principles.

At about this time, however, Darwin began to suffer the symptoms of a disease that was to plague him for most of the rest of his life. There has for many years been some medical controversy about the nature of this chronic illness, and in particular on the question of whether it was psychosomatic in origin. For some years, the prevailing opinion was that Darwin was suffering from the so-called Chagas disease, acquired through his having been bitten by the 'Benchuca bug' when he was travelling over the Pampas. This disease produces severe heart pains due to the activity of a parasitic trypanosome. However, Darwin recorded that he had suffered some manifestations of a heart condition before he sailed on *Beagle*, and the opinion now favoured is that the illness was of a neurotic character, serving as a kind of 'camouflage' which enabled him to retire from the glare of publicity and get on with his scientific investigations with as little disturbance as possible.[18]

The Darwins, therefore, after only a short period of residence in London, retired to the village of Down in North Kent. Ten children were born to them, but three died young. Darwin gradually became more and more a recluse, although it was doubtless as a result of his retiring disposition that he succeeded in getting through such an enormous amount of work, both experimental and literary. He maintained a world-wide correspondence, sought information that might have a bearing on the problem of evolution and the origin of species from such people as pigeon fanciers, gardeners and cattle breeders, and read widely in the biological literature. According to a famous paragraph in his *Autobiography*:

> I worked on true Baconian principles,[19] and without any theory collected facts on a wholesale scale, more especially with respect to domesticated productions, by printed enquiries, by conversation with skilful breeders and gardeners, and by extensive reading.[20]

For several years, Darwin made a detailed study of the natural history of barnacles. It might seem that this would have been a serious distraction from his principal interest in evolution and the origin of species, yet it appears that the detailed attention that he gave to one animal group was an essential feature of his self-education as a naturalist. And he made fundamental contributions to an understanding of the cirripedes. He noted particularly that lodged within the mantles of some types were small organisms that could be identified as the *male* barnacles, rather than parasites as had previously been supposed. 'Little husbands', Darwin called them. His publications on barnacles are still standard works of reference, although now extremely scarce.[21]

The turning point of Darwin's career was, of course, the publication of *The Origin of Species* in 1859[22] (which work will be discussed in the following chapter). After *The Origin*, Darwin wrote a number of further important works (discussion of which will also be postponed until a subsequent chapter).

Darwin's later years were not marked by outward events of any great import. Under the excellent care of his devoted wife he was able to give himself almost entirely to his work and to family affairs. But he gradually lost almost all interest in literature, art and music, becoming a kind of machine for grinding out scientific generalisations from masses of data.[23] He also lost his religious faith — a loss that greatly pained his devout wife. Darwin's religion did not disappear suddenly, but seems to have just withered away. He never declared himself an atheist, but preferred to see himself as an agnostic — the term coined by his fellow evolutionist, Thomas Henry Huxley.[24] However, Darwin was reluctant to speak on religious questions, although he did not consider that his evolutionary theory and religion were incompatible.[25] His final expressed opinions on the religious question were:

> The safest conclusion seems to me that the whole subject is beyond the scope of man's intellect; but man can do his duty;[26]

and:

> I cannot pretend to throw the least light on such abstruse problems. The mystery of the beginning of all things is insoluble by us; and I for one must be content to remain an Agnostic.[27]

Darwin was an almost archetypal liberal Victorian gentleman. In personality he was exceptionally tidy-minded and well ordered. He was notable for his modesty, although this probably was in part a reflection of the English social preference for unassuming amateurism rather than professional vainglory. Darwin's own assessment of his personal qualities provides us with a suitable conclusion to this brief sketch of his life and work. He wrote:

> I have no great quickness of apprehension or wit which is so remarkable in some clever men, for instance, Huxley. I am therefore a poor critic: a paper or book, when first read, generally excites my admiration, and it is only after considerable reflection that I perceive the weak points. My power to follow a long and purely abstract train of thought is very limited; and therefore I could never have succeeded with metaphysics or mathematics. My memory is extensive, yet hazy: it suffices to make me cautious by vaguely telling me that I have observed or read something opposed to the conclusion which I am drawing, or on the other hand in favour of it; and after a time I can generally recollect where to search for my authority. So poor in one sense is my memory, that I have never been able to remember for more than a few days a single date or a line of poetry.
> Some of my critics have said, "Oh, he is a good observer, but he has no power of reasoning!" I do not think that this can be true, for the 'Origin of Species' is one long argument from the beginning to the end, and it has convinced not a few able men. No one could have written it without having some power of reasoning. I have a fair share of invention, and of common sense or judgement, such as every fairly

successful lawyer or doctor must have, but not, I believe, in any higher degree. On the favourable side of the balance, I think that I am superior to the common run of men in noticing things which easily escape attention, and in observing them carefully. My industry has been nearly as great as it could have been in the observation and collection of facts. What is far more important, my love of natural science has been steady and ardent . . . Therefore my success as a man of science, whatever this may have amounted to, has been determined, as far as I can judge, by complex and diversified mental qualities and conditions. Of these, the most important have been: the love of science, unbounded patience in long reflecting over any subject, and a fair share of invention as well as of commonsense. With such moderate abilities as I possess, it is truly surprising that I should have influenced to a considerable extent the belief of scientific men on some important points.[28]

NOTES CHAPTER 6

1   There is still no definitive biography of Darwin, although he has become the subject of a vast and ever-expanding literature. For general accounts of Darwin's life and work, the following may be recommended: W. Irvine, *Apes, Angels and Victorians: A Joint Biography of Darwin and Huxley*, Weidenfeld & Nicolson, London, 1955; G. de Beer, *Charles Darwin: Evolution by Natural Selection*, Nelson, London, 1963; C. C. Gillispie, 'Biology comes of age', in *The Edge of Objectivity*, Princeton University Press and O.U.P., Princeton & London, 1960, pp.303-351; L. Eiseley, *Darwin's Century*, New York, 1961; M. T. Ghiselin, *The Triumph of the Darwinian Method*, California University Press, Berkeley & Los Angeles, 1969; G. Himmelfarb, *Darwin and the Darwinian Revolution*, Chatto & Windus, London, 1959; H. E. Gruber, *Darwin on Man: A Psychological Study of Scientific Creativity . . . Together with Darwin's Early and Unpublished Notebooks Transcribed and Annotated by Paul H. Barrett*, Dutton, New York, 1974. Essential source material for the study of Darwin's life and work is to be found in: F. Darwin (ed.), *The Life and Letters of Charles Darwin, including an Autobiographical Chapter*, 3 vols, John Murray, London, 1887; F. Darwin & A. C. Seward (eds), *More Letters of Charles Darwin: A Record of his Work in a Series of Hitherto Unpublished Letters*, 2 vols, John Murray, London, 1903. For general surveys of the 'Darwin' literature, see B. J. Loewenberg, 'Darwin and Darwin studies', *History of Science*, Vol. 4, 1965, pp.15-54 and J. C. Greene, 'Reflections on the progress of Darwin studies', *Journal of the History of Biology*, Vol. 8, 1975, pp.243-73.
2   On Erasmus Darwin (1731-1802) see D. M. Hassler, *Erasmus Darwin*, Twayne, New York, 1973, and D. King-Hele, *Doctor Darwin: The Life and Genius of Erasmus Darwin*, Faber, London, 1977.
3   Quoted in G. de Beer, *op. cit.* (note 1), p.25.
4   A. G. Werner (1750-1817), lecturer at the celebrated Freiberg Mining Academy in Saxony, preferred the term 'geognosy' rather than 'geology', claiming that in his hands the study of the Earth had become an exact science rather than a series of fanciful speculations. Jameson studied under Werner and became the leading exponent of his views in Britain.
5   An Edinburgh natural history society.
6   In particular, he developed a theory of coral reef formation which has proved to be of permanent value. But Darwin's greatest 'mistakes' were mostly of a geological nature, arising from his placing over-emphasis on the effects of marine erosion and denudation. Thus he ascribed the so-called Parallel Roads of Glen Roy in Scotland (the shore lines of ancient glacial lakes) to marine action, and an over-large estimate for the time taken for the denudation of the Weald of Kent was given (important for giving a general idea of the age of the Earth) on the assumption that it had been eroded by the sea. In Australia, Darwin suggested that the great valleys of the Blue Mountains were produced by marine erosion – an idea that has not found subsequent favour.
7   It should be noted that J. W. Gruber has argued that the position of ship's naturalist was initially filled by the surgeon, Robert McCormick, and that Darwin was really a supernumerary appointment. (J. W. Gruber, 'Who was the *Beagle*'s naturalist?', *British Journal for the History of Science*, Vol. 4, 1969, pp.266-282.)

8   N. Barlow (ed.), *Charles Darwin's Diary of the Voyage of H.M.S. "Beagle" Edited from the MS*, Cambridge University Press, Cambridge, 1933, pp.39-40 (republished Kraus, Millwood, 1969).

9   *Ibid.*, p.132.

10 C. Darwin, *Journal of Researches into the Geology and Natural History of the Various Countries Visited by H.M.S. Beagle*, London, 1839, p.381 (republished International Publications Co., New York, 1969). Darwin's ideas on this matter were evidently descended from the vulcanism of James Hutton, refracted through the lens of Lyell's *Principles of Geology*.

11 For a detailed discussion of the Galapagos finches and Darwin's studies of these interesting creatures, see D. Lack, *Darwin's Finches*, Cambridge University Press, Cambridge, 1947.

12 C. Darwin, *Journal of Researches*, 2nd edn, London, 1845, p.380.

13 C. Darwin, *The Structure and Distribution of Coral Reefs. Being the First Part of the Geology of the Voyage of the Beagle, under the Command of Capt. Fitzroy, R.N. During the Years 1832 to 1836*, London, 1842 (republished Scholarly Press, Saint Clair Shores, 1977).

14 See above p.80.

15 See above p.80. For a definitive discussion of Darwin's geological researches in this area, see M. J. S. Rudwick, 'Darwin and Glen Roy: a "great failure" in scientific method?', *Studies in History and Philosophy of Science*, Vol. 5, 1974, pp.97-185.

16 Darwin's notes from the period when he was first trying to give a clear formulation to his theory have been published by Sir Gavin de Beer et al.: G. de Beer (ed.), 'Darwin's notebooks on transmutation of species Part I – First notebook (July 1837 – February 1838)', *Bulletin of the British Museum (Natural History) Historical Series*, Vol. 2 (No. 2), 1960, pp.25-73; 'Darwin's notebooks . . . Part II – Second notebook (February to July 1838)', *ibid*, Vol. 2 (No. 3), 1960, pp.75-118; 'Darwin's notebooks . . . Part III – Third notebook (July 15th, 1838 – October 2nd, 1838)', *ibid*, Vol. 2 (No. 4), 1960, pp. 119-150; 'Darwin's notebooks . . . Part IV – Fourth notebook (October, 1838 – 10 July, 1839)', *ibid*, Vol. 2 (No. 5), 1960, pp.151-183; G. de Beer & M. J. Rowlands (eds.), 'Addenda and corrigenda', *ibid*, Vol. 2 (No. 6), 1961, pp.185-200; G. de Beer, M. J. Rowlands & B. M. Skramovsky (eds.), 'Darwin's notebooks . . . Part VI: Pages excised by Darwin', *ibid*, Vol. 3 (No. 5), 1967, pp.129-176. See also G. de Beer (ed.), 'Darwin's journal', *ibid.*, Vol. 2 (No. 1), 1959, pp.1-21. Here we read (p.7): 'In July opened first notebook on "Transmutation of Species" – Had been greatly struck from about month of previous March [1837] on character of S. American fossils & species on Galapagos Archipelago. These facts origin (especially latter) of all my views'.

17 J. D. Hooker, *The Botany of the Antarctic Voyage of H.M. Discovery-Ships Erebus and Terror, in . . . 1839-1843, Under the Command of . . . Sir J. C. Ross. 1. Flora Antarctica. 2 pt.-II. Flora Novae Zelandicae. 2 pt.-III Flora Tasmaniae*, London, 1844-1860.

18 See G. Pickering, *Creative Malady: Illness in the Lives and Minds of Charles Darwin, Mary Baker Eddy, Sigmund Freud, Florence Nightingale, Marcel Proust and Elizabeth Barrett Browning*, O.U.P., London, 1974.

19 Needless to say, Darwin did not mean by this that he followed exactly the methodology recommended by Francis Bacon in his *Novum Organum*, drawing up tables of positive and negative instances, making rejections and exclusions, drawing the 'first vintage', and so on. Presumably he wished to claim that he was working 'inductively' from a large mass of empirical data rather than in some aprioristic manner. Bacon was highly regarded as a philosopher of science in Britain in the early nineteenth century, although people never followed his program precisely. It is in no way surprising that Darwin proclaimed an allegiance to Bacon, without, in fact, being a 'true Baconian'.

20 F. Darwin (ed.), *The Life and Letters of Charles Darwin, including an Autobiographical Chapter*, 3 vols, John Murray, London, 1887, Vol. 1, p.83.

21 C. Darwin, *A Monograph of the Fossil Lepadidae, or Pedunculated Cirripedes of Great Britain*, London, 1851; *A Monograph of the Fossil Balanidae and Verrucidae of Great Britain*, London, 1854 (with index to the latter published separately in 1858); *A Monograph of the Sub-Class Cirripedia . . . The Lepadidae; or, Pedunculated Cirripedes*, London, 1851; *The Balanidae (or Sessile Cirripedes); the Verrucidae, etc.*, London, 1853.

22 *The Origin* ran to six editions and Darwin was kept busy with emendations through much of the latter part of his life. The six editions were published on November 26, 1859 and December 26, 1859, and in 1861, 1866, 1869, 1872 and 1876 respectively. For a detailed discussion of the history of the publication of *The Origin* and a composite representation of the various versions of the text, see M. Peckham (ed.), *The Origin of Species by Charles Darwin: A Variorum Text*, Pennsylvania University Press, Philadelphia, 1959.

23 For a discussion of this, see D. Fleming, 'Charles Darwin, the anaesthetic man', *Victorian Studies*, Vol. 4, 1961, pp.219-236, and J. A. Campbell, 'Nature, religion and emotional response: a reconsideration of Darwin's affective decline', *Victorian Studies*, Vol. 18, 1974-1975, pp.159-174.

24 For Huxley's account of his coining of the term, see T. H. Huxley, *Science and Christian Tradition (Collected Essays, Volume 5)*, London, 1895, p.239.

25 For some of Darwin's remarks on religious matters see F. Darwin, *op. cit.* (note 20), Chapter 8.
26 *Ibid.*, p.307.
27 *Ibid.*, p.313.
28 *Ibid.*, pp.102-103 & 107.

7

The Origin of Species

In this chapter, we will be concerned with three topics: a brief account of the events that led up to the publication of the first edition of *The Origin of Species* in 1859; a general exposition of the doctrines of Darwin's major work; a suggested account of the steps that may have led Darwin to the formulation of his theory.

The *Origin of Species*: its composition and publication

We have already seen, from a passage in Darwin's *Autobiography* reproduced in Chapter 5, that he prepared provisional written sketches of his theory in 1842 and 1844.[1] It should be noted, however, that quite recently the Darwin scholar Peter Vorzimmer has examined a document among the Darwin archives at Cambridge which he considers may represent an even earlier version of parts of the theory, probably from 1839.[2]

The pencil sketch of June, 1842, was only 35 pages long. It was discovered late in the nineteenth century, and was first published by Darwin's son, Francis, in 1909. The fuller ink version of 1844 ran to 230 pages. It was not intended for publication, although instructions were given that it should be published in the event of Darwin's death. The theory of 1844 was substantially the same as that of *The Origin of Species* in 1859.

After the completion of the 1844 sketch, Darwin spent some time revising his *Journal* of the *Beagle* voyage for its second edition,[3] and writing up the *Geology of South America*.[4] He then gave his attention to the study of barnacles for a number of years, finding that their investigation required considerably more time and effort than was originally anticipated, though ultimately he was rewarded for his labours with these smelly animals[5] when he won the coveted Royal Society Medal for biology in 1853.

Despite the distraction presented by the barnacles, Darwin continued to collect information that bore on his evolutionary theory and the problem of the origin of species in the 1840s and '50s. He discussed his ideas in detail with his friends Hooker and Lyell, and in 1857 sent a summary statement of his theory to the American botanist Asa Gray (1810-1888), but requested that he should not make the theory known publicly. Nevertheless, despite Darwin's apparent reticence on the subject, it is clear that a number of other prominent scientists were aware that he was working out a general theory of evolution at this time.

In 1856, Darwin started work on a definitive statement of the ideas that had been gradually fermenting in his mind ever since the voyage of *Beagle* — 'my big book', as he referred to it in his correspondence.[6] This work was to have been entitled *Natural Selection*. It is well known that it was never completed, but the manuscript fortunately survived and has recently been edited and published by R. C. Stauffer.[7]

Work on *Natural Selection* was well advanced by mid-1858,[8] when, on June 18, Darwin was shattered to receive a manuscript from A. R. Wallace (1823-1913), an English naturalist who was at that time working in the East Indies.[9] The title of Wallace's paper, which he had sent to Darwin for his evaluation, was 'On the law which has regulated the introduction of new species'. It was immediately clear to the recipient that the author had arrived quite independently at essentially the same theory as Darwin's doctrine of the evolution of organisms by means of natural selection.

Darwin, of course, had been in possession of the theory for many years, but he had not established his 'right' to it by formal publication.[10] Consequently, his first impulse on receiving Wallace's communication was to give up entirely any claims to priority in the matter. However, he was dissuaded from this action by Lyell and Hooker, and eventually it was arranged that a 'joint paper' should be presented to the Linnean Society in London, consisting of Wallace's quite short essay, with extracts from Darwin's sketch of 1844 and from his letter to Asa Gray of 1857.[11] The joint contribution was communicated to the Society by Lyell and Hooker on July 1, 1858,[12] but neither Darwin nor Wallace were present at this first public exposition of the new doctrine.

It is curious that the paper apparently aroused negligible interest at the meeting, and the President of the Linnean Society, Thomas Bell, in commenting subsequently on the year's activities made the extraordinary statement that 'The year which has passed . . . has not . . . been marked by any of those striking discoveries which at once revolutionise, so to speak, the department of science on which they bear'.[13] It is hard indeed to account for this initial lack of interest on the part of the scientific establishment, when one considers the excitement that surrounded the publication of *The Origin of Species* only a year later.

After the public presentation of the Linnean Society joint paper, Darwin changed his intentions entirely and decided to bring out a shortened and more popular version of his theory, without the massive erudition and parade of footnotes that had been planned for *Natural Selection*. The original plan was to bring out a quick series of papers with the Linnean Society, but *The Origin* proved too bulky for this format, although not by any means reaching the projected size of *Natural Selection*. Consequently, it was determined that the theory should be presented in the form of a book. The holograph was ready by March, 1859, and by September *The Origin of Species* had been printed and the proofs corrected. The first edition of 1250 copies was presented to the public on November 26, 1859. All copies were immediately sold and Darwin's early fears that the book would be a failure and a financial embarrassment to the publisher, John Murray, proved quite false.[14]

It is not usually very fruitful to speculate what *might* have happened in history *if* . . . ; but in this instance it is an interesting thought that the whole reception of the theory and the subsequent aberrations of 'Social Darwinism' might have been very different if Darwin had chosen to complete the full version of his theory, with all the paraphernalia of footnotes and references, for its readership would assuredly have been much smaller, and its wider influence correspondingly less. If Wallace had not sent his manuscript to Darwin, therefore, the history of Western culture might very well have been rather different in the last hundred years!

Darwin's Evolutionary Theory: the general argument of *The Origin of Species*

The first edition of *The Origin of Species*,[15] although very much shorter than the projected work on *Natural Selection*, was made up of fourteen chapters – about 155,000 words. The first four chapters – dealing respectively with 'Variation under domestication', 'Variation under nature', 'The struggle for existence', and 'Natural selection' – contain the core of Darwin's argument. The fifth chapter dealt with the laws of variation of organisms, but it was less successful than the rest of the book, for Darwin did not possess an adequate theory of inheritance, and as will be demonstrated subsequently it was at this point that the theory ultimately broke down, only to be resuscitated, with the help of Gregor Mendel's particulate theory of inheritance,[16] early in the twentieth century.

Chapter 6 ('Difficulties on theory') was written, no doubt, with the intention of pre-empting the attacks of potential critics. The remaining chapters were devoted to a discussion of the many observations which could find a simple and satisfactory explanation in terms of the Darwinian theory: the stratigraphical record, the geographical distribution of organisms, morphological and embryological observations, rudimentary organs, problems of taxonomy, instincts and the phenomena of hybridism. What had in many cases been isolated or inexplicable facts in the theory of special creations – the 'gill slits' observed in the early stages of the development of human embryos, for example – were shown by Darwin to be readily comprehensible in terms of his evolutionary theory.

Darwin's long argument began in Chapter 1 with a discussion of the phenomena of variation among living organisms. It was, he claimed, an obvious empirical fact that organisms in a species vary, and that the variations are inherited. Moreover, variation was obviously associated with sexual reproduction. For example, where plants reproduce asexually or vegetatively the offspring resemble the parents exactly. Darwin also claimed that the environment has some effect upon variation. He asserted, for example, that domestic animals are more prone to vary than wild types, and he ascribed this difference to the stimulus of the environment. In fact, we find in the very first chapter of *The Origin* clear instances of 'Lamarckian' thinking[17] – a point that is often overlooked by people who believe the Darwinian and Lamarckian theories to be antithetical. Darwin admitted that the laws governing inheritance were quite unknown to him.[18]

The remainder of Chapter 1 was devoted to a detailed discussion of *artificial* selection, chiefly using pigeons as the example for discussion. Darwin was unable to demonstrate the formation of new varieties or species in the wild state, but he *was* able to show how man had produced new varieties by artificial selection, and he could then claim by analogy that varieties and species could have been produced by some kind of selection process in nature. It is, I think, important to emphasise the considerable role played by analogical reasoning in the total structure of Darwin's argument.

It should be realised that Darwin was never able to trace the ancestry of domestic pigeons back to the common rock pigeon (from which they were supposedly derived), for the breeders' records did not go back far enough. So not only was the total argument of *The Origin* based to a considerable extent on analogical reasoning, but also there was a significant lacuna in the actual analogue that was chosen as the basis for discussion. However, there were occasional 'throwbacks' among domestic pigeons to the presumed ancestral rock pigeons, so it seemed not unreasonable to suggest that the domestic breeds were in fact derived from such forebears.

It is important also to note that in his first chapter Darwin was at pains to emphasise that there is no fundamental difference between varieties and species; he wished to maintain a kind of continuum between them. This point is significant, for it marked a departure from the traditional essentialist view of species. We will refer to it again below.[19]

The argument about the blurring of the classical distinction between varieties and species is carried further in Chapter 2. Varieties, says Darwin, are merely incipient species.[20] He notes that the groups which contain the dominant species (e.g., the *Compositae*, or the Eucalypts) are larger than the less predominant groups, and reveal the greatest degree of variation. He suggests that the species of the large genera are analogous to the varieties within a species, which suggests that they have a similar origin. Moreover, the larger genera tend to break up into smaller genera and thus 'the forms of life throughout the universe become divided into groups subordinate to groups'.[21]

In the first two chapters of *The Origin*, then, Darwin had convinced readers that organisms vary, and transmit the variations to their offspring, but that there is no fundamental difference between varieties and species. And selection was the key to biological change.

Chapter 3, as we have said, deals with the idea of struggle for existence among living organisms. Darwin refers to the arguments of Malthus, claiming that the tendency for organisms to increase their numbers in geometrical ratio, coupled with the limitations in food supply, will necessarily lead to a struggle for existence. Of course, this need not always be in a literal 'tooth and claw' sense, like two dogs fighting for a bone. It might, for example, be competition for light and space among plants, or 'competition' between them for the attention of birds that might disseminate their seeds.

Here is Darwin on the struggle for existence:

A struggle for existence inevitably follows from the high rate at which all organic beings tend to increase. Every being, which during its natural lifetime produces several eggs or seeds, must suffer destruction during some period of its life, and during some season or occasional year, otherwise, on the principle of geometrical increase, its numbers would quickly become so inordinately great that no country could support the product. Hence, as more individuals are produced than can possibly survive, there must in every case be a struggle for existence, either one individual with another of the same species, or with the individuals of distinct species, or with the physical conditions of life. It is the doctrine of Malthus applied with manifold force to the whole animal and vegetable kingdoms; for in this case there can be no artificial increase of food, and no prudential restraint from marriage. Although some species may be now increasing, more or less rapidly, in numbers, all cannot do so, for the world would not hold them.[22]

And in a famous passage, Darwin likened the pressure of populations on the available resources to:

ten thousand sharp wedges packed close together and driven inwards by incessant blows, sometimes one wedge being struck and then another with greater force.[23]

This simile had been used by Darwin through the various earlier versions of his theory.

Chapter 3 of *The Origin* is also interesting as a means of displaying his understanding of the ecological inter-relationships between organisms living in association with each other in a biological community. On one particularly well-known page[24] he showed that the number of red clover plants growing in a given region could be proportional to the number of cats living in that area. For clovers are pollinated by bumble bees; the nests of bumble bees are destroyed by field mice; and mice are destroyed by cats.[25] But such relationships, as envisaged by Darwin, are not to be confused with Linnaeus's version of the balance of nature. Even today, we sometimes hear the expression that one must not upset the balance of nature, the implication being that if we do the whole set of inter-relationships of living organisms will fall to pieces. But such was not Darwin's view. He envisaged that all the parts of a community 'interlock' with each other in a state which may be compared with the 'dynamic equilibrium' of physical chemistry. Changes could occur within the system, and new conditions of equilibria be produced as a result. Moreover, the whole system might gradually evolve in the course of time. This was a very different picture from Linnaeus's view of a static hierarchical system of inter-relationships, with no changes in these relations other than a continuing expansion of organic forms over the Earth.[26] Darwin's fourth chapter on 'Natural selection' formed the core of his whole book. This quotation gives the real nub of his argument:

> Can it, then, be thought improbable, seeing that variations useful to man have undoubtedly occurred, that other variations useful in some way to each being in the great and complex battle of life, should sometimes occur in the course of thousands of generations? If such do occur, can we doubt (remembering that many more individuals are born than can possibly survive) that individuals having any advantage, however slight, over others, would have the best chance of surviving and of procreating their kind? On the other hand, we may feel sure that any variation in the least degree injurious would be rigidly destroyed. This preservation of favourable variations and the rejection of injurious variations, I call Natural Selection.[27]

This, in all its simplicity, was the basic mechanism that Darwin used to account for the evolution of organisms. The pressure of population upon available resources led to selection. This was the analogue of the selection process used by man to breed various varieties of pigeon, for natural selection was not a random process. It tended to operate so as to produce organisms that showed the optimum fit to the conditions of existence. Darwin put forward this concept with considerable literary skill:

> It may be said that natural selection is daily and hourly scrutinising, throughout the world, every variation, even the slightest; rejecting that which is bad, preserving and adding up all that is good; silently and insensibly working, whenever and wherever opportunity offers, at the improvement of each organic being in relation to its organic and inorganic conditions of life. We see nothing of these slow changes in progress, until the hand of time has marked the long lapse of ages, and then so imperfect is our view into long past geological ages, that we only see that the forms of life are now different from what they formerly were.[28]

This argument, however, only brings us to the conclusion that natural selection, operating through the vast ages of geological history, will result in biological improvement, or better adaptation of organisms to their environments. It does not lead us to conclude that species formation will occur. And because Darwin believed in what is called the blending theory of inheritance,[29] it was difficult to see how natural selection could in fact cause species to break up into varieties, then into sub-species, and finally into new species. However, Darwin was able to account for this more or less satisfactorily by two subsidiary components of his theory: the principle of divergence and the principle of geographical isolation.

In discussing the principle of divergence, Darwin made use once again of the analogy of selection among domestic animals to form new breeds. For example, a breeder who wishes to produce two different breeds from a single stock, breeds from the extreme forms that are available to him, eliminating the intermediate forms. But, Darwin argued,[30] there is an analogous process in nature, for the competition for resources is always greatest between the most similar forms. Consequently, there is always a tendency for varieties to diverge and occupy different 'niches'[31] in the world — for the most distinct forms have the best chance of survival, if they can escape from competition with their fellows.

Darwin was able to bring forward some direct experimental evidence which supported the idea of the principle of divergence. He showed, for example, that if a plot of grass is sown with one species of grass, and a similar plot is sown with several different genera of grasses, then in the latter case one finds that there is a greater number of plants growing successfully, and a greater weight of dry vegetable matter produced. As Darwin put it: 'The greatest amount of life can be supported by great diversification of structure'.[32] On this principle we might say (speaking in twentieth-century terms) that the principle of divergence encourages the formation of new species by the occupation of different ecological niches.

Darwin believed that geographical isolation was the second phenomenon that could offset the effects of blending inheritance. During the voyage of *Beagle*, he had noticed that when animal and plant communities were geographically isolated from each other, small differences could often be discerned — as he had seen in the Galapagos Islands, or on opposite sides of the Andes. These observations could be generalised to the principle of geographical isolation. Fortuitous variations might occur in isolated populations, so that in time the course of evolution might run in different directions in the isolated areas, since the different variations might be sifted by natural selection in slightly different ways if interbreeding were prevented — even if the environmental conditions were almost identical. If the conditions differed, then the formation of new varieties, and eventually new species, might occur even more easily.

At the end of Chapter 4, Darwin gave a summary statement of his great principle of natural selection: the motor of evolutionary change. Because this was really what the whole book was about, and because it was Darwin's theory that led to such remarkable changes in such subjects as social theory, literature and philosophy in the latter part of the nineteenth century — the Darwinian Revolution in fact — it is worth repeating Darwin's words here, to give full emphasis to the nature of the theory and the way Darwin saw it:

> If during the long course of ages and under varying conditions of life, organic beings vary at all in the several parts of their organisation, and I think this cannot be disputed; if there be, owing to the high geometrical powers of increase of each species, at some age, season, or year, a severe struggle for life, and this certainly cannot be disputed; then, considering the infinite complexity of the relations of all organic beings to each other and to their conditions of existence, causing an infinite diversity in structure, constitution, and habits, it would be a most ex-

traordinary fact if no variation ever had occurred useful to each being's own welfare, in the same way as so many variations have occurred useful to man. But if variations useful to any organic being do occur, assuredly individuals thus characterised will have the best chance of being preserved in the struggle for life; and from the strong principle of inheritance they will tend to produce offspring similarly characterised. This principle of preservation, I have called, for the sake of brevity, Natural Selection.[33]

Finally, Darwin completed his great fourth chapter, the core of the book, the heart of the Darwinian Revolution, by referring to the ancient metaphor of the 'tree of life' as a means of describing the evolutionary development of organisms through the operation of natural selection. However, as he suggested elsewhere, it would really be more apt to refer to a 'coral of life'[34] since the lower parts of a coral and the lower parts of the evolutionary history of organisms are no longer living.

Chapter 5, dealing with the 'Laws of variation', was perhaps the least successful part of the whole work. As Darwin admitted quite bluntly: 'Our ignorance of the laws of variation is profound'.[35] And later it was this part of the total theory, with the problems of inheritance, which gave him by far the most difficulties. He was quite willing to include the doctrine of inheritance of acquired characteristics as a component of his theory,[36] although he did not acknowledge it as an idea associated particularly with the theories of Lamarck, and as we have seen his private remarks in his correspondence about Lamarck were far from complimentary. This chapter is interesting, however, in that Darwin was now able to give a simple explanation, in terms of his theory, for Cuvier's principle of the correlation of parts,[37] whereas for Cuvier it had been more like an unproven axiom in his biological theory.

Chapter 6 dealt with Darwin's attempts to forestall criticisms of his doctrines by considering various possible 'Difficulties on theory'. These will not be dealt with here, though some of them will be considered in our tenth chapter. We may note, however, that Darwin emphasised again how his theory could give an explanation of the Cuvierian principle of 'conditions of existence'.[38]

Darwin's seventh chapter on 'Instinct' is of considerable interest, and he brought forward numerous instances, drawn from his very wide knowledge of natural history, of instinctive behaviour. His basic idea, of course, was that organisms showed variations in innate behaviour patterns, which — like actual bodily structures — might be acted upon by the mechanism of natural selection. He again used the analogy of animals under domestication. Some dogs might display a predisposition to 'point', others to 'retrieve', others to run around a flock of sheep rather than at them. These apparently innate tendencies might be selected by breeders. Similarly, argued Darwin, natural selection might act so as to enhance or eliminate certain behaviour patterns among animals.

Darwin considered in some detail the interesting case of bees. There is considerable variation in the kinds of cells made by bees, from the clumsy and crude edifices of the bumble bees to the almost perfect hexagonal combs of domestic bees. But it takes about fifteen pounds of sugar and pollen to make a pound of wax, and consequently there is a considerable advantage in the struggle for existence if the minimum quantity of wax consistent with a mechanically sound structure is used in the making of the combs. It is easy to show by elementary mathematics that if the combs are constructed with hexagonal cells this produces the maximum space from a given amount of wax; or, putting it another way, it uses the minimum quantity of wax for the construction of a particular volume of cells. Thus the instinctive behaviour that favoured the construction of perfectly hexagonal combs would tend to be favoured by natural selection. Darwin maintained that it was irrelevant that the bees which performed the comb-building operations were themselves infertile insects. One had to think of the whole hive as a kind of 'super-organism'. If the queen laid eggs that produced workers that varied either in physical structure or behaviour in ways that favoured the hive as a whole then that hive would be more likely to survive. By this line of argument, then, Darwin was able to account very satisfactorily for the apparent 'design' of the honeycomb. One still meets people who argue that only God could have given bees the almost miraculous power to construct their combs.[39] But Darwin offered an acceptable naturalistic explanation of the phenomenon back in 1859. Of course, the proponents of design may be right, as far as logical arguments can show. God *may* have designed bees in such a way that they are able to construct their combs in the way they do. But Darwin's naturalistic explanation certainly took much of the wind out of the sails of those who argued for some divine, omniscient and omnipotent, transcendent creator of the universe, responsible for all the apparent design that we see around us.

Darwin's eighth chapter was concerned with 'hybridism'. As is well known, a great many interspecific hybrids such as mules, 'zedonks', 'geeps', 'tigrons' are sterile. On the other hand, crosses between varieties of the same species tend to produce 'mongrels', which are usually highly fertile. It might appear at first sight that the sterility of hybrids would place a severe limitation upon the evolutionary process. If mules, for example, were fertile, this would give a quick and easy way of producing new species from horses and donkeys. And if one were contemplating basing a doctrine of evolutionary change through the formation of hybrids — as Linnaeus had to some degree envisaged in the latter part of his career[40] — then certainly it would be a severe objection if it could be shown that hybrids were always infertile. But Darwin's mechanism simply did not operate through the formation of hybrids, or the 'convergence' of species. Rather, he was concerned with the 'divergence' of species, according to the mechanisms that we have outlined above. So the question of whether hybrids were fertile was almost irrelevant to Darwin's argument. And he was able to show that in a number of important instances, particularly among plants, interspecific hybrids were in fact fertile. So he could argue that there was no fundamental or ontological difference between species and varieties, as far as one could tell from the evidence provided by an examination of hybrids. This, it should be noted, was the theoretical position that Darwin constantly emphasised. Species were not supernaturally imposed, or God-given, special creations.

Chapters 9 and 10, 'On the imperfection of the geological record' and 'On the geological succession of organic beings', contain some very interesting material. Obviously one of the strongest arguments in Darwin's favour was that he could give a general account of the appearance of the stratigraphical column in terms of his doctrine of evolution by natural selection. But in points of detail there were difficulties. It was not possible in 1859 to point to any really good examples of obviously graded evolutionary trends among fossils,[41] and there were many instances of apparently sudden appearance or disappearance of organic forms. Consequently, Darwin was forced to plead that the stratigraphical record was as yet known very incompletely, and was in any case itself a very incomplete record, for according to the Lyellian doctrine, to which Darwin strongly adhered, rocks were constantly being removed by weathering and erosion, or altered by metamorphism, just as much as they were being formed, and fossils preserved. One has to admit that Darwin was perfectly correct in his claims about the incompleteness of the stratigraphical record, as known in his day, but it certainly weakened his argument that he was unable to point to any single instance of a definite graded evolutionary sequence of organisms among the whole of the paleontological record.

Chapter 9 contained an important discussion about the possible age of the Earth. Here Darwin gave an estimate of three hundred million years as the time that would have been taken for the denudation of the valley of the Weald in Kent — an estimate based upon the assumption that the erosion had chiefly been performed by the action of the sea, cutting into the strata at a rate of one inch per century. If this figure were correct, it would give an immense age for the Earth as a whole, for the strata of Kent stand as quite recent rocks in the stratigraphical column. It is natural that Darwin would wish to argue for as great an age for the Earth as possible, so that the very slow process of evolution by natural selection would have sufficient time to operate. However, he was — we now believe — mistaken in his estimate. The erosion of the Weald is thought to have been chiefly due to sub-aerial agencies, rather than the sea, so that the very basis of Darwin's calculation was utterly false. It is worth noting that three of the most prominent scientific 'mistakes' that he made in the course of his career were all associated with this erroneous emphasis on marine erosion: the fiasco of the theory of the Parallel Roads of Glen Roy; the suggestion about the possible causes of the formation of the valleys of the Blue Mountains in Australia; the case of the erosion of the Weald that we have just been considering. This was probably due in part to Darwin's youthful experiences on the voyage of *Beagle*, where he must surely have been greatly impressed by the erosive powers of the sea. But he was also psychologically committed wholeheartedly to all the geological doctrines of

Lyell's *Principles of Geology*. And Lyell also placed undue emphasis on the doctrine of marine denudations.[42]

Darwin's estimate for the time taken to erode the Weald was withdrawn from the later editions of *The Origin*, and it is worth noting that the problem of geological time caused him very great difficulty in his later years. For the physicist, Lord Kelvin (William Thomson) (1824-1907), maintained that if the Earth were to lose heat at the rate at which it was observed to be losing it for as long as the geologists demanded, then either it could not possibly be as old as they said, or the Earth would be much colder than at present. Necessarily, therefore, the Earth had to be thought of as a relatively youthful object — perhaps about one hundred million years old.[43] Needless to say, this placed a severe strain on the Darwinian argument, and all that Darwin and the geologists could do was to hope that something would turn up to vindicate their position and nullify Kelvin's calculations. As is well known, something did eventually turn up, namely the discovery of the phenomenon of radioactivity, and of heat-generating radioactive minerals within the Earth. But this discovery occurred too late to be of any assistance to Darwin, under attack from a somewhat unexpected quarter — the mathematical physicists.

Chapters 11 and 12 are concerned with the problems of the 'Geographical distribution' of organisms and the bearing of the doctrine of evolution by natural selection on such problems. Darwin argued that the best explanation of the facts was to assume that new species arose in certain places, and then might be distributed and modified subsequently by migrations, the possible mechanisms for which he discussed at some length. This, he thought, provided a more comprehensible account of the facts than was offered by the assumption of the multiple creation of the same species in different situations.

It was in Chapter 13, on the 'Mutual affinities of organic beings: morphology; embryology; rudimentary organs' — the last to introduce new material into the general argument of the book — that Darwin took up the question of the relation of his theory to problems of taxonomy. As we have seen above, it was commonly believed by taxonomists — working within the long tradition of the Aristotelian theory of naming and classifying — that classification should reveal the *essential* differences between natural kinds. But the nature of the essences revealed by the various systems of classification that were devised remained exceedingly obscure. The eighteenth-century taxonomists had sought a single character which would successfully mark off a whole group of similar organisms, and would bring together things which could be recognised intuitively as forming a natural kind. Just occasionally such single characteristics were found successfully, as for example the milk glands of mammals which seemed to be linked with a group of common characteristics such as the possession of hair, warm red blood and viviparous birth. Seemingly the possession of mammary glands was a definite mark serving as a criterion for the recognition of a particular natural kind. But was it the *essential* feature of mammalian character? Or should the possession of hair, or viviparous birth, be the criterion? It was very difficult to answer such questions with any degree of conviction or unanimity.

Darwin was able to resolve such difficulties at the theoretical level (although practical difficulties often remained) by maintaining that the classification of organisms should be based on the study of their genealogies, or, as he put it, on the 'propinquity of descent, the only known cause of the similarity of organic beings'.[44] This, he said, is 'the bond, hidden as it is by various degrees of modification, which is ... revealed to us by our classifications'.[45]

Darwin shifted attention away from the search for single essential characters which might serve as marks of whole groups. Rather, he said, one should consider clusters or aggregates of characters when attempting to identify natural kinds, and taxonomic distinctions should be made on the basis of genealogical differences. Then systematists 'will not be incessantly haunted by the shadowy doubt whether this or that form be in essence a species'.[46] And, he continued, 'This I feel sure, and I speak after experience, will be no slight relief'.[47] His whole approach to taxonomic problems becomes comprehensible in the light of the famous fan-shaped diagram, showing the evolutionary divergence of species, which was included in his chapter on 'Natural selection'.[48]

Examination of this diagram will readily show how Darwin might account for the map-like representation of the families of the vegetable kingdom, such as had been put forward by Linnaeus/Giseke in the eighteenth century, or systems such as that of Cuvier's four *embranchements* in the early nineteenth century. These were, so to speak, horizontal time-slices through a Darwinian evolutionary or genealogical system of taxonomy. But there was an even more fundamental difference between the Linnaean system based on the appraisal of visible characters and the Darwinian system based on genealogies.

Let us recall Lyell's notion of environmental determinism, and his supposition that if the appropriate circumstances were to recur the iguanodon might once again be found roaming in the forests. If this creature were in all physical, mental and behavioural respects identical with the ancient reptiles, then according to Linnaeus, Cuvier or Lyell, they would necessarily be placed in the same species. But according to Darwin, the 'old' and the 'new' iguanodons, though identical in appearance, would necessarily have different genealogies, and should, therefore, be regarded as different species.

Thus the Darwinian theory gave a perfectly clear account of the theoretical approach that should be pursued by taxonomists. But for practical purposes it must be admitted that more often than not it made absolutely no difference to the taxonomists' puzzles and problems. A naturalist is faced with the problems of classifying and naming animals and plants in a zoo, botanical

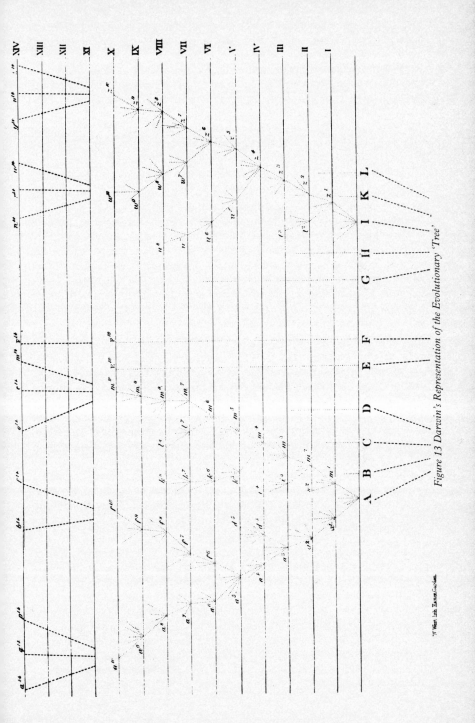

Figure 13 Darwin's Representation of the Evolutionary 'Tree'

garden or museum, or specimens in their native habitats. He does not normally have the opportunity to dig down in to the stratigraphical column to reveal the genealogies of the organisms he is attempting to classify. Nevertheless, Darwin maintained that 'descent' had in fact been used unconsciously by taxonomists, and that the various rules and guides they had established in order to build up their classifications had been directed towards identifying organisms with common genealogies. And we might say that because the stratigraphical column has now been more thoroughly explored, all that Darwin asserted as a theoretical basis for taxonomic practice seems to have been sufficiently confirmed.

To put the matter in a somewhat clearer light, we might say that it would have been quite outside the way of thinking of the Linnaean taxonomist — the eighteen-century man of the Enlightenment — to have looked into the *past* condition of things as a guide to the classification of the *present* scheme of existence. It simply would not have occurred to Linnaeus[49] to have done this, for if all creatures were originally created in their kinds by a single divine act, to have looked at the past development of organisms as a guide to the understanding of their present existences would have seemed quite futile. But for Darwin the historical, evolutionary genealogies of organisms provided the key to the understanding of the way they should be classified.

As noted above,[50] the first attempt to use the principles of Darwinian taxonomy for the purpose of systematising a biological investigation was made in J. D. Hooker's *Flora of Tasmania*, published in 1860. Hooker, of course, had been a confidant of Darwin for a considerable time, so we have no reason to suppose that he suddenly rewrote his book after the publication of *The Origin of Species*. The chief problem that Hooker set out to solve was the geographical distribution of plants, but he was by no means entirely successful in this attempt, despite the insight provided by the Darwinian theory. Hooker, needless to say, did not know anything about the theory of continental drift or the eustatic control of sea levels associated with the coming and going of the glacial epochs.[51] Such knowledge is really needed if one is to make some sense of all the problems of animal and plant distributions in the southern continents. Nevertheless, Hooker was able to gain a considerable degree of insight into his problems, despite his lack of these extra pieces of theoretical information.

The only other aspect of *The Origin of Species* that need be mentioned here briefly is the section from Chapter 13 on embryology and recapitulation. It will be recalled that Chambers, the anonymous author of *Vestiges*, had previously made a great deal of the embryological argument, and it had also been an important feature of the work of Nature Philosophers such as Oken, or those influenced by this movement such as Geoffroy Saint-Hilaire. To explain the facts of embryology, Darwin, as always, had recourse to analogies drawn with domesticated animals. He pointed out, for example, that puppies of dogs of different breeds were much more alike than were the adult dogs. Among humans, it may only become apparent in quite late childhood whether a person is ultimately going to be tall or short. Young children are much more similar than adults in all sorts of ways, such as intelligence, physical strength and sexuality. By analogy, then, the morphological similarities in the forms of embryos might perhaps be anticipated. Darwin's total theory, simple as it is, may now be given in his own words:

> The embryo is the animal in its less modified state; and in so far it reveals the structure of its progenitor ... Community in embryonic structure reveals community of descent ... The embryo [can be seen as] a picture, more or less obscured, of the common parent-form of each great class of animals.[52]

It must be admitted that Darwin was not really *explaining*, in any very satisfactory way, exactly how the phenomena of embryological recapitulation might occur. What he was doing, however, was to show how the facts of embryology were at least compatible with evolution, no longer appearing as a peculiar and idiosyncratic feature of the world, perhaps only to be understood through some metaphysical doctrine such as that of the archetypal *Urtier*.

With this, we may complete our brief sketch of the general outline of the arguments of *The Origin of Species*. In Chapter 9, we shall look more closely at the logical structure of Darwin's argument, but for the time being it will be sufficient to note here the general way Darwin sought to bring conviction to the minds of his readers by accumulating a vast mass of small items of information, which, individually, would not convert one from being a special creationist, but which, taken together, certainly presented an extremely convincing case. It was the great number of hitherto isolated bits and pieces of information that all fitted nicely into place when viewed through the glass of Darwin's theory of evolution by natural selection that made the totality of the argument so attactive, even though, as we shall see, individual segments of the argument were often far from plausible or convincing from a logical standpoint.

Let us now look at the steps that led Darwin to the formulation of his theory.

The Origin of *The Origin*

Despite the fact that we have an explicit statement in Darwin's *Autobiography* that he arrived at his explanation of the origin of species through his reading of Malthus,[53] it is clear that this by no means represents the whole of the story, and historians of science of recent years have exerted a quite remarkable amount of energy in attempting to pin down with perfect precision the exact steps that led to the establishment of the theory. But the task is a complex one, and even now we do not, perhaps, have the full story. It is not really essential that we should trace all the discussions that have gone on in the academic literature in recent years on this tangled question. I will, therefore, confine myself to a highly condensed account of the matter, presenting only a few of the points of controversy but offering references to some of the more recent papers that have considered this interesting question.

Several stages in the development of Darwin's thought seem to be distinguishable. As a young man, under the influence of Paleyism and the general intellectual milieu within which he had been nurtured, Darwin was undoubtedly a special creationist, despite the fact that his grandfather Erasmus was one of the eighteenth-century evolutionists. But during the course of the *Beagle* voyage, Darwin apparently came across a considerable amount of evidence that was difficult to reconcile with the special creationist thesis, and he became aware of evidence that suggested the evolution of organisms. The evolutionary hypothesis seems to have gradually taken hold, but initially Darwin was probably seeing his explanation in terms of a *quasi*-Lamarckian mechanism. Later, he began to think of the analogy between artificial selection and selection processes in nature, which would lead to the formation of new species. And finally, on reading Malthus, Darwin quite suddenly came to realise how population pressure and the concomitant struggle for existence could give rise to natural selection, which in course of time would result in evolutionary development. It should be noted that the principle of divergence did not appear in the sketches of the theory written in 1842 and 1844, and at that time Darwin had to rely on the principle of geographical isolation to account for the formation of new species through natural selection.

Let us now add a little detail to this outline. There is some evidence in the journal and notebooks of the *Beagle* voyage that Darwin's thoughts were beginning to turn towards evolutionary views as early as 1832 or 1833. He was, for example, considerably impressed by the similarity of the extinct giant quadrupeds of South America to their modern counterparts.[54] He noted also that the forms of some of the animals, such as the rheas, changed quite significantly as he travelled south down the continent.[55] On Rat Island, near Montevideo, he noted a lizard with rudimentary limbs, which seemed to mark 'the passage by which Nature joins the Lizards to the Snakes'.[56] And he noted three kinds of South American birds which used their wings for purposes other than flight: the penguin for swimming as if they were fins; the 'steamer' duck for paddling; and the ostrich or rhea as sails.[57]

On the other hand, it is known that Darwin received a copy of the second volume of the first edition of Lyell's *Principles* in Montevideo in November, 1832. This gives a detailed account of Lamarck's evolutionary theory, but expressed a firm preference on Lyell's part for the doctrine of the fixity of species. It is noteworthy that Darwin made no protest at this in his marginalia,[58] but this negative evidence could perhaps be discounted since he was intellectually very much overawed by Lyell, and was attempting to model his work on Lyell's methodological and theoretical principles.

Darwin seems to have been considering the problems of island populations when he visited the Falkland Islands in March, 1834. It was in 1835 that he noted the different flora and fauna on the opposite sides of the Andes, and it was in this year that he visited the Galapagos Islands. In a letter to a sister in England, Darwin tells us that he was expecting to make biological discoveries of importance when he arrived at the Islands.[59] But it was not until late in the visit to the archipelago that he realised the significance of the variations in birds and tortoises from one island to another, for at first he made his collections without recording which island each particular specimen came from.[60] To me, this has always seemed somewhat surprising, considering that Darwin was obviously expecting to discover something of special significance when he got to the Galapagos Islands. However, he was quick to notice that animals and plants were generally similar to but in some ways different from the mainland types. This had also been noted much earlier at the Cape Verde Islands and elsewhere. Towards the end of the voyage, Darwin noted in his field note book that his observations in the Galapagos Islands seemed to undermine the doctrine of the stability of species.[61]

In Lyell's *Principles*, one may find the suggestion that organisms can respond to changing environmental conditions in three ways: extinction, migration, and 'accommodation' − this last implying a limited degree of adaptation, though not such as to amount to evolutionary change. During the course of the voyage, and presumably under the influence of Lyell's ideas, Darwin gave special attention to the questions of extinction, geographical distribution and adaptation. Lyell's work, therefore, provided a kind of framework for investigation within which Darwin found it congenial to operate.[62] But he was disposed to substitute adaptation for the more limited 'accommodation' of Lyell.

Beagle returned to England in October, 1836, but Darwin did not have time to attend immediately to evolutionary problems. By March, 1837, however, he was reading the four-volume fifth edition of Lyell's *Principles*, and, at a point where Lyell asserted that the variation of organisms was limited, Darwin scribbled in the margin: 'If this were *true adios* theory,[63] − which is good evidence that he had some kind of evolutionary theory in his mind by this stage. But this is not to say that it was the theory of evolution by natural selection. An entry in Darwin's so-called 'Red Notebook', dated by Sandra Herbert as early 1837, envisaged non-progressive, saltatory changes in animal species.[64]

It was in July 1837 that Darwin opened the first of his four celebrated notebooks in which he accumulated all information available to him that might have a bearing on the question of species formation and evolution.[65] It appears from these notebooks that the approach favoured by Darwin was to adopt the uniformitarian methodology of Lyell. He did this by looking at contemporary examples of change in plant or animal forms; that is, he examined especially the work of plant and animal breeders[66] sought information on the question of plant crossings and animal hybridisations and the effects of isolation and environment. As Darwin says in his *Autobiography*, he collected facts 'wholesale'. The notebooks also reveal that Darwin was using the model or analogue of a tree, or better still a coral, as a means of representing his ideas on the development of organisms.[67]

The plant and animal breeders were obviously able to induce biological change by the action of artificial selection. The problem, then, for Darwin was to determine the analogue of *artificial selection* in *nature*. In other words, what was the mechanism of *natural selection?* Today, this phrase rolls so easily off our tongues that we sometimes forget exactly what it means, or what it meant to Darwin. His problem was to find out how 'nature' selects in order to produce biological change.

The answer to this question could, one may reasonably assume, have been given to Darwin by his reading of Malthus in September-October, 1838.[68] It was the pressure of population, and the consequent struggle for existence, coupled with the fact that organisms within a species show a considerable degree of variation, that led to the occurrence of natural selection. Thus, by an analogical shift from artificial selection to natural selection, mediated by his reading of Malthus, Darwin was able to arrive at a theory to account for the evolution of organisms. This, in simple terms, is the account of the matter as given by Peter Vorzimmer.[69]

However, the historian and philosopher of biology, Michael Ruse, has presented us with a somewhat different picture.[70] Ruse points out that Lyell had emphasised that artificial selection was incapable of giving rise to new species. By any kind of uniformitarian argument, therefore, Darwin would probably have been reluctant to use the case of artificial selection as a basis for thinking that natural selection might be capable of producing species. Moreover, Ruse has claimed, from his examination of the marginalia of copies of various breeders' pamphlets that Darwin was reading about six months before his perusal of Malthus's *Essay*, that Darwin was *not* at that time thinking that artificial selection would provide the key to the problem of an evolutionary mechanism. But after the reading of Malthus, the situation changed radically. Only then did the role of selection become clearly apparent to Darwin, to the extent that he was fully prepared to accept the analogy between natural and artificial selection processes and ignore the fact that artificial selection had shown itself incapable of giving rise to new species.

The difference of opinion between Vorzimmer and Ruse on this question is not, perhaps, as great as may appear at first sight. Both concur with Darwin's assertion in his *Autobiography* that the reading of Malthus was a crucial element in the discovery of the theory of natural selection.[71] The difference between the two commentators merely rests on whether Darwin was looking for the natural analogue of artificial selection and found it in the idea of population pressure through reading Malthus (Vorzimmer's interpretation); or whether, on reading Malthus, Darwin became aware of the relevance of the material on artificial selection that he had recently been examining. Then, with the help of Malthus, Darwin could have perceived the full force of the analogy between natural and artificial selection, and could believe that the failure of artificial selection to produce new species could be disregarded (Ruse's view).

Whatever the exact truth of this matter,[72] a point made by Ruse should be emphasised – in the early stages, Darwin's views contained strong Lamarckian elements, with the assumption that variation occurred in direct response to the environment and the effect of geographical isolation. This Lamarckian component of Darwin's theory persisted right through to the end of Darwin's career, though it was at its lowest ebb at about the time of the publication of the first edition of *The Origin*, where it is not particularly prominent. Perhaps because of the low profile of Darwin's Lamarckism in 1859 there has been a tendency to overlook it altogether. But to do this would be a serious misinterpretation of Darwin's thought and the overall structure of his theory.

NOTES CHAPTER 7

1   These have subsequently been republished in F. Darwin (ed.), *The Foundations of the Origin of Species; Two Essays Written in 1842 and 1844*, Cambridge, 1909; G. de Beer (foreword), *Evolution by Natural Selection*, Cambridge University Press, Cambridge, 1958.

2   P. J. Vorzimmer, 'An early Darwin manuscript: The "Outline and Draft of 1839" ', *Journal of the History of Biology*, Vol. 8, 1975, pp.191-217.

3   C. Darwin, *Journal of Researches into the Natural History and Geology of the Countries Visited During the Voyage of H.M.S. Beagle Round the World, under the Command of Capt. Fitz Roy, R.N.*, 2nd edn, London, 1845.

4   C. Darwin, *Geological Observations of South America, Being the Third Part of the Geology of the Voyage of the 'Beagle', Under the Command of Capt. Fitzroy, R.N. During the Years 1832 to 1836*, London, 1846.

5   An amusing anecdote relating to Darwin's study of barnacles has been recounted by William Irvine: 'As the years passed this pursuit – the barnacle study – became so familiar and inevitable to the Darwin family that one of the little boys, born into the midst of it, inquired about a neighbour, "Then where does he do his barnacles?" ' (W. Irvine, *Apes, Angels & Victorians: A Joint Biography of Darwin & Huxley*, Weidenfeld & Nicolson, London, 1955, p.53).

6   F. Darwin (ed.), *The Life and Letters of Charles Darwin, including an Autobiographical Chapter*, 3 vols, John Murray, London, 1887, Vol. 2, p.85.

7   R. C. Stauffer (ed.), *Charles Darwin's Natural Selection: Being the Second Part of his Big Species Book Written from 1856 to 1858*, Cambridge University Press, London, 1975.

8   Eleven chapters, comprising about 130,000 words, had been written.

9   Wallace's covering letter has not survived, but in a letter to Lyell of June 18th, 1858, Darwin records his dismay at being forestalled (F. Darwin (ed.), *op. cit.* (note 6), pp.116-117).

10   Scientists are not normally given any direct emoluments for their publications, but their standing within the intellectual community and often (as an indirect result) their financial rewards are related to their success in achieving priority of publication. Darwin, the amateur gentleman naturalist, was not much interested in financial considerations, but he was interested in achieving recognition for his work by means of his publications.

11   'C. Darwin to A. Gray, Down, Sept. [5th, 1857]' in F. Darwin (ed.), *op. cit.* (note 6), Vol. 2, pp.120-125.

12   'On the tendency of species to form varieties; and on the perpetuation of varieties and species by natural means of selection. By Charles Darwin, Esq., F.R.S., F.L.S., & F.G.S., and Alfred Wallace, Esq. Communicated by Sir Charles Lyell, F.R.S., F.L.S., and J. D. Hooker, Esq., M.D., V.P.R.S., F.L.S., &c.', *Journal of the Proceedings of the Linnean Society*, Vol. 2, August 20, 1858, pp.45-62.

13   T. Bell, Presidential Address to the Linnean Society on the anniversary of Linnaeus's birth, 24 May, 1859, *Proceedings of the Linnean Society of London*, Vol. 4, 1858-1859, pp.viii-xx (at p.viii). For a description of the events of the Linnean Society meeting, see J. W. T. Moody, 'The reading of the Darwin and Wallace papers: an historical "non-event" ', *Journal of the Society for the Bibliography of Natural History*, Vol. 5, 1971, pp.474-476.

14 The exact day of publication has not been established with complete certainty. Copies were distributed to booksellers on November 22, the publisher's stocks being cleared at once. One cannot be certain that all retail copies were sold on the first day of issue.

15 C. Darwin, *On the Origin of Species by Means of Natural Selection, or the Preservation of Favoured Races in the Struggle for Life. By Charles Darwin, M.A., Fellow of the Royal, Geological, Linnaean, etc. Societies; author of 'Journal of Researches During H.M.S. Beagle's Voyage Round the World'.*, John Murray, Albermarle Street, London, 1859. The most readily available reissue of the first edition is J. W. Burrow (ed.) *The Origin of Species [by] Charles Darwin*, Penguin, Harmondsworth, 1968. Subsequent references will be to this Penguin edition.

16 See below, Chapter 12.

17 For example: 'I believe that the conditions of life, from their action on the reproductive system, are so far of the highest importance as causing variability', C. Darwin, *op. cit.* (note 15, 1968), p.99. See also page 74.

18 *Ibid.*, p.76

19 See below, pages 106-107.

20 C. Darwin, *op. cit.* (note 15), p.107. Darwin's views on this question have subsequently been amply confirmed, for example by the well-known 'ring species'. The herring gull and the lesser black-backed gull are separate species in western Europe, but are joined by a continuous series of forms, forming a circle occupying similar climatic conditions right around the globe. For a discussion of this and many related topics, see A. J. Cain, *Animal Species and their Evolution*, Hutchinson, London, 1954.

21 C. Darwin, *op. cit.* (note 15), p.113.

22 *Ibid.*, pp.116-17.

23 *Ibid.*, p.119.

24 *Ibid.*, p.125.

25 A wag once suggested that the web of connections might be carried a step further to a consideration of the number of widows in a district. Widows commonly keep cats; so the clover population might be tenuously related to the number of widows.

26 But see R. C. Stauffer, 'Ecology in the long manuscript version of Darwin's *Origin of Species* and Linnaeus's *Oeconomy of Nature*', *Proceedings of the American Philosophical Society*, Vo. 104, 1960, pp.235-241.

27 C. Darwin, *op. cit.* (note 15), pp.130-131.

28 *Ibid.*, p.133.

29 This somewhat simplistic theory later took on a considerable number of forms. We may simply say, however, that the theory supposed that the characteristics of each individual were — more often than not — an 'average' of the characteristics of its parents.

30 C. Darwin, *op. cit.* (note 15), pp.155-159.

31 This word is highly convenient here for our purposes. But it was not used by Darwin, who employed phrases such as 'many and widely diversified places in the polity of nature'.

32 C. Darwin, *op. cit.* (note 15), p.157.

33 *Ibid.*, pp.169-170.

34 C. Darwin: 'The tree of life should perhaps be called the coral of life, base of branches dead, so that passages cannot be seen' (G. de Beer [ed], 'Darwin's Notebooks on Transmutation of Species Part I. First Notebook [July 1837–February 1838]', *Bulletin of the British Museum [Natural History] Historical Series*, Vol.2 [No. 2], 1960, p.44).

35 C. Darwin, *op. cit.* (note 15), p.202.

36 *Ibid.*, p.175.

37 C. Darwin, *op. cit.* (note 15), pp.182-188.

38 *Ibid.*, p.233. Darwin also discusses the law of the 'unity of type', rather than the Cuvierian principles of correlation and subordination of parts. 'Unity of type', he says, 'is explained by unity of descent'. In other words, the Cuvierian correlations are accounted for by Darwin from a 'genetic' point of view.

39 Anon., 'Creation or chance?', *Herald of the Coming Age*, Vol. 16, 1966, pp.81-96 (p.94). (This journal is a publication of the Christadelphian Church.)

40 See page 21 above.

41 Even now such sequences among macrofossils are uncommon, although many are known among microfossils and are much used for stratigraphical correlations by petroleum geologists. The classic nineteenth-century investigations of evolutionary sequences were those of O. C. Marsh on North-American horses, and A. W. Rowe on British sea-urchins (*Micraster* or 'heart-urchins'): O. C. Marsh, 'Polydactyle horses, recent and extinct', *American Journal of Science*, 3rd series, Vol. 17, 1879, pp.499-505; A. W. Rowe, 'An analysis of the genus *Micraster*, as determined by rigid zonal collecting from the zone of *Rhynconella Cuvieri* to that of *Micraster cor-anguinum*', *Quarterly Journal of the Geological Society of London*, Vol. 55, 1899, pp.494-547.

42 For a general discussion of the history of the theories of marine and fluvial erosion in Britain in the nineteenth century, see G. L. Davies, *The Earth in Decay: A History of British Geomorphology 1578-1878*, Macdonald, London, 1969, particularly Chapters 7 and 9.

43 For an account of Kelvin's work on the age of the Earth, and the controversies it created, see J. D. Burchfield, *Lord Kelvin and the Age of the Earth*, Science History Publications, New York, 1975.

44 C. Darwin, *op. cit.* (note 15), p.399.

45 *Ibid.*

46 *Ibid.*, p.455. (It should be noted, however, that in this early notebooks Darwin did regard 'non-interbreeding' as a criterion for the reality of species. See M. J. Kottler, 'Charles Darwin's species concept and theory of geographic speciation: the Transmutation Notebooks', *Annals of Science*, Vol. 35, 1978, pp.275-298.)

47 *Ibid.*

48 *Ibid.*, pp.160-161.

49 Strictly, this remark applies only to the earlier work of Linnaeus. As we have seen, in his later investigations he contemplated a gradual elaboration of new genera and species by the process of hybridization

50 Page 78.

51 This is the hypothesis that during the ice ages the sea levels fell because much water was locked up in the polar ice-caps. And the sea supposedly rose when the ice melted. But the land under the ice-caps may also be supposed to have risen after the melting of the ice load. The whole situation and its effect on animal and plant populations is therefore one of considerably complexity. (The glacio-eustatic theory was first adumbrated by S. V. Wood in 1865: *The Reader*, 9 September, 1865, p.297.)

52 C. Darwin, *op. cit.* (note 15), pp.427-428.

53 See above p. 66.

54 C. Darwin, *op. cit.* (note 3), p.173.

55 *Ibid.*, p.93.

56 C. Darwin, *Charles Darwin's Diary of the Voyage of H.M.S. "Beagle": Edited from the MS by Nora Barlow*, Cambridge University Press, Cambridge, 1933, p.83.

57 C. Darwin, *op. cit.* (note 3), p.200.

58 See S. Smith, 'The origin of 'The Origin' as discerned from Charles Darwin's notebooks and his annotations in the books he read between 1837 and 1842', *Advancement of Science*, Vol. 16, 1960, pp.391-410 (at p.396).

59 *Ibid.*

60 C. Darwin, *op. cit.* (note 3), p.394.

61 See N. Barlow (ed.), 'Darwin's ornithological notes', *Bulletin of the British Museum (Natural History) Historical Series*, Vol. 2 (No. 7), 1963, pp.201-278. Darwin's words were: 'When I see these Islands in sight of each other, & possessed of but a scanty stock of animals, tenanted by these birds, but slightly differing in structure & filling the same place in Nature, I must suspect they are only varieties . . . If there is the slightest foundation for these remarks the zoology of Archipelagoes will be well worth examining; for such facts undermine the stability of Species' [p.262, 1835 Sep-Oct].

62 For discussion of the inter-relationships between the work of Lyell and Darwin at this point, see P. Vorzimmer, 'Darwin, Malthus, and the theory of natural selection', *Journal of the History of Ideas*, Vol. 30, 1969, pp.527-542 (p.530).

63 S. Smith, *op. cit.* (note 58), p.397.

64 S. Herbert, 'The place of man in the development of Darwin's theory of transmutation Part I. To July 1937', *Journal of the History of Biology*, Vol. 7, 1974, pp.217-258 (at pp.247-249).

65 For references to the modern publications of these see above, Chapter 6, note 16.

66 See M. Ruse, 'Charles Darwin and artificial selection', *Journal of the History of Ideas*, Vol. 36, 1975, pp.339-350.

67 G. de Beer (ed.), *op. cit.* (chapter 6, note 16, Part 1), pp.43-47.

68 See G. de Beer, M. J. Rowlands & B. M. Skramovsky (eds), *op. cit.*, pp.162-163 (see above Chapter 6, note 16). Here a cryptic section from Darwin's notebooks, dated September 28, gives an explicit reference to Malthus: 'Population is increase at geometrical ratio in FAR SHORTER time than 25 years – yet until the one sentence of Malthus no one clearly perceived the great check amongst men . . . The final cause of all this wedging, must be to sort out proper structure, & adapt it to changes – to do that for form, which Malthus shows is the final effect (by means however of volition) of this populousness on the energy of man. One may say there is a force like a hundred thousand wedges trying [to] force every kind of adapted structure into the gaps in the oeconomy of nature or rather forming gaps by thrusting out weaker ones'. The crucial date for Darwin's reading of Malthus is now set at September 28, 1838

69 P. Vorzimmer, *op. cit.* (note 62).

70 M. Ruse, *op. cit.* (note 66).

71   This has not been the opinion of some other commentators. For example: G. de Beer, *Charles Darwin: Evolution by Natural Selection*, Nelson, Melbourne, 1968, p.100; G. Himmelfarb, *Darwin and the Darwinian Revolution*, Norton, New York, 1968, p.161; L. Eiseley, *Darwin's Century: Evolution and the Men Who Discovered it*, Anchor, New York, 1961, pp.181-182. These commentators do not, however, claim that Malthus taught Darwin nothing about the intensity of the struggle for existence in the animal and plant kingdoms.

72   For further discussion (which supports the importance of the role of Malthus in Darwin's discovery of natural selection), see S. Herbert, 'Darwin, Malthus and selection', *Journal of the History of Biology*, Vol. 4, 1971, pp.209-217. Other important writings dealing with the origins of Darwin's theory are: C. Limoges, *La Sélection Naturelle: Etude sur la Première Constitution d'un Concept (1837-1859)*, Presses Univ. de France, Paris, 1970; S. Herbert, 'The place of man in the development of Darwin's theory of transmutation Part I. To July 1837 [and] Part II', *Journal of the History of Biology*, Vol. 7, 1974, pp.217-258 & Vol. 10, 1977, pp.155-227; H. E. Gruber & P. H. Barrett, *Darwin on Man: A Psychological Study of Scientific Creativity . . . Together with Darwin's Early and Unpublished Notebooks.* Dutton, New York, 1974; E. D. Kohn, 'Charles Darwin's path to natural selection', Ph.D. dissertation, University of Massachusetts, 1975; E. Mayr, 'Evolution through natural selection: how Darwin discovered this highly unconventional theory', *American Scientist*, Vol. 65, 1977, pp.321-328; S. S. Schweber, 'The origin of the *Origin* revisited', *Journal of the History of Biology*, Vol. 10, 1977, pp.229-316; E. Manier, *The Young Darwin and his Cultural Circle: A Study of Influences which Helped Shape the Language and Logic of the First Drafts of the Theory of Natural Selection*, Reidel, Dordrecht & Boston, Mass., 1978.

8

Wallace: The Problem of Simultaneous Discoveries

Although this book is concerned with the *Darwinian* Revolution some consideration should also be given to the work of Alfred Russel Wallace (1823-1913), the co-discoverer of the theory of evolution by natural selection.[1] Wallace was a man of extraordinary intellectual energy — as was Darwin — and certainly he warrants discussion 'in his own right', so to speak. Had Darwin not lived, Wallace probably would still have discovered the principle of evolution by natural selection quite independently, and today we should be accustomed to speak of the Wallacian theory — though not perhaps of a Wallacian Revolution. But quite apart from the question of doing justice to Wallace's position in the history of biology, the almost simultaneous discovery of the same theory, by almost the same pathway, is in itself a matter of considerable interest, and may tell us much about the intellectual climate in mid-nineteenth-century Britain, as well as raising certain philosophical, psychological and sociological problems of considerable interest and complexity.

Wallace did not have Darwin's advantage of being born with a silver spoon in his mouth. He came from an impoverished middle-class family in Monmouthshire and although he attended the grammar school at Hereford, he received no higher education, and left school at the age of thirteen. His first occupation was that of a surveyor, by which he was introduced to the rudiments of geology, and was able to satisfy his love for country life. In 1844, Wallace was working as a teacher in Leicester, and there he had the opportunity to read Malthus's *Essay*, as well as popular works of natural history and exploration, such as Alexander von Humboldt's *Personal Travels*.[2] It was in the town library at Leicester that Wallace met H. W. Bates (1825-1892), the well-known entomologist, with whom he was later to carry out arduous and important explorations in South America. In 1848, Bates and Wallace set out for the Amazon region on an expedition supported by the American naturalist, W. H. Edwards, whose acquaintance they had made in London; their objective was to collect botanical and zoological materials for sale on their return. Wallace stayed in South America for four years, Bates for a further seven, eventually producing his notable work, *The Naturalist on the River Amazons*, in 1863.[3]

Wallace's Amazon exploration ended in disaster, however, when the vessel in which he was returning was destroyed by fire, together with nearly all the collection that had been accumulated in the four years of work in the jungle. Wallace himself was fortunate to escape in a small boat and was later picked up by a passenger boat returning to London. He was taken in, almost penniless, by his sister, but was able to redeem his position to some degree by publishing a book on his travels,[4] and from the insurance money raised for the lost materials. In this period, Wallace attended meetings of the Zoological and Entomological Societies in London, and made the acquaintance of some of the leading scientists of the day, including the geologist, Sir Roderick Murchison, then President of the Royal Geographical Society, who supported Wallace in his request for financial assistance from the government towards the cost of further explorations in the Malayan archipelago.

For eight years, beginning in 1854, Wallace, with the help of an assistant, worked assiduously in the East Indies collecting material of botanical and zoological interest, and exploring parts of the world that were then almost unknown to Western man. He travelled about fourteen thousand miles in this period.

It seems that as early as 1845, well before he journeyed to the East, Wallace had already accepted the idea of evolution, from his reading of Chambers's *Vestiges*;[5] and — as did Darwin — he was constantly turning over in his mind the problem of the origin of species. Moreover, as Darwin did through his experiences of the *Beagle* voyage, Wallace was able to bring to bear on the problem his very wide experience of the geographical distribution of plants and animals, acquired through his travels in Brazil and Malaya. And although Darwin and Wallace were so far apart from one another they were able to keep in touch to some degree by letter. Darwin, however, did not tell Wallace the details of his theory.

In 1855, Wallace published a paper in the *Annals and Magazine of Natural History* entitled 'On the law which has regulated the introduction of new species',[6] which was noticed by Lyell and Darwin, and seemingly influenced them both to a considerable degree. This paper maintained that the facts of the distribution of species were only compatible with an evolutionary hypothesis, but Wallace did not offer the mechanism of natural selection to account for this. We should note, however, that as early as the period of his Amazon explorations he had observed that different species were often separated from each other by geographical barriers, such as large rivers, even though the conditions of existence on the different sides of such barriers might seem substantially the same.

It should also be noted that well before he actually arrived at the principle of natural selection, Wallace was attuned to the notion of the struggle for existence, which is to be found, for example, in Lyell's *Principles of Geology*,[7] with which Wallace was fully familiar. Indeed, well before 1858, when Wallace eventually arrived at an understanding of the mechanism of evolutionary change through natural selection, he had all the main ingredients of the theory, except an understanding of the actual selection process – the survival of the fittest. His Malayan notebooks show that he was working on a book that was to be called [*On the*] *Organic Law of Change*,[8] and clearly this work was to be concerned with evolutionary change. However, it was never completed under that title.

In the years 1855 to 1858, then, Wallace was undoubtedly giving a great deal of thought to the central problem of a suitable mechanism to account for the origin of species. And he kept Darwin abreast of the development of his ideas through their correspondence. So both Darwin and Lyell were aware that Wallace was getting very close to a solution to the problem, and Lyell urged Darwin to publish a provisional statement of his ideas, so that he would not be forestalled.[9] Eventually, Wallace came to a solution of the problem when he was staying at the island of Gilolo, ten miles from the larger island of Ternate, near the western end of New Guinea. For convenience, we may give his account of how the idea came to him:

> I was then [February, 1858] living at Ternate[10] in the Moluccas, and was suffering from a rather severe attack of intermittent fever [malaria], which prostrated me for several hours every day during the cold and succeeding hot fits. During one of these fits, while again considering the problem of the origin of species, something led me to think of Malthus's Essay on Population (which I had read about ten years before), and the "positive checks" – war, disease, famine, accidents, etc. – which he adduced as keeping all savage populations nearly stationary. It then occurred to me that these checks must also act upon animals, and keep down their numbers; and as they increase so much faster than man does, while their numbers are always very nearly or quite stationary, it was clear that these checks in their case must be far more powerful, since a number equal to the whole increase must be cut off by them every year. While vaguely thinking how this would affect any species, there suddenly flashed upon me the idea of *the survival of the fittest* – that the individuals removed by these checks must be, on the whole, *inferior* to those that survived. Then, considering the *variations* continually occurring in every fresh generation of animals or plants, and the changes of climate, of food, of enemies always in progress, the whole method of specific [i.e., species] modification became clear to me, and in the two hours of my fit I had thought out the main points of the theory. That same evening I sketched out the draft of a paper; and in the two succeeding evenings I wrote it out, and sent it by the next post to Mr Darwin.[11]

We have already considered the repercussions of Wallace's action in sending his paper to Darwin, and there is no need for a repetition of the story here.

Wallace gave three other published accounts of the origin of his theory, and it has been noticed by H. L. McKinney that in each case Wallace stressed that he shifting his thinking from reference to mankind to a consideration of animals at the moment when he eventually grasped the theory.[12] This has led McKinney to emphasise the relevance of Wallace's interest in ethnology or anthropology as a focus for his thinking about evolutionary problems. And this aspect was undoubtedly a stimulus to the formulation of the theory, just as much as Wallace's concern with the problems of the geographical distribution of organisms.

Wallace always maintained his interest in man as a special kind of animal, and although he continued to maintain the most cordial relations with Darwin, and the two of them agreed with each other on almost all aspects of the theory of evolution, there was, nevertheless, one area where they differed substantially. As will be reiterated in our discussions of *The Descent of Man* below,[13] Darwin always wished to smooth over the apparent gulf between men and animals, maintaining that the phenomenon of man could be accounted for purely naturalistically, without invoking any non-material, spiritual, or psychic causes. Wallace, on the other hand, repudiated Darwin's agnosticism, and became deeply interested in spiritualism and psychic phenomena, maintaining that one could not account satisfactorily for all aspects of the world of living organisms — particularly those relating to man's mental powers and social characteristics — by a purely naturalistic description such as that implied by the doctrine of evolution by natural selection. Wallace's later ideas on psychic phenomena are of very considerable interest, but an account of them need not be entered into here.[14]

Apart from the difference between Darwin and Wallace about man,[15] we may also ask whether there were any substantive differences between them in their views on the theory of evolution by natural selection as applied to animals and plants. For example, can one discern significant differences, in their papers presented to the Linnean Society in 1858?

The fundamentals of the two expositions were substantially the same, but there are some interesting differences in emphasis. Wallace, for example, stresses that it is the observable constancy in the population numbers of most species over a limited period of time, coupled with the geometric ratio of increase in the numbers of organisms, that necessarily entail a struggle for existence.[16] Darwin, on the other hand, maintains that it is the limitation of resources, coupled with the geometrical ratio of increase, that lead to the struggle. But this is merely a difference in emphasis in the manner of presenting the argument, rather than a real point of theoretical difference.

On the other hand, whereas Darwin always gave great emphasis to the analogy between domesticated creatures and those living in their natural environments, and led off his argument in *The Origin* by a consideration of the domestic pigeon, Wallace minimised the importance of this analogy, stating that:

No inferences as to varieties in a state of nature can be deduced from the observation of those occurring among domestic animals. The two are so much opposed to each other that what applies to the one is almost sure not to apply to the other.[17]

His argument, therefore, did not place any great weight on the analogy with artificial selection. It is true, of course, that if we try to give a purely skeletal version[18] of Darwin's theory, then the analogy of artificial selection may be omitted without loss. But in Darwin's exposition — involving his attempt to persuade the somewhat sceptical reader of the truth and adequacy of the theory — the analogy with animals and plants under domestication plays a role of very considerable importance.

We have seen in our previous chapter that the principle of divergence was an important component in the argument of *The Origin*, helping one to move from the notion of natural selection as a cause of biological improvement or evolutionary change to the view that *new species* will come into being in the course of time. The principle of divergence is also prominent in Wallace's 1858 paper. But is it to be found in Darwin's sketches of 1842 and 1844 or his letter to Asa Gray of 1857? It is certainly to be found stated quite clearly and explicitly in the Gray letter[19] and also in the incomplete work, *Natural Selection*;[20] but we do not find it in the 1842 or 1844 sketch, and this might lead one to ask whether Darwin may have gleaned the idea of the principle of divergence from his correspondence with Wallace.[21] This suggestion is scarcely conceivable, however, from Darwin's statement in his *Autobiography*, where, in the account of his work leading up to the publication of *The Origin*, we read:

> At that time I overlooked one problem of great importance; . . . This problem is the tendency in organic beings descended from the same stock to diverge in character as they became modified. That they have diverged greatly is obvious from the manner in which species of all kinds can be classed under genera, genera under families, families under sub-orders, and so forth; and I can remember the very spot in the road, whilst in my carriage, when to my joy the solution occurred to me; and this was long after I had come to Down. The solution, as I believe, is that the modifed offspring of all dominant and increasing forms tend to become adapted to many and highly diversified places in the economy of nature.[22]

From the foregoing discussion, I think it may reasonably be concluded that the theories of Darwin and Wallace were essentially the same — yet they were discovered quite independently, at about the same time.

This raises the interesting general point about the occurrence from time to time of virtually simultaneous discoveries in the history of science.[23] It surely cannot have been merely coincidental that Darwin and Wallace arrived at the theory of evolution by natural selection as and when they did. Yet, if it were not a matter of coincidence, are we to conclude that the two naturalists were in some manner subservient to the 'external' social pressures, which should be accounted the chief determinants of the advent of new ideas?

Attention has been given to questions of this kind by the sociologist and social historian of science, R. K. Merton, well known for his advocacy of the so-called 'externalist'[24] approach to the study of the history of science. Merton has argued that far from being the exception, multiple discoveries are almost the rule, and are to be expected 'once science has become institutionalised, and significant numbers are at work on scientific investigation'.[25] He asserts that one should not attempt to attribute scientific discoveries to 'environmental' factors alone, or solely to the role of individual genius. The two are complementary, rather than incompatible. There will always be men of genius in science, but when such 'great men' work within a cohesive social framework it will be natural that they will address themselves to the problems of the day, which are customarily defined by the scientific literature of a period. And it is clear from their correspondence, if from no other line of evidence, that Darwin and Wallace were most certainly working within the same social milieu of scientific inquiry, despite considerable other differences between them.

A similar conclusion might be reached by the application of Thomas Kuhn's well-known thesis of the scientific 'paradigm',[26] which claims that under 'normal' circumstances scientists in the same field operate in accordance with the same general set of theoretical presuppositions, and there is mutual agreement between them on the kinds of problems that are relevant and potentially solvable, and general agreement about the way in which such problems may most profitably be tackled.[27] And although the science of biology (or natural history) was not solidly professionalised in the middle years of the nineteenth century, with specific programs of education and instruction for its practitioners, there was nevertheless a sufficient community of interest to account for the independent and almost simultaneous discovery of natural selection by Darwin and Wallace, without suggesting that they were, for example, both dominated by the Victorian belief in the virtues of free enterprise and the economic struggle for existence, with this social characteristic acting as the fundamental cause of the theory's formulation — or that one filched his ideas from the other.

Yet the explanations offered by Kuhn and Merton do not exhaust the possibilities, and I may mention briefly here a more recent and radical suggestion about the phenomenon of multiple discoveries, without attempting to evaluate the thesis with authority. I am referring to the 'structuralist' account of the phenomenon of multiple discovery, as advocated, for example, by Gunther Stent.[28] Stent sees the 'structuralist' account of the mind as providing a resolution of the age-old philosophical debate between the proponents of materialism and the advocates of idealism. Materialism (or realism) maintains that reality is mirrored in the mind. Idealism claims that reality is constructed or created by the mind. But structuralism suggests that there is a more satisfactory middle view. According to this interpretation, the sense organs are stimulated, but the information received by the mind is *abstracted* from the sensations. That is to say, as mental structures are built up, information is successively weeded out; the creation of mental patterns entails a selective destruction of the information received. The mind, then, is 'a set of structural transforms of primary data taken from the world'. And 'this transformation process is hierarchical, in that "stronger" structures are formed from "weaker" structures through selective destruction of information'.[29] If this view — which derives from theories of psychologists such as Piaget[30] — is correct then observations are only meaningful when organised or structured according to the already existing mental structures. So data which cannot be transformed successfully into a structure that is congruent with the already existing 'strong' mental structures are meaningless. In this way, one might explain how it may come about that various scientists are receptive to particular items of observational evidence at particular times, and thus simultaneous discoveries can occur. Conversely, one might account for the non-acceptance of some scientific theories at certain periods in the history of science by saying that the majority of scientists at the time did not possess the appropriate mental structures for the reception of the new doctrines. The obvious instance relevant to the theme of this book might be the tardy recognition of the importance of Mendel's work.[31]

Such explanations, at a psychological level, to account for phenomena such as simultaneous discoveries, or the non-acceptance of particular scientific theories at particular times, are obviously of very considerable interest, though bristling with difficulties. One may object, for example, that it leaves wide open the whole question of how sudden changes in theoretical explanations may occur. And it may well be that we will continue to prefer explanations couched in the more strictly empirical terms of sociology, rather than in terms of the hypothetical mental structures of the structural psychologists. Nevertheless, such approaches should not be ruled out in any aprioristic manner. The history of science is at least logically compatible with such psychological interpretations. And, conceivably, the great changes that we have discerned earlier in this volume, such as the shift away from the classical world of order of the eighteenth-century Enlightenment to the evolving, organismic, historically based, Romantic world-view of the nineteenth century, may yet best be interpreted in terms of some kind of major shift in mental structures in the Western world.[32] But these are deep and muddy waters and we shall probably be wise if we refrain from approaching them more closely.

NOTES CHAPTER 8

1   On Wallace, see particularly A. R. Wallace, *My Life: A Record of Events and Opinions*, 2 vols, London, 1905 (reprinted Gregg, Farnborough, 1969); J. Marchant (ed.), *Alfred Russel Wallace: Letters and Reminiscences, A Study of the Life and Writings of Alfred Russel Wallace*, Abelard-Schuman, London, 1964; H. L. McKinney, *Wallace and Natural Selection*, Yale University Press, New Haven & London, 1972. For a more succinct account, refer to L. Eiseley, 'Alfred Russel Wallace', *Scientific American*, Vol. 200, 1959, pp.70-83.

2   F. H. A. von Humboldt, *Personal Narrative of Travels to the Equinoctial Regions of the New Continent during the Years 1799-1804, by A. de Humboldt and A. Bonpland; with Maps, Plans*, written in French by A. de H., and translated into English by H. M. Williams, 7 vols, London, 1814-1829.

3   H. W. Bates, *The Naturalist on the River Amazons. A Record of Adventure, Habits of Animals, Sketches of Brazilian and Indian life, and Aspects of Nature under The Equator, During Eleven Years of Travel*, 2 vols, London, 1863.

4   A. R. Wallace, *A Narrative of Travels on the Amazon and Rio Negro, with an Account of the Native Tribes, and Observations on the Climate, Geology, and Natural History of the Amazon Valley*, London, 1853.

5   H. L. McKinney, 'Alfred Russel Wallace and the discovery of natural selection', *Journal of the History of Medicine and Allied Sciences*, Vol. 21, 1966, pp.333-357 (at p.335).

6   A. R. Wallace, 'On the law which has regulated the introduction of new species', *Annals and Magazine of Natural History*, Vol. 16 (n.s.), 1855, pp.184-196.

7   C. Lyell, *Principles of Geology*, 8th edn, London, 1850, pp.647-648. Here Lyell was citing earlier ideas of the Swiss botanist A. P. de Candolle on the struggle for existence.

8   H. L. McKinney, *op. cit.* (note 5), p.342.

9   According to Darwin's *Autobiography* (F. Darwin (ed.), *The Life and Letters of Charles Darwin, Including an Autobiographical Chapter*, 3 vols, John Murray, London, 1887, Vol. 1, p.84), Lyell wrote to Darwin in 1856, urging him to publish his ideas as soon as possible.

10 See note 11, below.

11 A. R. Wallace, *The Wonderful Century: its Successes and its Failures*, New York, 1898, pp.139-140. It is curious that although this is a highly circumstantial and seemingly authentic account of Wallace's discovery, it may be incorrect in certain particulars. McKinney has recently shown (from a study of Wallace's original *Journal*) that the flash of inspiration probably occurred on the island of Gilolo, rather than Ternate (H. L. McKinney, *op. cit.* [note 1], pp.131-138).

12 H. L. McKinney, *op. cit.* (note 5), p.354.

13 See pages 144 to 147.

14 But see M. J. Kottler, 'Alfred Russel Wallace, the origin of man, and spiritualism', *Isis*, Vol. 65, 1974, pp.144-192.

15 Recent opinion on this question seems to be favouring Darwin, rather than Wallace. (See above, Chapter 1, note 2.)

16 See below p.117.

17 A. R. Wallace, 'On the tendency of varieties to depart indefinitely from the original type', *Journal of the Proceedings of the Linnean Society*, Vol. 2, 1858, pp.53-62 (p.61).

18 See below, page 117, for an example of this.

19 C. Darwin, 'Abstract of a letter from C. Darwin, esq., to Prof. Asa Gray, Boston, U.S., dated Down, September 5th, 1857', *Journal of the Proceedings of the Linnean Society*, Vol. 2, 1858, pp.50-53 (at p.52).

20 R. C. Stauffer (ed.), *Charles Darwin's Natural Selection*, Cambridge University Press, London, 1975, pp.231, 234-235, 245, 247.

21 H. L. McKinney (*op. cit.*[note 1] pp.138-146) raises some interesting questions on this issue, suggesting that the legend that Darwin wished to pass over all credit to Wallace (only being dissuaded from this by Lyell and Hooker) is to some degree an oversimplification or idealisation of the situation.

22 F. Darwin (ed.), *op. cit.* (note 9), p.84.

23 Some well-known examples are the almost simultaneous discovery of the composition of water by Watt, Cavendish, and Lavoisier; the principle of conservation of energy by Mayer, Joule, Colding and Helmholtz. The race for the discovery of the so-called genetic code between Watson and Crick and Linus Pauling is also well known.

24 This approach to the study of the history of science places considerable emphasis on 'external' factors, particularly of a socio-economic nature, as opposed to 'internal' considerations involving the actual thoughts and actions of particular scientists. For further discussions of this point, see below, pp 365-366.

25 R. K. Merton, 'Singletons and multiples in science, 1961', in N. W. Storer (ed.), *Robert K. Merton: The Sociology of Science – Theoretical and Empirical Investigations*, Chicago University Press, Chicago & London, 1973, pp.343-370 (at p.264).

26 Originally, as we have seen, this term referred to a Platonic 'form' or 'exemplar'. But Kuhn has used it to refer to a set of theoretical presuppositions to which a scientist adheres in the course of his or her professional activities, together with the methods (both practical and theoretical) which he or she employs in attempting to find solutions to the problems that are being investigated. (See T. S. Kuhn, *The Structure of Scientific Revolutions*, Chicago University Press, Chicago, 1962.) The term is convenient and is widely used today. It is, however, fuzzy, and has been employed by Kuhn in a variety of ways. (See M. Masterman, 'The nature of a paradigm', in I. Lakatos & A. E. Musgrave (eds), *Criticism and the Growth of Knowledge*, Cambridge University Press, Cambridge, 1970, pp.59-89.)

27 Kuhn uses the term 'normal science' to refer to the situation in which scientists carry on their research under the aegis of a particular 'paradigm', solving the 'puzzles' that present themselves within the particular theoretical framework of their 'paradigm'. A 'revolutionary' situation develops when a particular 'paradigm' breaks down and is replaced by its successor.

28   See G. S. Stent, 'Prematurity and uniqueness in scientific discovery', *Scientific American*, Vol. 227, 1972, pp.84-93.

29   *Ibid.*, p.93

30   See J. Piaget (tr. C. Maschler), *Structuralism*, Routledge & Kegan Paul, London, 1971 (1st French edn, 1968).

31   See below, pages 167-171.

32   This seems to be the theme implicit in the writings of the contemporary French philosopher, Michel Foucault, although he strenuously denies that he is a 'structuralist' or that his descriptions of past phases of European culture are concerned with general changes in 'world-view'. His interest is directed chiefly to the analysis of discourse recorded in the texts of different periods; the similarities and differences in the texts of different intellectual domains; what they contain *and* what they omit.

9

The Structure of the Darwin/Wallace theory

We have already given a fairly extended account of the theory of evolution by natural selection in Chapter 7, and it may seem superfluous at this point to submit the theory to any further analysis. But a considerable number of points of interest emerge if we look more closely at the theory and try to say concisely and exactly what its assumptions are, what it attempts to explain, and how it purports to do so. In other words, what is the logical 'skeleton' of the theory? If this can be determined and the real logical structure of the theory identified, then perhaps we may have some hope of saying exactly what the theory *is*, and thereby we may have some means of appraising its merits and deficiencies and considering its adequacy as a basis for the scientific explanation of the phenomena of living organisms. To this end, it will be convenient to look at a selection of the several attempts that have been made to analyse the Darwin/Wallace theory. But before making such an examination it will be helpful to make a few preliminary remarks about the general question of the structure of scientific theories, and the associated problem of scientific explanation.

In Chapter 1, I gave a very brief sketch of the general structure of the deductive logical system known as Euclidian geometry, and I mentioned that this was so great a success that the kind of deductive thinking that it epitomised gained quite extraordinary influence in the history of Western thought, standing at the very centre of the whole essentialist tradition. Major instances of the successful application of the deductive 'geometrical' system of explanation in science were provided in the seventeenth century by the work of Galileo (1564-1642)[1] and Newton (1642-1727).[2] Newton, in his celebrated *Principia*, based his argument and reasoning on eight definitions, three axioms (the well-known 'laws of motion'), four 'rules of reasoning in philosophy', six statements of 'phaenomena', and two 'hypotheses'.[3] Starting from these, or making use of them as required in the course of the argument, Newton found it possible to deduce rigorously a whole host of theorems, lemmas, and corollaries (i.e., deductions, derived from the postulates of the theory). Today, by inserting appropriate items of observational evidence (so-called 'boundary conditions') into the Newtonian system, one can use it to make extraordinarily accurate predictions about the way the solar system, for example, will behave in the future – predictions that can be and have been amply confirmed by experimental observations. Very precise predictions about the time when an eclipse will occur can be made.[4] Moreover, by putting this observation about the time of the eclipse within the context of the deductive structure of the Newtonian theory, it is possible to offer a definite *explanation* of how and why the eclipse occurred as and when it did. In other words, explanations of phenomena may be achieved by their prediction, using deductive reasoning from certain general laws of nature, and certain 'boundary conditions'. An individual phenomenon is seen to be a special instance of the workings of a general physical system, or (in the case we are considering) an exemplification of one of the theorems of Newton's theory.

In the case of Euclidian geometry, the starting points for the deductive structure – the Euclidian axioms – remain unexplained, and not logically proven or justified, though intuitively they may seem to be correct, or even 'necessarily' true.[5] In Newton's system, however, the three laws of motion – the first steps of the deductive structure of the theory – were supposedly inductive generalisations (that is generalisations drawn from the observational evidence of experience), and Newton maintained with some vigour that *this* made all the difference. His work was supposedly an example of experimental or natural philosophy and was not, therefore 'hypothetical'. By contrast, Euclid's geometry was a mathematical system, with *a priori* postulates, and therefore in no way open to experimental falsification.

Whether Newton was right in claiming that his three axiomatic laws of motion were inductive generalisations from experience rather than products of his intuition is an immensely complex matter, which has provided employment for philosophers of science for many years.[6] Fortunately, however, the satisfactory resolution of this problem is quite irrelevant to our present concerns. The point that I wish to emphasise is simply that the deductive structure that we find in Newton's *Principia* – a system that has proved to be so extraordinarily successful and influential in the history of science – came to be seen as an ideal exemplar for all sciences. Moreover, it suggested to philosophers of science what the structure of a *bona fide* scientific theory 'ought' to look like.

In the seventeenth and eighteenth centuries, for example, one may find a number of instances of scientific works presented in *quasi*-mathematical or 'geometrical' form, often in cases where the deductive style was very far from appropriate.[7] Philosophers, also, have on occasion attempted to set out their arguments as if they were exemplifications of some branch of pure mathematics, though such 'deductive' philosophical systems have roots in the logic-chopping exercises of the mediaeval scholastics as much as the mathematics of Euclid or systems of mathematical physics such as those of

Newton or Galileo.

In the twentieth century, then, when philosophers of science have attempted to give some account of the general structure of scientific theories, they have readily turned to the venerable model of Euclid and Newton. Consider, for example, what R. B. Braithwaite had to say on the matter:

> A scientific system consists of a set of hypotheses which form a deductive system; that is, which is arranged in such a way that from some of the hypotheses as premisses all the other hypotheses logically follow. The propositions in a deductive system may be considered as being arranged in an order of levels, the hypotheses at the highest level being those which occur only as premisses in the system, those at the lowest level being those which occur only as conclusions in the system, and those at intermediate levels being those which occur as conclusions of deductions from higher-level hypotheses and which serve as premisses for deductions to lower-level hypotheses.[8]

The author then proceeds to give an example drawn from Galilean mechanics in illustration of his model of a science.

To be sure, Braithwaite does not see the starting points for the deductive systems of scientific theories as some kind of *a priori* truths, or as true inductions from experience. He accepts that they simply have hypothetical status. But the overall structure of scientific theories that he presents is clearly very much beholden to that which one finds so admirably exemplified in Newton's *Principia*; Braithwaite's choice of Galileo as an illustration for his thesis is also suggestive in this regard.

So, we may ask, is the general structure of Darwin's theory in some way similar to that of our Newtonian or Braithwaitian model — the model of scientific theories that is commonly presented by philosophers of science? Is the general argument of *The Origin of Species* such that it can be pared down to reveal a tidy deductive, 'geometrical' structure? There are passages in Darwin's text that suggest quite strongly that he was indeed trying to present a deductive argument, though not, of course, in a rigorous mathematical form. Consider, for example, the following well-known summary of Darwin's argument that occurs at the end of his chapter on natural selection:

> If during the long course of ages and under varying conditions of life, organic beings vary at all in the several parts of their organization, and I think this certainly cannot be disputed; if there be, owing to the high geometrical powers of increase of each species, at some age, season or year, a severe struggle for life, and this certainly cannot be disputed; then, considering the infinite complexity of the relations of all organic beings to each other and to their conditions of existence, causing an infinite diversity in structure, constitution, and habits, to be advantageous to them, I think it would be a most extraordinary fact if no variation ever had occurred useful to each being's own welfare, in the same way as so many variations have occurred useful to man. But if variations useful to any organic being do occur, assuredly individuals thus characterised will have the best chance of being preserved in the struggle for life; and from the strong principle of

inheritance they will tend to produce offspring similarly characterised. This principle of preservation, I have called, for the sake of brevity, Natural Selection.[9]

One might paraphrase this passage so that it reads: the *variation of organisms*, coupled with the *struggle for existence*, gives rise to *natural selection*. And by judicious reading of other portions of *The Origin* one may come up with a small number of propositions which, taken together, seem to provide a kind of deductive argument leading to the conclusion that evolution of organisms occurs as a result of the process of natural selection.

Although there is no single page in *The Origin* where the total argument is presented in its barest essentials, it is interesting to note that Wallace thought it worthwhile to provide his readers with a brief summary of the structure of the argument as a whole. This is represented in Figure 14.[10]

Figure 14 'A Demonstration of the Origin of Species by Natural Selection', according to A. R. Wallace

PROVED FACTS	NECESSARY CONSEQUENCES (afterwards taken as Proved Facts)
RAPID INCREASE OF ORGANISMS (*Origin of Species*, p.75, 5th ed.) TOTAL NUMBER OF INDIVIDUALS STATIONARY.	STRUGGLE FOR EXISTENCE, the deaths equalling the births on the average (*Origin of Species*, chap. iii.)
STRUGGLE FOR EXISTENCE. HEREDITY WITH VARIATION, or general likeness with individual differences of parents and offsprings (*Origin of Species*, chaps, i, ii, v.)	SURVIVAL OF THE FITTEST, or Natural Selection; meaning, simply, that on the whole those die who are least fitted to maintain their existence (*Origin of Species*, chap. iv.)
SURVIVAL OF THE FITTEST. CHANGE OF EXTERNAL CONDITIONS, universal and increasing. – See Lyell's *Principles of Geology*.	CHANGES OF ORGANIC FORMS, to keep them in harmony with the Changed Conditions; and as the changes of conditions are permanent changes, in the sense of not reverting back to identical previous conditions, the changes of organic forms must be in the same sense permanent, and thus originate SPECIES.

In this summary of Wallace, as in his other expositions of the theory, we discern a point of emphasis that is slightly different from that given by Darwin. That is, Wallace emphasises that the total number of individuals within a species is approximately stationary, whereas Darwin does not give this point special emphasis. Nevertheless, this is but a minor matter, and we can see that the pattern of Wallace's presentation is essentially the same as that of Darwin. Now, if one were trying to structure the theory of evolution by natural selection along the lines of the Euclidian or Newtonian models, we might choose to compare the 'proved facts' at the left hand of Wallace's table with, say, the putative inductive generalisations of Newton's three laws of motions. And by the fact that Wallace refers to the right-hand items of his table as '*necessary* consequences', if we attribute the full deductive sense that is usually given to the word *necessary* by philosophers, it would appear that he considers that *deductive* inferences are being made as one makes the three moves from the left to the right of the table. For example, it seems that he is claiming that STRUGGLE FOR EXISTENCE, together with HEREDITY WITH VARIATION, logically entail the SURVIVAL OF THE FITTEST. At first sight, therefore, it appears that one *can* press the Darwin/Wallace theory into the mould of a deductive structure.

Since Wallace's day, several other commentators have attempted to expose the bones of the deductive structure that supposedly lies concealed within the fleshy text of *The Origin of Species*. Perhaps the best-known attempt to do this has been carried out by A. G. N. Flew, in a paper published in the Penguin *New Biology* in 1959.[11] Flew criticises earlier attempts by Julian Huxley to give a succinct statement of the deductive structure of the theory,[12] and claims that he can do better, offering the following three 'equations':

G[eometrical] R[atio] of I[ncrease] + L[imited] R[esources] $\rightarrow$ S[truggle] for E[xistence]
S[truggle] for E[xistence] + V[ariation] $\rightarrow$ N[atural] S[election]
N[atural] S[election] + T[ime] $\rightarrow$ B[iological] I[mprovement].

Or, in brief, and as actually presented by Flew:

GRI + LR $\rightarrow$ SE
SE + V $\rightarrow$ NS
NS + T $\rightarrow$ BI[13]

Flew is cautious about claiming that this skeletal representation is the beginning and end of the whole matter. He writes:

Of course to make this core, and the equations used to represent it schematically, ideally rigorous [,] one would have to construct for all the crucial terms definitions to include explicitly every necessary assumption.[14]

And he says that he will not 'attempt here to develop Darwin's argument quite rigorously or to formalize the result', though to do so 'might be instructive'.[15] Nevertheless, he seems convinced that the total argument is deductive, that there is a *bona fide* 'deductive core' in *The Origin*, and that the arguments can, with care and when spelt out in detail, be given in rigorously deductive form. Flew has maintained the view that there is a deductive core to Darwin's argument, in a later volume, *Evolutionary Ethics*.[16]

It might appear, then, that in Flew's three simple equations we do have the logical skeleton of the Darwin/Wallace theory. And by examination of the equations one can see exactly what is being assumed in the theory and what supposedly follows from its assumptions. Thus, it would appear that GRI, LR, V and T serve as the premises or assumptions of the argument. Of these,

GRI, LR and V are evidently true on the basis of commonplace observations; and T can be borrowed from the science of geology with some confidence. Then from these four premises we can swiftly deduce BI, and this may be confirmed by examination of the paleontological record.

Flew's analysis might well be challenged, however. For example, it might be questioned whether the arrows of his 'equations' do in fact represent strict logical entailments. Thus, if NS followed *deductively* from SE and V, then there would be a *logical* contradiction involved in asserting that struggle for existence and variation *did* both occur while natural selection (or survival of the fittest) did *not* occur — even if this situation supposedly arose on one very special and specific occasion only. Put it this way: *if* it is true that SE + V entails NS, then, given SE and V, it would be a logical contradiction to suppose that NS did not occur concomitantly. It simply could not happen; one can never find empirical counter-instances to logical truths.

But it is not particularly difficult to envisage a situation in which SE and V occur but are not accompanied by NS. The fattest and healthiest of goats might be the ones most keenly sought by the lion in search of prey. Or, for all Flew's equations can show to the contrary, a population or species might 'choose' to save the less fit and sacrifice the strong and fit. Indeed, something rather like this probably happens in human wars, as, for example, when the flower of English youth was riddled with machine-gun bullets in the battle-fields of Flanders during the First World War. And the care given in our various hospitals is not obviously reconcilable with the edicts of Flew's equations. Again, the mushrooms that I grow under my house seem to offer some empirical refutation of Flew's first equation, for as their nutriment runs out they do not seem to falter in their geometrical rate of increase, but respond by becoming successively smaller and smaller. For a short time, if no more, one can apparently observe a situation in which GRI and LR are *not* accompanied by SE.

Several authors have been aware of criticisms of this general nature, and have made strenuous efforts to improve the presentation of the logical structure of the Darwinian theory. But such moves are fraught with difficulty. For example, Mary Williams, in a complex and sophisticated paper published in the *Journal of Theoretical Biology*, has provided what she claims to be a representation of: 'Darwin's theory of evolution as a deductive system[,] in which a few fundamental principles of the theory are used as axioms from which the remainder of the principles of the theory can be deductively derived'.[17] And the paper bristles impressively with all the apparatus of modern symbolic logic. But, in my view, it is questionable indeed whether such a schema can in any way be said to be a representation of *Darwin*'s theory, no matter how logically coherent the reconstruction may be. It is a different kind of animal altogether.

Much less extravagant is a representation of the theory given by Michael Ruse.[18] I will reproduce a figure from his paper here, to give an idea of the general view of the theory that he offers.

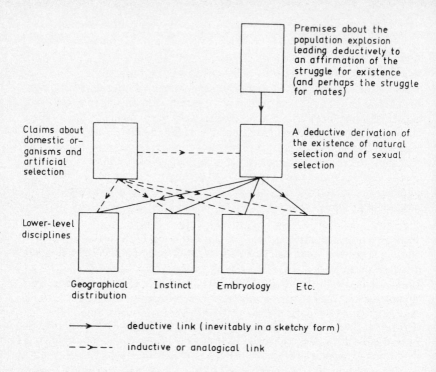

Figure 15 The General Structure of Darwin's Theory of Evolution by Natural Selection, according to Ruse.[19]

This is certainly recognisable as a legitimate reconstruction and representation of Darwin's theory, whereas one might be forgiven for failing to recognise Darwin altogether when he comes clothed in Mary Williams's logical apparatus. Besides offering this pictorial representation of the structure of the theory, Ruse polishes up the putative deductive steps in the argument, so that they do represent, he claims, genuine cases of logical entailment. For example, he gives the deduction that leads to 'SE' as follows:

Premise i: Organic beings tend to increase at a high (geometrical) rate.

Premise ii: If organic beings tend to increase at a high rate, then either there must be a struggle for existence or the numbers of organisms go up without limit.

Premise iii: If the numbers of organisms go up without limit, then the world must have unlimited room.

Premise iv: The world does not have unlimited room.

Conclusion: There is a struggle for existence.[20]

Certainly, this looks more logically secure than Flew's equations, and less daunting than Mary Williams's algebra. But the owner of the mushroom farm, while not, perhaps, wishing to question the legitimacy of drawing this particular conclusion from the four premises, would probably wish to argue that the second premise is not true — not an adequate representation of our world. This is not necessarily an overwhelming objection, however, for as may be seen from Figure 15, Ruse is happy enough to agree that the various links in the line of argument need not be rigorously deductive, such as would satisfy the demands of the mathematically-minded logician. The whole structure may be built on 'semi-deductive' inferences, rather than strict logical entailments.

Ruse's paper has the merit of emphasising the importance of analogical reasoning in the argument provided in *The Origin*, and cognizance of this kind of argument is taken in the dotted lines of his diagram. He sees the argument of the book as being partly inductive, partly deductive, with inductive analogies being highly important components of the total theoretical structure. In *The Origin*, many empirical instances are adduced in support of each of the inductive generalisations and 'deductive' inferences that are made in the course of the argument. And numerous additional observations are shown to be comprehensible when viewed in the light of the theory of evolution by natural selection. As Ruse rightly maintains, the whole argument of the book 'is that of a *very fine network*, where many different threads mesh together to make the whole'.[21] It might be said, then, that the overall aim of the book is to *persuade* the reader that evolution does occur through the medium of natural selection, and that the theory of evolution is capable of accounting satisfactorily for a multiplicity of otherwise disconnected 'facts'.

But where does this get us, if we are trying to display the Darwinian theory as a logical structure, analogous to the Euclidian or Newtonian systems, or the general structure of scientific theories as represented by Braithwaite? Or putting the question in a rather different way, and in a broader context, can non-mathematical theories such as the Darwinian theory of evolution by natural selection, or the geological theory of Lyell's *Principles*, be represented in such a way that they conform to the hypothetico-deductive model of the logical-empiricists? The problem is obscured in cases such as Darwin's *Origin* or Lyell's *Principles* by the fact that these books play two roles virtually simultaneously. On the one hand they seek to justify the acceptance of their theories; and on the other they seek to explain phenomena by means of their theories. And these two activities go on side by side, with the result that we sometimes have difficulty in seeing exactly what the theory is intended to be. So we may have considerable doubt about whether we have teased out the structure of the theory correctly when we offer our reconstruction of the argument.

But here we may have recourse once again to the tabular representation of the argument given by Wallace.[22] He, after all, was one of the co-authors of the theory. And he, if anyone, should have had a pretty clear idea of what the theory was. In Wallace's table, we find the theory stripped of all its analogies, all its illustrative examples, all its rhetoric. Can this succinct statement of the theory be viewed as a logically coherent structure, such as might be required by those who adhere to Braithwaite's ideas on the structure of scientific theories? Is Wallace's version of the theory such that it can really be fitted satisfactorily into the top right-hand corner of Ruse's pictorial representation of Darwin's theory (Figure 15)? (And let it be noted that by the very manner in which Ruse portrays the theory, as a kind of hierarchical deductive structure, he reveals himself as a supporter of a *quasi*-Braithwaitian view of scientific theories, with a long and highly distinguished tradition standing behind the two of them, extending back to classical antiquity.)

It does not seem that any simple representation of the theory — whether it be by Wallace, Flew, Ruse or whoever — can persuade the theory to take on a *strictly* deductive form. Or, if it is made rigorously deductive, as Mary Williams has seemingly achieved, it is no longer recognisable as Darwin's theory. So what are we to do in this situation? Several avenues seem to offer themselves for consideration. Let us take them in turn.

We could say, as Ruse did, that the putative deductive links in the theory are 'inevitably in a sketchy form'. (See Figure 15.) Possibly then, with some ingenuity, one could add sufficient extra premises to the theory to cause the links to become truly deductive. But the trouble with this approach is that it immediately leads one into the jungle of Mary Williams's symbolic logic and away from the pleasant pastures of Darwin's own theory.

As a second suggestion, we might say that there *is* a truly deductive structure in *The Origin*, but so far we have failed to find it. Flew's equations, for example, may simply be tackling the matter from the wrong starting point. Perhaps, by completely reshuffling the terms of the 'equations' (say, by starting with evolution as a premise instead of finishing with it), and working hard at the problem, we might be able to get out a new deductive structure successfully. This may possibly be achieved, but I have yet to see any representation of the theory that carries it through satisfactorily. To date, all published versions I have encountered follow essentially the same lines as those mapped out by such as Wallace, Flew and Ruse. And if we did succeed in putting the pieces together in some new way that was unambiguously coherent from a logical point of view, it would not, I think, have much utility, for surely it would be some other theory altogether, not the Darwin/Wallace theory, as conceived by its authors. For we know exactly what Wallace believed the logical structure of his theory to have been. Figure 14 has told us this as clearly as one could wish.

As a third possibility, we might say that there is something peculiar or defective about the theory of evolution by natural selection; that it is in some way different from other theories in that it does not conform to the logical requirements of scientific theories as represented by Braithwaite's description of their structure, and their exemplification by (say) Newton's *Principia*. Perhaps the theory of evolution by natural selection is not really 'scientific' in the true sense, because it is 'illogical'. If this is so, perhaps one cannot use the Darwin/Wallace theory for the purposes of scientific explanation and prediction.

There *may* be some truth in this, for as we will see below a number of commentators have raised the objection that the Darwinian theory is unscientific because it is unfalsifiable. Or perhaps the theory is not one that will enable predictions to be made; perhaps it *is* deficient. But let us leave this aside for the moment, and take it up again shortly.

Another possibility is that the requirement of strict deducibility within scientific theories is too exacting, and that while the general shape of Braithwaite's model may be essentially correct for physical theories it is not exactly applicable to the non-mathematical sciences such as geology or biology. In such cases, one must be satisfied with '*quasi*-deductive' reasonings within the theory.

Finally, and more radically, though related to our fourth suggestion, it might be said that the deductive model, beloved by philosophers of science (usually with initial training as philosophers, logicians, mathematicians, or one or other of the physical sciences), is simply irrelevant, or inapplicable to many branches of science, and the questions that have been raised are simply straw men that have reared their heads because of the baneful influence of mathematics and physics on the philosophy of science, aided and abetted by the long (and generally successful) tradition in the Western world of offering scientific explanations of phenomena by their incorporation within a deductive or logical structure. If such an iconoclastic view be followed, then one might say that we have run into difficulties simply because we have attempted to make use of a false or inappropriate model for the depiction of scientific theories. And such a critic might well point to the very long tradition in Western thought that has sought to link science with logic,[23] and claim that the link between the two is really illusory and that the sooner this is realised by philosophers of science the better it will be.

On the whole, I think I am inclined to adopt this fifth, iconoclastic, point of view. For if one examines the history of the non-mathematical sciences, one finds very few (if any) instances of theories that have rigorously deductive structures. And when one finds a geological or biological theory presented in 'geometrical' form, as occasionally one does in the early literature,[24] then it appears quite incongruous — almost silly, in fact. And one cannot help feeling some sympathy for the author who felt constrained by the conventions of his day to present a theory in a manner that was so inappropriate.

Moreover, examination of the history of science shows that scientists have constantly had recourse to the use of analogy, metaphor and simile,[25] not only as aids towards the formulation of hypotheses and the construction of theories, but also in the presentation of their ideas. This, of course, is now being increasingly appreciated by philosophers of science, who have come to place considerable emphasis upon the use of models and analogical reasoning, both in theory construction, and within the framework of theories themselves.[26] And here I should emphasise that I am not speaking merely of the use of models for didactic purposes; I am referring to the role played by models (which are themselves analogical in character) in scientific reasoning. My opinion, then, is that the Darwin/Wallace theory cannot be recast as a rigorously deductive structure, without turning it into something quite other than the Darwin/Wallace theory, but this, I suggest, need be no cause for alarm. For many — in fact most — non-mathematical theories of the natural sciences are simply not, by their very nature, rigorously deductive structures. This does not, however, prevent their being scientific theories, and it does not prevent their offering quite acceptable explanations. Though if one finds counter-instances to what is expected on the basis of these theories (e.g., the behaviour of the mushrooms under my house, or the actions of the youthful public-schoolboy second-lieutenants bravely sacrificing themselves to the German gunners) this need be no cause for alarm. It simply illustrates the fact that GRI + LR on most, but *not all*, occasions lead to SE; and SE + V much more often than not result in NS. And despite the fact that these 'equations' do not represent strict logical entailments, we can use them with some confidence to offer explanations of phenomena — to help us account for the appearance of the paleontological record, for example.

I conclude, then, that the reconstructions of the theory of evolution by natural selection given by Wallace and Flew, and (more thoroughly) by Ruse, *do* give reasonable representations of the structure of the theory, as it was understood by its originators. On the other hand, the theory that is revealed in the analyses of these authors, does not conform to the rigorous standards of logic favoured by the philosophers of the mathematical sciences. But this does not mean that the Darwin/Wallace theory is in some way inadequate or unscientific, owing to its lack of logical rigour. It means, rather, that the model of a scientific theory prescribed by the philosophers of the logical-empiricist tradition is inappropriate in many cases, for it fails to be applicable to a substantial number of theories of the non-mathematical type, which, by common agreement, are regarded as scientific and are capable of furnishing acceptable and worthwhile scientific explanations of phenomena. In other words, I regard the doctrine of evolution by natural selection as a genuine example of a scientific theory; and at the same time I reject the claim that the logical-empiricists' model is applicable to *all* scientific theories. The scientificity of Darwinian theory should be sufficiently revealed during the course of this book, where we find illustrated its explanatory power in a variety of ways.

But now let us return to the third point given above, where the spectre was raised that there may possibly be something specially peculiar, odd, aberrant, defective or deficient about the theory of evolution by natural selection — something that makes it quite different from other theories. From what I have said in the preceding pages, it should be apparent that I do not subscribe to this view. However, when we survey the critical literature that has grown up around the Darwinian theory over the years it soon becomes apparent that a number of commentators have made claims suggesting that there *is* something unusual and unsatisfactory about the Darwinian theory. These critics have frequently raised points of some substance and interest, and because these are intimately related to the question of the logical structure of the theory it will be convenient and appropriate to deal with them here.

The usual criticism of the Darwinian theory has not run along the lines that we have been considering above — namely, that the theory is 'illogical'. Rather, the objection more commonly raised is that it is unfalsifiable in that it does not make predictions that can can be tested experimentally. This, so it is claimed, makes the Darwinian doctrine quite unlike the Newtonian theory, which can be used to make such extraordinarily accurate predictions about the times and places of eclipses, or other physical phenomena.

It is usually objected that the Darwinian theory is unfalsifiable, because there is no criterion of the 'fitness' of organisms other than their survival. The group of organisms that survives *must*, by definition so to speak, have been the fittest. Putting it another way, it is claimed that the expression 'survival of the fittest' is tautological.[27]

At first sight one may be inclined to brush such objections aside rather lightly. It might be said, for example, that the expression 'survival of the fittest' is not really Darwin's at all, having been coined by the philosopher Herbert Spencer, and taken up by Darwin only in the later editions of *The Origin*.[28] But this is barely sufficient as a reply, for Darwin *did*, after all, employ Spencer's phrase, and he gave the expression 'survival of the fittest' essentially the same standing as 'natural selection'. Natural selection simply means that there is a process going on among living organisms in which those that are best suited to the conditions of the environment tend to survive. This really is essentially the same as saying that the fittest survive. So the question comes back to the problem of whether there are, or can be, criteria for fitness other than that of survival. Can we set up any kind of experimental situation whereby we may test whether the fittest do in fact survive? For if this cannot be done, it would seem that this part of the theory is unfalsifiable, and according to the well-known criterion of Sir Karl Popper this would mean that the principle is not a component of a *bona fide* scientific theory.[29] In Popper's language, the theory of evolution would be pseudo-scientific.

One might respond to this in a number of ways. K. K. Lee, for example, has simply taken this case as an indication that Popper's criterion is unsatisfactory, and that it fails to provide an acceptable way of distinguishing between sciences (such as physics) and pseudo-sciences (such as astrology).[30] Or, according to what is sometimes called the 'conventionalist' position in the philosophy of science, it might be held that the principle of natural selection provides a convenient way of ordering and interpreting phenomena, and it is effectively taken to be true by definition for the purposes of evolutionary biology. On this view, the principle of natural selection might be regarded as unfalsifiable, though not necessarily correct as a description of the affairs of the world. One could not falsify it, any more than one could falsify the

Newtonian equation: Force = Mass × Acceleration. But such a view may seem not a little strange as an interpretation of the status of a biological (as opposed to a physical) principle.

A more useful approach, I think, is to consider whether any independent criterion of fitness *can* be found, other than survival. As has been said above,[31] a number of authors have come to the conclusion that this is not possible, so that the principle of survival of the fittest is indeed a tautology. And this has led some non-scientific commentators to complain that the whole theoretical structure of modern evolutionary theory is in a state of ruin.[32]

But consider a simple case of natural selection arising from the struggle for existence: the struggle between Aborigines and Europeans in Tasmania that occurred towards the end of the nineteenth century, when the whole Aboriginal population of the island was eventually exterminated. One group (to their lasting *moral,* but not biological, shame) survived; another group failed to survive. Surely it is perfectly clear that this may be explained in terms of some criterion of fitness (say, the possession of fire-arms) that is quite separate from the *contingent* fact that the Europeans *did* survive. Thus we can readily see this example as an empirical exemplification of the principle of natural selection or the survival of the fittest. It may be noted, by the way, that on the Australian mainland, where resources were less limited, it being a roomy continent, the struggle for existence was less intense, and both black and white populations survived (although a number of mainland Aboriginal tribes have become extinct).

The principle may also be used to a limited degree in a *predictive* sense, as well as for a retrospective explanation, in cases where there are clear criteria for fitness for survival. An excellent example has been provided by the well-known case of the English peppered moth, studied in detail by H. B. D. Kettlewell.[33] This case is quoted so often that it is probably unnecessary to describe it again in detail here. The point is simply that there was, in this instance, an obvious independent criterion of fitness. Putting it in an utterly basic way: black moths are 'fit' on 'black' trees; white moths are 'unfit' on 'black' trees; black moths are 'unfit' on 'white' trees; white moths are 'fit' on 'white' trees. Because of this independent criterion of fitness, Kettlewell was able to predict what might happen when mixtures of black and white moths were released in separate 'black' and 'white' areas of woodland. And his predictions were duly supported by his observations.[34] In addition, one can predict what may be expected to happen to moth populations as the colours of woods change according to the vicissitudes of social change which manifest themselves in Britain by the passing of 'environmental' legislation.[35]

However, even this kind of argument may fail to satisfy the critic who regards the principle of natural selection as a tautology, or a mere truism. Suppose, the critic might say, Kettlewell had found that the white moths survived best on black trees. Would not he have dreamed up some *ad hoc* hypothesis to explain away this unexpected event, rather than admitting that a falsification of the principle of natural selection had occurred? Well, I cannot speak for Dr Kettlewell on this matter, but from what one knows of the history of science, and the descriptions given by writers on the sociology of science and the philosophy of science, one might anticipate that he would indeed have introduced some *ad hoc* hypothesis, rather than abandoning the principle of natural selection.[36] Would he not defend the principle at all costs, believing it to be incontrovertible? Perhaps, but this would best be explained by sociological considerations, not by the alleged tautological character of the principle of natural selection. For to throw over natural selection, and all that goes with it in the way of the general theory of evolution in biology, could have involved far more upheaval of theory than would be entailed in the formulation of some suitable *ad hoc* hypothesis to explain away the unexpected observations. As Kuhn would say, an anomaly would have emerged,[37] but this in itself would not have been sufficient to bring about a scientific revolution in biology, and would have been dealt with in the routine manner by the introduction of some special hypothesis, brought in for the occasion. If, however, when natural selection is put to the test it always fails to meet the expectations based upon independent criteria of fitness, then one would wish to reject the principle as a major component of biological theory, and a scientific revolution might be inaugurated. Yet to date this has not been found necessary.

Nevertheless, a considerable number of problems remain, for the theory of evolution has great difficult in predicting future events successfully, or for accounting for the particular details of the paleontological record. Thus, whereas the Newtonian theory can be used to predict eclipses well into the future, we can hardly suppose that the Darwinian theory will tell us with similar precision which species are going to survive in the future; which will become extinct; and how when and where such biological changes will occur. But there are several good reasons for this. For one thing, the variations that are postulated in Darwin's theory — now thought to be caused by genetic mutations[38] — happen randomly, so we can have no very definite idea of the course that evolution will take, though a good deal is now known about what happens at the molecular level when mutations occur. Secondly, the whole evolutionary process is linked with the changing conditions of the physical environment, and the precise future course of these is unknown. We do not know, for example, whether another ice age is to be expected, and if so when it will come. So we cannot tell in advance which particular varieties or species are going to be the fittest in the future.

In the case of Kettlewell's experiments with the peppered moths, he was dealing with a presently-occurring process of natural selection, and the reasons for the relative fitness of the varieties could readily be identified. But in cases relating to the past this is not generally possible, and the experimental testing of the hypothesis is not feasible. For example, one might seek to propose an hypothesis as to why the dinosaurs became extinct, or ammonites became less coiled in the latter stages of their evolutionary history. But such hypotheses as one may propose, to account for such phenomena, can never be tested experimentally, and the view that prevails today is that they are speculative, unfalsifiable, and ultimately ascientific or metaphysical.[39]

For such reasons, recent workers have tended to concentrate on general theories of population genetics, which avoid historical questions such as the why and the wherefore of the lineages of dinosaurs or ammonites. They seek, rather, to find mechanisms whereby equilibrium states of populations may be sustained in relation to the conditions of the environment. They are concerned to explain, for example, how a balance between different kinds of genes is maintained, a good case being provided by the well-known existence of genes producing sickle-celled anaemia in human populations in countries where malaria is prevalent.[40] And despite my remarks about the non-tautological character of the principle of natural selection, and the identification of independent criteria of biological fitness, it must be acknowledged that population biologists do frequently *define* fitness in terms of survival![41] But since their attention is now directed to testable population genetic theories, rather than particular historical evolutionary developments, the study of population genetics does not necessarily belong to the domain of speculative metaphysics. One can explore the possible relationships between gene (or nucleo-protein) frequencies and the distribution of phenotypic[42] characters in populations in a proper empirical manner, without using unfalsifiable hypotheses.

The evolutionary biologist may also point out that the failure of his science to make precise and accurate predictions about the future evolutionary development of organisms does not make it peculiarly different from other branches of science. In making risky, falsifiable predictions, astronomy is the atypical science — for it deals with a frictionless physical system such as is rarely encountered. The astrophysicist cannot predict and test the future evolution of the cosmos; the geographer cannot predict with certainty what will happen during the erosion of a particular coastline; the geophysicist cannot say exactly when and where the next earthquake will occur; the economist cannot predict with certainty the future monetary value of the pound or the dollar; the meteorologist cannot make precise long-range weather forecasts. So the theory of evolution is on all fours with a number of other disciplines that claim scientific status. Its problems are in no way unique. In fact, accurate and precise prediction is normally only possible when experimental conditions can be created artificially. Needless to say, this is impossible in many branches of science, not just in evolutionary biology.

The theme of explanation and/or prediction was taken up some years ago in an interesting paper by Michael Scriven, 'Explanation and prediction in evolutionary theory', which had the pertinent sub-heading, 'Satisfactory explanation is possible even when prediction of the future is impossible.'[43] Scriven freely admitted that the Darwinian theory did not enable one to make precise quantitative forecasts about future evolutionary developments, in some *quasi*-Newtonian style. But this, he said, is because the theory is probabilistic in character, and does not employ universal laws of total generality. The physicist, we might say, cannot countenance two heavenly bodies *not* attracting each other according to the equation

$$F = G \cdot \frac{m_1 m_2}{d^2}$$

The law of gravitation is a *universal* generalisation. By contrast, Kettlewell would have been in no way dismayed to discover that a significant proportion of 'white' moths had managed to survive in trees badly affected by industrial pollution. And, as Scriven rightly points out, not all explanation relies on the application of universal laws. As he says, if you have a general law it may be helpful for the purposes of explanation, but if you do not you may still be able to say a good deal about the possible and actual causes of events whose explanations are being sought. And this is the sort of task that a theory such as that of Darwin and Wallace is well able to perform. It can enable us to understand (or explain) the general features of the past — as revealed by the paleontological record — without enabling us to predict the future. As Darwin wrote:

> It can hardly be supposed that a false theory would explain, in so satisfactory a manner as does the theory of natural selection, the several large classes of facts [that it does explain].[44]

Of course, evidence in support of a theory is no logical proof of the truth of that theory,[45] and the colligation[46] of phenomena achieved by Darwin's theory does not give it canonical status. But the theory's inability to make precise predictions about the future course of evolution should not in itself lead us to reject it as an example of scientific reasoning. So at the present time there is an almost universal acceptance among biologists of the main features of the Darwinian theory, but attention is now chiefly directed to such matters as genetic mechanisms and their chemical foundations; studies of the structures of populations and their mathematical modelling; and ecological relationships. Modern biology has taken us far from the point to which Darwin brought us, but the basic principles that he enunciated have survived, the criticisms of philosophers notwithstanding.[47]

NOTES CHAPTER 9

1   See Galileo Galilei, *Discorsi e Dimonstrazioni Matematichè, intorno à due nuoue scienze*, Leyden, 1638 (*Dialogues Concerning Two New Sciences* . . . translated by Henry Crew & Alfonso de Salvio, London, 1914; reprinted Dover, New York, 1954).

2 See I. Newton, *Philosophiae Naturalis Principia Mathematica*, London, 1687 (*Sir Isaac Newton's Mathematical Principles of Natural Philosophy and his System of the World: Translated into English by Andrew Motte in 1729*. The translations revised, and supplied with an historical and explanatory appendix, by Florian Cajori [California University Press, Berkeley, 1934]).

3 This was the situation as it was presented in the third edition of *Principia* (1726). In the first edition there were no less than nine hypotheses, but these were gradually shunted off into the 'rules of reasoning' or 'phaenomena'.

4 Recently, there was a total eclipse of the sun in the southern part of Australia, and we were able to observe the phenomenon on television in Sydney. It was impressive indeed to be told by the commentator the exact moment at which the sun's disc would be fully obscured, and to see the prediction confirmed before our eyes to the very second.

5 According to Kant, the Euclidean view of (three-dimensional) space and the uniform flow of time are necessary for us, our minds being such that we cannot but 'see' the world in this way. Space and time, he says, are *a priori* intuitions, or *a priori* representations which necessarily underlie outward appearances.

6 See, for example, E. Nagel, *The Structure of Science*, Routledge & Kegan Paul, London, 1961, Chapters 7 and 8.

7 For example, Nicolaus Steno attempted (1669) to set out his geological theory, starting from a small number of simple and seemingly obvious principles. (*Nicolaus Steno (1631-1686) The Prodromus of Nicolaus Steno's Dissertation Concerning a Solid Body Enclosed by Process of Nature within a Solid*, Hafner, New York & London, 1968.)

8 R. B. Braithwaite, *Scientific Explanation: A Study of the Function of Theory, Probability and Law in Science*, Cambridge University Press, Cambridge, 1953, p.12.

9 C. Darwin, *The Origin of Species* (ed. J. W. Burrow), Penguin, Harmondsworth, 1968, pp.169-170.

10 A. R. Wallace, *Natural Selection and Tropical Nature: Essays on Descriptive and Theoretical Biology*, New edn, London & New York, 1891, p.166 (republished Gregg, Farnborough, 1969).

11 A. G. N. Flew, 'The structure of Darwinism', *New Biology*, Vol. 28, 1959, pp.25-42.

12 J. S. Huxley, *Evolution in Action*, Chatto & Windus, London, 1953, p.34.

13 A. G. N. Flew, *op. cit.* (note 11), p.28.

14 *Ibid.*

15 *Ibid.*

16 A. G. N. Flew, *Evolutionary Ethics*, Macmillan, London & Basingstoke, 1967, p.8.

17 M. B. Williams, 'Deducing the consequences of evolution: a mathematical model', *Journal of Theoretical Biology*, Vol. 29, 1970, pp.343-385 (at p.343). (Dr Williams's account has been clarified in her subsequent article 'The logical status of the theory of natural selection and other evolutionary controversies' in M. Bunge [ed.], *The Methodological Unity of Science*, Reidel, Dordrecht, 1973, pp.84-102, which also makes important contributions to the debate about whether the Darwinian theory is 'circular'.)

18 M. Ruse, 'Charles Darwin's theory of evolution: an analysis', *Journal of the History of Biology*, Vol. 8, 1975, pp.219-241.

19 *Ibid.*, p.241.

20 *Ibid.*, p.222.

21 *Ibid.*, p.241 (italics in original).

22 See page 117 above.

23 This tradition may readily be traced back to Aristotle, but many twentieth-century publications still treat logic and scientific method within the same covers. For example: M. R. Cohen & E. Nagel, *An Introduction to Logic and Scientific Method*, Routledge & Kegan Paul, London, 1934.

24 See above, note 7.

25 For a detailed review of the literature on this topic, see W. H. Leatherdale, *The Role of Analogy, Model and Metaphor in Science*, N. Holland, Amsterdam, Oxford & New York, 1974.

26 The classic statement of the 'modelist' position in the philosophy of science is to be found in N. R. Campbell, *Physics, the Elements*, Cambridge, 1920, Chapter 6 (republished as *Foundation of Science*, Dover, New York, 1957). See also M. B. Hesse, *Models and Analogies in Science*, Notre Dame University Press, Notre Dame, 1966, Chapter 1.

27 This view has been taken by both philosophers and scientists. For example: A. R. Manser, 'The concept of evolution', *Philosophy*, Vol. 40, 1965, pp.18-34; A. D. Barker, 'An approach to the theory of natural selection', *Philosophy*, Vol. 44, 1969, pp.271-289; J. B. S. Haldane, 'Darwinism under revision', *Rationalist Annual*, 1935, pp.19-29; C. H. Waddington, 'Evolutionary adaptation', in Sol Tax (ed.), *Evolution after Darwin*, Vol. 1 (*The Evolution of Life*), Chicago University Press, Chicago, 1960, pp.381-402; P. B. Medawar & J. S. Medawar, *The Life Science: Current Ideas of Biology*, Wildwood House, London, 1977, p.44.

28 The use of Spencer's term was recommended to Darwin by Wallace in 1866 (F. Darwin & A. C. Seward (eds), *More Letters of Charles Darwin*, 2 vols, John Murray, London, 1903, Vol. 1, p.268). Wallace maintained that the term 'natural selection' suggested some kind of conscious choice (or purposiveness)

on the part of Nature. By contrast, 'survival of the fittest' did not seem to have this connotation, and Darwin took up Wallace's suggestion, introducing the term as a sub-heading to the fourth chapter (on natural selection) of the fifth edition of *The Origin* (1869). This was, perhaps, a tactical mistake, for the fear that the whole theory is simply a glorified tautology has clung to the Darwinian doctrine ever since.

29   K. R. Popper, 'The demarcation between science and metaphysics', in *Conjectures and Refutations: The Growth of Scientific Knowledge*, Routledge & Kegan Paul, London, 3rd ed., 1969, pp.253-292.

30   K. K. Lee, 'Popper's falsifiability and Darwin's natural selection', *Philosophy*, Vol. 44, 1969, pp.291-302.

31   See note 27, above.

32   For example: N. Macbeth, *Darwin Retried*, Garnstone Press, London, 1974.

33   H. B. D. Kettlewell, 'Selection experiments on industrial melanism in the *Lepidoptera*', *Heredity*, Vol. 9, 1955, pp.323-342.

34   A film of Kettlewell's work has been made, which enables the viewer to see the process of selection in operation (*Evolution in Progress*, 1956).

35   Observations have already shown that the moth populations are changing in the way that would be anticipated according to the theory of natural selection. See L. M. Cook, R. R. Askew & J. A. Bishop, 'Increasing frequency of the typical form of the peppered moth in Manchester', *Nature*, Vol.227, 1970, p.1155. For a more general review of the problem of industrial melanism, see E. B. Ford, *Ecological Genetics*, 4th edn, Chapman & Hall, London, 1975, Chapter 14.

36   Speaking generally, evidence conflicting with particular theories is *not* usually sufficient to persuade scientists to discard those theories, for the power of a particular paradigm (using Thomas Kuhn's terms) is usually such that scientists are loth to throw away their theoretical guide-lines or frameworks. Rather, various '*ad hoc*' theoretical adjustments can usually be made. Only when a considerable mass of conflicting evidence has accumulated and an alternative theoretical structure is available do scientists make major shifts in their conceptual allegiances.

37   T. S. Kuhn, *The Structure of Scientific Revolutions*, Chicago University Press, Chicago & London, 1962, p.52 & *passim*.

38   That is, discrete changes in the hereditary constitutions of organisms, arising from a variety of causes, including such things as cosmic rays or radioactivity.

39   For further discussion of this thesis, see G. D. Wassermann, 'Testability of the role of natural selection within theories of population genetics and evolution', *The British Journal for the Philosophy of Science*, Vol. 29, 1978, pp.223-242.

40   Here a recessive allele(s) causes an alteration in the shape of the red blood corpuscles. If an individual is homozygous with respect to this allele he or she usually dies. There is some defect in the heterozygous (Ss) case and none in the presence of the dominant homozygous pair (SS). However, heterozygous individuals are much more resistant to malaria than those with 'SS' allele pair. Consequently, in malarial countries, there are many 'Ss' individuals, and although the 'ss' case is usually lethal a high proportion of 's' alleles remain in the population. So a balance of 'S' and 's' alleles may be established. The 's' alleles are very much less common in populations not subject to malaria.

41   For example: E. O. Wilson & W. H. Bossert, *A Primer of Population Biology*, Sinauer, Sunderland, Mass., 1971, pp.50-51.

42   See below, p. 162.

43   M. E. Scriven, 'Explanation and prediction in evolutionary theory', *Science*, Vol. 130, 1959, pp.477-482.

44   C. Darwin, *The Origin of Species by means of Natural Selection . . .* Introduction by Sir Julian Huxley, 6th edn, Mentor, New York & Toronto, 1958, p.442.

45   To suppose that it *is*, is to commit the well-known logical fallacy of 'affirming the consequent'.

46   I use a term (meaning the 'binding together' of empirical evidence by means of a suitable theoretical construction) introduced by the nineteenth-century historian and philosopher of science, William Whewell.

47   It is noteworthy that Sir Karl Popper, who was at one time of the opinion that the principle of natural selection is tautologous, has recently changed his views on the matter, pointing out that one cannot *explain* anything with a tautology. In fact, he says, it is not universally true; sometimes organs evolve that are *not* contributors to the fitness of organisms. (K. R. Popper, 'Natural selection and the emergence of mind', *Dialectica*, Vol. 32, 1978, pp.339-355.)

10

Some Criticisms of the Theory of Evolution by Natural Selection

Since 1859 there has been an almost incredible amount of ink spilt in criticism of the theory of evolution by natural selection, and it is quite impossible to give due account of all of it in a work of limited scope and intent such as this book. Consequently, this chapter will merely offer some account of what I can take to be a few of the more important and interesting criticisms from the point of view of the history of biology, and I will not attempt to go beyond these to more general questions such as those related to scientific methodology, to scriptural exegesis or criticisms relating to various sociological aspects of the theory. Rather, I will emphasise those questions that relate particularly to criticisms that Darwin himself took seriously, and which to a greater or lesser extent influenced the development of his thinking in the post-1859 period. Certain other objections to the theory have, of course, already been considered in particular places in our preceding pages; and we shall have occasion to refer to certain further criticisms in succeeding chapters.

In all, there were six editions of *The Origin*, the last appearing in 1872. Even the first edition contained the sixth chapter ('Difficulties on theory') in which Darwin answered in advance the points that he thought would be made by his critics. The last edition is strengthened by a whole new chapter (numbered seven), 'Miscellaneous objections to the theory of natural selection', in which some of the objections Darwin encountered in the reviews of *The Origin* were answered. But the really significant criticisms that we shall consider in this chapter were not met adequately in the sixth edition, and, as will become apparent, the whole theory began to be increasingly difficult to sustain in the latter years of the nineteenth century.

One of the most central problems for Darwin's theory was raised shortly after *The Origin* was first published, by Bishop Samuel Wilberforce (1805-1873), in an article in the influential *Quarterly Review* in 1860.[1] Today, Wilberforce is chiefly remembered for the drubbing that he supposedly received at the hands of T. H. Huxley in the celebrated 'Oxford

Debate' of 1860.[2] And this alleged crushing defeat at the hands of 'science' (in the guise of Huxley) has no doubt led to the popular view of Wilberforce as a man of somewhat insufficient intellectual powers.[3] But as early as 1860, Wilberforce drew attention in the aforementioned article to very considerable lacunae or weaknesses in Darwin's argument. Consequently, although the comparative anatomist Richard Owen[4] – perhaps Darwin's chief intellectual foe in the evolutionary debate – probably provided Wilberforce with a number of arguments, I do not think it correct to brush Wilberforce casually aside as a mere intellectual lightweight.

In his *Quarterly Review* article, Wilberforce reminded his readers that Darwin wished to argue by analogy from domestic breeds to wild animals. But, Wilberforce emphasised, in no cases had artificial selection succeeded in producing new breeds incapable of forming fertile crosses with each other. Artificial selection was never able to produce new *species*. So, we might say, if Darwin was really trying to employ the uniformitarian methodology of Lyell, that method had seemingly broken down at the very beginning. For the observations of contemporary circumstances (i.e., the work of plant and animal breeders) suggested that new species could *not* be produced by selection. Moreover, domestic breeds, when they become feral, usually revert to wild types after two or three generations. Therefore, selection seemed to be incapable of producing new permanent breeds, let alone permanent species. Darwin never really solved this problem successfully, despite the fact that it struck at the very roots of his theoretical and methodological systems.

A second related criticism put forward by Wilberforce was that although he was perfectly willing to allow that selection operates in nature, arising from a combination of variation and struggle for existence, he did not see how a resultant evolutionary change could occur indefinitely, since Darwin had given no account of how there might be a continuous source of new variations, upon which natural selection might act. In Wilberforce's pleasantly rhetorical words:

We must be shown ... [that the] law of competition has in nature to deal with favourable variations in the individuals of any species, [so] as truly to exalt those individuals above the highest type of perfection to which their least imperfect predecessors attained – above, that is to say, the normal level of the species – that such individual improvement is, in truth, a rising above the highest level of any former tide, and not merely the return in its appointed season of the feebler neap to the fuller spring-tide; and then, next, we must be shown that there is actively at work in nature, co-ordinate with the law of competition and with the existence of such favourable variations, a power of accumulating such favourable variation through successive descents.[5]

We may illustrate the point being made here in Figure 16, which shows how a population of organisms of a particular species might be expected to change in time: (a) as the Darwinian theory of evolution by natural selection might require; and (b) as Wilberforce would have suggested, if there were no new source of variations — remembering that the theory of natural selection, *per se*, gave no account of the origin of new variations.

Figure 16 Possible Changes in the Character of the Population of some Species under Selection

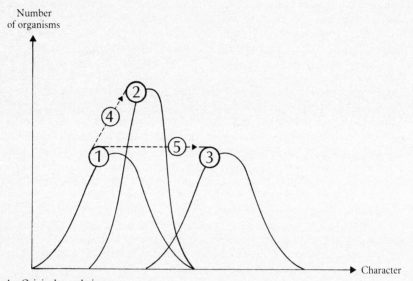

1 Original population
2 Population subsequent to action of natural selection if (as claimed by Wilberforce) there is no new source of variation.
3 Population subsequent to action of natural selection, if (as required by Darwin) there is some new source of variation.
4 Population shift asserted by Wilberforce.
5 Population shift required by Darwin, if his theory were to be viable.

I think it will be agreed that if Darwin could give no reason (either theoretical or empirical) for the argument that new variations were constantly arising in populations of organisms, then there was every justification for rejecting his theory. Darwin, however, did offer some account of the origin of variations, and this, of course, arose from the 'Lamarckian' aspects of his theory.

As has been noted above, he was disdainful towards the work of Lamarck; but from very early in his career, Darwin believed in the notion of the inheritance of acquired characteristics. At certain periods of his career the doctrine was very prominent; sometimes it receded into the background; but it was always there. So, remembering also that Darwin adhered to the Lyellian theory of slow, constantly fluctuating changes in the physical environment, if the character of organisms were causally linked to the environmental conditions by 'Lamarckian' means, then Darwin would indeed have an explanation of the source of new variations, and he could seemingly dismiss Wilberforce's criticism. It should be noted, however, that while Lamarck believed that organisms responded directly to changing environmental conditions, Darwin supposed that a changing environment stimulated random variations among organisms.

But Darwin's answer was not apparently sufficient, according to an important critique of his theory presented by the Scottish engineer, Fleeming Jenkin (1833-1885),[6] in *The North British Review* in 1867.[7] Jenkin's article was of considerable interest, and it is worthwhile giving it some special consideration here. In the first place he considered once again the analogy that Darwin wished to draw between wild and domesticated organisms. Jenkin pointed out that when selection is applied to domestic animals, there is always a definite limit to the changes that can be wrought by the breeder. Supposing, for example, one tries to breed pigeons with longer beaks. This can be done perfectly successfully for a few generations, and soon one has birds with considerably longer beaks. But it quickly becomes evident that this program cannot be continued indefinitely. Very soon the breeder finds that he is baulked, and cannot produce any further extension of the beaks. This, it is now believed, is due to the limitations of the 'gene pool' available for the pigeon fancier to use. If he wishes to proceed further, he must wait for genetic mutations to occur that will enable a beak-lengthening process to be continued — and this may entail a very long wait. In other words, Jenkin was claiming that according to empirical evidence, changes tended to resemble the situation indicated by '4' in Figure 16, rather than '5', as Darwin would have desired.

But this was not Jenkin's only significant argument. He is best remembered today for having drawn attention to the difficulties encountered by the Darwinian theory because of Darwin's attachment to the theory of blending inheritance. Jenkin engagingly presented his criticism in the form of a little story, which is worth reproducing here:

Suppose a white man to have been wrecked on an island inhabited by negroes, and to have established himself in friendly relations with a powerful tribe, whose customs he has learnt. Suppose him to possess the physical strength, energy, and ability of a dominant white race, and let the food and climate of the island suit his constitution; grant him every advantage which we can conceive a white to possess over the native; concede that in the struggle for existence his chance of a long life will be much superior to that of native chiefs; yet from all these admissions, there does not follow the conclusion that, after a limited or unlimited number of generations, the inhabitants of the island will be white. Our shipwrecked hero would probably become king; he would kill a great many blacks in the struggle for existence; he would have a great many wives and children, while many of his subjects would live and die as bachelors; an insurance company would accept his life at perhaps one-tenth of the premium which they would exact from the most favoured of the negroes. Our white's qualities would certainly tend very much to preserve him to a good old age, and yet he would not suffice in any number of generations to turn his subjects' descendants white. It may be said that the white colour is not the cause of the superiority. True, but it may be used to bring before the senses the way in which qualities belonging to one individual in a large number must be gradually obliterated. In the first generation there will be some dozens of intelligent mulattoes, much superior in average intelligence to the negroes. We might expect the throne for some generations to be occupied by a more or less yellow king; but can anyone believe that the whole island will gradually acquire a white, or even yellow population, or that the islands would acquire the energy, courage, ingenuity, patience, self-control, endurance, in virtue of which qualities our hero killed so many of their ancestors, and begot so many children; those qualities, in fact, which the struggle for existence would select, if it could select anything.[8]

I have mentioned this passage to students on a number of occasions in presenting lectures on the Darwinian Revolution. And from time to time I have been faced with the objection that white skins are *not*, in fact, related to 'fitness' in the struggle for existence in the manner that Jenkin implied! But this, of course, misses the point entirely. What Jenkin, or anyone else in the nineteenth century, felt about the relationship between skin colour and mental and/or physical prowess is totally irrelevant to the point at issue. What Jenkin is really saying is that if useful variations turn up from time to time (whether they be black, white, or any other colour) they will rapidly get swamped by their possessors breeding with the bulk of the population – *if*, that is, the theory of blending inheritance (or the 'paint-pot theory', as it has sometimes been called) is correct.

As we shall see below, Darwin was never able to produce a satisfactory theory of inheritance, or heredity. He always held to his ideas on blending, which were widely accepted in the nineteenth century, largely because of the common observation of what happens when humans of different skin colours breed together.[9] And if Jenkin were right in his suggestion, and the evolutionary process did in fact occur through the occasional appearance of specially favoured variations, then the Darwinian theory would indeed be faced with a most serious difficulty. Let us, therefore, look further at the cogency of Jenkin's criticisms and the extent to which Darwin was able to meet them.

There seems to be no doubt that Darwin took Jenkin's point seriously. In a letter to Hooker, dated January 16, [1869], Darwin wrote:

It is only about two years since last edition of *Origin*, and I am fairly disgusted to find how much I have had to modify, and how much I ought to add; but I have determined not to add much. Fleeming Jenkins [sic] has given me much trouble, but has been of more real use to me than any other essay or review.[10]

And on the basis of such evidence a number of authors[11] have suggested that when Darwin presented his new theory of inheritance in 1868, in his *Variation of Animals and Plants under Domestication*,[12] this new theory had been devised specifically to meet the problems raised in Jenkin's review. This interpretation has, however, been shown to be unsatisfactory, for it has been demonstrated[13] that the proofs of *Variation* were ready before Jenkin's review was actually published, and also that Darwin had been looking into the question of the mechanism of inheritance for some time, quite independently of any influences that may have emanated from Jenkin. In fact, what Jenkin did was to persuade Darwin that he should *not* think of the evolutionary process as occurring through the action of selection on populations that are largely homogeneous, with occasional especially well-endowed members. Rather, one should envisage a whole spectrum of characters in a population, with these being constantly 'scrutinised'[14] by the process of selection, there being a constant tendency for the less fit to be sifted out while the more fit tended to survive. This can be put another way: if we adopt the paint-pot simile,[15] we may say that according to Darwin it was not a case of occasional drops of white paint being added to a large quantity of black paint which would hopefully all turn white in time. Rather, the model was that of black paint constantly being drawn from the pot, and white paint constantly being added. Furthermore, the paint was not stirred perfectly either, because of the effects of geographical isolation. In other words, Darwin did have an answer ready, by which he could meet Jenkin's criticism. And the effect of the Scotsman's criticism was not, as has been supposed, the cause of Darwin suddenly and somewhat desperately dreaming up the *ad hoc* theory of *pangenesis* (the theory of inheritance that Darwin put forward in *Variation*). Rather, it had the effect of confirming his view that evolution did *not* proceed by the action of selection on more or less uniform communities that were favoured by the occasional appearance of well-fitted individuals.

This view of the matter, however, still leaves open the question of the source of the new (non-saltatory[16]) favourable variations. The theory has not yet explained how the paint-pot is able to acquire any new addition of white paint whatsoever. In other words, we still seem to be at the stage represented by move '4' in Figure 16, although we have hinted at Darwin's solution to the problem through the offices of a 'Lamarckian' theory. The way Darwin attempted to resolve this problem with the help of the theory of pangenesis is taken up in our next chapter.

NOTES CHAPTER 10

1   S. Wilberforce, 'Darwin's *Origin of Species*', *Quarterly Review*, Vol. 108, 1860, pp.225-264.

2   On this, see below, pages 193-194.

3   He was commonly referred to as 'Soapy Sam' by his detractors.

4   Richard Owen (1804-1892) was a leading spokesman in Britain of the ideas of the German 'Romantic' biologists. As such, he might have been expected to have been receptive to evolutionary concepts. But he was not; at least not to such concepts in their Darwinian form. On Owen, see R. M. MacLeod, 'Evolutionism and Richard Owen, 1830-1868: an episode in Darwin's century', *Isis*, Vol. 56, 1965, pp.259-280.

5   S. Wilberforce, *op. cit.* (note 1), pp.233-234.

6   Pronounced 'Fleming'.

7   [F. Jenkin,] 'The Origin of Species', *The North British Review*, Vol. 46, 1867, pp.277-318. The review is reprinted in D. L. Hull, *Darwin and his Critics: The Reception of Darwin's Theory of Evolution by the Scientific Community*, Harvard University Press, Cambridge, Mass., 1974, pp.303-350.

8   *Ibid.*, pp.315-316.

9   This phenomenon can be explained today by postulating that skin colour is determined not by a single pair of genes, but by several pairs. (See below, Chapter 12.)

10   F. Darwin & A. C. Seward (eds.), *More Letters of Charles Darwin*, 2 vols, John Murray, London, 1903, Vol. 2, p.379.

11   For example, G. Hardin, *Nature and Man's Fate*, Jonathan Cape, London, 1960, pp.117-118; L. Eiseley, *Darwin's Century: Evolution and the Men Who Discovered It*, Anchor, New York, 1961, p.217.

12   C. Darwin, *The Variation of Animals and Plants under Domestication*, 2 vols, London, 1868, Vol. 2, Chapter 27 ('Provisional hypothesis of pangenesis').

13   P. Vorzimmer, 'Charles Darwin and blending inheritance', *Isis*, Vol. 54, 1963, pp.371-390; P. Vorzimmer, *Charles Darwin: The Years of Controversy − The Origin of Species and its Critics 1859-82*, London University Press, London, 1972.

14   This term was one employed by Darwin in *The Origin*: 'It may be said that natural selection is daily and hourly scrutinising, throughout the world, every variation, even the slightest; rejecting that which is bad, preserving and adding up all that is good . . .' (C. Darwin, *The Origin of Species*, [ed. J. W. Burrow], Penguin, Harmondsworth, 1968, p.133).

15   G. Hardin, *op. cit.* (note11), p.115; P. Vorzimmer, *op. cit.* (note 13, 1972), p.110.

16   A 'saltation' is a 'jump', or sudden transition.

11

Darwin's Later Work

The full list of books Darwin published after *The Origin* is:

(i)   *On the Various Contrivances by which British and Foreign Orchids are Fertilized by Insects, and on the Good of Intercrossing . . . with illustrations*, London, 1862.

(ii)   *On the Movements and Habits of Climbing Plants . . . From the Journal of the Linnean Society*, London, 1865.

(iii) *The Variation of Animals and Plants under Domestication . . . with illustrations*, 2 volumes, London, 1868.

(iv)   *The Descent of Man, and Selection in Relation to Sex . . . with illustrations*, 2 volumes, London, 1871.

(v)   *The Expression of the Emotions in Man and Animals . . . with . . . illustrations*, London, 1872.

(vi)   *Insectivorous Plants . . . with illustrations*, London, 1875

(vii) *The Effects of Cross and Self Fertilization in the Vegetable Kingdom*, London, 1876.

(viii) *The Different Forms of Flowers on Plants of the Same Species . . . with illustrations*, London, 1877.

(ix)   *The Power of Movement in Plants. By C. Darwin . . . assisted by F. Darwin. With illustrations*, London, 1880.

(x)   *The Formation of Vegetable Mould, Through the Action of Worms, with Observations on their Habits . . . with illustrations*, London, 1881.[1]

In this chapter, we shall look particularly at *Variation* and *The Descent of Man*, and also make a few remarks about each of the other late works, showing how these related to the general program of Darwin's enquiries, and to his overall theory of evolution by natural selection.

In the previous chapter, it will be recalled, the reader was left in the position of knowing that Darwin found it necessary to invoke the hypothesis that variation could be induced by the effects of the environment, and that the resulting 'acquired characteristics' could supposedly be transmitted to succeeding generations. Also, it was believed that the environmentally-stimulated variations could be acted on by natural selection to further the evolution of organisms. In other words, in terms of our metaphor, the source of the 'white paint', constantly being added to the paint pot, was the *environment*, acting directly on living bodies. However, apart from referring briefly to the theory of pangenesis, developed in *Variation*, no indication has yet been given of the mechanism that Darwin had in mind for this supposed general hereditary process. Let us, therefore, make a few remarks about the rather interesting theory of pangenesis.

What Darwin hypothesised was this. He suggested that each cell of the body threw off minute particles, which he termed 'gemmules'. These, he said, could:

> Circulate freely throughout the system, and when supplied with proper nutriment multiply by self-division, subsequently becoming developed into cells like those from which they were derived.[2]

The gemmules, after circulating through the body, supposedly collected in the sex organs, and thus formed components of the sperms and eggs or pollen grains and ovules. The idea, then, was that the gemmules were transmitted in reproduction and consequently they were responsible for determining the particular characters of the offspring. Moreover, since gemmules were received from both parents, the offspring would tend to resemble them both. In other words, the theory would posit the *blending* of characters, as is so often observed. Children *do* normally resemble both their parents. The black mother and the white father *do* customarily produce brown babies.

Of course, as is well known, children sometimes resemble their grandparents or great-grandparents more than their parents. 'Throwback' to earlier generations (atavism) is by no means uncommon. Darwin thought that this might reasonably be accounted for by the supposition that the gemmules sometimes get handed on from one generation to the next in a 'dormant' state, only becoming active after one or two generations pass by. Also, there are normally more gemmules than are needed to determine the character of particular parts of the bodies of the offspring. Consequently, the loss of a given part — say a finger — by one or both of the parents would not be expected to result in the offspring being deficient in that part. The normal number of fingers might be expected quite confidently.

Darwin believed that the theory of pangenesis could explain the phenomena of variation reasonably satisfactorily. Variability, he maintained, depends:

> Firstly, on the deficiency, superabundance, fusion, and transposition of gemmules, and on the redevelopment of those which have long been dormant . . . [and] Secondly, in the cases in which the organization has been modified by

changed conditions, the increased use or disuse of parts, or any other cause, the gemmules cast off from the modified units of the body will be themselves modified, and, when sufficiently multiplied, will be developed into new and changed structures.[3]

Obviously, if the gemmules are characteristic of the part from which they are derived and if that part is modified in some way by the acquisition of new characteristics, through the influence of the environment, then new gemmules should be passed on accordingly. And so Darwin would have a hypothetical mechanism to support his 'Lamarckian' belief in the acquisition and transmission of new characteristics.

So the theory had some merit in Darwin's eyes. It accounted more or less satisfactorily for the facts of crossing as he understood them, and provided the sort of background support that was required for his general theory of evolution. But Darwin was probably never entirely happy with his hypothesis. It offended against the positivist/empiricist philosophy that characterised British science in the nineteenth century, in that it required the postulation of hypothetical entities (the gemmules) that could not be seen with the microscope or detected in any other way. They were simply dragged in, so to speak, in order to account for that which needed to be accounted for.[4] There was no independent way of confirming that they actually existed. Indeed, it was not difficult to produce experimental evidence that threw considerable doubt on their existence. Darwin's cousin, Francis Galton (1822-1911), for example, performed blood transfusions from animals of one colour to others of the same species, but of different colour. And he showed that there was no discernible change in the colour of the subsequent offspring.[5] Of course, Darwin had never definitely claimed that the gemmules circulated in the blood, and obviously they could not do so in plants. But if they did not pass through the blood of animals from the tissues to the gonads it was really rather difficult to imagine how they did in fact move through the body.

It should be realised that the theory of pangenesis was a very ancient one. Indeed, it had been considered (and rejected) by Aristotle,[6] who thought that it was an unacceptable doctrine because the characteristics of parents are not found consistently in their offspring. A grey-haired father, for example, does not produce grey-haired children. For Darwin, however, this was not a particularly significant objection. All he had to do was to suppose that the gemmules would be responsible for giving rise to the particular characteristics at the appropriate times in the development of the offspring. If, for example, the parents began to go grey at forty five, according to Darwin's view of the matter, the offspring, under the influence of the appropriate gemmules from the scalps of the parents, would also begin to go grey at about the same age. Later, in *The Descent of Man*, Darwin maintained that there was generally (though not universally) a: 'tendency in characters acquired at a late period of life by either sex, to be transmitted to [offspring of] the same sex at the same age, and of characters acquired at an early age to be transmitted to both sexes . . . ' .[7]

As we shall see below, this idea was associated with Darwin's somewhat curious views on the relative mental capacities of men and women. In *The Descent of Man* he did not specifically link the idea exhibited in this quotation to the doctrine of pangenesis. But it will be seen that it accords with it reasonably well. In other words, the theory, though put forward somewhat hesitantly and apologetically in *Variation*, apparently cohered quite satisfactorily, for Darwin, with other general aspects of his theory.

Variation, a massive and thoroughly documented work, running through two volumes to a total of eight hundred and ninety seven pages, was intended as one of a series of publications, each of which was to expand on one of the chapters of *The Origin*. However, as can be seen from the list of books at the beginning of this chapter, much of Darwin's effort in the later part of his career was given over to rather specialised monographs on particular aspects of botany and zoology, rather than the broader themes that were adumbrated in *The Origin*. But in *Variation* there is the full and detailed treatment of one particular aspect of the theory of *The Origin*. It would be beyond the scope of our present exposition to attempt to give a detailed account of even a fraction of the rich material that is to be found in *Variation*, and we must be content here with a few very cursory remarks about some of its more interesting features, other than what has already been said about the doctrine of pangenesis.

The Introduction to *Variation* is of interest if only for its admirably concise statement of the theory of evolution by natural selection and for its statement of some of the pieces of evidence that Darwin believed were highly significant in the first formulation of his theory. The Introduction also provides some passing remarks about his views on scientific method which are worth our attention. Following the views of the leading philosophers of science of his day,[8] Darwin defined laws as 'the ascertained sequence of events'.[9] But there was more to science than the mere conversion of observations into law-like inductive generalisations. Hypotheses were important, and if well confirmed they might rise to the rank of well-grounded theories.[10] Thus, Darwin wrote about the major theoretical component of his evolutionary biology:

> The principle of natural selection may be looked at as a mere hypothesis, but rendered in some degree probable by what we positively know of the variability of organic beings in a state of nature, by what we positively know of the struggle for existence, and the consequent almost inevitable preservation of favourable variations, and from the analogical formation of domestic races. Now this hypothesis may be tested . . . by trying whether it explains several large and independent classes of facts; such as the geological succession of organic beings, their distribution in past and present times, and their mutual affinities and homologies. If the principle of natural selection does explain these and other large bodies of facts, it ought to be received.[11]

Darwin was saying that if his hypothesis were successful in accounting satisfactorily for a wide range of otherwise disparate pieces of information, there was a good chance of its being true, and so it should be accepted. This is an exemplification of the so-called doctrine of the 'consilience'[12] of inductions of William Whewell.

Variation offered the reader a seemingly endless stream of empirical data on observed variants, and recorded genealogies and pedigrees. In the second volume, however, Darwin turned to somewhat more theoretical matters, considering, for example, the problems of inheritance, atavism, hybridisation, selection, and the causes of variability — all of which were tentatively accounted for by means of the hypothesis of pangenesis. The chapter 'On crossing' is of special interest, for it was here that Darwin gave some account of his investigations of plant hybridisation which were at least compatible with the earlier experimental findings of Mendel,[13] although the two investigations were conducted independently. Darwin described his experiments in this way:

> I crossed the peloric snapdragon (*Antirrhinum majus*) . . . with pollen of the common form; and the latter, eciprocally, with peloric pollen. I thus raised two great beds of seedlings, and not one was peloric . . . I carefully examined the flowers of ninety plants of the crossed Antirrhinum in the two beds, and their structure had not been in the least affected by the cross, except that in a few instances the minute rudiment of the fifth stamen . . . was more fully or even completely developed. . . . The crossed plants, which perfectly resembled the common snapdragon, were allowed to sow themselves, and, out of a hundred and twenty-seven seedlings, eighty-eight proved to be common snapdragons, two were in an intermediate condition between the peloric and normal state, and thirty-seven were perfectly peloric, having reverted to the structure of their one grandparent.[14]

The ratio of 90 (88 + 2) to 37 is 2.43 to 1. As we shall see in Chapter 12, if the theory of Mendel is correct a ratio of about 3 to 1 might have been anticipated as an outcome of this experiment. So Darwin's results were at least statistically compatible with what might be expected on the basis of the Mendelian theory. But Darwin was quite unable to penetrate the veil of the figures to perceive any kind of theoretical pattern. When the first set of crosses was performed, all plants were normal according to their external appearances. The 'peloric' character temporarily disappeared. Mendel would have said that the normal form was 'dominant', the peloric form 'recessive'. Darwin, however, said that the normal form was 'prepotent' compared to the peloric form, and he called the phenomenon of one character masking that of another 'prepotency'. He imagined that the prepotency gradually 'wore off', so to speak, in the succeeding generations, so that when the peloric snapdragons turned up again in the second generation[15] this was due to the diminishing prepotency of the normal character. In other words, the reappearance of the peloric form was regarded as a kind of 'throwback', or an instance of atavism. Darwin believed that it could be accounted for in a general way by means of his theory of pangenesis. He described many other experiments similar to those with the snapdragons in his *Effects of Cross and Self Fertilization in the Vegetable Kingdom*, but was unable to make any real progress with the problem.

In all this Darwin was very far from gaining a true understanding of the situation, and perhaps for this reason *Variation* has sometimes been regarded as something considerably less than a success. There seems, however, to be very little point in attempting to form 'judgements' of this kind. It is more profitable, I think, to attempt to see how *Variation* — a most remarkable and interesting book — fitted into the total context of Darwin's investigations.

Let us now look at Darwin's second most important work, *The Descent of Man*. In *The Origin*, Darwin only made a very cursory pronouncement on the question of the inclusion of man in the evolutionary process, though his readers and critics were quick to assume that the general theory could be taken to refer to man as well as animals. And as is well known, when *The Origin* was first published there was much talk of apes evolving into man, though needless to say this involved a serious misunderstanding of the actual theory, which postulated the divergence of men and apes from common ancestors, rather than the direct transmutation of apes into men.

In 1871 Darwin published *The Descent of Man*, which tried to set the record straight on this point, applying the general doctrines of *The Origin* to man and also elaborating considerably on another aspect of the theory which had only been touched on in the earlier work:[16] the doctrine of sexual selection.[17] Darwin was encouraged to work on *The Descent of Man* by the publication by Lyell in 1863 of an important volume covering the interface between geology and archaeology, *The Antiquity of Man*.[18] In this, Lyell had decided to apply the general geological theory of the *Principles of Geology* to the study of the paleontological history of mankind. In so doing, he brought forward an impressive array of evidence to show that man had most certainly been an inhabitant of the Earth for very much longer than the traditional six thousand years[19] — although he believed that there was a distinct gap between man and the rest of the animal kingdom, man's intellect being God-given. Huxley, on the other hand, confidently maintained that man was an animal, just like any other.

In 1864, Wallace published a paper dealing with the origin of human races.[20] This attracted no widespread or popular notice, though Darwin read it with great interest. Another paper by Wallace, touching on the same topic, appeared in 1869, and in this he drew for the first time a sharp distinction between men and animals,[21] arguing that human intelligence and culture could only be accounted for by postulating some kind of 'cosmic' intelligence. Darwin objected strongly to this,[22] and he and Wallace thereafter gradually drifted apart on the question of the status of man in nature. Wallace, as he grew older, became increasingly interested in spiritualism, but this held little attraction for Darwin, who never relinquished his wholly naturalistic attitude in his accounts of organic nature and always wished to maintain the view that there was no essential difference between men and animals.

The Descent of Man is rather like two books in one. The first, shorter part offers an essay on the origins of man, while the second, in many ways the more interesting part, deals with the concept of sexual selection. At the outset, Darwin points out that man is subject to the same factors of geometrical ratio of increase, limited resources, struggle for existence, variation and natural selection, as other animals, so that man, like animals, might be expected to be subject to the evolutionary process. In fact, his principal thesis is that the 'survival of the fittest' provides the motor for evolutionary change in man, just as much as in animals and plants. A number of interesting comparisons may be made between men and animals: they may have the same diseases (e.g., syphilis); their tissues seem similar; medicines may yield similar effects; often they have similar internal parasites; their wounds heal similarly; courtship among men and monkeys is in some ways rather similar; the embryos of men and apes are more similar than are the adult forms. Darwin also discussed the many vestigial organs of man which suggest an affinity with animals – for example the muscles that enable one to raise one's eyebrows (most animals can twitch their skins all over their bodies); the muscles of the ears; the convolutions of the ear; hair; wisdom-teeth; the sense of smell; the appendix; the coccyx; the prostate gland; and so on. By the presentation of such an array of evidence in Darwin's usual manner, the reader is urged to the apparently irresistible conclusion that man is indeed just one natural component of the total economy of nature.

In the succeeding chapters, Darwin discussed at length the question of the evolution of man's mental characteristics, his religious and moral feelings, and his powers of language. Many of the ideas he put forward are now regarded as commonplace although they must have seemed daring and iconoclastic to Victorian readers. Darwin tried to show inductively that the difference between human and animal mental powers was not as great as had traditionally been supposed. He maintained that some of the higher animals apparently had simple means of communication or even primitive languages. They used stones as weapons or sticks as tools. Moreover, some animals seemed to possess a rudimentary sense of beauty, or the beginnings of aesthetic sensibilities – as supposedly evidenced by the plumage and the singing of certain birds. On the other hand, remembering the inhabitants of Tierra del Fuego, Darwin denied that all men have a religious sense. In any case, the origin of religious sentiments might perhaps be attributed to primitive men having formed the idea of supernatural beings as a means of accounting for things that could not otherwise be explained in a natural way. Somewhat naively, perhaps, Darwin gave the instance of his own dog, which, when lying on the lawn on a hot still day, growled slightly when a breath of wind stirred a sun-shade. It was suggested that the dog might have 'thought' that a strange living agent was causing the movement.

Darwin offered a most interesting discussion of the possible origins of ethical and social behaviour, raising questions that are still by no means fully answered. Working as usual within the general framework of his evolutionary theory, he proposed that there could be advantage in the struggle for existence when men banded together in groups. Then the common opinion of the group would tend to urge each member to act to the advantage of the group as a whole, and the consequent altruistic behaviour would become reinforced by habit, and later by training and example. Subsequently, to the moral philosopher ruminating on the question of the source of men's ethical behaviour, it might appear that man had an *a priori* knowledge of right and wrong. But, in Darwin's view, 'The imperious word *ought* seems merely to imply the consciousness of the existence of a persistent instinct, either innate or partly acquired, serving him as a guide, though liable to be disobeyed'.[23]

To support his contentions, Darwin pointed out how an ethical code in primitive man is always directed towards the customs of his own tribe. For example, while it is held to be wrong to kill a member of one's own family or tribe, it may be permissible to kill a person from a neighbouring tribe. I might add the obvious comment here that the traditional ethical code of Western nations is not so different in this matter. It is held to be wrong to kill one's neighbour, though it may be acceptable to kill a man from a foreign country in time of war. Obviously, the inhabitants of the countries of the Christian West, despite their traditional claims to be followers of the Christian ethic of loving one's enemy,[24] have always obeyed a much older and cruder moral code, as epitomised in the writings of Machiavelli.[25] It is only in recent years, in the period of the Vietnam War, that a whole generation of military age has revolted against the dictates of 'might is right' in the field of international military contests, and in this movement non-Christian members of the community were as prominent as Christian pacifists.

Darwin also emphasised the importance of parental love and care as one of the sources of altruistic behaviour, arguing that mother love is something that has 'survival value'. The children of parents who display special care of their offspring will have more chance of surviving. If parental care is an inheritable trait, then clearly it can be enhanced over a period of time by the normal process of natural selection.

In his sixth chapter, Darwin attempted to give an account of the way man might have descended from animals, suggesting that the origin of man probably occurred in Africa, and certainly in the Old World, for men's teeth are much more like those of Old-World monkeys than those of the American continent.

It must be remembered that at the time Darwin published *The Descent of Man*, it was still widely believed that man had been specially created in the Garden of Eden. The following passage must, therefore, have appeared utterly abhorrent to many of his less sophisticated readers:

The early progenitors of man were no doubt once covered with hair, both sexes having beards; their ears were probably pointed and capable of movement; and their bodies were provided with a tail, having the proper muscles. Their limbs and bodies were also acted on by many muscles which now only occasionally reappear, but are normally present in the Quadrumana.[26] The great artery and nerve of the humerus ran through a supra-condyloid foramen.[27] At this or some earlier period, the intestine gave forth a much larger diverticulum[28] or caecum[29] than that now existing. The foot, judging from the condition of the great toe of the foetus, was then prehensile;[30] and our progenitors, no doubt, were arboreal in their habits, frequenting some warm, forest-clad land. The males were provided with great canine teeth, which served them as formidable weapons.

At a much earlier period the uterus was double; the excreta were voided through a cloaca;[31] and the eye was protected by a third eyelid or nictitating membrane.[32] At a still earlier period the progenitors of man must have been aquatic in their habits; for morphology plainly tells us that our lungs consist of a modified swim-bladder, which once served as a float. The clefts on the neck in the embryo of man show where the branchiae[33] once existed. At about this period the true kidneys were replaced by the corpora wollfiana.[34] The heart existed as a simple pulsating vessel; and the chorda dorsalis[35] took the place of a vertebral column.[36]

The impact of a passage such as this on the minds of Victorian readers may readily be imagined, regardless of whether the details Darwin imagined were right or wrong.

Darwin considered differences in climate were important in accounting for the development of the different human races, but he believed the process of 'sexual selection' was the chief causal agency. This led Darwin into a detailed discussion of the whole question of this supposed adjunct to natural selection and his discussion was then widened to encompass all animals, not just man.

As mentioned above, the concept of sexual selection had been briefly adumbrated in *The Origin*, but the reader of this earlier work might well have been surprised to see the way in which the hint of 1859 grew to form a major component of the total theory of 1871. The theory of sexual selection is easily explained. It simply proposes that in some instances the competition between the members of a species is chiefly for mates, rather than for food or for living space. By such means, thought Darwin, might evolve the considerable number of species with otherwise inexplicable characters such as the antlers of deer, the coloured anal regions of baboons, the tail feathers of peacocks, the beautiful blue colour of the bower birds, or the large breasts of humans — features that might seem non-adaptive, or at least unexpected, if considered purely from the point of view of 'orthodox' natural selection.

It will be noticed that Darwin is proposing not only that sexual selection might account for such features as deer antlers (which would seemingly have an obvious advantage in a struggle for mates), but also features such as peacock feathers which, it might be conjectured, are in some way 'attractive' to the peahens. On the basis of this latter consideration, Darwin suggested that sexual selection might in fact be the origin of *aesthetic* sensibilities. The peahen does the 'selecting' according to her 'judgement' of the relative 'beauty' of the peacock feathers that are presented for her delectation; the female nightingale may find the 'song' of her mate in some measure aesthetically attractive; highly coloured male baboon posteriors excite the visual sensibilities of the females. This view of the matter is not now generally accepted.[37] Clearly, the relevant anatomical parts may be related to a form of sexual selection, but it is no longer believed that this can be held responsible for the origins of the aesthetic dimensions of man. More likely, the brilliant posterior of the male baboon sexually stimulates or excites the female; there is no need to invoke an aesthetic component in the process, imagining that the female exerts a conscious choice. To do so is to think in unwarranted anthropomorphic terms. However, Darwin's views on the matter are worth noting.

Darwin gave considerable attention to ways in which sexual selection appeared to act in man. He noted that there are very different standards of beauty in different parts of the world. Round faces are much admired in Thailand; slanted eyes meet with approval in Japan. Hottentots like large bottoms; Australians (so far as my observations have revealed) seem to be fond of large tops. Negroes admire black skin; American Indians delight in long hair, but races deficient in hair do not admire it. Man, said Darwin, seems to use sexual selection to exaggerate all kinds of physical features — and, we might add, modern fashions seem to carry these exaggerations a step further into the inorganic dimension. Moreover, variety and divergence apparently characterise evolution by sexual selection just as much as evolution by natural selection. As Darwin said:

> If all our women were to become as beautiful as the Venus de Medici, we should for a time be charmed; but we should soon wish for variety; and as soon as we had obtained variety, we should wish to see certain characters in our women a little exaggerated beyond the then existing common standard.[38]

The whole of Darwin's theory of sexual selection has come in for much criticism since he first put forward the idea,[39] particularly that part which seemed to imply some kind of conscious preference on the part of animals in the formation of their mating pairs. It is possible that he was allowing some of the mores of Victorian middle-class society to influence his discussions of animal behaviour and evolution by sexual selection, although this cannot unambiguously be shown to have been the case by examination of the text of *The Descent*.

In considering the question of sexual selection among humans, Darwin gave a fairly brief but interesting discussion of the relative mental powers of men and women. He maintained that there were indeed inherent differences in mental capacities:

> The chief distinction in the intellectual powers of the two sexes is shewn by man attaining to a higher eminence, in whatever he takes up, than woman can attain —

whether requiring deep thought, reason, or imagination, or merely the use of the senses and hands. If two lists were made of the most eminent men and women in poetry, painting, sculpture, music comprising composition and performance, history, science, and philosophy with half-a-dozen names under each subject, the two lists would not bear comparison.[40]

And to account for the alleged inherent or innate mental differences between men and women, Darwin made a suggestion which seems to be based on several of the many pieces that made up the mosaic of his thought, notably: the ideas on the acquisition of characteristics and the transmission of these to succeeding generations; the ideas on recapitulation among embryos, including the extension of these to the post-embryonic developments of childhood and youth; and perhaps also the pangenesis theory.

As we have noted above,[41] Darwin believed that there was a tendency for characters acquired late in life to be transmitted to offspring of the same sex at about the same age as that at which the characters were acquired by the parents. If this view of the situation were correct, men who acquired particular mental characteristics in adult life would tend to pass these on to their *sons*, who might be expected to reveal these characteristics at the same period of their lives as that at which they were acquired by their fathers. Similarly, women would pass on the characteristics that they acquired in maturity to their *daughters*, although these characteristics would also only show up in adulthood. How, then, might women become equal to men in mental development? Darwin answered:

> In order that woman should reach the same standard as man, she ought, when nearly adult, to be trained to energy and perseverance, and to have her reason and imagination exercised to the highest point; and then she would probably transmit these qualities chiefly to her adult daughters.[42]

But here the difficulty arose. For to raise the individual mental powers of a woman much time and effort would be required. And such a woman would probably not have time for child bearing. Consequently, it would be rather unlikely that the woman's mental skills, so painfully acquired, would be transmitted in good measure to succeeding generations. Those women with highly developed intellectual capacities, would, it was thought, leave few offspring and could make little contribution to the evolution of mental powers. Darwin, therefore, did not look forward to a gradual equalisation of the mental powers of men and women. Indeed, if he were right in his thinking, it would be a waste of resources to give women an education equal to that of men.

Needless to say, Darwin's theory about the relative mental powers of men and women has not survived to the present day, for the biological assumptions on which it rests have long since been superseded. But taking a somewhat broader perspective, there was and is[43] the question of whether the average mental power of humans is decreasing because more able people tend to have less children than average, a situation that probably would not be anticipated *a priori*, and one that apparently contradicts the normal state of affairs in which the 'fittest' tend to have the most surviving offspring.

Darwin, of course, in reaching his conclusions about the relative mental powers of men and women, was largely ignoring the whole question of the influence of social factors. No doubt it was, and is, true that women do not compare favourably with men when lists of persons of special excellence are drawn up and comparisons are made. But to assume, therefore, that the differences are innate and not at all influenced by social factors was, I think, a grave misunderstanding on Darwin's part. In this respect he seems to have been less perceptive than John Stuart Mill (1806-1873) and Harriet Taylor Mill (1808-1858) in their *Subjection of Women* (1869), who argued that it was simply not possible to determine at that time the *innate* relative mental capacities of men and women, for the social circumstances to which they were subjected were so entirely different.[44] Darwin, by contrast, linked his biological theory of the mental powers of men and women to the prevailing social attitudes of the well-to-do Victorian gentleman.[45]

During the year following the publication of *The Descent of Man*, Darwin issued his major work on psychological questions and the problem of mental evolution, *The Expression of the Emotions in Man and Animals*. The previous important work on this topic[46] had been by the British anatomist, Charles Bell (1774-1842), well known as the author of one of the Bridgewater Treatises.[47] Bell had argued that man had been specially created with particular muscles that might be useful and appropriate for expressing emotion — the muscles for raising the eye-brows, for example. Needless to say, Darwin found this Paleyesque view of the question utterly unacceptable. As we might expect from what we now know of his methods, he gave a detailed qualitative survey of the way in which men and women of various races express their 'emotions': suffering, anxiety, grief, despair, joy, love, devotion, reflection, meditation, bad-temper, determination, hatred, anger, disdain, surprise, fear, horror, disgust, loathing and contempt. He observed animals, attempting to see indications of parallel emotions among them also. The dog's tail gaily wagging, or drooping dolefully between the legs, makes an obvious example. The conclusion he reached was that many emotions are expressed in ways that seem innate. Darwin attempted to show that certain ways of displaying emotions may be accounted for in evolutionary terms, though they are now merely vestigial. For example, the raising of the corners of the upper lip to reveal the canine teeth — an action not uncommonly used by the sneering and supercilious — might be seen as a remote evolutionary descendant of the action of a wild animal baring its teeth in order to deter its enemy. Darwin, however, did not wish to suggest that all behaviour patterns have (or had) some adaptive significance, conferring special advantage in the struggle for existence.

Darwin attempted to set his observations within a theoretical framework of three major principles: (a) 'the principle of serviceable associated habits'; (b) 'the principle of antithesis'; (c) 'the principle of actions due to the constitution of the nervous system, independently from the first of the will, and independently to a certain extent of habit', or the 'principle of the direct action of the nervous system'.[48] An example of the first of these would be the unsheathing of a cat's claws in times of danger. The second would be illustrated by a dog that stiffens when angry, while becoming relaxed and mobile (tail wagging) when pleased. In the third category, Darwin grouped a variety of behaviour patterns which seemed to result from particular 'accidents' in the way in which the nervous system is organised — for example, the actions of trembling or crying. But this three-fold manner of classifying the phenomena was not especially revealing or fruitful. The important thing about *Expression* was Darwin's attempt to account for simple behaviour phenomena in naturalistic terms, invoking the evolutionary hypothesis and completely repudiating earlier attempts to employ the teleological argument from design. However, although Darwin's work in this area was to provide one of the major foundation stones for the twentieth-century science of animal behaviour (ethology),[49] it cannot be said that *Expression* had a very deep influence on psychology in the application of the principle of natural selection, although the naturalism that now characterises psychological investigations was an important feature of Darwin's approach. The question of the relationship between Darwin and psychology will be considered further in Chapter 20.

Darwin's remaining investigations chiefly related to two major questions. Firstly, there were his works that dealt with the problems of cross-fertilisation and all that this implied for the problems of variation and the general theory of evolution: *On the Various Contrivances by which British and Foreign Orchids are Fertilized by Insects . . . ; The Effects of Cross and Self Fertilization in the Vegetable Kingdom; The Different Forms of Flowers on Plants of the Same Species . . .* Secondly, there were the four works concerned with the problems of the 'behaviour' of relatively simple organisms: *Insectivorous Plants . . .; On the Movements and Habits of Climbing Plants . . . ; The Power of Movement in Plants . . . ; The Formation of Vegetable Mould, Through the Action of Worms, with Observations on their Habits . . .* Just a few words will be said about these various publications, with but one intention in mind, namely to show how they fitted into the general program of Darwin's investigations and his overall theory of evolution.

The work on orchids was to a considerable degree a polemic against the venerable argument from design. As everyone knows, orchids are usually regarded as plants of considerable beauty, and before Darwin's time they had frequently been thought of as plants especially created by God to give pleasure to mankind; or by their peculiarly intricate construction, they could provide means whereby — to use Linnaeus's words — 'the observer of the wonderful work might admire and praise its Maker'.[50] But Darwin's observations suggested that the often quite bizarre structures of orchids could in fact confer advantage in the struggle for existence, since the structures were such that in many cases they could be recognised as facilitating cross-pollination. And in *Cross and Self Fertilization* Darwin was able to show that plants were generally more healthy when cross fertilised than when self pollinated. Darwin's work on the cross fertilisation of polymorphic plants such as *Primula* (cowslip) — in which he showed that the existence of the two forms was apparently a device that ensured cross pollination — was related to the same question, and seemed to show that natural selection had acted in such a way as to generate the two polymorphs.

Darwin first began his remarkable investigations on insectivorous plants in 1860, and he continued with this work for many years, eventually publishing his detailed monograph on the subject in 1875.[51] He first examined the common sun-dew, or *Drosera*, having noticed that small insects became stuck to the leaves of this inconspicuous little plant of infertile heath and moorland habitat. The insects first became stuck to the sticky material on the leaves and then the small leaf tentacles curled over to trap the victims. Darwin showed that the same effect could also be produced by small pieces of raw meat, and a dilute solution of ammonia (a nitrogenous substance) also caused motion of the tentacles. He further investigated the effects of a wide range of different substances (such as adder poison, curare, strychnine, digitalin, morphia) in a typical 'Baconian' series of experiments. And, displaying a considerable flair for delicate experimentation, he showed that the tentacles were sensitive to a piece of human hair weighing no more than 0.0008 mg.

Darwin maintained that the insectivorous plants were 'disguised animals', which obtained the nitrogenous matter required for their growth, not by using humus, as do most plants, but by 'eating' animals. Later, one of his sons showed that plants well fed with flies were in every way healthier than those deprived of animal nutriment. The whole exercise displayed Darwin's considerable experimental skill, and his results revealed an unusual form of plant adaptation to particular environmental conditions. They also suggested a somewhat remote analogy between animals and plants.

Darwin's interest in climbing plants, and their special adaptations of coiling round supports and having tendrils and suckers, was stimulated by a paper published by Asa Gray in 1858.[52] Darwin investigated the rates at which the growing parts circled round (a hop plant taking just two hours and eight minutes for one complete cycle),[53] and he compared the process to the South American device for catching bulls (the *bolos*) which he had seen during the *Beagle* voyage. He went on to show that other kinds of climbing plants (e.g., leaf curlers, or those with tendrils) have properties that can be explained as derivatives by adaptation from the more 'primitive' type such as the hop or the runner bean. On the other hand, it seemed that the specialised types could not have evolved one from another. All this could be integrated into the general theory of evolution by natural selection yielding divergence from common ancestors.

Darwin's later book, *Power of Movement in Plants*,[54] described investigations into many other aspects of plant movement, such as the 'sleep' movement of leaves, the arching of the hypocotyl during the emergence of the plumule from the seed, the spreading of leaves to catch the sunlight, the turning of flower stalks, the burying of seed capsules, the evasion of stones by roots, and in general the influence of light, gravity and moisture in orienting plants for optimum growth conditions.

The general theory of phototropism[55] in Darwin's day was that of the German botanist, Julius Sachs (1832-1897). It may be illustrated by means of the sketch in Figure 17.

Figure 17 Illustration of Phototropism

Light from all directions   Light

But Darwin showed that if the tips of the shoots were covered with small cups, the bending did not occur, even if the bending parts were illuminated as usual. This is shown in Figure 18.

Figure 18 Illustration of Darwin's Experiments on Phototropism

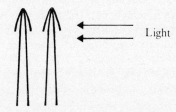

Light

On the other hand, when the tip was illuminated, and the growing part covered up, bending *did* occur as usual. Darwin concluded that there is 'some matter in the upper part which is acted on by light, and which transmits its effects to the lower part'.[56] This was a fundamental discovery, and gave a very considerable encouragement to subsequent studies in plant physiology (i.e., the investigation of growth hormones).

Darwin's last work, *The Action of Worms*, was in many ways his most unexpected, being almost incongruous as a serious scientific publication by a major author. Yet it was a most interesting work, and highly popular with his literary admirers. In *Worms*, Darwin began to turn his attention away from the behavioural characteristics of plants to those of simple animals. He had been interested in these 'humble' animals for many years, and had the famous so-called 'worm stone' constructed in his garden at Down, by which he could measure the slow rate at which it sank into the ground through the constant actions of worms. Worms, he realised were largely responsible for the slow mantling of archaeological relics by soil, and they also performed the important ecological role of aerating the soil, taking humus down to the lower layers, and generally circulating and mixing the materials of which the soil consists. By measuring the weight of worm-castings thrown up on a square yard of pasture in a year, Darwin calculated that the animals bring to the surface about eighteen tons of material per acre per year. And large stones seemed to be buried at the rate of about a quarter of an inch per year.

But it was what we might loosely call the 'psychological' or 'mental' aspects of worms, as revealed by Darwin's investigations, that excited the greatest interest among his readers. He noted that the animals used small leaves to block up the entrances to their burrows, and they generally seemed to 'choose' the narrow end of the leaf first for this purpose. Darwin prepared small slips of paper of various shapes for the worms, and laid the pieces out on the ground to see what action the worms took when offered a free choice of material for their use. And it seemed to Darwin that the worms did in fact exercise some rudimentary sense of judgement as to shape when picking up the pieces of paper for hole blocking. He wrote:

> We may therefore infer — improbable as is the inference — that worms are able by some means to judge which is the best end by which to draw triangles of paper into their burrows.[57]

Darwin's argument, therefore, was that the worms actually possessed a very primitive form of intelligence. This meshed well with his belief in the existence of a continuum of characters through all the species of the animal kingdom. In our first chapter we saw how early discussions of the relationships between man and animals supposed a great unbridgeable gulf between the two. Here, in this last of Darwin's published writings, we find him placing yet another stone in the bridge that *was* slowly coming to join the two.

Darwin's publications were all beautifully phrased and comprehensible to both laymen and specialists alike. They were always characterised by a certain modesty and diffidence about the truth of the opinions they advanced, and also to some degree they seemed to wish to give the impression that the mental powers of their author were in no way remarkable. But they were not notable for any very obvious flashes of humour. Yet in several passages in *Worms*, the aged Darwin was surely writing with something of a twinkle in his eye. Let us, therefore, conclude this chapter with one such passage, not because it is of any special significance in the history of science (except possibly as an illustration of the 'Baconian' approach to the investigation of phenomena so much favoured in Darwin's day), but simply for the light that it throws on Darwin's rather puckish sense of humour and engaging personality. His little *jeu d'esprit* was as follows:

> Worms do not possess any sense of hearing. They took not the least notice of the shrill notes from a metal [tin?] whistle, which was repeatedly sounded near them; nor did they of the deepest and loudest tones of a bassoon. They were indifferent to shouts, if care was taken that the breath did not strike them. When placed on a table close to the keys of a piano, which was played as loudly as possible, they remained perfectly quiet.
> Although they are indifferent to undulations in the air audible to us, they are extremely sensitive to vibrations in any solid object. When the pots containing two worms which had remained quite indifferent to the sound of the piano, were placed on this instrument, and the note C in the bass clef was struck, both instantly retreated into their burrows. After a time they emerged, and when G above the line in the treble clef was struck they again retreated. Under similar circumstances on another night one worm dashed into its burrow on a very high note being struck only once, and the other worm when C in the treble clef was struck ... [The worms] often showed their sensitiveness when the pot in which they lived, or the table on which the pot stood, was accidentally and lightly struck; but they appeared less sensitive to such jars than to the vibrations of the piano; and their sensitiveness to jars varied much at different times.[58]

Here, then, on this engaging note, we may leave Darwin for the time being. The reader will now have a general conspectus of his method of working, his scientific interests, the broad outlines of his theory, and its strengths and weaknesses. In fact, as Darwin grew older, the deficiencies of this theory became increasingly clear. He was pressed on the one hand by the problem of the age of the Earth, and on the other he found that he was unable to solve to his real satisfaction the problems of heredity and the sources of variation; and we have found him coming to place ever-increasing reliance on 'Lamarckian' doctrines (i.e., the environment acting as a source of variation and evolutionary change) in the later part of his career. The whole network of problems is highlighted by the perhaps somewhat desperate conjecture of the theory of pangenesis. In the latter part of the nineteenth century there were not many practising scientists who placed whole-hearted reliance on the Darwinian theory, despite the fact that by that time it was being used and abused in a whole plethora of related or unrelated disciplines, ranging from music to sociology or from politics to moral philosophy. As is well known today, the basis of a solution to Darwin's problems was already available in the work of his contemporary, the Moravian monk, Gregor Mendel. But Darwin never got to hear of Mendel's work, and so he remained troubled and uneasy about the sufficiency of his theory through most of his later years. In any case, we cannot be certain that he would have understood Mendel's work, or realised its relevance for him, even if he had encountered it. But it was Mendel who eventually provided the basis of an answer to the problems that plagued the ageing Darwin. Accordingly, we shall now give a fairly cursory account of Mendel's achievements, attempting also to show in a general way how modern evolutionary theory has developed from a synthesis of Darwinian and Mendelian systems.

NOTES CHAPTER 11

1   Only the first editions are listed here, although most of Darwin's books ran through several editions. The standard bibliography of Darwin's work is R. B. Freeman, *The Works of Charles Darwin: An Annotated Bibliographical Handlist*, 2nd edn, Dawson & Archon, Folkestone & Hamden, 1977.

2   C. Darwin, *The Variation of Animals and Plants under Domestication*, 2 vols, London, 1868, Vol. 2, p.374.

3   *Ibid.*, pp.396-397.

4   Using the term popular with philosophers of science, we may say that the hypothesis of pangenesis was distinctly '*ad hoc*'.

5   F. Galton, 'Experiments in pangenesis, by breeding from rabbits of a pure variety, into whose circulation blood taken from other varieties has previously been largely transfused', *Proceedings of the Royal Society*, Vol. 19, 1870-1871, pp.393-410.

6   Aristotle, *De Generatione Animalium I*, 722a-724a (*Aristotle's De Partibus Animalium I and De Generatione Animalium I*, translated with notes by D. M. Balme, Clarendon Press, Oxford, 1972, pp. 35-40).

7   C. Darwin, *The Descent of Man, and Selection in Relation to Sex . . . With Illustrations*, 2 vols, London, 1871, Vol. 2, p.329.

8   For a discussion of the influence of contemporary philosophy on Darwin, see M. Ruse, 'Darwin's debt to philosophy: an examination of the influence of the philosophical ideas of John F. W. Herschel and William Whewell on the development of Charles Darwin's theory of evolution', *Studies in History and Philosophy of Science*, Vol. 6, 1975, pp.159-181.

9   C. Darwin, *op. cit.* (note 2), Vol. 1, p.6.

10 *Ibid.*, p.8.

11 *Ibid.*, p.9.

12 See above, page 129. 'Consilience', it may be noted, is defined by the *Oxford English Dictionary* as 'the fact of "jumping together" ', or 'concurrence'.

13 See below, Chapter 12.

14 C. Darwin, *op. cit.* (note 2), Vol. 2, pp.70-71.

15 Now known as the 'Second filial generation'. See below, page 161.

16 C. Darwin, *The Origin of Species by Means of Natural Selection*, (ed. J. W. Burrow), Penguin, Harmondsworth, 1968, pp.136-138.

17 In Darwin's words: 'This depends, not on a struggle for existence, but on a struggle between the males for possession of the females; the result is not death to the unsuccessful competitor, but few or no offspring' (*ibid.*, p.136).

18 C. Lyell, *The Geological Evidences of the Antiquity of Man with Remarks on Theories of the Origin of Species by Variation*, London, 1863.

19 By the 1860s a very considerable amount of archaeological evidence which clashed with the traditional age of the Earth (6000 years) had been brought forward. The work during the 1830s and 1840s of Boucher de Perthes, particularly on the flint implements found near Abbeville, was of special significance.

20 A. R. Wallace, 'The origin of human races and the antiquity of man deduced from the theory of natural selection', *Journal of the Anthropological Society of London*, Vol. 2, 1864, pp.clvii-clxxxvii.

21 [A. R. Wallace,] 'Art. III. - 1. Principles of Geology; . . . By Sir Charles Lyell, . . . Tenth . . . edition . . . 2. *Elements of Geology*; . . . By Sir Charles Lyell, . . . Sixth edition . . .', *The Quarterly Review*, Vol. 126, 1869, pp.359-394. Wallace wrote (p.391): 'Neither natural selection nor the more general theory of evolution can give any account whatever of the origin of sensational or conscious life'.

22 F. Darwin (ed.), *The Life and Letters of Charles Darwin*, 3 vols, John Murray, London, Vol. 3, 1887, p.116. Darwin wrote to Wallace: 'I differ grievously from you, and I am very sorry for it'.

23 C. Darwin, *op. cit.* (note 7), Vol. 1, p.47.

24 *The Gospel According to St Matthew*, Chapter 5, Verses 43-44.

25 See N. Machiavelli, *The Prince:* translated with an introduction by George Bull, Penguin, Harmondsworth, 1961. (*Il Principe* was completed by Machiavelli in 1514.)

26   *Quadrumana* is the mammalian group that includes monkeys, apes, baboons and lemurs.

27   *Supra-condyloid foramen* is a hole through the humerus just above the elbow joint, found in reptiles and human embryos.

28   *Diverticulum* is a side-branch of a cavity.

29   *Caecum* is a 'cul-de sac' of the alimentary canal, branching off at the junction of the small and large intestines.

30   *Prehensile* means capable of grasping or taking hold of something.

31   *Cloaca* is the common passage by which alimentary and urinary excretion occurs in birds, reptiles, fish and the monotremes (egg-laying mammals).

32   *Nictitating membrane* is the third eyelid present in some animals (particularly birds) to protect the eye from dust. (For Paley's description of the organ, see above, page 64.)

33   *Branchiae* are gills.

34   *Corpora wollfiana* is a primitive kidney, as it appears in the intermediate embryonic stages of development.

35   *Chorda dorsalis* (or notochord) is a cartilaginous rod found in vertebrate embryos, running between the main dorsal nerve-cord and the gut. It does not persist in adult development, except in the case of primitive vertebrates such as the lancelet or *Amphioxus*.

36   C. Darwin, *op. cit.* (note 7), Vol. 1, pp.206-207.

37   Current opinion favours the view that secondary sexual characters help to arouse sexual interest, but it is doubted whether there is any aesthetic component to the process.

38   C. Darwin, *op. cit.* (note 7), Vol. 2, p.354. (Note the way Darwin talks of '*our* women'!)

39   The idea of sexual selection is to be found in Darwin's very early statements of his theory: F. Darwin (ed.), *The Foundations of the Origin of Species: Two Essays written in 1842 and 1844 by Charles Darwin*, Cambridge, 1909 (Kraus, New York, 1969), pp.10 and 92-93.

40   C. Darwin, *op. cit.* (note 7), Vol. 2, p.327.

41   See note 7.

42   C. Darwin, *op. cit.* (note 7), p.329.

43   On this, see P. B. Medawar, *The Future of Man*, Methuen, London, 1960.

44   J. S. Mill (introduction by W. R. Carr), *The Subjection of Women*, Harvard University Press, Cambridge, Mass. & London, 1970, p.57 and *passim*.

45   I am indebted to my colleague, W. R. Albury, for some suggestions about Darwin's and Mill's views on women.

46   C. Bell, *The Anatomy and Philosophy of Expression, as connected with the Fine Arts*, 3rd edn, London, 1844.

47   C. Bell, *The Hand, its Mechanism and Vital Endowments, as Evincing Design*, London, 1833. (The Bridgewater Treatises formed a series of works, financed by the will of the Duke of Bridgewater, which were intended to prove the existence and attributes of God by means of the so-called 'argument from design'.)

48   C. Darwin, *The Expression of the Emotions in Man and Animals ... With Photographs and other Illustrations*, London, 1872, p.28 (republished Chicago University Press, Chicago, 1965).

49   The term has been appropriated (by Konrad Lorenz) for studies of animal behaviour. It was coined by John Stuart Mill in the nineteenth century for a subject that would be concerned with 'the science of [human] character'. It was hoped that it would be able to form a bridge between the theoretical work of the psychologists and the studies of human behaviour carried out by sociologists or historians. (See A. M. McBriar, 'Human nature in historical explanation', *Search*, Vol. 6, 1975, pp.167-174.)

50   C. Linnaeus, *Systema Naturae 1735, Facsimile of the First Edition With an introduction and first English translation of the "Observations" by Dr. M. S. J. Engel-Ledeboer and Dr H. Engel*, B. de Graaf, Nieuwkoop, 1964, p.18.

51   C. Darwin, *Insectivorous Plants*, London, 1875 (republished A. M. S. Press, New York, 1972).

52   A. Gray, 'Note on the coiling of tendrils of plants', *Proceedings of the American Academy of Arts and Sciences*, Vol. 4, 1858, pp.98-99.

53   C. Darwin, *The Movement and Habits of Climbing Plants*, 2nd edn, London, 1875, p.3 (republished A. M. S. Press, New York, 1972).

54   C. Darwin (assisted by F. Darwin), *The Power of Movement in Plants*, London, 1880 (republished A. M. S. Press, New York, 1972).

55   That is, plant movement stimulated by light.

56   C. Darwin, *op. cit.* (note 54), p.486.

57   C. Darwin, *The Formation of Vegetable Mould through the Action of Worms with Observations on their Habits*, 13th thousand, London, 1904, p.85 (republished A. M. S. Press, New York, 1972).

58   *Ibid.* (1904), pp.24-25.

12

The Work of Mendel: The Synthetic Theory of Evolution

In the previous two chapters the reader has been made aware of the various difficulties encountered by Darwin's theory after its presentation to the public in 1859, and some account has been given of the way Darwin hoped the objections might be overcome, chiefly by recourse to the thesis that the environment might be a source of or stimulus to variation, and also by emphasising that geographical isolation could to some degree offset the effects of blending inheritance.

As already stated, the first step on the long road towards a solution of the problems facing the simplistic theory of evolution by natural selection was taken by the Moravian monk Gregor Mendel (1822-1884),[1] Abbot of the Monastery of Altbrünn in the town of Brünn (or Brno), in what is now part of Czechoslovakia. Mendel worked initially as a school-teacher. He attended Vienna University, where he studied philosophy, mathematics and physics, and also botany. But he never completed his degree, having become nervously ill at the time of the examination ordeal. Consequently, until he became Abbot at Brünn in 1868, he was employed merely as a 'supply' teacher. Apparently, however, he was a considerable success in this role.

It appears that Mendel was brought into contact with the problem of what actually happens in the process of plant hybridisation by Fritz Unger, his botany teacher at Vienna. And it was probably through his university studies in mathematics and physics that Mendel realised that it would be necessary to solve the problem of plant hybridisation by mathematical and statistical analysis. He started his famous series of investigations on the pea plant (*Pisum sativum*) in the monastery gardens at Brünn in 1856, and concluded the experimental work in 1863. An account of the results of the investigations was given in a paper presented to the Brünn Natural History Society in two parts, on February 8 and March 8, 1865. This was published the following year in the *Proceedings* of the Society for 1865.[2]

After the publication of his results, Mendel sent out a number of reprints, and copies of the journal were received by many of the major European scientific libraries, including those of the Linnean Society and the Royal Society in London. But the journal in which the work was published was not particularly prestigious and it is clear that Mendel's paper went almost unread on its first publication. Mendel did correspond with the Swiss botanist, C. W. Nägeli (1817-1891),[3] but it seems that the eminent professor (at Munich) had little real understanding of what the unknown monk and supply school-teacher was arguing for and what he had achieved. Nägeli himself was at the time particularly interested in the group of plants known as hawkweeds (*Hieracium*) and he tried to persuade Mendel to develop a similar interest, and repeat his experiments on these plants. This proved to be a very ill-judged piece of advice. Compared with the large pea flowers, the 'composite' hawkweeds are extremely difficult to work with and do not show the clear-cut distinctions that one finds in the peas that Mendel investigated. Moreover, their behaviour is now known not to follow the hybridisation rules that Mendel discovered with peas. Mendel did make some attempt to follow up Nägeli's suggestion that he should try to extend the findings with *Pisum* to the case of *Hieracium*, but he was unable to do this successfully and he probably became discouraged in his work, and perhaps even began to doubt the truth of his earlier findings. Eventually he gave up his scientific investigations altogether, and devoted himself exclusively to work in the monastery. And it was not until the end of the nineteenth century that Mendel's paper was eventually 'rediscovered', quite independently, by three separate investigators. Something further will be said about this coincidence of discovery below.

What Mendel achieved, basically, was an experimental and theoretical understanding of what happens when *varieties* of a particular species of plant are crossed with each other under controlled conditions. He was, therefore, investigating whether blending occurred; and by using different varieties rather than different species he was able to breed from the crossed offspring and trace out the results of the crossings. If he had used separate species, rather than varieties, the experiments would probably have been impossible since the crosses would almost certainly have been sterile.

From the many possibilities that were open to him,[4] Mendel chose for his investigation seven pairs of differing characters in *Pisum sativum*. These were:

1 round or wrinkled seeds
2 yellow or green seeds
3 white or grey seed coats
4 smooth or wrinkled pods
5 yellow or green pods
6 axillary or terminal flowers
7 tall or short plants.

For the purposes of elementary exposition, we shall confine our discussions to just one of these pairs of characters, tallness or shortness.

The first task was to obtain a set of plants that were 'pure tall' and another set that were 'pure short'. This could be done by arranging plants to be generated by self-pollination for two years, and weeding out any of the 'wrong' kind, until so-called 'pure lines'[5] were obtained. Then a set of 'pure tall' plants was deliberately crossed with a set of 'pure short' plants. According to the theory of blending inheritance, this should have yielded plants that were intermediate in height. But none of them were: all were tall. The short character had seemingly disappeared entirely. But, presumably from preliminary experiments not described in his paper, or from his general knowledge, Mendel was aware that the disappearance of shortness was by no means permanent. The next step, therefore, was to recover the shortness, so to speak. This was done by taking the tall *hybrid* plants and causing them to *self-pollinate*. The results were most interesting, though the degree to which they were *unexpected* to Mendel is still a matter of some dispute. The ratio of tall plants to short plants obtained by the self-pollination of the hybrids was 787 : 277, or 2.84 : 1, which is fairly close to a simple integral ratio of 3 : 1. When the results for all the seven pairs of characters were collated, the final ratio was 2.98 : 1, which was even closer to an integral 3 : 1 ratio.

At this stage, all that Mendel had achieved was to show that with peas, the theory of blending inheritance could no longer be sustained. But he was able to go far beyond this by offering a remarkable theory to account for the results that he had obtained. He introduced the terms *dominant* and *recessive*, tallness, for example, being apparently dominant over shortness, and shortness being recessive relative to tallness. Also, he suggested — although not entirely explicitly — that each character was determined by a pair of 'factors', which separated when the germ cells (pollen grains and ovules) were formed, and recombined when the fertilisation of the ovules by the pollen grains occurred. Suppose, then, we choose to let 'A' represent the tallness factor, and we let 'a' represent shortness. Then a plant possessed of the double pair of factors, 'AA', would be tall; 'aa' would give shortness; and 'Aa' or 'aA' would impart tallness, since (by experiment) it appears that tallness is dominant relative to shortness. The course of Mendel's experiments could therefore be represented by the following diagram — although I emphasise that this is a twentieth-century reconstruction, not Mendel's original representation.

It is to be hoped that this puts the matter, as it is broadly understood in modern terms, with sufficient clarity. It must be remembered particularly that the whole process should be thought of in statistical terms. Suppose, for example, at the last stage given in Figure 19, we think of the process as being analogous to two coins being tossed together repeatedly. There are four possibilities, with equal probabilities: head/head, head/tail, tail/head, and tail/tail. If the first three are considered as giving rise to the same effect (tallness), and the last one to shortness, then on average there will be a 3 : 1 ratio of tallness to shortness.

Unfortunately, however, we cannot be exactly sure, from the words used by Mendel, that he had the idea of 'internal factors' in the cells determining the 'external' characters precisely as suggested in Figure 19.

Figure 19 A Modern Representation of Mendel's Theory

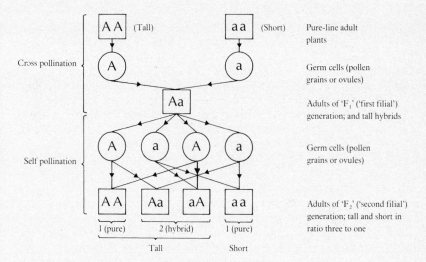

He represented the last line shown in this figure as:

$$\frac{A}{A} + \frac{A}{a} + \frac{a}{A} + \frac{a}{a},$$

which corresponds pretty closely with what we have given. But he also gave it as:

$$A + 2Aa + a,$$

which is by no means exactly the same as the modern representation. If he had written 'AA + 2Aa + aa' throughout his paper, his meaning might well have been considerably clearer to his readers, and I am inclined to think that the theory might possibly have been taken up more quickly and escaped its thirty-five years of neglect or misunderstanding. But this, of course, is pure speculation. It should be noted, however, that Mendel wrote 'the product of their A and A, or a and a association must be constant, namely A and a'.[6] In other words he *seems* to equate 'AA' and 'aa' with 'A' and 'a'. This is not quite the modern view and Mendel does not seem to make the modern distinction between 'genotype' and 'phenotype'. It is not as if he were simply writing 'A' as a *shorthand* for 'AA'.

Mendel also worked out the ratios that might be expected if two or three pairs of characters were investigated simultaneously. For example, Figure 20 shows a modern representation for two pairs.

Figure 20 A Modern Representation of Mendel's Theory, Applied to Two Characters

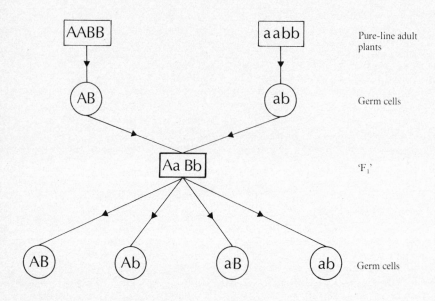

The statistical recombination of these is most easily derived with the help of the chequerboard diagram shown in Figure 21.

Figure 21 Representation of the Statistical Recombination of Two Pairs of Mendelian 'Factors'

	AB	Ab	aB	ab
AB	AABB	AABb	AaBB	AaBb
Ab	AAbB	AAbb	AabB	Aabb
aB	aABB	aABb	aaBB	aaBb
ab	aAbB	aAbb	aabB	aabb

This gives the ratio of numbers of plant forms (or 'phenotypes') as 9 : 3 : 3 : 1, as the reader may readily confirm. Mendel was able to support this experimentally. However, instead of setting out the situation in this clear pictorial manner, he described it as a mathematical combination of the two expressions $(A + a)^2$ and $(B + b)^2$. We would choose to represent this by: $(AA + 2Aa + aa)(BB + 2Bb + bb)$. But unfortunately Mendel described it as the product of $(A + 2Aa + a)$ and $(B + 2Bb + b)$. So instead of working it out to yield AABB + AAbb + aaBB + aabb + 2ABbb + 2aaBb + 2AaBB + 2Aabb + 4AaBb, as does our chequerboard calculation, Mendel gave the expression: AB + Ab + aB + ab + 2ABb + 2aBb + 2AaB +

2Aab + 4AaBb. I have never been surprised that the members of the Brünn Natural History Society went home somewhat puzzled after hearing Mendel present his paper, and that Nägeli never really understood what his correspondent was talking about.

There has been considerable discussion in the literature, about exactly how Mendel knew what to do in order to carry out his experiments successfully. From a reading of his paper, one might be led to imagine that he did it by some kind of inductive process – he just did the experiments and the integral ratios popped out, so to speak. But this is scarcely feasible. It would be most improbable that the experiments were carried out in a purely Baconian manner – in the style of 'Let's see what happens if we . . . ' . And even if the experiments had been performed in this way, it would have been very difficult to have moved from them directly to the Mendelian theory, as represented in his algebra.

In 1936, the celebrated geneticist, R. A. Fisher, carefully re-examined Mendel's results[7] and showed that the figures that had been obtained were *too* good; that is to say, they were suspiciously better than what might have been expected from the 'law of averages'. This led to the question of whether the results obtained were really all pretence, and whether Mendel was merely making up results that would agree with a preconceived idea. The question has still not been answered entirely satisfactorily, but current opinion has it that Mendel was probably working with some kind of hypothetico-deductive methodology. Perhaps he worked out (either on the basis of preliminary inquiries, or on the basis of some 'thought experiment') what might be expected to happen. Then he could have tested his expectations carefully. Of course, if he had been anticipating a particular result, there was always the possibility that he would lean towards such a result. Or, quite unknown to Mendel, his gardener-assistant might have shown some predisposition towards obtaining a particular set of observations.[8]

It has often been emphasised that Mendel was one of the first persons to look for statistical or probabilistic results in a biological experiment. He was probably able to do this because of his fairly advanced training in mathematics and physics at the University of Vienna. In the mid-nineteenth century it was rather unusual for 'naturalists' to receive a good grounding in mathematics. In his *Autobiography*, Darwin bemoaned his ignorance of mathematics, and as we have seen, although he carried out experiments with *Antirrhinum* plants that were compatible with Mendel's theory, he was not able to infer from the results any 'particulate' theory of inheritance such as that of Mendel, and he was forced to hobble along with the qualitative theories of 'prepotency' and 'pangenesis' though the 'pangenes' themselves were, it would appear, conceived as being in some manner particulate.

But there was more to Mendel's theory than its expression in mathematical terms. His approach was markedly different from that of his contemporaries in that it did not concern itself at all with the problem of the origin of *species*. His work was not related to questions of classification, the dominating problem in natural history ever since antiquity. It was in no way concerned with the specific essences, or the essential characters, of organisms. As has been pointed out by Elizabeth Gasking,[9] Mendel was looking for the laws of the inheritance of particular characters, and by turning attention to *this* problem he left behind entirely the question of the study of specific essences – the problem of what were the essential features of species.

Darwin did likewise, of course, in *The Origin*, but presumably Mendel, starting his experiments before 1859, did it quite independently. Earlier workers on the problem of the hybridisation of organisms[10] had been concerned with what happens when a species of one supposed essence is crossed with another, assuming that each species is marked by essential characteristics, with the various 'accidents' that constituted the attributes of the varieties of the species being of no scientific interest.[11] This philosophical 'essentialist' view stood in the way of understanding the phenemena of inheritance. But Darwin and Mendel, by their two separate roads, helped to bring about a break with this kind of thinking, albeit a break already mediated in part by Cuvier. Of course, Darwin, as the very title of his book testifies most clearly, was still concerned with the problem of the origin of species. On the other hand, he envisaged a temporal continuity between different species, and supposed that competition between *individuals* rather than species led to evolutionary change. In this sense he was not concerned with the supposed 'essences' of species.

Darwin never got to hear of Mendel's work in any definite way, although Vorzimmer has shown[12] that a brief notice of the Brünn paper by one Heinrich Hoffmann[13] containing the words 'Hybrids possess the inclination, in the following generation, to revert to the parental [or specific] form' was owned and probably read by Darwin. But this tiny clue was insufficient to excite his interest, and as far as we know, no further contact was ever forged between the two naturalists. So Darwin struggled on with the problems plaguing his theory, believing that the environment could serve as the source of the variations upon which natural selection could act, thereby permitting evolutionary development, yet without precise knowledge of how the variations were transmitted from one variation to the next.

Towards the end of the nineteenth century, however, even the possibility that the external environment could be the cause of variation was questioned by the German cytologist, August Weismann (1834-1914). Weismann is remembered for an experiment which – so he believed – provided a definite refutation of Lamarckism. He cut off the tails of mice for several generations, and showed that this produced no tendency towards decreased tail size in the succeeding generations.[14] It might appear, therefore, that the acquired characteristics were *not* inheritable.

This conclusion could, of course, be disputed by a confirmed Lamarckian, who might simply deny that Weismann had carried on with his experiments for a sufficient length of time for the predicted effect to be discernible. Or, with a greater degree of sophistication, the Lamarckian might claim that the removal of the tails was in no way related to the 'needs' (*besoins*) of the mice as determined by the conditions of the environment, so that the experiment was quite irrelevant as a test of Lamarckism. Most commentators, without necessarily being Lamarckians, have agreed that such objections are valid and that Weismann did not succeed in refuting Lamarckism. Nevertheless, late nineteenth-century biology did come to reject Lamarckism, and the hypothesis of Weismann known as the 'doctrine of the continuity of germ-plasm'[15] was widely accepted. This hypothesis can readily be understood by considering Figure 22.

Figure 22 Illustration of Weismann's Doctrine of the Continuity of the Germ-Plasm

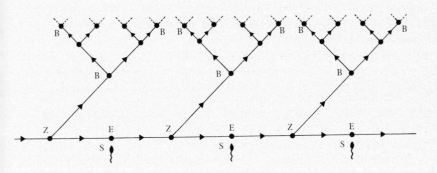

B = Body cells (somatic cells)
Z = Zygote (cell formed by fusion of sperm and egg)
S = Sperm cell }
E = Egg cell   } Germ cells

If the sketch shown in Figure 22 illustrating Weismann's doctrine is in fact a correct representation of the biological situation, then it can readily be seen that no mechanism is provided whereby the body (somatic) cells, which may be changed by the effects of the environment, can influence the germ cells. Consequently, if Weismann's picture is correct, Lamarckism must be a false doctrine. But in the nineteenth century Weismann's thesis was more a hypothesis, or perhaps even a kind of major metaphysical assumption governing a whole system of biological thought, than an empirically established principle. Nevertheless, many biologists, finding absolutely no empirical evidence in favour of the inheritance of acquired characteristics, began to favour the hypothesis of the continuity of the germ-plasm, and this placed great difficulty in the way of accepting the Darwinian theory of evolution by natural selection, because Darwin required the environmentally produced inheritable variation as the raw material on which natural selection could operate. (It should be noted, however, that Weismann regarded himself as a Darwinian, and was trying to purify the Darwinian doctrine of Lamarckian features.)

On the other hand, evolutionism *per se* was very widely adopted during the late nineteenth century, and a great deal of attention was devoted to attempts to elucidate the family trees or genealogies[16] of various organisms — indeed of the whole of the animal and plant kingdoms. This could be approached in two ways: either by direct study of the paleontological record or by examination of the development of embryos, which, according to the principle of recapitulation (now called Haeckel's 'biogenetic law'),[17] passed successively through the adult stages of their various ancestors. And such studies were remarkably successful in piecing together the general evolutionary history of organisms. But the whole edifice had a rather shaky theoretical foundation. On the one hand, Lamarckism was rejected, though not necessarily refuted. On the other, Darwinism, in order to be theoretically feasible, still required that the inheritance of acquired characteristics could occur, for without this, natural selection lacked the raw material of new variation on which it could operate.

It will not be surprising, therefore, to learn that biology was characterised by a great deal of speculative thinking in the late nineteenth century, with many suggestions involving various kinds of hypothetical hereditary units being put forward, and bold attempts being made to link ideas of evolution, embryology, cytology and heredity. Neo-Lamarckians, orthogenesists,[18] supporters of emergent evolution,[19] and mutationists were all offering their ideas and receiving acceptance to a greater or lesser degree. It was chiefly through the mutationists that an indication of the way the dilemma could be resolved first came to be discerned. Here we can give only the briefest sketch of what happened, for to treat the matter in the detail it deserves is a task far beyond the scope of this book.[20] The following, then, is necessarily the merest outline of a complex story, offered so that the reader may have a general understanding of the way the dilemma was eventually resolved. But it would be unfortunate if we had to leave Darwinism hanging uncomfortably in the air, so to speak, neither fully accepted by the community of biologists, nor totally rejected.

Darwin had never been well disposed to thinking of large saltatory 'sports' as the source of variation on which natural selection might operate to yield evolutionary change, and this view had been considerably strengthened by Fleeming Jenkin's famous review of 1867. Darwin preferred to emphasise the effect of selection pressures acting on whole populations, thereby giving rise to evolutionary developments. And the British school of mathematically-minded biologists, who styled themselves 'biometricians',[21] grew up in the late nineteenth century, working on the assumption that the best way to approach biological and specifically evolutionary problems was by statistical analysis of populations displaying 'continuous' variations according to the well-known 'Gaussian' bell-shaped curve of the 'normal' distribution. To these men, as to Darwin, the idea that evolution might be beholden to the occasional appearance of 'sports', or large discrete variations, was quite repugnant.

On the Continent, however, a markedly different approach was taken by the so-called 'mutationists', led by the Dutch plant breeder, Hugo de Vries (1848-1935). In 1886, de Vries found in an abandoned potato field near Hilversum large numbers of a plant named the Evening Primrose, (*Oenothera Lamarckiana*), probably escaped from a garden. Among these and other plants that he observed were several new varieties, each of which differed from the normal form of the species in a number of ways. And these new forms, de Vries found in a series of controlled experiments, bred true when self-pollinated. Subsequently, he bred some fifty thousand *Oenothera* plants, and obtained eight hundred mutants of seven specifically different kinds.[22]

What de Vries had discovered may have been something like the new variety (*Peloria*) noticed by Linnaeus in the eighteenth century.[23] But instead of referring the discovery to the phenomenon of hybridisation, de Vries supposed that macro *mutations* were occurring, giving rise to wholly new species. In fact, many of the claims made by de Vries have not been sustained by subsequent investigators; but enough has survived to allow that mutations (albeit miniscule compared with the large-scale changes discovered by de Vries) can occur and that they can be the source of the variations on which selection can operate. Today, the large-scale changes observed by de Vries are attributable to 'polyploidy', that is, multiplication of the number of chromosomes in the cells above that which is normal for the species. The mutations which provide the raw material for natural selection, according to the modern theory, are not of this large-scale character but arise from small chemical changes in the genetic material of the chromosomes.

De Vries was supported by Wilhelm Johannsen (1857-1927), who showed experimentally, by measuring the weights of bean seeds, that selection alone was incapable of producing new species and although 'pure lines' could readily be obtained, these rapidly reverted when artificial selection was no longer applied.[24] This seemed to confirm the view that selection alone could not be the motor for evolutionary change, and something like de Vries' macro-mutations seemed to be required. The Dutchman's *Mutationstheorie* achieved considerable acclaim in the first decade of the twentieth century.

In 1900, no less than three workers — E. von Tschermak (1871-1962), C. Correns (1864-1933), and de Vries himself — quite independently came across Mendel's long forgotten paper on pea hybrids, and immediately realised its great significance.[25] The paper soon became widely known among biologists, in Britain chiefly owing to the proselytising activities of William Bateson (1861-1926). There was some initial opposition to the Mendelian theory, mainly from the biometricians, but breeding experiments did seem to confirm Mendel's observations. In America, the geneticist Thomas Hunt Morgan (1866-1945) was initially sceptical, objecting, for example, that there were several known instances where dominance and recessiveness were by no means clearly evident. And Morgan had qualms about the invisible Mendelian 'factors', which seemed to be dragged in as theoretical entities merely to account for what was observed in the pea-breeding experiments. But after working with experiments on fruit-flies (*Drosophila melanogaster*) for a time, Morgan changed his mind, and became an enthusiastic convert to the Mendelian theory.[26] Johannsen made an important contribution in 1909[27] by making the theoretical distinction between what is now referred to as the *genotype* (the hereditary genetic characteristics of an organism) and the *phenotype* (the visible physical characteristics of the organism).[28] This removes the ambiguity or uncertainty about this distinction that is to be found in Mendel's own paper. Johannsen also coined the term 'gene' in its modern sense.

By application of the Darwinian theory of selection, the Mendelian theory of inheritance, and the theory of mutations (though in terms of micro-mutations, not the macro-mutations of de Vries), Morgan found it possible to bring together the three major components required for a reasonably satisfactory account of evolution. Small mutations, although not accounted for causally, could be viewed as the prime source of the variations on which might operate the Darwinian natural selection — itself aided by the principles of divergence and geographical isolation, as Darwin and Wallace originally envisaged. Mendelism removed the problems associated with a theory of blending inheritance, for it allowed variations to be 'carried' in the alleles (equivalent to Mendel's 'factors') and preserved in a population, even when the phenotypic variations were adversely affected by natural selection.

To explain this, let us take a particular example, even though it is one that is perhaps oversimplified. Let us suppose a given phenotype is governed by a particular pair of alleles, which we may choose to represent by 'AA'. Then let it be supposed that a mutation occurs to one of the alleles, yielding 'Aa'. By the mechanism illustrated in Figures 23 and 24, further organisms bearing this pair of alleles may arise in the population, without this fact becoming in any way apparent in the phenotypes.

Figure 23

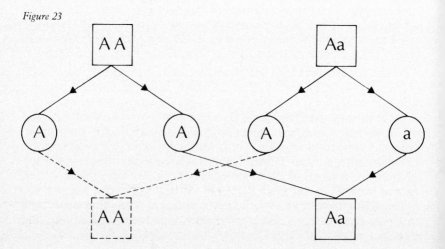

Several such organisms, equipped with the 'Aa' genotype may therefore be produced. Some of these may fortuitously cross with each other, thus generating the three-to-one Mendelian ratio in the offspring.

Figure 24.

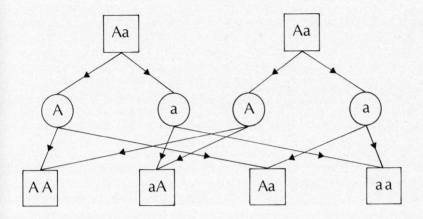

Only the 'aa' organism would display the new phenotype, whatever that might be, and this might or might not be eliminated by natural selection. But either way, the 'a' alleles could be preserved in the population. In principle, once the recessive 'a' alleles have been formed by mutation,[29] they may, in later generations, serve as a source of variation upon which natural selection may operate. Moreover, one can conceive a situation in which the external environmental conditions change. Then, perhaps, the phenotype corresponding to the 'aa' genotype may be *favoured* by selection, and 'AA' and 'Aa' may be adversely affected. If this happens, then the whole phenotypic character of the population may change – perhaps quite quickly. Doubtless, something rather like this occurred when the celebrated English peppered moths changed their characteristic phenotypic colouration after the Industrial Revolution.

What has been said above is necessarily schematic and crude, and by no means does justice to the subtleties of modern genetics, totally ignoring, for example, the question of the relationships between genes and the chromosomal structures of cells, and the phenomenon of 'crossing over', whereby there is a considerable re-sorting of genetic material during the process of germ cell formation.[30] Nevertheless, enough has been said to give a general conspectus of the way twentieth-century biology can give a solution to the dilemma which faced evolutionary theorists in the late nineteenth century.

The general theory, sketched and illustrated above, is usually referred to as the 'synthetic theory of evolution', the 'synthesis' being the amalgam of Darwinism, Mendelism and mutation theory.[31] Broadly speaking, this has become the paradigm for evolutionary theory in the twentieth century. It is this *synthetic* theory that critics revile when they attack modern evolutionism, although on occasions they greatly conflate nineteenth-century Darwinism with the twentieth-century synthesis.[32] But it should be noted that what is given in the preceding paragraphs is the merest sketch of the 'synthetic theory', which does nothing to show how it is connected to the modern chemical theories of molecular biology, where an attempt is made to give chemical descriptions of what occurs in the processes of mutation.[33] Also, we have ignored the fact that modern biology seeks to link studies of inheritance with statistical studies of the phenotypic characteristics of organisms, and the ecological relationships between organisms and the environments, in the discipline known as 'population genetics' or 'population biology'. Such matters, however, lie beyond the scope of this book.

Finally, we may refer once again to the remarkable coincidence in 1900 of the three independent rediscoveries of Mendel's work. If we follow arguments such as those of Gunther Stent, referred to in Chapter 8, it may appear that a great *mental* 'mutation' occurred among biologists in the late nineteenth century, which somehow made it possible for Mendel to be appreciated in 1900, whereas he was ignored or rebuffed in 1865. Had some great change of mental 'structure' occurred which at last permitted Mendel's work to receive the recognition it merited?

Such a question is difficult to answer, and it would require a very detailed historical analysis, covering a wide range of disciplines, for any sort of meaningful answer to be supplied. It is, of course, fairly obvious that by 1900 mathematical and statistical analysis were widely used in the biological sciences — even though the biometricians were subsequently reluctant to accept Mendelism because it proposed discrete changes, rather than continuous spreads of variation. It is also interesting to note that the similarity of offspring to their parents in certain characteristics in the first generation and the separation of the characteristics in the second generation was known well enough in the second half of the nineteenth century,[34] although scientists failed to take theoretical advantage of this knowledge. Yet can we say, from this, that the mental structures of 1900 were in some significant way different from those of the 1860s or 1870s, as perhaps the structuralist thesis of Stent might imply?

I will not attempt to answer this question, except by a little thought experiment. Suppose Darwin and Mendel had been able to meet and Mendel had had the opportunity of explaining to Darwin the rationale of the *Pisum* experiments, and the theory that he employed in order to account for the observations he made. From what we know of Darwin's character, interests, and abilities, what kind of response might he have made to Mendel's work?

I am inclined to think that Darwin would have been receptive to Mendel's interpretations. Certainly he would have understood the experimental part of the work. He would have been willing to think of invisible, hypothetical entities, contained within the organisms, which could be postulated in order to account for the observations, because the theory of pangenesis was a system of this kind. I see no reason to suppose that Darwin, an Englishman from the land of Dalton's chemical atomic theory, would have been averse to a 'particulate' theory of inheritance such as that of Mendel. As for the vaunted 'mathematical' character of Mendel's theory, it really amounts to no more than a knowledge of binomial expansions, such as Darwin probably learnt at school. There remains, then, the 'statistical' approach of the 1865 paper. This might have caused a problem, but one can imagine that Mendel, using a couple of coins, could readily have made his meaning clear to Darwin.

All this is not to say that Darwin would have understood Mendel's paper if he had read it alone. But I believe Darwin would have recognised its importance, and its potential relevance to his interests. And if he had then shown the paper to his colleagues and discussed it with them, I do not doubt that they could have been converted to Mendel's views. There seems to be no reason to believe that the mental structures of Darwin, Hooker, Huxley or Lyel, on the one hand, and Mendel, de Vries, Correns and Tschermak, on the other, were so different that they would have been unable to communicate. Rather, I suggest, the failure of Mendel's work to be appreciated in his own day can largely be attributed to fortuitous historical circumstances, such as have been briefly described at the beginning of this chapter.

This argument, however, presupposes that we have an accurate understanding of Mendel's theory as it was understood by him in his own day. It *may* be that this is not so. A recent paper by Robert Olby[35] has suggested that Mendel did not in fact, have the concept of pairs of 'factors' determining pairs of phenotypic characters. Such a view is a twentieth-century misrepresentation of the nineteenth-century theory, according to Olby's arguments. We shall not enter into this controversy here, but readers should note the direction that modern historical research is taking on this question. Some of the difficulties of the traditional interpretation of Mendel's paper have, of course, been adumbrated in my foregoing account.

NOTES CHAPTER 12

1   For a general account of Mendel's life and work, see H. Iltis, *Life of Mendel*, Allen & Unwin, London, 1932 (republished 1966). For a general history of genetics, including some account of Mendel's work, see L. C. Dunn, *A Short History of Genetics: The Development of Some of the Main Lines of Thought: 1864-1939*, McGraw-Hill, New York, 1965. See also R. C. Olby, *Origins of Mendelism*, Constable, London, 1966.

2   G. Mendel, 'Versuch über Pflanzen-Hybriden', *Verhandlungen des Naturforschenden Vereines in Brünn*, Vol. 4, 1865, *Abhandlungen*, pp.3-47. Various English translations of this are available. A convenient source is C. Stern & E. R. Sherwood (eds), *The Origin of Genetics: A Mendel Sourcebook*, Freeman, San Francisco & London, 1966, which, as the title suggests, contains translations of Mendel's major papers in genetics, the papers of his twentieth-century 'discoverers', and papers by R. A. Fisher and Sewall Wright giving statistical analyses of Mendel's experiments.

3   Translations of Mendel's letters to Nägeli may be found in C. Stern & E. R. Sherwood (eds), *op. cit.* (note 2), pp.56-102.

4   It is a remarkable fact that Mendel chose for investigation seven pairs of characters which are (we now believe) determined by seven pairs of alleles residing on the seven pairs of chromosomes which occur in each of the cells of the *Pisum* plants. Thus, all problems of 'linkage' were eliminated. It is most unlikely, therefore, that the seven pairs of characters were chosen at random. But Mendel tells us nothing about the preliminary experiments that (we presume) he must have conducted before he began the experiments that are described in his 1865 paper.

5   This is a modern term, not Mendel's.

6   C. Stern & E. V. Sherwood (eds.), *op. cit.* (note 2), p.30.

7   R. A. Fisher, 'Has Mendel's work been rediscovered?', *Annals of science*, Vol. 1, 1936, pp.115-137.

8   The question has recently been reviewed by Margaret Campbell: 'Explanations of Mendel's results', *Centaurus*, Vol. 20, 1976, pp.159-174. She concludes that Mendel may have tended to select vigorous plants which would be heterozygous. And in some cases observation of the plants themselves could give indications of whether they were homozygous or heterozygous, despite the dominance of one of the genes.

9   E. B. Gasking, 'Why was Mendel's work ignored?', *Journal of the History of Ideas*, Vol. 20, 1959, pp.60-84.

10   For example, J. G. Kolreuter, C. F. Gaertner and C. Naudin. For accounts of the work of these three, see R. C. Olby, *op. cit.* (note 1), Chapters 1-3.

11   This outlook had its roots in Aristotle's theory of science. Aristotle believed that the '*properties*', but not the '*accidents*', of things could be deduced from their defining formulae, or '*essences*'. Linnaeus thought that the study of plant varieties (groupings below the level of the species) was not the concern of the natural historian, but was merely of interest to florists.

12   P. J. Vorzimmer, 'Darwin and Mendel: the historical connection', *Isis*, Vol. 59, 1968, pp.77-82.

13   H. Hoffman, *Untersuchungen zur Bestimmung des Werthes von Species und Varietät: Ein Beitrag zur Kritik der Darwinischen Hypothese*, Giessen, 1869, pp.136-137.

14   A. Weismann, *Essays upon Heredity and Kindred Biological Problems*, Oxford, 1889, pp.431-433.

15   A. Weismann, 'The continuity of the germ-plasm as the foundation of a theory of heredity 1885', *ibid.*, pp.161-249.

16   Also called phylogenetic trees – representations of the evolutionary development of types of organisms.

17   Ernst Haeckel ('the German Darwin') stated this law succinctly: 'Ontogenesis is a brief and rapid recapitulation of phylogenesis' (E. Haeckel, *The Riddle of the Universe*, Watts, London, 1929, p.66).

18   '*Orthogenesis*. Gradual evolution of related groups of organisms in the same direction over a prolonged period of time due to working out of inherent trends within the inherited material' (M. Abercrombie, C. J. Hickman & M. L. Johnson, *A Dictionary of Biology*, Penguin, Harmondsworth, 1951, p.162). The view is that once evolution is proceeding in a particular direction it cannot deviate from this – it is like a tram on **ɪs** tram-lines. Orthogenesis (not widely accepted today) has been invoked to account for the existence of certain seemingly 'non-adaptive' characters, such as the giant antlers of the extinct Irish elk, which would appear to have been more of a nuisance than a help to their owners.

19   *The Shorter Oxford English Dictionary* defines 'emergent' as 'that which is produced by a combination of causes, but [which] cannot be regarded as the sum of their individual effects'.

20   For a fuller treatment, see, for example: G. E. Allen, *Life Science in the Twentieth Century*, Wiley, New York, 1975.

21   The leading members of the school were Darwin's cousin, Francis Galton, Karl Pearson (also a noteworthy philosopher of science) and W. F. R. Weldon.

22   For descriptions of de Vries's work, see his *Species and Varieties, Their Origin by Mutation*, Open Court, Chicago, 1905; or *The Mutation Theory; Experiments and Observations on the Origin of Species in the Vegetable Kingdom*, 2 vols, Open Court, Chicago, 1909-1910.

23   See above, p.21.

24   W. Johannsen, *Ueber Erblichkeit in Populationen und in reinen Linien*, Jena, 1903, Part of this is to be found in English translation in J. A. Peters (ed.), *Classic Papers in Genetics*, Prentice-Hall, London, 1959, pp.20-26. See also F. B. Churchill, 'William Johannsen and the genotype concept', *Journal of the History of Biology*, Vol. 7, 1974, pp.5-30.

25   For a discussion of this episode, see J. S. Wilkie, 'Some reasons for the rediscovery and appreciation of Mendel's work in the first years of the present century', *British Journal for the History of Science*, Vol. 1, 1962, pp.5-18.

26   T. H. Morgan, 'Sex limited [or 'linked' in modern terminology] inheritance in *Drosophila*', *Science*, Vol. 32, 1910, pp.120-122; J. A. Peters, *op. cit.* (note 24), pp.63-66.

27   W. Johannsen, *Elemente der Exakten Erblichkeitslehre*, Jena, 1909, pp.123 & 130.

28   Two organisms having different genes (which we may represent by 'Aa and 'AA' respectively' can have similar external appearances (phenotypes) because of the phenomenon of Mendelian dominance; hence the necessity for drawing a clear distinction between genotype and phenotype.

29   For de Vries and the early mutationists, no satisfactory explanation of mutations was forthcoming; they just happened. Today it is believed that they can be induced by phenomena such as radioactive disintegrations and cosmic rays, or certain chemicals such as mustard gas.

30   The phenomenon of 'crossing over' was first described by the Belgian, F. A. Janssens, in 1909: 'La théorie de la chiasmatypie, nouvelle interprétation des cinéses de maturation', *La Cellule*, Vol. 25, 1909, pp.387-406.

31   See J. S. Huxley, *Evolution: The Modern Synthesis*, Allen & Unwin, London, 1942.

32   A particularly egregious example recently published in the Australian Press is T. Bethell, 'Evolution is bunk: all change is not progress', *The National Times*, 13-18 September, 1976, pp.8-10.

33   For a survey of some of the more recent literature on the subject, which draws attention to some of the difficulties of the orthodox views, and points to some of the interesting possible alternatives, see M. de I. Wolsky & A. Wolsky, *The Mechanism of Evolution: A New Look at Old Ideas*, Karger, New York, 1976.

34   In a paper published in 1877, Francis Galton described his investigations with the transmission of the character of the seed weight of peas from one generation to the next, but, although noting 'reversion' at the first generation and 'deviation' at the second generation, did not come close to Mendel's solution of the problem. (F. Galton, 'Typical laws of heredity', *Proceedings . . . of the Royal Institution of Great Britain*, Vol. 8, 1875-1878, pp.282-301.)

35   R. C. Olby, 'Mendel no Mendelian?', *History of Science*, Vol. 17, 1979, pp.53-72.

13

Neo-Lamarckism

From what has been said in the previous chapter, it might be thought that with the acceptance of the Weismann principle, the extension of the geological time-scale, the rediscovery of Mendel's work, and the establishment of the paradigmatic synthetic theory of evolution, an adequate theory of evolution would have been formulated which could gain further support as the discoveries of biochemistry (or molecular biology) gradually permitted a chemical explanation of the genetic and the evolutionary theories. And Lamarckism, one might think, would disappear altogether from the scene, at least after the successful establishment of the synthetic theory, if not before.

But, in fact, the history of biology has not been nearly as tidy and simple as this — an important reason being, I suggest, that the fields of genetics and evolutionary biology are inextricably tangled with social questions of the most intense interest, and ultimately with politics and vexatious problems of race. The whole question of nature *versus* nurture is at issue here; and rightly or wrongly the correct solution of this problem has been seen as an important consideration in relation to the way the social system ought to be organised.

In Chapter 17, it will be shown that in broad terms the 'left' of the political spectrum during the earlier part of the twentieth century found a 'Lamarckian' version of the evolutionary theory particularly attractive, while the 'right' favoured the Darwinian version. This is an extremely crude generalisation, which obviously requires considerable qualification, but taken as an approximation, it has some truth. The reason is not hard to find. The left hopes to improve society by ameliorating the conditions of the social environment and diminishing the struggle for existence, believing that mankind will adapt itself to the new conditions. Obviously, if Lamarckism (as defined at the end of the section on Lamarck in Chapter 3) is a correct biological theory, this process will be so much the simpler.

The right, on the other hand, accepts with equanimity the doctrine that people are intrinsically unequal in their inherent characteristics, and that these inherent differences are little susceptible to change by so-called 'social engineering'. Traditionally, their argument has been that progress in society is made possible by giving free rein to well-endowed individuals, even at the expense of those less favoured by nature. If Lamarckism is false, there is little hope that planned changes in the social environment will yield beneficial changes in actual human endowments — or so the argument runs. For example, better education facilities would not be expected to make people inherently more intelligent. Broadly speaking, then, the political right has found the Darwinian doctrines more attractive than those of Lamarck.

It is evident, therefore, that the question of the scientific truth or otherwise of the Lamarckian doctrine is a matter of deepest concern, and consequently, in this last chapter of the second part of this book, it will be useful to look at some of the later developments of Lamarckism in the writings of the so-called Neo-Lamarckians.

Darwin himself, of course, can in a sense be referred to as a Neo-Lamarackian, for although he firmly rejected some of the speculative elements in Lamarck's thinking, such as the doctrine of subtle fluids, he did accept and employ the idea of inheritance of acquired characteristics, and the theory of pangenesis allowed the environment to act as an agent producing new variations on which natural selection might operate in a *quasi*-Lamarckian fashion. Some of Darwin's most ardent admirers, such as the German philosopher/biologist, Ernst Haeckel,[1] were also Neo-Lamarckians. In the previous chapter, however, it has been said that the anti-Lamarckism of Weismann, with his theory of the continuity of the germ plasm and the famous tail-cutting experiments with mice, seemed to make Lamarckism untenable. But Weismann did not really refute Lamarck. The doctrine of the continuity of the germ plasm, and the inability of the soma (body) cells to influence the germ cells, while a useful guide to research and perfectly reasonable as a hypothetical biological principle or axiom, was not an experimental fact. No one in Weismann's day had ever shown that it was chemically, biologically or logically impossible for the somatic cells to act in some way on the germ cells, or that this did not happen. All Weismann could say was that no one could think of a causal mechanism whereby such an interaction might take place. In the last analysis, his doctrine was purely dogmatic.

It is not perhaps surprising, therefore, that Lamarckian ideas were still widespread in the late nineteenth century among both biologists and social scientists, and this has been confirmed by the investigations of a number of historians. In fact, according to E. J. Pfeifer,[2] Neo-Lamarckism was a strongly supported doctrine in America as early as 1866, when A. Hyatt presented a paper showing distinct Neo-Lamarckian tendencies to the Boston Natural History Society. He was subsequently supported by E. D. Cope, A. S. Packard, W. H. Dall, T. Meehan, C. King, H. F. Osborne, and J. LeConte. Not many of these are well known today, but together they formed a fairly powerful Neo-Lamarckian 'lobby'. In Europe, Darwin himself (especially in his later works as we have seen), Richard Owen, Ernst Haeckel, St George Mivart (1827-1900), and Herbert Spencer (1820-1903), may all be regarded as Neo-Lamarckians in various guises, even though Darwin, Haeckel and Spencer in particular, laid great emphasis on the idea of struggle for existence.[3] And, as will be shown further in Chapter 16, men such as Lester F. Ward, writing in America in the late nineteenth century as a 'liberal' or 'reform' Social Darwinist, found it necessary to emphasise the Lamarckian side of the Darwinian theory, to combat the notion that all social progress was actuated by a pitiless struggle for existence. The idea was developed that *social habits might in time become fixed*, by some kind of Lamarckian process, *as instincts*.[4] This has some analogy with the earlier Spencerian doctrine of 'equilibration';[5] but it would provide a wonderful fillip for social planners, if true. The question, however, was whether it was true that habits could evolve into instincts. Was there any experimental evidence to support such a contention?

There was quite intense debate on this question for about twenty years from around 1890. Gradually the Weismannists, or Neo-Darwinians, gained the upper hand. The Neo-Lamarckians seemed unable to produce any concrete experimental evidence to support their side of the question, and with the rediscovery of Mendel and the demonstration that the Mendelian theory could be applied successfully to such a wide range of phenomena, biologists, psychologists and sociologists began to desert the Neo-Lamarckian cause. By 1915, the anthropologist A. L. Kroeber was stating emphatically that '*Heredity by acquirement is equally a biological and historical monstrosity*'.[6]

One result of this decline of faith in Lamarckism was the opening up of a schism between social scientists and biologists — between those who wished to develop their social science independently of the results obtained in experimental biology, and those who stuck to biology, treating with sometimes ill-concealed disdain the investigations of the allegedly 'softer' sciences such as sociology or psychology.

In the 1920s, however, it seemed at last as if some experimental evidence had been found to show that learned behaviour might be inherited, and also that physical characteristics acquired as a result of environmental changes might be inherited. The Russian psychologist, I. P. Pavlov (1849-1936), trained mice to run to their food trough at the sound of a bell, and claimed that while the first generation required about three hundred repetitions to learn the task, by the second generation this had dropped to a hundred, and by the fifth generation only five lessons were needed.[7] But he soon withdrew this striking claim.[8]

Then in 1927 the eminent psychologist William McDougall (1871-1938) reported what seemed at first to be something more positive.[9] He trained rats to escape from a tank of water set up with two alternative escape ramps. One was brightly lit and was equipped with a device to give the rats an uncomfortable electric shock as they ventured to escape. The other ramp was dimly lit and provided no such unpleasant sensations to the would-be escapers.

The rats soon learned how to perform their task successfully. McDougall then bred from these rats; ... ; ... We have not space to give a detailed account of all his experimental work, but the result was that McDougall believed he was able to show that the acquired characteristic (knowledge of how to escape from the tank) *was* inherited in succeeding generations.

Figure 25 McDougall's Apparatus for Testing the Lamarckian Hypothesis

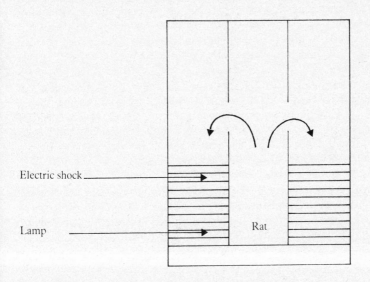

This was indeed an exciting result. As McDougall wrote:

> If the Lamarckian hypothesis be valid, if it be true that modifications of function and structure, acquired by the individual organism in consequence of its efforts to adapt itself to its environment, may be in some degree, however slight, transmitted to its descendants, then we have in outline an adequate theory of organic evolution; and, further, we are able to assign to mind, or, in other words, to purposive, teleological, or hormic[10] activity, an intelligible and leading role in the drama. On the other hand, if we can find no warrant for accepting the Lamarckian hypothesis, then we remain utterly in the dark as to the nature of the evolutionary process; we have no theory of it, and the place of mind in the scheme of nature remains utterly unintelligible.[11]

Of course, the lack of a Lamarckian dimension to evolutionary theory has not, since McDougall's day, proved an insuperable difficulty. But on the other hand the question of whether mind can, even to a minor degree, control the evolutionary process was, and is, a matter of central concern — although one might smile a little to think that a question of such import might be settled by the use of small rodents in a water tank. McDougall also wrote:

> I believe that, if the Lamarckian principle is valid, the social outlook, the prospect before our civilization, is very much brighter than if it be illusory. For if it be valid, eugenics[12] can work harmoniously with euthenics.[13] If it be not valid, the conflict between eugenists and euthenists would seem destined to continue while our western civilization declines and decays, it will then remain for some non-Christian people to carry on the torch of civilization.[14]

It is scarcely surprising that his paper was eagerly read, and a considerable amount of effort was put into trying to corroborate or falsify the claims of a discovery of a form of Lamarckian inheritance effect, even though McDougall put forward such claims very tentatively and with many qualifications.

The general opinion about the results of McDougall's experiments is that the claims made were not justified.[15] McDougall admitted that he had a natural propensity towards finding a positive result in his experiments, and that he had possibly overlooked certain significant factors, such as the general health of the animals in the colony with which he was working (which showed unexplained cycles), or the fact that he might unconsciously have chosen the 'brighter' specimens in a litter for his experiments.

The final negativeoutcome of the experiments initiated by McDougall caused considerable disappointment, and needless to say more especially among those who favoured the nurture side of the nature/nurture controversy. This was especially so among those with affiliations to the left of the political spectrum. However, support for *their* cause had seemed to be forthcoming much earlier from the results of the investigations conducted shortly after the First World War by the Austrian zoologist, Paul Kammerer (1880-1926).

The 'Kammerer affair', as it is now usually called, was certainly a most strange episode in the history of science, and well worth some consideration. A number of differing accounts have been given by various authors, and it is noteworthy that the accounts have differed substantially according to the political affiliations of the raconteurs.[16]

Kammerer claimed that he had been able to breed creatures called midwife toads (*Alytes obstetricans*) that displayed the inheritance of acquired characteristics. This toad mates on land, and, unlike the normal water-breeding species, the males do not possess 'nuptial pads' on their forelegs that enable them to cling to the slippery females in water. But according to Kammerer's account, the toads could be induced to breed in water, and after several generations they developed nuptial pads and transoitted this character to succeeding generations. The nuptial pads showed a darkening of the skin, and it was this feature that later became a critical focus for the discussions.

Kammerer also worked with yellow spotted salamanders (*Salamandra maculosa*) and showed that if they were reared on dark soil the spots disappeared, whereas if they were bred on yellow soil the spots grew to form yellow bands. These, of course, are adaptive colour changes. Kammerer made the further claim that the acquired characteristics could be handed on to succeeding generations. He also did work of a similar character with sea squirts (*Ciona intestinalis*).

It is difficult to know what to make of Kammerer's results, but as far as I am aware they have never been repeated successfully. However, he published his results,[17] and gave verbal accounts of them at various public meetings, including a lecture tour to Britain in 1923. He was assailed with perhaps undue spleen by William Bateson, one of Britain's leading Mendelian geneticists, but the descriptions of the experiments and the material displayed do not seem to have led to accusations of forgery at that time. Nevertheless, some American biologists, particularly G. K. Noble, the Curator of Reptiles at the American Museum of Natural History, were suspicious, and Noble asked to be allowed to see Kammerer's specimens. Kammerer, however, was apparently reluctant to allow this. The crisis came when Noble visited Kammerer in Vienna in 1926, and found that the specimens on which the Lamarckian claims had been based were seemingly doctored, the nuptial pads of the toads apparently having been darkened artificially with Indian ink.

Noble promptly attacked Kammerer's work and reputation in the columns of *Nature* on August 7, 1926.[18] And on September 23 of the same year the Austrian was found shot dead on a mountain path, with a suicide note in his pocket.

It must be realised that Kammerer was a man whose political affiliations leaned rather strongly to the left. He had lost all his money in the financial crash of the great inflation in Germany and he was intending to move to Russia. He had also written shortly before his death to the Praesidium of the Communist Academy in Moscow stating that he had *not* added the black ink marking, and that the (admitted) forgery must have been carried out by a laboratory assistant who wished to protect his employer from Noble's inquiries. Kammerer then shot himself because of the great disgrace to his scientific career.

For a good many years it was believed, following the accounts of Noble,[19] Conway Zirkle,[20] and J. S. Huxley,[21] that Kammerer was simply an apologist for Marxism and the inheritance of acquired characteristics, and that he had grossly falsified his results for political purposes. The whole question has, however, been looked into again in considerable detail by Arthur Koestler in his *Case of the Midwife Toad*, and the case against Kammerer seems to be by no means clear-cut.[22] Possibly, like McDougall, he *thought* he had obtained positive results, which others, looking from a different theoretical stance, would not be prepared to accept. And today it is thought that he may have been investigating an instance of what is called 'genetic assimilation'.[23] But not the least curious part of the affair was that — according to Koestler's account — Kammerer was found shot through the left temple, while his pistol was held in his right hand.[24]

It seems that Lamarckism was also one of the major driving forces behind the notorious 'Lysenko affair', another episode in which the theory of evolution became inextricably tangled with political matters in Russia, from the nineteen twenties right through to the end of the Khrushchev era in 1964. Consequently, it is a moot point whether this episode should be dealt with here or in Chapter 17, where the interaction of evolutionary doctrines and political theories is discussed. However, since the matter may be linked quite conveniently with a discussion of the Kammerer affair, we will consider it here.[25]

In the early part of the twentieth century, the paradigmatic evolutionary theory of Darwinism/Mendelism/Morganism was accepted in Russia, as other countries, and genetical research and plant-breeding experiments of a high order were carried out there, most notably by Nicolai Vavilov (1887-1943), with his important work directed towards improving the strains of Russian wheats for increasing food production. 1927, however, saw a disastrous harvest in Russia, and there was widespread famine. The authorities turned almost desperately to some form of escape, and some of the ideas of I. V. Michurin (1855-1935), an idiosyncratic plant breeder and nurseryman, a former *protégé* of Lenin, were taken up, as well as ideas of T. D. Lysenko (1898-1976), a man of peasant stock and little formal education in genetics, who was working in a plant-breeding station at Azerbaidzhan.

Basically, what Michurin and Lysenko were preaching was a crude kind of Lamarckism,[26] and a bland denial — not an experimental refutation — of the results of Mendelian genetics. In this, they received the fullest support of the political authorities, chiefly emanating from Stalin. Lysenko, something of a demagogue, was promoted to positions of administrative and political power, while 'traditional' Western-type geneticists were demoted or deposed. It is believed that Vavilov died of starvation in prison early in 1943. The climax came in 1948, when Lysenko presented a celebrated address to the Lenin Academy of Agricultural Sciences of the U.S.S.R.[27] A resolution was formally passed condemning the 'reactionary-idealistic *Weismann* (Mendel-Morgan) trend', and acclaiming the 'progressive, materialist, *Michurin* trend'.[28] From then on, until the end of the Khrushchev era — although with some lifting of the gloom shortly before 1964 — Soviet biology moved into the 'dark ages', and developed on principles quite different from those accepted in the West. The whole affair was a classic instance of the baneful influence of politics on science, although this is not to deny that there is also a constant interplay between science and politics, or science and ideology, in the Western world. And I do not wish to pretend that any science is ever entirely value-free.

The link between science, politics, and the nature/nurture controversy is fully evident from the following quotation from the 1948 Lenin Academy declaration:

The Mendelist-Morganist trend in biology propounds the idealistic and meta-physical theory of Weismann that the nature of an organism is independent of its external environment, the theory of the so-called immortal "hereditary sub-stance". The Mendelist-Morganist trend is divorced from life and its researches are practically fruitless.[29]

Clearly, Soviet biology, for ideological reasons, had chosen to turn its back on the theories which, rightly or wrongly, were thought to characterise the capitalist West, and it sought to develop its own brand of 'practical' science. Partly what was involved was a repudiation of the employment of invisible, hypothetical scientific entities such as the Mendelian 'factors', or the genes proposed by Johannsen, as part of a system of scientific explanation. Not without some reason, such explanatory principles were thought to be 'idealistic and metaphysical'. However, it appears that Lysenko had rather little understanding of what the Mendelian theory was actually about. Indeed, his understanding seems to have stopped short at the point of grasping the concept of the three-to-one ratio obtained in the pea experiments.

The *quasi*-Lamarckian doctrine which first excited the interest of Lysenko, and brought him into political prominence, was concerned with what was called the 'vernalisation' of wheat.[30] In this process, wheat seeds were watered, and the water allowed to freeze, thus simulating the conditions of winter. By this means, wheat could apparently be sown in the spring, and, growing rapidly, could reach a state of maturity before the summer droughts occurred. This avoided the need for autumn sowing, and thereby helped to reduce the normal losses of wheat struggling to survive through the winter. The system has some possibilities in Russia with its short growing season and very severe winters. But it is not a good method, for the watered grains can readily go bad, especially when the process is conducted on a large scale, and in the West, under the auspices of the 'Mendelist-Morganist trend', it is customary to select strains that have short growing periods and breed from these. Vavilov, in fact, was engaged in work of this kind.

In the period of Lysenko's dominance, the whole of Russian biology, including, of course, what was taught in the schools and universities, as well as what was done at the research bench, was restructured. The doctrine of genes and chromosomes as carriers of hereditary material was denied, and replaced by the notion that heredity was a general property of living matter. In fact, in some of his later publications, Lysenko began to return to the pangenesis theory of Darwin. Lysenko's work largely disregarded the usual canons of scientific method, as these are understood in the West. His initial experimental evidence for vernalisation, for example, was based on results from a single plant, of unknown genetic history. And the use of control techniques was ill-understood, or ill-applied.

It is often believed that the troubles in mid-twentieth-century Russian agriculture were due to organisational problems, such as the coercive collectivisation of the peasantry. But this was only part of the story. The biological theories of the Lysenkoist school, given the political support of Stalin's regime and thrust upon the country's agronomists, may be held responsible to a very considerable degree. To take an extreme example, in 1948 re-afforestation schemes were being established in Siberia. Following Lysenko's ideas, there could be no intra-specific competition. So seeds were planted in groups, which, by some supposed analogy with the notion of class solidarity, were intended to produce clusters of saplings which would protect the best tree in each group from competition by neighbouring plants of other species, all the supportive trees eventually sacrificing themselves for the good of the species — or the 'cause'. The trees, needless to say, died in thousands.

Lysenko even believed that he could provide evidence for the transformation of biological species:

> When experiments were started to convert hard wheat into winter wheat it was found that after two, three or four years of autumn planting (required to turn a spring into a winter crop) durum becomes vulgare, that is to say one species is converted into another. Durum wheat with 28 chromosomes is converted into several varieties of soft 42-chromosome wheat, nor do we, in this case, find any transitional forms between the durum and the vulgare species. *The conversion of one species into another takes place by a leap.*[31]

Lysenko found barley growing in wheat fields and fir trees in pine forests — but he was, we think, utterly deceiving himself in believing that new species were formed. He also praised the work of Lepeshinskaya, who was supposedly able to generate cells from egg albumen, saying that this was a refutation of the chromosome theory of heredity.[32]

The whole bizarre system seems today like some gigantic hoax, and the Russians themselves have now left it well behind. Yet much of this happened within the lifetime of many of the readers of this book. Man is certainly a strange animal, especially when his metaphysics begin to impinge on his physics.

Yet several points should be emphasised before a historical judgement on this episode is reached. Firstly, the Lysenkoist biology was the product of an ill-educated, peasant-stock political activist who rose to power in peculiarly difficult social circumstances, and it came to the fore at a time of terrible crisis in Russian life — the famines of the late 1920s. In other circumstances, Lysenko might not have been taken up so enthusiastically, or might have been disregarded entirely. The Russians at that time were grasping at anything that might offer a solution to their problems. Secondly, the Western world has had equally peculiar political and social characteristics in its twentieth-century history, the Nazi racial theories being perhaps the outstanding example.[33] Indeed, it was in part the Nazi's corrupt and distorted versions of Western biology that led to the terrible confrontation between Russia and Germany in the Second World War. And the U.S.S.R. was trying to build up a new political and social system that would be the antithesis of the Western capitalist system, which drew so much comfort from the biology of its day. Little wonder, then, that the Russian government sought to foster the work of the 'agrobiologists' of the Lysenko school, which would produce a quick solution to the country's agricultural problem and would not need the years of painstaking experimentation demanded by the orthodox geneticists. And thirdly, when allowances have been made for differences in soil and climate between Russia and the West, the agricultural productions of the two systems are not so favourable to the capitalist system as is sometimes supposed.[34] Besides, during the Second World War, it appears that Lysenko did much to encourage food production among the peasant farmers, through his energetic support for 'proletarian production'.

Perhaps the most interesting instance of an interplay between biological science and social and political ideologies in the West in recent years is revealed by the public response to the psychological investigations of A. R. Jensen and H. J. Eysenck and others, who have suggested that there may be inherent or genetic differences in mental powers between blacks and whites in America, such that the various programs of 'compensatory education' that have been instituted in that country for young black children are essentially worthless.[35]

Such claims have led to a considerable amount of academic debate[36] and some more concrete forms of political activity, with campaigns of tyre-slashing in America and physical attacks on Eysenck in Britain. And once again political opinion has polarised over the long-drawn-out debate on the question of nature and nurture. Jensen and Eysenck have claimed that experimental investigations (chiefly the twin studies of Sir Cyril Burt[37]) reveal that about 80 per cent of intellectual performance (as revealed by standard IQ tests) may be attributed to hereditary factors and only about 20 per cent to environmental circumstances. Consequently, it has been argued, the expensive American 'headstart' programs of compensatory education – which seemingly have had little success in boosting the IQs of black children – are not worth pursuing.

These assertions have been vehemently denied by many critics,[38] who argue that IQ tests are far from culturally neutral, and that Jensen's and Eysenck's claim that measured intelligence can be split up into separate genetic and environmental components is based on faulty reasoning and fallacious scientific evidence. Indeed, it has been alleged[39] fairly recently that Burt's evidence on twins, which underpinned Jensen's and Eysenck's arguments, was probably 'doctored' and was quite untrustworthy. Moreover, putative scientific claims such as those of Jensen and Eysenck and their supporters may be (and have been) taken up all too willingly by politicians eager to cut down on expensive social-welfare programs. Jensen's and Eysenck's arguments, it is said, do nothing but harm when presented with an air of scientific authority that is far from justified by the facts.

It is extremely interesting to note something of the intellectual ancestry of this debate. Jensen was himself a student of Eysenck, who in turn was a student of Burt. Burt was a student of the biometrician Karl Pearson (1857-1936) who was a co-worker of Francis Galton, who was one of the first psychologists to investigate 'individual differences' and did much work in the nineteenth century on the hereditary transmission of particular skills and aptitudes. And Galton, it will be recalled, was no less than Darwin's cousin, and was greatly influenced by his views. So one may readily trace the intellectual ancestry of the present-day advocates of the nature side of the nature/nurture controversy to the nineteenth-century Darwinian theories.[40] Moreover, a recent study has shown that there is a strong correlation between the political affiliations and the intellectual positions taken up by the disputants in this purportedly purely scientific controversy of nature and nurture.[41] Clearly, therefore, we have a notable example of extra-scientific considerations impinging on a debate that is supposedly being conducted on scientific grounds alone.[42] Moreover, recent studies have shown that some programs of compensatory education have in fact been quite effective,[43] so at present the tide seems to be running against the hereditarians. But all this does not provide any evidence for the 'Lamarckian' inheritance of acquired characteristics, *per se*.

So, we may ask, is there any remaining evidence, accepted in the West, for Lamarckian evolutionism, or for the rejection of the Weismann hypothesis? What I have to say on this question cannot be regarded as authoritative. But there seems to me to be no generally-accepted evidence for Lamarckian inheritance — of phenotypic changes having influence on genotypes, or somatic changes becoming directly inheritable through the genes.[44] Experiments suggesting changes of this kind have been reported from time to time,[45] but they do not seem to have been confirmed successfully; or, with a little ingenuity, they can be given 'orthodox' interpretations. Modern proponents of Lamarckism such as H. G. Cannon have concentrated chiefly on pointing up difficulties that the synthetic theory may encounter in explaining particular phenomena[46] — and there are such of course[47] — rather than identifying solid experimental evidence for Lamarckian inheritance.

But this does not leave us in a totally non-Lamarckian world. There is, in the first place, an interesting phenomenon known as 'simulated Lamarckism' or the 'Baldwin effect',[48] first discussed by the American Neo-Lamarckian, J. M. Baldwin (1861-1934), at the end of the nineteenth century,[49] and which has been taken up in recent years by a number of writers, perhaps most notably by the Oxford zoologist, Alister Hardy (1896-).[50]

The phenomenon of simulated Lamarckism can perhaps best be explained by means of a hypothetical example. Suppose a fox-like creature alters its habits under the pressure of the circumstances of the environment. It might, for example, take to 'fishing' if its supply of rabbits or chickens begins to run out, and move to a partially aquatic habitat. If such a change in behaviour occurs, *subsequently* occurring variations (or mutations) which favour the new aquatic habit will tend to be preserved by natural selection. And in time, then, the creature will evolve to something better adapted to the aquatic environment. It might, for example, become something resembling an otter. All this can take place by mechanisms lying entirely within the purview of the orthodox synthetic theory of evolution. But it will give the appearance of being a case of the environment causing the adaptive changes. In other words, it will be an instance of *simulated* Lamarckism.

Hardy believes that this sort of situation arises very commonly in the evolutionary histories of organisms, and that it may be one of the major determinants of evolutionary change. He goes beyond this, however, to point up considerable difficulties in orthodox evolutionary theory, as, for example, when it is faced with the problem of explaining the correlation of small mutational changes to produce seemingly co-ordinated, or even 'directed', adaptations. Hardy also emphasises the difficulties posed for orthodox theory by observations of the behavioural characteristics of very simple single-celled organisms, which seem to display some kind of 'memory' capacity.

In the closing chapters of his book, *The Living Stream*, Hardy reveals the religious import of his argument, suggesting that some of the phenomena that he has described (including a good deal of discussion of telepathic communication) can best be accounted for by the supposition that organisms are somehow able to 'plug in' to a kind of psychic flux (the 'living stream', in Hardy's phrase), standing apart from the normal 'mechanical' processes proposed by the orthodox Darwinian/Mendelian synthetic theory, and in some manner guiding the evolutionary process. We might call this a kind of externally mediated, purposive, 'psychic Lamarckism'.

At this point, of course, we have retreated from standard positivistic science, and are being introduced to Hardy's metaphysical suppositions. But the overall arguments he presents are of considerable interest, and should be consulted further by the reader with an interest in psychic matters. But Hardy has failed – as has everyone else – to bring forward hard experimental evidence for Lamarckian inheritance.

Somewhat related to the question of 'simulated Lamarckism' is a phenomenon which C. H. Waddington (1905-1975)[51] has called 'genetic assimilation', for which there seems to be plenty of solid empirical evidence. Waddington showed some years ago that if specimens of the *Drosophila* fruitfly were heated to 40°C at a certain stage of their early development, some of them developed an unusual vein pattern on their wings. One could breed from those flies that showed this effect, selecting for this character at every generation. It was then shown that after the twelfth generation the flies began to show the unusual venation, even when they had *not* been exposed to the unusually high temperature.[52] Thus it appeared that the newly acquired characteristics had become inherited.

Waddington believed this phenomenon of genetic assimilation, which appears to occur quite commonly, to be an important aspect of evolutionary change. However, he did not believe that it was an indication of some kind of Lamarckian phenomenon. The important point to note is that selection was accompanying the alteration of the environmental circumstances. Some organisms had a pre-existing, genetically-determined propensity to respond to the new environmental conditions in the way they did. Selection could preserve these and eliminate (or separate out, in the experimental set-up) the others. But how could the effect occur, in time, without the special environmental stimulus? How could this apparently Lamarckian effect occur?

To answer this, Waddington used his hypothesis of 'canalisation'.[53] He pointed out that wild animals of a given species, despite their considerable genetic differences, all have very similar external characteristics, or phenotypes. Their development seems to be canalised in a particular direction, regardless of varied inheritable genetic characteristics. So he suggested that under the influence of selection, an optimum canalised response to the conditions of the environment might occur, even though there might be a considerable variety of external stimuli acting (say different levels of temperature stimulus). While the external stimuli were applied, triggering the organisms to produce the new canalised response, and while natural selection was acting, a re-sorting of the genetic material could occur, to the extent that the triggering effect of the environment might become superfluous. And so genetic assimilation would occur.

Such an interpretation may, however, conveniently be supplemented by the idea of 'threshold selection',[54] which seems to be seeking to account for the same kind of phenomena as those considered by Waddington, without making so much of 'canalisation'. Suppose a character is controlled by several allele pairs, e.g., 'Aa, Bb, Cc, Dd, Ee, Ff' − if we consider a purely heterozygous case. Also, let us suppose that the presence of six dominant alleles is sufficient to produce the character when the special external stimulus is applied. But if (say) ten dominant alleles are present, then the character will appear *without* the external stimulus. Now if the organism moves into a new environment, and is subjected to natural selection, the number of dominant alleles in the population will rise, the others tending to be culled out by the pressure of selection. In time, then, organisms endowed with allele complements such as 'Aa, BB, CC, Dd, EE, FF' will become commonplace and these will produce the special character *without* the environmental stimulus. By this model, the Baldwin effect and Waddington's 'genetic assimilation', or processes of simulated Lamarckism, can be accounted for quite satisfactorily without going beyond the standard Darwin/ Mendel/ Morgan theory of evolution. Again we find we can manage well enough without dragging in any Lamarckian ideas.[55]

Yet there is, of course, one vast segment of the evolutionary process which may reasonably be called Lamarckian, and that is in the area of human culture. Because every time we build a house, write a poem, make a tool, or discover a new mathematical theorem, in a sense we may be said to *acquire* a new characteristic, which may be transmitted to subsequent generations. Needless to say, this is why the process of human evolution is so utterly different from that of other organisms, and why it is proceeding at such breakneck speed. An animal may acquire new characteristics, as when the race-horse is trained to run fast, or the circus lion learns to jump through the hoop. But such acquired characteristics are not heritable — at least not according to the views of orthodox Western geneticists. By contrast, the learning of one generation of humans is, to a considerable degree, handed on to subsequent generations, as the reader in any library well knows. And artefacts, though ultimately perishable, can often be handed on for a considerable number of years. So, while animals and plants run the evolutionary race with the handicap of having to return almost to the starting point at each generation,[56] humans have secured the inestimable advantage of taking a forward step at every generation. It is no wonder that our social evolution is proceeding at such a frenetic rate, and that the whole may very well culminate in a mighty explosion. This is what the 'Lamarckian' inheritance of acquired characteristics in the cultural domain seems likely to yield.

NOTES CHAPTER 13

1   On Haeckel, see page 274.
2   E. J. Pfeifer, 'The genesis of American neo-Lamarckism', *Isis*, Vol. 56, 1965, pp.156-167.
3   For a detailed discussion of the Lamarckian aspects of Spencer's thought, see D. Freeman, 'The evolutionary theories of Charles Darwin and Herbert Spencer', *Current Anthropology*, Vol. 15, 1974, pp.211-237.
4   For an account of the development of this hypothesis in early American sociology, see G. W. Stocking, 'Lamarckism in American social science: 1890-1915', *Journal of the History of Ideas*, Vol. 23, 1962, pp.239-256. Essentially this hypothesis lay at the base of the thinking of British writers such as Samuel Butler and George Bernard Shaw on evolutionary questions. (See Chapter 22, below.)
5   See page 207 below.
6   A. L. Kroeber, 'Eighteen professions', *American Anthropologist*, Vol. 17 (n.s.), 1915, pp.283-288 (at p.285).
7   See E. W. MacBride, *An Introduction to the Study of Heredity*, Williams & Norgate, London, 1924, pp.107-108.
8   I. P. Pavlov, *Conditioned Reflexes: An Investigation of the Physiological Activity of the Cerebral Cortex*, Dover, New York, 1960, p.285.
9   W. McDougall, 'An experiment for testing the hypothesis of Lamarck', *The British Journal of Psychology*, Vol. 17, 1927, pp.267-304.
10 'Hormic' means 'purposive'.
11 W. McDougall, *op. cit.* (note 9), p.268.
12 A discipline, influential in the late nineteenth and early twentieth centuries, which sought to improve the characteristics of human populations by the implementation of suitable programs of selective breeding. Eugenics fell from grace in the 1930s after the work of Nazi scientists became known, but it is rising in a new form with the current work in so-called 'genetic engineering'.
13 Euthenics is the study of the scientific control of the environment.
14 W. McDougall, *op. cit.* (note 9), p.304.
15 See G. C. Drew, 'McDougall's experiments on the inheritance of acquired characteristics', *Nature*, Vol. 143, 1939, pp.188-191; W. E. Agar, F. H. Drummond, O. W. Tiegs & M. M. Gunson, 'Fourth (final) report on a test of McDougall's Lamarckian experiment on the training of rats', *Journal of Experimental Biology*, Vol. 31, 1954, pp.307-321.
16 For a right-wing view, unsympathetic to Kammerer, see, for example, C. Zirkle, *Death of a Science in Russia*, Pennsylvania University Press, Philadelphia, 1949, pp.16-20. For a left-wing view, see E. W. MacBride, 'The inheritance of acquired characteristics', *Nature*, Vol. 129, 1932, pp.900-901.

17 Most of Kammerer's publications were, of course, in German. One that was not was 'Breeding experiments on the inheritance of acquired characters', *Nature*, Vol. 111, 1923, pp.637-640.

18 G. K. Noble, 'Kammerer's *Alytes*', *Nature*, Vol. 118, 1926, pp.209-210.

19 *Ibid.*

20 C. Zirkle, *op. cit.* (note 16).

21 J. S. Huxley, *Soviet Genetics and World Science: Lysenko and the Meaning of Heredity*, Chatto & Windus, London, 1949.

22 A. Koestler, *The Case of the Midwife Toad*, Random House, New York, 1971.

23 See above, page 185.

24 A. Koestler, *op. cit.* (note 22), p.121.

25 For a 'cold-war' American view of the Lysenko affair, see C. Zirkle, *Evolution, Marxian Biology, and the Social Scene*, Pennsylvania University Press, Philadelphia, 1959. For a British view from the same period, see J. Langdon-Davies, *Russia Puts the Clock Back: A Study of Soviet Science and Some British Scientists*, Gollancz, London, 1949, or J. S. Huxley, *op. cit.* (note 21). For an 'eye-witness' account by an expatriate Russian scientist, see Z. A. Medvedev, *The Rise and Fall of T. D. Lysenko*, Columbia University Press, New York & London, 1969. For a detailed analysis by an American historian, see D. Joravsky, *The Lysenko Affair*, Harvard University Press, Cambridge, Mass., 1970. For recent inter-pretations by Western Marxists, very different from earlier Western accounts, see R. Lewontin & R. Levins, 'The problem of Lysenkoism' in H. Rose & S. Rose (eds.), *The Radicalisation of Science: Ideology of/in the Natural Sciences*, Macmillan, London & Basingstoke, 1976, pp.32-64, and D. Lecourt, *Proletarian Science? The Case of Lysenko*, New Left Books, [London,] 1977.

26 It should be noted that this interpretation is given from a 'Western' point of view. Lysenko did not accept the Neo-Lamarckian label, preferring to regard himself as an exponent of 'Soviet Darwinism'. Nevertheless, he maintained that the Michurin teaching proved the inheritance of acquired characte-ristics. Moreover, the Soviet 'agrobiologist' could supposedly 'train' plants, by alterations of the conditions of their environments, to develop in new ways. See T. D. Lysenko, *Agrobiology: Essays on Problems of Genetics, Plant Breeding and Seed Growing*, Foreign Languages Publishing House, Mos-cow, 1954, pp.518-522 and *passim*.

27 T. D. Lysenko, *The Situation in Biological Science: Address delivered at the Session of the Lenin Academy of Agricultural Sciences of the U.S.S.R., July 31, 1948*, Foreign Languages Publishing House, Moscow, 1951.

28 *Ibid.*, p.96.

29 *Ibid.*, p.98.

30 Literally, the 'Springization', 'Springification' or 'Springifying' of wheat!

31 T. D. Lysenko, *op. cit.* (note 27), pp.69-70.

32 On this, see Z. A. Medvedev, *op. cit.* (note 25), p.182.

33 See pages 217-218 below.

34 See R. Lewontin & R. Levins, *op. cit.* (note 25).

35 The article by Jensen that first generated the recent controversy was 'How much can we boost IQ and scholastic achievement?', *Harvard Educational Review*, Vol. 39, 1969, pp.1-123.

36 Jensen has provided a bibliography of the controversy to 1972 in his book *Genetics and Education*, Methuen, London, 1972. Since then the controversy has been taken up with enthusiasm by philo-sophers (A. G. N. Flew, 'The Jensen uproar', *Philosophy*, Vol. 48, 1973, pp.63-69; M. Scheifer, 'The Flew-Jensen uproar', *Philosophy*, Vol. 48, 1973, pp.386-390; O. A. Ladimeji, 'Flew and the revival of Social Darwinism', *Philosophy*, Vol. 49, 1974, pp.97-101; A. G. N. Flew, 'Jensen: the uproar continues', *Philosophy*, Vol. 49, 1974, pp.310-314; T. R. Miles, 'The Jensen debate', *Philosophy*, Vol. 51, 1976, pp.216-218). Recently a Marxist writer, Stephen Rose, has thrown considerable light on the question by showing the political ramifications of the controversy, and exposing the intellectual antecedents of the disputants: 'Scientific racism and ideology: The IQ racket from Galton to Jensen', in H. Rose & S. Rose (eds.), *The Political Economy of Science: Ideology of/in the Natural Sciences*, Macmillan, London & Basingstoke, 1976, pp.112-141. An interesting selection of essays relevant to the controversy is to be found in M. F. A. Montagu (ed.), *Race and IQ*, O.U.P., New York, 1975.

37 C. Burt, 'The genetic determination of differences in intelligence: A study of monozygotic twins reared together and apart', *British Journal of Psychology*, Vol. 57, 1966, pp.137-153.

38 See, for example, the articles published in Ashley Montagu's volume (*op. cit.*, note 36).

39 For a review of the allegations, see N. Wade, 'IQ and Heredity: Suspicion of fraud beclouds classic experiment', *Science*, Vol. 194, 1976, pp.916-919. Even Jensen has admitted recently that Burt's data may be unsatisfactory, although he maintains that other independent studies confirm Burt's findings.

40 See S. Rose, *op. cit.* (note 36), pp.130-135.

41 J. Harwood, 'The race-intelligence controversy: A sociological approach; I — Professional factors', *Social Studies in Science*, Vol. 6, 1976, pp.369-394; II — 'External factors', *ibid.*, Vol. 7, 1977, pp.1-30. (Earlier studies arrived at similar conclusions. See N. Pastore, *The Nature-Nurture Controversy*, King's Crown Press, New York, 1949.)

42 Traditionally, Western scientists have claimed that their work is value-free and ideologically neutral. But this view is now being widely questioned, following critiques by Marxist analysts.

43 For a good recent review of the problem (although written by 'committed' authors) see P. R. Ehrlich and S. S. Feldmann, *The Race Bomb: Skin Colour, Prejudice and Intelligence*, Time Books, New York, 1977, Chapter 6.

44 For a review of the question, see P. B. Medawar, *The Uniqueness of the Individual*, Methuen, London, 1957, Chapter 4 ('A commentary on Lamarckism').

45 A list of some of the earlier literature which indicated experimental evidence in favour of the inheritance of acquired characteristics (mostly published in the first four decades of the twentieth century) is to be found in R. Lewontin & R. Levins, *op. cit* (note 25), pp.179-180. See also R. Glavinic, 'L'hybridation végétative comme méthode dans la selection des tomates', *Report of the XIVth International Horticultural Congress*, Netherlands, 1955, Section 1A, pp.440-445.

46 H. G. Cannon, *The Evolution of Living Things*, Manchester University Press, Manchester, 1958; *Lamarck and Modern Genetics*, Manchester University Press, Manchester, 1959.

47 The most serious are what appear to be instances of 'non-adaptive' evolutionary changes, or changes that seemingly confer absolutely no advantage in the struggle for existence. But such cases can be accounted for by the supposition that one gene or set of genes is responsible for more than one phenotypic character. Selection may be acting on one of these characters, and changes occur concomitantly in the others.

48 This is also sometimes known as 'organic selection'.

49 See J. M. Baldwin, 'A new factor in evolution', *The American Naturalist*, Vol. 30, 1896, pp.441-451 & 536-553.

50 A. Hardy, *The Living Stream: A Restatement of Evolution Theory and its Relation to the Spirit of Man*, Collins, London, 1965.

51 A convenient collection of Waddington's papers is to be found in his volume, *The Evolution of an Evolutionist*, Edinburgh University Press, Edinburgh, 1975.

52 *Ibid.*, pp.22-24. (From C. H. Waddington, 'Selection of the genetic basis for an acquired character', *Nature*, Vol. 169, 1952, p.278.)

53 C. H. Waddington, 'Canalization of development and the inheritance of acquired characteristics', *Nature*, Vol. 150, 1942, pp. 563-565.

54 See P. A. Moody, *Introduction to Evolution*, 3rd edn, Harper & Row, New York, Evanston & London, 1970, pp.434-437.

55 But it may be objected (and this objection is often made by critics of modern genetics) that this explanation merely drags in as many hypothetical genes as necessary to satisfy the requirements of the observational situation. The hypothesis does indeed seem to be uncomfortably '*ad hoc*'.

56 Some animals have limited powers for handing on 'possessions' such as nests or burrows from one generation to the next, and there is evidence that learned behaviour can also be transmitted 'socially' rather than genetically. An example of this latter is provided by the British blue-tits which seemingly learned how to peck the aluminium tops from milk bottles. This 'knowledge' did not disappear from the blue-tit tribe when the bird that first performed the exploit died!

Part 3
The consequences of Darwinism

14

The Public Reception of *The Origin of Species*

We have seen that the first public reaction to Darwin's theory was remarkable chiefly for its lack of excitement. The Linnean Society meeting of 1858 did not erupt in wild debate. But after the publication of *The Origin* matters quickly came to a head when in 1860 the new theory was debated at the Oxford meeting of the British Association for the Advancement of Science, held in the Library of the University's new Museum. The debate did not form part of the official program of the Association's meeting. However, after Charles Daubeny (1795-1867), the doyen of the Oxford science professors, had read a paper 'On the final causes of sexuality in plants, with particular reference to Mr Darwin's work *On the Origin of Species*',[1] Richard Owen, commenting on the paper, asserted that the size difference between the brain of a gorilla and that of a man was greater than that between the brain of a gorilla and the lowest primate. In the ensuing discussion, T. H. Huxley questioned this statement and promised to publish a paper on the subject, which he did a year later in the *Natural History Review*.[2] A further, and more generally known, clash occurred after the presentation of a paper by an American, J. W. Draper (1811-1882),[3] entitled 'On the intellectual development of Europe, considered with reference to the views of Mr Darwin and others that the progression of organisms is determined by law'.[4] People in Oxford were expecting something of a pitched battle to take place between the proponents and opponents of the Darwinian theory, and about seven hundred turned up to hear Draper's paper. Those who anticipated something exciting were not to be disappointed.

Oxford, needless to say, stands at the very heart of the British 'establishment'. It is in this wonderful city that so many of the lines of power and influence interconnect in the British scene. And in the 1860s it stood at the centre of Christian orthodoxy — the place where young men were trained, chiefly in the Classics, to move on to positions in country parishes, overseas missions, higher ranks of the ecclesiastical hierarchy, or to positions in the legal profession, government or the army. Everyone knew that the arguments of *The Origin* could readily be extrapolated to include man, and that the very foundations of Anglican orthodoxy, as entrenched in Oxford, were at risk — and all that this entailed for the social hierarchy of English life was transparently clear. It is not surprising, then, that although it was not strictly a public meeting, undergraduates scrambled in to catch a place, many dons were there, some with their wives, as also were members of the general public, in addition to the scientists attending the British Association meeting. Samuel Wilberforce (1805-1873), Bishop of Oxford, primed (it appears) by Owen, led the attack on behalf of the religious establishment. Huxley and Hooker were the chief spokesman for the evolutionary theory. Chambers, and Lyell were also there, but Darwin was not.

There is no completely objective account of the events during the debate. Apart from a rather sedate report in the *Athenaeum*,[5] all we have is a series of individual reminiscences.[6] However, it appears that Wilberforce spoke with his usual eloquence, using many of the arguments that appeared in his article in *The Quarterly Review* shortly afterwards.[7] Doubtless he used his wit and sarcasm to the full. According to an oft-repeated (although not properly documented) story, he concluded his speech by turning to Huxley to inquire whether it was 'through his grandfather or his grandmother that he claimed descent from a monkey'.[8]

Words such as these are thrown about now in public life in Australia almost every day, but things were different in Britain in the 1860s, and Huxley immediately realised that Wilberforce had overstepped the narrow bounds of conventional Victorian etiquette, and Huxley is said to have slapped his knee with glee and murmured: 'The Lord hath delivered him into mine hands'.[9] In his reply, Huxley is reported to have said that he was only there in the interests of science. He wished to defend Darwin's theory since it was the best explanation of the existence of species yet put forward and was much more than a crude hypothesis. He showed up Wilberforce's misunderstandings of the theory — his belief, for example, that Darwin was saying that man was directly descended from some ape (rather than that apes and men have common ancestors) — and he gave a clear exposition of Darwin's views. Then — somewhat pompously as it appears to us today — he said:

> If the question is put to me 'Would I rather have a miserable ape for a grandfather, or a man highly endowed by nature and possessed of great means and influence, and yet who employs these faculties and that great influence for the mere purpose of introducing ridicule into a grave scientific discussion', [then] I unhesitatingly affirm my preference for the ape.[10]

This bold advance on Wilberforce's position apparently led to uproar, and one lady 'employing an idiom now lost, expressed her sense of intellectual crisis by fainting'.[11] Wilberforce seems to have perceived that Huxley, reinforced by arguments from Hooker, had got the better of the argument, and he did not reply.

At this point it may be useful to interpolate some information about T. H. Huxley (1825-1895), for after 1860 he became best known as a tireless advocate of the Darwinian theory, constantly working to achieve its acceptance in Victorian Britain, in both scientific and lay circles.

Huxley started his career as a medical student, served as surgeon aboard the exploration vessel H.M.S. *Rattlesnake* in Australian waters (he married a girl he met in Sydney), and ultimately he became Professor of Paleontology and Natural History at the Government School of Mines in South Kensington, the institution that later evolved into the influential Imperial College.

Besides being an eminent naturalist, Huxley was also an amateur philosopher of some distinction. He was a skilled lecturer and organiser, and worked with extreme energy in the cause of education reform in Britain, particularly in his efforts to bring about the introduction of science teaching at both the secondary and tertiary levels, and in his lectures to members of the artisan class.[12] He was an indefatigable polemicist on behalf of the Darwinian theory, and this earned him the sobriquet of 'Darwin's bulldog'.

Following his clash with Owen at Oxford, Huxley, as promised, published his paper on the relative brain sizes of men and apes in 1861,[13] and a monograph on the subject, *Man's Place in Nature*, appeared two years later.[14] This contained a detailed discussion of the comparative anatomy of man and apes, and a refutation of Owen's claim. Huxley showed, for example, that the *range* of brain capacity in man was substantially greater than the difference between that of the average man and the average gorilla.

But, as sometimes happens in discussions of this kind, the debate between Owen and Huxley became focussed on what might seem at first to have been a somewhat trivial detail — a point which came to be regarded as a kind of *experimentum crucis* for the debate as a whole. Owen claimed that no ape's brain contains a part well known in humans: the so-called *hippocampus minor*, a lobe of the cerebral hemispheres overlapping the cerebellum. Huxley, however, brought forward ample evidence to falsify Owen's claim, and Owen later had to admit his error. This was considered a great triumph for the Darwinian party, though in fact it did not settle the whole question once and for all, and could not have been expected to do so. The debate over the *hippocampus minor* question was subsequently parodied in Charles Kingsley's *Water Babies*, where there is much talk of 'hippopotamus majors'.[15]

Yet despite Huxley's extreme enthusiasm for Darwin's theory, and his great reputation for his work as a populariser and general protagonist of the new doctrine, the view which Huxley held of the theory is open to some question. Huxley tells us that his immediate thought 'when I first made myself master of the central idea of the 'Origin', was, "How extremely stupid not to have thought of that!" '.[16] Yet a recent paper by Michael Bartholomew[17] has examined this question with some care, and has reached somewhat unexpected conclusions. Bartholomew draws attention to

Huxley's quite strong anti-evolutionist stance until the publication of *The Origin*, as exemplified by his biting attack on Chambers in a review of the tenth edition of *Vestiges*.[18] And even after 1859, Huxley seems to have made little use of the concept of natural selection or classification by genealogies according to the Darwinian method, and he seems to have found one of the most attractive features of the theory to be the fact that it could explain retrogression, and 'no change' as well as evolutionary development. In the *Athenaeum* report of the Oxford debate he is reported as having spoken of the 'short-legged sheep of America' having 'originated in the birth of an original parent of the whole stock, which had been kept up by a rigid system of artificial selection'.[19] Perhaps the feature of the Darwinian theory that most appealed to Huxley was that it accounted for phenomena in a purely *naturalistic* manner, totally eliminating any notion of final causes. This, in Huxley's view, was how science should be conducted, and what scientific theories should look like. His whole defence of Darwinism was really as much a battle on behalf of scientific naturalism as for evolutionism.

A convenient way to follow the public debate in Britain following the publication of *The Origin of Species* is by an examination of the various reviews in newspapers, magazines, and literary and scientific journals. An exhaustive study on these lines has been published by A. Ellegard, in his *Darwin and the General Reader*.[20] Drawing on Ellegard's analysis, we may prepare the table shown in Figure 26.

This analysis reveals that the first reaction to the new theory was anything but favourable. However, it should be noted that the reviews considered here formed only the *initial* response to the theory, and during the years following 1859 opinion gradually warmed towards Darwin. *The Times* newspaper, it should be noted, provided an exception to this generalisation, for after Huxley's initial enthusiastic review the paper gradually turned against the theory, and was quite antagonistic towards *The Descent of Man* when this was published in 1871. The difference in attitude between the dailies and the more serious quarterlies is also noteworthy. It may suggest that when men had time to sit down for a while and ponder the implications of the theory it appealed to them less than it did at a first quick appraisal. But this can scarcely be the whole story, for the weeklies were also less than enthusiastic towards the theory. The special case of Huxley having been invited to compose *The Times'* first review contributes to an impression that the dailies were especially sympathetic to the theory, and this somewhat distorts the picture.

Figure 26. Attitudes towards the Darwinian Theory, as Expressed in British Press in the Period Immediately Following the Publication of The Origin of Species *(after Ellegard)*

PRO	NEUTRAL	ANTI
DAILIES		
Daily Telegraph	Standard	Daily News
Echo		Globe
Manchester Guardian		Morning Advertiser
Morning Post		Record
Pall Mall Gazette		
St. James' Chronicle		
(thrice weekly)		
Times (Huxley)		
WEEKLIES		
All the Year Round	Critic	Athenaeum
Chambers' Journal	English Independent	British Medical Journal
Gardener's Chronicle	Examiner	British Standard
(Hooker)	Guardian	Church Review
John Bull	Illustrated London News	English Churchman
Leader	Inquirer	Family Herald
Nature	London Review	Freeman
Observer	Parthenon	Good Words
Reader	Patriot	Lancet
Sunday Times	Press	Leisure Hour
	Spectator	Literary Churchman
		Methodist Recorder
		News of the World
		Nonconformist
		Public Opinion
		Saturday Review
		Tablet
		Vanity Fair
		Watchman
		Weekly Review
MONTHLIES		
Cornhill	Dublin University	Annals and Magazine of
Macmillan's (Huxley)	Magazine	Natural History
Month	Fraser's Magazine	Blackwood's Magazine
	Geological Magazine	Christian Observer
	London Society	Contemporary Review
	Temple Bar	Ecclesiastic
		Eclectic Review
		Friend
		New Monthly Magazine
		Progressionist
		Recreative Science
		St. James' Magazine
		Tait's Edinburgh
		Magazine
		Tinsley's Magazine
		Zoologist

PRO	NEUTRAL	ANTI
QUARTERLIES		
National Review	*Dublin Review*	*British and Foreign*
Natural History Review	*Friend's Quarterly*	*Evangelical Review*
Theological Review	*Examiner*	*Christian Remembrancer*
Westminster Review	*Journal of Sacred*	*Edinburgh New*
(Huxley)	*Literature*	*Philosophical Journal*
	Popular Science Review	*Edinburgh Review* (Owen)
	Quarterly Journal of	*London Quarterly Review*
	Science	*Quarterly Review*
		(Wilberforce)
		North British Review
		(Jenkin)
		Rambler

As might be expected, better-educated readers (gauged by the opinions expressed in articles published in the more sophisticated newspapers and journals) came to accept the theory fairly quickly, whereas the 'gutter press' (or its Victorian equivalent) continued to revile Darwin for a long time, and it seems likely that this represented the views of uneducated opinion quite accurately. The relationship between 'level of brow' and attitudes towards Darwinism may be seen from Figure 27, based on date assembled by Ellegard.[21]

Figure 27 Attitudes Towards Darwinian Evolution and the Evolution of Man in the Period 1859 to 1871, According to Educational Standards (after Ellegard).

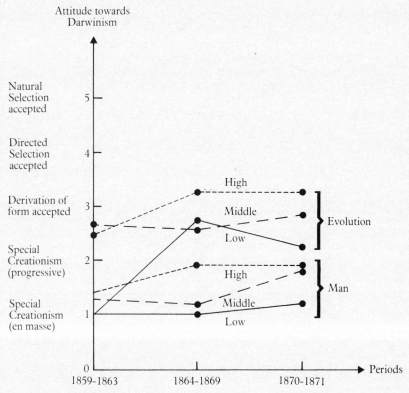

1 Here it is supposed that all kinds of living organisms were created by a single Divine act.

2 Here a series of Divine creations of organisms is supposed, each more 'advanced' than its predecessor.

3 Here some kind of evolution or development of organisms is accepted, but not necessarily by any kind of selection process.

4 Here it is supposed that evolution proceeds by some kind of selection mechanism, but the process is in some manner 'guided' by a supernatural being.

5 Here the full Darwinian scheme of evolution by natural selection is accepted.

It should be noted, however, that these 'average' opinions reveal that even among educated men and women there were few who accepted the doctrine of evolution *by natural selection* wholeheartedly. And the extent of belief in the unique creation of organisms — in the Garden of Eden, say — seems truly remarkable today. But the scientific journals, while initially hostile in many cases, moved quite quickly towards an acceptance of the new theory. Scientists could appreciate the way in which the new theory could handle biological problems successfully, whereas the 'man in the street' thought more of the implications of the theory for his own personal standing in the cosmos and for the possible undermining of established religion.

Shades of political opinion affected acceptance of Darwin's theory and some correlation may be found between degree of radicalism and the nature of the response to the theory. As *Blackwood's Magazine* put it:

> The hypothesis is clamorously rejected by the conservative minds, because it is thought to be revolutionary, and not less eagerly accepted by insurgent minds, because it is thought destructive of old doctrines.[22]

The truth of this is revealed by Figure 28, also derived from Ellegard's data.[23]

Figure 28 Attitudes Towards Darwinian Evolution and the Evolution of Man, in the Period 1859 to 1871, Among the 'Highbrow' Reading Public, According to Political Affiliations (after Ellegard).

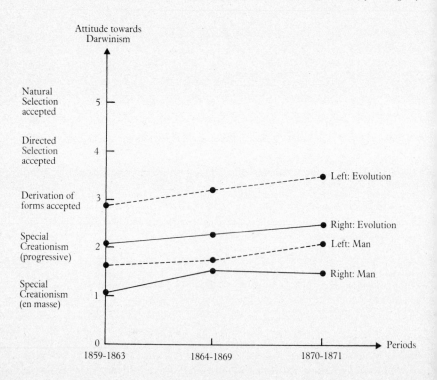

However, as will be discussed in Chapters 16 and 17, after Darwin's theory became fairly widely accepted, right-wing opinion soon took up the theory with considerable enthusiasm, particularly the idea of evolutionary progress through the mediation of the struggle for existence. And thus there arose the bleak doctrine of Social Darwinism that so disfigured social theorising in the late nineteenth century. But further discussion of this issue will not be attempted here.

Ellegard has also provided an interesting analysis of the responses of several religious groups to the new Darwinian theory, again basing his contentions on the known religious affiliations of the various journals in which the reviews that he has analysed appeared. Thus, the information in Figure 29 may be culled from Ellegard's data.[24]

Figure 29 Attitudes Towards Darwinian Evolution and the Evolution of Man, in the Period 1859 to 1871, According To Religious Affiliations (after Ellegard).

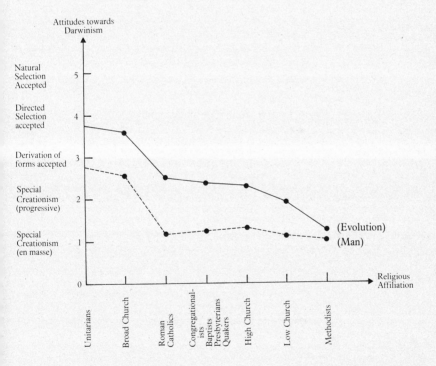

The question of the religious response to Darwinism will be discussed further in Chapter 18, and we need not pause to consider this data further at this stage, beyond noting that although opinion was prepared to countenance the doctrine of evolution as a whole, substantially less enthusiasm was shown for the idea of the evolution of man by the same naturalistic mechanism as was supposed to hold for other living organisms.

To consider further the reactions of individuals or organisations to Darwin's theory would not be profitable at this stage. The reader will note that the influence of Darwinism on various distinct aspects of thought or culture will be considered separately in the subsequent chapters of this book. But for those who seek further information on the question of the general public response to the Darwinian theory, I refer them to the publications of A. Ellegard,[25] G. Himmelfarb,[26] W. Irvine,[27] D. L. Hull,[28] G. de Beer,[29] P. Vorzimmer,[30] L. Eiseley,[31] or the various papers in T. F. Glick's volume, *The Comparative Reception of Darwinism.*[32]

NOTES CHAPTER 14

1   C. J. B. Daubeny, 'Remarks on the final causes of the sexuality of plants, with particular reference to Mr Darwin's work "On the Origin of Species by Natural Selection . . ." ', *Report of the Thirtieth Meeting of the British Association for the Advancement of Science; held at Oxford in June and July 1860*, London, 1861, pp.109-110.

2   T. H. Huxley, 'On the zoological relations of man with the lower animals', *The Natural History Review*, Vol. 1, 1861, pp.67-84.

3   Draper is still remembered today for his influential volume, *History of the Conflict between Religion and Science*, New York, 1872. This ran through eight editions between 1872 and 1877, and was subsequently reprinted many times.

4   *Op. cit.* (note 1), pp.115-116.

5   *The Athenaeum: Journal of English and Foreign Literature, Science and the Fine Arts*, No. 1707, July 14, 1860, pp.64-65.

6   Some of these are to be found in G. Himmelfarb, *Darwin and the Darwinian Revolution*, Norton, New York, 1968, pp.286-293 and 482-483.

7   [S. Wilberforce,] 'Art. VII — *On the Origin of Species, by means of Natural Selection; or the Preservation of Favoured Races in the Struggle for Life.* By Charles Darwin, M.A., F.R.S., London, 1860', *The Quarterly Review*, Vol. 108, 1860, pp.225-264.

8   Quoted in G. Himmelfarb, *op. cit.* (note 6), p.290.

9   L. Huxley, *Life and Letters of Thomas Henry Huxley*, 2 vols, Macmillan, London, 1900. Vol. 1, p.188.

10   Letter from Huxley to F. D. Dyster, 9 September, 1860, cited in G. de Beer, *Charles Darwin: Lecture on a Master Mind, Henrietta Hertz Trust of the British Academy*, O.U.P., London, 1958, p.18. According to another version, however, Huxley wrote: 'I would rather be descended from an ape than a bishop.' (R. G. Wilberforce, *Life of the Right Reverend Samuel Wilberforce, D.D. . . . with selections from his diaries and correspondence*, 3 vols, London, 1880-1882, Vol. 2, p.451.)

11   W. Irvine, *Apes, Angels & Victorians: A Joint Biography of Darwin & Huxley*, Weidenfeld & Nicolson, London, 1955, p.6.

12   Huxley gave a well-known series of lectures on evolutionary theory to working men, not long after the publication of *The Origin*. (*Professor Huxley's Lectures to Working Men: On our Knowledge of the Causes of the Phenomena of Organic Nature*, London, 1862.)

13   See note 2 above.

14   T. H. Huxley, *Evidence as to Man's Place in Nature*, London, 1863 (republished University of Michigan Press, Ann Arbor, 1959).

15   C. Kingsley, *The Water Babies* [and] *Glaucus*, London & New York, 1908, p.92: 'Nothing is to be depended on but the great hippopotamus test. If you have a hippopotamus major in your brain, you are no ape, though you had four hands, no feet, and were more apish than the apes of all aperies. But, if a hippopotamus major is discovered in one single ape's brain, nothing will save your great-great-great-great-great-great-great-great-great-great-great-greatest grandmother from having been an ape too'.

16 T. H. Huxley, 'On the reception of the 'Origin of Species'', in F. Darwin (ed.), *The Life and Letters of Charles Darwin*, 3 vols, London, 1887, Vol. 2, pp.179-204 (at p.197).

17 M. Bartholomew, 'Huxley's defence of Darwin', *Annals of Science*, Vol. 32, 1975, pp.525-535.

18 [T. H. Huxley,] '*Vestiges of the Natural History of Creation*. Tenth edition, London, 1853', *British and Foreign Medico-Chirurgical Review*, Vol. 13, 1854, pp.425-439.

19 Darwin did admit the occasional occurrence of large-scale variations, but he treated them as atypical: C. Darwin (ed. J. W. Burrow), *The Origin of Species*, Penguin, Harmondsworth, 1968, pp.89-90. However, as we have seen in our discussions of Fleeming Jenkin's critique of Darwin's theory, Darwin did not favour large-scale variations as the motor of evolutionary change.

20 A. Ellegard, *Darwin and the General Reader: The Reception of Darwin's Theory of Evolution in the British Periodical Press, 1859-1872*, University of Göteborg, Göteborg, 1958.

21 *Ibid.*, p.352.

22 *Blackwood's Magazine*, Vol. 89, 1861, p.166.

23 A. Ellegard, *op. cit.* (note 20), p.363.

24 *Ibid.*, p.367.

25 A. Ellegard, *op. cit.* (note 20).

26 G. Himmelfarb, *op. cit.* (note 6).

27 W. Irvine, *op. cit.* (note 11).

28 D. L. Hull, *Darwin and his Critics: The Reception of Darwin's Theory of Evolution by the Scientific Community*, Harvard University Press, Cambridge, Mass., 1973.

29 G. de Beer, *Charles Darwin: Evolution by Natural Selection*, Nelson, London, 1963.

30 P. Vorzimmer, *Charles Darwin: The Years of Controversy: The Origin of Species and its Critics 1859-82*, London University Press, London, 1972.

31 L. C. Eiseley, *Darwin's Century: Evolution and the Men Who Discovered it*, Gollancz, London, 1959.

32 T. F. Glick (ed.), *The Comparative Reception of Darwinism*, Texas University Press, Austin & London, 1972.

15

Herbert Spencer

In the remaining chapters of this book we shall be considering a number of areas of thought or culture where the idea of evolution in general and the work of Darwin in particular exerted their influence in a variety of interesting ways. It was this particularly wide-reaching spread of influence that was so characteristic of the Darwinian Revolution. And in no area was the impact felt more strongly than in theories of society, both descriptive and prescriptive — in the social sciences as they are called today.

The movement known as Social Darwinism was made up of people who tried — in many different or even contradictory ways — to apply the theories of Darwinian evolutionism to descriptions of the way society is constituted, or, more riskily, to say how they thought it *ought* to be structured. Our broader discussion of Social Darwinism will be given in Chapter 16, for which the present short chapter may serve as a kind of foreword.

Among the many who may be described as Social Darwinists — for the term is a very loose one — the outstanding figure was the influential English philosopher and critic, Herbert Spencer (1820-1903).[1] And because Spencer's work was to some degree quite independent of Darwin's theories, having been worked out in part well before 1859, and because in some ways Darwin drew from Spencer rather than *vice versa*, it seems reasonable to detach Spencer from our general discussion of the Social Darwinist movement and give him individual consideration.

Spencer was the son of a Derby schoolmaster. As a young man, he worked as an engineer in the construction of the London to Birmingham and Birmingham to Gloucester railways — no doubt the kind of experience that would have encouraged his later keen advocacy of free enterprise, private competition, and the virtues of the economic struggle for existence. Subsequently, Spencer gave up engineering and devoted himself to serious writing and popular journalism. In the latter part of his life, his books became sufficiently widely read to provide him with a reasonable income, so that his total effort could be devoted to writing.

Spencer was an autodidact, with enormous capacity for work and extraordinary intellectual range. But like so many other men and women of the mid-nineteenth century, he suffered a relapse during the middle years of his life, which left him a partial invalid, although it appears that his illness was chiefly psychosomatic in character. Spencer never married, but he seems to have had some emotional relationship with the eminent female novelist, George Eliot.

The scope of Spencer's work is remarkable indeed, as may be gauged from the following list of his major productions:

Social Statics, 1851
The Principles of Psychology, 1855
Education: Intellectual, Moral and Physical, 1861
First Principles, 1862
The Principles of Biology, 2 vols, 1864-1867
The Study of Sociology, 1873
Descriptive Sociology, 1873-1934 (completed posthumously)
The Principles of Sociology, 3 vols (in 8 parts), 1876-1897
The Principles of Ethics, 2 vols (in 6 parts, including *The Data of Ethics,* 1887), 1879-1893
The Man Versus the State, 1884
An Autobiography, 2 vols, 1904 (posthumous).

Also important for our study was a paper published in 1852 entitled, 'A theory of population, deduced from the general law of animal fertility',[2] which is noteworthy for having come very close to establishing the principle of natural selection.

The corpus of Spencer's philosophical works, and his philosophical system as a whole, is usually referred to as the 'Synthetic Philosophy', the general title given to some of the works listed above, which formed an overarching philosophical argument. What Spencer was trying to accomplish was the formulation of a general synthesis of all knowledge under the aegis of a single explanatory concept — the idea of *evolution.* But this scheme was not at first directly indebted to Darwin. As has been said above, Spencer had already established the broad outlines of his doctrines well before 1859. In forming the initial framework of his system, he drew on ideas derived from his lower middle-class background in industrial England; on the popular non-conformist theology of his day; on Malthus, Lamarck and Lyell; on *laissez-faire* economics;[3] and certain principles of physics such as the principle of conservation of energy.[4] Nevertheless, despite this eclecticism, running right through Spencer's work there was the single grand principle of evolution — in an all-embracing cosmic sense, not merely the specific notion of the evolution of living organisms, which was the focus of Darwin's work.

Spencer gave several definitions of what he meant by the term 'evolution', but they all said basically the same thing, that is:

Evolution is a change from an indefinite, incoherent homogeneity, to a definite, coherent heterogenity; through continuous differentiations and integrations.[5]

This statement may well appear scarcely intelligible on a first reading, and it has for long been considered as something of a joke by certain commentators. The mathematician T. P. Kirkman, for example, once rephrased Spencer's leading principle so that it became:

> Evolution is a change from nohowish, untalkaboutable, all-alikeness, to a somehowish and in-general-talkaboutable not-all-alikeness, by continuous somethingelseifications, and sticktogetherations.[6]

On reading this, one may be forgiven for imagining that Spencer was talking arrant nonsense. But this is by no means a just view of the matter, as the following examples should readily show.

By 'differentiation', Spencer meant a process in which a specialisation of functions occurs. By 'integration', he meant the process in which the various structurally differentiated parts with their several specialised functions maintain their mutual interdependence but also attain a suitable co-ordination of their functions. Moreover, in Spencer's view, there is a universal or cosmic tendency for these processes to go on all the time and throughout the universe in all its aspects. A couple of examples may help to make the operation of his principle clearer.

Consider, for example, an amoeba and a man; and let us suppose for the sake of argument that man has actually evolved from the amoeba. An amoeba might reasonably be said to lack many specialised parts, or be undifferentiated. It is a relatively *homogeneous* entity. A man, on the other hand, is *differentiated* into many specialised parts. He is very much a *heterogeneous* entity. But his various parts all 'interlock' with each other, or are correlated and co-ordinated together. In Spencer's language, they are *integrated* or *cohere*. So, according to his general principle, the gradual change from amoeba to man would be just one aspect or instance of the overall cosmic evolutionary process, with homogeneity giving way to heterogeneity, and with a concomitant increase in differentiation and integration.

As our second example, consider the 'evolutionary' development of a particular business organisation. As the business expands, it becomes more differentiated, opening more branches for example. This entails an increase in *heterogeneity*. But at the same time the firm has to set up a system of co-ordination of the separate branches, with each other and with some central office. More and more sophisticated systems of intercommunication are required to link the component parts of the system. It must become better *integrated* as the *differentiation* proceeds, otherwise the business will surely founder.

Thus, although at first Spencer's pronouncement on the general principle of evolution may seem somewhat bizarre, on closer inspection it appears as quite a plausible generalisation. It would seem, however, that Spencer's basic reason for holding to his maxim was a metaphysical belief in the *idea of progress*,[7] although he attempted to present it as a generalisation derived from fundamental laws of physics.

Having said this, however, we find on looking into the matter further that there was something rather odd about Spencer's view of the evolutionary process in society, for instead of supposing that it would carry on indefinitely, as might be expected if it were really just an aspect of the general physical laws of the universe, he believed that it would finally reach a plateau or limit, which he called a state of *'equilibration'*.[8] This condition was somewhat similar to that which is described today by engineers as 'dynamic equilibrium', although for Spencer the concept was to denote something wider than the mere mechanics of physical systems. One could refer also to the 'equilibration' of organisms *vis-à-vis* the conditions of the environment. And the laws of supply and demand in commerce could in time be expected to produce a state of economic 'equilibration'. In politics, it might be supposed that a state of balance would be achieved between the forces of reaction and reform, with a stable, harmonious and perfectly adapted state coming into being, yielding the greatest good for the greatest number. Such a view may seem utopian to the twentieth-century mind, and scarcely compatible with Spencer's more basic evolutionary premise. Nevertheless, we must note Spencer's position, recognising it as a characteristic product of nineteenth-century thought.

In 1852, in the essay, 'A theory of population, deduced from the general law of animal fertility', Spencer coined his famous phrase 'Survival of the Fittest' — the phrase that Darwin chose to adopt and add to the heading of Chapter 4 of the fifth edition of *The Origin*, and which led subsequently to the charge that the theory of evolution by natural selection was non-scientific, being tautological or unfalsifiable. Thus Spencer came very close indeed to offering a statement of the principle of natural selection. In fact, one might reasonable say that he *did* discover the principle independently of Darwin, although not quite in its general form, for he seems to have applied it principally to the development of organisms of higher intelligence.

Following Malthus, Spencer recognised the importance of population pressures on resources. This, he said, leads to a struggle for existence and the *survival of the fittest*, with the more *intelligent* organisms surviving. This, so he supposed, produces an improvement in stock and an accompanying *decrease in fertility*. So there is a self-correcting mechanism in the population, with evolution as a by-product. In man, it is population pressure that forces people to be more efficient, or become better adapted:

> From the beginning, pressure of population has been the proximate cause of progress . . . It forced men into the social state; made social organization inevitable; and has developed the social sentiments . . . It is daily pressing us into closer contact and more mutually-dependent relationships.[9]

So, quite differently from Malthus, Spencer drew a highly optimistic conclusion from the principle of population pressure. In his view, it was the very motor of progress.

Let us consider, then, how Spencer envisaged that his general evolutionary principle could be applied to society in a prescriptive sense. His fundameal maxim was that there should be no interference with the general evolutionary process and the social and economic struggle for existence. So he was unequivocally opposed to such things as state education, state regulation of housing conditions, poor laws, factory acts, state banking or postal system and tariff barriers. On the contrary, following the precepts of an arch-individualist, he advocated free trade, or, as it is sometimes known, *laissez-faire* economics. He was a member of the British Liberal Party.

Thus, in Spencer's view, the weakest members of society *ought* to go to the wall, for only in this way could one hope to see some improvement in society. Welfare programs were of illusory value. They only disuaded people from helping themselves. What was required — so Spencer supposed — was a keener prosecution of the struggle for existence, for this would enable man to become better adapted to his environmental conditions, through his own exertions and the elimination of the socially unfit. Here, Lamarckian elements in his thinking may be discerned.

Such views were stressed right through Spencer's career, as may be seen from the following quotation from the late *Man Versus the State* (1884), itself citing opinions published in *Social Statics* in 1851:

> To become fit for the social state, man has not only to lose his savageness, but he has to acquire the capacities needful for civilised life. Power of application must be developed; such modification of the intellect as shall qualify it for its new tasks must take place; and, above all, there must be gained the ability to sacrifice a small immediate gratification for a future great one. The state of transition will of course be an unhappy state. Misery inevitably results from incongruity between constitution and conditions. All these evils which afflict us, and seem to the uninitiated the obvious consequences of this or that removable cause, are unavoidable attendants on the adaptation now in progress. Humanity is being pressed against the inexorable necessities of its new position — is being moulded into harmony with them, and has to bear the resulting unhappiness as best it can. The process *must* be undergone, and the sufferings *must* be endured. No power on earth, no cunningly-devised laws of statesmen, no world-rectifying schemes of the humane, no comm unist panaceas, no reforms that men ever did broach or ever will broach, can diminish them one jot. Intensified they may be, and are; and in preventing their intensification, the philanthropic will find ample scope for exertion. But there is bound up with the change a *normal* amount of suffering, which cannot be lessened without altering the very laws of life.[10]

Thus Spencer's general view was that a struggle for existence in society was inevitable and any relaxation of it would necessarily lead to social dissolution.

This contention was prominent also in the earlier *Study of Sociology* (1873). Here it was argued that human nature would slowly adapt to circumstances, provided the struggle for existence was maintained. If this struggle were relaxed there would be a cessation of adaptive changes and the 'social dissolution' to savage life would follow. Doubtless, adaption to the new conditions would then occur, so in effect it was being argued that nothing less than the very destruction of civilisation would follow on the introduction of measures of social welfare. At first, this seems quite absurd. However, if one looks at the recent histories of some Western European countries, there may be some truth in what Spencer was saying. In any case, it should not be forgotten that he was talking about the introduction of welfare measures to countries that were ideologically committed to the virtues of competition and contest. He was not talking about their introduction into a social system that was built on the principles of co-operation, social cohesion, and mutual aid.

It has already been noted that Spencer believed the evolutionary process would, in some way that was by no means clear, lead to a condition of 'equilibration'. This seems somewhat incongruous; but there was a further curious feature about Spencer's doctrines, in that he was both a pacifist and an internationalist. He believed that the early conditions of society, with many small groups in armed conflict, would give way to large groups at peace. Militarism would disappear in favour of a unified industrial state. Egoism would supposedly give rise to altruism, for men would come to value the well-being of the social group rather than their personal interests. Spencer's thinking displayed clearly the characteristic optimism of the Victorian period; but to us it seems somewhat naive.

Spencer played a considerable role in the establishment and development of the discipline of sociology. He did not found the subject or give it its name, but his contribution in suggesting that it is useful to examine society from an evolutionary perspective — which is more than saying merely that change is occurring — was of considerable significance. He compared society to an organism, the parts of which perform different functions. His attitude to the study of society may therefore be described as that of a functionalist — an approach which has played an important role in the subsequent development of sociology.

It is worth drawing attention to a few points of comparison between Darwin and Spencer,[11] and to consider the extent to which they may be thought of as manifestations of a single unified evolutionary *Weltanschauung* or 'world view'. Spencer's idea of survival of the fittest was very similar to Darwin's principle of natural selection: but Spencer's attitude to evolution was fundamentally Lamarckian in that individual effort was of paramount importance. In his *Autobiography*, Spencer explicity informs us of his interest in and adherence to the Lamarckian doctrine,[12] and in *The Principles of Psychology* (1855) one may read the unequivocal assertion that 'a modified form of constitution produced by new habits of life, is bequeathed to future generations'.[13] This Lamarckian principle provided Spencer's chief motive power for the evolutionary development of living organisms. The survival-of-the-fittest doctrine was, by comparison, a subsidiary matter although an important feature of the theory. And later critics have tended to associate Spencer chiefly with doctrines of intra-specific struggle.

We have also noted Spencer's utilisation of ideas drawn from the physics of his day — the principle of conservation of energy. He spoke of the 'persistence of force' as a determinant of evolutionary change. But the nature of the 'force' was never spelt out in precise terms. In his *Autobiography*, Spencer informed his readers that the force was an aspect of a 'power' that transcended human knowledge and powers of conception.[14] But this was really an explicit admission of ignorance, and Spencer had clearly shifted from science to the realms of speculative metaphysics. And this, of course, gives us the core of the difference between Darwin and Spencer. Spencer's cast of mind was — as Darwin noted in his *Autobiography*[15] — essentially deductive in character, and the deductions that he made were based upon an all-embracing metaphysical postulate that was by no means of certain truth or validity, although he sought to verify or support deductions by countless instances of empirical evidence. The principle of natural selection was simply subsumed under his general evolutionary principle.

Darwin's thinking never achieved quite the scope and grandeur of Spencer's attempted universal synthesis. By contrast, no matter what modern commentators may think his method was, Darwin sought to base his theory on inductions from a vast array of 'established facts'. In a sense he really did work on 'true Baconian principles', and did so with consummate success. The general structure of his argument — with its observational evidence for artificial selection, variation, struggle for existence and all the rest — was built on a strong empirical basis. Spencer was a deductivist philosopher; Darwin was an inductivist naturalist.

This argument does not, however, refute the thesis that both Darwin and Spencer, in their different ways, were important representatives of the same evolutionary world-view that characterised thinking in the nineteenth century. Clearly they were, even though Darwin's system was conceived under the stimulus of his observations during the *Beagle* voyage. In many ways Spencer was as influential as Darwin, particularly in America. Moreover, the distinction in the public mind between Spencerism and Darwinism was not always clear. And although, as we have seen, the basic framework of Spencer's system was distinctly Lamarckian in character, he was not slow to embrace Darwin's evolutionism after 1859. Darwin, of course, was a highly respected, virtually apolitical naturalist, author of one of the most influential scientific theories of all time. Spencer, therefore, was able to absorb some respectability from the success and popularity of the Darwinian theory. Consequently, perhaps for somewhat unexpected reasons, Spencer's ideas on social and political questions were heard with considerable respect in his day, and nowhere more than in America.

The way Spencer's thinking came to make itself felt so very widely in the capitalist world in the latter part of the nineteenth century will be the subject of our next chapter.

NOTES CHAPTER 15

1   A valuable analysis of Spencer's life and work is given in J. D. Y. Peel, *Herbert Spencer: The Evolution of a Sociologist*, Heinemann, London, 1971. A useful anthology of Spencer's writings is S. Andreski (ed.), *Herbert Spencer: Structure, Function and Evolution*, Nelson, London, 1972.
2   H. Spencer, 'Art. IV − A theory of population, deduced from the general law of animal fertility', *Westminster Review*, Vol. 57, 1852, pp.468-501.
3   For a discussion of this term, see below, pp.226-227.
4   But Spencer spoke of 'persistence of force' rather than 'conservation of energy'. For a discussion of Spencer's use of models drawn from physics for the purpose of developing theories about human society, see H. I. Sharlin, 'Herbert Spencer and scientism', *Annals of Science*, Vol. 33, 1976, pp.457-480.
5   H. Spencer, *First Principles*, London, 1862, p.216. This was the wording given by Spencer in the first edition of his book. In later editions it became: 'Evolution is an integration of matter and concomitant dissipation of motion; during which the matter passes from an indefinite, incoherent homogeneity to a definite, coherent heterogeneity; and during which the retained motion undergoes a parallel transformation' (*First Principles*, 5th edn, London & Edinburgh, 1887, p.396).
6   This is cited by Spencer himself, *op. cit.* (note 5, 1887) p.565.
7   The 'idea of progress' had formed an important component of European culture at least as far back as the seventeenth-century scientific revolution, although it rose to special prominence in the nineteenth century under the aegis of the evolutionary philosophy. The literature on the 'idea of progress' is considerable. See, for example, J. B. Bury, *The Idea of Progress: An Inquiry into its Origin and Growth*, New York, 1932 (republished Dover, New York, 1955); S. Pollard, *The Idea of Progress: History and Society*, London, 1968 (republished Penguin, Harmondsworth, 1971); C. van Doren, *The Idea of Progress*, Praeger, New York, Washington & London, 1967.
8   H. Spencer, *op. cit.* (note 5), Chapter 22.
9   H. Spencer, *op. cit.* (note 2), p.501.
10   H. Spencer, *The Man Versus the State: with Four Essays on Politics and Society*, Penguin, Harmondsworth, 1969, p.140.
11   Here we may usefully draw on the arguments contained in a valuable paper by Derek Freeman: 'The evolutionary theories of Charles Darwin and Herbert Spencer', *Current Anthropology*, Vol. 15, 1974, pp.211-237.
12   H. Spencer, *An Autobiography*, 2 vols, London, 1904, Vol. 1, pp.176-177.
13   H. Spencer, *The Principles of Psychology*, London, 1855, p.526.
14   H. Spencer, *op. cit.* (note 12), Vol. 1, p.554.
15   N. Barlow (ed.), *The Autobiography of Charles Darwin*, Collins, London, 1958, pp.108-109. Darwin's remarks on Spencer were thought to be too critical by his contemporaries, and were carefully excised from the earlier editions of *The Autobiography*. But Darwin wrote: 'Herbert Spencer's conversation seemed to me very interesting, but I did not like him particularly, and I did not feel that I could have become intimate with him. I think he was extremely egotistical. After reading any of his books, I generally feel enthusiastic admiration for his transcendent talents, and have often wondered whether in the distant future he would rank with such great men as Descartes, Leibniz, etc., about whom, however, I know very little. Nevertheless, I am not conscious of having profited in my own work by Spencer's writings. His deductive manner of treating every subject is wholly opposed to my frame of mind . . . His fundamental generalizations (which have been compared in importance by some persons with Newton's laws!) − which I daresay may be very valuable under a philosophical point of view, are of such a nature that they do not seem to me to be of any strictly scientific use. They partake more of the nature of definitions than of laws of nature. They do not aid one in predicting what will happen in any particular case. Anyhow they have not been of any use to me'.

16

Social Darwinism

In the previous chapter it was stated that the term 'Social Darwinism' referred to attempts to utilise the evolutionary theory of Darwin to give descriptions of society or prescriptions for its best constitution. It is to this second aspect, however, that the term is most usually applied, so that the general connotation of Social Darwinism is of a loose amalgam of doctrines such as conservatism, militarism, racism, rejection of social welfare programs, eugenics, *laissez-faire* economics and unfettered capitalism.

This is a pretty disparate collection of often mutually antagonistic views – and their diversity is one of the reasons why it is somewhat difficult to talk about Social Darwinism succinctly without introducing unjustifiable distortions into the discussion. Broadly speaking, however, the arguments of the Social Darwinists can be stated in a few sentences.

Darwin's theory is, for Social Darwinists, to be accepted. There is a struggle for existence among animals and plants and this results in evolutionary change. But this 'change' is not to be interpreted in a neutral sense. It entails evolutionary 'development', which may be regarded as 'progressive'. Thus a value judgement immediately intrudes. The term 'progress' has a pleasant ring to it. It sounds as if it is a *good* thing for progress to take place. Therefore, evolutionary change should be cultivated, encouraged, or otherwise nurtured. And this, so the Social Darwinists believed, could be achieved by the more intense prosecution of the struggle for existence.

Darwin and Wallace said that evolutionary change, according to the mechanism they envisaged, gave rise to a 'better' adaptation of organisms to their environment. They also agreed that the evolutionary process produced a constantly increasing 'complexification' of organisms. But they wholly rejected the idea that the evolutionary 'progress' of organisms had any kind of moral dimension. To say that the world of Tertiary organisms, for example, was in way morally or socially 'better' than that of Primary or Secondary times, or that the change from one to the other involved any kind of moral progress, would have seemed quite grotesque.[1] The use of the word progress was permissible, but the term referred to 'goodness' in a functional, rather than an ethical, moral, or social sense.

Social Darwinists, on the other hand, placed no such limitations on their thinking. Drawing on Darwin, they believed the struggle for existence in animals and plants produced evolutionary progress in the structural or physical sense. By analogy, then, the struggle for existence among humans might be expected to yield social progress. And this was deemed to be a good thing *per se*, not merely a morally neutral process leading to a complexification of society, with better adaptation of people to the circumstances of their environment — assuming (for the sake of argument) that 'struggle' among human communities does produce such evolutionary adaptive results.[2] Herbert Spencer was one of the people whose work might be considered illustrative of such an approach, for as we have seen he believed that population pressure served as a stimulus to mental and intellectual development. In fact, what is customarily referred to as Social Darwinism might in many cases better be described as Social Spencerism.

Social Darwinism received some of its widest support in the United States, and it is worth considering why this was so. One of the most important concepts that motivated the writing of the new Constitution in America after the War of Independence was the notion of the inalienable right of the individual to personal freedom, and in particular to freedom from interference by government. Indeed, the major function of government was thought to be the preservation of individual freedoms. This was perhaps the main strand that led to the ready acceptance of Social Darwinism in America.

A second strand, not unrelated to the first, derived from the ideas of the classical political economists writing in England and France in the late eighteenth century. These writers believed that certain 'natural laws' governed economic processes, and that one interfered with these laws at one's peril.[3] So, it was argued, legislation should be framed to allow full freedom to the operation of the 'natural laws' of economics. According to Adam Smith (1723-1790), for example, one of these laws was that the individual naturally seeks his own economic interest, and this, Smith argued, naturally gives rise to the general economic interest of the whole community.[4] So, with characteristic eighteenth-century optimism, Smith supposed that the system of natural liberty in economic affairs would be conducive to the general good.

We thus have the general doctrine of *laissez-faire*[5] economics, which advocated complete freedom from interference by governments in economic matters and was very widely accepted by American writers in the nineteenth century — although, somewhat inconsistently, tariff barriers were believed necessary to protect the new American industries from competition with established British industries. It will cause the reader no surprise, therefore, to learn that the writings of Spencer and Darwin were acclaimed with such enthusiasm in the New World.

The leading Social Darwinist among American academic circles was

William Graham Sumner (1840-1910), Professor of Political Economy and Social Science at Yale. Under Sumner's influence, this university became a kind of pulpit for Social Darwinism. The general line of argument advocated was similar to that outlined above, although there were some points of difference, and Sumner's ideas were derived chiefly from Herbert Spencer, rather than directly from Darwin himself. It should be noted also that there were some important differences between the nineteenth-century Social Darwinist views of *laissez faire* and the views of the eighteenth-century physiocrats. The former advocated freedom from government legislation because this would permit economic development and dynamic *progress*. The eighteenth-century view, on the other hand, was that it was ill-advised to interfere with the beautifully balanced and harmonised economy of nature. They did not suppose that leaving things alone would of itself produce desirable *change*.

Sumner distinguished between the 'competition of life' and the 'struggle for existence'.[6] The latter involved the struggle with nature to yield means of subsistence; the former referred to the competition between men for the available resources, the competition arising between groups of various sizes such as families, tribes and states. The capitalist system, which Sumner viewed with such favour, might be thought of as one that allowed the free play of the 'competition of life'. Thus he could maintain that:

> Millionaires are a product of natural selection, acting on the whole body of men to pick out those who can meet the requirement of certain work to be done. . . . They get high wages and live in luxury, but the bargain is a good one for society. There is the intensest competition for their place and occupation. This assures us that all who are competent for this function will be employed in it, so that the cost of it will be reduced to the lowest terms; . . .[7]

Obviously, we have here the unqualified assertion that competition and struggles have beneficial effects, or are positively 'good'. The comparison with the process of natural selection given in this passage is also noteworthy.

Sumner believed that the rise of the capitalist system had marked a great step forward in history. The accumulation of capital enabled labour to become more productive. Moreover, it was highly desirable that wealth be inherited, since by this means a man might preserve in his children the favourable characteristics that had enabled him to enrich the community. Thus, for Sumner, the social analogue of the biological inheritance of acquired characteristics was the passing on of acquired capital from one generation to the next. It will be noted here that he was conflating Lamarckism and Darwinism, and, although there was certainly some justification for this in Darwin's own writings, it would seem that the advocacy of such *quasi*-Lamarckian doctrines on Sumner's part sprang chiefly from the fact that he was preaching the gospel of Social Darwinism on the basis of ideas initially derived from Spencer.[8]

It would not perhaps be fair to suggest that Sumner positively revelled in the notion of economic and social struggle for its own sake. Rather, he was inclined to think that the importance of struggle lay in the fact that it gave rise to 'societal organization'.[9] Above all, Sumner's message was that government interference in social questions could do nothing but harm. He referred to socialists as 'social meddlers' and objected that their social planning was not merely a waste of time, but was positively harmful: 'It is the greatest folly of which a man can be capable, to sit down with a slate and pencil to plan out a new social world'.[10] Competition, Sumner believed, was a law of nature. He gloried in the achievements of the capitalist system, and claimed that socialist schemes were the greatest danger to society:

> We can take the rewards from those who have done better and give them to those who have done worse. We shall thus lessen the inequalities. We shall [thereby] favour the survival of the unfittest, and we shall accomplish this by destroying liberty. Let it be understood that we cannot go outside this alternative: liberty, inequality, survival of the fittest; not liberty, equality, survival of the unfittest. The former carries society forward and favours all its best members; the latter carries society downwards and favours all its worst members.[11]

But in many ways, Sumner's thinking was profoundly pessimistic. Unlike Spencer, he did not look forward hopefully to a future state of 'equilibration'. On the contrary, he was concerned that there would be a great conflict between the proletariat and the capitalistic middle-class or bourgeoisie. He was immensely distrustful of politicians, and while it seemed to him that mankind in some degree benefited from war, unlike some of his contemporaries he was not an uninhibited war-monger. He believed that 'what is wanted is a peaceful and rational solution of problems and situations'.[12] Fundamentally, Sumner was something of a puritan. He believed that the only way to social progress lay through sobriety, industriousness, prudence and wisdom. If men would cultivate these qualities, then perhaps poverty might be eliminated.

Whereas Sumner represents the best-known 'academic' position on Social Darwinism, the classic statement by a successful industrialist is presented in the writings of the business tycoon, Andrew Carnegie (1835-1919), perhaps chiefly remembered today for his considerable acts of philanthropy, and the author of a volume engagingly called *The Gospel of Wealth*.[13] Carnegie held the view that individualism, private property, the 'law' of accumulation of wealth and the 'law' of competition, were the 'highest result of human experience, the soil in which society, so far, has produced the best fruit'. In Carnegie's view:

> The price which society pays for the law of competition, like the price it pays for cheap comforts and luxuries, is also great; but the advantages of this law are also greater still than its cost — for it is to this law that we owe our wonderful material development, which brings improved conditions in its train. But, whether the law

be benign or not, we must say of it, as we say of the change in the conditions of men to which we have referred: it is here; we cannot evade it; no substitutes for it have been found; and while the law may be sometimes hard for the individual, it is best for the race, because it ensures the survival of the fittest in every department. We accept and welcome, therefore, as conditions to which we must accommodate ourselves, great inequality of environment; the concentration of business, industrial and commercial, in the hands of a few; and the law of competition between these, as being not only beneficial, but essential to the future progress of the race.[14]

Carnegie maintained, therefore, that the best way to benefit the community was a social system that allowed the accumulation of large quantities of money in private hands, which money might be returned to the community in the form of generous benefactions for purposes chosen by the donors. This would supposedly yield much more effective results than could be achieved by allowing money to be frittered away in small quantities, either by small acts of individual charity, or through government taxation schemes.[15]

Other businessmen liked to see themselves as the successful survivors in the struggle for existence, and drew unsophisticated analogies between the business community and the world of plants and animals. J. D. Rockefeller (1839-1937), for example, maintained that:

The growth of a large business is merely a survival of the fittest . . . The American Beauty rose can be produced in the splendor and fragrance which bring cheer to its beholder only by sacrificing the early buds which grow up around it. This is not an evil tendency in business. It is merely the working-out of a law of nature and a law of God.[16]

Hofstadter has referred to other businessmen of the period who thought in similar terms.[17] But since Hofstadter's interpretation was put forward, doubt has been cast on the idea that the majority of American businessmen were consciously Social Darwinists.[18] Rather, they attributed such success as they had to their industry and virtue, rather than their achievement in trampling on their less successful competitors.[19] After all, most of them saw themselves as Christians, adhering to the rules of 'love thy neighbour' and 'do as you would be done by'. So, even though they sought to achieve the impossible by serving God and Mammon simultaneously, they found no difficulty in accommodating Christianity to the Darwinian ideas of struggle for existence and survival of the fittest, and by no means all of them consciously thought of themselves as being in a state of economic warfare with their fellow manufacturers.

Turning now from economic matters, it does not require much stretching of the imagination to appreciate that the arguments of Social Darwinism might readily be extrapolated to the conclusion that the evolutionary progress of mankind may be furthered by inter-racial or international struggles. In other words, the theory of evolution could be and was used in justifications of war and struggles for racial supremacy. Perhaps the best-known writer in this vein was the German historian, Heinrich von Treitschke (1834-1896). Consider, for example, the following quotation from his *Politics*:

> Brave peoples alone have an existence, an evolution or a future; the weak and cowardly perish, and perish justly. The grandeur of history lies in the perpetual conflict of nations, and it is simply foolish to desire the suppression of their rivalry.[20]

Von Treitschke spoke with enthusiasm of 'the moral majesty of war' and 'the sublimity and grandeur of war', and he held quite unabashedly to the unappealing ethical doctrine that might is right: 'Between civilized nations . . . war is the form of litigation by which States make their claims valid'.[21] He believed that war should be conducted in a spirit of chivalry, and that it should be 'conventionalized' or regulated by acts of international law. Nevertheless, he was, without qualification, an exponent of the virtues of war – a warmonger.

It would be totally unrealistic to claim that arguments such as those of von Treitschke derived solely from Darwinism. They show strong evidence of the influence of the theories of Hegel, of the Prussian or Teutonic militaristic traditions, and the idea of the virtues of individual *Völker* that is to be found in the work of the eighteenth-century historian-philosopher, J. G. von Herder (1744-1803).[22] On the other hand, it would seem that von Treitschke was drawing also on ideas that had been given a degree of intellectual respectability (because of their seeming scientificity) through the success of the Darwinian theory.

It is not difficult to perceive parallels between the writings of von Treitschke and the later fulminations of Adolf Hitler (1889-1945). Von Treitschke objected to the international character of Judaism, for Jews, instead of belonging tidily to a single geographically unified *Volk*, were, so to speak, of dual nationality, owing allegiance both to their nation of domicile and to Jewry as a whole.[23] Hitler, in his infamous *Mein Kampf,*[24] whipped up an infinitely more diabolical creed, drawing facile analogies from the world of animals in his diatribes against the Jews. Each animal, he said, mates only with animals of its own species. Then, using the erroneous theory of blending inheritance, and the ideas of struggle for existence and survival of the fittest, he was able to give a *quasi*-scientific argument for the need for racial purity, the fundamental philosophical underpinning of the Nazi movement:

> Any crossing of two beings not at exactly the same level produces a medium between the level of the two parents. This means: the offspring will probably stand higher than the racially lower parent, but not as high as the higher one. Consequently, it will succumb in the struggle against the higher level. Such mating is contrary to the will of Nature for a higher breeding of all life. The precondition for this does not lie in associating superior and inferior, but in the total victory of the former. The stronger must dominate and not blend with the weaker, thus sacrificing his own greatness . . .

> In the struggle for daily bread all those who are weak and sickly or less determined succumb, while the struggle of the males for the female grants the right and opportunity to propagate only to the healthiest. And struggle is always a means for improving a species' health and power of resistance and, therefore, a cause of its higher development . . .
>
> No more than Nature desires the mating of weaker with stronger individuals, even less does she desire the blending of a higher with a lower race, since, if she did, her whole work of higher breeding over perhaps hundreds of thousands of years, might be ruined with one blow.[25]

On the basis of such pseudo-biological arguments, Hitler could call for the preservation of the purity of the so-called 'Aryan' race,[26] and ultimately for the attempted extermination of all Jews. At the very best, of course, such an argument would only be persuasive if it could be shown that the 'Aryans' were in some sense 'higher', 'superior', or 'fitter' than the other races, while Jews were 'lower', 'inferior', or less 'fit'. And it goes without saying that Hitler was never able to produce a tittle of evidence to show that this was so. Indeed, the notion of an 'Aryan' race as a distinct anthropological entity was largely a figment of imagination. Nevertheless, we can see in this abhorrent Hitlerian doctrine a kind of Darwinism carried to a madly illogical conclusion — although as far as I am aware Hitler never stated *explicitly* that he was drawing on Darwin's theory of evolution by natural selection.

Darwin, we may suppose, would have utterly repudiated the racism of Hitler, yet even Darwin occasionally put forth a remark that gives some indication of racist tendencies, as for example when he wrote:

> The more civilized so-called Caucasian races have beaten the Turkish hollow in the struggle for existence. Looking to the world at no very distant date, what an endless number of the lower races will have been eliminated by the higher civilized races throughout the world.[27]

Here he does not seem to shrink from the prospect of a continual struggle for existence at an inter-racial, or perhaps an international level. It is not, therefore, altogether surprising — if the gentle Darwin himself gave some hint of racist thinking — that the evolutionism of the biological theory of natural selection became distorted to yield a significant component of the ugly philosophy of the Nazi movement, and that its contagion was only finally suppressed by the holocaust of the Second World War, surviving now in some corners of the world such as South Africa, and often present to a limited degree in nations such as Britain and America, but no longer forming the basis of a major political philosophy, at least not in Europe.

The high-water mark of Spencerian Social Darwinism was reached in America in 1882 when Spencer himself paid a visit to that country, giving an extensive lecture tour. But by then the pendulum had already begun to show some signs of swinging in the opposite direction, with a number of writers beginning to question the wisdom of permitting utterly unfettered competition within the framework of the capitalist economy. Leading the reaction against Spencerian Social Darwinism was Lester Frank Ward (1841-1913), initially a government geologist, but later turning his attention to sociology, of which he eventually became a professor at Brown University.[28]

Ward[29] underlined the tremendous waste of resources inherent in a competitive industrial society. Moreover, he argued, free enterprise does not necessarily lead to 'efficiency', keeping down prices, for example. A multitude of small factories, all producing the same articles, may be highly inefficient. On the other hand, if one company really succeeds in the economic struggle for existence, swallowing all its competitors, a monopolistic situation will result, in which there is no competition, and consequently no stimulus to efficiency.[30] Ward argued that man's greatest achievements often occurred without significant competition. (The artistic achievements of the monks of the Middle Ages provide us with a convenient example.) And, if it is really necessary to force analogies with the world of animals and plants, the critic of Spencerism might well ask why it is that domestic organisms often do best when competition is minimised. Why, if competition is such an excellent thing, does the gardener weed his garden?

Ward also emphasised some important differences between men and animals, pointing out that man is possessed of intellect, though this was, of course, supposedly acquired through the Darwinian process of evolution by natural selection. Consequently, because man had the power of intellect, ideas of struggle for existence were no longer strictly applicable to man, a social and rational animal. Ward maintained that Malthus, somewhat paradoxically, was quite mistaken in applying his doctrine to man – the very case where the theory of struggle was inapplicable. For man often shows himself willing to protect the weak.

More importantly, Ward rejected the notion that poverty is a proof of indolence and vice. Poverty could equally be attributed to the surrounding social circumstances. Ward did not consider himself a socialist, but he saw fit to point out that some state-run enterprises might be just as efficient or successful as private enterprises. The trans-Atlantic cable and the Belgian State Railways were cited as examples.[31]

From what has been said above, it might appear that a man such as Ward was no Social Darwinist at all, and certainly, in his trenchant critique of the doctrine of *laissez-faire*, he was at odds with the 'classical' Social Darwinists such as Spencer or Sumner. In fact, however, there was much in Ward that paralleled Spencer's effort to construct a synthetic philosophy based on the single principle of cosmic evolution. As did Spencer, Ward sought to establish a unified evolutionary system, but one that revealed a sharp distinction between plants and animals on the one hand and man on the other – man's possession of intellect marking the crucial line of demarcation. Intellect enabled man to 'meliorate' the grip of the struggle for existence. By exercising choice and will, man might alter the circumstances of the environment to better the conditions of society. In this, Ward was basically propounding a *quasi*-Lamarckian thesis — but a warrant for this may be found in the writings of both Darwin and Spencer.

Ward took his stand on the side of nurture in the growing controversy of nature *versus* nurture. He rejected the schemes of the Neo-Darwinian eugenicists to reform the world by the breeding of selected humans. 'The only way', he wrote, 'in which effort can be profitably expended is upon the environment. This is plastic. It can be indefinitely modified or completely transformed'.[32] Accordingly, in his *Applied Sociology*, Ward undertook a detailed study of the conditions of the environment as they affected human societies, considering successively the physical, ethnological, religious, local, economic, social and educational aspects of the environment, suggesting how they might be variously ameliorated for the purposes of social improvement.

Ward was a Social Darwinist seeking to provide a framework for the betterment of society through evolution based on environmental factors[33] — the Lamarckian segment of the Darwinian theory. Ward's ideas coincided with the rising aspirations of the socialist movement (to be considered in the next chapter) although he did not specifically regard himself as a socialist. But Ward did not formulate a political program or work through a political party. He was attempting to achieve an intellectual analysis of the social problems of mankind in the light of an evolutionary theory, and he sought to offer his suggestions for reform. His purpose was chiefly analytical rather than political, and this is why I have chosen to discuss him here as a representative of the intellectual/academic reaction against the *laissez-faire* version of Social Darwinism, rather than in our next chapter where he might be treated as a political philosopher or politician. But the border-line between philosophy, sociology and politics is extremely hazy at this point, and it would not be unreasonable to regard Ward equally as some kind of political theorist, as a social philosopher, or as a sociologist.

Ward provides us with an excellent example of what B. J. Loewenberg has referred to as 'reform' or 'liberal' Social Darwinism,[34] repudiating the 'struggle' doctrines of the *laissez-faire* school in favour of emphasis on social improvement through attention to the conditions of the social environment. Other writers who may be seen as representatives of this stance were men like E. A. Ross,[35] William James[36] and various representatives of the British Fabian movement such as George Bernard Shaw or H. G. Wells. It will not, however, be profitable to treat each of these in turn — although the Fabian socialists will be given some consideration in the next chapter on Darwinism and literature. Ward provides us with sufficient exemplification of the views of the 'reform' Social Darwinists. Let us, therefore, as we happen to be writing from an antipodean position, switch somewhat abruptly to describe some of the ways in which the ideas characteristic of the Social Darwinist movement manifested themselves in Australia in the nineteenth century, for it is quite remarkable how closely they paralleled developments in America.[37]

As in America, so in Australia: the period from about 1860 to about 1885 saw the most frequent advocacy of Spencerian evolutionary ideas. But the succeeding period of economic depression of the late nineteenth century appreciably dampened the enthusiasm of exponents of extreme *laissez-faire* economics, and as in America criticisms of such views began to develop and make themselves felt in the 1880s.

An obvious instance of the appearance of Spencerian ideas on the Australian academic scene was provided by the writings and lectures of Edward Hearn (1826-1888), the foundation Professor of History and Political Economy at the University of Melbourne. In his *Plutology*, published in 1864, the economic society was compared to an organism in strongly Spencerian terms:

> The homogeneous structure gradually becomes heterogeneous; and the unifor-
> mity of function gives way to variety. The division of employments is established
> between the several parts of the organism. Their separate existence is merged in
> the larger collective life; and they become component parts of an organized
> whole.[38]

Then, following Spencer, Hearn confidently arrived at the conclusion that *laissez-faire* economics provided the optimum conditions for social growth. It is noteworthy that a number of politicians, such as Alfred Deakin and H. B. Higgins, apparently acquired their faith in the virtues of free trade from Hearn's teaching. Spencer's ideas were also apparently taught at the University of Sydney, although less actively than in Melbourne.

Just as American businessmen such as Carnegie and Rockefeller found themselves attracted to Social Darwinism and tried to rationalise their activities by claiming that they were of general benefit to the development of the community, so in Australia we find businessmen − although of lesser wealth and fame − arguing along similar lines. H. K. Rusden (1826-1910) and H. G. Turner (1831-1920), for example, advocated *laissez-faire* ideas on the basis of Spencer's teachings and grounded their arguments on evolutionary principles. Rusden displaying as well a liking for somewhat Malthusian ideas, maintained that:

> The positive checks to population are the only other means which are not fatally
> invidious of determining who should give place to the others in the struggle for
> existence. Some must be pressed out or down; and who should they be, if not the
> criminal, the lunatic, the stupid, the weak, the diseased, and the incompetent? The
> survival of the fittest is best.[39]

Many other quotations of a similar character might be given from politicians, businessmen, academics and journalists.[40]

But the situation began to look rather different as the economic depression deepened towards the end of the century. And, just as in America, we find in Australia a questioning of the application of the law of the jungle − the survival of the fittest — to economic affairs; yet at the same time evolutionary concepts were used as a means of comprehending society and as a basis for action directed towards its improvement.

George Lacy (1844-?), for example, in his *Liberty and Law* (1888),[41] maintained that systems of government legislation were themselves the product of evolutionary processes, and therefore had just as much or as little right to be called 'natural' as had conditions of unfettered economic competition. In the same year, an article in *The Bulletin*[42] drew attention to the tremendous waste and loss to humanity that occurs during the process of uninhibited competition. The journal argued for tariff protection and immigration restrictions — particularly against the Chinese — as a means of nurturing Australian enterprises.[43] Thus, although critical of *laissez-faire* principles, the article was certainly not socialistic or collectivist in outlook and displayed distinct elements of racist thinking. Its purpose was to secure protection of the interests of local manufacturers and entrepreneurs. Nevertheless, arguments similar to those of Ward were being applied.

In the early years of the twentieth century, we again find authors attempting to argue for particular social theories in biological-evolutionary terms. The future Prime Minister, W. M. Hughes (1864-1952), for example, in an address to the Australian and New Zealand Association for the Advancement of Science in 1907, denied the *laissez-faire* conclusions of Social Darwinism, yet employed evolutionary theory to justify state intervention in economic affairs. Society might be thought of as a developing organism that required extensive government attention, regulation and maintenance; in Hughes's words:

> Competition, perhaps, is the primary law of life, but co-operation is certainly that of society. Amongst primitive communities the State generally protects the individual but slightly. With civilization the restraint of the individual for the benefit of the community becomes more marked. Life and property are protected from the operations of the strong and unscrupulous. The weaker individuals by co-operation prevent the stronger from exercising their strength against the rest of the community.[44]

The biological metaphor was used despite the repudiation of unbridled *laissez-faire* doctrines.

By such arguments, economic collectivists (the antithesis of the free-trade individualists) sought to use the still powerful evolutionary thesis in support of their views. The doctrine of 'mutual aid' (to be discussed further in our next chapter) was employed here in support of government economic action.

These few examples should be sufficient to give weight to the claim that the discussions over the application of Darwinism and evolutionary theory that excited such interest in the nineteenth century in Europe and America had almost exact parallels in the antipodes. And it should be apparent that we are dealing here with something quite central to the whole development of economic and political philosophy in the Western world in the nineteenth and twentieth centuries. I will not, however, pause here to appraise these attempted uses of a biological theory for 'extra-biological' purposes. This we shall attempt in the concluding section of our next chapter on Darwinism and politics — a topic that interlocks with the problem of Social Darwinism at many points, and from which it can only be separated at the risk of some distortion of the history of ideas. But such a separation is useful, I suggest, if clarity of exposition is a leading consideration. Accordingly, I choose to cut off the discussion of Social Darwinism at this point and turn to the somewhat broader question of the influence of Darwinism on politics and political theory.

NOTES CHAPTER 16

1   T. H. Huxley pointed out that morality was often concerned with *combating* the struggle for existence and the survival of the fittest: *Evolutionary Ethics and other Essays*, London, 1894, p.83.
2   As we are now living under the shadow of the hydrogen bomb, this may well be questioned.
3   This followed from the seventeenth- and eighteenth-century confusion between laws of nature and civil laws.
4   See below, p.226.
5   Literally 'Allow to do'. The full maxim is: '*Laissez faire, laissez passer*'. It is usually attributed to the French physiocrat, J.-C.-M. Vincent de Gournay, though it has also been ascribed to an earlier writer, the Marquis d'Argenson.
6   A. G. Keller & M. R. Davie (eds), *Essays of William Graham Sumner*, P. H. Macmillan Memorial Publishing Fund, New Haven & London, 1934, p.142.
7   S. Persons (ed.), *Social Darwinism: Selected Essays of William Graham Sumner*, Prentice-Hall, Englewood Cliffs, 1963, p.157.
8   Sumner's route to Darwin, via Spencer, is described by Richard Hofstadter in his well-known volume, *Social Darwinism in American Thought*, Beacon Press, Boston, 1955, p.55 (1st edn, 1944).
9   W. G. Sumner, *Folkways: A Study of the Sociological Importance of Usages, Manners, Customs [,] Mores, and Morals*, Ginn, Boston, 1940, p.16 (1st edn, 1906).
10 W. G. Sumner, 'The absurd effort to make the world over', *Forum*, Vol. 17, 1894, pp. 92-102 (at p.102).
11 S. Persons (ed.), *op. cit.* (note 7), pp.76-77.
12 *Ibid.*, p.53.
13 A. Carnegie, *The Gospel of Wealth*, London, 1890 & New York, 1900.
14 E. E. Kirkland (ed.), *The Gospel of Wealth: And Other Timely Essays by Andrew Carnegie*, Belknap, Cambridge, Mass., 1962, pp.16-17. Very similar arguments were put forward in Britain at about the same time by the conservative apologist, W. H. Mallock, in his volume, *Aristocracy & Evolution: A Study of the Rights, the Origin, and the Social Functions of the Wealthier Classes*, London, 1898.
15 Such an argument is not entirely without substance. But it ignores the fact that the *private* benefactor may choose to spend his money in the form of frivolous or socially undesirable benefactions.
16 Cited in R. Hofstadter, *op. cit.* (note 8), p.45. (The original source of this quotation has not been authenticated entirely satisfactorily.)
17 *Ibid.*, pp.44-45.
18 See I. G. Wylie, 'Social Darwinism and the businessman', *Proceedings of the American Philosophical Society*, Vol. 103, 1959, pp.629-635.
19 See C. E. Russett, *Darwin in America: The Intellectual Response 1865-1912*, Freeman, San Francisco, 1976, p.94.
20 H. von Treitschke, *Politics . . .* translated from the German by Blanche Dugdale & Torben de Bille with an Introduction by the Rt. Hon. Arthur James Balfour, 2 vols, Constable, London, 1916, Vol. 1, p.21.
21 *Ibid.*, pp.65-66.
22 For a discussion of Herder's social and political theories, see F. M. Barnard, *Herder's Social and Political Thought: from Enlightenment to Nationalism*, Clarendon Press, Oxford, 1965.

23   *Selections from Treitschke's Lectures on Politics* translated by Adam L. Gowans, Gowans & Gray, London, 1914, p.60.

24   A. Hitler, *Mein Kampf* with an Introduction by D. C. Watt, Translated by Ralph Manheim, Hutchinson, London, 1969. (Hitler's book was first published in two volumes in 1925 and 1926.)

25   *Ibid.*, pp.258-260.

26   See below, page 300. For an extended discussion, see L. Poliakov, *The Aryan Myth: A History of Racist and Nationalist Ideas in Europe*, Chatto & Heinemann, London, 1974.

27   C. Darwin, Letter to W. Graham, 3 July, 1881, in F. Darwin (ed.), *The Life and Letters of Charles Darwin, including an Autobiographical Chapter*, 3 vols, John Murray, London, 1887, Vol. 1, p.316. For a discussion of Darwin's Social Darwinist proclivities, see J. C. Greene, 'Darwin as a social evolutionist', *Journal of the History of Biology*, Vol. 10, 1977, pp.1-27.

28   On Ward, see particularly S. Chugerman, *Lester F. Ward, The American Aristotle: A Summary and Interpretation of his Sociology*, Durham (N.C.), 1939 (republished Octagon Books, New York, 1965).

29   L. F. Ward, *The Psychic Factors of Civilization*, 2nd edn, Boston, 1901 (1st edn, 1892), Chapter 33.

30   There is some analogy to be drawn here with plants and animals. Once an organism has successfully occupied an 'ecological niche' it is very difficult for other types to evolve to occupy that niche. On the other hand, a highly specialised adaptation to a niche may be followed by extinction if the environmental circumstances change for some reason.

31   L. F. Ward, *Glimpses of the Cosmos*, 6 vols, Putman, New York & London, 1913-1918, Vol. 2, pp.336-348.

32   L. F. Ward, *Applied Sociology: A Treatise on the Conscious Improvement of Society by Society*, Ginn & Co., Boston, 1906, p.128.

33   At one part of his career, however, he was influenced by the 'conflict' school of sociologists headed by Ludwig Gumplowicz and Gustav Ratzenhofer. (See R. Hofstadter, *op. cit.* [note 8], pp.77-78.)

34   B. J. Loewenberg, *Source Problems in World Civilization: Darwinism Reaction or Reform?*, Holt, Reinhart & Winston, New York, 1957. (It should be noted that not all scholars accept Loewenberg's classification of Social Darwinism into 'reaction' and 'reform' categories. Some prefer to apply the term Social Darwinism only to those who believe that social struggle is the chief motor of social progress.)

35   See, for example, E. A. Ross, *Social Control: A Survey of the Foundations of Order*, Macmillan, New York, 1901; *Social Psychology: An Outline and Source book*, Macmillan, New York, 1909; *Sin and Society: An Analysis of Latter-day Iniquity*, Houghton, Mifflin & Co., Boston & New York, 1907.

36   See W. James, *The Will to Believe, and Other Essays in Popular Philosophy*, New York, 1897.

37   For discussions of Social Darwinism in Australia, see P. D. Marchant, 'Social Darwinism', *The Australian Journal of Politics and History*, Vol. 3, 1957, pp.46-59; P. D. Marchant, 'Darwin and social theory', *The Australian Journal of Politics and History*, Vol. 5, 1959, pp.213-217; A. Mozley, 'Evolution and the climate of opinion in Australia, 1840-1876', *Victorian Studies*, Vol. 10, 1967, pp.411-430; C. D. Goodwin, 'Evolution theory in Australian social thought', *Journal of the History of Ideas*, Vol. 25, 1964, pp.393-416.

38   W. E. Hearn, *Plutology: or the Theory of the Efforts to Satisfy Human Wants*, Melbourne, 1864, p.383.

39   H. K. Rusden, 'Labour and capital', *Melbourne Review*, Vol. 1, 1876, pp.67-83 (at p.79).

40   Goodwin, *op. cit.*, (note 37), cites the opinions of H. G. Turner, C. Fairfield, A. Garran, H. A. Ellis, R. A. Woodthorpe, W. McMillan, W. H. Chard and C. H. Pearson (although Pearson took an unusually bleak view of the future of social evolution).

41   G. Lacy, *Liberty and Law: Being an Attempt at the Refutation of the Individualism of Mr Herbert Spencer and the Political Economists; an Exposition of Natural Rights, and of the Principle of Justice, and of Socialism; and a Demonstration of the Worthlessness of the Supposed Dogmas of Orthodox Political Economy. Addressed to the Youth of Great Britain and the Colonies*, London, 1888. (Lacy spent several years in South Africa, New Zealand and New South Wales. His arguments were not specifically based on antipodean experiences and political circumstances, and the book was written in Cornwall. He was, however, active in public affairs for three years in Sydney.)

42   Editorial, 'The brutality of competition', *The Bulletin*, Vol. 8, 1888 (No. 415), p.4.

43   Editorial, 'Protection – a national necessity', *The Bulletin*, Vol. 9, 1888 (No. 433), p.4. (The argument in this Australian periodical was based on ideas put forward by T. H. Huxley in an article entitled 'The struggle for existence: a programme', *The Nineteenth Century*, Vol. 23, 1888, pp.161-180.)

44   W. M. Hughes, 'The limits of state interference', *Report of the Eleventh Meeting of the Australasian Association for the Advancement of Science held at Adelaide, 1907*, Adelaide, 1908, pp.622-632 (at p.627). (Hughes was Prime Minister of Australia during the First World War.)

17

Darwinism and Politics

The story of the interactions of Darwinian and Spencerian evolutionism with political theory and practice in the nineteenth and twentieth centuries is one of considerable complexity and its full investigation is a task that lies well beyond the scope of the present work. I will therefore content myself with giving what must necessarily be a somewhat superficial account of the various ways in which politicians and political theorists of all parts and colours of the political spectrum found something in Darwinism to support their manifold political positions. Darwin was, so to speak, all things to all men, or as George Bernard Shaw put it: 'He had the luck to please everybody who had an axe to grind'.[1] And this simple fact is a matter of significance, for it reveals once again the quite remarkable degree and range of influence that evolutionism has had on the Western world over about the past one hundred and fifty years. What is offered in this chapter, then, is not intended as a formal account of the development of political theory and political activity since (say) 1859. I will simply attempt to display the various ways in which Darwinism was utilised by various political groupings. In doing this it is impossible to avoid some overlap with what has already been said in the previous two chapters.

The 'liberal' view

To give even our cursory account of the matter, it is necessary to go back at least as far as the eighteenth century, but by doing so we may with advantage give further attention to the seemingly ubiquitous doctrine of *laissez faire*, a concept central to this part of our inquiry.

The economic system operating in France and elsewhere in Europe in pre-Revolutionary days was what is customarily referred to as 'mercantilism',[2] resting on the philosophy that money alone is wealth. The idea was simply that a state should attempt to accrue wealth by selling as much as possible and buying and using as little as possible. The system was characterised by the development of various devices of tariff control and subsidies, which sought to ensure favourable trade balances and the protection of domestic manufactures. But government showed little interest in agriculture — rural conditions deteriorated in eighteenth-century France, for example, under the aegis of Colbert's ministry, which was seeking to employ mercantilist policies.

From about 1750 onwards, however, a group of philosophers led by François Quesnay (1694-1774), Louis XV's court physician, began to criticise the assumptions of the mercantilist policies, arguing that the real sources of wealth in the economy were those derived from the land — forestry, fishing, hunting, mining, and agriculture, the so-called 'natural' trades. Reforms, they said, should be instituted so as to protect the interests of the ultimate producers of wealth — the rural peasantry. Their enrichment would ultimately enrich the whole nation. The 'civic order' (or state) should be brought into line with the 'natural order' by the removal of restrictions to trade such as were characteristic of the mercantilist system. And taxes should only be levied on land, the ultimate source of wealth.

All these suggestions were supported by arguments based on general considerations of human freedom and natural law doctrines. The movement was known as *physiocracy*[3] and its supporters were referred to as *physiocrats*, their idea being that *nature* should have primacy. The catch phrase of the physiocrats was *laissez faire*, meaning that government policy should be complete non-interference in economic affairs. This could be linked, for example, with John Locke's earlier pleas for religious toleration, or non-interference in religious affairs.[4] Despite the fact that the agrarianism of the physiocrats did not long survive after the coming of the Industrial Revolution, their ideas formed one of the major strands leading to the complex of nineteenth-century liberalism.

A further highly significant strand was added by Adam Smith's celebrated *Wealth of Nations*, first published in 1776.[5] Smith (1723-1790) also believed in the significance of ideas of natural law and the doctrine of free trade, but he questioned the physiocrats' contention that agricultural production was the natural and sole source of wealth.[6] Anyone performing work, he said, is generating wealth. And everyone should be entitled to the fruits of his labours. The division of labour would help to generate wealth, by enabling work to be carried out more efficiently and productively. But all must be allowed to function without any interference by government in the operations of manufacture and trade. Every man, so it was supposed, would work to further his own interests, but the net result of this would be the benefit of the whole community. The natural laws of commerce, so Smith believed, would function in such a way as to promote the common good of the community. This was expressed in his *Theory of Moral Sentiments* (1759) by the celebrated simile of the 'invisible hand':

The rich only select from the heap what is most precious and agreeable. They consume little more than the poor, and in spite of their natural selfishness and rapacity, though they mean only their own convenience, though the sole end which they propose from the labours of all the thousands whom they employ be the gratification of their own vain and insatiable desires, they divide with the poor the produce of all their improvements. They are led by an invisible hand to make nearly the same distribution of the necessaries of life which would have been made had the earth been divided into equal portions among all its inhabitants; and thus, without intending it, without knowing it, advance the interest of the society, and afford means to the multiplication of the species.[7]

Yet a third strand in the liberal tradition was provided by the utilitarianism of Jeremy Bentham (1748-1832) and James Mill (1773-1836).[8] According to their view, society should be constituted to allow everyone to maximise his or her happiness, to the general benefit of the community as a whole. Individual freedom should be given maximum scope. Laws should protect private property, but otherwise should permit the maximisation of human freedom. The views of Bentham and Mill retained much of the optimism of the eighteenth century, in contrast to the bleaker outlook of men such as Ricardo and Malthus. Nevertheless, despite the growing evidence of the dire results of the unfettered exercise of free-trade practices in the earlier years of the Industrial Revolution, the so-called Manchester School of economics[9] (noting at least the rising wealth of the entrepreneurial classes) eulogised the doctrines of free trade and the virtues of individual initiative and enterprise. This movement of economic liberalism, with its eighteenth-century principles applied to the industrial practices of the nineteenth century, achieved its greatest degree of influence in Britain in the 1830s and 1840s.

The doctrines of British liberalism were substantially modified by ideas presented by John Stuart Mill (1806-1873), notably in his book *On Liberty,*[10] which appeared in the same year as *The Origin of Species*. Mill warmly applauded all doctrines of freedom of thought and expression. But he questioned whether the state should stand back from economic regulation entirely. By the middle of the nineteenth century, it was quite obvious that the doctrines of *laissez-faire* liberalism were leading to anything but the hoped-for maximisation of human happiness. The capitalist system was signally failing to offer freedom to those who lacked the advantage of the possession of some form of capital, and despite the belief among some Victorian writers — perhaps most notably Samuel Smiles (1812-1904) with his well-known doctrine of 'self-help'[11] — that individual initiative and effort would allow anyone to rise to conditions of economic security, it was all too evident that this was an illusory doctrine. So Mill urged the enactment of suitable social legislation and popular educational reform to enable the weaker members of society to rise to somewhat improved standards of living. Thus there arose the basic concepts of 'modern' or 'social' liberalism, as these are understood today. The state should take some control over the distribution of the fruits of production and should regulate trade to some degree by such means as progressive taxation systems, the imposition of tariffs and the provision of limited schemes of public welfare. But it should make no moves towards state control of the means of production. In this area economic freedom should prevail. All this Mill sought to encourage through the exercise of universal franchise and parliamentary democracy. He also supported the notion of international peace and co-operation and improved social rights for women.

I suppose that, in theory, vast numbers of people today subscribe to a political view of the world that approximates quite closely to these views of that archetypal Victorian, John Stuart Mill. The Australian Liberal Party, for example, professes doctrines that in broad outline seem to be quite Millian.[12] In political practice, of course, such doctrines are constantly moulded by pragmatic considerations, or, to put it less politely, sheer expediency. But in terms of *theory* they are Millian, no matter what the *practice* may be.

This discussion can now be related fairly directly to what we know already about that somewhat quixotic representative of British liberalism, Herbert Spencer. It is evident that the roots of his ideas on freedom and responsibility supposedly leading to the general benefit of the community can be found in the arguments of the classical political economists such as Adam Smith. And as we have seen, Spencer persuasively integrated this with his general evolutionary principles. But he lacked Mill's wiser realisation that wholly unfettered competition led to anything but 'equilibration', the greatest good of the greatest number or the maximisation of happiness. Nevertheless, if we are looking for evidence of the influence of Darwinian principles on political theory, we cannot do better than refer again to Spencer's version of nineteenth-century liberalism. The biological arguments of the Darwin/Wallace theory seemingly fitted the venerable arguments of classical political economy like hand and glove. We can see, therefore, how liberalism drew much strength from the new evolutionary doctrines.

Conservatism

Of all contemporary political philosophies, that of conservatism perhaps drew less on evolutionary doctrines than did any other. But even in this area one may find some evidence for arguments based on evolutionary considerations. The classic case for conservatism is stated in Edmund Burke's (1729-1797) well-known *Reflections on the Revolution in France*,[13] in which this Irish statesman reacted strongly against the proclaimed ideals of the Enlightenment. He was something of a conservative romantic, and had a good deal in common with the German romantics of the same period, influencing their opinions considerably.

Conservatism is the political doctrine that advocates the careful maintenance of existing political institutions or other systems of authority such as that of the Church. Needless to say, it is usually advocated most strongly by those who have, for whatever reason, some advantageous position in society. In such cases it is not usually associated with any carefully thought-out political philosophy, but it is quite often, if stated in any coherent way at all, a mere expression of romantic nostalgia for the virtues of

Burke opp to schem of french Philosophes

the past. But it can be given a philosophical base, and it was chiefly Burke who laid this foundation.

Burke believed that the French Revolution was a social disaster, simply because its leaders sought to change a whole social system in a single sweep. This, he claimed, was bound to lead to an impossible situation, for by changing all parts of society simultaneously in such a radical manner one could not know which of the changes brought about were beneficial and which were deleterious. But in even broader terms Burke objected in principle to men trying to formulate new, rationally devised social structures. He distrusted reformers who came forward with more or less hare-brained schemes for the reconstruction of society. He was, in short, wholly opposed to the schemes devised by the Enlightenment *philosophes* and he believed that what he saw as the disaster of the French Revolution came about as a direct result of trying to put such plans into practice.

In contrast to the arguments of the would-be revolutionists, Burke, like the German romantics and the members of the historicist school of law whom we have mentioned previously, believed that states and societies are products of imperceptible, natural and *organic* growth. This growth could only be interfered with at society's peril. Constitutions should not be written down *a priori*. They should be allowed to emerge gradually through the natural process of historical development. A nation, so Burke supposed, is not something to be created by arbitrary *fiat*; it is an entity that grows naturally, like an organism, developing its own traditions in its own ways. So any well-established organisation is to be cherished for its characteristics, the products of time and history. Order, unity, continuity and authority are of paramount importance for the man of conservative temper.

The Englishman's innate conservatism is apparent to any outside observer of Britain: the love of ceremonial, the reverence for traditional forms of behaviour, the obeisance to authority and the cherishing of ancient buildings, works of art, manners of speech, dress and social institutions and the belief that there is a right and proper way of behaving that only true-blue Englishmen can know or understand. Other conservative, hierarchical societies such as those of Japan or India have similar deeply-ingrained attitudes and resistance to change.

The link between this conservatism and Darwinian evolutionism is doubtless somewhat difficult to discern at first, but it is there. It has been argued by conservative political philosophers, for example, that the systems that have survived the long sifting of the historical process must be 'good' ones — otherwise they would not have survived. Their very act of survival is in a sense a guarantee of their worth, and this argument can be used against those who seek their change.

The general terms of this argument were developed by Burke well before Darwin's day, yet it has been applied with renewed force since the widespread acceptance of the Darwinian doctrine. It should be no surprise, then, that when we examine a modern statement of conservative political philosophy we find it replete with organic metaphors, with society being explicitly compared with biological organisms. Thus the British Conservative politician, Quintin Hogg (Lord Hailsham) (1907-   ), wrote soon after the Second World War:

> Instead of a clear-cut conception of an ideal society to which all nations should attempt to the best of their ability to conform [as, broadly, was advocated by the socialist parties of the day], Conservatives believe in a somewhat more mature conception of the nature of political organisation. This theory may be described as the organic theory of society . . . Conservatives . . . believe that a living society can only change healthily when it changes naturally — that is, in accordance with its acquired and inherited character, and at a given rate.[14]

Hogg spoke in favour of variety in social forces, changing only at rates appropriate to healthy living organisms. Variety, indeed, was allegedly a mark of social well-being. And change and growth were also esteemed, provided they were not accompanied by political upheavals.

Thus, although conservatism made rather less use of arguments from biological/evolutionary considerations than did some other forms of political philosophy, it may be seen from the foregoing that it also occasionally employed arguments characteristic of a Social Darwinist frame.

Militarism, colonialism, racism, Nazism

Theoretical defences of the conservative political stance can and have been formulated, but conservatives generally tend to be uninterested in theoretical issues. Typically, in nineteenth-century Britain, conservative politicians were chiefly interested in questions of international politics, rather than internal domestic affairs, and they sought to build up the strength of the country's armed forces. This meshed well with evolutionary concerns, and whole nations could be regarded as struggling for existence, one with another. In Germany, as we have seen, such views were advanced in the romantic jingoism of Heinrich von Treitschke. In Britain, when the holocaust of the First World War began, writers returned again — seemingly with renewed enthusiasm — to the use of biological analogies as a means of stirring up enthusiasm and resolve for the conflict. An article published in the second month of the War contained the following enthusiastic call for self-sacrifice:

> Amidst the chaos of domestic politics and the wavelike surge of contending social desires the biological law of competition still rules the destinies of nations as of individual men. And as the ethical essence of competition is sacrifice, as each generation of plants or animals perishes in the one case, or toils or dares in the other, that its offspring may survive, so with a nation, the future of the next generation is determined by the self-sacrifice or the absence of self-sacrifice of that which precedes it.
> The bud flowers and the flower dies, and, dying, flings its seeds on the winds to produce, if it may be, a wider re-creation of itself. And in the animal world the sacrificial impulse of maternal love fronts all peril and endures all suffering that its

young may live.

That impulse, in the later manifestations of evolution, is the root source of all human families, and of all human morality. And it finds its crown in patriotism, in the sacrifice which a nation makes to fulfil the trust which it has inherited from its fathers, and to hand down that heritage, not diminished but increased, to the generations that succeed.[15]

The British could also seek to validate their empire-building by the claim that a 'superior' social order was being imparted to those who lacked the advantages of the British social and political system. The British were 'called' to carry 'the white man's burden' on behalf of the lesser, as yet uncivilised races, to whom the manly virtues and respect for law and order might be taught. Joseph Chamberlain (1836-1914), an archetypal nineteenth-century politician, believed that the many different races benefited immeasurably from their tutelage under the political and social system of the British Empire. Their intercourse with white men was supposedly wholly to their advantage.[16]

The British never reached the heights of absurdity and nastiness of the German racial theories, but everyone knows their colonial attitude to 'wogs', 'kaffirs', 'chinks', 'niggers', or for that matter 'frogs' and 'huns'. In Australia and New Zealand, of course, the tables are turned now, with supposedly effete Englishmen referred to as 'Brits' or 'poms'. All these puerilities are themselves simple latter-day manifestations of nineteenth-century social and racial prejudices which were fanned by crude Darwinistic arguments. The final stages of the tragic side of colonialism are now being enacted in countries such as Rhodesia and South Africa.

The way in which the extreme right wing of the political spectrum took up *quasi*-Darwinistic doctrines in the bizarre racial theories of the Nazi movement has already been considered in our chapter on Social Darwinism. But I would like to remind readers that there were at least three major pathways leading from Darwin to Hitler. Firstly, there was the route that ran *via* the overt militarism and imperialism of writers such as von Treitschke, drawing on racist doctrines, but who were not directly concerned with the practice or theory of science. Secondly, there was the biological tradition passing more directly from Darwin through Ernst Haeckel to the German Monist League[17] and thence to their culmination in the doctrines of the Nazi theorists. And related to this were certain anthropological beliefs that encouraged racist tendencies. These matters are taken up elsewhere.[18]

Marxism

The relationship between Darwinism and Marxist or Fabian socialism is by no means easy to unravel. But let us start with a few remarks about Karl Marx (1816-1883).

Marx drew his ideas from many sources, but particularly from the doctrines of the British political economists such as Adam Smith, and the German idealist philosophy of Hegel, as well as from his knowledge of economic conditions in the capitalist countries of Europe.[19] As it seemed to Marx, the application of *laissez-faire* economics had given rise to a large class of wage labourers who were working diligently in factories or fields, producing wealth which was not accruing to them, the front-line producers. They were paid subsistence wages and the 'surplus value' of their labour was skimmed off by the capitalists or bourgeois class, who were gaining all the material and social benefits of the great wealth generated by the scientifically-based Industrial Revolution. As a rough approximation to the nineteenth-century situation, there was much truth in this criticism. Despite the many cases that Samuel Smiles could quote to the contrary,[20] the majority of the wage labourers lacked the capital required to escape from their unfortunate situations and were quite unable to take practical advantages of the system of unfettered free-enterprise. There seemed to be no escape from their drudgery, poverty, ill-health and death, within the fearful system of industrial manufacture that the system of economic liberalism had spawned. The state, said Marx,[21] was the instrument whereby the bourgeoisie — the economic rulers of the nation — sought to manipulate society to their advantage in their constant struggle with the working classes.

The solution, as Marx saw it, was for the workers to rise in revolution against the ruling bourgeoisie, establishing a new social system in which the state would take over all the instruments or means of production, in a system of state socialism.[22]

As a radical program for political action, the proposals of Marx and Engels had much to recommend them, at least as a possible answer to the appalling social conditions that so disfigured the nineteenth-century industrial West. But Marx also sought to show that what he urged would happen naturally, for the progress of history was patterned according to the dialectical mode of change described (in an idealist/historical, not a materialist/historical, context) by Hegel.[23] For Marx the 'material mode of production' was the analogue of Hegel's 'world spirit'.[24] According to the changing modes of production in society, so history would change, the social system accommodating itself to the changing modes of production. These changes were supposed to follow a 'dialectical' pattern, as with Hegel's thesis, antithesis and synthesis. So the workers might be encouraged in their revolutionary fervour by the thought that they must inevitably be successful, for according to Marx's analysis the general future development of society could be foretold.[25]

Both Marx and Engels were much interested in Darwin's work, and thought highly of *The Origin*. At one time, it was believed that Marx sought to dedicate the second volume of *Capital* to Darwin, but this view has been refuted in a recent paper by Margaret Fay.[26] The collapse of the supposed historical connection between Marx and Darwin notwithstanding, Darwinism has always been an important component of the Soviet education system, even at periods when Mendelian genetics has been quite out of favour.

One of the reasons for the appeal of Darwin's work to Marx and Engels was that it could be used to give scientific sanction to the notion of class struggle, and it is clear that this aspect of Darwin's work did have interest for them for this very reason. Thus we find Marx writing to Lassalle on January 16th, 1861:

> Darwin's book is very important and it suits me well that it supports the class struggle in history from the point of view of natural science. One has, of course, to put up with the crude English method of discourse.[27]

But there were wider issues involved than the simple question of inter-class struggles for existence. Engels placed Darwin and Marx on equal thrones in a speech delivered at Marx's graveside in Highgate in 1883:

> Just as Darwin discovered the law of development of organic nature, so Marx discovered the law of development of human history.[28]

And a similar comparison was also made in Engels' preface to the English edition of the *Manifesto of the Communist Party* in 1888.[29]

One particular reason why Darwin held so much appeal to Marx and Engels was that he had effectively eliminated teleology and design from biology, substituting a naturalistic materialism for earlier vitalistic or teleological modes of explanation. Darwin's historical or genetic approach to the phenomena of nature also attracted the communists' attention, and Marx stated that *The Origin* would provide a foundation in natural history for their whole outlook.[30] In other words, they believed that Darwin provided a means of achieving a unified science encompassing both man and nature.

However, Marx and Engels never made much real use of the doctrine of natural selection. Engels defended Darwin's theory in his *Anti-Dühring*,[31] but in his *Dialectics of Nature* he drew attention to the fact that in humans certain groups may be 'fit' from a social or economic point of view, while being 'unfit' in biological terms, for, as he rightly pointed out, 'the bourgeoisie breed more slowly than the workers, and even if they win the struggle for wealth, [they] lose the struggle for life'.[32] Marx scarcely referred to either natural selection or Darwin's evolutionism in *Capital*. At one point he drew a rather tentative analogy between the specialisation in nature arising from natural selection and adaptation and the processes of manufacture in which various specialised tools may be produced by a kind of process of differentiation and adaptation.[33] And because the use of tools of varying kinds or the different means of production formed a vital component of Marx's understanding of social and economic evolution, it is not perhaps surprising that he should suggest the need for a history of technology which would be comparable in importance to Darwin's study of the history of the organs of plants and animals — 'which organs serve as instruments of production for sustaining life'.[34] But Marx's economic and social writings are not permeated by Darwinian theory or Darwinistic metaphor. Nevertheless, the theory, in its naturalistic repudiation of teleology, was thought a significant support to the theoretical framework of the Marxist movement.

Fabian Socialism

An alternative nineteenth-century solution to the evils of capitalism – a solution which also preached the take-over of the means of production and distribution by the state – was proposed by the various social-democrat and labour parties of the industrialised West. In Britain their philosophical spearhead was provided by the writings of the Fabians such as George Bernard Shaw, Beatrice and Sidney Webb, Graham Wallas, Annie Besant, Herbert Bland, William Clarke and Lord Olivier. They sought a reformation of society, and held as an ultimate goal the idea of a classless system not unlike that of the Marxists. But they deplored the suggestion that this should be achieved through revolutionary means. Rather, they maintained that the changes should be brought about by the legal, constitutional procedures of parliamentary democracy.[35] Fabian socialism drew much from the doctrines of Marx, but perhaps even more from earlier ideas of Saint-Simon in France, the collectivism of Robert Owen in Scotland, and also the liberalism of John Stuart Mill.

Basically, the Fabians presented arguments about evolutionism similar to those of Lester Ward. That is, they advocated the diminution of the pitiless struggle for existence so exalted by the Spencerians. They sought an amelioration of the conditions of existence – to be brought about by state-directed planning of society – and they hoped that the social, moral and intellectual condition of man might be improved thereby.

The Fabians experienced some difficulty in appealing to the Darwinian principles of struggle for existence and natural selection as a means of support for Fabian social philosophy. When the Fabians did appeal to Darwinism, it was largely to the Lamarckian aspects of the total theory that they turned. Their general line of argument is to be found, stated with typical Shavian *élan*, in the Preface to *Back to Methuselah*. As Shaw said:

> Perhaps the strongest moral bulwark of Capitalism is the belief in the efficacy of individual righteousness . . . If you were rich, how pleasant it was to feel that you owed your riches to the superiority of your character! The industrial revolution had turned numbers of greedy dullards into monstrously rich men. Nothing could be more humiliating and threatening to them than the view that the falling of a shower of gold into their pockets was as pure an accident of our industrial system as the falling of a shower of hail on their umbrellas. Nothing could be more flattering and fortifying to them than the assumption that they were rich because they were virtuous.[36]

But, continued Shaw, pointing up the Lamarckian aspect of the Darwinian doctrine:

> Darwinism made a clean sweep of all such self-righteousness . . . It implied that

street arabs are produced by slums and not by original sin: that prostitutes are produced by starvation wages and not by feminine concupiscence. It threw the authority of science on the side of the Socialist who said that he who would reform himself must first reform society. It suggested that if we want healthy and wealthy citizens we must have healthy and wealthy towns . . . It could be led to the conclusion that the type of character which remains indifferent to the welfare of its neighbours as long as its own personal appetite is satisfied is the disastrous type, and the type which is deeply concerned about its environment the only possible type for a permanently prosperous community. It shewed that the surprising changes which Robert Owen had produced in factory children by a change in their circumstances which does not seem any too generous to us nowadays, were as nothing to the changes — changes not only of habits but of species, not only of species but of orders — which might conceivably be the work of the environment acting on individuals without any character or intellectual consciousness whatever. No wonder the Socialists received Darwin with open arms.[37]

Unfortunately, this is largely a misrepresentation of the Darwinian theory. And, if the socialists really had to rely on the Lamarckian component of Darwinism in order to justify their social doctrines they would be in a sorry state today, now that Lamarckism is virtually rejected as a biological theory. Nevertheless, the way social democrats sought to invoke the Darwinian theory in support of their political program is clear enough from Shaw's exegesis.

Moreover, the Fabians were astute enough to realise that the whole nature of the analogy that might be drawn (if any were to be drawn at all) from biological theories of the animal kingdom to political and economic programs was radically altered by the recognition of the *social* nature of man's being. So the struggle for existence could be transferred to a higher dimension. Sidney Webb (1859-1947) put the matter clearly when he wrote:

We know now that in natural selection at the stage of development where the existence of civilized mankind is at stake, the units selected from are not individuals, but societies. Its action at earlier stages, though analogous, is quite dissimilar.[38]

The struggle for existence continued to operate, but at the level of whole societies rather than individuals. Webb suggested, for example, that:

The French nation was beaten in the last war [the Franco-Prussian War], not because the average German was an inch-and-a-half taller than the average Frenchman, or because he had read five more books, but because the German social organism was, for the purposes of the time, superior in efficiency to [that of] the French.[39]

Thus it could be argued that the mutually co-operative and cohesive social system would be the one that would triumph in the struggle for existence. With this line of reasoning one might hope to refute the arguments for the economic individualism of the *laissez-faire* state. Men should subordinate their individuality to fulfil their 'humble function in the great social machine'.[40]

There is something a little incongrous and perhaps somewhat poignant here, in that such a man as Sidney Webb, the preacher of social co-operation, sympathy and understanding should resort to considerations of struggle for existence at the international level in order to give weight to his political credo. The Marxists did at least see international worker co-operation as an attainable goal.

Anarchism

Finally, in this cursory survey of the various colours of the political spectrum we may say a few words about the philosophical presuppositions of anarchism, for these had something in common with the doctrines of social co-operation preached by the Fabians, although the anarchists rejected the belief in the efficacy of state enterprises — a belief that formed such a vital component of the utopianism of the parties of social democracy.

Anarchism is today a doctrine that is largely disregarded as a potentially useful political program in the capitalist West, and it is usually somewhat vaguely associated in people's minds with wild and hairy young men hurling bombs in public places; and to most people the term 'anarchist' is pejorative in the extreme. Yet anarchism was and is a carefully thought-out political doctrine with extensive historical roots, and expressive of a deep concern with the ills of society.[41]

The first anarchist philosopher is generally reckoned to have been William Godwin (1756-1836), author of the important volume, *Political Justice*,[42] and one of the eighteenth-century optimists against whom Malthus directed his critical attacks.[43] Godwin had been directing his criticisms against the doctrine of the hypothetical 'social contract' expounded by Thomas Hobbes (1588-1679) in his celebrated *Leviathan*.[44]

According to Hobbes, men lived together in civil society because — despite all the objectionable features of life in a rule-bound, regimented, civil structure — this was a lesser evil than life in a savage society lacking any central government, a condition that would be tantamount to perpetual civil war. Thus according to Hobbes's argument it is preferable to live under a strong government, even a wholly despotic regime, provided the ruler or government is powerful enough and willing to 'keep the peace'. It is for this reason only that the citizen of a country owes allegiance to its ruler or rulers. The appeal of such an argument in the century of civil war in England must be quite evident.

Of course, Hobbes's argument is predicated on the assumption that men are by nature inherently selfish, brutal, lustful, warlike, and aggressive — all that is summed up in the Christian notion of evil. But a less pessimistic outlook, perhaps more idealistic than realistic, might lead one to assert that men are by nature co-operative and good, and imbued with natural sympathies towards one another. From this standpoint, then, the state or government might appear as an oppressor rather than a protector — an instrument for interfering with the private desires and freedom of individuals within the community. And it might be argued that sovereignty should be vested in the individual rather than in the state. In fact, according to this way of thinking, the evils of war — which Hobbes believed provided a justification for seeking security within the framework of a civil system of government — could arise from the mere existence of predatory national states. If there were no such national systems of government, there could be no such thing as international war. In rough outline, this was the basis of Godwin's argument, and of other anarchists such as Tolstoy in the following century.[45] In brief, they simply denied that there was a need for the complex structures of government control of society. One might rely on man's innate sympathies for his fellow-man to procure the well-being of the social fabric. This, of course, was *laissez-faire* liberalism carried to its ultimate extreme. And the hairy young men with their grenades and bombs were, one must suppose, trying to break the control of governments over the sovereignty of the people and allow a new anarchistic utopia to arise spontaneously.

The history of anarchism in the nineteenth and twentieth centuries and its relationship with Marxist and social democrat movements and the workers' internationals are complex subjects which we need not explore here. All that need concern us is the way anarchist philosophy might try to draw on the arguments of the Darwinian theory. The best-known attempt to do this was put forward by the celebrated Russian anarchist, Prince Peter Kropotkin (1842-1921), in his widely read volume, *Mutual Aid*.[46] Kropotkin, as so many other social theorists, sought to give his theoretical doctrines a firm scientific base, and Darwinism was ostensibly capable of providing this.

Kropotkin was himself a naturalist of some reknown, with specialised interests in geology. He spent a number of years in Siberia, and it was on the basis of his observations there that he sought to argue that if one looked carefully at the animal kingdom just as much evidence for mutual co-operation between animals could be found as of pitiless struggles for existence. He saw plenty of evidence for struggle with 'Nature' — with the rigours of the elements; but he failed to find much evidence for actual physical contest between animals of the same species:

> On the other hand, wherever I saw animal life in abundance, as, for instance, on the lakes where scores of species and millions of individuals came together to rear their progeny; in the colonies of rodents; in the migrations of birds . . . and especially in a migration of fallow-deer which I witnessed on the Amur,[47] and during which scores of thousands of these intelligent animals came together from an immense territory, flying before the coming deep snow, in order to cross the Amur where it is narrowest — in all these scenes of animal life which passed before my eyes, I saw Mutual Aid and Mutual Support carried on to an extent which made me suspect in it a feature of the greatest importance for the maintenance of life, the preservation of each species, and its further evolution.[48]

The tenor of Kropotkin's argument should be clear enough from this single extract, although it should be added that quite rightly he referred also to evidence provided by Darwin in *The Descent of Man* — for example, evidence about the origins of social altruism or ethical behaviour in man, or the co-operative behaviour of social insects such as bees and ants — in further support of his doctrine of 'mutual aid'. There can be no doubt that Kropotkin *could* find analogies in the animal world that might persuade the 'doubting Thomas' to agree with Godwin's optimistic conclusions about human nature, just as the 'tooth and claw' Social Darwinists could draw on *The Origin of Species* for arguments about social progress arising from the ceaseless struggle for existence.

We have been able to show that all shades of political opinion were able to draw support from the Darwin/Wallace theory. Shaw was correct in saying that Darwin 'had the luck to please everybody who had an axe to grind'. So we must now face the question of whether *any* of these Janus-faced Social Darwinists were really justified in their assumptions.

The question of the use of a biological analogue as a basis for the formulation of social theories was considered in a perceptive way in 1875 by Marx's colleague Friedrich Engels (1820-1895). Engels rightly pointed out that historically what had happened was that the supporters of the Darwin/Wallace theory had transferred the Hobbesian/Malthusian idea of struggle (in the social and economic sphere) to the world of nature; and then the Social Darwinists had brought it back again to man when they argued in favour of their social policies. So, logically, one was moving in an almost perfect circle.[49]

There is certainly some force in what Engels had to say on this point; but one could object with some justice that for Darwin the Malthusian doctrine was merely a clue he used on the journey to his theory, and that the theory, once developed and displaying the might of its explanatory power, could with some justification be used subsequently as a basis for theories about the social problems of mankind. But leaving this point aside, we should refer to Engels' second major point of argument. He wrote:

> The essential difference between human and animal society consists in the fact that animals at most *collect* while men *produce*. This sole but cardinal difference alone precludes the simple transfer of laws of animal societies to human societies.[50]

This point, so characteristically Marxist, with its concern with the question of the material production of wealth, we may link with our discussion at the end of Chapter 13, where it was pointed out that human societies *could* inherit acquired characteristics, and thus social evolution might proceed by a *quasi*-Lamarckian mechanism. Men *can* make things, and hand these on to their successors. For animals, this is scarcely ever possible. Or, as Engels put it, animals merely *collect*, but men *produce*. Consequently, there is a

Lamarckian component to human evolution that almost entirely destroys the putative analogies between animal and human societies. The Social Darwinists, in their eagerness to argue their theories with the help of the prestige of Darwin's science, usually overlooked entirely this 'cardinal difference' and all it entailed.

None of the political theories we have looked at in this chapter actually developed directly from the Darwin/Wallace theory. They all arose from some other source; and I have tried to show in an approximate manner what some of these sources were. What all these theories did do, however, was to seek *corroboration* from the Darwinian system. The Darwinian theory is a many-faceted affair. Some competition in the animal and plant worlds takes place at the inter-species level; and some occurs at the intra-species level. There are well-authenticated instances of symbiosis[51] and commensalism,[52] as well as parasitism. And, if one so desires, analogies can be drawn with all of these. All in a sense are legitimate; or, if one prefers, all are invalid. Certainly, none of the arguments have any deductive strength. And the measure of the *degree* of positive and negative analogy in each case never has been and cannot be determined. There is no reason humans should have to turn to animals and plants when considering the kind of social system they desire. The rationality of the human being enables him – in principle – to make independent decisions on questions of this kind, although decisions need to be made in the light of an understanding of the ecological interactions between men and other living organisms,[53] and human rationality does not allow man to transcend the laws of physics.

Despite this, many of the political battles of today still follow lines essentially the same as those drawn up in the nineteenth century, and the tired arguments about co-operation versus struggle and social planning versus individual enterprise still persist. In Australia, for example, the Federal Labor Government of 1972-1975 sought to ameliorate the conditions of society by prodigal programs of social welfare, urban renewal, public transport reorganisation, and so on, through the medium of a benevolent, planning, centralised government bureaucracy. This was very much a program that would have appealed to the early Fabians. The Liberal/National Country Party Government which succeeded Labor in 1975, however, eschews (in theory) government interference in social affairs, urges individual initiative and enterprise, and tells us that life is not meant to be easy. Indeed, a modern political commentator sees the Prime Minister as a latter-day Social Darwinist (Figure 30).[54]

And a former Premier of New South Wales, Sir Eric Willis, fairly recently expressed his opinion that the next State election would be fought on the issue of 'the conflict between stifling socialism and vigorous free enterprise'.[55]

The political battle-lines have become a little fuzzy over the years, but essentially the categories of thought are the same as those that prevailed in the late nineteenth century. In Britain, the Heath (Conservative) and Wilson

(Labour) Governments sought to solve the problems of the ailing British economy, the former through emphasis on 'struggle', the latter through talk of co-operation — the 'social contract' doctrine revived by Mr Wilson. There was some sense in what both said. But both, I believe, failed in what they set out to do; and largely, I suggest, for reasons that Malthus would surely have understood: the competition of too many people for too few resources.

Figure 30 The Australian Prime Minister, Mr Malcolm Fraser (1977), perceived as a Social Darwinist

Published by *courtesy of the* Sydney Morning Herald.

NOTES CHAPTER 17

1   Bernard Shaw, *Back to Methuselah, A Metabiological Pentateuch*, Brentano, New York, 1921, p.1xv.

2   For a useful collection of writings setting out the leading features of the mercantilist doctrines, see W. E. Minchinton (ed.), *Problems in European Civilization: Mercantilism, System or Expediency?*, Heath, Lexington, 1969. For a useful brief survey of mercantilist doctrines, see C. Wilson, *Mercantilism*, Historical Association Pamphlet No. 37, London, 1958.

3   Cf. aristocracy, democracy, meritocracy, etc.

4   J. Locke, *Epistola de Tolerantia*, Gouda, 1689; *Letter Concerning Toleration*, London, 1689. Locke also wrote on *political* freedom in his celebrated *Essay Concerning the True, Original, Extent, and End of Civil Government* (1689): 'The end of law is not to abolish or restrain but to preserve and enlarge freedom'.

5   A. Smith, *An Inquiry into the Nature and Causes of the Wealth of Nations*, 2 vols, London, 1776. For a general description of Smith's economic philosophy, see, for example, J. Cropsey, *Polity and Economy: An Interpretation of the Principles of Adam Smith*, Nijhoff, The Hague, 1957.

6   Smith also rejected the basic assumptions of mercantilism. He repudiated the equation of wealth and gold, and the identification of a favourable trade balance with the annual balance of income over consumption. Moreover, argued Smith, mercantilism favoured the interests of traders and manufacturers and not necessarily the nation as a whole.

7   A. Smith, *The Theory of Moral Sentiments: Or an Essay towards an Analysis of the Principles by Which Men Naturally Judge Concerning the Conduct and Character, First of Their Neighbours, and Afterwards of Themselves*, Part IV, Chapter 1, in H. W. Schneider (ed.), *Adam Smith's Moral and Political Philosophy*, Harper & Row, New York, Evanston & London, 1970, p.215.

8   For a statement of the opinions of these authors, see, for example, J. Plamenatz, *The English Utilitarians*, 2nd edn, Blackwell, Oxford, 1958.

9   On the Manchester School, see E. Helm, 'The Manchester School' in R. H. I. Palgrave (ed.), *Dictionary of Political Economy*, 3 vols., London & New York, 1894-1899, Vo. 2, 1896, pp.678-680.

10   J. S. Mill, *On Liberty*, London, 1859.

11   S. Smiles, *Self-Help; with Illustrations of Character and Conduct*, London, 1859.

12   For example, the Australian Liberal Party platform for the 1946 General Election contained the assertion that the Liberal Party stood for an Australian Nation:
'In which an intelligent, free, and liberal Australian democracy shall be maintained by
(a)   Parliament controlling the Executive and the Law controlling all;
(b)   Freedom of speech, religion, and association;
(c)   Freedom of citizens to choose their own way of life, subject to the rights of others;
(d)   Protecting the people against exploitation;
(e)   Looking primarily to the encouragement of individual initiative and enterprise as the dynamic force of re-construction and progress'.
(R. G. Menzies, *Afternoon Light: Some Memories of Men and Events*, Penguin, Harmondsworth, 1969, p.292.) See also D. M. White, *The Philosophy of the Australian Liberal Party*, Hutchinson, Richmond (Victoria), 1978.

13   E. Burke, *Reflections on the Revolution in France, and on the Proceedings in Certain Societies in London Relative to that Event. In a Letter Intended to have been sent to a Gentleman in Paris*, London, 1790 (republished Penguin, Harmondsworth, 1968).

14   Q. Hogg, *The Case for Conservatism*, Penguin, Harmondsworth, 1947, pp.24-25.

15   H. F. Wyatt, ' "God's test by war": a forecast and its fulfilment', *The Nineteenth Century and After*, Vol. 76, 1914, pp. 489-510 (at pp.489-490). (This article had previously been published in the same journal in 1911 [Vol. 69, pp.591-606], but the editor believed its contents to be so relevant to the new wartime circumstances that he chose to republish it on the occasion of the outbreak of war.)

16   See J. Chamberlain, 'The true conception of empire', in C. W. Boyd (ed.), *Mr Chamberlain's Speeches*, 2 vols, Houghton, Mifflin & Co., Boston & New York, 1914, Vol. 2, pp.1-6.

17   See below, page 274.

18   See below, page 305.

19   As is well known, Marx's work while in Britain was carried out chiefly in the Library of the British Museum. But his colleague, Engels, carried out first-hand investigations of the social conditions of the working classes within the capitalist system: F. Engels, *The Condition of the Working Class in England in 1844*, New York, 1887 (first German edition, Leipzig, 1845).

20   S. Smiles, *op. cit.* (note 11).

21   C. J. Arthur (ed.), *Karl Marx and Frederick Engels: The German Ideology Part One with selections from Parts Two and Three, together with Marx's "Introduction to a Critique of Political Economy"*, Interna-

tional Publishers, New York, 1970, p.80.

22   K. Marx & F. Engels, *Manifesto of the Communist Party*, Progress Publishers, Moscow, 1967, p.76 (first German edition, 1848).

23   G. W. F. Hegel, *The Philosophy of History*, Dover, New York, 1956, pp.47, 53, 63, 72 and *passim*,

24   In a famous passage in the Preface to *A Contribution to the Critique of Political Economy* (1859), Marx wrote: 'It is not the consciousness of men that determines their existence, but their social existence that determines their consciousness' (M. Dobb [ed.], *Karl Marx: A Contribution to the Critique of Political Economy*, Progress Publishers, Moscow, 1970, p.21).

25   There has been much discussion in the literature about whether Marx believed that the course of history was knowable in advance because of its law-like character. In the view of 'liberal' anti-Marxists, such as has been sketched above, this *was* the view of Marx and Engels and one of the chief reasons why their doctrines were politically and socially obnoxious. (See, for example, K. R. Popper, *The Open Society and its Enemies, Volume II, The High Tide of Prophecy: Hegel, Marx, and the Aftermath*, 4th edn, Routledge & Kegan Paul, London, 1962, pp.135-198.) Certainly, one can find some evidence within the corpus of Marx's writings which supports the view that the future course of history can be foretold in the light of the Marxist social analysis. For example, in an 'Afterword' to the second German edition of *Kapital*, Marx quotes at length a critic who had attributed such a view to him. Far from repudiating this, Marx wrote: 'Whilst the writer pictures what he takes to be actually my method, in this striking and (as far as concerns my own application of it) generous way, what else is he picturing but the dialectic method?' (K. Marx, *Capital: A Critique of Political Economy, Volume 1, The Process of Capitalist Production*, International Publishers, New York, 1967, pp.17 & 19.) But this is not a positive assertion of the doctrine; rather, it is an acceptance of it when it is attributed. Later Marxist writers have tended to repudiate any doctrine of 'historical inevitability'. Lenin, for example, wrote: 'No Marxist has ever regarded Marx's theory as some universally compulsory philosophical scheme of history' (*Collected Works*, 45 vols, Foreign Languages Publishing House, Moscow, 1960-1970, Vol. 1, p.192). For further argument against viewing Marxism as a purely deterministic analysis of society, see B. Easlea, *Liberation and the Aims of Science*, Chatto & Windus, London, 1973, pp.164-167.

26   See M. A. Fay, 'Did Marx offer to dedicate *Capital* to Darwin? A reassessment of the evidence', *Journal of The History of Ideas*, Vol. 39, 1978, pp.133-146. The author convincingly demonstrates that Darwin's literary contact was Edward Aveling (the *de facto* husband of Marx's daughter Eleanor), not Marx himself.

27   K. Marx & F. Engels, *Selected Correspondence*, 2nd edn, Foreign Languages Publishing House, Moscow, 1965, p.115.

28   K. Marx & F. Engels, *Selected Works in One Volume*, Lawrence & Wishart, Moscow & London, 1968, p.429.

29   K. Marx & F. Engels, *op. cit.* (note 22), p.21.

30   K. Marx, Letter to Engels, 19 Dec., 1860, in K. Marx & F. Engels, *Werke*, Dietz, Berlin (1967-1971), Vol. 30 (1964), pp.130-131 (at p.131).

31   F. Engels, *Anti-Dühring: Herr Eugen Dühring's Revolution in Science*, Progress Publishers, Moscow, 1947, pp.85-93.

32   F. Engels (C. Dutt, translator and editor), *Dialectics of Nature*, Lawrence & Wishart, London, 1941, p.209 (footnote).

33   K. Marx, *op. cit.* (note 25), p.341.

34   *Ibid.*, p.372.

35   The name of the Fabian movement is derived from that of the Roman general, Fabius Maximus, who foiled Hannibal by *delaying* tactics rather than by direct battle.

36   G. B. Shaw, *op. cit.* (note 1), pp.1xv-1xvii.

37   *Ibid.*, p.1xvii.

38   S. Webb, 'Historic', in G. B. Shaw *et al.* (eds), *Fabian Essays*, 6th edn, Allen & Unwin, London, 1962, p.89 (1st edn, 1889).

39   *Ibid.*, p.90.

40   *Ibid.*, p.90.

41   For a good introduction to anarchist political theory, see A. Carter, *The Political Theory of Anarchism*, Routledge, London, 1971, or G. Woodcock, *Anarchism*, Penguin, Harmondsworth, 1963.

42   W. Godwin, *An Enquiry Concerning Political Justice and its Influence on General Virtue and Happiness*, 2 vols, London, 1793 (republished Penguin, Harmondsworth, 1976).

43   See above, page 69.

44   T. Hobbes, *Leviathan Or the Matter, Forme and Power of A Commonwealth Ecclesiastical and Civil*, London, 1651 (republished Penguin, Harmondsworth, 1968).

45   See L. Tolstoy, 'Patriotism and government', in *The Complete Works of Count Tolstoy*, 24 vols, AMS Press, New York, 1968, Vol. 23, pp.141-166.

46   P. Kropotkin, *Mutual Aid*, London, 1902 (republished Penguin, Harmondsworth, 1939).

47   The Amur River runs parallel with the Trans-Siberian Railway for a considerable distance, and forms part of the boundary between Mongolia and Siberia.

48   P. Kropotkin, *op. cit.* (note 46, 1939), p.13.

49   The point is made by Engels in a letter to P.L. Lavrov, November 12 [-17], 1975. (K. Marx & F. Engels, *op. cit.* [note 27], pp.283-285.)

50   *Ibid.*, p.284.

51   Symbiosis is 'Association of two different organisms which live attached to each other, or one as a tenant of the other, and contribute to each other's support' (*Oxford English Dictionary*).

52   Commensalism is the living together of members of different species 'in close association, e.g. in same burrow, shell or house, without much mutual influence, i.e. not symbiotic' (M. Abercrombie, C. J. Hickman & M. L. Johnson, *A Dictionary of Biology*, Penguin, Harmondsworth, 1951, p.57).

53   There is also the problem that it is very difficult to undertake 'scientific', closely controlled, experimental investigations of human societies. This is one reason why animal subjects are so often used; it is then hoped that valid transference can be made from animal to human populations.

54   *The National Times*, 3-8 January, 1977, p.1.

55   Quoted in *The National Times*, 31 January-5 February, 1977, p.44.

18

Darwinism and Theology

The popular conception of the Darwinian Revolution is, I suggest, that Darwin's work 'undermined' (whatever that may mean) religious beliefs and was one of the major steps leading to the pervasive agnosticism of the twentieth century. It marked a great 'battle' between science and religion, of cultural enlightenment against benighted obscurantism, and perhaps (paradoxically) of good against evil. Moreover, the celebrated 'Oxford Debate' which we discussed in Chapter 14 is often regarded as the epitome of some kind of intellectual duel between Darwinism and the Church.

Darwinism did have an impact on religion. But it is a grave historiographical solecism to judge the participants in the evolutionary debate in terms of black and white — the evolutionists pure as driven snow; the theologians foolish bigots. Such a dichotomy does no justice to the complexities of the total situation. And now that the dust of the 'battle' has largely cleared it should be possible to present a reasonably balanced picture.

The reason Christian theology and evolutionary doctrine came into conflict is not difficult to discern. The leading principle of the Reformation was the establishment of the authority of the Scriptures against the authority of the established Church. Calvin, for example, is quoted as having written:

They whom the Holy Ghost hath inwardly taught do wholly rest upon the Scripture, and . . . the same Scripture is to be credited for itself sake, and ought not to be made subject to demonstration and reason: but yet the certainty which it getteth among us, it attaineth by the witness of the Holy Ghost. For though by the only majesty of itself it procureth reverence to be given to it, yet then only it thoroughly pierceth our affections when it is sealed in our hearts by the Holy Ghost. So, being lightened by its virtue, we do then believe, not by our own judgement or other men's, that the Scripture is from God . . .[1]

Whether the Scriptures were to be understood in an entirely literal manner was, needless to say, a vexed question; but certainly Darwinism was incompatible with a literal reading of the Old Testament. In the second chapter of *Genesis*, for example, one finds the famous words:

> And the LORD God formed man *of* the dust of the ground, and breathed into his nostrils the breath of life; and man became a living soul.[2]

The idea of the breath of life has parallels in (pagan) Stoic doctrine of the universal *pneuma*, and a considerable number of other early beliefs, but we need not worry about the historical pedigree of this notion here.[3] The simple point to notice is that if this Biblical passage is taken literally it simply *cannot* be reconciled with the evolutionism of the Darwinian theory. There is an utter logical incompatibility. Of course, as we know, *The Origin* hardly refers to man at all. In 1859, all that Darwin said on this question was: 'Light will be thrown on the origin of man and his history'.[4] But it was clear to all that the theory might be extrapolated forthwith to encompass man, and it caused not the slightest surprise to anyone when this extrapolation made its formal appearance in 1871, with the publication of *The Descent of Man*. So some kind of clash with religious opinion was inevitable as long as the literal truth of the Bible was strictly adhered to. For if it were admitted by the criteria of evolutionary science that even *one* passage of the scriptures – supposedly *divinely* inspired – was false, then *all* might be called in question. Thereby, the whole basis of authority of the Protestant churches would begin to be eroded.[5] As with any politician today who is loth to show anything less than infallibility on any issue whatsoever, for fear of having the validity of all of his pronouncements questioned, the Church was obviously reluctant to admit the falsehood of even one Biblical passage, and needless to say the evolutionary theory threw doubt on much more than the seventh verse of the second chapter of *Genesis*.

No doubt it may be objected that literalist theology had already had to give up several of its choicest Biblical passages long before 1859. Had not the theories of Copernicus and Galileo been incompatible with a literal reading of *Joshua*, where the Lord told the *Sun* to stand still upon Gibeon?[6] And had not the work of Lyell called in question the whole of the Old Testament history of the Earth, with its miniscule time-scale? Certainly, there had been considerable heart-searching over both these issues, and both the revision of physics and astronomy known as the Copernican Revolution and the uniformitarianism of Lyell had, in their different ways, excited considerable opposition. But the evolutionary issue was seen as far more critical, for it focussed on man himself and on his nature – and the nature of man's being was a question that stood at the very heart of all religious matters.

But it was not only the questions raised by science that created difficulties for religious orthodoxy in the middle of the nineteenth century. Ever since the Renaissance there had been questioning of the authenticity of certain passages in the Bible, and critics had pointed to the numerous inconsistencies and incompatibilities that may be found between different sections of the holy scriptures;[7] and doubts were raised about whether the Bible was really a single coherent revelation of God's will or a synthesis of a vast range of ancient texts and sources.

By the nineteenth century, in Protestant Germany and Holland at least, this work of literary criticism of the Bible, which subjected the sacred texts to critical scrutiny (from a literary point of view), just as any other set of ancient documents such as the *Odyssey* or the *Iliad*, had grown to a movement known as 'higher criticism'.[8] But such iconoclasm had not made much headway in Britain, where the traditional ways of thinking were deeply entrenched and linked with the whole social fabric of the country; and nowhere was the traditional opinion stronger than in Oxford, where the politician, W. E. Gladstone (1809-1898), chose to speak for the orthodox, literalist view.[9] The 'Oxford Declaration' of 1864, signed by eleven thousand Anglican clergymen, was adamant that if any part of the Bible were admitted to be in error all might be doubted.[10] The signatories, therefore, stood for the absolute inerrancy of the Bible.

It is not at first sight apparent why Britain should have been so reluctant to accept a liberal interpretation of the Bible, for it was, after all, a country that nominally espoused toleration and freedom of religious thought and expression, in the tradition of John Locke. And Britain had been a stronghold of deism in the eighteenth century. However, one of the reasons was undoubtedly the conservative reaction that had taken place at the end of the eighteenth century after the excesses of the French Revolution. This helped to suppress deism, although allowing or even encouraging the continuance of the tradition of natural theology. And while the religion of the aristocracy and bourgeoisie was simply conservative and antipathetic towards any thoughts that seemed to threaten the established order in any way whatsoever, the religion of the new urban working classes – chiefly the non-conformism of the Methodists or Wesleyans – was largely fundamentalist in character. A few groups, most notably the Unitarians, were disposed to accept quite radical alterations to traditional ways of thinking, but the majority of the population was far from willing to accept any substantive changes to their beliefs. Putting it in somewhat simplistic terms, it might be said that the upper classes were antagonistic towards changes that might diminish their social advantages and the working classes did not wish to have dashed their hopes of some better kind of existence in the after-life. So, as we have seen, Darwinism was reviled with almost equal vigour on the one hand by the gutter press, speaking for the working classes, and on the other hand by 'saponaceous' Samuel Wilberforce, speaking on behalf of the privileged classes, orthodoxy and traditionalism. Nevertheless, the fundamentalism of so many men in the nineteenth century is something of an historical curiosity. For if the eighteenth-century trend towards deism or even outright atheism had continued, one might have expected the nineteenth century to have been predominantly a period of 'free-thought'. But this was far from the case. It was a period of great religious revival and a period in which fundamentalist thinking was very widely adhered to. These changes in religious alignment are probably linked in some causal way with the shift from the eighteenth-century Enlightenment views to nineteenth-century romanticism and historicism. But it would be inappropriate to attempt to analyse this causality here.

We see, then, why the evolutionary doctrine posed such a profound challenge to religious thought when *The Origin* was published in 1859. And we can see why the threat seemed strongest at first for Protestants, rather than Catholics. The very truth of the Bible in what it taught about the *nature* of man was in question. But matters did not stop there. For Darwin's theory, as we have seen on numerous occasions, was purely *naturalistic*. It made no use of any kind of *design* argument; it made no use of teleology (or arguments couched in terms of purpose or 'final' causes). Yet it was *design* that the proponents of natural theology had used as one of their chief arguments in favour of the existence of God. It was *design*, plus the revelation of God supposedly provided by the scriptures, that formed the fundamentals of Christian theology and the basis or springboard for the acts of faith of the members of the Christian community. Clearly, Darwin cast grave doubt on the design argument, as well as the plausibility of the literal truth of the scriptures.

Since 1859, there has been a slow and painful process of accommodation to the idea of evolution by various Churches and people of faith. Today, there are still religious groups such as the Plymouth Brethren and the Christadelphians who subscribe to fundamentalist views in relation to evolutionary theory and they have at least the merit of logical consistency in their thinking. But such groups are today generally regarded as at least a little odd. The majority of Christians has finally come to terms with the evolutionary doctrine and some have not merely accommodated it with reluctance but have embraced it with a positive enthusiasm, building it up into the very core of a new theism.

So let us try to trace, albeit briefly, the various ways in which Christians have sought to accommodate their views to the challenge of the Darwinian theory. In the first place, they simply tried to show that Darwinism was unsound from a biological point of view, and this was what critics such as the Anglican, Wilberforce, and the Catholic, St George Mivart,[11] attempted to do and with some success. For a brief period, they were able to hold back the flood of opinion. But gradually, as more and more evidence for evolutionism was gathered, and more and more biologists chose to accept the evolutionary theory, the *scientific* arguments that might be mustered on behalf of the theologians grew less plausible, and, even though the natural selection mechanism of Darwin and Wallace was in difficulty in the late nineteenth century, biological evolutionism came to be widely accepted.

Nevertheless, a number of writers sought to hold evolutionism in one compartment of the mind, and biology and evolutionary theory in another, with a somewhat schizophrenic world view emerging as a result. This is well illustrated by a review article in *Frazer's Magazine*, published shortly after the appearance of *The Origin*. Here we have what may be called a 'God-of-the-gaps' solution to the problem:

> Where the reasonings and methods of science are no longer applicable . . . the candid and earnest investigator of truth will turn to any other source [*viz.*, God] from which he conceives that further knowledge is to be derived.[12]

Or, as the *Edinburgh New Philosophical Journal* put it: 'Here revelation steps in'.[13] The trouble with this response, however, is that as scientific knowledge expands, the area left over to be accounted for by God's personal activity gets gradually whittled away. This can hardly be an acceptable long-term solution to the problem of reconciling science and religion, and today the 'God-of-the-gaps' view has few advocates.

We have noted above that it was Darwin's displacement of design from biological theory that acted as a special challenge to the received views of nineteenth-century natural theology. It will not surprise us, therefore, that as religious men sought to accommodate their ideas and beliefs to the impact of the new Darwinian ideas, they made considerable effort to reconstruct the design argument, not in its old Paleyesque form, but in a refurbished version that might incorporate the new biological theory.

One way in which an attempt was made to do this is illustrated in a proposal put forward by Darwin's correspondent, the American botanist, Asa Gray (1810-1888), who, although agreeing that the main outline of the Darwinian theory might be accepted, suggested that one should add the extra hypothesis that God was responsible for the occurrence of the favourable variations.[14] This would allow the full explanatory power of the Darwinian theory to come into operation but would still retain a role for God in shaping the progress of the world and of mankind. In this way, there would still be an important element of design in the system.

Such a scheme is, I suggest, unattractive, both from biological and theological points of view. Must one suppose that God (or even the Devil?) must also be responsible for producing the unfavourable variations? In effect, Gray was merely postulating a divine cause for the commonplace phenomenon of variation. This simply brought back the element of supernaturalism into biology, whence it had recently been driven by Darwin. But it also did it in an implausible way. It is by no means easy to see why an omnipotent and omniscient being should employ the Darwinian method of 'higgledy-piggledy' in the revelation of the divine plan. An outright creation of forms would appear a much more obvious way of proceeding.[15]

This objection notwithstanding, various versions of design argument continued to find favour in the nineteenth century. The overall cosmic evolutionary process could be construed as a revelation of Divine Will, a mark of God's beneficence, wisdom and power. Such a view was apparent in the ideas of the American theologian, Henry Ward Beecher (1813-1887),[16] and more significantly in the thought of the liberal Anglican divine,

Frederick Temple (1821-1902), who lectured on the subject at Oxford in 1884. Temple supposed that God's design might be recognised in the original act of creation, and he suggested also that the chemical elements were originally endowed with properties suitable for the formation of the world, as it is known to us, by an evolutionary process.[17]

Perhaps such arguments do permit a reasonable *rapprochment* between evolutionism and theology. But it is really a question of *faith* whether we interpret what we see around us — the product of a long evolutionary process — as a manifestation of the activity of a supernatural architect employing an evolutionary process for the revelation of His purpose. Beecher or Temple could say that it was so; Huxley could disagree. The issue could not be settled either empirically or logically. It was a matter of faith.

It is important to remember that Temple was appointed Archbishop of Canterbury in 1896, and although this event did not pass without protest it effectively marked the Anglican acceptance of the evolutionary theory that had emerged in biology. Temple, besides being an exponent of an 'evolutionary theology', had earlier been one of the authors of the controversial *Essays and Reviews* (see note 10). Consequently, the appointment of this spokesman of the liberal view to the archepiscopate was a clear indication of the Anglican Church's reconciliation with both the liberal approach to Biblical criticism and the evolutionary theory of man's development.

In America, however, the reconciliation took longer to effect, and even today certain fundamentalist groups are still very active.[18] A law banning the teaching of biological evolutionism in public schools was passed in Tennessee in 1925, and was challenged in the celebrated Scopes Trial in the same year.[19] Although the teacher, John Thomas Scopes, was found guilty of breaking the law by instructing his pupils in the theory of biological evolution, the moral victory lay with the defendant and his able counsel, Clarence Darrow. After the farce of the Scopes Trial, biology has generally been taught on evolutionary lines in America without interference, although in recent years — in the pluralistic mood of contemporary America — a number of classes teach the non-evolutionary view and special-creationist textbooks have been published fairly recently.[20] The Tennessee law was repealed in 1967.

In the twentieth century, apart from a few exceptions such as have been indicated above, Protestant theologians have largely come to terms with evolutionism and evolutionary biology. This has been made possible by regarding substantial sections of the Bible, and particularly *Genesis*, as *allegorical* in character, as a series of poetical utterances, or as a form of myth. This is by no means an entirely new approach. Several of the early Church fathers, and even St Augustine himself, were prepared to accept certain Biblical passages as allegorical.[21] And in the seventeenth century, Sir Thomas Browne (1605-1682), in his widely read and admired *Religio Medici* (1643), maintained that:

> Unspeakable mysteries in the Scriptures are often delivered in a vulgar and illustrative way; and being written unto man, are delivered, not as they truly are, but as they may be understood.[22]

But it is only in the twentieth century that there has been a fairly general acceptance of the doctrine. Clearly, it was Darwinism that helped Christianity to move in this direction — that gave it perhaps its strongest impetus.

Thus the orthodoxy of the present-day Protestantism asserts that it is *faith* that forms the ultimate basis of religion, and that rational argument is not the way to an acceptance of Christianity or any other kind of theism. *Natural* theology, then, has almost died and Darwinism has helped to dig its grave.

The neo-orthodoxy does not reject the Bible, of course, but it is no longer thought of in any way as a text-book of science or of history. Rather, the Bible, as the old adage says, tells not how the heavens go, but how to go to heaven. Or, more seriously (but again in somewhat metaphorical terms), the Bible throws light on an important dimension of reality — the spiritual dimension — which is ignored by science. The Bible supposedly 'points towards' some kind of spiritual reality underlying human history, without giving explicit and factually correct accounts of the historical events in the creation of the world — perhaps not even of the life of Jesus. Faith is paramount. And God (for Karl Barth, for example) is held to be the 'ground of man's being' — or his ontological basis, as the philosophers would say.[23]

It is rather difficult to write a satisfactory account of the Protestant response to Darwinism because the Church of England, for example, never took any official 'line' on the question which might be regarded as marking the generality of views on the subject within the Anglican Church.[24] Indeed, it would not have been appropriate for a Church that preached that each member should seek personal grace and salvation through personal faith and piety to lay down a series of official pronouncements on the question of evolutionary theory. Therefore, for Protestantism — that religion so very appropriate to, and intimately bound up with, the individualism and *laissez-faire* doctrines of the West — the history of the reconciliation with Darwinism is represented by a series of separate personal decisions and separate intellectual accommodations — or individual weakenings of the faith to agnosticism or a more forthright atheism.

But in the Roman Catholic Church, the historical development may be traced by means of a series of official pronouncements such as the various papal encyclicals.[25] As we have seen, the initial Catholic reaction to *The Origin* was quite subdued, for although the literal veracity of the Bible was impugned, the question of man's nature was only touched on somewhat obliquely. But the publication of *The Descent of Man* drew strong opposition from the Catholic press and from the Church itself.

It is a matter of considerable doctrinal importance for Catholics that each man and woman is possessed of an immortal soul, and that there was originally just one human pair thus equipped. But the Darwinian theory said nothing about entities such as immortal souls. In fact, as we know, Darwin believed in a wholly naturalistic explanation of mental phenomena, and although one could maintain the idea of the corporeal creation of mankind through the process of Darwinian evolution, together with the idea of a special and unique creation of man when Adam became imbued with the Holy Spirit, such a view was rather implausible.

So, after an initially quiet reaction to *The Origin*, over about the last thirty years of the nineteenth century the Catholic Church adopted a substantially fundamentalist position, and by official decree the members of the Church were positively discouraged from taking up theological issues that might be related to the question of evolutionism. Indeed the authors of one or two works dealing with evolutionary themes[26] were formally advised by the Holy Office that their opinions had been judged untenable, although the writings were not placed on the Index of forbidden books.

Catholicism in the latter part of the nineteenth century became one of the world's most conservative institutions. The infallibility of the Pope, for example, was pronounced at the Vatican Council in 1870; it is not by any means a doctrine of venerable tradition. And generally speaking there was a strong reaffirmation of the ancient Augustinian and Thomistic roots of the Church. This precluded admission of Darwinian evolutionism, especially about man and his immortal soul. The papal encyclical, *Providentissimus Dei*, issued in 1893 by Pope Leo XIII, preached an uncompromising literalism, asserting that:

> All the books, which the Church receives as sacred and canonical, are written wholly and entirely, with all their parts, at the dictation of the Holy Ghost; and so far is it from being possible that any error can co-exist with inspiration, that inspiration not only is essentially incompatible with error, but excludes and rejects it as absolutely and necessarily as it is impossible that God Himself, the supreme Truth, can utter that which is not true.[27]

Protestantism, by its very individualistic inchoate nature, could never have made an official pronouncement such as this, setting up an almost impenetrable barrier between evolutionary science and theology.

However, by 1909, with decrees issued by the Pontifical Biblical Commission, a middle way was already being sought between the dogma of unbending fundamentalism on the one hand and a totally allegorical interpretation of the Bible on the other.[28] It was maintained that *Genesis* contained elements of history, although it did not choose to use the literary forms of modern historiography. But despite this element of liberality, and an admission that an absolutely strict literalism was not required, it was asserted that the first three chapters of Genesis did contain a 'narrative which corresponds to objective reality and historic truth'.[29]

In 1943, in the encyclical of Pope Pius XII entitled *Divine Afflante Spiritu*, it was urged that those trying to interpret the Old Testament should seek to do so by trying to understand the ways and thinking and expression of the Near East in Biblical times.[30] This was clearly moving away further from a strict literalism, and would allow an element of allegorical interpretation.

Then in 1951, in a celebrated encyclical of Pope Pius XII entitled *Humani Generis*,[31] the following points were made:

1   In any discussion of evolution, the Catholic must take for granted the spiritual soul of man.
2   Otherwise, such a discussion is left open by the Church.
3   However, such a discussion is for experts in science and theology, and reasons for and against must be gravely weighed. The Catholic must be ready to submit to the judgement of the Church.
4   People should not take it for granted that evolution is a proved fact and should not act as if there were no theological reasons for reserve and caution in their discussions.[32]

This cleared away any remaining official obstacles to the discussion of evolutionary questions by Catholic scholars. The idea of books on this subject being placed on the Index today seems far-fetched indeed. The result of this relaxation has been a considerable heightening of Catholic interest in evolutionary questions in the post-war years, and the idea of an allegorical interpretation of the *Genesis* account of the creation of the Earth and man is now widespread in Catholic circles. However, the question of whether there was a single creation of a first pair of humans is still a point of some delicacy. Clearly, 'polygenism' is scarcely compatible with the doctrine of original sin as it is customarily understood. And most Catholics subscribe to the monogenist view.[33]

With this relaxation and the assumed allegorical interpretation of *Genesis*, the Catholic Church, as the Protestant Churches several decades earlier, has retreated from its besieged fundamentalist position which was in theory open to some kind of empirical test and might be regarded as a component of a natural theology with a bond between science, historical scholarship and faith, to a more strictly fideist position. For no one can produce any kind of empirical test to distinguish between the claims of monogenism and polygenism. How can we know empirically whether Adam and Eve (or some equivalent) were the first human pair, endowed with some (by definition) non-material entity known as an immortal soul? In the days of dominance of fundamentalist thinking, the Bible — God's Revelation to man — could be supposed to supply a kind of 'empirical' means of knowing that the monogenist doctrine was the correct one. But with the dissolution of the sacred texts into a collocation of writings more or less allegorical, this test no longer holds and we are left with faith as the sole arbiter. Earlier, I wrote of the gradual decline of the Protestant Churches, but stated that the Catholic Church was managing to maintain its support with greater success. I am inclined to think, however, that when the 'modernist' movement that has influenced Church intellectuals percolates down to the less well educated laity, we will see a similar fall-off in support for the Catholic Church. Faith alone may move mountains; but by itself it is not always equal to the task of imparting a sense of intellectual conviction to educated people.

So far in the discussions of this chapter we have been looking mainly at the negative side of the coin – at the various accommodations, reconciliations and admissions that religion and theology have had to make in response to the challenge of the biological theory of evolution. But in some quarters there was a much more positive response, with new *quasi*-religious systems of a curious secular character being built on the foundation provided by the new evolutionism.

Such systems did not all originate in Darwin's theory. The French positivist philosopher, Auguste Comte (1798-1857), for example, had sought to transform his philosophy into what he called a 'Religion of Humanity', with its own ceremonies, sacraments, priests and temples, and a list of saints made up of the great contributors to the progress of mankind. Comte sought to establish his bizarre new religion as a secular equivalent of the Roman Catholic Church (for which he expressed a considerable admiration), and he achieved some success in this endeavour in his native France, and more particularly in South America. There was even a Positivist temple in Melbourne at one time. Also, it was Comtean ideas that led to the establishment of the world's first chair in History of Science, at the Collège de France in 1892.[34] And in the twentieth century one of the first professional historians of science, George Sarton, believed that the study of the history of science had a kind of therapeutic value, helping to bridge the gulf between the arts and the sciences and establish what he termed the 'new humanism'.[35]

It was not, however, through establishment of Comtean positivist replicas of the Catholic Church that Western culture moved towards its present pervasive secularism. Much more widespread, and of far greater significance, was the general philosophical movement known as *humanism*; and this – also a kind of secular religion – drew very considerably on evolutionism in general and the Darwin/Wallace theory in particular.

Humanism is not a new philosophical movement, but it has only come into wide esteem and prominence in the twentieth century. It draws on a variety of ethical systems, on the philosophies of naturalism and materialism, on the methods of the sciences, on ideals of democracy and liberty, on earlier traditions of Renaissance humanism and on the values of art and literature. Corliss Lamont has listed ten of the major tenets of the humanist movement as:

naturalism;
the idea that man is an evolutionary product of nature;
the belief that human beings have within themselves the power of solving their own problems;
an acceptance of the doctrine of free-will and a denial of predestination;
the belief that the highest ethical goal is happiness, freedom and progress in this world;
the idea that the good life is arrived at through self-development and work contributing to the development of the community;

the policy that art and awareness of beauty should be given special encouragement;
the establishment of a world democracy;
the widespread use of scientific method as a means of solving problems, with full freedom of expression permitted;
the belief in the constant necessity of questioning one's basic assumptions.[36]

It will be appreciated from this list that although most Western men and women may not choose to identify themselves explicitly as philosophical humanists or spend their time at humanist society meetings, these ten points do encapsulate many of the basic assumptions of educated, Western, liberal society. Clearly, the humanist creed represents a major component of the thinking of many of us.

The first two items on the list of Lamont's articles of faith are intimately related to the Darwinian Revolution. Naturalism was a major premise of Darwin's thinking and the success of his theory gave strong sanction to the validity of naturalism, showing that the supernatural account of the world's seeming design was a superfluity. And the belief in the evolutionary origin of man's body and mind draws enormous strength from the Darwinian theory. Obviously, without an intellectually cogent theory of biological evolution there could be no place for the second item on Lamont's list, bearing in mind the requirement of the tenth humanist 'commandment' — the constant testing of basic assumptions.

So a metaphysical system, although naturalistic and secular, has been built up by modern humanists around the nucleus of biological evolutionism. Such a system may be seen to the best advantage in the writings of the well-known biologist, Julian Huxley (1887-1975), grandson of Darwin's 'bulldog', Thomas Henry Huxley. Really Julian Huxley espoused a new religion, rather than a mere metaphysical system. Accepting with enthusiasm the doctrine of evolutionism, he maintained that the future evolutionary process on Earth is to be carried out almost exclusively by man. Thus man's destiny has become that of realising his evolutionary potentialities and furthering the evolutionary process, which for Huxley is a notion that may be contemplated with a kind of religious enthusiasm:

> Instead of worshipping supernatural rulers, . . . [the new evolutionary humanism] will sanctify the higher manifestations of human nature, in art and love, in intellectual comprehension and aspiring adoration, and will emphasize the fuller realization of life's possibilities as a sacred trust.[37]

The use of words such as 'sanctify', 'adoration' and 'sacred' is indicative of the elevation of evolutionary theory to the religious plane. Huxley sees the evolutionary emergence of intellectual powers in man as something inherently good and worthy of esteem. The process of the realisation of the possibilities of man (through the application of the methods of science, but with due regard to aesthetic considerations) has become the object of his faith.[38]

Unfortunately, however, in attempting to use evolution as a basis for some kind of ethical code, Huxley is, I believe, falling into the trap which philosophers are pleased to call the 'naturalistic fallacy', and his system is unstable at its very foundations. But we shall not pause here to discuss this point, which is taken up in more detail in the next chapter. All that needs emphasis here is the fact of the existence of evolutionary humanism as a philosophical system and its affinities with religious modes of thinking.

The tenets of the humanist movement mesh well with the generality of beliefs in the contemporary liberal West even though the number of people specifically calling themselves humanists is quite small. In other words, in one direction at least, the evolutionary doctrines of Darwinism have emerged as a point of wide consensus in the secular world of the twentieth century. But it should be noted that this was by no means a necessary development. In Germany, the evolutionary doctrine was taken up with zeal and enthusiasm by the influential zoologist Ernst Haeckel (1834-1919), who developed what he called the 'monist' philosophy from Darwin's evolutionary naturalism. In Haeckel's view, ideas and spiritual values were mere epiphenomena[39] with respect to matter. Hence we have the name *monism*, which became the *Leitmotif* of the Monist League, established in Germany in the late nineteenth century to propagate the monist viewpoint. This movement, like that of the gentle British humanists, with their Fabian affiliations, took on a *quasi*-religious character. But in Germany it became a leading platform of right-wing Social Darwinism, and, as Daniel Gasman has recently shown in an important study,[40] it provided the chief intellectual basis of Hitler's National Socialism. Evolutionary humanism did not always lead in directions that one would wish to commend.

We may complete this chapter by considering briefly a couple of twentieth-century examples of writings that have sought to employ evolutionary concepts, although certainly not by using the methodology of investigations in evolutionary biology — to yield religious systems that are highly mystical in character, and can not be regarded as scientific. They are also very remote from the evolutionary humanism of men such as Julian Huxley. It will be quite impossible to do proper justice to these modern mystics, for the systems they have propounded are of considerable complexity; so it is necessary to refer the reader who has a particular interest in such matters to the original texts for a full and satisfactory exposition. Our purpose here is the very limited one of seeking to show yet another dimension of the impact of evolutionism on modern thought.

Rudolf Steiner (1861-1925) is well known in many parts of the world for the system of education which he founded, and the many schools, now well established, that bear his name. He is also becoming widely known in recent years for his admirable ideas on 'natural' agriculture, nutrition and health. And many persons who do not subscribe to the general metaphysics of his system find much of value in Steiner's ideas on education and health. But it was the general religious system known as 'anthroposophy' which was perhaps his chief concern.

Steiner's system was not directly connected with Darwin's evolutionism. It would be much more accurate to see it as an eclectic blend of Christianity, Nature Philosophy, Rosicrucianism, Gnosticism, Eastern religions, Pythagoreanism, Stoicism, and much else. But the overall picture of the cosmos that he presented was evolutionary in character. Perhaps one should say developmental, rather than evolutionary, although his English translators have chosen to render his German term *'Entwicklung'* by 'evolution'.

Steiner wrote as a kind of seer or clairvoyant and claimed that he had a special mystical intuition into the nature of man's being and essence, into his evolutionary past, and into the history of the Earth. He believed that human beings are constituted in a seven-fold aspect: 1 Physical body; 2 Etheric body or life-body; 3 Astral body; 4 I or Ego; 5 Spirit-Self; 6 Life-Spirit; 7 Spirit-Man. Man gradually 'evolved', from the condition in which he was a mere 'physical body' to the condition of conscious selfhood, the 'I' or 'Ego', through the intermediate conditions of Etheric body and Astral body, by means of the successive additions of Spirit-Self, Life-Spirit and Spirit-Man. Each stage supposedly corresponded to a particular stage of the development (or evolution) of the cosmos — stages which Steiner designated as Saturn, Sun, Moon and Earth, respectively, and which were characterised, he claimed, by the attributes of warmth (fire), air, water, and earth.[41]

Put in this bald way, the system seems merely cranky, and I am strongly inclined to see it that way. One cannot, of course, argue with anthroposophists about the truth or falsehood of their assertions. For Steiner maintained that he had esoteric knowledge of such matters by means of his privileged powers of clairvoyance. One cannot argue a person out of an intellectual position if he was not argued into it in the first place by some kind of rational process. Those who have ever had discussions on politics or religion with anyone will know the broad truth of this. But Steiner's ideas are really no more obscure intellectually speaking than, say, the doctrine of the Holy Trinity. And if one evaluates the worth of his religion from the quality of the lives of some of those who profess it, then one might say with some confidence that his intellectual system was wholly admirable.

Also of interest and importance and perhaps more directly related to the evolutionary doctrines of modern biology is the work of the Jesuit priest, archaeologist, paleontologist, and scholar, Pierre Teilhard de Chardin (1881-1955).[42] Chardin is remembered for his contributions to the discovery of Peking Man (*Sinanthropus*), but his metaphysical speculations on the future course of evolution of man, presented in a number of books, chiefly *The Phenomenon of Man* (1959),[43] have attracted considerably greater attention.

Chardin's ideas were uncharacteristic of the religious order to which he belonged and his metaphysical work was given little official encouragement during his lifetime. However, he has been read widely in the post-War period, although having considerably more appeal to evolutionary humanists such as Julian Huxley than to Catholic orthodoxy.[44] Doubtless one reason for Chardin's appeal to the post-War generation was his immense optimism, which gave much comfort to men in the distressful conditions of the Cold War. Yet he has been assailed with but little kindness by hard-nosed critics such as Sir Peter Medawar,[45] and his ultimate position in intellectual history is still somewhat uncertain.

Chardin's work was acknowledged to be indebted to a considerable degree to the ideas of the French evolutionary philosopher, Henri Bergson, whose work is described briefly in the following chapter. But Chardin denied that his scheme had the character of metaphysical speculation, and he maintained rather that it was strictly scientific in character. No doubt it was this somewhat grotesque claim that so offended Medawar's sensibilities.

In some respects Chardin's major thesis had something in common with that of Spencer's leading evolutionary principle. Chardin supposed that the whole cosmos is an evolving entity, the evolutionary process entailing a constant increase of complexity, accompanied by a corresponding increase in level of consciousness. But matter, even in its lowest level — what we would normally think of as inanimate or inorganic substance — had for Chardin, a minimal level of consciousness. This is able to express itself when higher levels of matter complexity are gradually developed during the evolutionary process.

We are normally accustomed to think of the lithosphere, the hydrosphere, the atmosphere, and the biosphere. In addition, said Chardin, since the advent of man there has come into being the 'layer' of mind or consciousness. This, he designated the '*noosphere*' — or the sphere of the '*νοῦς*' (*nous*) — which has supposedly 'emerged' as the complexification of matter has taken place. But this, he says, is not yet the culmination of the whole process. One may look forward to a further stage of evolution, when consciousness may transcend altogether its present connections with matter. In this further evolutionary step, the process is convergent rather than divergent, and consciousness in some way focusses to a single point of cohesion. This is the celebrated 'omega point' (Ω) of Chardin's theology, which by some curious piece of exegesis he manages to identify with Christ or one of the Persons of the Trinity. Thus the final level of evolution — beyond that of the *noosphere* — is supposedly what Chardin refers to as the 'Christosphere'.

One must agree wholeheartedly with Medawar that claims that Chardin's system is in any way scientific are utterly absurd. It is obviously an exercise in metaphysics, and the poetical language in which the arguments are presented is appropriate enough to this end. Medawar, therefore, would perhaps have been wiser to have seen the matter in this light, and been kinder or more courteous in his criticism.

But this is not to say that Chardin is talking in a way that bears much relationship to the actuality of the universe that we happen to inhabit. He is telling us of his personal faith and his vision of the cosmos. He was optimistic for the future, as he believed that out of the great seething mass of humanity arising from the natural processes of population growth there would emerge the matter-independent levels of the *noosphere* and ultimately the 'Christosphere'. He could therefore contemplate the possible physical destruction of the world in some atomic Armageddon with a certain equanimity. But this optimism, I suggest, arose from the recesses of Chardin's noble personality, and was not warranted by the nature of the evolutionary process.

In this chapter, we have wandered far from the prosaic 'higgledy-piggledy'[46] theory of Darwin and Wallace, and it is obvious that much of what we have been describing utterly transcends that which may legitimately be inferred from the biological theory of evolution. There is no need to labour this point. What we have discerned is, however, admirable evidence for the extraordinary diversity of thinking about evolutionary themes that the Western world has seen since the days of Darwin and Wallace. The whole of our civilisation has seemingly been in the grip of an evolutionist *Zeitgeist*.[47] Evolutionism jumped over the boundaries that might have limited it to a biological paradigm. It thrust into theology, upsetting established systems of metaphysics and spawning some bizarre substitutes. Perhaps only in the last ten years or so has the Western world seriously questioned the possibility, the propriety, or the wisdom of a constant forward evolutionary thrust. For such prognostications as science is able to make do not foretell a coming convergence to a divine Omega Point, but rather an exhaustion of world resources and much hunger and misery, a situation which will not be mitigated by metaphysical speculations of an evolutionary cast of mind.

NOTES CHAPTER 18

1   From C. Beard, *The Reformation of the 16th Century in its Relation to Modern Thought and Knowledge*, University of Michigan Press, Ann Arbor, 1962 (1st edn, 1883), p.123.
2   *The First Book of Moses, called Genesis*, Chapter 2, Verse 5.
3   See B. Gandevia, 'The breath of life: an essay on the earliest history of respiration', *The Australian Journal of Physiotherapy*, Vol. 16, 1970, pp.5-23.
4   C. Darwin (ed., J. W. Burrow), *The Origin of Species*, Penguin, Harmondsworth, 1968, p.458.
5   As we will emphasise further below, the Catholic Church was not at first as antagonistic towards the evolutionary theory as were the Protestants, for the source of Catholic authority was to some degree independent of the scriptures. But Catholic opinion hardened against evolutionism after the appearance of *The Descent of Man*, where the doctrine of man's immortal soul was seemingly impugned.
6   *The Book of Joshua*, Chapter 10, Verse 12.
7   These criticisms were traced in A. D. White's notorious book, *A History of the Warfare of Science with Theology in Christendom*, 2 vols, New York, 1896, Vol. 2, Chapter 20 (republished Dover, New York, 1960).
8   For a description of the aims and methods of this movement, see C. Beard, *op. cit.* (note 1), pp.351-353.
9   Gladstone (MP for Oxford) made a detailed study of the writings of Homer, and sought to show that the contents of *The Odyssey* and *The Iliad* were compatible with the accounts of the early history of mankind given in the Peutateuch (W. E. Gladstone, *Studies on Homer and the Homeric Age*, 3 vols, Oxford, 1858). Gladstone continued his anti-evolutionist and literalist stance for many years. See, for example, his volume *The Impregnable Rock of Holy Scripture*, London, 1890.

10 The Declaration was directed against the authors of a theological volume by seven liberal theologians, entitled *Essays and Reviews* (1860), rather than biological evolutionism *per se*. But the two issues became interlocked in the public mind. For an outline of the *Essays and Reviews* controversy, see A. R. Vidler, *The Church in an Age of Revolution*, Penguin, Harmondsworth, 1961, Chapter 11.

11 St George Jackson Mivart (1827-1900) was a Catholic naturalist of some distinction. He reviewed *The Descent of Man* in 1871 (*The Quarterly Review*, Vol. 131, 1871, pp.47-90), and also wrote against Darwin in *On the Genesis of Species* (London, 1871). Mivart accepted biological evolution of a saltatory kind, but disallowed its extension to man's rationality. He was eventually excommunicated because of his opposition to papal infallibility rather than from his unorthodoxy in matters of evolutionary theory. He made a number of pertinent objections to the Darwinian version of the evolutionary theory which Darwin thought it necessary to seek to rebut in the 6th edition of *The Origin*.

12 W. Hopkins, 'Physical theories of the phenomena of life', Part 1, *Frazer's Magazine*, Vol. 61, 1860, pp.739-752; Part 2, *ibid.*, Vol. 62, 1860, pp.74-90 (at p.89).

13 *Edinburgh New Philosophical Journal*, Vol. 16, 1862, p.285. (This remark is contained in a review of Darwin's work on the fertilisation of orchids [1862], but it relates to the general naturalistic argument of *The Origin of Species*.)

14 A. Gray, *Darwiniana: Essays and Reviews pertaining to Darwinism*, New York, 1876 (republished, Cambridge, Mass., 1963). Gray's opinion was first expressed publicly in his review of *The Origin*, published in *Atlantic Monthly* in 1860. He wrote: 'We should advise Mr Darwin to assume, in the philosophy of his hypothesis, that variation has been led along certain beneficial lines' (1963, pp.121-122).

15 But such a view was clearly fraught with difficulty. If all organisms had been created 'at one go', so to speak, this would clash with the well-known observations of the fossil record. One could, of course, suggest that God had created fossils so that the world *looked* as if it had a long geological history, and one writer did seriously make this somewhat bizarre suggestion (P. H. Gosse, *Omphalos: An Attempt to Untie the Geological Knot*, London, 1857), although critics merely laughed at him. It has recently been shown, however, that the relationship between Darwin and Gosse has been partially misunderstood (F. C. Ross, 'Phillip Gosse's *Omphalos*, Edmund Gosse's *Father and Son*, and Darwin's theory of natural selection', *Isis*, Vol. 68, 1977, pp.85-96). Incidentally, readers may care to consider why Gosse chose the word *Omphalos* (meaning navel) as the title of his book.

16 H. W. Beecher, *Evolution and Religion . . .* [twenty six] *Sermons discussing the Bearings of the Evolutionary Philosophy on the Fundamental Doctrines of Evangelical Christianity*, 2 vols, London & New York, 1885-1886, Vol. 1, p.115. Here, among other interesting statements, we find the profound observation that: 'Design by wholesale is grander than design by retail'! Beecher was not, perhaps, the most reputable spokesman for the new evolutionary theology. Earlier, he had become involved in a highly publicised law-suit in relation to an accusation of adultery with one of the members of his congregation. (See R. Shaplen, *Free Love and Heavenly Sinners: The Story of the Great Henry Ward Beecher Scandal*, Knopf, New York, 1954.)

17 F. Temple, *The Relations between Religion and Science: Eight Lectures preached before the University of Oxford in the Year 1884*, London, 1885, p.119 (republished Gregg, Farnborough, 1972).

18 There is, for example, a 'Creation Science Research Center' based in San Diego, and a 'Creation Research Society' in Ann Arbor. In Australia, the 'Evolutionary Protest Movement (Australian Branch)' produces a small *News Gazette*.

19 For a transcript of part of the proceedings of this trial, see P. Appleman (ed.), *Darwin: A Norton Critical Edition*, Norton, New York, 1970, pp.533-544.

20 For example, H. M. Morris *et al.*, *Scientific Creationism*, Creation Life, San Diego, 1974. In relation to the controversies associated with the recent revival of special creationism, see, D. Nelkin, 'Creation vs. evolution: the politics of science education', in: E. Mendelsohn, P. Weingart & R. Whitley (eds), *The Social Production of Scientific Knowledge*, Reidel, Dordrecht, 1977, pp.265-287.

21 St Augustine wrote: 'We can . . . interpret the details of paradise with reference to the Church, which gives them a better significance as prophetic indications of things to come in the future. Thus paradise stands for the Church itself, as described in the *Song of Songs*; the four rivers represent the four Gospels; the fruit trees, the saints; and the fruit, their achievements; the tree of life, the Holy of Holies, must be Christ himself; while the tree of knowledge of good and evil symbolises the personal decision of man's free will; (Augustine, *Concerning The City of God against the Pagans*: a new Translation by Henry Bettenson with an introduction by David Knowles, Penguin, Harmondsworth, 1972, p.535 (Book XIII, Chapter 21).

22 W. A. Greenhill (ed.), *Sir Thomas Browne's Religio Medici . . .*, Macmillan & St Martin's Press, London & New York, 1966, p.72.

23 In Barth's words: 'The *ground* of creation is God's grace, and the fact that there is a grace of God is real and present to us, alive and powerful in God's Word' (K. Barth, *Dogmatics in Outline*, S.C.M. Press, London, 1966, p.57).

24   For a further account of Protestant attitudes towards evolutionary theory, see, for example, J. Dillen-berger, *Protestant Thought and Natural Science: A Historical Interpretation*, Collins, London, 1961, Chapter 8.

25   For an account of these, see J. C. Greene, *Darwin and the Modern World View*, Louisiana State University Press, Baton Rouge, 1961; Z. Alszeghi, 'Development in the doctrinal formulations of the Church concerning the theory of evolution', *Concilium*, Vol. 6, 1967, pp.14-17.

26   M. D. Leroy, *L'Evolution Restreint aux Espèces Organiques*, Paris & Lyon, 1891; J. A. Zohm, *Evolution and Dogma*, Chicago, 1896.

27   Cited in D. Lack, *Evolutionary Theory and Christian Belief*, Methuen, London, 1957, p.32.

28   Z. Alszeghi, *op. cit.* (note 25), p.15. And see 'On the historical character of the first three chapters of Genesis (June 30, 1909)', in *Rome and the Study of Scripture: A Collection of Papal Enactments on the Study of Holy Scripture together with the Decisions of the Biblical Commission*, 6th edn, Grail Publications, St Meinrad, Indiana, 1958, pp.120-122.

29   *Ibid. (Papal Enactments)*, p.120.

30   'Encyclical letter of His Holiness, Pius XII, Divino afflante spiritu: On the promotion of Biblical studies', in *Foundations of Renewal: Four Great Encyclicals of Pope Pius XII*, Deus Books, Paulist Press, Glen Rock, 1961, pp.64-87.

31   'Encyclical letter of His Holiness, Pius XII, Humani generis: Concerning some false opinions which threaten to undermine the foundations of Catholic doctrine', *ibid.*, pp.171-186.

32   As summarised by J. F. Ewing, 'Current Roman Catholic thought on evolution; in S. Tax (ed.), *Evolution after Darwin: The University of Chicago Centennial, Volume III: Issues in Evolution*, Chicago University Press, Chicago, 1960, pp.19-28 (p.26).

33   For further discussion of the polygenist/monogenist controversy in the nineteenth century, see below, pages 298-299.

34   See H. W. Paul, 'Scholarship versus ideology: the chair of the general history of science at the Collège de France, 1892-1913', *Isis*, Vol. 67, 1976, pp.376-397.

35   See T. Frängsmyr, 'Science or history: George Sarton and the positivist tradition in the history of science', *Lychnos*, 1973-1974, pp.104-144.

36   C. Lamont, *The Philosophy of Humanism*, Vision, London, 1962, pp.10-11.

37   J. S. Huxley, 'The humanist frame', in J. S. Huxley (ed.), *The Humanist Frame*, Allen & Unwin, London, 1961, pp.11-48 (p.26).

38   J. S. Huxley, *Religion without Revelation*, Parrish, London, 1957, p.239.

39   'Epiphenomenon' meant originally in medicine a 'secondary symptom'. To illustrate the philosophical meaning of the term, we may consider the following example. In physics, it may be supposed that the particular vibrations of particular atomic particles give rise to the appearance of yellowness, but the atomic particles are not themselves yellow. Then one may say that the yellowness is an epiphenomenon with respect to atoms' motions. Similarly, it might be suggested that mental processes are mere epiphenomena with respect to the electrical and chemical changes taking place in the nerve cells of the brain; that there is no such thing as 'mind' independent of body.

40   D. Gasman, *The Scientific Origins of National Socialism: Social Darwinism in Ernst Haeckel and the German Monist League*, Macdonald, London & New York, 1971.

41   See R. Steiner, *Occult Science – An Outline*, Rudolf Steiner Press, London, 1969.

42   For a brief but clear and sympathetic account of Chardin's work, see E. Delfgaauw, *Evolution: The Theory of Teilhard de Chardin*, Fontana, London & New York, 1969.

43   P. Teilhard de Chardin, *The Phenomenon of Man*, Collins & Harper, London & New York, 1959. This was written in Peking in the years 1938-1940. For a more concise and coherent account of Chardin's system, see his *Man's Place in Nature: the Human Zoological Group*, Fontana, London & New York, 1966.

44   Huxley wrote a complimentary introduction to the English translation of *The Phenomenon of Man*.

45   P. B. Medawar, *The Art of the Soluble: Creativity and Originality in Science*, Penguin, Harmondsworth, 1969, pp.81-92. (Medawar's review first appeared in *Mind* in January, 1961.)

46   This term was suggested by the physicist, Sir John Herschel. Darwin did not like it. In a letter to Lyell he wrote: 'I have heard, by a roundabout channel, that Herschel says my book "is the law of higgledy-piggledy". What this exactly means I do not know, but it is evidently very contemptuous. If true this is a great blow and discouragement' (F. Darwin (ed.), *The Life and Letters of Charles Darwin*, 3 vols, John Murray, London, 1887, Vol. 2, p.241).

47   Literally, 'time-spirit'. For further discussion of this concept, see below, pages 346-347.

19

Darwinism and Philosophy

The influence of Darwinism on philosophical thinking has been considerable and many-sided, but the precise way this influence has acted is by no means easy to state in simple terms. So in this chapter I will deal with a number of facets of the problem in a fairly compartmentalised manner, despite the fact that this will to some extent have a distorting effect on the discussion, for philosophy, while by no means a wholly seamless garment, is perhaps a more coherent and integrated discipline than the present exposition may tend to suggest.[1]

Questions about the relationships between Darwinism and religious, social and political philosophy have already been treated in previous chapters. We may move on immediately to consider the relationship between Darwinism and essentialism.

Darwinism and Essentialism

In Chapter One some account was given of the ancient doctrine of essentialism. But it may be helpful to remind the reader that in the Aristotelian tradition scientific inquiry consisted of a search for the definitions of the so-called 'essences' of things, stated in terms of genus and species. From these definitions the properties of the things might hopefully be determined by deduction.

Platonism, likewise, subscribed to an essentialist theory of knowledge, the essences being thought to reside in the transcendent Platonic world of 'forms', which the intellect might try to apprehend with the aid of 'dialectic'. But the net result was much the same as that yielded by the Aristotelian program, for by the dialectical method Plato simply meant talking round a problem until an acceptable 'essential' definition of a thing or concept had been reached.[2] This supposedly allowed one to apprehend the 'forms' of things or concepts. Plato also explored the possibility that words expressed essences directly by various onomatopoeic links,[3] although he never acquired much following in this aspect of his philosophy.

It should be appreciated, however, that the doctrine of essentialism, as Sir Karl Popper calls it in his various writings,[4] is of wider application than just the epistemologies and ontologies of Platonism or Aristotelianism, even in all their many ramifications. Indeed, Popper dubs all supposed 'ultimate' explanations as being essentialist in character. For the chemist John Dalton, for example, the ultimate explanations of chemical phenomena were to be given in terms of the various atoms hypothesised in his atomic theory. These atoms were the *essential* feature of Dalton's theory – the essence of the matter, in his view. For Newtonian mechanics, mass, length and time served were as 'ultimates'. One cannot, in terms of the Newtonian theory, analyse the concept of mass and say what it is caused by. It just 'is'; mass is the essential characteristic of matter. For a Christian theist the ultimate explanation of the cosmos is God. The Christian does not seek to explain God's existence or attributes in terms of something yet more fundamental or essential.

So, in their various ways, the Daltonian, the Newtonian and the Christian are all essentialists according to Popper's usage of the word. It may be noted that Popper does not believe that science is ever satisfied with ultimate, or essentialist, explanation; and he believes that it *ought* not to be. Whether he is right in this is an interesting and difficult question, but not one that need concern us here.

In Chapter 2 we noted that the essentialism of the Aristotelian tradition was strongly attacked in the seventeenth century by John Locke, in favour of the doctrine of nominalism. And we saw Buffon in the eighteenth century trying to treat the natural history of the animal kingdom from a nominalist standpoint. But such views did not achieve a particularly wide acceptance or application and Buffon himself quickly gave up his more radical nominalism. Thus the Linnaean view, standing in the Aristotelian tradition, prevailed in the eighteenth century and naturalists of the early nineteenth century were still seeking the *essential* characteristics of animals and plants, which would enable them to be pigeon-holed satisfactorily within a taxonomic system. It should be noted that this approach meshed well with the natural theology and the various forms of design argument that were so widely held in the nineteenth century. For in the popular view God supposedly created the various species of creatures in the Garden of Eden, making each kind *essentially* different from all the others.

As David Hull has pointed out,[5] there were really three areas where essentialism seemed to be particularly successful: in Euclidian geometry, chemistry and natural history. In Euclidian geometry the essentialist doctrine worked pretty well – and still does. A triangle is a three-sided plane figure; a quadrilateral is a four-sided plane figure. They have different definitions – different 'essences'. It would be absurd to suppose that a triangle could change its essence and 'evolve' into a quadrilateral. Likewise, in the nineteenth century, it was thought equally absurd that gold might transmute or 'evolve' into silver, or a dog might turn into a cat, or an ape into a man. One divinely created species could not change into another — at least not according to the orthodox theory of knowledge and the ontology of Christian theism.

But this was what the Darwin/Wallace theory and other evolutionary theories such as that of Lamarck were suggesting. Euclidian triangles cannot change into squares. Of this there was, and is, no doubt. But if Darwin were correct it seemed that some ape-like creature *could* evolve into man. So after Darwin, biological species became *historical* entities determined by their genealogies.[6] As a result, the doctrine of *essentially* different natural kinds was driven out of natural history by the Darwin/Wallace theory. And the subsequent discovery of radioactivity has displaced it from chemistry by destroying the doctrine of the immutability of elements, although it tends to re-assert itself in this science in the guise of whatever 'fundamental' sub-atomic particles are fashionable at any given time — such as protons, neutrinos, quarks, or what have you. Moreover, it might be said that relativity theory has even driven essentialism out of geometry, although this does not mean that Euclidian geometry cannot stand on its own when regarded as a deductive axiom system with arbitrarily chosen axioms.

The point to be made out of all this is that Darwin, perhaps unwittingly, fatally injured the ancient doctrine of philosophical essentialism by showing that the most popular instance on which it rested — the alleged *essential* differences between various kinds of animals or plants — was basically unsound. Creatures did not possess particular characteristics because God had willed that this should be so, or because there was a kind of necessary, changeless connection between the environment and animal or plant characteristics as Cuvier had supposed. Although the process was very slow, animals and plants could change their characteristics. The essences of organisms, therefore, were seemingly mere phantasms.

The case presented so far may not seem so serious for philosophy. But consider the following remark of the eminent British philosopher, William Whewell, in his *Philosophy of the Inductive Sciences* (1840):

> Our persuasion that there must needs be characteristic marks by which things can be defined in words, is founded on the assumption of *the necessary possibility of reasoning.*[7]

For Whewell, therefore, if evolutionary theory were true, essentialism would be false and natural kinds might slide around, so to speak, from one sort into another. No kind would be marked off clearly from all other kinds. And if Whewell was right, knowledge itself would seemingly be impossible or at least would lack all *certainty*. One would be left with a disquieting relativism; it would be impossible to gain a firm epistemological purchase on the world.

John Stuart Mill's canons of induction,[8] the basis of his inductive methodology of science, also presupposed the existence of natural kinds, and would seemingly slide into confusion if the essentialist view of kinds were disallowed. For example, Mill's 'method of agreement' may be represented in the following way. If:

A, B, C are followed by E
A, D, F are followed by E
A, G, H are followed by E
A, I, J are followed by E
etc.,

then according to the 'method of agreement' it may be said that A is the cause of E. But, if A, B, C, etc., could not be stated in essentialist terms, it would appear that Mill's method and his other canons would not be viable.

All this may seem a little odd for surely, one might say, the natures of animals and plants do not, according to the Darwin/Wallace theory, change so quickly that one cannot get a grip of understanding on the world at a particular time sufficient for practical purposes. Surely the theory of evolution is not suggesting anything so silly as cats changing into dogs before our very eyes!

This is true enough. For *practical* purposes, the advent of the Darwinian theory did not, and does not, make very much difference to taxonomic precedures.[9] But it considerably alters our view of the world — the way we conceptualise things and what we think we are doing when we conduct our investigations. It means that we recognise that we are not discovering final, ultimate, timeless or absolute truths. In natural history, we realise that we are merely ascertaining how things are now and with less certainty how they may have come to their present circumstances. We realise that we can have no certain knowledge of the course of evolution in the future. The absolute knowledge of the essentialist is foresworn; relativism takes its place.

It would not, of course, be true to say that the Darwinian theory was solely responsible for the decline of essentialism and the concomitant rise of relativism in many branches of philosophy (e.g. ethics) since Darwin's day. But there is no doubt that the evolutionary theory did make a significant contribution to the fundamental change in philosophical outlook that we have been outlining. The doctrine of essences has been driven out of philosophy and despite many years of subsequent effort it has not been possible to find a substitute that retrieves the 'absolutist' characteristics of the earlier theories of knowledge.

Darwinism and pragmatism

Let us now turn our attention to a consideration of the influence of Darwinism on the American school of philosophy known as *pragmatism*.[10] This group of philosophers was roughly contemporary with the high tide of Social Darwinism and many of the political questions that have troubled America since the nineteenth century may be seen as disputes between the heirs of pragmatism and the heirs of Social Darwinism.

The school of pragmatism developed from the meetings in the 1870s of a group of brilliant young Harvard intellectuals — members of the so-called Metaphysical Club. The leading members of the group were:

Chauncey Wright (1830-1875) — employed doing computations for the *Nautical Almanac*, but a spare-time philosopher of some distinction;
Charles Peirce (pronounced 'purse') (1839-1914) — a surveyor, occasional lecturer at Harvard and philosopher;
William James (brother of the novelist, Henry James) (1842-1910) — psychologist and philosopher;
John Fiske (1842-1901) — historian, librarian and philosopher;
Oliver Wendell Holmes (not the novelist, of the same name) (1841-1935) — lawyer;
John Dewey (1859-1952) — educationist and philosopher.
All were influenced in one way or another by Darwinism.

Pragmatism is difficult to define precisely because the various members of the pragmatist school differed even among themselves about the exact nature of the philosophy they espoused. Indeed at one stage Peirce claimed that James had woefully misrepresented his opinions and by labelling them with the term pragmatism had quite distorted the meaning of the word. So he coined yet another word, pragmaticism, to represent his own views. Because of such differences and divergences, we will have to treat each person in our list separately.

Wright accepted the Darwinian theory and to Darwin's considerable pleasure[11] defended it [12] against the perceptive attacks of the able Catholic scholar and naturalist, St George Mivart.[13] Wright denied determinism, which, as we have seen from our previous discussions, is incompatible with Darwinian evolutionism. So Wright believed that it would never be possible to account for all phenomena in the universe by means of a unique metaphysical formula. Consequently, a variety of explanations must be given to account for the varied kinds of phenomena that are experienced. No single controlling law can be discovered. Wright used the metaphor of 'cosmic weather' to describe such a situation.[14] It appears that his attraction to this point of view was in part influenced by his acceptance of the Darwinian 'law of higgledy-piggledy'.

Wright's ethical ideas were derived from the early nineteenth-century utilitarian doctrines of Jeremy Bentham and James Mill: actions are morally right if they lead to the greatest good of the greatest number. Actions should be calculated so as to maximise pleasure and minimise unhappiness. Pleasure, thought Wright, has *survival value*.[15] Consequently, those actions and beliefs which tend to give pleasure (such as good-neighbourliness, for example) have become 'imbedded' in mankind through the evolutionary process. In this manner Wright sought to account for the origin of man's ethical sensibilities. Darwin had said much the same thing when he spoke of the evolutionary advantages of sociable behaviour.[16]

Wright's chief epistemological principle may be summed up in the maxim: an idea is equivalent to a plan of action; and the truth or otherwise of that idea must be judged by the practical results of that action. To offer an unsophisticated example, the adequacy (or truth) of my ideas about bridge-building may be gauged by seeing whether the bridges that I build stand up successfully. Or, as the Biblical adage has it: 'Wherefore by their fruits ye shall know them'.[17]

This view, that the truth of ideas may be judged by their practical consequences, was perhaps the principal *Leitmotiv* of the pragmatist movement. For example, Peirce simply cut through the Gordian knot that had surrounded the problem of induction ever since the time of Hume by stating that inductive inferences may be accepted as true provided the practical outcomes of such generalisations are successful. According to this view, one need not worry whether previous risings of the Sun will be repeated tomorrow. We can assume that the past evidence does give a guarantee of the future behaviour of the Earth and Sun, and plan our lives accordingly. If the inductions turns out to be false, practical experience will very soon make this clear to us.

Peirce's views on this question were similar to those of Wright. But Peirce claimed he had first derived the viewpoint from his reading of Immanual Kant (1724-1804). He also tells us that the name 'pragmatism' was derived from this source. In the *Critique of Pure Reason*, Kant had given the example of a doctor trying to cure a patient. He makes his diagnosis as best he can and prescribes a medicine, even though he is quite aware that the diagnosis may be incorrect. Nevertheless, he has no option but to act on the diagnosis, faulty though it may be. Whether the diagnosis (or 'idea') is correct will become apparent as a result of the success or otherwise of the treatment. In such a situation, said Kant, the doctor has *pragmatic* ('practical') belief.[18]

This idea of pragmatic belief formed the very core of Peirce's philosophy. A concept, he maintained, is to be understood by its practical consequences. The concept of weight, for example, is arrived at through the experience of objects falling to the ground. In a well-known essay entitled 'How to make our ideas clear',[19] Peirce stated that an idea is clear when we understand its conceivable effects properly, or the logical consequences of adopting it as a rule for the resolution of a problem. This was his theory of the meaning of concepts.

The connection of this with the Darwinian theory of natural selection is not difficult to understand. Peirce made a careful study of Darwin's work[20] and it appears that he envisaged a kind of natural selection process acting on ideas. The various ideas or concepts that a person may come up with are tested in the external world. Those that are true survive; those that are false are eliminated.[21]

Peirce believed that by such a process of elimination of false ideas, systematic habits and conscious methods gradually come to prevail over random trial-and-error efforts and thus an evolution of consciousness is to be expected. It is worth noting that according to the Kantian view the principles of knowledge were fixed and immutable, but for Peirce they were only habits, certified by experience yet in principle capable of being changed or improved. Such a stance might be anticipated from one influenced by evolutionary considerations. It is interesting to note that in his *Objective Knowledge*, Popper has fairly recently been reviving ideas rather similar to those of Peirce:

> The growth of our knowledge is the result of a process closely resembling what Darwin called 'natural selection'; that is, *the natural selection of hypotheses*: our knowledge consists, at every moment, of those hypotheses which have shown their (comparative) fitness by surviving so far in their struggle for existence; a competitive struggle which eliminates those hypotheses which are unfit.[22]

As with Wright, Peirce was influenced by utilitarianism, for he maintained that *true* belief is that which leads to the greatest happiness of the greatest number — this provides the *pragmatic* test of true belief.

William James also developed a 'pragmatic' theory of truth. He wrote:

> *True ideas are those that we can assimilate, validate, corroborate, and verify. False ideas are those that we can not* . . . The truth of an idea is not a stagnant property inherent in it. Truth *happens* to an idea. It *becomes* true, is *made* true by events. Its veracity *is* in fact an event, a process: the process namely of its verifying itself, its veri-*fication*. Its validity is the process of its valid-*action*.[23]

The true ideas are the 'fit' ones — the ones that survive the process of validation, corroboration and verification.

James was a pluralist in his outlook — as Wright was — believing also that the efforts of individuals resulted in the progress of society. Following Darwin, he agreed that there was a great spread in the mental capacities of men and women, from men of genius to imbeciles. James adhered to what is called the 'great man' theory of history, ascribing major historical changes to the acts of the very few men of genius (sometimes evil genius) that are born from time to time (for example, Napoleon, Bismarck), just as most of the erosion of a valley is brought about by occasional great floods. But in James's view such great men are not, as Hegel would have us believe, passive vehicles for the transmission of the 'Absolute Idea'. They are simply the beings at one extreme of the spectrum of abilities that the Darwinian theory would lead us to expect.

Oliver Wendell Holmes is interesting because of his influence on the development of legal theory in the United States, through his judgements on the Supreme Court and his legal classic, *The Common Law*.[24] Holmes denied that law should be based on precedents and deductions made from earlier legal decisions. Rather, he thought of the law as an *evolving* institution — evolving, that is, from being an agent of vengeance or retribution to a means of ensuring public safety. 'The life of the law', he said, 'has not been logic: it has been experience'.[25] And following a typically pragmatic approach he maintained that the *meaning* of the law is to be gauged by its practical operation — by what the courts actually do. For example, the law in New South Wales states that it is illegal to bathe naked on the beaches. But in *practice*, that is in pragmatic terms, it is illegal to bathe thus on Manly beach but it is perfectly legal on any quiet cove up or down the coast! Similar examples relating to pollution, homosexuality, or truancy at school will readily occur to the reader. Holmes stressed that a sound body of law should correspond with the feelings and demands of the community.[26] If the law departs significantly from these feelings then it will be brought into disrepute.

The growing influence of relativism and pluralism may be discerned again in Holmes's legal philosophy. It would not be correct to ascribe the advent of such views wholly to the influence of Darwinian evolutionism. The classical view of legal doctrines had been that they might be known by mental introspection by any right-thinking person.[27] If one looked into the contents of one's mind one might find there a criterion of what was morally right or wrong. This was the so-called doctrine of 'natural law',[28] which served as an inspiration for the American Declaration of Independence. But by the beginning of the nineteenth century the acceptability of this approach was questioned by the proponents of the 'historical' school of law, led by F. C. von Savigny (1779-1861). Von Savigny spoke against the introduction to Germany of formal legal codes on the Napoleonic model with their supposed basis in natural law.[29] He maintained that the law should be understood through a study of its historical development. It will be appreciated that the pragmatic approach to law such as was espoused by Holmes had a good deal in common with this earlier 'historicist' attitude epitomised by von Savigny. Nevertheless, the direct link from Darwinian evolutionism through to Holmes, *via* the association with the Harvard pragmatists, cannot be gainsaid.

John Dewey, the influential educationist, is also remembered for his philosophy of *instrumentalism*. Thought, Dewey supposed,[30] is like an instrument for solving problems and it should be appropriate to the solution of those problems in the same way as a screwdriver should be appropriate to the crew that it is to turn. Thoughts, according to Dewey's understanding of the matter, are not static or constant at all times. They gradually *evolve* to meet the exigencies of the problems posed by the environment. Thought evolves so as to be an instrument equal to the requirements of the problems of the time.

As with Peirce, Dewey drew from the traditions of utilitarianism. He supposed that thoughts or ideas were good and true if they led to the greatest good of the greatest number. But for Dewey, unlike the original utilitarians, it was growth and evolutionary development that was in itself conceived as good — not some hypothetical ultimate goal. He advocated the testing of experience by experiment and the application of the lessons learned to the attainment of more creative activity. This provided him with the basis of his general philosophy of education.

At first sight, the discussions of the pragmatists may seem to be nothing more than common-sense dressed up in philosophical garb. But they do probe ethical questions of considerable philosophical depth — questions not susceptible to any kind of ultimate resolution. For if one denies ethical or moral 'absolutes', then (obviously) relativism enters promptly. According to the pragmatist view, 'success' is the measure of what is right and wrong. That which is acceptable to a community is, for that community and at that time, right. That which is unacceptable is wrong. That which yields the greatest good of the greatest number is right — the ends justify the means. Or, as the pragmatist would phrase it: 'A thing is right if it works'.

But needless to say this can lead to the most horrendous political and social consequences. An S.S. guard at Belsen, for example, might readily have justifed his actions by appeal to maxims of the pragmatists, for what he was doing received the social sanctions of his peers. Yet almost anyone would agree that the acts of Nazis were morally wrong even in some kind of absolute sense. Most people today do not subscribe to any kind of ethical absolutism, and Holmes's pragmatist view of the law is widely accepted. Yet the outcome of such views is not always very pleasing. It is compatible with the 'might is right' doctrines of the Social Darwinists. And one may hanker after some kind of natural law doctrine, even though fully aware that it is only a chimera. It is noteworthy, however, that ideas of natural law are most persuasive on international questions, on which one can scarcely appeal to the consensus of a populace. Unfortunately, this area is one of considerable philosophical confusion, and it would not be wise for us to attempt to penetrate it further.[31] Let us simply note the fact that evolutionary considerations entered the argument at a number of significant points.

Darwinism and ethics

In the previous section we have been touching on the question of finding generally acceptable ethical or moral codes, and we have noted in passing some of the difficulties that one encounters when questions of this kind are looked into. Discussions of such questions may be traced back to antiquity; they did not suddenly break out in the middle of the nineteenth century. Many attempts have been made to set down the distinctions between right and wrong, good and evil, or to stipulate how people ought to behave. The Stoics, for example, maintained that the good action is that which is natural. The Platonist believed that one would know what was good by successful apprehension of the transcendent 'form' of goodness, with the aid of dialectic. A hedonist would say that the good is that which gives pleasure. The Christian theist maintains that God's personal revelation (attained through the medium of the Bible, for example) provides him with a knowledge of what is right and wrong. The utilitarian likes to maximise happiness. Kant believed that the right action is that which one would wish to see universalised. Charles Kingsley (1819-1875) reminds us of the excellent rule of 'do-as-you-would-be-done-by'.[32] And the pragmatist and the twentieth-century sociologist agree that the notion of goodness is relative and depends on what is acceptable to a community, the *mores* being changeable from one generation to the next.

All such views — and others besides — present considerable difficulties. The masochist, for example, may enjoy being flagellated. But seemingly it would not be right for him (or her) to apply the 'do-as-you-would-be-done-by' rule to the person living next door. I leave it to the reader to think out objections to the various other ethical systems that have been listed above. All have severe difficulties, and indeed no general agreement has ever been achieved among philosophers on the question of a universally acceptable ethical code. But people have continued the search, and what is particularly interesting to us is that a number of attempts have been made to employ the *evolutionary* doctrine for the purpose of establishing ethical codes or ethical norms. Let us have a look at some of these attempts.

Darwin himself was one of the first to consider the relationship between ethical theory and evolutionary doctrines, as when he argued that altrusim might have had an evolutionary origin. He sought to show how ethical behaviour would have survival value, and thus might become established in human societies.[33] But Darwin did not take the further step and say that one might distinguish between right and wrong by considering what had happened during the course of evolution, or where it was going in the future. Evolution *per se* did not provide an ethical code.

Herbert Spencer, however, went beyond Darwin and hinted that this would be a possibility, as when he wrote:

> The conduct to which we apply the name good, is the relatively more evolved conduct; and ... bad is the name we apply to conduct which is relatively less evolved.[34]

And:

> That which we ... [find] to be highly-evolved conduct, is that which ... we find to be what is called good conduct; and the ideal goal to the natural evolution of conduct ... we here recognize as the ideal standard of conduct ethically considered.[35]

This just manages to hold back from saying that 'the good' *is* that which is the most highly evolved, but it comes very close to this. It might also be said that writers such as Sumner, Carnegie or von Treitschke, who were advocates of social policies based on evolutionary theory, were in effect giving their opinions about ethical norms in the social sphere. They were, on the basis of evolutionism, saying how things *ought* to be. Struggle, for example, was justified since it was the motor for evolutionary 'progress'. In the judgement of such men evolution provided a philosophical sanction for particular courses of human action.

Such opinions were countered long ago by T. H. Huxley, in his essay entitled 'Evolution and ethics' of 1893:

> There is another fallacy which appears to me to pervade the so-called "ethics of

evolution". It is the notion that because, on the whole, animals and plants have advanced in perfection of organization by means of the struggle for existence and the consequent 'survival of the fittest'; therefore men in society, men as ethical beings, must look to the same process to help them towards perfection. I suspect that this fallacy has arisen out of the unfortunate ambiguity of the phrase 'survival of the fittest'. 'Fittest' has a connotation of 'best'; and about 'best' there hangs a moral flavour. In cosmic nature, however, what is 'fittest' depends apon the conditions . . . If our hemisphere were to cool again, the survival of the fittest might bring about, in the vegetable kingdom, a population of more and more stunted and humbler and humbler organisms, until the 'fittest' that survived might be nothing but lichens, diatoms, and such microscopic organisms as those which give red snow its colour; while, if it became hotter, the pleasant valleys of the Thames and Isis might be uninhabitable by any animated beings save those that flourish in a tropical jungle.[36]

Clearly, what Huxley is saying here is that one cannot possibly draw any moral or ethical conclusions from a consideration of the course of evolution. Evolution and ethics are quite distinct, even antithetical:

Social progress means a checking of the cosmic process at every step and the substitution for it of another, which may be called the ethical process.[37]

Thus, said Huxley, ethical behaviour 'repudiates the gladiatorial theory of existence'. Then, in a well-known aphorism, he wrote:

The ethical progress of society depends, not on imitating the cosmic process, still less in running away from it, but in combating it.[38]

It might be thought that such arguments would be quite sufficient to dissuade subsequent authors from attempting to derive ethical norms from the evolutionary process. But this has been far from true. A number of writers, biologists more often than professional philosophers, have in quite recent years attempted to establish ethical norms on the basis of evolutionary theory. Indeed, this has been an important concern for persons in the humanist movement, such as were considered briefly in the previous chapter. Hopefully, evolutionism might provide a substitute for the traditional ethical norms given in orthodox Christian theology. For example, in Julian Huxley's very interesting book, *New Bottles for New Wine* (1957), we find the following passage:

Man's most sacred duty [i.e., what he *ought* to do], and at the same time his most glorious opportunity, is to promote the maximum fulfilment of the evolutionary process on this earth; and this includes the fullest realization of his own inherent possibilities.[39]

This, of course, parallels the ancient parable of the talents.[40] But the concern with the evolutionary process is to be remarked upon. We do not find *that* in the Bible.

A more detailed presentation of the position of evolutionary ethics is to be found in an earlier book, *Science and Ethics* (1942), by the British biologist, C. H. Waddington.[41] Waddington maintained that ethical statements were *not* merely exhortatory, or expressions of social conventions, but might be given the same status as scientific propositions. He wrote:

> In the world as a whole, the real good cannot be other than that which has been effective, namely that which is exemplified in the course of evolution.[42]

and:

> We must accept the direction of evolution as good simply because it *is* good according to any realist definition of that concept.[43]

I take it that what Waddington meant was something like the following. Evolution could have taken any number of different courses, but in fact it took one particular direction. The *actual* course of evolution must, in Waddington's view, have been the 'good' course. That which has been effective is good, he said.

Waddington also tried to argue by analogy. His argument was not set out in detail, but it seems to have been as follows:

(i) Food is good for promoting nutrition.
(ii) Good food is that which promotes nutrition most successfully.
(iii) Hence we have a criterion for the goodness of food.

This may be compared with:

(i) Ethical behaviour is good for promoting evolution.
(ii) Good ethical behaviour is that which promotes evolution most successfully.
(iii) Hence we have a criterion for the goodness for ethical behaviour.[43]

Unfortunately, however, this analogy rests on a 'slide' between the use of the word 'good' in a *functional* sense, and its use in a *moral* or *ethical* sense. Consequently, the analogy proposed is simply unacceptable.

In 1960, Waddington was still trying to extract an ethical code from the course of evolution,[44] but with no better success, and despite the fact that his argument had been effectively demolished by C. E. M. Joad (1891-1953) in 1942. Joad's treatment of the question has pleasant touches of humour, and I take pleasure in quoting at some length:

> I cannot understand how anything can be measured without a ruler which is external to and other than what it measures. Now to adjudge a movement as good or bad — witness in this connexion Dr Waddington's talk about 'the "good" direction of evolution' — entails that some meaning is understood to be conveyed

by the words good and bad which serves as a standard of measurement by reference to which the movement is evaluated. Now this meaning cannot itself be part of the process which it is invoked to evaluate, any more than a ruler can be part of the length which it measures, or a man can lift himself by his own braces. Dr Waddington points out that the later stages of evolutionary development include the earlier. Certainly they do, but what of it? The later stages of a travelling snowball include the earlier, but this does not mean that the snowball's journey is ethically valuable or worthy of praise. It may not even be well advised; if it is heading for a precipice it is ill advised. When Dr Waddington affirms that evolution is moving in the right direction or is progressive – it is 'good', he says, 'simply because it *is* good' – he is applying ethical standards to it. Now all progress implies movement in a direction and direction implies a goal. If I put myself in the Strand and set my legs in motion, there is movement or process, but until I know whether I want to go to Charing Cross or Temple Bar I cannot say whether I am progressing or not.[45]

This, I believe, effectively dismisses all arguments such as those of Waddington and Julian Huxley. Who, after all, would wish to say that the course of human evolution, as it is known to us, has been ethically good? If Hitler had won the war, would this have made Nazism a morally praiseworthy political philosophy?

A. G. N. Flew has pointed out[46] that all attempts to derive ethical norms or social or political systems from evolutionary principles are vitiated by what G. E. Moore (1873-1958) referred to in his *Principia Ethica* as the 'naturalistic fallacy'.[47] In simple terms, this claims that any attempt to derive '*ought*' statements from '*is*' statements is logically fallacious. Now to describe the course of evolution is to say something about how the world *is* and how it came to be as it is. But this tells us nothing about how the world *ought* to be, that is to say, how mankind might wish it to be. An ethically ideal world would probably be totally different from ours. Thus I agree with Flew that a satisfactory ethical code cannot justifiably be extracted from the theory of evolution. But the attempts that have been made to do this are not without interest and they provide further evidence of the extraordinarily far-reaching effects of the Darwin/Wallace theory.

Darwinism, materialism and naturalism

The Darwinian theory was purely naturalistic: it made no appeal to entities such as God, divine spirits, hypothetical entelechies,[48] final causes, souls or Platonic Ideas.[49] And, as we have seen in our discussion of evolution and theology, the advent of Darwinism coincided with a considerable decline in religious beliefs and adherence to religious doctrines. By providing an alternative naturalistic explanation of 'design', Darwin made it seem less necessary to construct a view of the world that invoked some kind of supernatural being. Not that Darwin wished to positively deny the existence of God; he was agnostic on this question.

But Darwin's theories did give considerable support to 'materialist' interpretations of the world. Ideas could be regarded as mere 'epiphenomena',[50] compared with the actions and interactions of matter. The old mind/body dualism of Descartes and his followers would be replaced by a monistic materialism. As mentioned in the previous chapter, this attitude proved particularly attractive in Germany, in the writings of the members of the so-called 'Monist League', the work of the philosopher/biologist, Ernst Haeckel (1834-1919), being particularly prominent.

Haeckel, a leading systematic zoologist and embryologist, and professor at the University of Jena, was the chief spokesman for Darwin's ideas in Germany in the nineteenth and early twentieth centuries. He has traditionally been regarded as a progressive liberal opposed to the excesses of arbitrary state power[51] but this interpretation has been almost completely overthrown in recent years by the work of Daniel Gasman,[52] who sees Haeckel as one of the principal intellectual influences leading to German Nazism.

According to Gasman,[53] there were three main strands in Haeckel's thought: German romantic idealism; scientific positivism and materialism; and Darwinism. But these were synthesised into the monistic doctrine that *all* phenomena may be accounted for by the actions of atoms operating in a vast cosmic evolutionary process. This doctrine became a kind of religion for Haeckel, and the Monist League, inaugurated in 1906, may well be regarded as his Church.

But Haeckel's materialism was very different from, say, the mechanistic materialism of the eighteenth-century *philosophes* such as d'Holbach or de la Mettrie whose schemes were purely materialistic in character — or what one might expect from a direct employment of Darwin's naturalistic evolutionism. For Haeckel's atoms were endowed with souls! His doctrine was really a variant of 'pan-psychism'[54] or 'hylozoism'.[55] So his evolutionism was a kind of manifestation of the creative energy with which nature in every atom is imbued. In a quite *a priori* manner he simply drove together the mind and matter of traditional dualistic philosophers. But the Monists were not in any sense theists of the Christian tradition.

Darwinism and the will: Friedrich Nietzsche

Also drawing on biological evolutionism, although less directly than Haeckel and his followers, was the philologist and nihilist philosopher, Friedrich Nietzsche (1844-1900), particularly in his obscure and poetic work *Thus Spake Zarathustra*.[56]

Nietzsche lost his religious faith as a young man, but instead of turning away from Christianity to a quiet agnosticism, he adopted an uncompromising hatred of the religion. Also, after being rejected in love, he came to hate all women. He ended his days in a lunatic asylum, allegedly as a result of a venereal infection, inherited, or contracted when he was a young man.

Nietzsche thought the world as he knew it was quite meaningless and chaotic, and he tried to show that all things in which men take pleasure and pride have no *intrinsic* worth. This was summed up in his celebrated dictum:

'God is dead'.[57] There are no absolute moral principles. Morality is merely a weapon in the struggle for power. But there was also a positive aspect to the Nietzschean doctrine, which may be found in *Zarathustra*. He believed in the ancient Stoic doctrine of 'eternal recurrence'; but he also looked forward to the time when man would be 'overcome' or transcended, with the advent of the '*Ubermensch*' or 'Superman'. He detested and despised the common herd of humanity, the 'proles' as Orwell later called them,[58] the 'masses' in Marx's terminology, or the 'great unwashed' as the clubman of St James or Piccadilly would say. He abhorred the Christian morality that said: 'Blessed are the meek'. This was ignoble – fit for slaves. Nietzsche believed that by a proper exercise of *will* certain men might *evolve* to give a world-élite of '*Ubermenschen*'. The Superman would be his own master, and might succeed to the position originally occupied by God. That which increases power is good; evil proceeds from weakness.

Precisely what Nietzsche meant by all this is not easy to determine. He certainly did not mean that ordinary man would evolve into Superman by the commonplace Darwinian mechanism of natural selection. (In fact, in a number of passages, Nietzsche specifically attacked the Darwinian theory.[59]) But, following Copleston, we may say that Nietzsche's concept of the Superman was

> The highest possible development and integration of intellectual power, strength of character and will, independence, passion, taste and physique.[60]

Zarathustra (who was supposed to refer to the ancient Persian prophet or seer, Zoroaster) is – rather as John the Baptist – the prophet for the coming of this semi-divine being. But the Superman was a goal towards which mankind might aspire by exercise of what Nietzsche called the 'Will to Power', rather than a being that might be expected to turn up in due course through the 'higgledy-piggledy' mechanism of Darwinian selection. Evolutionism, rather than Darwinism, was the inspiration of Nietzsche's doctrine; or Lamarckian striving, rather than Darwinian selection.

Most Anglo-Saxons have a certain revulsion from the idea of the *Ubermensch*, with war being the instrument whereby the visionary new world would come into being, and we may condemn or despise the 'futurology' of Nietzsche's writings. Yet it must be acknowledged that many of the features of human existence that he foresaw in the nineteenth century have come to pass in the present century. Nietzsche, a man of aristocratic or 'Apollinian'[61] disposition, loathed the herd-like features of human existence. And he correctly foresaw the uniformity of thought and existence of the common man of the twentieth century, with his mediocre talents, distrust of intellectuals and elites, and his lowest-common-denominator aesthetic sensibilites.

The Nietzschean doctrine of 'will' is a somewhat indistinct one. It derives from Schopenhauer,[62] who saw it as a resolution of Kant's problem of the noumenal reality of a person: the body was but the phenomenal appearance, the epiphenomenon of the will, one might say. The will, according to Schopenhauer's view, was the real 'motor' of mankind. Clearly, this is quite unlike Haeckel's view, in which the will would be regarded purely as a 'by-product' of the activity of matter.

In Nietzsche's version of this doctrine we have the idea that the 'will' may be able to drive men on to evolve into the 'Superman'. This suggestion is more Lamarckian than Darwinian. But the idea of struggle (to be sure, common to both Lamarckism and Darwinism) is plainly there. And so is the idea of evolution to some higher kind of being. In a way, the ideas of Nietzsche have something in common with Plato's theory of the ideal state, as portrayed in *The Republic*. But Nietzsche wrote in nineteenth-century terms and saw the attainment of his vision as occurring through an evolutionary process. Plato, by contrast, sought to counter all forms of social change.

Darwinism and the Anglo-Hegelians

So far in our discussions we have looked for positive instances of Darwinian influence in philosophy. But the matter may be looked at from an alternative point of view. Were there any negative philosophical responses to the Darwinian doctrine? In a valuable article published in the centenary year of the publication of *The Origin*,[63] J. A. Passmore has pointed to the late nineteenth-century group of British philosophers known as the Anglo-Hegelians, who sought to oppose the intransigent materialism of Haeckel's monistic philosophy and turned to the philosophy of Hegel as a shield against the threat of naturalism and materialism and the usurpation of philosophy by science. The leading members of this group were T. H. Green, Edward Caird, Bernard Bosanquet, J. H. Stirling and F. H. Bradley.

Like the materialists, the Anglo-Hegelians (or Absolute Idealists) wished to deny the distinction between matter and spirit. But whereas materialism taught that matter is the only reality, with spirit and ideas as mere epiphenomena, the Absolute Idealists saw things the other way round, presenting Spirit as the ultimate reality and matter as the epiphenomenon. The laws of science become mere manifestations of the human mind, rather than independent self-existent truths.

It would distract us too far from our present purpose to enter into further exposition or appraisal of this doctrine. The unrepentant monism should be noted, however. Passmore believes that this may in part have been a further side-effect of Darwinian naturalism, and the nineteenth-century desire to close the gap entrenched in the Cartesian mind/body dualism.

Darwinism and grand cosmic philosophies

Finally, in this somewhat breathless scamper through a number of the important nineteenth and twentieth-century philosophies that displayed the influence of Darwinism (or evolutionism in general) to a greater or lesser degree, we may mention a few of the several grand cosmic philosophical schemes employing the evolutionary *Leitmotif* that were propounded in the post-Darwinian period, and consider one of them in a little detail, as illustrative of the whole.

Good examples are provided by S. Alexander's *Space, Time and Deity* (1920),[64] with its interest in the evolution of concepts of value, seen in the context of the new relativist theories of Einstein and Minkowski; A. N. Whitehead's *Science and the Modern World* (1926),[65] with its doctrine of 'organism'; and H. Bergson's *Évolution Créatrice* (1907),[66] with its idea of *élan vital*. The work of Haeckel, Spencer or Nietzsche would also fit in here quite comfortably.

Bergson (1859-1941) was born in that auspicious year, 1859, and his whole life-work was developed under the aegis of an evolutionary *Zeitgeist*. Like the Anglo-Hegelians, Bergson allotted primacy to spirit and intuition, rather than matter and analysis. Mataphysics was concerned with spirit and intuition. Bergson sided with the metaphysicians.

Bergson's evolutionism, although all-pervasive in his system, was very different from Darwin's naturalistic, mechanistic or materialistic doctrine of evolution by natural selection.

Like many others before and since, Bergson could not see how mere chance could account for the evolutionary development of organisms into the higher forms of life. This is indeed difficult to comprehend, and we know that even Darwin had some doubts as to the adequacy of his theory on this score. A commonplace response to this problem has been to invoke some kind of teleological explanation such as Driesch's 'entelechy'.[67] But Bergson would not accept teleology as an escape from the dilemma. Teleological explanation (that is, to use Aristotle's terminology, explanation couched in terms of 'the cause for the sake of which a process advances') was unacceptable to Bergson. He regarded it as entailing some kind of pre-ordination; it was, for him, *quasi*-mechanical.

So let us reject pure mechanism, said Bergson. Let us disregard the possibilities of teleological explanation. But let us look into our own inner lives and consciousness and see what we find there. When we do this, we become aware of the existence within us of an inner 'vital impetus' (the *élan vital*). So it may be, he suggested, that there is:

> An *original impetus* of life, passing from one generation of germs to the following generation of germs through the developed organisms which bridge the interval between the generations.[68]

It is the meeting of the 'explosive' activity of the *élan vital* and the resistant matter that leads to the many lines and levels of evolution. To express his idea, Bergson used the simile of an exploding shell, the fragments of which themselves explode in their turn.[69]

Thus Bergson used the intuition we have of our own freedom of will — our own free activity — as a key to the nature of universe as a whole. He employed also the simile of a jet of steam issuing from some container at high pressure, condensing in drops, and falling groundwards: 'So, from an immense reservoir of life, jets must be gushing out unceasingly, of which each, falling back, is a world'.[70]

The movement of life in the world is the analogue of the upward-moving steam. Matter corresponds to the falling back of the water droplets — a process of 'unmaking'. God, for Bergson, is not the Judaeo-Christian transcendent creator of the universe, but rather a kind of immanent cosmic vital impulse, using matter as its (not His) instrument for the creation of fresh forms of life.

The evolutionism of Bergson is apparent to even his most casual reader. But it is clear that he has far transcended the hard ground of Darwinian science and has moved on to the lusher fields of speculative metaphysics. It is noteworthy, for example, that he exercised a considerable influence on Teilhard de Chardin, whom we considered in Chapter 18. Today such grand metaphysical systems are not held in much esteem, and Bergson's *Creative Evolution* is now a dusty occupant of the lumber-room of speculative philosophy. But in its time, his work aroused considerable excitement and enthusiasm (as also did Chardin's), for he was breaking into new philosophical regions, and providing a fresh alternative to the mechanistic, positivistic science of his day. So Bergson developed a double-edged weapon from Darwinian evolutionism. On the one hand he drew his whole philosophy from the groundwork of evolutionary theory. But on the other he sought to establish a new non-mechanistic, non-materialistic, non-teleological kind of evolutionism. Schopenhauer and Nietzsche, no doubt, would have approved such a venture, though we, with our contemporary Olympian vision, may be inclined to regard it as a philosophical aberration.

NOTES CHAPTER 19

1   For discussions of the influence of Darwinism on philosophy, see J. Dewey, 'Darwin's influence on philosophy', *The Popular Science Monthly*, Vol. 75, 1909, pp.90-98; J. H. Randall, Jr, 'The changing impact of Darwin on philosophy', *Journal of the History of Ideas*, Vol. 22, 1961, pp.435-462; J. A. Passmore, 'Darwin's impact on British metaphysics', *Victorian Studies*, Vol. 3, 1959, pp.41-54; P. P. Wiener, *Evolution and the Founders of Pragmatism*, Harvard University Press, Cambridge, Mass., 1949; A. G. N. Flew, *Evolutionary Ethics*, Macmillan, London & Basingstone, 1967; W. H. Marnell, *Man-Made Morals: Four Philosophies that Shaped America*, Doubleday, New York, 1966; D. Daiches Raphael, 'Darwinism and ethics', in S. A. Barnett (ed.), *A Century of Darwin*, Heinemann, London, 1958, pp.334-359; T. H. Huxley & J. Huxley, *Touchstone for Ethics: 1893-1943*, Harper, New York, 1947; J. Collins, *Crossroads in Philosophy: Existentialism, Naturalism, Theistic Realism*, Regnery, Chicago, 1962; F. S. C. Northrop, 'Evolution in its relation to the philosophy of nature and the philosophy of culture', in S. Persons (ed.), *Evolutionary Thought in America*, Braziller, New York, 1950, pp.44-84; J. S. Fulton, 'Philosophical adventures of the idea of evolution', *The Rice Institute Pamphlet*, Vol. 46, 1959, pp.1-31. For the influence of philosophy on Darwin, see M. Ruse, 'Darwin's debt to philosophy: an examination of the influence of the philosophical ideas of John F. W. Herschel and William Whewell on the development of Darwin's theory of evolution', *Studies in History and Philosophy of Science*, Vol. 6, 1975, pp.159-181.

2   See above, page 12.
3   Plato, *Cratylus*, 426c-427d and *passim*.
4   For example, K. R. Popper, 'Three views concerning human knowledge', in his *Conjectures and Refutations*, 3rd edn, Routledge & Kegan Paul, London, 1969, pp.97-119.
5   D. L. Hull, *Darwin and his Critics: The Reception of Darwin's Theory of Evolution by the Scientific Community*, Harvard University Press, Cambridge, Mass., 1973, pp.70-71. (Hull's book gives a good general account of the influence of the doctrine of essentialism in biology and natural history. See also his paper 'The metaphysics of evolution' in *The British Journal for the History of Science*, Vol. 3, 1967, pp.309-337.)
6   See above, page 94.
7   W. Whewell, *The Philosophy of the Inductive Sciences, Founded upon their History*, 2nd edn, 2 vols, London, 1847, Vol. 1, p.476.
8   J. S. Mill, *A System of Logic, Ratiocinative and Inductive, Being a Connected View of the Principles of Evidence, and the Methods of Scientific Investigation*, 2 vols, London, 1843, Book III, Chapter 8 (republished Routledge, London, 1974).
9   In *practice*, classifications are still related to visible characteristics rather than genealogies. For example, by genealogy crocodiles are seemingly more closely related in some respects to birds than to lizards or turtles. Nevertheless, crocodiles are customarily classified with the other reptiles, rather than with birds. (See R. S. Bigelow, 'Monophyletic classification and evolution', *Systematic Zoology*, Vol. 5, 1956, pp.145-146.) However, recent work is leading to some major restructuring of vertebrate taxonomy because of genealogies revealed by paleontological investigations. (For an interesting popular account of these developments, see A. J. Desmond, *The Hot-Blooded Dinosaurs*, Futura Publications, London, 1977.)
10 For more detailed discussions of this, see particularly the volumes by Wiener and Marnell referred to in note 1 above.
11 Darwin wrote to Wright (July 14, 1871): 'I have hardly ever in my life read an article which has given me so much satisfaction as the review which you have been so kind as to send me. I agree to almost everything which you say. Your memory must be wonderfully accurate, for you know my works as well as I do myself, and your power of grasping other men's thoughts is something quite surprising . . .' (F. Darwin (ed.), *The Life and Letters of Charles Darwin*, 3 vols, John Murray, London, 1887, Vol. 3, p.145).
12 C. Wright, 'The genesis of species', *The North American Review*, Vol. 113, 1871, pp.63-103.
13 [St George Jackson Mivart,] 'Darwin's Descent of Man', *The Quarterly Review*, Vol. 131, 1871, pp.47-90. (The articles by both Mivart and Wright are reprinted in: D. L. Hull, *op. cit.* [note 5].)
14 C. Wright (ed. C. E. Norton), *Philosophical Discussions*, New York, 1877, p.7.
15 E. H. Madden (ed.), *The Philosophical Writings of Chauncey Wright: Representative Selections*, Liberal Arts Press, New York, 1958, pp.59-60.
16 C. Darwin, *The Descent of Man, and Selection in Relation To Sex*, 2 vols, London, 1871, Vol. 1, p.80.
17 *The Gospel According to St Matthew*, Chapter 7, Verse 20.
18 N. K. Smith (translator and editor), *Immanuel Kant's Critique of Pure Reason*, 2nd edn, Macmillan, London & New York, 1933, pp.647-648.
19 C. S. Peirce, 'How to make our ideas clear', *Popular Science Monthly*, Vol. 12, 1878, pp.286-302.
20 There are numerous references to Darwin and to evolutionary theories in Peirce's *Collected Papers*. His probabilistic interpretation of the theory of *The Origin* is to be found, for example, in C. Hartshorne & P. Weiss (eds), *Collected Papers of Charles Sanders Peirce*, 6 vols (in 3), Belknap, Cambridge, Mass., 1960, Vol. 1, pp.214-218.
21 *Ibid.*, Vol. 2, p.47. Here Peirce sees the method of hypotheses of the scientist as being analogous to the evolutionary development of living organisms.
22 K. R. Popper, *Objective Knowledge: An Evolutionary Approach*, Oxford, 1972, p.261. (A recent volume by Nicholas Rescher — *Methodological Pragmatism: A Systems-Theoretic Approach to the Theory of Knowledge*, Blackwell, Oxford, 1977 — explores issues in 'evolutionary epistemology' in a very interesting way. The author gives particular attention to what he calls 'methodological Darwinism'. Popper, on the other hand, is concerned with the evolution of knowledge, rather than method.)
23 W. James, *Pragmatism: A New Name for Some Old Ways of Thinking together with Four Related Essays from the Meaning of Truth*, Longmans, Green & Co., New York, London & Toronto, 1949, p.201 (1st edn, 1907).
24 O. W. Holmes, *The Common Law*, Boston, 1881 (republished Little Brown, Boston, 1963).
25 *Ibid.*, p.1.
26 *Ibid.*, p.36.
27 This, for example, was the view of John Locke: '[The law of nature] binds men, for it *contains in itself* all that is requisite to create an obligation. Though no doubt it is not made known in the same way as positive laws [i.e., by revelation] it is sufficiently known to men (and this is all that is needed for the

purpose) because it can be perceived by the light of nature alone'. (J. Locke [W. von Leyden, ed.], *Essays on the Law of Nature* [1660-1664], O.U.P., Oxford, 1954, p.113.

28 There was for a long time conflation of laws of nature (for example, the inverse square law of gravity) and moral laws (for example, 'thou shalt not kill'), for both were thought to emanate from a Divine Will.

29 F. C. von Savigny, *Of the Vocation of our Age for Legislation and Jurisprudence*, translated from the German by A. Hayward, London, 1831.

30 J. Dewey, *Reconstruction in Philosophy*, New York, 1920 (enlarged edition, Beacon, Boston, 1948). Dewey wrote: 'Conceptions, theories and systems of thought are always open to development through use . . . They are tools. As in the case of all tools, their value resides not in themselves but in their capacity to work shown in the consequences of their use' (1948, p.145).

31 For a good general introduction to the philosophy of law, see D. Lloyd, *The Idea of Law*, Penguin, Harmondsworth, 1964.

32 We meet the good fairy, Mrs Doasyouwouldbedoneby, in Kingsley's *The Water Babies*. But she had her Victorian opposite number, Mrs Bedonebyasyoudid. (C. Kingsley, *The Water-Babies: A Fairy Tale for a Land-Baby*, London & Cambridge, 1863.)

33 C. Darwin, *op.cit.* (note 16), Book I, Chapter 5.

34 H. Spencer, *The Data of Ethics*, Williams & Norgate, London, 1907, p.19.

35 *Ibid.*, p.36. (It should be noted, however, that Spencer's ethical system was, in the last analysis, grounded on a utilitarian premise).

36 T. H. Huxley, *Evolution & Ethics and Other Essays*, London, 1894, pp.80-81. (The quotation is from Huxley's 'Romanes Lecture', presented in 1893.)

37 *Ibid.*, p.81.

38 *Ibid.*, p.83.

39 J. S. Huxley, *New Bottles for New Wine*, Chatto & Windus, London, 1957, p.293.

40 *The Gospel according to St Matthew*, Chapter 25, Verses 14-30.

41 C. H. Waddington, *Science and Ethics*, Allen & Unwin, London, 1942, p.18.

42 *Ibid.*

43 *Ibid.*, p.41.

44 C. H. Waddington, *The Ethical Animal*, Allen & Unwin, London, 1960.

45 C. M. Joad, commenting on Waddington's paper, in C. H. Waddington, *op. cit.* (note 41), pp.28-29.

46 A. G. N. Flew, *op. cit.* (note 1), pp.31-51.

47 G. E. Moore, *Principia Ethica*, Cambridge, 1902, p.10 and *passim*. (It should be noted that it was David Hume who first drew attention to the fact that there is no logical connection between 'is' and 'ought' statements.)

48 Entelechy is that which gives form or perfection to anything. The concept was used by Aristotle, and the term was revived in the twentieth century by Hans Driesch, who suggested that the development of embryos was impossible to comprehend as a purely mechanical process, but had to be 'supervised' by some guiding 'entelechy'.

49 The gemmules of the theory of pangenesis were invisible hypothetical entities. But they were not thought to be supernatural.

50 See above, page 260.

51 A. E. Nordenskiold (tr. L. B. Eyre), *The History of Biology: A Survey*, Knopf, New York, 1928, pp.505-507 (republished Tudor, New York, 1942).

52 D. Gasman, *The Scientific Origins of National Socialism: Social Darwinism in Ernst Haeckel and the German Monist League*, Macdonald, London & New York, 1971.

53 *Ibid.*, p.xvii.

54 Pan-psychism is the doctrine that there are universal forces, related to spiritistic phenomena, which cannot be explained by physical science.

55 Hylozoism is the doctrine that *all* matter is endowed with life to a greater or lesser degree.

56 F. Nietzsche, *Also Sprach Zarathustra. Ein Buch für Alle und Keiner*, Chemnitz, 1883-1891; *Thus Spoke Zarathustra: A Book for Everyone and No One*, Penguin, Harmondsworth, 1961.

57 *Ibid.* (1961), p.41. For Nietzsche's polemics against Christianity, see *Twilight of the Idols and The Anti-Christ*, Penguin, Harmondsworth, 1968.

58 G. Orwell, *Nineteen Eighty-Four*, London, 1949 (republished Penguin, Harmondsworth, 1970).

59 F. Nietzsche, *The Will to Power*, §§647, 684-685. Nietzsche wrote (§647): 'The influence of "external circumstances" is overestimated by Darwin to a ridiculous extent: the essential thing in the life process is precisely the tremendous shaping, form-creating force working from within which *utilizes and exploits* "external circumstances" '. (W. Kaufmann [ed.], *The Will to Power: Friedrich Nietzsche*, Vintage Books, New York, 1968, p.344).

60 F. Copleston, *A History of Philosophy: Volume VII, Fichte to Nietzsche*, Burns Oates, London, 1963, p.414.

61 To explain Nietzsche's distinction between the so-called 'Apollinian' and 'Dionysian' aspects of life, we

may quote from a work on Nietzsche by Crane Brinton: 'According to Nietzsche, art — and therefore, of course, everything in human life — has two poles, the Dionysian and the Apollinian. The Dionysian is A Good Thing: it is God's and Nature's primal strength, the unending turbulent lust and longing in men which drives them to conquest, to drunkenness, to mystic ecstasy, to love-deaths. The Apollinian is A Bad Thing — though not unattractive in its proper place: it is man's attempt to stop this unending struggle, to find peace, harmony, balance, to restrain the brute in himself. But the brute is life, and cannot be long restrained. Greek life and art, as we can find if we go back to the sources, was originally Dionysian. With Socrates and Euripedes, however, the Apollinian element won a too-conclusive victory. The living springs of Dionysian strength were cut off. Greek culture became restrained, harmonious, gentlemanly, reasonable, beautiful — and dead'. (C. Brinton, *Nietzsche*, Harper & Row, New York, 1965, p.39.)

62   See A. Schopenhauer, *Die Welt als Wille und Vorstellung*, Dresden, 1818 (*The World as Will and Idea*, Trübner, London, 1883). Nietzsche's materials for the book that was to be entitled *Der Wille zur Macht* (*The Will to Power*) were published posthumously by his sister in 1909-1910.

63   J. A. Passmore, *op. cit.* (note 1).

64   S. Alexander, *Space, Time and Deity, The Gifford Lectures at Glasgow, 1916-1918*, Macmillan, London, 1920.

65   A. N. Whitehead, *Science and the Modern World*, Cambridge, 1926 (republished Free Press, Riverside, 1967).

66   H. Bergson, *L'Evolution Creatrice*, Paris, 1907; *Creative Evolution*, London & New York, 1911.

67   See above, note 48.

68   H. Bergson, *op. cit.* (note 66, 1911), p.92.

69   *Ibid.*, p.103.

70   *Ibid.*, p.261.

20

Darwinism and Psychology

According to the historian of psychology, Gardner Murphy:

> The influence of Darwinism upon psychology during the last quarter of the nineteenth century probably did as much as any single factor to shape the science as it exists today.[1]

This may be something of an exaggeration, but it should offer us sufficient warrant for giving our attention to some of the historical connections between evolutionism and studies of mental phenomena.

Psychology began to emerge as an independent scientific discipline in the last quarter of the nineteenth century, the period when Darwin's work was exerting its maximum influence. Before this time, psychology – or the study of mental phenomena – was chiefly a branch of philosophy rather than experimental science. There was no clearly recognisable discipline of psychology, with its own distinctive theoretical system and associated set of experimental techniques; no psychological paradigm, in Kuhn's terminology.[2]

Before the period of Darwin's ascendancy, mental phenomena were treated primarily from a philosophical point of view, so that studies were undertaken chiefly by what may be called mental introspection. That is to say, the philosopher, instead of approaching the study of mind through some kind of experimental technique, was disposed to try to analyse the contents of his own mind, asking himself how he came to acquire the particular ideas and information with which he was endowed or had acquired, and what was the character of the contents of his mind. It was this approach that gave rise to the psychological theory known as *associationism*, which was widely adhered to in Britain in the early years of the nineteenth century.

The doctrine of associationism can be traced back to the Greeks,[3] but it became entrenched in British philosophy chiefly as a result of the writings of the well-known empiricist school of Locke, Berkeley and Hume, and subsequently the Mills, father and son.

According to Locke,[4] the mind at birth was like a blank tablet or sheet of white paper.[5] As a result of the sensations received through the sense organs, simple ideas were successively 'engraved' upon this mental 'tablet', and then mentally 'synthesised' to form a series of complex ideas, or mental pictures. To take a simple example, if one looks at an orange, one may sense successively an orange colour, a round shape, a particular smell, a particular feel, and so on. According to Locke's view of the matter, the mind is capable of synthesising all these separate 'simple' ideas in order to form the 'complex' idea of the orange. It may be noted that such a view of the workings of the mind has negligible support today, although a latter-day version of it was still to be found in the writings of Bertrand Russell (1872-1970) in the early years of this century.[6]

A leading exponent of associationism in the eighteenth century was the British philosopher and physician, David Hartley (1705-1757).[7] Suppose, said Hartley, a particular set of sensations (or Lockian 'simple ideas') are commonly found in association one with another, as, say, with the orange. According to the doctrine of associationism, the presentation of one of the sensations would promptly stioulate mental images of the other ideas that are normally found in association (spatially and temporally) with the first.

Suppose, for example, the 'qualities' 'A', 'B', 'C', 'D', and 'E' normally occur in association. And these, it may be supposed, give rise to the mental images 'a', 'b', 'c', 'd', and 'e', from which the mind is accustomed to construct a particular complex idea. Then if, on some occasion, the 'quality' 'A' (say 'orangeness') is presented to the sensory experience of some observer, and the simple idea 'a' occurs consequently, according to the associationist doctrine the ideas 'b', 'c', 'd' and 'e' might be expected to arise concomitantly in association with 'a', following the presentation of 'A' to the observer's senses. Hartley supported this doctrine with a complicated theory of vibrations of minute medullary particles in the brain (rather pleasingly named 'vibratiuncles') to serve as a mechanical explanation of the association of ideas. This idea, based upon the musical analogue of the interactions of vibrating strings, was, however, purely speculative, as indeed was the whole doctrine.

The leading exponent of associationism in the early nineteenth century was James Mill (1773-1836).[8] The associationist principle was linked with the ethical doctrine of utilitarian hedonism, the supposition being that every experience could be reduced to sensory components under the guidance of the pleasure/pain principle. John Stuart Mill, however, maintained in his *Logic* (1843) that the associative whole (or 'complex idea') is really much more than the sum of its psychic components, just as the colour white is more than the sum of its constituent colours of the spectrum.[9]

The point that should be noted is that the associationist psychology was profoundly un-evolutionary in character. It did not present a picture of one man, or a whole generation, making mental advances relative to predecessors.

Moreover, it had nothing to say about mental differences; about why some men or women should display greater degrees of mental capacity than others. Rather, it was thought that suitable mental application, and adherence to the appropriate methodological procedures, would in principle enable any person to display a considerable degree of mental skill. This belief was one of long standing. Descartes's rules for procedure, for example, in his celebrated *Discourse on Method* (1637), suggested that anyone, by careful systematic enquiry, might achieve the intellectual feats for which Descartes became renowned.[10]

The associationists made little attempt to consider evidence that might throw light on the way in which mental development occurs among children, or the adult mind in different stages of development, or different kinds of minds in different environments. They merely sought to examine the supposed workings of an already functioning adult mind, and took no cognizance of individual mental differences. Increased emphasis was laid on inborn or instinctive ideas by Alexander Bain (1818-1903),[11] but the basic suppositions of his system were still those of associationism. He described learning in terms of (1) random movements, (2) the retention of pleasurable actions and the rejection of unpleasurable ones, and (3) fixation through repetition.

But with the coming of Darwinism, the old doctrines of associationist psychology were discarded fairly quickly. After Darwin, psychology could be viewed in biological terms, with the insights provided by the concepts of variation, heredity and adaptation as prime considerations. The Darwinian emphasis on variation led people to consider mental differences; considerations of heredity focussed attention on uniformities of mental powers; and adaptation could be related to studies of changes in mental structures.

However, even before Darwin, mental studies had begun to shift from the fixism of the associationists, most notably in Spencer's attempt to subsume psychological phenomena under the framework of his general evolutionism (*Principles of Psychology*, 1855).[12] Spencer emphasised the importance of the environment in mental development, with the evolution of the mind being only one manifestation of the general doctrine of cosmic evolution. But his actual theory of the functioning of the brain still owed much to associationist psychology/physiology. Indeed, his model was not unlike that of Hartley's speculative mechanism of the 'vibratiuncles'. Thus Spencer supposed that nerve fibres were developed in an organism by the habitual passage of stimulus waves along particular paths — after the first path was cut, the subsequent stimuli followed the same route, taking the 'line of least resistance'. Reflex arcs were supposedly established first, then nerve ganglia which directed the nervous tremors in particular channels. The progressive elaboration of these was presumed to correspond to the progressive rise of intelligence. Consciousness supposedly arose when internal motions of the brain began without the presentation of external stimuli. Spencer sought[13] to interpret his theory of the mind through his general formula of evolution — increasing heterogeneity, definiteness and integration.

It will be appreciated that despite the willingness to entertain mental evolutionism, Spencer's investigations were still primarily philosophical rather than scientific. His ideas tended towards aprioristic speculation rather than the results of experimental investigations. Much of his system depended upon *quasi*-Lamarckian principles.

Darwin was not solely responsible for giving investigations of mental phenomena an experimental basis. If any single person is to be awarded such an accolade (an unnecessary act for an historian), then it should probably go to Wilhelm Wundt (1832-1920) in Germany.[14] Nevertheless, Darwin certainly directed attention towards the possibility of an experimental and observational approach to the problem of understanding mental phenomena through his two major works dealing with psychological matters, *The Descent of Man* (1871) and *The Expression of the Emotions in Man and Animals* (1872), and his less well-known paper published in *Mind* in 1877, entitled 'A biographical sketch of an infant'.[15]

Darwin sought to subsume the evolution of mental powers under his general evolutionary theory, supposing, that is, that there was variation in mental capacity among humans and other animals, that being well endowed mentally was advantageous in the struggle for existence and consequently would be encouraged by the usual natural selection process. By this characteristically Darwinian explanation one might be led to the conclusion that both instincts and the 'higher mental powers' (moral sensibilities, for example) could have arisen through natural selection, assisted also by the inheritance of acquired characteristics. The argument was that there was no fundamental or qualitative difference between men and animals in mental attributes, although there was a vast quantitative difference. Language appears to mark a fundamental distinction between men and animals, but Darwin argued that it arose quite naturally from instinctive animal noises and imitation with the greater use of vocal organs being inherited in a Lamarckian fashion. Thus conceptually, at least, if not in terms of strict experimental proof, Darwin finally closed the gap which since antiquity had supposedly existed between men and animals. Or, recalling the discussions of our first chapter, we may say that Darwin eliminated the great chasm which, according to Descartes, separated rational man from the irrational automata of the animal kingdom. We might add here in parenthesis that twentieth-century research has supported the view that thought can take place without the aid of language;[16] so the gap has been closed further in recent years by an approach from a rather different direction.

Darwin's *Expression of the Emotions* begins with three major principles:
1 The principle of serviceable associated habits;
2 The principle of antithesis;
3 The principle of the direct action of the nervous system.
The first of these envisages various kinds of emotional expression as being

evolutionary residues of behaviour patterns that were once appropriate in a different context. For example, the sneer of disdain (of a duchess towards a flower-girl perchance) in which the upper lip is raised somewhat, partially revealing the upper canine teeth, may be seen as an evolutionary vestige of the action of an animal (a baboon perhaps) baring its teeth to deter some potential aggressor. This principle is still quite widely accepted. It may have had some origin in Darwin's mind in the associationism of James Mill's psychology.

One can find many illustrations of the second principle: for example, the smile, with the turning up of the corners of the mouth to display happiness, which may be contrasted with the down-turning of the lips to denote misery; or the wagging tail of the pleased dog, which is the very antithesis of the drooping, listless tail of the frightened or miserable hound. This principle may also have been derived from James Mill, who had tried to extend his theory to account for contrasted associations. It does not have the support today that is given to the first principle. An angry man may turn either red or white.

The third principle, which seems to have a Spencerian ring, is illustrated, for example, by emotion being displayed by a general action of the nervous system not directly related to the emotion concerned — for example, trembling caused by anger, joy, fear or cold. Darwin was not always able to explain instances of this third category in any very satisfactory way in terms of his theory of evolution by natural selection. Trembling, for example, seemed to be disadvantageous, and probably did not arise through the action of the will. But the trembling of muscles in a state of anger might be an evolutionary vestige of a physical preparation for attack or defence.

In Darwin's view, these three principles, stated almost with axiomatic force at the beginning of the first chapter of *Expression of the Emotions*; sufficed to account satisfactorily for most of the expressions and gestures involuntarily used by man and animals when under the influence of various emotions and sensations. But it was not the theoretical framework provided by these three broad categories that made the book important. It was, rather, the method employed by Darwin that was particularly significant. He conducted a kind of 'natural historical' survey of the emotions, showing in great detail how the different emotions are expressed, usually instinctively, by particular sounds or gestures. And in many instances he was then able to suggest hypotheses on how the particular means of conveying or expressing the emotion might have arisen in the evolutionary history of organisms — as with, for example, our disdainful duchess. Such a program was certainly innovative in that it offered a new method for explaining psychological phenomena in genetic or evolutionary terms. On the other hand, Darwin's work in this field was to a large degree anecdotal in character and did not depend on the results of carefully planned experimental investigations. And on occasions he was (it is thought today) prone to anthropomorphise his interpretations of animal behaviour to an unwarranted degree, as for example when he wrote: 'Even insects, by their stridulation, express anger, terror and love'.[17] But the point of over-riding importance that should be noted was that Darwin believed that his investigations of expression and behaviour showed that mental or psychological phenomena, like all other biological questions, were to be explained in purely naturalistic terms.

Let us turn now to look at some of the results of Darwin's theories as they impinged on the development of psychology as a science. A good way to begin is with the work of Francis Galton (1822-1911), Darwin's highly gifted cousin.

Galton sought to examine the characteristics of human behaviour in a practical and experimental way, looking particularly into the question of variations, and also selection and adaptation; considering both different individuals and different races. As we have seen, earlier investigators had tended to treat all men as if they were essentially the same, although women perhaps were considered to be substantially different. Galton set out with the specific intention of investigating human *differences*. His first work in this field resulted in the publication of his celebrated *Hereditary Genius* in 1869.[18] In this remarkable book, he showed how some families were sometimes endowed with gifts that were seemingly inheritable, for example, special musical, mathematical, linguistic, or sporting talents. The Darwin family provided a fine example of an apparently inherited expertise in scientific inquiry. The Bachs, likewise, provide the most celebrated instance of great musical gifts in one family.

There seems little doubt that Darwin's interest in heredity and individual similarities and differences provided the source of inspiration for Galton's work. But, by present-day criteria, Galton is open to criticism in that he tended to ascribe almost everything to heredity and virtually nothing to environment. He believed, for example, that some men belonged to the 'criminal type' and that no amount of environmental improvement would serve to alter this. It is true that Galton was able to support his contentions for the nature side of the nature/nurture[19] controversy to a considerable degree by the results of his pioneering work on identical twins. But on the question of talents being concentrated within families, one could readily argue that Galton's observations were compatible with their being a product of environmental causes rather than genetic or hereditary factors, and it appears that he was introducing a number of the social prejudices of his class into his scientific investigations. Galton's work did provide considerable support for the conservative Social Darwinists and his remarks in several places in *Hereditary Genius* have much of the flavour of Samuel Smiles's *Self Help*.

It was in his *Inquiries into Human Faculty* (1883)[20] that Galton at last began to subject the principles of associationism to experimental inquiry. He prepared a number of cards with words on them, and then asked his subjects to say what they spontaneously and freely associated with these words. He later tried to establish what had been the cause of the association and the time when the connection might have been established. He found that in most cases the associations were established in certain childhood experiences. This seemed to indicate the considerable importance of the very early life of the child for later adult life and personality. Also in his *Inquiries into Human Faculty* Galton gave the results of experiments that he had carried out by means of questionnaires, trying to establish the similarities and differences between mental images and direct perceptions or sensations. He found that there were remarkable differences in the capacities of different persons to form mental images – a point that would never have been recognised by the methods of mental introspection of the associationists.

Galton, claiming the primacy of 'nature' as opposed to 'nurture' in the development of organisms (including humans) was the founder of the so-called 'eugenics' movement, in which it was hoped that human stocks might be radically improved, not by culling out mentally or physically 'unfit' persons, but by offering special inducements to certain selected people to encourage them to procreate freely. Such a scheme, although it had certain attractive features, had never been attempted on a large scale, except for moves in this direction in Hitler's Germany, in the so-called 'camps of joy'.[21] Aldous Huxley's *Brave New World*[22] proved singularly effective in focussing protest against the eugenics movement in the English-speaking world, and the collapse of Nazi Germany prevented the further development of eugenics in Europe.

Following the publication of *The Origin*, *The Descent of Man*, and *Expression of the Emotions*, a considerable number of writers took up the general idea of mental evolution and published volumes that sought to account for psychological phenomena in evolutionary terms.[23] We have insufficient space to deal with all of these, but will consider briefly the work of William McDougall (1871-1938), to whom reference has already been made in our chapter on Neo-Lamarckism.

McDougall was an English psychologist who later took up an appointment at Harvard. He was the author of a well-known volume, *Psychology: the Study of Behaviour* (1912),[24] the title of which has often linked him with the so-called behaviourist school, although his ideas differed substantially from those of the leader of the behaviourists, J. B. Watson. McDougall wished to get away from all connections with introspectionist psychology and treat the subject empirically and in a positivistic manner. In this he was at one with the behaviourists. But he is usually regarded as a 'purposivist' rather than a behaviourist. He stressed that the behaviour of the body is a result of the interactions between mind and body; he saw behaviour as a mark of purposiveness on the part of an organism. Behaviour, so he supposed, when considered from an objective point of view, clearly displays goal-seeking activity. Goal seeking implies that organisms possess some kind of motivation, and this, so McDougall supposed, is supplied by instincts. Moreover, instincts are handed down by heredity and consequently have an evolutionary base. McDougall also stressed the link between the instincts and the emotions, and in discussing problems of social psychology he emphasised the need to consider the gradual building up of intellectual and social traditions which would influence men as they grew up in their social frameworks.

Although McDougall wrote much on behaviour, it is not correct to refer to him as a behaviourist. This school is intimately connected with the work of J. B. Watson (1878-1958). The theoretical presuppositions of the school were crystallising in America just before the First World War and being strongly influenced by positivist philosophy of science.[25] In his *Behaviour* (1914),[26] Watson did not deny the phenomenon of consciousness, but he considered it a theoretical superfluity that might usefully be excised with the help of Ockham's razor.[27] Psychology, for Watson, should eschew all dealings with introspection as a tool for the investigation of mental phenomena and should concern itself solely with empirically observable and testable behavioural characteristics of organisms.

In *Behaviour*, Watson explained the Darwinian theory (as resuscitated after the rediscovery of Mendel's work) and considered its possible role in the origin of instincts. He suggested that if new behaviour patterns were inherited this would form 'a ready method of evolution',[28] but he admitted that this had not so far been demonstrated. And he was forced to conclude that:

> The application of either the selection or the direct adaptation theory to behaviour complexes is as yet impossible, owing to the lack of any very definite concepts of the structural basis of behaviour.[29]

It must be admitted that by the time we get to Watson in the history of psychology the direct links with Darwin are becoming somewhat tenuous. Nevertheless, it may fairly be claimed that the emphasis on the experimental approach, set strongly in motion by Darwin's investigations, reached its zenith in Watson, who, with an almost crass positivism, was unwilling to seek below the level of observable phenomena to uncover the workings of the brain or the nature of thought and consciousness.

The work of the celebrated Russian psychologist, I. P. Pavlov (1849-1936), on conditioned reflexes is, among behavioural studies, perhaps the best known. Pavlov worked chiefly with dogs. His procedure was to set a metronome ticking for a minute and then put food in a dog's mouth. The procedure was repeated several times. In time, the dog would begin to salivate while the metronome was ticking, and before the presentation of the food. Eventually, the salivation occurred when the metronome ticked, even when no food was provided. But if the experiment was carried further in this way, the effect would wear off after a time. On the other hand, if the conditioning was carried out on successive days, the number of trials needed to establish the flow of saliva gradually decreased.

From experiments such as these, Pavlov sought to establish a general theory of the working of the brain, claiming that all learned behaviour is established by means of conditioned reflexes. He wrote:

It is obvious that the different kinds of habits based on training, education and discipline of any sort are nothing but a long chain of conditioned reflexes.[30]

Using such a model, Pavlov and his colleagues offered a kind of mechanism whereby the evolutionary process might take place.

As a kind of precursor to the behaviourist school was the *functionalism*[31] of William James and John Dewey, who have already been mentioned in connection with the pragmatist movement in philosophy. James's chief psychological publication was his *Principles of Psychology* of 1890.[32] Its whole approach was profoundly influenced by evolutionary considerations. For example, James listed and discussed a long list of instincts that may be found in animals and others that may be found in man. Instincts, he said,[33] are the functional correlatives of structure. And these instincts were clearly all of adaptive value in the evolutionary process. Then, in his last chapter, on 'Necessary truths and the effects of experience', James discussed the problem of what he called psychogenesis, and maintained that ideas that seem to us necessarily true (such as geometric relations or logical principles) have acquired their apparent necessity through the long process of evolutionary development of the human mind. Thus Kant's problem, considered in the eighteenth century, about how certain synthetic propositions[34] appeared to be knowable *a priori*,[35] could, in James' view, be answered in evolutionary terms. Such knowledge had become embedded in the human psyche by a *quasi*-Darwinian mechanism.[36] However, not all human knowledge is of this kind. Most synthetic propositions can only be known *a posteriori*.[37] The mind, therefore, must also have the capacity to learn everyday facts, as well as those that are supposedly knowable *a priori* by courtesy of the evolutionary process. James sought to explain both functions of the mind in evolutionary terms.

Related to the psychological theories of James was the work of John Dewey (1859-1952). Dewey considered thought as a product of the active relationship between an organism and its environment and that thought should be regarded as purely naturalistic in origin. It could be seen as a particularly highly developed form of the normal biological relationship between stimulus and response. Thought, for Dewey is a kind of 'instrument', with a special practical function, and is to be considered therefore as a form of activity. Moreover, according to this view, thought is a kind of evolutionary product of the relation between an organism and its environment. Personality is not just 'given'; it is built up during the evolutionary history of organisms and in the development of particular beings.[38] The link with nineteenth-century evolutionism should be apparent here, although it is rather more subtle than the suggestion that a kind of natural selection process acts on thoughts or ideas, as Dewey's pragmatist predecessor, C. S. Peirce, was inclined to suppose.[39]

Close links with evolutionism can be found in the work of the animal psychologists and comparative psychologists of the late nineteenth century.

George Romanes (1848-1899), for example, though still making some use of associationist principles, made important contributions in his *Animal Intelligence* (1882),[40] *Mental Evolution in Animals* (1883),[41] and *Mental Evolution in Man* (1888).[42] As with Darwin, Romanes's treatment was somewhat anecdotal and he tended to anthropomorphise animals, but his emphasis on the continuity in mental faculties between men and animals was important. His evolutionism is clearly demonstrated by his attempt to portray the evolutionary development of the intellect by means of an evolutionary tree. (See Figure 31.) The right-hand column suggests that Romanes was applying the old doctrine of recapitulation (or Haeckel's 'biogenetic law') to mental phenomena. Also, Romanes's tree may be compared with the diagram prepared by Chambers for his *Vestiges*, illustrated above on page 56.

Romanes's work was carried further by the Bristol psychologist, C. Lloyd Morgan (1852-1936), who made considerable efforts to distinguish satisfactorily between innate and acquired behaviour, attempting to approach the problem from an experimental point of view and looking particularly at the processes of animal learning. He found, for example, that chickens discovered which kinds of food were good to eat by a kind of 'trial and error' process, without displaying any evidence of intelligent behaviour, although they seemed to display a rudimentary form of consciousness.

In his *Introduction to Comparative Psychology* (1894), Lloyd Morgan gave some attention to the problem of the origin of consciousness (which he associated with energy) and found himself driven to the startling conclusion that 'all modes of energy of whatever kind, whether organic or inorganic, have their conscious or infra-conscious aspect'.[44] And he toyed with the idea of a kind of principle of conservation of consciousness, analogous to the conservation of energy. It was not possible, however, to give a clear picture of what was meant by the infra-consciousness of matter and in talking about it we see that Lloyd Morgan, despite all his objective experimentation, was far from being a positivist behaviourist. We should note, also, that he stated explicitly that he did not think that the phenomenon of the evolution of consciousness could be explained satisfactorily by natural selection alone.[45]

In his later *Emergent Evolution* (1923),[46] Lloyd Morgan considered that there were different 'levels' of organisation and consciousness which emerged successively in the evolutionary process.[47] L. T. Hobhouse (1864-1928) developed this idea and investigated abilities of different kinds of animals to solve problems of different levels of difficulty. The results obtained could be correlated with the supposed levels of the different kinds of animals in the evolutionary hierarchy. Investigations of this kind were continued by E. L. Thorndike (1874-1948) in America, but his work merged with that of the behaviourist school.

Finally, in this brief survey, we may say a few words about the influence of Darwin's ideas on the work of Sigmund Freud (1856-1939), founder of the celebrated psycho-analytic movement of psychology.[48] It would be far

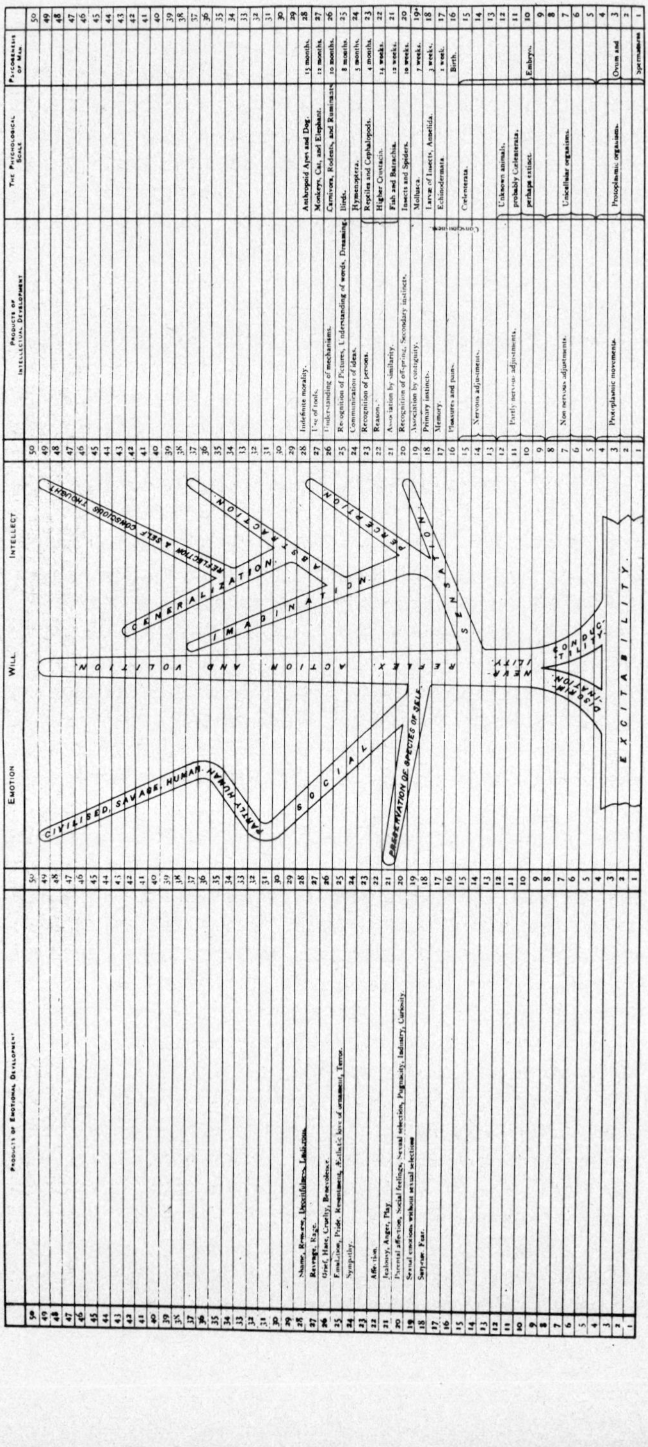

Figure 31 A Representation of the Evolutionary Development of Mental Powers, according to G. J. Romanes[43]

beyond the scope of the present work to give a general exposition of the work and theories of Freud. Suffice it to say that his investigations of neurotic patients, conducted initially through studies of hypnosis, led him to the conclusion that their neuroses might often be ascribed to forgotten experiences (frequently sexual) in early childhood which had left an indelible mark on their personalities but only existed in adulthood at the unconscious level. Freud sought to expose these unconscious components of the psyche, chiefly by analysis of patients' dreams and overt behaviour. And he found that the patients could often be cured of their neuroses once their causes at the unconscious level had been revealed.

To account for his findings, Freud eventually worked out a highly original and controversial theory of human psychic processes. He proposed that a fundamental driving force in man was the need for the satisfaction of what he called the *libido* − a core of instinctive urges, chiefly sexual. The libidinal instincts supposedly originate in and through the part of the psychic system which in Freud's terminology is called the *id*. But owing to the demands of social life, the drives emanating from the *id* come to be repressed through the operations of the part of the psychic system called the *ego*. Related to this latter, the agency of the *super-ego* censures and judges this process of repression. This corresponds to the moral conscience, about which theologians and others have long been accustomed to discourse. The human subject feels his moral conscience to be part of the *ego*, yet also as something foreign and superior to it.[49] The psychological drama of all humans concerns the actions and interactions of these three aspects of the psyche. By analysis of such phenomena as dreams, neurotic behaviour, the patterns of jokes and slips of the tongue, Freud sought to explore everyday mental life and penetrate also into the hitherto unexplored realms of the unconscious. It may well be that his theory of the psyche is far from adequate, but the program of inquiry he initiated − the probing of the deeper structures of human unconsciousness (depth psychology) − is surely one of the most important aspects of the whole of twentieth-century culture.

There are several indications in Freud's writings that he was considerably influenced by Darwin as a young man, and as Freud grew up Darwin was becoming widely known in the German-speaking world through the work of Ernst Haeckel. Darwin's theory formed an important component of the curriculum to which Freud was exposed when he was working as a medical student in Vienna. It has been recorded that Freud's teacher in psychiatry, T. H. Meynert, emphasised that Darwin had shown in his *Expression of the Emotions* that one might gauge the inner workings of the mind by an examination of outward expressions, and it is not unreasonable to suppose that Freud used this as an important clue for the later development of his theory. But it appears that Meynert was critical of Darwin's theory of instinct.

It should also be noted that the systems of both Freud and Darwin sought historical explanations of psychiatric and biological phenomena respectively.

But this mode of explanation was commonplace in the nineteenth century, and it cannot be proved that Freud's approach was in this respect directly derived from Darwin.

It has been suggested that Freud's discussion of sexual repression may have owed something to Darwin, paralleling the following passage from Darwin's *Expression of the Emotions:*

> Some actions ordinarily associated through habit with certain states of the mind may be partially repressed through the will, and in such cases the muscles which are least under the separate control of the will are the most liable still to act, causing movements which we recognize as expressive.[50]

But this comparison may be no more than an act of 'free association' and not an indication of some definite causal link between the doctrines of Darwin and Freud.

Freud probably took from Darwin the idea of the 'primal horde' (which appears in *The Descent of Man*,[51] and Darwin's idea that the social formations of primitive man — with a single male ruling a small community and discouraging promiscuous interbreeding within groups — was used by Freud in his discussion of the origins of incest taboos.[52] The idea of 'struggle', which played such a fundamental role in Darwin's theory, emerged for Freud as the doctrine of 'conflict' between the different parts of the personality. On the other hand, as far as I am aware we do not find the idea of natural selection *per se* playing a role of any special significance in Freud.

It should also be noted that Freud, contrary to the view prevailing at the period when he began his investigations in the 1880s, tended to play down the role of heredity in accounting for mental disorders, preferring to offer explanations in terms of specific events that occurred in patients' life-times. In this sense his system ran counter to the general program developed by the evolutionary psychologists. It has been suggested that Freud, a Jew, may have been reluctant to embrace any idea of hereditary mental degeneracy, since such theories — as deployed in the late nineteenth century — commonly contained certain racist elements.[53] On the other hand, some of Freud's later writings did make use of the hypothesis of inherited racial memories.[54]

In general, I think it may be said that interesting points of comparison may be drawn between the work of Darwin and Freud, but Freud's work, disregarding entirely the question of whether his ideas were correct, was of such striking originality that we would not expect to find him operating as a mere elaborator of the Darwin theory, applying the evolutionary doctrine to the particular instance of mental evolution. Freud struck out in entirely new directions. Nevertheless, as we have seen, there was certain common ground with the work of Darwin and his school.

It is not by any means easy to find a common thread running through all the work of psychological investigations in the late nineteenth and early twentieth centuries, and, as has been noted by a number of authors, the discipline of psychology tended at that time to break up into a number of separate, often mutually antagonistic, 'schools',[55] a situation that is atypical in the history of the 'harder' sciences, and which might lead some critics to question whether psychology could, at that period, properly be regarded as a science. Fortunately, we need not concern ourselves too much with this question. I hope I have achieved a sufficient demonstration of the fact that Darwin's work and theories permeated almost all of the various schools that proliferated at that time.[56] Darwin stood very close to the birthplace of scientific (experimental) psychology. And clearly his subsequent influence on this science was considerable.

NOTES CHAPTER 20

1   G. Murphy, *An Historical Introduction to Modern Psychology*, 5th edn, Routledge & Kegan Paul, London, 1949, p.116.
2   T. S. Kuhn, *The Structure of Scientific Revolutions*, Chicago University Press, Chicago, 1962.
3   Plato, *Phaedo*, §73.
4   J. Locke, *An Essay Concerning the Human Understanding*, London, 1690, Book II, Chapter I, §2.
5   The doctrine of the '*tabula rasa*' was satirised by Sterne in his eccentric novel, *Tristram Shandy*, where we encounter a page printed entirely black, and another depicting a tablet of marble. One can also read *Tristram Shandy*, with its crazy juxtaposition of events and ideas, as a critique of associationism.
6   B. Russell, *Our Knowledge of the External World as a Field for Scientific Method in Philosophy*, Open Court, London & Chicago, 1914.
7   D. Hartley, *Observations of Man his Frame, his Duty, and his Expectations*, 2 vols, London, 1749.
8   J. Mill, *Analysis of the Phenomena of the Human Mind*, 2 vols, London, 1829.
9   J. S. Mill, *A System of Logic*, 2 vols, London, 1843, Vol. 2, p.502.
10   R. Descartes, *Discourse on Method and Other Writings*, Penguin, Harmondsworth, 1960, pp.50-51.
11   A. Bain, *The Senses and the Intellect*, London, 1855.
12   H. Spencer, *The Principles of Psychology*, 2 vols, London, 1855.
13   *Ibid.* (3rd edn, 1881), Vol. 1, pp.186-190.
14   See W. Wundt (tr. J. Creighton & E. Titchener), *Lectures on Human and Animal Psychology*, London, 1894.
15   C. Darwin, 'A biographical sketch of an infant', *Mind*, 1877, No. 7, pp.285-294.
16   See L. S. Vygotskii, *Thought and Language*, M.I.T. Press, Cambridge, Mass., 1962.
17   C. Darwin, *The Expression of the Emotions in Man and Animals*, revised and abridged by C. M. Beadnell, Watts, London, 1934, p.167.
18   F. Galton, *Hereditary Genius, an Inquiry into its Laws and Consequences*, London, 1869 (republished Collins, London, 1962). For a useful discussion of Galton's life and his contributions to science, see D. W. Forrest, *Francis Galton: The Life and Work of a Victorian Genius*, Elek, London, 1974. Also of importance is R. S. Cowan, 'Nature and nurture: the interplay of biology and politics in the work of Francis Galton', *Studies in History of Biology*, Vol. 1, 1977, pp.133-208.
19   Galton introduced this term (referring to inheritable genetic characteristics and environmental influences respectively) into the title of one of his works: *English Men of Science: their Nature and Nurture*, London, 1874.
20   F. Galton, *Inquiries into Human Faculty and its Development*, London, 1883.
21   For an account of this bizarre aspect of German history, see H. P. Bleuel, *Strength through Joy: Sex and Society in Nazi Germany*, Secker & Warburg, London, 1973.
22   A. L. Huxley, *Brave New World*, London, 1932 (republished Longman, London, 1976).
23   See, for example, the writings of Henry Maudsley (1835-1918), James Sully (1842-1923), James Ward (1843-1925), Charles Mercier (1852-1914), or George Stout (1860-1944).
24   W. McDougall, *Psychology: the Study of Behaviour*, H. Holt, London & New York, 1912.
25   The term 'positivism' has received an extraordinary number of different interpretations. But here I am using it in reference to a scientific methodology which maintains that science should not concern itself

with hypothetical explanatory entities (such as genes, atoms or germs) but should be content with the accurate determination of the laws of nature and the inter-relations of phenomena. For a more detailed discussion of the denotations and connotations of 'positivism', see L. Kolakowski, *Positivist Philosophy: From Hume to the Vienna Circle*, Penguin, Harmondsworth, 1972.

26 J. B. Watson, *Behavior: An Introduction to Comparative Psychology*, H. Holt, New York, 1912.

27 A principle of 'simplicity', often employed in discussions of the philosophy of science. It is attributed to the scholastic philosopher, William of Ockham (*circa* 1285-1349), and is traditionally expressed by the maxim: 'Entities are not to be multiplied unnecessarily' (entities here referring to means of explanation).

28 J. B. Watson, *Behavior: An Introduction to Comparative Psychology*, with an Introduction by R. J. Herrnstein, Holt, Rinehart & Winston, New York, 1967, p.181.

29 *Ibid*, p.182.

30 I. P. Pavlov (tr. G. V. Anrep), *Conditioned Reflexes: An Investigation of the Psychological Activity of the Cerebral Cortex*, Oxford, 1927, p.395 (republished Dover, New York, 1960).

31 This school emphasised the need to examine and interpret experience and behaviour in terms of the functions that they play for the effective life of organisms within the conditions of their environment.

32 W. James, *The Principles of Psychology*, 2 vols, New York, 1890 (republished Dover, New York, 1950).

33 *Ibid*. (1950), Vol. 2, p.383.

34 A synthetic proposition, according to Kant, is one in which the predicate is not 'contained within' the subject of the proposition, but adds something to it: for example, 'This apple is green'. An analytic proposition, on the other hand is one in which the predicate is 'contained within', or equivalent to, the subject: for example, 'A green apple is an apple'.

35 *A priori* knowledge is that which is not derived from experience and is (supposedly) knowable 'prior' to experience. According to Kant (by arguments which will not be entered into here) certain propositions are knowable *a priori*, even though they are synthetic: for example, 'The shortest distance between two points is a straight line'. This claim has exercised philosophers' attention almost continuously since Kant's day.

36 W. James, *op. cit.* (note 32, 1950), Vol. 2, p.618.

37 That is, after, or 'posterior' to, experience.

38 Dewey was an extremely prolific writer and one cannot give an adequate exposition of his opinions here. The comparison between thought and a tool or instrument appears in his *Essays in Experimental Logic* (1916), reprinted in J. Ratner (ed.), *Intelligence in the Modern World: John Dewey's Philosophy*, Modern Library, New York, 1939, pp.929 ff.

39 See above, p.266.

40 G. J. Romanes, *Animal Intelligence*, London, 1882.

41 G. J. Romanes, *Mental Evolution in Animals . . . With a Posthumous Essay on Instinct, by C. Darwin*, London, 1883.

42 G. J. Romanes, *Mental Evolution in Man. Origin of Human Faculty*, London, 1888.

43 *Ibid.*, frontispiece.

44 C. Lloyd Morgan, *An Introduction to Comparative Psychology*, London, 1894, p.329.

45 *Ibid.*, p.355.

46 C. Lloyd Morgan, *Emergent Evolution: The Gifford Lectures . . . 1922*, Williams & Norgate, London, 1923.

47 Morgan also made significant contributions to theories of instinct, developing them to meet the demands made by Weismann's total rejection of Lamarckism. See R. J. Richards, 'Lloyd Morgan's theory of instinct: from Darwinism to Neo-Darwinism', *Journal of the History of the Behavioural Sciences*, Vol. 13, 1977, pp.12-32.

48 For discussions of the relationship between Darwin and Freud, see A. Comfort, *Darwin and the Naked Lady: Discursive Essays on Biology and Art*, Braziller, New York, 1962, Chapter 2; L. B. Ritvo, 'The impact of Darwin on Freud', *Psychoanalysis Quarterly*, Vol. 43, 1974, pp.177-192.

49 For Freud's diagrammatic representation of his theory, see his *New Introductory Lectures on Psycho-Analysis*, in *The Standard Edition of the Complete Psychological Works of Sigmund Freud* (ed. J. Strachey *et al.*), Vol. 22, Hogarth Press, London, 1964, p.78.

50 C. Darwin, *op. cit.* (note 17), p.4.

51 C. Darwin, *The Descent of Man, and Selection in Relation to Sex*, 2 vols, London, 1871, Vol. 2, pp.362-363. Freud wrote: 'If we associate the translation of the totem as given by psychoanalysis, with the totem feast and the Darwinian hypothesis about the primal state of human society, a deeper understanding becomes possible and a hypothesis is offered which may seem fantastic but which has the advantage of establishing an unexpected unity among a series of hitherto separated phenomena. [But] the Darwinian conception of the primal horde does not, of course, allow for the beginning of totemism' (A. A. Brill [ed. and tr.], *The Basic Writings of Sigmund Freud*, Modern Library, New York, 1938, p.915).

52   *Ibid.*, p.903.
53   See L. Stewart, 'Freud before Oedipus: race and heredity in the origins of psychoanalysis', *Journal of the History of Biology*, Vol. 9, 1976, pp.215-228.
54   See S. R. Heyman, 'Freud and the concept of inherited racial memories', *The Psychoanalytic Review*, Vol. 64, 1977, pp.461-464.
55   See R. S. Woodworth, *Contemporary Schools of Psychology*, Methuen, London, 1931.
56   It does not appear to have had much influence on the so-called '*Gestalt*' school.

21

Darwinism and Anthropology

The question of the influence of Darwinism on the development of anthropology (the scientific study of man) or on ethnology (the scientific study of human races) is by no means easy to unravel. On the one hand, we find a writer such as R. R. Marett enthusing that:

> Anthropology is the child of Darwin; Darwinism makes it possible. Reject the Darwinian point of view, and you must reject anthropology also.[1]

But on the other, we find a more sober assessment provided by the contemporary Darwin scholar, J. W. Gruber, who has argued,[2] for example, that the acceptance of the antiquity of man was independent of the advent of the Darwin/Wallace theory, with the implication that studies of man were beginning to find their feet without Darwin's help at all. So opinion is divided on the question of the influence of Darwin's ideas on the study of man. We also have the problem that the subject runs in such a variety of directions. Studies of human races, cultures and physical and mental characteristics are all relevant here. And the scientific questions are conflated with religious and political controversies, with all the confusion that this entails. There are also Darwin's own views on anthropological matters to consider. Clearly, our task at this point is not an easy one.

Let us make a start by sketching the orthodox view of man's place in nature, as it was generally and popularly perceived in Britain in the first half of the nineteenth century. It was an amalgam of traditional Biblical opinion and the catastrophist geological theory of Cuvier and Buckland. God had created the first pair of humans in the Garden of Eden. The various races of man were supposed to have descended from the several sons of Noah after the Flood, and the different languages originated when the Tower of Babel was built. The eastern Mediterranean was thought to be the sole centre from which mankind had subsequently spread. (This corresponded to what is known as the *monogenist* hypothesis. *Polygenism* advocated a number of separate foci of human creation.) A number of people still believed in the chronology of Bishop Ussher (1581-1656), which postulated 4004 BC as the year of the Creation.

As we have noted previously,[3] William Buckland identified the last of Cuvier's catastrophes with the Noachian Flood and his detailed investigations of cave deposits, which revealed a variety of remains of creatures now no longer extant in Britain, were thought to provide concrete evidence for the occurrence of the Deluge and the veracity of the Biblical account of the history of the globe.[4] On one well-known occasion when Buckland investigated a cave at Paviland in Glamorganshire he discovered what he took to be the remains of a female skeleton and ascribed it to the 'postdiluvian' period, suggesting that it might have been the remains of a woman of easy virtue, as the cave was adjacent to a British camp where she might have been able to find employment. Subsequent research has shown that the 'lady' in question was a young palaeolithic male. Buckland, however, believing in the recent creation of mankind, could not have countenanced any great antiquity for his discovery, and sought to interpret it as fairly recent. The case admirably illustrates the manner in which metaphysical presuppositions may influence men's scientific judgement.[5]

Yet even in the first half of the nineteenth century, a considerable amount of evidence was accumulated which suggested an early antiquity for man. Old folklore had interpreted flint implements as the work of fairies, and the Renaissance scholars Agricola and Gessner had suggested that neolithic implements might be interpreted as thunderbolts.[6] But John Frere (1740-1807), had discovered flint implements in a brick-put at Hoxne, Suffolk, in 1797, and suggested that they derived from a very remote period – from a people who did not have the use of metals.[7] In 1830, human remains (the famous 'Engis' skull) associated with bone and flint implements in geological cave deposits of considerable antiquity were discovered near Liège in Belgium by P.-C. Schmerling (1791-1836).[8] But his correct interpretation of their great age found little acceptance. Then in 1836, J. Boucher de Perthes (1788-1868) discovered flint implements *in situ* in the gravels of the River Somme near Abbeville in northern France and spoke out strongly for the existence of 'antediluvian man' in his country.[9] His views were derided. Eventually, the excavations at a cave at Brixham in Devon, in 1858, by Hugh Falconer, William Pengelly and Joseph Prestwich finally convinced the scientific public in Britain of the great age of some human remains,[10] and Lyell publicly announced his conversion to the notion of the great antiquity of man in an address to the British Association in 1859. During the next three years he studied the question in detail and published his notable *Antiquity of Man* in 1863.[11] The celebrated 'Neanderthal' man was discovered by H. Schaaffhausen (1816-1893) in the Neanderthal district near Dusseldorf in Germany in 1857[12] and was a creature apparently of ape-like features with a considerable brain capacity. And the well-known 'Cro-Magnon' man – who gave the world his remarkable cave-paintings –

was reported by Louis Lartet (1840-1899) in the Dordogne district of France in 1868.[13] Thus, quite independently of *The Origin*, a good deal of empirical work on man's pre-history was accomplished in the first part of the nineteenth century.

There were also certain theoretical contributions that should be noted. In the eighteenth century, Sir William Jones (1746-1794) had pointed to the linguistic similarities of Sanskrit, Greek, Latin, Celtic and other European languages and suggested that this might be an indication that these languages derived from some common source, perhaps no longer extant.[14] This proposal, obviously not in accord with the story of the Tower of Babel,[15] opened up a whole field of inquiry into the affinities of the various languages and their possible historical connections; it also raised again the question of the origin of language – a popular topic for philosophical speculation in the eighteenth century.[16] Jones's ideas were confirmed by the German philologist, Franz Bopp (1791-1867) in 1835, and F. Max Müller (1823-1900) adopted the name 'Aryan' to describe the Indo-Iranian group of languages from which the European languages were supposed to have evolved.[17] Regrettably, and despite Müller's protests that he was talking only about a *linguistic* (rather than an anthropological) grouping, later commentators chose to assume that there was a common racial affinity associated with this unified linguistic heritage, and so there arose the vulgar German prejudice that there was a distinct Aryan race, superior to the Jewish race which was associated with the Semitic group of languages.

The Danish government set up a geological and natural historical commission in 1806, and the stone implements and shell middens of Denmark were investigated early in the nineteenth century. The curator of the 'Museum of Northern Antiquities' in Copenhagen, Jürgensen Thomsen (1788-1865), classified the newly acquired collections and suggested the names 'Stone Age', 'Bronze Age', and 'Iron Age' in 1836.[18] The terms 'Neolithic' and 'Palaeolithic' were suggested by Sir John Lubbock (1834-1913) in 1865.[19]

The first half of the nineteenth century also saw a considerable increase in empirical knowledge about the physical characteristics of the various races of modern man. In the eighteenth century, the Göttingen naturalist, J. F. Blumenbach (1752-1840), had begun to assemble a considerable collection of human skulls which he classified into Caucasian, Mongolian, Ethiopian, American and Malay types.[20] His collection has been increased until the present day, and the skulls are still on display. Various scales were devised by later workers for comparing the physical characteristics, such as shape and brain capacity, of different skulls, the best known being the so-called 'cephalic index'[21] of the Swedish investigator Anders Retzius (1796-1860) who also introduced the terms 'dolichocephalic' (long-headed) and 'brachycephalic' (short-headed), the first of these being supposedly a superior racial variety.[22] F. J. Gall (1758-1828) in his new science of phrenology attempted to divine people's psychological and intellectual characteristics from examination of the shape of their crania.[23] But although phrenology was an important precursor of modern psychology it is not considered today that it has any scientific legitimacy. Besides these comparative investigations of the physical characteristics of humans, there was also a very considerable flow of information in the early nineteenth century on the habits and customs of distant civilisations such as those of China and India, and primitive races such as those of Brazil or Australia.

In all this, particularly with respect to the study of languages, there were undoubtedly strong presentiments of the evolutionary doctrine. Indeed, in the work of J. C. Prichard (1786-1848), a Bristol physician and author of a volume entitled *Researches into the Physical History of Mankind*, there was a partial anticipation of Darwin's theory of natural selection, although it achieved little public notice.[24] But the study of man failed to crystallise around an evolutionary hypothesis before 1859.

There was, however, even in the first half of the nineteenth century, a degree of 'institutionalisation' of anthropological studies, a sure sign that the discipline was beginning to become professionalised and a step that is normally accompanied by the establishment of an agreed pattern of theoretical views. An Ethnological Subsection of the British Association for the Advancement of Science was established in 1846, with Prichard as its first president, three years after the founding the Ethnological Society of London. The earlier Aborigines Protection Society, which grew from the concerns of the anti-slavery movement, had had some interest in anthropological matters. The Anthropological Society of London held its first meeting in 1863. And the Ethnological Society combined with the Anthropological Society in 1871 to form the Anthropological Institute. The *Société Ethnologique de Paris* and the *Société d'Anthropologie de Paris* were founded in 1839 and 1859 respectively.

There were substantial theoretical and social differences between the members of the Ethnological and Anthropological Societies.[25] The former, of evangelical and philanthropic affiliations, displayed interests in archaeology, linguistic and cultural anthropology, and the physical characteristics of man. The latter, who at times tended to adopt somewhat ugly racist views, were chiefly interested in the physical description and classification of man and showed little historical concern. It is interesting, therefore, and in some ways paradoxical, that the evolutionists were mostly to be found in the Ethnological Society, with its strong Christian connections.

But in theory this was the natural place for them, for evolutionism was most readily compatible with the monogenist hypothesis, rather than polygenism. And the 'Anthropologicals', with racist proclivities, were typically advocates of polygenism with its notion of the distinctiveness and individuality of the different human races. It was on this question of monogenism versus polygenism that debate was focussed in professional circles at about the time of the publication of *The Origin*.

Monogenism is the view most readily reconcilable with the Darwinian theory. It would be highly unexpected, although not logically impossible, for the evolutionary process to occur along similar lines and produce creatures with man's intellectual powers in separate parts of the globe. Nevertheless, one could have it both ways, and Wallace tried to do so. He differed from Darwin on one fundamental point, in his belief that the theory of natural selection was inadequate to account for the phenomenon of the intellect, for which some kind of divine creation had to be invoked. Thus one could suppose that the different races of man had a common *animal* ancestor from which the several human races had diverged in the normal evolutionary way, only developing human intellects at differing stages of these later evolutionary courses.[26] But positivistic polygenists could object that there was no empirical evidence for the monogenist hypothesis in any form. It was a gratuitous conjecture.[27]

Huxley, however, as with Wallace, believed that the Darwinian theory provided a satisfactory reconciliation of the monogenist and polygenist positions.[28] The ability of all human races to interbreed successfully implied mongenism, while the distinctive characteristics of the different races could be accounted for by the usual mechanisms described by the principles of divergence and geographical isolation. And in his celebrated essay, *Man's Place in Nature* (1863),[29] written as an outcome of the notorious Oxford Debate in 1860, Huxley drew together a considerable weight of evidence to reveal man's close anatomical and genealogical relationship with the higher apes. But in this publication he did not speak out clearly on the monogenism/polygenism controversy. Eventually, Darwin in *The Descent of Man* spoke tentatively for the monogenist view, although in a characteristically circumspect and guarded manner.[30]

It was the Oxford anthropologist, Edward B. Tylor (1832-1917), who is customarily regarded as the first leading scholar to have used the Darwinian theory as a *guide* to anthropological researches and as the basis of a general anthropological theory. The way he did this may be understood by thinking of his position as one version of the monogenist hypothesis. In his two major publications,[31] Tylor sought to synthesise the empirical knowledge of individual human cultures and civilisations — which seemed to have reached different levels of sophistication and complexity in different parts of the world — unifying this knowledge of the contemporary situation with the results of archaeological investigations — all considered within the framework of evolutionary theory. It was supposed that all human races and cultures had sprung from the same root, but that the diverging branches had not all reached the same level of development — although all were destined in time to pass through approximately the same evolutionary course.

Such a viewpoint, implausible though it may appear today, was by no means unusual in the nineteenth century. We are reminded, for example, of the Comtian or the Marxist theories of history. As envisaged by Tylor, it meant that if one looked around at the contemporary world to races or tribes of different customs and levels of cultural development one might gain a general idea of the typical pathway of human cultural evolution. If each group evolved in approximately the same manner, then one might have an idea of where each had come from and, apart from the highest cultures, where they might be going. Moreover, if, for example, one came across a present-day, stone-age culture and ascertained the kind of marriage system it employed, then it might be possible to have a reasonable idea of what the marriage systems of the former stone-age tribes of Europe might have been like. Tylor believed in a psychic unity of mankind, consequent on the monogenist hypothesis. This kind of argument, shaky as it may seem to us, formed the basis of the so-called 'comparative method'.

We may also put the argument in an alternative form. Because one knew from stratigraphical evidence (employing the principle of superposition[32]) which kinds of archaeological relics were the oldest, the *contemporary* social institutions could be arranged in supposed evolutionary sequence. Then hypotheses might be formulated about why and how one level of society had evolved into the next.

As a good example of the application of this supposedly evolutionary method, one may quote the suggestions of American lawyer, businessman, sociologist and anthropologist, Lewis Henry Morgan (1818-1881).[33] The following levels of cultural evolution were proposed:[34]

Lower Savagery	fruit and nut subsistence;
Middle Savagery	fish subsistence and fire used;
Upper Savagery	bow and arrow used as weapon;
Lower Barbarism	pottery used;
Middle Barbarism	animals domesticated, maize cultivated with irrigation, adobe and stone architecture;
Upper Barbarism	iron tools used;
Civilisation	phonetic alphabet and writing employed.

Similarly, general developmental patterns for kinship systems and socio-political organisations were recognised and attempts were made to interconnect the separate sets of evolutionary sequences.

It will be noted that Morgan's thesis had as much in common with the theories of ecapitulation in embryology as with the branching evolutionary tree of the Darwinian theory. Nevertheless, he is normally regarded as one of the anthropologists who was most strongly influenced by Darwinian ideas. Unfortunately, however, the system of explanation that Morgan proposed was too rigid to be reconciled adequately with all the information then available. For example, it was found necessary to relegate the aborigines of Hawaii to the period of Middle Savagery — in part because they lacked the bow and arrow, despite their practising a simple kind of agriculture. And the Aztecs and Iroquois Indians had to be placed at the same level of cultural development because they were both using iron tools. The biological emphasis of Morgan's work is worth noting. For example, he studied both American Indians and beavers in detail, publishing a volume entitled *The American Beaver and His Works* in 1868.[35] The imputed connection between man and beast is obvious in this title. Incidentally, it is worth noting here that many of Morgan's ideas were taken over by Engels in his *Origin of the Family* (1884),[36] and consequently became established in the Marxist canon. (There is some irony in this, for Morgan was a staunch Republican and arch-capitalist.)

It was not long before the 'evolutionist' school of anthropology of men such as Tylor and Morgan was subjected to rigorous critical scrutiny, and the leader of the new movement which grew up in opposition to it was the German/American anthropologist Franz Boas (1858-1942).[37] Boas did not seek to deny that there were many parallels in geometric designs, tools and religious beliefs in many widely separated cultures. But he claimed it is easy to show that such parallels do not necessarily imply a universal sequential pattern of development. It was possible to show, for example, that in some Indian communities, clans had arisen through the fusion of different groups; in others they had arisen from splitting up. Boas therefore urged careful study of individual cultural communities and avoidance of the over-arching generalisations of the anthropologists of the evolutionist school. His work has been characterised as 'historical particularism'.[38]

An obvious alternative way of explaining the cultural parallels that are to be found in so many parts of the World is by employing a hypothesis of *diffusion* rather than that of a universal pattern of cultural evolution. Such an approach has been widely followed in the earlier years of the twentieth century, particularly in Germany and America, but it is beyond the scope of our present inquiry to follow up the details of the diffusionist school. We may note in passing, however, that emphasis on diffusionism has been superseded by a rising interest in the French 'structuralist' anthropology of Claude Lévi-Strauss and his followers.[39]

Returning to the nineteenth century, it is worth emphasising the way anthropological theories reflected the prevailing social attitudes of the day. Perhaps the most fundamental unspoken assumption was that Victorian social institutions were natural, good and healthy, whereas primitive societies were in some sense abnormal, degenerate or unhealthy. On occasions, this led to somewhat absurd theoretical twists. For example, anthropologists found difficulty in understanding the complex kinship systems of the Australian Aborigines. But instead of regarding this complexity as a mark of sophistication and evolutionary development, the systems — so different from the ways of nineteenth-century Europe — were regarded as over-complicated and a mark of irrationality rather than cultural sophistication. It was believed that there was a natural evolutionary trend towards the typical monogamous family of Western bourgeois society, and the progress towards this stage was thought to parallel evolutionary development towards 'higher' moral codes and more highly developed mental powers.

The nineteenth century also was accustomed to regard 'savages' (primitive peoples) as analogues of social deviants — such as lunatics, the deaf and dumb, criminals, and even children! Indeed it was commonly believed that criminals possessed overt physical characteristics that were marks of criminality. The criminal could be regarded as a primitive 'throwback'. Childhood, although a curable disease, required severe treatment. The poor and unemployed might also be seen as having primitive or savage characteristics which no amount of social amelioration could eradicate. There was frequent reference to deviant 'types'. The early sociological investigations of the London poor were influenced by prejudices derived from anthropological theories. Henry Mayhew's celebrated *London Labour and the London Poor* (1851),[40] for example, began with a discussion of wandering tribes and a reference to the opinion of J. C. Prichard that people fall into two distinct moral and physical types, according to whether they are settled or migratory.[41] Mayhew even went so far as to maintain that in London the wandering poor had an exceptional development of the jaw and cheekbone compared with the cranium.[42]

Anthropology in the nineteenth century was striving to establish itself as a rigorous positive science and the theory of evolution contributed to the development of this science. However, apart from helping to give a more appropriate understanding of 'man's place in nature' and ensuring a naturalistic approach to the study of mankind, the way evolutionism was applied in the doctrine of cultural parallelism of Tylor and Morgan and their school was not (it now appears) entirely satisfactory or appropriate and was superseded fairly rapidly. Moreover, the new science suffered to a considerable degree from the influences of the social mores of its practitioners. Inevitably, the notions of social evolution that so dominated nineteenth-century Western thought impinged on the new science to no small degree. But the flow of ideas (or prejudices) was not merely a question of social doctrines moulding the new science of man. It may be argued that the upheavals of the First and Second World Wars and the racial disturbances that continue to this day in countries like South Africa are partly attributable to ideas emanating from nineteenth-century anthropological studies. Thus we find ourselves returning yet again to the problems of Social Darwinism and the influence of Darwinism on political thought.

Let us recall once more the controversy of monogenism versus polygenism. The idea of the separate (divine) creation of the human races is to be found in the writings of the eighteenth-century Scottish jurist and philosopher, Lord Kames (1696-1782).[43] And through the early nineteenth century, before the impact of Darwin's theory was felt, this polygenist viewpoint was quite widely held, despite its incompatibility with the orthodox Biblical account of the origin of the different races. The notion of racial differences could quickly lead to the notion of relative racial superiorities and inferiorities and thence to the view (on the part of the representatives of the allegedly 'superior' races) that racial purity ought to be maintained, since miscegenation would lead to the deterioration of the supposedly superior groups. So the American anthropologist Josiah Nott

(1804-1873) could maintain that 'superior races ought to be kept free from all adulterations, otherwise the world will retrograde, instead of advancing in civilisation'.[44] And the French scholar, P. P. Broca (1824-1880), believed that unions between different human races tended to be infertile. This was congenial to the polygenist hypothesis and the doctrine of racial inequality.[45]

As we have seen, the monogenist view was generally favoured by the Darwinian school, but the point that must be emphasised is that polygenism was not by any means repudiated following the triumphs of the Darwin/Wallace theory, and so one may find a strong continuation of the early racist ideas associated with polygenism in the second half of the nineteenth century, and such ideas continue to some degree to the present day.

Paul Topinard (1830-1911), for example, in his *Élements d'Anthropologie Générale*[46] (1885), recorded a vast amount of anthropometric data, sought to establish the idea of different anthropological 'types' characteristic of each race and claimed that there was good scientific evidence for the idea of a hierarchy of 'superior' and 'inferior' human races. Similar ideas became well established in America through the work of W. Z. Ripley (1867-1941).[47] In Europe, the writings of Otto Ammon (1842-1916)[48] and Georges Vacher de Lapouge (1854-1936)[49] fanned the flames of racial hatred. The Negro question in America, racial hatred in England, the present race laws and violence in South Africa, even the squalid racism of parts of outback Australia and the earlier fears of the so-called 'Yellow Peril' — all have some connection with the anthropological speculations of the nineteenth century. The corruptions of science of the Nazi theoreticians provide us with the most tragic consequence of all. The desperate fears of racial suicide, miscegenation, 'all becoming grey', declining birth rates, and other phantasms of the early twentieth century drew strength from these strange racial speculations without necessarily being caused by them alone. Only in the last twenty years or so have these fears begun to recede with the greater spread of education and, I believe, with the dominance of television and the vast increase in tourism and international trade.

In all this we do not find that Darwinism itself was directly responsible for all the varied twists and turns that anthropological theory followed in the late nineteenth and early twentieth centuries, and the opinion of R. R. Marett quoted at the beginning of this chapter seems to be considerably exaggerated. The direction taken by evolutionary anthropologists, after *The Origin* was published, proved to be rather unsatisfactory and their theoretical orientation changed fairly quickly. And in anthropology the more extreme views that were propounded do not seem to have been put forward specifically under the aegis of the Darwinian theory. Nevertheless, here, as in the various other aspects of late nineteenth and early twentieth-century thought that we have examined, the role played by Darwin's work was of real significance. We have identified yet another important building-block contributing to the structure of the present-day thought of Western man.

NOTES CHAPTER 21

1   R. R. Marett, *Anthropology*, H. Holt, London, 1912, p.8.
2   J. W. Gruber, 'Brixham Cave and the antiquity of man', in M. E. Spiro (ed.), *Context and Meaning in Cultural Anthropology*, Free Press, New York & London, 1965, pp.373-415 (at p.375).
3   See above, page 42.
4   W. Buckland, *Vindiciae Geologicae; or the Connexion of Geology with Religion*, Oxford, 1820; *Reliquiae Diluvianae; or, Observations on the Organic Remains contained in Caves, Fissures, and Diluvial Gravel, and on other Geological Phenomena, attesting the action of an Universal Deluge*, 2nd edn, London, 1824.
5   See F. J. North, 'Paviland Cave, the "Red Lady", the Deluge, and William Buckland', *Annals of Science*, Vol. 5, 1942, pp.91-128.
6   A. C. Haddon, *History of Anthropology*, Watts, London, 1934, p.80.
7   J. Frere, 'Account of flint weapons discovered at Hoxne in Suffolk', *Archaeologia*, Vol. 13, 1800, pp.204-205.
8   P.-C. Schmerling, *Recherches sur les Ossemens Fossiles Découverts dans les Cavernes de la Province de Liège*, 2 vols., Liège, 1833-1834.
9   J. Boucher de Perthes, *De l'Homme Antédiluvien et de ses Oeuvres*, Paris, 1860, partly translated in R. F. Heizer (ed.), *Man's Discovery of his Past: Literary Landmarks in Archaeology*, Prentice-Hall, Englewood Cliffs, 1962, pp.1-18.
10 See J. W. Gruber, *op. cit.* (note 2).
11 C. Lyell, *The Geological Evidences of the Antiquity of Man with Remarks on Theories of the Origin of Species by Variation*, London, 1863.
12 G. Busk, 'On the crania of the most ancient races of man. By Professor D. [*sic*] Schaaffhausen of Bonn. (From Müller's Archiv., 1858, pp.453.) With remarks, and original figures, taken from a cast of the Neanderthal cranium . . .', *Natural History Review*, Vol. 1, 1861, pp.155-176.
13 L. Lartet, 'Mémoire sur une sépulture des anciens troglodytes du Périgord (Cro-Magnon)', *Annales des Sciences Naturelles*, Zoologie, 5th Ser., Vol. 10, 1868, pp.133-145.
14 See W. Jones, 'Discourse the ninth. On the origin and families of nations. Delivered 23 February, 1792', in, *The Worke of Sir William Jones in Six Volumes*, London, 1799, Vol. 1, pp.129-142. (Jones, it should be noted, still subscribed to the doctrine of the Noachian flood, and the idea that the different races of mankind were descended separately from Noah's sons.)
15 *The First Book of Moses, called Genesis*, Chapter 11, Verses 1-9.
16 For example, E. Bonnot (l'abbé Condillac), *Essai sur l'Origine des Connoissances Humaines*, Paris, 1746, Part II, Section 1, Chapters 1-2.
17 The name derives from an area of Central Asia: Ariana. It was the Romantic scholar Friedrich Schlegel who captured the German imagination with the idea of Europe being colonised and civilised by beautiful, masterful men, moving Westwards in antiquity from the roof of the world.
18 C. J. Thomsen, *Ledetraad til Nordisk Oldyndighed*, Copenhagen, 1836 (*A Guide to Northern Antiquities*, London, 1848). Thomsen suggested the tripartite archaeological classification in his correspondence as early as 1818.
19 J. Lubbock (Lord Avebury), *Pre-Historic Times, as Illustrated by Ancient Remains and the Manners and Customs of Modern Savages*, London, 1865, pp.1-3.
20 J. F. Blumenbach, *Decas . . . Collectionis suae Craniorum Diversarum Gentium, Illustrata*, Göttingen, 1790-1820; *The Anthropological Treatises of Johann Friedrich Blumenbach . . . Translated by Thomas Bendyshe*, London, 1865. Blumenbach, it may be noted, believed that the Caucasians were the 'highest' human type, and that the others had emerged by a process of 'degeneration'. Adam and Eve were supposedly white – being created in God's image!
21 The ratio of the breadth to the length of a skull.
22 A. Retzius, 'A glance at the present state of ethnology, with reference to the form of the skull . . .', *British and Foreign Medico-Chirurgical Review*, Vol. 25, 1860, pp.503-514 & Vol. 26, 1860, pp.215-230. (Retzius stated that his ideas were introduced at meetings of the Scandinavian Association of Naturalists in 1850 and 1852.)
23 F.-J. Gall, *Sur les Fonctions du Cerveau et sur Celles de Chacune de Ses Parties*, Paris, 1825.
24 J. C. Prichard, *Researches into the Physical History of Mankind*, 2nd edn, London, 1826, Vol. 2, pp.557, 565, 569-571, 581 and *passim*. For a discussion of Prichard's evolutionism, see: E. B. Poulton, 'A remarkable anticipation of modern views on evolution', *Science Progress*, Vol. 1, 1897, pp.278-296.
25 For discussion of this, see G. W. Stocking, 'What's in a name? The origins of the Royal Anthropological Institute (1837-71)' *Man*, Vol. 6, 1971, pp.369-390.
26 A. R. Wallace, 'The origin of human races and the antiquity of man deduced from the theory of "natural selection" ', *Journal of the Anthropological Society of London*, Vol. 2, 1864, pp.clviii-clxxxvii.

27 J. Hunt, 'On the application of the principle of natural selection to anthropology, in reply to views advocated by some of Mr Darwin's disciples', *The Anthropological Review*, Vol. 4, 1866, pp.320-340.
28 T. H. Huxley, 'On the methods and results of ethnology', *The Fortnightly Review*, Vol. 1, 1865, pp.257-277 (p.275).
29 T. H. Huxley, *Evidence as to Man's Place in Nature*, London, 1863 (republished University of Michigan Press, Ann Arbor, 1959).
30 C. Darwin, *The Descent of Man, and Selection in Relation to Sex*, 2 vols, London, 1871, Vol. 1, p.233. Darwin predicted (p.235) that when the theory of evolution became generally accepted the controversy between monogenists and polygenists 'would die a silent and unobserved death'.
31 E. B. Tylor, *Researches into the Early History of Mankind and the Development of Civilization*, London, 1865; *Primitive Culture: Researches into the Development of Mythology, Philosophy, Religion, Art, and Custom, etc.*, 2 vols, London, 1871 (republished Harper, New York, 1958).
32 That is, the geological principle (introduced by the Danish naturalist/physician/theologian, Nicolaus Steno, in the seventeenth century) that the upper layers of a series of strata are younger than those laying beneath them. The order of superposition of the strata provides an indication of the order of their deposition.
33 This man should not be confused with the geneticist, T. H. Morgan, or the psychologist, C. Lloyd Morgan.
34 L. H. Morgan, *Ancient Society, or, Researches in the Lines of Human Progress from Savagery through Barbarism to Civilization*, New York, 1877, p.12.
35 L. H. Morgan, *The American Beaver and His Works*, Philadelphia, 1868.
36 F. Engels, *The Origin of the Family, Private Property, and the State in the Light of the Researches of Lewis H. Morgan* ... with an Introduction and Notes by Eleanor Burke Leacock, Lawrence & Wishart, London, 1972 (1st edn, 1884).
37 Boas's major work was: *The Mind of Primitive Man*, Macmillan, New York, 1911. Many of his papers have been collerted in *Race, Language and Culture*, Macmillan, New York, 1940.
38 M. Harris, *The Rise of Anthropological Theory: A History of Theories of Culture*, Crowell, New York, 1968, p.250.
39 C. Lévi-Strauss, *Anthropologie Structurale*, Paris, 1958 (*Structural Anthropology*, Lane, London, 1968).
40 H. Mayhew, *London Labour and the London Poor: A Cyclopaedia of the Condition and Earnings of Those that Will Work, Those that Cannot Work, and Those that Will not Work*, 4 vols, London, 1851-1862 (republished Dover, New York, 1969).
41 *Ibid.*, Vol. 1, p.1.
42 *Ibid.*, p.3.
43 [H. Home (Lord Kames),] *Sketches of the History of Man*, 2nd edn, 4 vols, London & Edinburgh, 1778, Vol. 1, pp.75-76. Yet Home felt constrained to write, in direct opposition to his own polygenist theses: 'This opinion, however plausible, we are not permitted to adopt; being taught a different lesson by revelation, viz., that God created but a single pair of the human species' (p.76).
44 J. C. Nott & G. R. Gliddon, *Types of Mankind*, Philadelphia, 1854, p.455.
45 P. P. Broca, *On the Phenomenon of Hybridity in the Genus Homo*, London, 1864, p.16 and *passim*.
46 P. Topinard, *Eléments d'Anthropologie Générale*, Paris, 1885.
47 W. Z. Ripley, *The Races of Europe: A Sociological Study*, 2 vols, New York, 1899.
48 O. Ammon, *Die Naturaliche Auslese beim Menschen [Natural Selection in Man]*, Jena, 1893.
49 G. Vacher de Lapouge, *L'Aryen, son Rôle Social, cours ... professé à l'Université de Montpellier (1889-1890)*, Paris, 1899; *Les Sélections Sociales, cours ... professé à l'Université de Montpellier (1888-1889)*, Paris, 1896.

22

Darwinism and Literature

Evolutionism in general and the Darwinian theory in particular exerted a
very considerable influence on the literary world in the nineteenth century,
and to a lesser degree in the present century. Our problem in this section is
trying to do some justice to the rich diversity of material within a few pages.
Unfortunately, it is not possible to do this in a wholly satisfactory manner,
and I am forced therefore to refer the interested reader to some of the
relevant secondary literature[1] and thence to the primary literature. My aim
here can be no more than the very modest one of giving an approximate
sketch of some of the principal literary responses to evolutionary concepts in
their various manifestations. A division into poetry and prose writings seems
admissible, although somewhat arbitrary.

Poetry

Let us begin with poetry — always a mirror of the general thought of an age.
It should be emphasised at the outset that poets' consideration of
evolutionary themes did not begin suddenly in 1859. Many of the
nineteenth-century poets were acutely aware of the problems raised by the
new science and the Industrial Revolution, and the problems of materialism
and naturalism figure prominently in poetry long before the full impact of
Darwin's doctrines was felt. We also find some eighteenth-century figures
seeking to give expression to 'proto-evolutionary' ideas through poetry,
while earlier still, in the seventeenth century, we find the most orthodox of
special-creationist views expressed by John Milton (1608-1674) in his
celebrated *Paradise Lost*. This will give us a convenient starting place for our
present discussion.

Book VII of *Paradise Lost* tells us that:

> . . . The Earth obey'd, and strait
> Op'ning her fertil Woomb teem'd at a Birth
> Innumerous living Creatures, perfet formes,
> Limb'd and full grown: out of the ground up rose
> As from his Laire the wilde Beast where he wonns[2] . . .

> The grassie clods now Calv'd, now half appeer'd
> The tawnie Lion, pawing to get free
> His hinder parts, then springs as broke from Bonds,
> And Rampant shakes his Brinded[3] main; the Ounce,
> The Libbard,[4] and the Tyger, as the Moale
> Rising, the crumbl'd Earth above them threw
> In Hillocks; the swift Stag from under ground
> Bore up his branching head . . .[5]

This is the very antithesis of an evolutionary view.

But by the late eighteenth/early nineteenth century we find attempts to give early evolutionary ideas in verse form by Darwin's eccentric grandfather, Erasmus (1731-1802), noted physician, deist, naturalist, poet and philosopher. His *Temple of Nature* (1802), for example, contains the following lines:

> Organic life beneath the shoreless waves,
> Was born and nurs'd in Ocean's pearly caves;
> First forms minute, unseen by spheric glass,[6]
> Move on the mud, or pierce the watery mass;
> These, as successive generations bloom,
> New powers acquire, and larger limbs assume;
> Whence countless groups of vegetation spring,
> And breathing realms of fin, and feet, and wing.[7]

Erasmus Darwin's theory rested on the concept of evolution arising from the action of an inner 'life-force', which, starting with an original primal-filament of living substance, caused the gradual development of all varied forms of life by a process analogous to vegetative reproduction. He believed in a 'Lamarckian' role for the environment.

Darwin's poetic style bears some analogy to the rather four-square writing of Alexander Pope (1688-1744), such as found in the well-known verse *Essay on Man*. ('Know then thyself, presume not God to scan. The proper study of mankind is man.'[8]) But Darwin was scarcely a distinguished poet, and his science verse was rapidly exposed to parody.[9] Nevertheless, the German Nature Philosophers were impressed. Darwin's evolutionism was itself attractive to them, and the idea of presenting it in poetic form appealed to their belief that men should strive for an intellectual universalism, as realised in Goethe.

J. W. Goethe (1749-1832), the great polymath of Germany's intellectual renaissance, wrote much on science, particularly on plant morphology, theories of colour, comparative anatomy and geology. He sought to unify all knowledge; art and Nature were, for him, two faces of the same coin. And Nature's hidden law was that of development or *Entwicklung*. Thus the notion of *Entwicklung* dominates Goethe's famous *Metamorphose der*

Pflanzen,[10] and appears also in *Die Metamorphose der Thiere*. In the latter are the following lines (in translation), revealing Goethe's ideas as very like those of Cuvier in certain respects, yet moulded also by a developmentalist point of view:

> Truly's each creature itself its own purpose, for nature creates it
> Perfect; and in its turn begets progeny that will be perfect.
> Organs and members are shaped according to laws everlasting,
> Even the oddest formation its prototype latent preserveth.
> Thus is each mouth well adapted to seize the right food and to swallow
> That which is fit for its stomach — the one may be tender and toothless,
> While there are others with powerful jaws; but one organ will always
> Cooperate with the others for a wholesome and proper nutrition.
> Also the feet to the needs of the body are wisely adjusted,
> Some of them long, while others are short, yet in perfect proportion.
> Thus the kind mother assureth to each of her several children
> Health in good store; and the organized limbs of each animate being
> Always will work for the whole, and ne'er counteract one another.
> Therefore the shape of a creature determines its life and habits,
> While *vice versa* the habits of life will react on the organs
> Potently. Any formation possesses a definite order
> Which yet is subject to change through external effects and conditions.
> But in the innermost self of the noblest of nature's creations
> Lieth their power, confined to a holy mysterious circle.
> And these limits removeth no god; they are honoured by nature,
> For limitation alone maketh possible highest perfection.
>
> Yet in the innermost self a spirit titanic is also
> Stirring, which fain would arbitrarily break through the circle —
> Bold innovation begetting new forms! But in vain it aspireth.
> See how it swelleth one part, it endoweth with power
> One for all others, and lo the result! Those others must suffer.
> Thus a onesided preponderance taketh away the proportion —
> Yea, it destroyeth all beauty of form and harmonious motion.
> Seest thou then that a creature has preference gained over others,
> Look for the shortage at once and seek with confiding inquiry.
> Then thou at once will discover the key for the varied formations;
> As, for example, no animal beareth a horn on its forehead
> If in its jaw it possesseth its teeth in perfect completion;
> Wherefore our mother eternal e'en if she endeavoured to do so,
> Could not in all her creation engender such forms as horned lions.
> There's not enough in amount for constructing the horns on the forehead,
> And in the mouth the formation of teeth that are perfect in number.[11]

And for Goethe, the whole development of the cosmos was a process analogous to the gradual unfolding or unravelling of a seed.

But the early English romantic poets did not follow this lead directly, although in William Wordsworth's (1770-1850) *The Excursion* (1814) we find the following lines, which indicate a belief in the 'idea of progress':

> ... The vast Frame
> Of social nature changes evermore
> Her organs and her members, with decay
> Restless, and restless generation, powers
> And functions dying and produced at need, —
> And by this law the mighty whole subsists:
> With an ascent and progress in the main . . .[12]

Coleridge, Byron and Shelley were much concerned with the relationship between man and nature or man and the cosmos, and Coleridge was especially interested in German Nature Philosophy and romantic science, doing much to transmit such ideas to the English scene. However, these writers do not offer much evolutionary thinking in their poems. Tennyson, on the other hand is much more interesting in this respect.

Throughout his life (1809-1892), Alfred Tennyson maintained a deep interest in science. Indeed, T. H. Huxley described him as 'the first poet since Lucretius who has understood the drift of science'.[13] Although this does scant justice to many of Tennyson's forerunners, the comment is interesting. Evolutionist ideas of a general, cosmic kind appeared in Tennyson's poetry long before *The Origin*, and even before *Vestiges*. It is known that he was familiar as a young man with Buffon's writings with their somewhat tentative evolutionism, and with the ideas of Laplace's nebular hypothesis of the solar system, itself a product of Kant's developmental cosmogony. And Tennyson was tutored at Cambridge by the redoubtable historian and philosopher of science, William Whewell. There is also plenty of evidence to show that Tennyson maintained his interest in scientific matters through his later life.

Lionel Stevenson has identified many passages in Tennyson's poetry extending from 1829 to 1885 which suggest ideas of evolutionary change.[14] But it is his poem *In Memoriam*, written in memory of his close friend Arthur Hallam over a long period (1833-1850), in which concern with evolution stands out most clearly, and in which we find the famous line depicting nature as 'red in tooth and claw'[15] — a presentiment of Darwin's idea of struggle for existence. So *In Memoriam*, long before 1859, raises questions about the conflict between materialistic evolutionary science and orthodox belief; between the religious scepticism that evolutionism seemed to entail, and the certitude of intuitive faith.

The pessimistic side emerges in the third section of the poem:

> O Sorrow, cruel fellowship,
>   O Priestess in the vaults of Death,
>   O sweet and bitter in a breath,
> What whispers from thy lying lip?

'The stars,' she whispers, 'blindly run;
   A web is wov'n across the sky;
   From out waste places comes a cry,
And murmurs from the dying sun:

'And all the phantom, Nature, stands —
   With all the music in her tone,
   A hollow echo of my own —
A hollow form with empty hands'.[16]

And the poet's vision of the evolutionary process appears in section fifty-six:

Man, her last work, who seem'd so fair,
   Such splendid purpose in his eyes,
   Who roll'd the psalm to wintry skies,
Who built him fanes of fruitless prayer,

Who trusted God was love indeed
   And love Creation's final law —
   Tho' Nature, red in tooth and claw
With ravine, shriek'd against his creed —

Who loved, who suffer'd countless ills,
   Who battled for the True, the Just,
   Be blown about the desert dust,
Or seal'd within the iron hills?

No more? A monster then, a dream,
   A discord. Dragons of the prime,
   That tare each other in their slime,
Were mellow music match'd with him.

O life as futile, then, as frail!
   O for thy voice to soothe and bless!
   What hope of answer, or redress?
Behind the veil, behind the veil.[17]

But an optimistic outcome may be seen, for the evolutionary process may lead to higher spiritual forms of man. God is developing His Creation towards a state of harmonious perfection:

A soul shall draw from out the vast
And strike his being into bounds,

And, moved thro' life of lower phase,
   Result in man, be born and think,
   And act and love, a closer link
Betwixt us and the crowning race

Of those that, eye to eye, shall look
    On knowledge; under whose command
    Is Earth and Earth's, and in their hand
    Is Nature like an open book;

No longer half-akin to brute,
    For all we thought and loved and did,
    And hoped, and suffer'd, is but seed
Of what in them is flower and fruit;

Whereof the man, that with me trod
    This planet, was a noble type
    Appearing ere the times were ripe,
That friend of mine who lives in God,

That God, which ever lives and loves,
    One God, one law, one element,
    And one far-off divine event,
To which the whole creation moves.[18]

Thus, before the publication of *The Origin*, Tennyson had worked out what was to become a commonplace response to the challenge of evolutionism: the perception of the over-arching evolution of the cosmos as a manifestation of God's design, ultimately beneficent and leading to a higher state of human perfection despite present earthly miseries. His view was almost that of Teilhard de Chardin.

After 1859, Tennyson accepted the new theory, although he found its materialistic assumptions metaphysically repugnant. The world might evolve into a better place, and the main future evolutionary course would take place through the medium of the human soul. He was glad to receive Darwin's assurance that he did not perceive a conflict with Christianity; and he helped to create the Metaphysical Society in London for the discussion of these pressing issues of the inter-relations of science and religion.[19] The poem *De Profundis* (1880) expressed Tennyson's growing pantheism and his ideas on the duality of physical evolution and spiritual or mental evolution, the latter occurring through series of reincarnations.[20] But *Locksley Hall Sixty Years After* (1886) reveals the continuing spiritual anguish of his later years:

Is there evil but on earth? or pain in every peopled sphere?
Well be grateful for the sounding watchword, 'Evolution' here,

Evolution every climbing after some ideal good,
And Reversion ever dragging Evolution in the mud.[21]

Robert Browning (1812-1889) bears some similarity to Tennyson, though Browning did not evince a life-long interest in science. Nevertheless, in one important verse-play, *Paracelsus* (1835), he gave a fairly coherent statement of evolutionary ideas, well before the public appearance of the Darwinian or Spencerian theories.

The historical Paracelsus was a sixteenth-century Swiss/German philosopher/physician/scientist, with strong Neo-Platonist proclivities, remembered particularly today for his role in the history of chemistry. His approach was mystical, yet grounded in a wide knowledge of empirical practices. He believed in chemical transmutation and sought the artificial propagation of life — although he was not explicitly an exponent of evolutionary ideas. It was through this sage, standing at the threshold of the modern scientific movement, that Browning chose to present his ideas.

Browning's evolutionism was not mechanistic in the Darwinian sense. It was, rather, a kind of cosmic unfolding (or *Entwicklung*, as the Germans said), analogous also to the later doctrines of 'creative evolution' of Bergson and Chardin and somewhat similar to Samuel Butler's doctrine of life force which will be mentioned below. Some lines from the fifth section of *Paracelsus* may help to make Browning's feeling of evolutionary exuberance clear:

> God renews
> His ancient rapture! Thus He dwells in all,
> From life's minute beginnings, up at last
> To man — the consummation of this scheme
> Of being, the completion of this sphere
> Of life: whose attributes had here and there
> Been scattered o'er the visible world before,
> Asking to be combined, dim fragments meant
> To be united in some wondrous whole,
> Imperfect qualities throughout creation,
> Suggesting some one creature yet to make,
> Some point where all those scattered rays should meet
> Convergent in the faculties of man . . .[22]

> Hints and previsions of which faculties,
> Are strewn confusedly everywhere about
> The inferior natures, and all lead up higher,
> All shape out dimly the superior race,
> The heir of hopes too fair to turn out false,
> And man appears at least. So far the seal
> Is put on life; one stage of being complete,
> One scheme wound up: and from the grand result
> A supplementary reflux of light,
> Illustrates all the inferior grades, explains
> Each back step in the circle . . .[23]

And this to fill us with regard for man,
With apprehension of his passing worth,
Desire to work his proper nature out,
And ascertain his rank and final place,
For these things tend still upward, progress is
The law of life, man's self is not yet Man! . . .[24]

When all the race is perfected alike
As Man, that is; all tended to mankind,
And, man produced, all has its end thus far:
But in completed man begins anew
A tendency to God.[25]

These words Browning placed in the mouth of the Renaissance mystic. But they express, I think, Browning's nineteenth-century version of the essence of man and his place in the cosmos.

This quite early view was sustained by Browning through his life, even after the publication of *The Origin*. He acquiesced in the notion of the evolution of men from animals but not through the mechanism of natural selection. Indeed, Browning seemed to find some difficulty in distinguishing Darwinism from Lamarckism. His version remained anthropocentric; the world was expressly made for man. And Browning's theory of development even in his later poetry was essentially spiritual rather than physico-mechanical, such as the Darwinian doctrine might lead one to contemplate, and perhaps embrace.

As a third instance of pre-Darwinian Victorian poetry expressing evolutionary ideas, we may refer to the work of Matthew Arnold (1822-1888), which reflects an acutely pessimistic reaction to the struggle and cruelty of the world. Unlike Tennyson and Browning, who were able to find hope in a possible future existence or could see suffering as a necessary concomitant of progress, Arnold could find little joy and tended towards a position of pessimistic fatalism — a mood portrayed most clearly in the long dramatic poem *Empedocles on Etna* (1852),[26] in which Arnold chose to present his ideas through the man reputed to be the world's first evolutionist.[27]

Arnold believed in an immanent life-force of which man is ultimately a product. But the developmental process is not one designed or guided by a beneficent God. God is merely an invention of man, whom he may blame for the chances of ill-fortune. Man may come to imagine God as a beneficent or omnipotent creator, but this belief is nothing but the deluded product of the human imagination. The dream of immortality is a mere illusion. But Arnold's sense of spiritual desolation was formed well before 1859. No doubt it was the fear of such a world that led to much of the frenzy that surrounded Darwin's work after it was published. And Arnold's poetry is an indication that the intellectual problems raised by *The Origin* did not all suddenly spring into being in 1859–60. Rather, one must say that the book acted as a kind of catalyst or 'seed' for the spiritual crisis of the age brought about by the burden of the Industrial Revolution.

However, as we have seen, men soon began to recognise an optimistic side of Darwinian evolutionism. Was not natural selection the motor of social *progress* and better adaption? And poets, likewise, reflected this new view. Whereas Matthew Arnold found uncertainty, futility and bleakness, Swinburne (1837-1909) optimistically saw progress, emancipation and an escape from supernatural vengeance. The evolutionary concept could, in fact, supplant the notion of a creative God as a first cause. This appears in his poem *Hertha* (1871) (an Earth-goddess, in Norse mythology) — a eulogy to the creative power and fecundity of the Earth:

> First life on my sources
>   First drifted and swam;
> Out of me are the forces
>   That save it or damn
> Out of me man and woman, and wild beast and bird;
>   before God was, I am.[28]

It is the evolutionary process that Swinburne finds divine:

> Not men's but man's is the glory of god-
>   head, the kingdom of time, . . .
> Glory to Man in the highest! for Man is
>   the master of things.[29]

This is the Comtian, positivist 'religion of humanity' in poetic form. It looks forward to the twentieth-century godless religion of Julian Huxley and the humanists.

Somewhat similar to Swinburne's response was that of George Meredith (1828-1909). Unlike Tennyson and Browning, Meredith did not evince an interest in evolutionism until the public pronouncement of the Darwinian theory, but once this appeared it took a dominant grip upon the poet's whole philosophy of nature. He was, in fact, a 'nature poet' in the Wordsworthian tradition; and the biological theory of evolution was therefore naturally a matter of very considerable concern to him. He was, moreover, one of the rising generation of Victorians who were beginning to turn away from Christianity towards an agnostic stance. Indeed, one might almost describe Meredith as a poetical exponent of Social Darwinism, contemplating the struggle for existence with equanimity, or even a certain enthusiasm:

> Look in the face of men who fare
> Lock-mouthed, a match in lungs and thews
> For this fierce angel of the air,
> To twist with him and take his bruise.
> That is the face beloved of old

Of Earth, young mother of her brood:
Nor broken for us shows the mould
When muscle is in mind renewed:
Though farther from her nature rude,
Yet nearer to her spirit's hold:
And though of gentler mood serene,
Still forceful of her fountain-jet.
So shall her blows be shrewdly met,
Be luminously read the scene
Where Life is at her grindstone set,
That she may give us edgeing keen,
String us for battle, till as play
The common strokes of fortune shower. . .[30]

Behold the life at ease; it drifts.
The sharpened life commands its course.
She winnows, winnows roughly; sifts,
To dip her chosen in her source. . .[31]

For Meredith, the individual finds his immortality in the survival and evolutionary progress of the human race. The spiritual emerges from man's role in the evolutionary system; but only by close communion with nature can these spiritual qualities be developed. Nature, or the Earth, the 'mother' of man, provides the basis for all human activities, even those of a spiritual character.[32] But Meredith does not preach a fatalistic pantheism. It is by will and action, by contributing something to the evolution of the race, that man is able to escape the hideous cruelty that faces the weak. Nature endows man to take part in the struggle. But it is through his will that he must reach for the prize. Work, as the saying goes, brings its own reward. Meredith acted as a spokesman for the social ideals of the period of ascendancy of the Social Darwinist creed, after the darker implications of the theory had been shrugged aside to yield acceptance or positive enthusiasm for the value of the world of struggle and competition. By conforming to the law of evolution, one could live the moral life. Meredith, like the evolutionary humanists, was seeking to derive a kind of ethical code from evolutionary principles. Work and self-sacrifice — promoters of the evolutionary process — formed a basis for standards of conduct.

We have given some appraisal of this thesis from a logical standpoint in Chapter 19, and have found it wanting. But it would be an absurdity to demand that the poet should conform to the canons of deductive logic. Meredith's poems give us an idea of his vision of the desirable condition of the social system. It was not necessarily a logically coherent vision, but this does not prevent it from being what he took to be an adequate view of the world and man's place in it, attuned to the beliefs of the day with evolutionary doctrines a fundamental support for the whole.

In Thomas Hardy (1840-1928), we have an author whose whole adult life fell within the period when interest in Darwinian evolution and the Social

Darwinist movement were at their strongest. But whereas Meredith was able to draw a hopeful and optimistic verdict from his understanding of the new theory, Hardy, although accepting it fully, came to bleaker, gloomier, more despondent conclusions.

Some commentators have ascribed Hardy's system, invoking the doctrine of 'Immanent Will' in nature, to the influence of the philosophy of Schopenhauer.[33] But it has also been suggested that Hardy was receptive to such ideas because of his prior acceptance of the Darwinian concepts.[34]

As with Meredith, Hardy rejected the anthropomorphic God of Christian orthodoxy and the doctrine of the immortal soul. But unlike Meredith, he repudiated the hopeful idea that immortality might be achieved through the evolutionary process of descent through subsequent generations of mankind. One could only live on through the memories of still living men and women. When these memories fade, immortality shrivels. Thus the effort of a lifetime becomes a mere futility.

For Hardy, God is virtually synonymous with Mother Nature, both being symbols of the creative force of the universe. But God is not omniscient and omnipotent, or a beneficent designer of the cosmos. There is no purpose guiding the universe. The human intellect arose in the evolutionary process quite fortuitously. The immanent will or life force of the universe generates constant change, but there is no guarantee that intellect will be the outcome, any more than one might expect the fabled monkeys armed with an endless supply of time and paper, to type out the Bible. The 'Fore Scene' of *The Dynasts*, (a poetic drama illustrating the subordination of even the greatest of men to the vagaries of the Will) puts it thus:

> In the Foretime, even to the germ of Being,
> Nothing appears of shape to indicate
> That cognizance has marshalled things terrene,[35]
> Or will (such is my thinking) in my span.
> Rather they show that, like a knitter drowsed,
> Whose fingers play in skilled unmindfulness,
> The Will has woven with an absent heed
> Since life first was; and ever will so weave.[36]

This Will, as Lionel Stevenson has said,[37] causes evolution, but does not determine its direction.

Yet surprisingly, in his later years and also in a few of his earlier poems, Hardy showed some sympathy for the view more characteristic of his contemporaries: that evolution would ultimately yield some improvement in man's affairs and conditions. The early poem, *1967* (written in 1867), contains the lines:

> A century which, if not sublime,
> Will show, I doubt not, at its prime,
> A scope above this blinkered time.[38]

And events have surely confirmed this somewhat hopeful prognostication.

The late Armistice Day poem, *And There Was a Great Calm*,[39] also expresses a note of guarded optimism. Possibly, if the human race can unite in a common purpose, evolution will yield some progress. And poetry, maybe, is able to form a bridge between religion and science.

Evolution, for Hardy, could account for the origins of faith from a psychological point of view (without in any way guaranteeing or justifying this faith); it accounted for the cruelty of the conditions of existence; and the emergence of consciousness could be understood from an evolutionary stand-point. And possibly it might give a gleam of hope for the future.

This is as far as space will permit us to carry our consideration of the impact of evolutionary theory on the poetry of the nineteenth century, and although some twentieth-century examples may be cited,[40] our discussion has probably been taken far enough for the present purpose. By the 1890s the preoccupation with evolutionary concepts among British poets was beginning to diminish. Tennyson's later poems expressed a kind of evolutionary pantheism, and the hope of a future spiritual evolution towards God. Browning died believing that the onward struggle would be completed in the next life. Arnold gave up writing poetry. Swinburne seemed to lose interest in evolutionary speculations. And the younger poets simply accepted the doctrine as a matter of course, although, as we have seen, Meredith and Hardy took it as one of the principal foci of their interests.

Prose

Let us turn to prose writings. Right through the nineteenth century one may again find this reflection of scientific interests in the literary domain, and every twist and turn of the evolutionary doctrine seems to have been mimicked in the imaginary worlds of the novelists. Just as Ellegård has been able to reveal the progress of the evolutionary debate in Britain through his analysis of the articles appearing in the British press, so, in principle, one might achieve a similar understanding through an analysis of the British novel in the nineteenth century, although it would be difficult indeed to match the precise quantitative treatment that characterised Ellegård's work.

Reaching back to the early years of the nineteenth century, we find the slight, but engagingly entertaining, novels of Thomas Love Peacock (1785-1866) poking fun at science and manners at the same time. *Melincourt* (1817),[41] for example, recounts the story of an orang-outan being brought up in high English society, becoming known as Sir Oran Haut-ton through the purchase of a baronetcy. Sir Oran lacks the power of speech (or is unwilling to communicate) but in every other respect he is quite the equal of the gentry of his day, in matters of manner, decorum and gallantry. The text is supported by weighty footnotes from Linnaeus, Buffon and Monboddo to show that the putative human character of Sir Oran may be justified and is in no way atypical of his kind. Clearly, all this is based on the theories of Lord Monboddo,[42] and Peacock's intention is evidently to draw on the beginnings of evolutionary science, and the Rousseauian doctrine of the noble savage, as a means of berating the manners and customs of his peers. There are further jesting references to science and the idiosyncracies of scientists in some of Peacock's other stories, such as *Headlong Hall* (1816),[43] *Nightmare Abbey* (1818),[44] and *Gryll Grange* (1861).[45]

For a response to the furore of the publication of Chambers's *Vestiges* (1844), one may refer to Benjamin Disraeli's (1804-1881) novel of high society, *Tancred* (1847). Here, following the popular determination of the day, the evolutionary doctrine is derided, being placed in the mouth of one Constance Rawleigh, a young lady of scholarly pretensions but little intellectual worth.[46] Her pronouncements on the evolutionary hypothesis are sufficient to deter the hero (Tancred) from any kind of entanglement with this shallow flibbertigibbet. Clearly, Disraeli, the conservative politician/ novelist, was not sympathic to the evolutionary view, and accepted the public verdict on Chambers without demur. Evolutionism, Disraeli would have his readers believe, lies within the province of the feather-brained female.

We find some indication of evolutionism of a 'recapitulationist' variety, such as was espoused by Chambers, in an interesting novel by Charles Kingsley (1819-1875), *Alton Locke* (1850). In this, the hero, in a delirious dream, imagines himself evolving through the stages of sponge, crab, *Remora* (sucking fish), ostrich, *Myledon* (sloth), ape, and primitive man.[47] Kingsley was himself an amateur naturalist of some standing, and he was perhaps the first English clergyman to embrace publicly the evolutionary theory of *The Origin*. The reference to the *hippocampus minor* debate between Huxley and Owen in Kingsley's *Water Babies* has already been noted.[48]

Darwin was parodied for his taxonomic work with barnacles in a novel by E. Bulwer Lytton (1803-1873), published in 1859, appearing as the author of a two-volume tome on limpets.[49] After 1859, the novelists had a field-day, with numerous satires appearing that focussed on the evolutionary doctrine. A single instance will have to serve as an examplar for all the various works of this genre. In R. D. Blackmore's (1825-1900) *The Remarkable History of Tommy Upmore* (1884),[50] for example, the hero is represented as a living contradiction of the doctrine of descent. Although the son of exceptionally obese parents, Tommy Upmore himself has the curious quality of being so thin that he is actually capable of flight in an appropriate breeze. His case is examined by learned scientists. A Dr Chocolous (who hopes to restore the primordial tail to humans by making them desist from sitting – a Lamarckian view, perhaps?) thinks the case may have something to do with 'histic fluxion'. A Professor Brachipod offers an unhelpful diagnosis of 'organic levigation' which does little to assist the hero in his predicament! A Professor Jargoon diagnoses 'gaseous expansion'. A Professor Mullicles thinks that 'bacilli' may be the cause of the problem. And Professor Megalow, a wiser and kinder man, refrains from offering any definite opinion.

The celebrated French writer, Jules Verne (1828-1905), was one of the first to employ evolutionary ideas in what is now known as science fiction, in his widely-read *Journey to the Centre of the Earth* (1864).[51] Men enter the bowels of the Earth through the orifice of a volcano in Iceland and during the course of their adventures pass through all the layers of the stratigraphical column, encountering the living representatives of creatures only known in fossil form to those on the surface. A battle between an *Ichthyosaurus* and a *Plesiosaurus* forms a centre-piece of the tale. Verne's writings are always entertaining for the way they portray the popular understanding of the science of his day, although in some parts of the *Journey* his ideas are notably out-of-date. The action of volcanoes, for example, is accounted for according to the early nineteenth-century theory of Sir Humphry Davy that water percolates through to subterranean deposits of metallic sodium and potassium. Later works, such as Arthur Conan Doyle's (1859-1930) *The Lost World* (1912),[52] in which the reader is introduced to living specimens of *Pterodactylis*, are of the same genre as Verne's *Journey*. We may mention here also Henry Curwen's (1845-1892) *Zit and Xoe* (1886),[53] an imaginary account of Adam and Eve having evolved from monkeys; H. G. Wells's (1866-1946) short story 'A Story of the Stone Age' (1897),[54] dealing with the discovery of the flint axe; J. Compton Rickett's (1847-1919) *Quickening of Caliban* (1893),[55] concerned with the missing link between men and animals.

Then there were novels which speculated about the possibility of evolution taking unexpected directions in the future. Examples are provided by William Westall's (1835-1903) *A Queer Race* (1887),[56] dealing with the products of miscegenation by shipwrecked sailors on an island off South America; H. B. Marriott Watson's (1863-1921) *Marahuna* (1888),[57] which imagines a beautiful woman who has grown in isolation from the rest of mankind and thus totally lacks any kind of soul; H. G. Wells's *In the Abyss* (1896),[58] concerning a race of intelligent man-like creatures that have evolved at the bottom of the Atlantic and his *Island of Dr Moreau* (1896),[59] which envisages the acceleration of the evolutionary process by the help of artificial surgery; James de Mille's (1837-1880) *Strange Manuscript Found in a Copper Cylinder* (1888),[60] a novel of a race of beings which are in all respects — social, mental and moral — exactly the opposite of humans. Many of the novels of this category were of dubious quality, and seem to have been the intellectual ancestors of the deplorable television serials of the present day, such as *Planet of the Apes*.[61]

Closer to the poetic responses to the evolutionary doctrines were novels about the problem of the decline of religious belief consequent on the rise of the Darwinian doctrine. Edward Maitland's (1824-1897) *The Pilgrim and the Shrine* (1868),[62] recounts the story of a young man destined for the Church, filled with intellectual doubts arising from the problems posed by the evolutionary theory and ultimately settling into an acceptance of evolutionary naturalism in the environment of unsophisticated frontier life in America. This novel was partly autobiographical in character, as was Winwood Reade's (1838-1875) *The Outcast* (1875),[63] which portrayed the social ostracism suffered by those who abandoned their faith in favour of evolutionary belief. In *Under which Lord?* (1879),[64] Eliza Linton described an intellectual contest between a high-minded agnostic scientist and an objectionably scheming High-Church clergyman. The latter is triumphant and succeeds in destroying his adversary, but it is represented as a Pyrrhic victory, with the author working to gain the reader's sympathy for the loser. Many other novels of a similar character may be cited. Mrs Humphry Ward's (1851-1920) *Robert Elsmere* (1888)[65] was a best-seller. The number of novels attacking evolutionism because of its supposed evil influence on religious thought declined noticeably after about 1880. However, in the modern period, important novels such as John Fowles's (1926-   ) *The French Lieutenant's Woman* (1969)[66] have been written around the theme of the impact of Darwinian ideas on Victorian society, considering matters from a moral and social standpoint.

We should also notice the novels that drew on evolutionary theory to look forward in a serious way to the future possibilities of man's existence, often with a Utopian vision. In many ways these were the most interesting kinds of evolutionary novel for they meshed with the social Utopias that were being formulated at that time by the members of the Fabian movement. E. Bulwer Lytton's *The Coming Race* (1871)[67] provides a good example, portraying the evolutionary development of mankind into a 'calm, intellectual race'. The hero discovers a Utopian people living in the interior of the Earth, using a marvellous fluid, *vril*, which gives them limitless power — no doubt something like electricity. The *Vril-ya* people have special powers, apparently obtained through a combination of natural selection and the exercise of a Lamarckian will. They trace their ancestry back to a tadpole, just as the Victorians traced theirs to an ape. Among the *Vril-ya* there is no poverty, no crime, no misery, no government other than a benevolent patriarchy, and no war — for with *vril* they realise that war would mean the destruction of their civilisation. Perhaps the energy of the atom is our analogue of *vril*.

Better known, and possibly the best of these Utopian writings, was H. G. Wells's *A Modern Utopia* (1905).[68] He describes a planet that is the same as ours in physical characteristics and also has a one-to-one relation in respect of the inhabitants, but is Wells's idea of what a perfect world might be like. It was one that had evolved through the will and directed efforts of its inhabitants. It had not come into being simply by allowing the struggle for existence to carry it forward of its own accord to the visionary state of socialist perfection. Moreover, the planning that Wells envisaged was not of a social character alone. It entailed a positive program of selective breeding or eugenics — not, however, by killing the weak, but by laying down strict criteria as to who might serve as parents, just as Francis Galton and his followers had proposed. However, the idea of an *evolving*, dynamic Utopia (which Wells admitted on his opening page was entailed by the Darwinian theory) is hard indeed to sustain. It is, one might say in jest, a truly Utopian vision. And the combination of Huxley's *Brave New World*[69] and the experiences with Nazi ideas on eugenics seems effectively to have wiped out hopes of arriving at a better world through the application of programs employing the selective breeding of human populations. Yet such schemes may rise again one day. Many of Wells's other writings such as *The War of the Worlds* (1898),[70] *The Time Machine* (1895)[71] and *The Shape of Things to Come* (1933)[72] were concerned with evolutionary themes. We need not, however, pursue them here.

In many ways, the writings of H. G. Wells, George Bernard Shaw (1856-1950), and Samuel Butler (1835-1902) provide the most interesting illustration of the application of evolutionary ideas in the literary scene in the late nineteenth century, through the way they fused Lamarckism and Darwinism in their discussions of characteristics of possible future social systems. So let us say something about Butler and Shaw.[73]

Butler's life was not happy. He quarrelled with his father and spent a period pioneering in New Zealand, trying to escape from civilisation. But after a fairly short stay in the foothills of the Southern Alps he returned to Europe. As a young man he was wildly enthusiastic about *The Origin*, and evolutionary considerations played an important role in his two major novels, *Erewhon* (1872)[74] and *The Way of all Flesh* (1903),[75] both of which also contained autobiographical elements.

But Butler later came to disagree strongly with Darwin, at a personal level, and about ideas on the correct formulation of evolutionary theory. The personal antagonism arose through an unfortunate misunderstanding. An article on Erasmus Darwin had been published in Germany by Ernst Krause; Darwin thought it would be pleasant to have this translated into English and wrote a biographical introduction on Erasmus to accompany the translation.[76] Unfortunately, however, Krause introduced some changes into the translated version which were construed by Butler as attacks on him and his ideas on the evolutionary theory. And Darwin had apparently given his approval to those changes by failing to state that emendations had been made when the translation was prepared. It appears that this omission was merely an oversight on Darwin's part, but Butler took it as evidence of tacit approval of Krause's criticisms. The result was that Butler mounted a vigorous one-man campaign against Darwin in letters to the press and to Darwin. But the ageing naturalist simply did not deign to reply.

This emphasises the remarkable change that took place between the work of the earlier and the later Butler. *Erewhon*, written when Butler was still a Darwinian evolutionist, contains numerous instances of ideas inspired by the theory of natural selection. But in his *Luck, or Cunning?* (1887),[77] *Life and Habit* (1878),[78] and *Evolution, Old and New* (1879),[79] Butler's ideas moved strongly towards a Lamarckian interpretation.

Erewhon, the land of 'topsy-turvy' was a bizarre kind of Utopia, and it also served Butler as means of criticising the ideas and customs of his day. The section entitled 'The book of the machines' contains the most obviously evolutionary ideas. Supposedly, some five hundred years earlier, machines had themselves shown signs of evolving to a condition where they might take over from man, and the Erewhonians had therefore determined to destroy them all or place them in museums. So it is interesting to reflect that in the present day computers are showing some signs of 'evolving' as Butler had in a way foreseen. Today, each generation of computers is used to design the computers of the subsequent generation. Moreover, the progress of computer technology is accelerating at an almost terrifying rate, and there is no prospect (for economic and political reasons) of our switching off this process as the Erewhonians had chosen to do. At the time Butler may have seemed to have been presenting a mere *jeu d'esprit*, but his ideas now seem to be disquietingly accurate.

Of course, machines are objects of design, although to some degree they may also be products of trial and error.[80] So even in the fairly early work, *Erewhon*, Butler was apparently (perhaps unconsciously) rebelling against the notion of wholly fortuitous chance being the determinant of evolutionary change. Lamarckism was already a significant component of his thinking, and the doctrine of 'unconscious memory' was beginning to emerge.[81]

Besides the section on machines there are other interesting aspects of *Erewhon* that are suggestive of evolutionary ideas. The Erewhonians were vegetarians, for they did not wish to consume their animal relations. (Some indeed objected to eating plants for the same reasons, but it seemed better to sin than not to eat at all!) But it has been argued[82] that this section on the rights of animals and plants is a commentary on Old Testament asceticism, rather than on evolutionism. And certainly several parts of the book may best be seen in this light — and more widely as a critique of the hypocrisy of British evangelical religion. As the hero crosses the mountain pass to the happier land of Erewhon he encounters ten giant statues looming through the mist and moaning woefully. These represented no less than the Biblical ten commandments. And in the land of nowhere, many of the deadly sins of Victorian society were regarded as curable diseases — a view that the twentieth century, rightly or wrongly, has come to accept in many areas.

Butler's hatred of religion, in the bigoted nineteenth-century form with which he was well acquainted, is even more central to the autobiographical *The Way of All Flesh*. And although this novel does not deal explicitly with evolutionary themes, it is deeply concerned with the problems of heredity and the transmission of characteristics (whether acquired or not) from one generation to the next.

In *Evolution Old and New*, Butler made some pertinent criticisms of Darwin's theory, pointing out (quite reasonably, I think) that it rested to a considerable degree on Lamarckian ideas, even though Darwin ostensibly repudiated Lamarckism. But Butler went beyond this to say that many of Darwin's leading ideas were already to be found in Buffon, Erasmus Darwin, and Lamarck, and plagiarism was imputed. This latter claim was pretty far-fetched, and Butler found little sympathy — Darwin in old age was beginning to be deified.

The basic idea of Butler's later concept of evolution – arrived at by wide reading and ruminating on the problems, but not by personal experimentation – was that of an inner will and striving being responsible for the evolutionary process, rather than the 'higgledy-piggledy' method of natural selection. An internal life-force realised its pent-up potential through the evolutionary process. Acquired characteristics were inheritable; habits could evolve into instincts. In many ways, as we have seen, such ideas were being expressed in one way or another by various nineteenth-century poets. Wells's *Utopia* likewise suggested something of this kind. And it is a point of some interest that so many men – scientists and non-scientists, but particularly those with specialised literary interests – should emphasise the Lamarckian aspects of evolutionism, which seemed somehow so much more encouraging for the human psyche than the blind chance of the Darwin/ Wallace theory.

It is this Lamarckian view that was particularly characteristic of the thinking of George Bernard Shaw on evolutionary questions. The central 'philosophical' section of *Man and Superman* (1903)[83] proclaimed Shaw's somewhat curious notion of the 'Life Force', in conjunction with a somewhat distorted version of Nietzsche's doctrine of the Superman. The 'hero', Don Juan, is made to say:

> And I, my friend, am as much a part of Nature as my own finger is a part of me. If my finger is the organ by which I grasp the sword and the mandoline, my brain is the organ by which Nature strives to understand itself. My dog's brain serves only my dog's purposes; but my own labors at a knowledge which does nothing for me personally but make my body bitter to me and my decay and death a calamity. Were I not possessed with a purpose beyond my own I had better be a ploughman than a philosopher; for the ploughman lives as long as the philosopher, eats more, sleeps better, and rejoices in the wife of his bosom with less misgiving. This is because the philosopher is in the grip of the Life Force. This Life Force says to him 'I have done a thousand wonderful things unconsciously by merely willing to live and following the line of least resistance: now I want to know myself and my destination, and choose my path; so I have made a special brain – a philosopher's brain – to grasp this knowledge for me as the husbandman's hand grasps the plough for me'. And this, says the Life Force to the philosopher, 'must thou strive to do for me until thou diest, when I will make another brain and another philosopher to carry on the work'.[84]

An uncomfortable amalgam of Lamarck, Schopenhauer, Nietzsche, and Hegel, one might suggest! Thus did the literary Shaw envisage the progress towards the Superman; this was his way of achieving what the exponents of the eugenics movement were seeking at about the same period.

In *Back to Methuselah* (1921),[85] however, and more particularly in the Preface to this play, Shaw gives us his clearest ideas – and they were really rather bizarre – on the evolutionary process. The Preface is at once perceptive and extraordinarily naive, and it is sometimes difficult to know the extent to which it should be taken seriously:

> If you have no eyes, and want to see, and keep trying to see, you will finally get eyes. If, like a mole or subterranean fish, you have eyes and don't want to see, you will lose your eyes. If you like eating the tender tops of trees enough to make you concentrate all your energies on the stretching of your neck, you will finally get a long neck, like the giraffe. This seems absurd to inconsiderate people at the first blush; but it is within the personal experience of all of us that it is just by this process that a child tumbling about the floor becomes a boy walking erect; and that a man sprawling on the road with a bruised chin, or supine on the ice with a hashed occiput, becomes a bicyclist and a skater . . . And he has done it solely by willing. For here there can be no question of Circumstantial [i.e., natural] Selection, or the survival of the fittest. . . . The man has acquired a new habit, an automatic unconscious habit, solely because he wanted to, and kept trying until it was added into him.
> But when your son tries to skate or bicycle in his turn, he does not pick up the accomplishment where you left, any more than he is born six feet high with a beard and a tall hat. The set-back that occurred between your lessons occurs again. The race leaves exactly as the individual leaves. Your son relapses, not to the very beginning, but to a point which no mortal method of measurement can distinguish from the beginning.[86]

Basically this is the same theory as that of Samuel Butler.

It is difficult to know how seriously Shaw meant such passages. But I suggest that, despite the appearance of flippancy, they do represent his basic beliefs. And this is interesting, for much of the Preface to *Back to Methuselah* is concerned with showing, most ably, how various political theorists had all found something in Darwin which was to their liking, and could be used to support their views. Yet Shaw did this very thing. He looked at the evolutionary theory, and took from it just those aspects which suited his socio-political views. Fabianism, Shaw's political credo, sought slow evolutionary change by rational exercise of man's will and the appropriate modification of the environment to meet the needs and desires of the community, thereby feeding back onto the community or reinforcing the actions of the will by a *quasi*-Lamarckian process. Thus we find ourselves returning to the old socio-economic and philosophical concerns and interconnections of the theory of evolution. In Butler, Wells and Shaw the literary domain interlocks neatly with all the other ramifications of the evolutionary theory that we have traced in earlier chapters.

Before leaving the question of the influence of evolutionism on literature, something must be said about the alleged link between Darwin, and literary *naturalism*. This movement, the chief exponent of which was the French novelist, Emile Zola (1840-1902), sought to apply to literature the discoveries and methods of nineteenth-century science. Indeed the naturalistic novel was itself conceived as a kind of scientific study, a factual inquiry into man and society. Man was to be considered as a product of the evolutionary process and his animal (or physiological) aspects were to be portrayed as being determined by the effects of heredity and environment. Thus the novelists of this school claimed to offer a dispassionate analysis of observed facts, rather than concerning themselves with higher moral themes. So they often wrote about 'humdrum' matters, the doings of working-class people engaged in the bitter nineteenth-century struggle for existence, and portrayed 'warts and all' in this battle of life. An authentic representation of everyday activities became a worthwhile aim. The naturalistic philosophy of the day was thereby transferred to the literary idiom.

Good examples of works influenced by this approach were *Les Rougon-Macquart* novels of Zola, the short stories of Guy de Maupassant (1850-1893), or plays such as Henrik Ibsen's (1828-1906) *Ghosts* (1881),[87] and Shaw's *Mrs Warren's Profession* (1894)[88] or *Widowers' Houses* (1892).[89] In the twentieth century, novels such as Steinbeck's (1902-   ) *Grapes of Wrath* (1939)[90] may be classified as works of this genre.

But if Zola was the fountain-head of this movement, can it be said that he was explicitly indebted to Darwin for his literary program? His manifesto is to be found in the preface to the novel, *Thérèse Raquin* (1867):

> In *Thérèse Raquin*, I wished to study temperament and not character . . . I chose people entirely dominated by nerves and blood, without free will, drawn to each act of their lives by the fatality of their flesh. Thérèse and Laurent are human animals, nothing more. . . The scientific analysis that I have tried to apply in *Thérèse Raquin* would not surprise them [i.e., sympathetic critics]; they would find in it the modern method, the tool of universal enquiry that this century uses so feverishly for finding out the future . . . They would accept my starting point, the study of temperament and the modifications due to environment and circumstances.[91]

This shows well enough the kind of intentions that Zola had in mind when writing his novels. But it is believed that the direct inspiration for this 'scientific' approach to literature stemmed not from Darwin, but more particularly from the work of the notable French physiologist, Claude Bernard (1813-1878), in his *Introduction to the Study of Experimental Medicine* (1865).[92] Nevertheless, it can reasonably be maintained that the movement of literary naturalism sprang from the same soil as nineteenth-century philosophical naturalism. And Darwin did much to fertilise this soil.

Any reader of Zola's novels, or member of the audience at a performance of Ibsen's *Ghosts*, will know well enough the power of the writing which 'down-to-earth' themes may inspire. Yet it may be argued that the trite 'kitchen-sink' comedies of present-day television serials and 'pot-boiler' novels are themselves evolutionary descendants of nineteenth-century literary naturalism − if indeed they have any intellectual roots whatsoever. It would scarcely be worth developing a detailed argument on this point here, for the subject is not very edifying, but we may conclude this chapter with an amusing quotation from the Stow Persons volume, *Evolutionary Thought in America*, revealing perhaps the ancestry of some of the clichés that still clutter our thinking in the 1980s:

> Ideas about nature, science, and destiny led to the recurrent use of words and phrases by which early naturalistic fiction can be identified. 'The irony of fate' and 'the pity of it' are two of the phrases; 'pawns of circumstance' is another. The words that appear time and time again are 'primitive', 'primordial' (often coupled with 'slime'), 'prehensile', 'apelike', 'wolflike', 'brute' and 'brutal', 'savage', 'driving', 'conquering', 'blood' (often as an adjective), 'master' and 'slave' (also as adjectives), 'instinct' (which is usually 'blind'), 'ancestor', 'huge', 'cyclopean', 'shapeless', 'abyss', 'biological', 'chemic' and 'chemism', 'hypocrisy', 'taboo', 'unmoral'. Time and again we read that 'The race is to the swift and the battle to the strong'. Time and again we are told about 'the law of claw and fang', 'the struggle for existence', 'the blood of his Viking ancestors', and 'the foul stream of heredity evil'. 'The veneer of civilization' is always being 'stripped away', or else it 'drops away in an instant'. The characters . . . 'lose all resemblance to humanity', reverting to 'the abysmal brute'. But when they 'clash together like naked savages', or even like atoms and star dust, it is always the hero who 'proves himself the stronger'; and spurning his prostrate adversary he strides forward to seize 'his mate, his female'. 'Was he to blame?' The author asks his readers; and always he answers, 'Conditions, not men, were at fault'.[93]

Darwin, it seems, not only gave us a new philosophy; encouraged war, racial hatred and every shade of political opinion; destroyed religion; and led to Freud. He despoiled the English literary idiom as well. Poor Darwin! Did he perceive a fraction of all that he was to do to us?

NOTES CHAPTER 22

1   Some relevant publications are: R. B. Crum, *Scientific Thought in Poetry*, Columbia University Press, New York, 1931; J. W. Beach, *The Concept of Nature in Nineteenth-Century English Poetry*, Macmillan, New York, 1936; D. Bush, *Science and English Poetry: A Historical Sketch, 1590-1950*, O.U.P., New York, 1950; M. Cowley, 'Naturalism in American Literature' in Stow Persons (ed.), *Evolutionary Thought in America*, Braziller, New York, 1956, pp.300-333; W. Irvine, 'The influence of Darwin on literature', *Proceedings of the American Philosophical Society*, Vol. 103, 1959, pp.616-628; A. Dwight Culler, 'The Darwinian Revolution and literary form', in G. L. Levine & W. A. Madden (eds), *The Art of Victorian Prose*, O.U.P., New York, 1968, pp.224-246; L. Stevenson, *Darwin Among the Poets*, Russell & Russell, New York, 1963; L. R. Furst & P. N. Skrine, *Naturalism*, Methuen, London, 1971; L. Isaacs, *Darwin to Double Helix: The Biological Theme in Science Fiction*, Butterworths, London, 1977.

2   'Wonns' means 'dwells'.

3   'Brinded' means tawny coloured, with streaks of a different hue.

4   An ounce is a lynx; a libbard is a leopard.

5   *The Works of John Milton*, 18 vols, and indices, Columbia University Press, New York, 1931-1940, Vol. 2 (Part 1), pp.227-228.

6   Spheric glass means microscope.

7   D. King-Hele (ed.), *The Essential Writings of Erasmus Darwin*, MacGibbon & Kee, London, 1968, pp.90-91.

8   A. Pope, *An Essay on Man* (1733-1734), Epistle II, Lines 1-2 (republished Scolar Press, London, 1969).
9   See G. Canning, 'The loves of the triangles. A mathematical and philosophical poem, inscribed to Dr Darwin [written in 1798, parodying Darwin's *Loves of the Plants*]' in *Poetry of the Anti-Jacobin: Comprising the Celebrated Political & Satirical Poems, Parodies and Jeux d'Esprit of the Right Hon. George Canning*, London, 1854, pp.123-138, 143-149.
10 See Chapter 4, note 11.
11 P. Carus, *Goethe: with Special Considerations of his Philosophy*, Open Court, Chicago & London, 1915, pp.256-257. This book also contains German and English versions of the verse form of *Die Metamorphose der Pflanzen*, as well as the original German of *Die Metamorphose der Thiere*. The 'Metamorphosis of animals' was first published in Vol. 1 of Goethe's *Zur Morphologie* (1820), but it is believed to have been composed in 1806, or possibly earlier. (See *Goethe's Werke Hamburger Ausgabe in 14 Bänden*, Wegner, Hamburg, n.d., Vol. 1, pp.201-203 & 585-587.)
12 E. de Selincourt & H. Darbishire (eds), *The Poetical Works of William Wordsworth: The Excursion, The Recluse Part I Book I*, O.U.P., Oxford, 1959, p.263 (Book VII, lines 999-1005). Darwin, it may be noted, recorded in his *Autobiography* that he took 'much delight' in the poetry of Wordsworth and Coleridge, and he 'boasted' that he read *The Excursion* through twice.
13 L. Huxley (ed.), *Life and Letters of Thomas Henry Huxley*, 2 vols, Macmillan, London, 1900, Vol. 2, p.338.
14 L. Stevenson, *op. cit.* (note 1), pp.62-63. For further discussions of the impact of the idea of evolution on Tennyson, see, for example, W. R. Rutland, 'Tennyson and the theory of evolution', *Essays and Studies by Members of the English Association*, Vol. 26, 1940, pp.7-29; J. Harrison, 'Tennyson and evolution', *Durham University Journal*, Vol. 64, 1971, pp.26-31; M. Millhauser, *Fire and Ice: The Influence of Science on Tennyson's Poetry*, Tennyson Society, Lincoln (Nebraska), 1971; K. R. Chatterjee, *Studies in Tennyson as Poet of Science*, Chand, New Delhi, 1974.
15 A. Tennyson, 'In memoriam A. H. H.: Obit MDCCCXXXIII', Section 56, Stanza 4, in *The Works of Alfred Lord Tennyson Poet Laureate*, London & New York, 1887, pp.247-286 (p.261).
16 *Ibid.*, Section 3, Stanzas 1-3 (p.248).
17 *Ibid.*, Section 56, Stanzas 3-7 (pp.261-262). It has been suggested that the enigmatic phrase 'behind the veil' is a pointer to Tennyson's interest in mysticism, which might provide a hopeful outlet for man, contrary to the vision of 'Nature, red in tooth and claw'. By mystical insight, one might hope to lift the veil shrouding phenomena, to reveal the inner essence of things.
18 *Ibid.*, Epilogue, Stanzas 31-36 (p.286).
19 See A. W. Brown, *The Metaphysical Society: Victorian Minds in Crisis, 1869-1880*, Columbia University Press, New York, 1947, Chapter 2.
20 C. B. Ricks (ed.), *The Poems of Tennyson*, Longmans, London, 1969, pp.1281-1283.
21 *Ibid.*, pp.1359-1369 (p.1367).
22 R. Browning, *Paracelsus*, Section 5, in *Poems of Robert Browning*, Frowde, Oxford, 1910, p.495.
23 *Ibid.*, pp.495-496.
24 *Ibid.*, p.496.
25 *Ibid.*, p.496.
26 M. Arnold, *Poems: Dramatic and Later Poems*, Macmillan, London, 1885, pp.119-178.
27 G. S. Kirk & J. E. Raven, *The Presocratic Philosophers: A Critical History with Selections of Texts*, Cambridge University Press, Cambridge, 1957, pp.336-345.
28 *Swinburne's Collected Poetical Works*, 2 vols, Heinemann, London, 1935, Vol. 1, pp.732-740 (p.732).
29 A. C. Swinburne, 'Hymn of man (during the session in Rome of the Ecumenical Council)', *ibid.*, Vol. 1, pp.753-764 (at pp.756 and 764).
30 From the poem 'Hard Weather' (1888), in *Selected Poems by George Meredith*, Constable, Westminster, 1897, pp.24-25.
31 *Ibid.*, p.25.
32 See, for example, 'The Woods of Westermain', in G. Meredith, *op. cit.* (note 30), pp.225-245.
33 E. Brennecke, *Thomas Hardy's Universe: A Study of a Poet's Mind*, Unwin, London, 1924, Chapter 1 and *passim*.
34 L. Stevenson, *op. cit.* (note 1), p.240.
35 'Terrene' means earthy, or occurring on or inhabiting the Earth.
36 T. Hardy, *The Dynasts: An Epic-Drama of the War with Napoleon, in Three Parts, Nineteen Acts, & One Hundred & Thirty Scenes, The Time Covered by the Action being about Ten Years*, Macmillan, London, 1923, p.2 (1st publ. 1903-1908).
37 L. Stevenson, *op. cit.* (note 1), p.283.
38 '1967', in *The Collected Poems of Thomas Hardy*, 4th edn, Macmillan, London, 1932, p.204.
39 ' "And there was a great calm" (On the signing of the Armistice, Nov. 11, 1918)', *ibid.*, pp.557-558.
40 See L. Stevenson, *op. cit.* (note 1), Chapter 6.
41 T. L. Peacock, *Melincourt. By the author of Headlong Hall*, 3 vols, London, 1817.

42   See above, page 4.
43   T. L. Peacock, *Headlong Hall*, London, 1816 (republished Dent, London, 1961).
44   T. L. Peacock, *Nightmare Abbey*. By the author of *Headlong Hall*, London, 1818 (republished Penguin, Harmondsworth, 1969).
45   T. L. Peacock, *Gryll Grange*. By the author of *Headlong Hall*, London, 1861.
46   Benjamin Disraeli, *Tancred or The New Crusade . . . With an Introduction by Philip Guedalla*, Peter Davies, London, 1927, pp.112-113.
47   C. Kingsley, *Alton Locke, Tailor and Poet. An Autobiography*, 2 vols, London, 1850 (republished Scholarly Press, Saint Clair Shores, 1971).
48   See above, page 000.
49   E. G. E. Bulwer Lytton, *What Will He Do with It? By Pisistratus Caxton*, 4 vols, Edinburgh & London, 1859.
50   R. D. Blackmore, *The Remarkable History of Sir Thomas Upmore, Bart., M.P., formerly known as "Tommy Upmore"*, new and cheaper edition, London, 1889.
51   J. Verne, *Voyage au Centre de la Terre*, Paris, 1864 (English tr., Penguin, Harmondsworth, 1970).
52   A. Conan Doyle, *The Lost World. Being an Account of the Recent Amazing Adventures of Professor George E. Challenger, Lord John Roxton, Professor Summerlee and Mr E. D. Malone of the 'Daily Gazette'*, Hodder & Stoughton, London, 1912. (See also, *Professor Challenger Stories*, John Murray, London, 1952).
53   H. Curwen, *Zit and Xoe; Their Early Experiences*, 2nd edn, Edinburgh, 1887.
54   H. G. Wells, 'A Story of the Stone Age' in *Tales of Space and Time*, London & New York, 1899 (first published in *The Idler*, 1897).
55   J. Compton Rickett, *The Quickening of Caliban: a Modern Story of Evolution*, London, 1893.
56   W. B. Westall, *A Queer Race: The Story of a Strange People*, London, 1887.
57   H. B. Marriott Watson, *Marahuna: A Romance*, London, 1888.
58   H. G. Wells, 'In the Abyss', in *The Plattner Story: And Others*, London, 1897 (first published in *Pearsons's Magazine*, 1896).
59   H. G. Wells, *The Island of Doctor Moreau*, London, 1896 (republished Pan, London, 1975).
60   J. de Mille, *A Strange Manuscript found in a Copper Cylinder*, New York, 1888.
61   It should be noted, however, that the novel that served as a prototype for the various films and television serials was not without interest, making several perceptive observations on Western civilisation in general and Western science in particular. See P. Boulle, *Planet of the Apes*, Stacey, London, 1973 (1st French edn, 1963).
62   E. Maitland, *The Pilgrim and the Shrine: or, Passages from the Life and Correspondence of Herbert Ainslie, B.A., Cantab.*, London, 1868.
63   W. Winwood Reade, *The Outcast*, London & Edinburgh, 1875 (republished, Garland, New York, 1975).
64   E. Linton, *Under Which Lord?*, London, 1879.
65   Mary Augusta [Mrs Humphry] Ward, *Robert Elsmere*, 3 vols, London, 1888.
66   J. R. Fowles, *The French Lieutenant's Woman*, London, 1969 (republished Panther, London, 1971).
67   E. G. E. Lytton Bulwer, *The Coming Race*, Edinburgh & London, 1871 (republished as *Vril: The Power of the Coming Race*, Rudolf Steiner Publications, New York, 1972).
68   H. G. Wells, *A Modern Utopia*, London, 1905 (republished Nebraska University Press, Lincoln, Nebraska, 1967).
69   A. Huxley, *Brave New World*, London, 1932 (republished Panther, London, 1967). See also his *Brave New World Revisited*, Chatto & Windus, London, 1959.
70   H. G. Wells, *The War of the Worlds*, London, 1898 (republished Pan, London, 1975).
71   H. G. Wells, *The Time Machine: An Invention*, London, 1895 (republished Corgi, London, 1974).
72   H. G. Wells, *The Shape of Things to Come. The Ultimate Revolution*, London, 1933 (republished Corgi, London, 1974).
73   For a discussion of the relationship between Butler and evolutionary theory, see B. Willey, *Darwin and Butler: Two Versions of Evolution*, Chatto & Windus, London, 1960. On Shaw's ideas on evolution, see V. de Vahl Davis, *Shaw on Evolution: An Analysis of George Bernard Shaw's Preface to Back to Methuselah*, Unpublished Fourth Year Honours Dissertation, School of History and Philosophy of Science, University of New South Wales, 1969.
74   S. Butler, *Erewhon; or, Over the Range*, London & Edinburgh, 1872 (republished Penguin, Harmondsworth, 1970).
75   S. Butler, *The Way of All Flesh*, London, 1903 (republished Penguin, Harmondsworth, 1971).
76   E. Krause, *Erasmus Darwin*, translated from the German by W. S. Dallas, with a preliminary notice by Charles Darwin, London, 1879 (republished Gregg, Farnborough, 1971).
77   S. Butler, *Luck, or Cunning, as the Main Means of Organic Modification? An Attempt to throw Additional Light upon the late Mr Charles Darwin's Theory of Natural Selection*, London, 1887.

78 S. Butler, *Life and Habit*, London, 1878.
79 S. Butler, *Evolution, Old and New; or, the Theories of Buffon, Dr Erasmus Darwin, and Lamarck, as compared with that of Mr Charles Darwin*, London, 1879.
80 It has been said that modern aeroplanes are remarkably safe in part owing to the very great number of models that have been constructed – the inadequate versions having been eliminated by a process somewhat akin to natural selection.
81 See above, page 327.
82 E. Dwight Culler, *op. cit.* (note 1).
83 G. B. Shaw, *Man and Superman: A Comedy and a Philosophy*, London, 1903 (republished Penguin, Harmondsworth, 1971).
84 *Ibid.* (1971), p.179.
85 Bernard Shaw, *Back to Methuselah: A Metabiological Pentateuch*, New York, 1921 (republished Penguin, Harmondsworth, 1971).
86 *Ibid.*, (1921), pp.xxiii-xxiv.
87 H. Ibsen, *Ghosts: A Drama of Family Life, in Three Acts*, translated from the Norwegian by Henrietta F. Lord, new edition, revised, London, 1890.
88 G. B. Shaw, *Mrs Warren's Profession: A Play in Four Acts*, London, 1902 (republished Penguin, Harmondsworth, 1970).
89 G. B. Shaw, *Widowers' Houses: A Comedy*, London, 1893 (republished Penguin, Harmondsworth, 1970).
90 J. Steinbeck, *The Grapes of Wrath*, London & Toronto, 1939 (republished Penguin, Harmondsworth, 1976).
91 E. Zola, *Thérèse Raquin* (tr. P. G. Downs), Heinemann, London, 1955, pp.vii-viii & xi.
92 C. Bernard, *An Introduction to the Study of Experimental Medicine* (tr. H. C. Green), Dover, New York, 1957.
93 M. Cawley, in S. Persons (ed.), *op. cit.* (note 1), pp.318-319.

23

Darwinism and Music

Darwinism did not have as profound an effect on the arts as on the various sciences, philosophy and religion. Nevertheless, significant areas can be recognised in which Darwin's work, or the more general evolutionism of the nineteenth century, exercised an appreciable influence on artistic forms. In music, the main subject of this chapter, links may be noted with the political and social awareness of certain composers, in occasional uses of evolutionary themes for the purpose of 'program' music and in the interpretation of the historical development of music by various nineteenth-century musicologists.

The nineteenth century was the great period of Romanticism, though to a considerable degree the influence of the Romantic movement hangs over us to this day. Thus although many academic musicians now show a tendency to turn up their noses at nineteenth-century compositions and find greater solace in the inchoate noises of the contemporary musical scene, the niceties of the rhythmical structures of the music of the Renaissance, or the correct rendition of the *fortepiano* works of J. C. Bach, I think most concert-goers and amateur music lovers still find pleasure chiefly in the lush fields of Schubert, Brahms and Tschaikowsky.

The Romantic composers began to turn away from the careful, formal structures of the eighteenth century (so admirably exemplified, of course, by Haydn's 79th Symphony), producing the strange harmonies, outlandish keys and multitudinous tempo changes and movements of Beethoven's extraordinary late C# minor quartet (*op.*131), the frenzied abruptness of Berlioz's *Benvenuto Cellini* overture, the portrayal of nature in sound as in Mendelssohn's *Hebrides* overture or Smetana's *Vltava*, the eroticism of Wagner's *Tristan and Isolde*, the nationalistic writings of Brahms, Chopin, Dvorak, or the wild virtuosity of Paganini. All this, of course, occurred quite independently of Darwin. Yet there was common ground between the musicians, the political theorists and the evolutionists, as has been well shown by Jacques Barzun in his illuminating study, *Darwin, Marx, Wagner*.[1]

Barzun considers three major intellectual creations which first appeared in 1859: Darwin's *Origin*, Marx's *Critique of Political Economy*, and Wagner's *Tristan and Isolde*. And he succeeds in revealing significant common features in these three — at first sight — quite disparate works. For Darwin, Barzun writes:

History was a sieve that worked. Man was the residue.[2]

For Marx:

History was a sieve that worked. The proletarian Utopia was the residue.[3]

And about Wagner, Barzun writes:

With Wagner we take another half-step upwards and reach an uncertain twilight region — part biological, part social, and (this is the half-step) part esthetic. But the pattern is the same. Art has its evolution, which follows the development of races and nations, the progress of culture ultimately requiring the union of the arts in a popular synthesis of sociological import. The *Ring* accordingly celebrates in turn the superman-to-be, the fall of the old gods through the curse of gold, and the triumph of Germanism, in one long tale of blood, lust, and deceit . . . History is a sieve that works, and the residue is the artwork of the future.[4]

Barzun then goes on to explain the common factors underlying these three 'isms': Darwinism, Marxism and Wagnerism:

At bottom lay a simple principle. The survival of the fittest [Darwin], the theory of value and surplus value [Marx], the leitmotif and its function [Wagner], were the patent props of the three constructions. The public could thus enjoy the double pleasure of simpleness and profundity. The chaotic universe of change was made rational by the ordinary fact of struggle; the anarchy of social existence was organized around class hatred; the tumultuous sea of harmony in the music drama could be charted with a guide to the motifs. The beholder began with a matter of fact and could reach symbolism and true knowledge with only an effort of application and memory. Physical struggle led to survival, physical labour to value, physical object to musical theme, and at the end each system yielded the most exalted objects of contemplation; the adaptation of living forms; a perfect state; a religion of art and the regeneration of mankind.[5]

Clearly, if what Barzun says is correct, then a considerable similarity in the very broad structure of the thinking of his exemplars of the natural sciences, the social sciences, and the arts must be admitted. A general world-view or unified *Weltanschauung* seems to be manifested.

By the term 'artwork' Richard Wagner (1813-1883) meant much more than a 'work of art'. His operas were intended to yield a general synthesis of all the major art forms in unified or 'organic' wholes. All the senses were to be assailed simultaneously; the artist was to combine both orchestra and voices and the visual impact of the drama, which was to be both poetic and thematic. Thus Wagner sought to achieve an integration of all the arts into a synthetic whole — the 'artwork'. Wagnerian opera came close to the culmination of a particular line of evolutionary development of music, rather than forming the shape of things to come. No one has ever tried to emulate *The Ring!* Nevertheless, Wagner looked to the future and saw a vision of an ever-more-perfect union of the various art forms. No doubt he hoped that the senses of smell and touch might ultimately be included in the final perfect artistic and aesthetic synthesis. (It is known that in his old age he developed a kind of erotir urge to breathe perfume and to be in physical contact with satins, silks and velvets![6]) Thus Wagner, we might say, thought of music, or art in general, from an indubitably evolutionary or developmental perspective. The notion of the *Leitmotif* was central to his conception of musical form. His operas were not clearly marked out in successive stylised arias, choruses or recitatives. Each section flowed smoothly into the next. The *Leitmotif* was supposed to supply an internal coherence or organic unity to the work as a whole.

Wagner's operas were chiefly concerned with the ancient myths and legends of German folklore and folk-history. This we might expect. The Romantics always evinced a great interest in the past, and were concerned with the feelings and utterances of different nations and peoples. Thus Wotan, Siegfried, Brünnhilde and all the rest seem obviously appropriate subjects for Wagner's attention. It is not always realised, however, that *The Ring* may also be interpreted as a trenchant critique of the values of the bourgeois capitalist system of the mid-nineteenth century. Yet in a delightful study, *The Perfect Wagnerite* (1898), George Bernard Shaw was able to present some attractive evidence to support such an interpretation, and thereby reveal the common ground of political, scientific and artistic concern in Wagner's work.[7]

Wagner later became highly reactionary in his political views, but as a young man he had quite strong socialist leanings. He associated with the anarchist leader Michael Bakunin and took part in the abortive political disturbances in Germany in 1848/49, finding it necessary to seek political asylum in Switzerland.[8] And among Wagner's many minor writings may be found an item entitled 'Art and Revolution',[9] which sought to show a link between these two forms of human activity. So perhaps Shaw's claims are not so bizarre as might at first appear. But here are a couple of passages from *The Perfect Wagnerite*, giving *The Ring* a socio-economic interpretation. In the third scene of the *Rhine Gold*, one is introduced to a mine in which dwarfs are toiling to heap up treasure for their ungodly master, Alberic. Shaw sees it this way:

> This gloomy place need not be a mine: it might just as well be a match-factory, with yellow phosphorus, phossy jaw, a large dividend, and plenty of clergymen shareholders. Or it might be a whitelead factory, or a chemical works, or a pottery,

or a railway shunting yard, or a tailoring shop, or a little gin-sodden laundry, or a
bakehouse, or a big shop, or any other of the places where human life and welfare
are daily sacrificed in order that some greedy foolish creature may be able to hymn
exultantly to his Plutonic idol.[10]

Or again, in describing the magic helmet of invisibility, Shaw writes:

This helmet is a very common article in our streets, where it generally takes the
form of a tall hat. It makes a man invisible as a shareholder, and changes him into
various shapes, such as a pious Christian, a subscriber to hospitals, a benefactor of
the poor, a model husband and father, a shrewd, practical independent Englishman, and what not, when he is really a pitiful parasite on the commonwealth,
consuming a great deal, and producing nothing, feeling nothing, knowing nothing,
believing nothing, and doing nothing except what all the rest do, and that only
because he is afraid not to do it, or at least pretend to do it.[11]

Obviously, there is a good deal more of Shaw than Wagner in this.
Nevertheless, it does reveal some of the various interconnections that may be
found running between the political and social context of the times and
Wagner's compositions.

But in his later life, Wagner moved away from political radicalism towards
an ugly racism, and his anti-semitism is well known. In the twentieth century,
the Nazis made considerable use of Wagner's political writings, making
much of his unsavoury little pamphlet, *Jews in Music*,[12] and emphasising the
way the great composer advocated militarism and the glory of the German
Volk. The Nazis took pleasure in attending the performances of Wagner's
operas at Beyreuth. Hitler, in particular, revered Wagner's prose writings,
tried to emulate their style, and sought to enthrone him as the artistic god of
the Third Reich. The Nazis, in fact, put into practice many of the social
theories which the later Wagner, writing in the period of ascendancy of the
Social Darwinism movement, had preached in his essays. Consequently,
Beyreuth became a kind of temple for the worship of the new cult of
Germanism, with all its pagan heroes. Both Hitler and Wagner might be
construed by their admirers as kinds of 'Supermen' who had shown
themselves to be 'fittest' in the struggle for existence. Thus music and politics
finally coalesced in the depraved Social Darwinism of the Nazi movement.

As for evolutionism *per se* providing some source of direct inspiration for
musical compositions, there are not too many examples that may be
proposed, but an obviously telling case is to be found in Richard Strauss's
(1864-1949) tone poems, and most notably his *Thus Spake Zarathustra*,
which was based on Nietzsche's work of that name.[13] At one time, Nietzsche
had been a disciple of Wagner, but he later turned against him on musical —
not political or philosophical — grounds. Strauss's music was a natural
progression in terms of harmonic treatment and orchestral texture from that
of Wagner, and he also subscribed to Wagner's later political and social
theories, besides being enamoured of the philosophical doctrines of

Schopenhauer and Nietzsche. Schopenhauer had written of the 'will' as a blind, striving power; Nietzsche had written of the 'will to power' and had propounded the idea of the '*Ubermensch*'; Wagner revealed new techniques of orchestration and harmonisation; evolutionism (though not necessarily of the Darwinian variety) provided a further thread in the tapestry. The result, in Strauss, was the strange pagan music of *Thus Spake Zarathustra* (1896), in which the gradual *Entwicklung* of the human race is portrayed as a driving, forward-thrusting process from its origin, through the various phases of its development, religious and scientific, and culminating in the arrival of the 'Superman'.[14] This is *not* Darwinian evolutionsim — a random 'higgledy-piggledyness' fortuitously producing the seeming design of the world of living organisms. It is, rather, a realisation of the potentialities pent up within the bonds of the cosmos as originally conceived. If we must choose biological analogies, the parallel with Lamarckism would be much closer than with Darwinism. Or Spencer's evolutionism might provide a better fit. But neither does real justice to Strauss's vision. A primitive, hell-let-loose, saturnine world is revealed, yet also one of exaltation for the Utopian vision of the coming *Ubermensch*.

It is interesting to recall that Joseph Haydn (1732-1809) had sought to portray the origin of the Earth from its primaeval chaos in his well-loved oratorio, *The Creation* (1800).[15] This work, a product of Haydn's old age, is by no means a perfect example of Enlightenment music, and indeed it was composed some time after the Romantic movement was well launched. Nevertheless, the greater part of the oratorio displays the open clarity that one might expect from the 'enlightened' age and the kind of world that is portrayed may be compared with the ordered system of Linnaeus or the state of busy, happy activity conjured up by William Paley. On the other hand, Haydn did choose to pen some most un-Classical chords and modulations in his efforts to represent the formlessness of the original inchoate cosmos. Yet this has nothing of the dynamic power of Strauss's evolutionary vision. And the contrast between the way the eighteenth-century Haydn and the nineteenth-century Strauss sought to represent the coming of light in musical terms is most instructive.

Haydn reveals his orthodox, pious Christian understanding of the origin of the world, with God shaping formless matter according to His Will. For Strauss, it is as if a giant seed is beginning slowly and painfully to crack its shell and unleash the hidden energies within. He points to the violent paganism of the twentieth century, though with an optimism for the new visions that will be achieved. For Haydn, in contrast, the universe will calmly run its linear course, as St Augustine had supposed long before. There would be no new, unforeseen adventures, no climacterics, no new kinds of beings to inhabit this Earth. We can imagine Haydn saying, as Paley did, 'It is a happy world after all'.[16] For both of them the world was close-knit, safe and ordered according to some beneficent design.

In what we have said so far, the link between Darwinism and music doubtless seems a little tenuous although through the examples that have been given it should be possible to recognise certain affinities between musical ideas in the second half of the nineteenth century and the general evolutionism of the day. These affinities come into sharper focus when we look at attempts that were made in this period to theorise about music in the science of musicology.

Musicology as a distinct intellectual discipline is usually considered to have come into being in the late eighteenth century, with the writings on the history of music by the Göttingen scholar, J. N. Forkel (1749-1818).[17] His work was a natural concomitant to the investigations of the new breed of Göttingen historians such as Gatterer and Schlözer.[18] In England also, at the same period, Charles Burney (1726-1814) wrote his celebrated *General History of Music*.[19] But the new discipline did not really become widely established until the nineteenth century, particularly after about 1850 when music came to beseen as a kind of 'organism', exhibiting the characteristics of organic growth. Not unreasonably, it became popular in the nineteenth century to use categories established in social science as a means of attempting to conceptualise the development of music. Auguste Comte (1798-1857) and Herbert Spencer proved exceptionally popular in this regard. Comte, it may be recalled, had supposed that each science naturally progressed through three stages, which he termed the 'theological', the 'metaphysical', and the 'positive'.[20] And following Comte, a considerable number of tripartite divisions of musical history were suggested in the nineteenth and early twentieth century. For example, we have the German scholar, J. M. Fischer (1836), proposing the following three stages:

1 Antiquity	Simplicity; Pure melody
2 Christian era	Harmony; Brotherhood
3 Modern era	Many-sided union of harmony and counterpoint.[21]

And in the 1880s the poet, clergyman and amateur musicologist, Frederick Rowbotham, supposed that the three stages were:

1 Drum stage (rhythm only)
2 Pipe stage (simple consecutive sounds, or melody)
3 Lyre stage (harmony).

Even at the beginning of the twentieth century, the *Oxford History of Music* still favoured a three-fold division of musical history:

1 Use of simple consecutive sounds
2 Polyphony
3 Harmony.[22]

Clearly, these were idealised 'histories', saying as much about the human predilection for division in threes as the actual course of musical development. But they illustrate well enough the idea of musicologists seeking to model their interpretations on quasi-Comtian categories.

The influence of Spencer was even more pronounced. The English scholar and composer, Sir Hubert Parry (1848-1918), for example, wrote:

> The progress of this somewhat immature period shows the inevitable tendency of all things [to change] from [a condition of] homogeneity towards diversity and definiteness.[23]

And his treatment of the evolution of harmony offered an unashamedly Spencerian view:

> The early phase of the progress of harmony from homogeneity to heterogeneity is distinctly traceable . . . In the first stage there is no variety at all; all are fifths or fourths consecutively. A slight variety appears when fourths and fifths are mixed up with one another and with octaves . . . When the force of circumstances drove composers to use the less perfectly consonant combinations of thirds and sixths . . . their materials became more heterogeneous . . . [until] ultimately the composers with the higher instincts learnt to use the qualities of the different consonances . . . and then going a step still further, composers at last found out how to use real discords . . .[24]

It may be noted that whereas Spencer would have marked with approval the diversification and increasing heterogeneity of musical techniques that Parry believed (quite rightly) could be discerned, Wagner, at about the same time, was seeking to unify all art in one great synthesis grouped around the operatic stage. But this, the Spencerian might retort, corresponded to the process of 'integration' which always accompanied the 'differentiation'; and actually Spencer's formula fitted remarkably well. Parry, it may be noted, treated the early history of music very much from an anthropological standpoint.

Of course, the Victorians could hardly help but see the development of music as a kind of evolutionary progression. Music was becoming ever *better* as it grew grander in its proportions. Even harmony could be thought of as 'growing', as the interval of the seventh, the ninth, the eleventh and the thirteenth were successively employed. And then it became decorated with chromatic embellishments and lush suspensions. Instruments also multiplied: the contrabassoon appeared, the Sousaphone, and that remarkable invention of J. B. Vuillaume (1798-1875), the octo-bass, which was so large that one had to stand on a stool to play it, the fingers being replaced by mechanical stops.[25] Pianos, too, belied their name, and the delicate tracery of Mozart's concertos was superseded by the pounded opening chords of Tschaikowsky's First Concerto or the frenetic contests of Lizst's. Organs grew like Jurassic dinosaurs: witness the monster of the Sydney Town Hall. In Haydn's day, an orchestra had been content with about forty players, but the *Tuba Mirum* of Berlioz's *Grande Messe des Morts* demanded a gigantic orchestra, choir and four brass bands.[26] The close of the Civil War in America was celebrated in Boston with an orchestra of a thousand players and a chorus of ten thousand singers.[27] *Aïda* was incomplete without elephants. *The Ring* took four days to perform.

Likewise, instruments seemed to become extinct from time to time. The venerable 'serpent' made one of its last appearances in Wagner's *Rienzi*. The ophicleide fell into disuse. The clavicitherium and the harpsichord were heard no more. The arpeggione made a fleeting appearance in a sonata by Schubert, but no other composer of note followed up this lead. Early works were considered worthy of performance, but only if suitably arranged or modernised according to Victorian preferences. As with the cathedrals or parish churches of the Mediaeval period, they could be 'improved' in accordance with the putatively more sophisticated canons of contemporary taste.

It may well seem now that the nineteenth century was profoundly mistaken in its attempt to apply the Spencerian formula to the aesthetic dimension. We can discern many periods of musical history where progressive simplification seems to have been the order of the day. The bleak and stark quality of much twentieth-century chamber music can hardly be thought of as a Spencerian evolutionary development from the grand opera of the nineteenth century, and Wagner would hardly have been expected to appreciate it as the 'artwork' that he had been anticipating. And today we are happy to perform anything from Elizabethan madrigals, songs of Richard the Lion Heart, or Brahms quartets, to Vaughan Williams symphonies or electronically-composed music — striving only for 'authenticity' in the performance. It would seem that the evolutionary analogy can not well be applied to the history of music.

Yet I am not so sure that this is true. The nineteenth-century grand opera grew something like a dinosaur, filling the 'ecological niche' that was available to it. Then, when circumstances changed (that is, when its financial patrons withdrew their support), it no longer became viable within the conditions of the environment and became virtually extinct in its overblown, 'run-to-seed' form. Similarly, the trend towards ever-greater musical gymnastics at the expense of musical content, which Liszt and Paganini so encouraged has not been much pursued this century. On the other hand, the process of complexification (or 'differentiation', to use Spencer's term) has proceeded apace. Composers are constantly trying to explore new harmonic combinations, new rhythmic patterns, new tone colours, atonal music; and only fairly recently the whole new dimension of electronic music has been opened up. Moreover, people can to some degree hold all this in their minds by the 'integration' made possible by the inventions of radio, gramophone or tape-recorder.

So far, the examples I have presented have shown various analogies between evolutionism and musical theory and practice. But Darwin and the theory of evolution by natural selection have scarcely been mentioned. Yet a little searching will reveal what I hope the reader has been anticipating: instances of direct comparisons between survival of the fittest, natural selection, the evolution of living organisms, and the changes that have taken place in the history of music; also aesthetic theories based on evolutionary considerations.

Particularly good examples of this line of approach are to be found in a number of nineteenth-century French-speaking authors, possibly because the (unauthorised) first French translation of *The Origin* by Clémence-Auguste Royer[28] had been accompanied by a preface that gave Darwin's theory a strong Social Darwinist emphasis. Thus Hippolyte Taine (1828-1893), professor of aesthetics and history of art at the *Ecole des Beaux Arts* in Paris, specifically drew on the natural selection metaphor, offering an essentially mechanical and deterministic aesthetic theory. 'A work of art', he wrote, 'is determined by the condition of things, combining all surrounding social and intellectual influences'.[29] Moreover, a word of art can be compared to a plant, and just as the conditions of the environment exert a selection pressure on plants, so:

> There is . . . a *moral* temperature consisting of the general social and intellectual influences of a community . . . [And] we may conceive [this] moral temperature as *making a selection* among different species of talent, allowing only this or that species to develop itself, to the exclusion more or less complete of others.[30]

However, Taine emphasised that environmental conditions should not be supposed actually to *generate* the particular artistic variants; they merely selected among them.

Using this selection model, Taine could supposedly forge a direct link between the environmental conditions and the art forms of any period. Thereby he hoped to be able to offer a history of art with all the links in the historical chain given a theoretical support, thus yielding an essentially mechanical aetiology.

In the writings of the Belgian music historian and critic, F-J. Fétis (1784-1871), we find interesting links between studies of music history and contemporary researches in geology, anthropology and linguistics. He suggested that one should examine the characteristics of the music of various races and tribes, noting also the cranial characteristics of the men and women in those tribes. One might link particular crania with particular forms of music, after which archaeological investigations in a given region — showing a sequence of varied crania — might give a rough indication of the history of musical developments in that region.[31] Certainly this faith in the powers of craniometry shows a confidence in physical anthropology that we see as excessive. Nevertheless, we may note the way in which Fétis's proposed method of enquiry meshed well with the social and biological theories of his day.

However, of all the writers that I have examined, the work of the French musicologist, Jules Combarieu (1859-1916), in his *La Musique, ses Lois et son Evolution* (1907),[32] offers the clearest example of the employment of a Darwinistic model for the purposes of explanation in music history and in music theory. Combarieu drew so many analogies between the world of organisms and the world of music that there is no hope of dealing with all of them here. But we may look at a few interesting examples.

Organisms, said Combarieu, have all their parts inter-related and co-ordinated. So it is with music. The *Leitmotif* of a profound work, for example, enables the composer to organise a vast composition in a coherent manner. If it is possible to extract a few pages from a composition without seriously lessening its value, then this is a sure sign that 'the work is only of moderate value'.[33] In other words, a sense of organic unity is being suggested as a criterion of aesthetic judgement.

Following further his evolutionary line of thinking, Combarieu pointed out rightly that no composer or composition can properly be analysed in isolation. Each composer first assimilates the ideas of his immediate predecessors and contemporaries, before branching out to make his own original contributions. Each composer's new style may supposedly be compared with a biological variant, adapted to its own *milieu*. A work that is a success in Norway may fail in Paris. Shifts of music from one environment to another may be compared with 'graftings', which may be successful if applied to plants that are fairly closely related, but will be destined to fail if transferred to a host that is only remotely related. In addition, Combarieu supposed, there are 'extinct species' in music which cannot survive under changed environmental conditions.

Now, pulling out my trump card to complete the section, let me quote a passage from Combarieu in which the Darwinian principle of natural selection is given a direct application. We read that:

In the musical world, as with living beings, it is difficult not to recognize a 'struggle for life'. Among the composers who write, the virtuosi who perform, the masters who teach, the instrument makers who manufacture — among the forms of art themselves, whether in the secular or in the religious world — competition is as sharp as it is continuous. At all epochs there has been a conflict of talents unequally adapted: conflicts of schools, conflicts of theories, conflicts of kinds. The symphony has supplanted religious music; and the opera is now killing the symphony. In music, as in all else, the strongest triumph, only to recommence the struggle, and to be overcome in their turn. Thus is evolution produced.[34]

There is, assuredly, much truth in this. Yet it misses a vitally important factor. Music, like so much else, does gain something from competition. Yet it is also a co-operative endeavour, as any conductor or musical director knows very well. Mutual aid is a considerable factor. And sometimes it is the relaxation of competition that yields the finest results. With whom was Beethoven competing when he wrote his last quartets?

NOTES CHAPTER 23

1 J. Barzun, *Darwin, Marx, Wagner: Critique of a Heritage*, 2nd edn, Anchor, New York, 1958.
2 *Ibid.*, p.322.
3 *Ibid.*, p.322.
4 *Ibid.*, pp.322-323.
5 *Ibid.*, p.323.
6 See E. Newman, *The Life of Richard Wagner*, 4 vols, Knopf, New York, 1937-1946, Vol. 4, p.606.
7 G. B. Shaw, *The Perfect Wagnerite: A Commentary on the Ring of Niblungs*, London, 1898 (republished Dover, New York, 1967).
8 R. Wagner, *My Life*, 2 vols, Constable, London, 1911, Vol. 1, pp.465 ff.
9 R. Wagner, *Die Kunst und die Revolution*, Leipzig, 1849.
10 G. B. Shaw, *The Perfect Wagnerite: A Commentary on the Niblung's Ring*, 4th edn, London, 1923, p.17 (reprinted Dover, New York, 1967).
11 *Ibid.*, (1923) pp.17-18.
12 *Wagner on Music and Drama: A Compendium of Richard Wagner's Prose Works*, selected and arranged by Albert Goldman and Evert Sprinchorn, translated by H. Ashton Ellis, Dutton, New York, 1964, pp.51-59. However, Wagner's views on Jews have in part been misunderstood. For further discussion of the question (and an excellent general account of Wagner's music theory and philosophy of art), see B. Magee, *Aspects of Wagner*, Panther, London, 1972.
13 See above, page 275.
14 R. Specht (ed.), *Also Sprach Zarathustra: Tondichtung (frei nach Friedrich Nietzsche) for full Orchestra by Richard Strauss*, Eulenburg, London, Zurich, Mainz & New York, n.d. Strauss's tone-poem formed the theme-music for the film, *2001*. For a detailed explanation of the relationship between Strauss's music and the philosophical ideas of Nietzsche's *Thus Spake Zarathustra*, see N. del Mar, *Richard Strauss: A Critical Commentary on his Life and Works*, 3 vols, Barrie & Rockliff, London, 1962-1972, Vol. 1, pp.132-145. Other works inspired by Nietzsche's *Zarathustra* were Delius's *Mass of Life* and Mahler's mammoth *3rd Symphony*.
15 J. Haydn, *Die Schöpfung. Oratorium*, Peters, Leipzig, n.d.
16 See page 66, above.
17 V. Duckles, 'Johann Nicolaus Forkel: the beginnings of music historiography', *Eighteenth-Century Studies*, Vol. 1, 1968, pp.277-290.
18 For an account of the development of the Göttingen school of history, see H. Butterfield, *Man on his Past: The Study of the History of Historical Scholarship*, Cambridge University Press, Cambridge, 1955, pp.39-44.
19 C. Burney, *A General History of Music, from the Earliest Ages to the Present Period*, 4 vols, London, 1776-1789 (republished Foulis, London, 1935).
20 Comte wrote: 'Each of our principal conceptions, each branch of our knowledge, passes successively through three different theoretical states: the theological or fictitious, the metaphysical or abstract, and the scientific or positive. In other words, the human mind, by its nature, employs in all its investigations three methods of philosophising, of an essentially different and even opposed nature: first the theological, then the metaphysical, and finally the positive.' (S. Andreski (ed.) & M. Clarke (tr.), *The Essential Comte selected from Cours de Philosophie Positive by Auguste Comte First published in Paris 1830-1842*, Croom Helm, London & New York, 1974, p.20.
21 J. M. Fischer, *Die Grundbegriffe der Tonkunst in ihrem Zusammenhange nebst einer Geschichtlichen Entwickelung Derselben*, Leipzig, 1836, quoted in W. D. Allen, *Philosophies of Music History*, Dover, New York, 1962, p.94.
22 H. W. Hadow (ed.), *Oxford History of Music*, 6 vols, O.U.P., Oxford, 1901-1905, Vol. 1 (by H. E. Wooldridge), p.1.
23 C. H. H. Parry, *The Evolution of the Art of Music*, 5th edn, London, 1894, p.169. (The first edition of this work, published in 1893, was simply entitled *The Art of Music*, the word 'Evolution' being added in later editions.)
24 *Ibid.*, pp.107-108.
25 For an illustration of this bizarre (and useless) instrument, see P. A. Scholes, *The Oxford Companion to Music*, 6th edn, O.U.P., London, New York & Toronto, 1945, Plate 112, facing p.625.
26 For an amusing account of the first performance, illustrating the difficulties facing the people responsible for the 'integration' (in a Spencerian sense) of the executants, combating the remarkable heterogeneity of Berlioz's production, see *The Life of Hector Berlioz as written by himself in his Letters and Memoirs* (tr. K. F. Boult), Dent, London and Dutton, New York, 1903, p.147.

27   See W. D. Allen, *Philosophies of Music History: A Study of General Histories of Music 1600-1960*, Dover, New York, 1962, p.270.

28   C. R. Darwin, *De l'Origine des Espèces, ou des Lois du Progrès chez les Êtres Organisés... Traduit .. sur la troisième édition ... par Mlle Clémence Auguste Royer, Avec une Préface et des Notes du Traducteur*, Paris, 1862.

29   H. Taine, *The Philosophy of Art*, London, 1865, p.77 (1st French edn, Paris, 1865).

30   *Ibid.*, pp.85-86.

31   F.-J. Fétis, *Histoire Générale de la Musique depuis les Temps les Plus Anciens jusqu'à nos Jours*, 5 vols, Paris, 1869-1876, Vol. 1, p.10.

32   English translation: J. Combarieu, *Music: Its Laws and Evolution*, Kegan Paul, French, Trübner & Co., London, 1910.

33   *Ibid.*, p.302. Such a criticism might, for example, be levelled against the fourth movement of Schubert's second piano trio, *opus* 100.

34   J. Combarieu, *op. cit.* (note 32), p.308.

24

Concluding Remarks and Personal Reflections

The history of the Darwinian Revolution is complex, and it would be foolish to pretend that we have done more than scratch the surface of the story in this study. We have traced a number of lines of thought which converged on Darwin and Wallace; we have given some account of their work and looked at the structure of their theory; we have also looked at a selection of the manifold influences of their theory which ran in all sorts of unexpected directions. In many cases direct connections with the Darwin/Wallace theory were revealed. In other instances the new ideas could not perhaps be linked directly to the theory, but seemingly drew inspiration from the general evolutionism of the nineteenth century. But all may be regarded as manifestations, to a greater or lesser degree, of the Darwinian Revolution. So the overall structure of our exposition has something of the shape of an old-fashioned hourglass or egg-timer. It should be realised, of course, that this appearance arises as much from the manner in which we have chosen to present the exposition, as from the actual 'shape' of history. Nevertheless, it is a patterning that has considerable didactic utility. The work of Darwin and Wallace did serve as a watershed in biology, and — as Barzun informs us — 1859 marked a climacteric in three aspects of European culture that are customarily thought of as quite separate.

There can be little disagreement, even admitting the possibility that this study has been unduly partial in the material that has been chosen for discussion, that the Darwinian theory, and the evolutionism that it propounded, was utilised in quite an extraordinary number of ways, in widely disparate areas of Western thought. But this raises a number of general questions of considerable interest and importance, such as:

1 Did these non-biological areas of thought, which seemingly drew upon Darwinism with such enthusiasm, take their inspiration from Darwinism *per se*, or were they merely imbibing ideas from a general evolutionism such as characterised the whole of Western culture in the nineteenth century?

2 Were the uses that were made of Darwinism outside biology legitimate exten-
sions, extrapolations or modifications of the biological theory?
3 How could it be that in many instances mutually contradictory ideologies both
found that they could draw something to their liking from the same theory?

There is also the question of the extent to which present categories of thought
– in political and theological debate, for example – are the same as those that
were established in the nineteenth century under the aegis of the evolutionary
doctrines. And there is still the nice question of the satisfactory resolution of
the nature/nurture question, which so plagued men in the nineteenth century
and continues to trouble us today.

Let us consider the first of these questions. According to Hegel,[1] there is a
mysterious transcendent entity called the 'Absolute Spirit' or 'Idea', which,
so to speak, 'moves' in its own mysterious way and the gradual 'unfolding' of
which is manifested in the course of human history in a dialectical pattern of
repeated 'thesis', 'antithesis' and 'synthesis'. Certain great men such as
Napoleon, Alexander the Great, Peter the Great may be thought of as 'world
historical figures' who are vehicles, as it were, bearing for a time the
'Absolute Spirit' in the forward march of history. Then, when their day is
done, they may be tossed aside as the juggernaut of history rolls on and some
new figure takes on its burdens. Moreover, at certain periods in history,
particular nations embodying particular ideals hold the stage and permit the
physical manifestation of the 'Absolute Spirit' in the particular stage of its
development. Thus, according to the Hegelian doctrine, the material course
of history is dependent on the corresponding development of the 'Absolute
Idea'. In other words, for Hegel the whole of history is given an idealistic
interpretation. Hegel liked to speak of the 'spirit of the times' or *Zeitgeist* as
an *explanatory principle* to account for the characteristic values and ways of
thought of a particular historical epoch. In his view, we could regard
evolutionism as a major aspect of the nineteenth-century *Zeitgeist*.

If one subscribes to a Hegelian view of history, then, one would be likely to
say that thinkers such as Darwin, Wallace, Spencer, Sumner, Marx, Chardin
and Wells were all 'plugging in' to the evolutionary *Zeitgeist* of the nineteenth
and twentieth centuries. But such an interpretation is an anathema to
Marxists, who prefer to turn Hegel on his head, as they say,[2] retaining a
dialectical pattern in history but arguing that the motor of history
corresponds to changes in the means of production and the concomitant
economic order rather than the patterns of thoughts or ideas.[3] Social thought
is presumed to be a kind of epiphenomenon with respect to the material basis
of history.

Now it is to some degree a matter of taste or metaphysical preference
which of these alternatives one chooses; and in any case they do not by any
means exhaust all the logical possibilities. But let us consider for the moment
the Hegelian and Marxist positions, for if one or other of them is true we
should have an immediate solution to our first question: the many
manifestations of evolutionism that we have discerned might be ascribed to a

general evolutionary *Zeitgeist* or some particular mode of production and associated economic order rather than the special virtues and influences of the Darwinian theory.

It is not easy to disprove Hegel's thesis, any more than it is easy to disprove any general system of metaphysics. For if Hegel asserts that Napoleon, for example, is the temporary bearer of a mysterious entity that one may choose to call the 'World Spirit', by what logical or empirical means could we show Hegel to be in error? He may propose his system; I may deny its truth. But there seems to be no obvious way in which we might settle our disagreement without resorting to blows or some other quite inappropriate form of action. There seems to be no empirical criterion to which one might have recourse. All I can say on this is that what Hegel proposes seems to be far from plausible. According to all our everyday experience (not an infallible guide, of course), ideas are the products of brains. They may be actualised by spoken or written words, various works of art or in the formulation of scientific theories. But it is indeed difficult to see how they may exist in some way wholly independent of human intelligences or the intelligences of some other kind of living organisms. Thought, in this view, is a kind of epiphenomenon with respect to physical substance.

So, by the testimony of everyday experience and a general materialist metaphysic, the concept of the Hegelian *Zeitgeist*, with some kind of 'causal power', is to me implausible to say the least. But this is not to deny that there may be a common pattern of thought in any particular period of history. And if we so choose, we may perhaps refer to this by means of Hegel's term, without wishing to aver that there is in fact some kind of transcendent 'Spirit'. But this is likely to be misunderstood, and one may be falsely accused of subscribing to the totality of Hegel's metaphysics.

I do not wish to be thus accused, so it would seem prudent to avoid the use of the term *Zeitgeist*, with all its connotations. Nevertheless, I would like to suggest that the many manifestations of evolutionism that we have looked at in this study can hardly be ascribed solely to the influence of the Darwin/Wallace theory — the fact that the first formulation of Spencer's ideas preceded the publication of *The Origin* seems to preclude this. The great success of the Darwin/Wallace theory made a major contribution to the dissemination and acceptance of evolutionary views. Yet it was, I suggest, only the leading manifestation of nineteenth-century evolutionism, rather than its first cause. To what, then, might we ascribe the over-arching evolutionism of the period?

If we take a Marxist view, we do not look for some kind of intellectualist or idealist explanation at all, or anything in any way resembling the Hegelian *Zeitgeist*. One looks for some kind of economic determinant — perhaps some 'mode of production' that was particularly characteristic of the nineteenth century, and which might in some manner induce men, including Darwin, Wallace, Spencer and all the rest, to think in evolutionist terms, and perhaps also in terms of a theory shaped around the concept of struggle for existence.

Such a view has been put forward a number of times with the suggestion, for instance, that Darwin drew his ideas from the examples of struggle and competition that he saw around him in the world of nineteenth-century *laissez-faire* commerce.[4] Darwin was influenced to a very considerable degree in the formulation of his ideas by his reading of Malthus, but this in itself is insufficient to establish the connection with the economic base. The studies that have been made by a number of distinguished Darwinian scholars point to events that were peculiar to Darwin's own career — to his special interests, contacts and program of study — as the factors that led him to the formulation of this theory. Little hard evidence has ever been produced to suggest that he arrived at the theory by drawing directly some kind of analogy between the world of commerce and the world of animals and plants.[5] But this does not, in itself, meet the Marxist point. One could perhaps put the argument in the following way. The economic system in the early nineteenth century was such that certain members of the community did not have to work (in the customary sense of the word) for their living. Darwin was one of these fortunate few. Without the money made available by the 'surplus value' generated by the wage-labouring classes, Darwin would not have been able to live in the style to which he was accustomed and, although Wallace did not come from the well-to-do bourgeoisie, there would have been no money available to support his explorations to the Amazon or the Far East without the excess profits of the capitalist system. There were also good economic and social reasons why the voyage of *Beagle* occurred at all, making it possible for Darwin to carry out his vitally important work during his circumnavigation of the globe. The reasons Darwin was deemed acceptable to take part in the voyage were — in part at least — economic in origin.

To an extent, then, I accept the Marxist thesis. But it is not, I suggest, the whole story. For although I cannot accept the Hegelian doctrine of some transcendent cause of the spirit of an age, that is not to say that the suggestion that there may be a common pattern of thinking in any given period of history is illusory. And any such pattern is not, I believe, logically or necessarily tied to some economic base. Kuhn has shown well how this may be the case in a particular science at a particular time when he introduced the concept of a 'paradigm' to studies in the philosophy and sociology of science,[6] and common patterns of thought are also possible in many areas besides science — for example, the jingoism of the early twentieth century, the present concern with environmentalism, or the Platonism of the Renaissance. Sometimes such common patterns of thought seem to be little more than manifestations of the vagaries of fashion. Why, for example, did the architects of the 1930s and 1940s evince such an interest in curved walls? Why did the man of the eighteenth century choose to wear periwigs? Why have so many women recently taken to walking on stilts? Is it really rather difficult to answer such questions in any positive way, except to say that men and women are seemingly constantly seeking for variety and new patterns of experience. But this is coupled with the powerful tendency towards conformity. Thus some common patterns of thought may have no more remarkable origin than that which is displayed when a man looks up at the sky in a busy street, and soon has a whole crowd craning their necks upwards in rapt attention. So nineteenth-century evolutionism may, to some degree, have been a kind of self-generating phenomenon — a kind of band-wagon effect, or a mere fashion.[7] Because of man's very nature as a social animal — talking, reading books, and being exposed to formal systems of education — it is perfectly natural that an interesting and perhaps useful idea or concept, once propounded, may have a good chance of becoming widely disseminated within a community. Hegel might call this a *Zeitgeist*, but there is no need to invoke a *quasi*-mystical term of this kind with transcendental overtones.

So, without suggesting that evolutionism was a mere fad or fashion, we need have no difficulty in seeing how, once propounded, it might take on the appearance of a *Zeitgeist*. The different persons and groups that we have discussed in this study, therefore, could all draw on it and use it in their various ways. The great success of the Darwinian evolutionary theory as a system of explanation, together with the growing prestige of science in the nineteenth century, can account very well for the extraordinary zeal with which the theory was applied and misapplied in the post-1859 period.

But this leaves unanswered the question of the 'first cause'. What was the analogue of the man in the street who first gazed into the sky, and set all the other passers-by gazing upwards too? This is indeed a difficult question, and one that historians seem to be incapable of answering conclusively. In fact, there was probably a multiplicity of factors at work, rather than one prime cause.

One cause was undoubtedly the economic expansionism of the period, associated with the beginnings of the Industrial Revolution. But another factor of paramount importance seems to have been the rise of Romanticism and Nature Philosophy, and the collapse of the ideals of the Enlightenment with its associated natural-law doctrines. A full consideration of the cause or causes of the rise of Romanticism and Nature Philosophy requires a book in itself, rather than a few sentences appended to an introductory study of the Darwinian Revolution. Nevertheless, a few remarks will be offered here, albeit in a somewhat perfunctory manner.

In one sense, the pious, conservative German Nature Philosophy may be seen as a reaction to the ideals of the French Enlightenment in which a premium was placed on order, rationality, clear and distinct ideas and a public or collective solution of problems by scientific means. Thus, if the ideals of the Enlightenment are designated as the 'thesis', then their 'antithesis' is represented by the Nature Philosophy movement. But what caused this swing from the one to the other? If we had the answer to this question, we might have a solution to our problem, for the notion of *Entwicklung* was one of the leading features of the thinking of the Nature Philosophers.

I cannot pretend to offer any original solution to this conundrum, but some of the suggestions of Sir Isaiah Berlin seem to me to be most useful.[8] Berlin traces the rise of Nature Philosophy back to origins that may be located in the terrible Thirty Years War in seventeenth-century Europe. This war utterly devastated Germany, leaving it as a series of fragmented kingdoms, principalities and electorates united by a common language, but little else. France, by contrast, emerged from the War relatively unscathed, rich and prosperous and the dominant power in Europe, particularly in social and intellectual matters.

In the period of the Enlightenment, while Catholicism, a great monolithic 'public' religion, flourished in France, there grew up in Germany the religion of Pietism. This was a quiet, inward-looking version of Protestantism – a religion, moreover, that was nurtured by the non-aristocratic pastors of Germany, the intellectuals of that society.

Pietism was a religion that preached that each man should try to turn inwards spiritually, and quietly nurture and cherish the development of his soul rather than show outward forms of religious zeal. It was, no doubt, a religion highly appropriate to the psyche of a defeated, demoralised and fragmented people. Berlin has suggested that towards the end of the eighteenth century, when the Germans finally recovered from the catastrophe of the Thirty Years War, many of the characteristics of their thought – which had been working like a yeast in their minds during the long years of their eclipse as a Continental power – blossomed to form the dominant new intellectual movement of the post-Enlightenment period. One of the leading features of this new way of thinking was the notion of *Entwicklung*, which spread through European intellectual circles in the nineteenth century, becoming modified, in Darwin's theory, to become more than a process of 'self-fulfilment'. It grew into the characteristic evolutionism of his theory, predicated by the doctrine of 'higgledy-piggledy'.

This can hardly be regarded as a full and final solution to the motive cause of evolutionary doctrines in the nineteenth century. The very pace of social change may have become such by the end of the eighteenth century that an evolutionary world-view was a natural outcome. But Berlin's is an interesting and attractive thesis, and one that deserves to be looked at more thoroughly in the history of biology by students of intellectual history.

Let us turn now to a consideration of our second major question, the *legitimacy* of the uses that were made of the Darwin/Wallace theory in non-biological areas of thought. The general form of the extrapolations from the theory was that of argument by *analogy*. For example: there is a struggle for existence among plants and animals, which through natural selection yields evolutionary progress; similarly, there is a struggle for existence among humans; this ought to be encouraged for it will give rise to a progressive evolution of society.

It would, of course, be utterly foolish to disregard the great utility and importance of analogical arguments. Indeed, some writers claim that all creative thinking in science employs some kind of analogical reasoning.[9] But it should be emphasised that arguments by analogy never have any *deductive* force. They are always instances of inductive reasoning. Nevertheless, this does not in any way rule out the employment of arguments by analogy in science. It can be seen that analogies may usefully be employed in the *formulation* of hypotheses, which should then be tested by the experimental trial of their logical consequences, and if they successfully withstand these processes of experimental testing they may be taken, for the time being, to be acceptable. But it should be realised that in principle they are always open to falsification and may one day be found wanting and have to be discarded.[10]

If we follow this line of argument, the Social Darwinists would have to present their case along the following lines: there is a struggle for existence among animals and plants, which through natural selection yields evolutionary progress; humans in many respects are like animals and plants; it may well be the case, therefore, that a struggle for existence among humans, or between human societies, will – aided by natural selection – give rise to evolutionary progress. Let us, therefore, set up two experimental societies, one which encourages the maximisation of 'struggle' and the other which keeps this to a minimum and see which offers the greater degree of evolutionary progress. And let us decide which of the societies is, in general terms, the 'better'.

This would be the 'scientific' approach. But it is obvious that it is quite impracticable to set up such experimental conditions, although anthropologists have made interesting studies of various societies, some of which do, and some of which do not, exhibit 'struggle'.[11] I should like to emphasise that the nineteenth-century Social Darwinists of both conservative and liberal factions did *not* argue in this 'scientific' manner at all. Ostensibly, they perceived certain features within the animal and plant worlds and sought to argue from these to the world of human societies. Analogies were carried over directly but were not presented as arguments which were at best merely inductive in character with no probative force, or which should be regarded as scientific hypotheses only. The claims that were made were never subjected to rigorous empirical test; on the contrary, it was made to appear as if the arguments could legitimately be used without further ado for establishing or reinforcing particular social norms.

My feelings on all this will probably have been made apparent to the reader in earlier chapters. But they may be reiterated here. One cannot, I say, argue deductively from 'is' to 'ought'.[12] The arguments of the Social Darwinists and those who sought to build up systems of evolutionary ethics have no deductive force. All that may be said is that the Social Darwinists put forward interesting ideas which were most certainly worthy of appraisal and critical scrutiny, but which were virtually impossible to test in any rigorous scientific manner. Thus they have come and gone in the march of history and are today normally regarded as quite outmoded, although their influence lingers on. But they have never been scientifically tested, nor can they be, by their very nature. I conclude, therefore, that the arguments of the Social Darwinists were illegitimate judged by the canons of deductive logic. They were legitimate, in a loose sense, if thought of as hypotheses which might throw light on the nature of society, but they had not the slightest prescriptive force. The Social Darwinists never succeeded in establishing reliable social norms with their Darwinian arguments, although what some of them had to say may be acceptable enough from an independent point of view — that is, judged from the standpoint of some political or social philosophy, rather than political or social science.

All this raises the parallel question of how it came about that so many different facets of thought in the nineteenth century fell under the influence of the Darwin/Wallace theory or the general evolutionism of the period. The following argument is worth consideration. Evolutionism was one of the major categories of thought in the nineteenth century. Also popular was what is sometimes called 'scientism' — the belief in the efficacy of the scientific (preferably 'physical') approach to social problems or the claim that particular social views have scientific status. By adherence to the Darwin/Wallace theory, both these could be apparently satisfied simultaneously. In other words, the Darwin/Wallace theory — so remarkably successful in biology, despite the considerable number of unsolved problems that it faced in the late nineteenth century — was evidently a product of the researches of *bona fide* scientists, rather than speculative metaphysicians. It was indubitably a scientific theory. But what of studies of society and culture and political systems at that time? It would be hard to claim that these were sciences. However, by appealing to Darwinism they could hope to be credited, to some degree at least, with being scientific.[13] I suggest that this was probably the chief factor influencing the development of the Social Darwinist movement, to the extent that it purported to represent carefully thought-out plans, sanctioned by the findings of science, for the improvement of society rather than mere rationalisations of social inequalities for the benefit of those who had most to gain from such rationalisations.

This leads us to a consideration of the question of how it was that groups so far apart as, say, the Spencerians and the Fabians could both attempt to draw on the Darwin/Wallace theory in support of their views. We have seen *why* both of them might seek to do this, but *how* was it that both might give the appearance of having some justification for what they sought to do? This may appear to be something of a conundrum, but the difficulty lies in the way that I have posed the problem rather than in the nature of the case.

The Social Darwinists sought to draw analogies between men and animals, and then pass from descriptions to prescriptions — from 'is' to 'ought'. Men and women are just one kind of animal, albeit a rather peculiar and special kind. So we may find similarities between men and animals as well as differences. Animals compete with each other in a variety of ways. For some, it is a case of 'tooth and claw' in a real fighting sense, as when a cobra and a mongoose do battle with each other. Such competition is *inter*-specific. There is also the sort of competition that is exemplified by giraffes searching for the succulent leaves at the tops of trees, or plants competing for light in a forest. Such competition is *intra*-specific. Then there is the co-operative aspect of animal existence – a lioness caring for her cubs; bees co-operating in the construction of their hives; a male baboon leading the pack to safety; elephants herding together for mutual support. All these are instances that are repeated a thousand-fold in animal life. And, to the extent that it is legitimate to draw analogies with the world of animals or plants, it is legitimate to draw analogies with *any* of these.

But, one may ask, is one of the analogies 'better' or in some way more 'authentic' than the others? Logically: no. If the question *is* to be answered it must also be realised that the answer that is proffered will necessarily represent an expression of some personal preference. Besides, I would question the very assumption that evolution is, *per se*, a 'good' thing. Obviously, there has been a vast social evolution in the Western world in the last two thousand years and its effects are now spreading rapidly to the East but it is by no means clear that this has been marked by a corresponding progress in any ethical or moral sense. Leaving this aside, however, I incline to the view that the arguments of the Fabians, and Kropotkin's emphasis on mutual aid, form the 'best' of the analogies that are to be drawn. I say this simply because man is, quite obviously, a social animal and consequently the analogy that emphasises the co-operative aspects of life seems to me to be the most appropriate. We may remember that humans, through their various artefacts and their skills in language and writing have entered a *quasi*-Lamarckian phase of cultural evolution. Thus I am disposed to sympathise with the Fabians' emphasis on the virtues of improving the social environment. It agrees, after all, with the excellent maxim of do-as-you-would-be-done-by. Unfortunately, however, as we have seen, the Fabians were rather wide of the mark when they sought comfort in the Lamarckian elements of the Darwin/Wallace theory, which are now thought to be mistaken in animal and plant biology. It would also be wise for me to recognise that my Fabian proclivities can be traced readily to their source in parental upbringing. So they should, no doubt, be treated *cum grano salis*.

Our next question is to consider the extent to which the current categories of political debate may be seen as direct lineal descendants of the nineteenth-century debates clustering around the focus of the Darwinian theory. Certain new elements have entered the debate – most noticeably problems of environmentalism and the exhaustion of world resources; problems that were almost completely ignored in the nineteenth century. The feminist movement has grown, and, although certainly not wholly insignificant in the nineteenth century, has only come into its own in the post-War period. This movement has also coincided with greater educational opportunities and increased economic emancipation of women as well as major technological advances in contraceptive practices.

But the basic categories of political debate in most countries of the Western world still focus on the question of individualism *versus* egalitarianism, state planning *versus* private enterprise and capitalism *versus* socialism — all of which, as we have seen, focussed on the evolutionary debate. At every election in Australia, for example, we still hear the tired old arguments about the virtues and vices of such matters as social engineering, state capitalism, private industry and initiative, planning and *laissez faire*, and 'dole bludging'. The Labor Party when in office (1972-1975) introduced a national health scheme, coyly known as Medibank. Yet almost as soon as the Liberal Party took government, it sought to restore a system consisting of a multiplicity of competing private health insurance schemes. And this it did almost entirely for reasons related to basic political ideologies. It did not wait to see how the Medibank scheme operated in practice, or compare the health bill and the general health of the nation before and after the introduction of the new system. Rather extraordinary, one might say. But equally the Labor Government of 1972–1975 introduced many social welfare schemes, admirable in themselves without a doubt, but with little thought given to the cost of their implementation. The Sumner/Ward debate seems somehow to have set hard in Australia, some eighty or ninety years after the original controversy in America. And the tragedy of it is that both sides of the debate have virtually ignored some of the most important issues of the present day. Both seek to solve the social problems of the contemporary world with outworn categories: consumerism on the one hand, and large programs of public spending on the other. Both of these are predicated by the continuation of a profligate use of the world's resources. Our children and grandchildren will not thank us for this.

The last of the points which I promised for discussion at the outset of this concluding chapter was the perennial nature/nurture controversy. There is not perhaps any need to say a great deal about this. It is worth drawing attention, however, to the simple fact that the debate still continues so vehemently, often generating more heat than light owing to its conflation with political considerations. The left of the political spectrum, we recall, has generally been sympathetic to the nurture side of the controversy; the right has tended to emphasise nature. It might be thought, therefore, that since Lamarckism has been repudiated in biology, the right might have been able to claim some kind of victory in this rather sterile controversy. But this has by no means been so. As we have seen, human culture is in many respects highly Lamarckian. Consequently, the right wing, to claim victory in the debate, had to emphasise the animal nature of mankind — which was somewhat demeaning, to say the least. And the left wing could claim that in placing emphasis on the nurture side of things they were doing so with due recognition of the 'human' side of human nature, and were playing down the baser animal characteristics.

On the whole, it may be said that the left has been gradually winning the *political* debate in the last half century. More and more countries have come under Marxist dominion, and although the world abounds in military dictatorships, the idea of the paramount importance of government programs of social welfare seems to be widely accepted, even in capitalist America. Moreover, the relative success of the 'New Deal' of Franklin Roosevelt, and Keynesian economic theories, led to the acceptance of the need for, and the efficacy of, government manipulation of the market economy. Adam Smith, for all his genius, is not thought today to have provided a satisfactory program for the conduct of human affairs.

Thus the slogan of the French Revolution — 'liberty, equality, and fraternity' — which can be translated into the 'do-as-you-would-be-done-by' maxim without too much distortion, forms a strong component of the thought of the countries of the liberal West. Indeed, egalitarianism — at least, in the form of the doctrine of equality of opportunity — now constitutes a very significant element in our thinking, no matter how far the reality of the situation may differ from the mental image of it that liberals may profess. Yet the nature/nurture controversy continues to smoulder, moulding political thinking and erupting from time to time, as in the Jensen/Eysenck 'affair' which we considered briefly in Chapter 13. Darwinism *contra* Lamarckism is still an issue to contend with in the social sciences, if not in 'pure' biology.

The Darwinian Revolution, then, was unquestionably an episode of quite outstanding importance in the history of Western culture. It has touched every one of us, and the ripples it set in motion continue to disturb us today, although the huge waves of the nineteenth-century debate have largely subsided. In trying to understand our own being, and our own natures, we need to know as much as possible about the intellectual history of the times that have preceded our own — for those times have shaped our thinking in ways that one may at first be slow to suspect. Man should know his intellectual heritage. He may thereby become more aware of some of the innumerable factors that govern his opinions, tastes and passions. One of the strongest of such factors is found hooked untidily together by the threads of the Darwinian Revolution.

NOTES CHAPTER 24

1 See G. W. F. Hegel, *The Philosophy of History*, prefaces by Charles Hegel and the translator, J. Sibree, with a new Introduction by Professor C. J. Friedrich, Dover, New York, 1956, pp.1-102.

2 See the 'Afterword to the Second German Edition' of *Capital*: 'The mystification which dialectic suffers in Hegel's hands, by no means prevents him from being the first to present its general form of working in a comprehensive and conscious manner. With him it is standing on its head. It must be turned right side up again, if you would find the rational kernel within the mystical shell' (*Capital: A Critique of Political Economy by Karl Marx, Volume 1 The Process of Capitalist Production* translated from the third German edition by Samuel Moore and Edward Aveling, edited by Frederick Engels, International Publishers, New York, 1967, p.20).

3 Marx wrote: 'In the social production of their existence, men inevitably enter into definite relations, which are independent of their will, namely relations of production appropriate to a given stage in the

development of their material forces of production. The totality of these relations of production constitutes the economic structure of society, the real foundation, on which arises a legal and political superstructure and to which correspond definite forms of social consciousness. The mode of production of material life conditions the general process of social, political and intellectual life. *It is not the consciousness of men that determines their existence, but their social existence that determines their consciousness* [emphasis added]' (K. Marx, *A Contribution to the Critique of Political Economy*, Progress Publishers, Moscow, 1970, pp.20-21).

4   See, for example, B. G. Gale, 'Darwin and the concept of a struggle for existence: a study in the extrascientific origins of scientific ideas', *Isis*, Vol. 63, 1972, pp.321-344.

5   However, a recent detailed study by Edward Manier (*op. cit.*, Chapter 7, note 71) explores in detail some of the 'external' factors that may have influenced Darwin in the formulation of his theory. From this study it appears that 'external' considerations were of considerable importance for Darwin. (For a discussion of the historiographical categories of 'internal' and 'external', see below, page 365).

6   T. S. Kuhn, *The Structure of Scientific Revolutions*, Chicago University Press, Chicago, 1962.

7   The role of 'fashion' in science can not be dismissed out of hand. See W. O. Hagstrom, *The Scientific Community*, Basic Books, New York & London, 1965, pp.177-184; R. G. A. Dolby, 'The transmission of science', *History of Science*, Vol. 15, 1977, pp.1-43. It would seemingly be too weak a reed to have supported the whole of nineteenth-century evolutionism, and the Darwin/Wallace theory was empirically and conceptually successful in accounting for phenomena. Nevertheless, the social dimension of the evolutionary paradigm is an important factor.

8   Berlin's ideas were put forward in a series of lectures delivered at the National Gallery of Art in Washington under the aegis of the Bollingen Foundation, and broadcast by the Australian Broadcasting Commission in 1975. A summary statement of his views is to be found in his article 'The counter enlightenment' in P. P. Wiener (ed.), *Dictionary of the History of Ideas*, Vol. 2, Scribner, New York, 1973, pp.100-112. See also Berlin's *Vico and Herder: Two Studies in the History of Ideas*, Hogarth, London, 1976.

9   See W. H. Leatherdale, *The Role of Analogy, Model and Metaphor in Science*, N. Holland, Amsterdam, Oxford & New York, 1974, p.32 and *passim*.

10   Roughly speaking, this is the methodology of science described in the writings of Sir Karl Popper. (See K. R. Popper, *Conjectures and Refutations: The Growth of Scientific Knowledge*, 3rd edn, Routledge & Kegan Paul, London, 1969, pp.33-65, 253-292 and *passim*.) It is not difficult to bring forward objections to such an account, but it would not be appropriate to discuss the matter further here. A useful elementary discussion of Popperian methodology and its recent elaborations is to be found in A. F. Chalmers, *What is This Thing Called Science?* Queensland University Press, St Lucia, 1976.

11   See, for example, Margaret Mead's comparison of the peaceful Arapesh, the violent Mundugumor and the artistic Tchambuli tribes of New Guinea in *Sex and Temperament in Three Primitive Societies*, Routledge & Kegan Paul, London, 1935, or M. Mead (ed.), *Cooperation and Competition among Primitive Peoples*, McGraw-Hill, New York & London, 1937.

12   Many attempts have been made to do this, nevertheless. See W. D. Hudson (ed.), *The Is-Ought Question: A Collection of Papers on the Central Problem in Moral Philosophy*, Macmillan, London, 1969.

13   An example of a work seeking to place social theory on a scientific footing with the help of the Darwinian theory is found in W. Bagehot, *Physics and Politics: or Thoughts on the Application of the Principles of 'Natural Selection' and 'Inheritance' to Political Society*, London, 1867.

Appendix

Some historiographical considerations

It may be helpful to add here a few remarks concerning some of the problems that arise in connection with the writing of history, particularly intellectual history and history of science.

The word history has a three-fold meaning. It may refer to: (i) the events that occurred in the past; (ii) a text seeking to describe, understand or explain some aspect of man's past; (iii) the academic study of man's past.[1] There is also the term 'historiography', which can mean either the study of the history of historical writing or the act of writing works about the past. I shall use the term in the second of these senses.

Writing history might seem a relatively straightforward undertaking. All one has to do is to locate and read the historical documents relevant to a particular inquiry, abstract the portions that seem to be most important, and write a description of the past by synthesising the selected passages. But such a performance, although creating history of a kind, is usually regarded with little favour by professional historians, who refer to it contemptuously as 'scissors and paste' history or dismiss it as 'mere chronicle' rather than 'history proper'. Chronicle is obtained when events in the past are written down, usually in their chronological order, without any 'connective tissue' linking the separate events that are referred to or described. The chronicler makes little or no attempt to explain the events he describes and 'historical understanding' is not a major desideratum. History, on the other hand, is supposedly distinct from chronicle in that events are explained, the connections between them are given and, in the main, 'significant' events are selected for description and comment. 'Understanding' the past is an important consideration. Moreover, the historian may claim that the judicious selection of material, from the large amount that is available in the historical record, is something of an art for which special gifts are required. By appropriate selection and weaving of material into a smoothly flowing account, the historian may supposedly make the past comprehensible to his readers, the object of the exercise being both to explain and understand the past. And this, the historian would have us believe, requires gifts somewhat above those of the rank and file of humanity. However, it must be confessed that philosophers have found considerable difficulty in making a clear distinction between 'chronicle' and 'history',[2] and to some degree 'chronicle' is used today simply as a term of opprobrium by reviewers, in reference to historical works that for some reason displease them.

The position of history of science in the world of learning is still today somewhat ambivalent and insecure. Although science has obviously exerted a profound effect on the development of human culture, for many years professional historians have been chary about taking an interest in history of science, and even now links between general historians and historians of science are not as close as they should be. This is partly because general historians are not (in most cases) very familiar with the scientific disciplines and they feel ill at ease in the territory of the history of science. This can readily be understood, in view of the yawning gap between the humanities and the sciences that one commonly finds in the education systems of the English-speaking world. But there are, I believe, other possible explanations, arising from the way studies in the history of science first developed.

Much of the earlier work in the history of science was written by so-called 'scientist/historians' — men who were themselves practising scientists, or had been so in their younger days. They made many important contributions, but, as may be expected, they brought to their historical studies the value systems of research scientists rather than those of professional historians. What effect did this have? Until fairly recently most scientists were what one might call 'inductivist/empiricists' — particularly in the late nineteenth and early twentieth centuries, when the scientist/historians dominated history of science. According to the inductivist/empiricist philosophy of science, in its crudest and simplest form, a scientist operates by making observations and carrying out experiments, using the data thus obtained as a basis for formulating hypotheses, which may then be further tested. Well-confirmed hypotheses may in time be accorded the status of laws, and these may be explained by suitable theories. This is a caricature of an inductivist methodology, but it cannot be denied that many earlier writers on science supposed that scientific ideas could be educed more or less directly from experience; they spoke with some reverence of the inductive road to scientific truth.[3] It will not surprise us, then, if the scientist/historians looked at the history of science from the inductivist perspective and represented past science as if it had been conducted according to an inductivist methodology. That is, they represented the history of science as a grand accumulation of fact and theory, with each scientist making his individual contribution to the total structure.

There were also features of the scientist/historians that arose from the particular social system in which they were trained and in which they functioned. Scientists are concerned with pushing forward the boundaries of their subject,[4] so they must necessarily feel dissatisfied with the previous state of knowledge – otherwise there would not be much reason for conducting scientific research. Consequently, though not necessarily supposing that they have arrived at 'the truth', scientists usually believe that their knowledge offers an advance over the knowledge of their predecessors. They know more and have 'better' theories than their precursors. Moreover, they are rewarded (in terms of jobs and peer-group approval) according to their success in producing new knowledge. So for both philosophical and social reasons, the scientist is committed to the worth of the most advanced state of knowledge and he regards past knowledge as inadequate, insufficient or wrong.

Such presuppositions colour the work of the scientist/historian, giving him a simple recipe for writing the history of science. One looks back at the past and arranges events in an order such that ideas, theories and techniques are seen to evolve smoothly, culminating in the present state of affairs, which offers a suitable vantage point from which one may appraise the worth of earlier scientific achievements. Thus one highlights those earlier scientists whose contributions seemingly added directly to the present state of knowledge, but one plays down the role of those whose work has now been rejected or superseded or which led in a direction that is no longer favoured.

The work of the scientist/historians is often described by the somewhat unexpected term 'Whiggish', following an idea put forward in 1931 by Herbert Butterfield (1900-), in his influential essay *The Whig Interpretation of History*. Butterfield wrote of:

> the tendency in many historians to write on the side of Protestants and Whigs, to praise revolutions provided they have been successful, to emphasize certain principles of progress in the past and to produce a story which is the ratification if not the glorification of the present.[5]

According to this view, the Whig historians (such as Macaulay or Trevelyan) saw history as a grand evolutionary process culminating in the present, so that the historian occupied a privileged viewpoint from which he might appraise the past. It will be seen that the work of the scientist/historians, referred to above, fits Butterfield's description rather well. For this reason, much of the older historiography of science is often described as 'Whiggish'. We can see why it might now have rather little appeal to professional writers of general history.

For most historians of science as well, Whiggish historiography of science is now a complete anathema, for – taking their cue from general historians (such as Butterfield) – they have come to believe that it is unreasonable to judge the past by any standards other than those of the past.[6] If the historian's task is to seek to *understand* the past, he will not be able to do so if he seeks to use present criteria of evaluation. Rather, one should try to see past problems from the point of view of the men and women of the past. Or, in the context of the historiography of science, one should seek to understand how particular scientific investigations meshed with the context of their times, and how they fitted into the historical development of science. Historical anachronism should be avoided. But how *is* this anachronism to be avoided? How are the gulfs separating the centuries to be crossed?

An answer of a general kind to such questions has been provided by the Oxford historian and philosopher, R. G. Collingwood (1889-1943), in his posthumous work, *The Idea of History*. In this volume Collingwood claimed that historical inquiry required 'the re-enactment of past experience'. He wrote:

> When a man thinks historically, he has before him certain documents or relics of the past. His business is to discover what the past was which has left these relics behind it. For example, the relics are certain written words; and in that case he has to discover what the person who wrote those words meant by them. This means discovering the thought . . . which he expressed by them. To discover what this thought was, the historian must think it again for himself.[7]

Collingwood sought to make his view of the matter clear by means of this illustration:

> Suppose . . . [the historian] is reading a passage of an ancient philosopher . . . [He] must know the language in a philological sense and be able to construe; but by doing that he has not yet understood the passage as an historian of philosophy must understand it. In order to do that, he must see what the philosophical problem was, of which his author is here stating his solution. He must think that problem out for himself, see what possible solutions of it might be offered, and see why this particular philosopher chose that solution instead of another. This means re-thinking for himself the thought of his author, and nothing short of that will make him the historian of that author's philosophy.[8]

In other words, to write good history, the historian should seek to *empathise* with the subject about whom he is writing. He should seek to place himself in his shoes, so to speak; he should re-think his thoughts or re-enact his experiences. This will vivify the historical writing and will help prevent historical anachronism creeping in.

Collingwood's program for the historiographer has excited much critical discussion in the literature of philosophy of history.[9] But it does not now stand in very high favour. If I try to empathise with (say) the thought of Napolean, I cannot but help do so with my mind loaded with all its twentieth-century presuppositions. Just as it is not really possible for me to think like a Chinese person, because of our different cultural backgrounds, so it is impossible for me really to think in the manner of a man of the early nineteenth century. And even if I were successful by diligent soaking in the literature of Napoleonic France, or simply by chance, how could I *know* that I had been successful? What are criteria for successful Collingwoodian acts of empathy?

Such criticisms obviously have much strength, although with studies in the history of science they may lose some of their force. If, for example, I work my way through the geometrical proofs of Newton's *Principia* I must to some degree be re-thinking Newton's thoughts; but not entirely. In any case, in many ways more interesting for the history of science are the intellectual steps that led Newton to his new system, rather than the polished product, the *Principia* (although obviously that is important too). The historian of science is interested in all the factors leading to Newton's discoveries; the social and intellectual conditions for the production of *Principia*; the scientific and cultural effects of its publication; as well as the content of the work. So the task of the historian of science is much more than the intellectual comprehension of a particular text, and although a Collingwoodian program may be part of the story it cannot, I maintain, be the whole.

We may note that Collingwood's book is entitled *The* Idea *of History*, and the word 'idea' in the title is not, I suggest, a mere accident. For Collingwood as a philosopher stood squarely within the idealist camp, in opposition to the materialist view. Consequently, he was much concerned to trace out the development of ideas in history and his general approach might be described as 'intellectualist'. Indeed his whole approach to historical investigations was related to this concern with ideas, and philosophy and historiography merged in his work.

Somewhat akin to the work of Collingwood — certainly contemporary with it, but not, I believe, connected to form a single historical school — was the work of A. O. Lovejoy (1873-1962), founder of the 'history of ideas' movement and the *Journal of the History of Ideas*. This journal was established in 1940 to 'foster studies which will examine the evolution of ideas in the development and inter-relations of several fields of historical study — the history of philosophy, of literature and the arts, of the natural and social sciences, of religion, and of political and social movements . . .'.[10] Lovejoy taught at Johns Hopkins University in the United States, where in the 1920s and 1930s there was an active group of scholars interested in exploring intellectual history according to the program quoted above. Lovejoy's major work was *The Great Chain of Being: A Study of the History of an Idea*,[11] the introduction to which gives us a statement of his general program for studies in the history of ideas.[12]

The historian of ideas, said Lovejoy, is concerned to deal with categories such as:

(a) 'Implicit or incompletely explicit *assumptions*, or more or less *unconscious mental habits*, operating in the thoughts of an individual or generation';[13]
(b) 'Dialectical motives . . . much of the thinking of an individual, a school, or even a generation, dominated and determined by one or another turn of reasoning, trick of logic, [or] methodological assumption';[14]
(c) 'Susceptibilities to diverse kinds of metaphysical pathos';[15]
(d) 'Philosophical semantics';[16]
(e) 'Single specific proposition[s] or "principle[s]" expressly enunciated by the most influential or early European philosophers . . . and . . . the processes which constitute their history'.[17]

The doctrine of the Great Chain of Being was supposedly an example of category 'e'; and Lovejoy set out to give the history of this idea in detail in his book.

Lovejoy also referred to what he called 'unit-ideas'. It is sometimes said that all novels revolve round a very limited number of themes, such as love, revenge or ambition; the number of plots is finite. Similarly, Lovejoy supposed, the history of thought rings the changes on a very limited number of basic intellectual components, although these may manifest themselves at any given time in a whole range of apparently distinct fields. Thus the 'classical' conception of order in the eighteenth century might make itself felt in architecture, art, landscape gardening, military tactics, natural history, and many other areas. The task of the historian of ideas should be to seek to trace out these 'unit ideas' through the course of history and in all the disparate fields in which they appear. In the modern idiom, the history of ideas is an 'inter-disciplinary study' *par excellence*.

To be more precise, in Lovejoy's words the study of the history of ideas is:

> especially concerned with the manifestations of specific unit-ideas in the collective thought of large groups of persons, not merely in the doctrines or opinions of a small number of profound thinkers or eminent writers. It seeks to investigate the effects of the sort of factors which it has ... isolated, in the beliefs, prejudices, pieties, tastes, aspirations, current among the educated classes through, it may be, a whole generation, or many generations. It is, in short, most interested in ideas which attain a wide diffusion, which become a part of the stock of many minds.[18]

It will be appreciated that what has been attempted in this book falls broadly within the domain of the history of ideas as understood by Lovejoy. For evolutionism may indeed be described as one of the 'implicit or incompletely explicit *assumptions*, or more or less *unconscious mental habits*' that operated on a whole generation (or more) in the nineteenth century. Moreover, we have on occasions sought to show how particular patterns of thought manifested themselves in apparently disparate fields at particular periods of history. (See, for example, page 14.) So when this text has dealt with intellectual history — with the history of ideas — it has been doing so (partly at least) according to the program of a particular historiographical school. And it is only fair that this be stated now. This being the case, one should perhaps draw the reader's attention to some of the difficulties that the historian of ideas has to face and some of the criticisms that have been made of his school.

I think many readers will agree that the history of ideas is an inherently interesting area of inquiry, perhaps more so than older, more strongly established branches of historiography such as political or military history. But this does not mean that certain inherent difficulties associated with an historiographical program such as that envisaged by Lovejoy can be disregarded.[19]

The chief difficulty seems to be that the discipline of the history of ideas is prone to undue subjectivity on the part of the historiographer. It is, no doubt quite easy to discern a similarity between the ordered structure of the Linnaean taxonomy and the sonata form of a Haydn symphony; or between the evolutionary social and political philosophy of Herbert Spencer and the musicological theories of Parry. But are these supposed similarities really an expression of intellectual community in an objective sense, or manifestations of the psyche of the historiographer seeking to find graceful historical patterns and expressions of 'unit-ideas' come what may? It must be admitted that such patternings of thought, although pleasing, may, on occasions, be artefacts of the historian. But because mistakes may be made, it does not follow that there can be no intellectual community between disparate areas of thought or that it is technically impossible to identify this communality. In any case, critics will usually be pleased to point to the weak points in the arguments advanced, and the dialectical interplay between historian and critic should serve to generate a reasonable degree of verisimilitude.

Even so, objections to the history of ideas should not simply be brushed aside without careful consideration of their cogency. It is clear that when we see the same word in the texts of different centuries, it does not follow that the word had the same meaning in the separate cases, or that it had the same meaning as today. If, for example, we see the word 'natural' in an eighteenth-century text, it would be foolish to suppose that we can immediately give it a modern meaning such as 'normal'. Thus a Collingwoodian re-thinking of the eighteenth-century idea of 'natural' is not something that can be undertaken by the simplistic historiographer; and the historian of ideas must keep his wits about him if he is to avoid historiographical solecisms.

On the other hand, it would seem equally foolish to suppose that the thought of the past is wholly cut off from us, and that we have no way at all of rethinking past thoughts. Here the techniques of the philologist come into play. The past may be partly opaque to us, and the further back we go the more difficult the task of the historian of ideas may become and the less successful he may be. But it is not an enterprise that is totally illusory: we have some measure of access to past thoughts, as we do to past events.

An additional problem that makes the history of ideas a particularly slippery area of inquiry arises with 'causation'. In this text we have considered some of the 'influences' of Darwinism on political theory, literature, music, and so on. And the reader has perhaps been led to suppose that there were direct causal connections between the thought of Darwin and the thought of, say, Marx, von Treitschke or Thomas Hardy. But we have also spoken of the grand cosmic evolutionary philosophies of nature that were spawned in the nineteenth century, that of Herbert Spencer being perhaps the grandest and most cosmic of them all. Thus, as we have seen, the question arises of whether the evolutionism of the late nineteenth century sprang directly from Darwinism, or whether both were the product of some much more deep-seated causes. If so, what were these causes, and how, precisely, did they bring about the evolutionism about which we have spoken, in all its many forms?

These kinds of problems have been brought into focus by the work of the French scholar, Michel Foucault. He underscores the difficulty of demarcating the history of science from the history of opinions and belief, or the history of knowledge from that of imagination. He emphasises the difficulty, for the historian of ideas, of knowing what he is writing about. Is it, Foucault asks, the history of what has been known, acquired or forgotten, the history of mental forms or the history of their interference? Should one be writing the history of the thoughts shared by the men of a particular period or culture? Is the aim to describe a collective mind? Are the thoughts of a period to be regarded as the signs of something else (such as social relations, political or economic situations), or their results? Are they the 'refractions' of these other entities through human consciousness, or their symbolic expressions?[20]

These are pertinent questions, for which, I fear, the historian of ideas has no simple answers. They arise, I suggest, with particular force when one attempts to treat ideas as causes — which the historian of ideas, tracing supposed intellectual influences from one domain to another, may be particularly liable to do. And for the materialist philosophers, among whose ranks we may normally include the Marxist philosophers of history and Marxist historiographers, the notion of ideas exerting causal influences of this kind is peculiarly repugnant.

But do such criticisms totally invalidate the program of the historian of ideas, or can elements of it be maintained? I would agree that the notion of a finite set of unit-ideas is an unwarranted hypothesis, but the suggestion that ideas — through human agents — cannot be agents of historical change seems curious to me, no matter how metaphysically distasteful the notion may be to a materialist. This is not to suggest, of course, that I subscribe to some theory of autonomous 'ideas', in some Platonic or Hegelian sense. Clearly, a thought requires a thinker. Even if written in a book and preserved in a library, it will languish there for ever unless recovered and used again as a further spur to action. This much one may readily grant. But to suppose that thoughts or ideas cannot be transferred from one mind to another through written or spoken language seems patently absurd. And to suppose, therefore, that ideas expressed thrrough human actions cannot have a kind of life and history of their own, traceable (albeit imperfectly) through their expression in literary form, also seems quite contrary to what I understand of human nature and society. A man can have an idea and convey that idea to his fellow-man, whose actions may be effected as a result. And the idea may gradually spread through a community, taking slightly different forms in the minds of each of the members of the community.

All this leaves Foucault's questions as yet unanswered. I believe such difficulties did not unduly concern the early exponents of the history of ideas school such as Arthur Lovejoy, or did not occur to them. But I would say that the historian of ideas is *not* aiming to describe some kind of Jungian[21] collective mind. There is no such entity. Rather he *is* seeking to describe the history of thoughts shared by the people of a particular period or culture. The thoughts may be, in part, determined by social relations or political and economic situations. But reciprocally, they may have influence on these. It must be granted, however, as I have previously indicated, that at this point the situation is rather hazy.

Although one may disallow any Marxist/materialist claim that ideas cannot exert 'influence' in human history, this does not mean that one should overlook Marxist contributions of fundamental importance to the historiography of science. They have contributed chiefly through their legitimate emphasis on the social dimensions of scientific inquiry, and in recent years this has come to be a very significant area of the total domain of historiography of science. In the 1930s, for example, the academic world was somewhat startled to learn from the Russian academician, Boris Hessen (1883-1937?), that Newton's work could be much better understood if one recognised that it was in part directed towards certain socio-economic ends.[22] Thus Hessen went through Newton's *Principia*, showing how the different sections were relevant to such matters as gunnery (the calculations on projectiles), navigation, shipbuilding (the calculations on the statics of floating bodies) and other topics of social and economic significance.

Much of Hessen's case is now thought to be overstated, but enough of it remains to convince us that an adequate understanding of the history of science cannot be achieved if the social dimension is ignored. His work was followed by other Marxist historians of science, most notably J. D. Bernal (1901-1971) in his massive volume *The Social Function of Science* (1939),[23] and since the War many more writers have sought to investigate the social structure of science and the role (dare I say influence?) of social factors in the history of science. Science has become an object of sociological scrutiny by non-Marxist sociologists such as R. K. Merton (1910-),[24] as much as Marxist writers.

This interest in the social *milieu* within which science operates has led to a fairly long-drawn-out controversy between the advocates of so-called 'internal' historiography of science, and the 'externalists'. At first the more traditionally-minded historians of science maintained that they need take no account of factors 'external' to the development of scientific knowledge (such as economic imperatives and questions of social control within the scientific community). These questions might be interesting but, the 'internalists' maintained, there was no need to take them into account as one sought to understand the science of the past. It was enough to go through the early scientific papers and monographs and show how scientific theories gradually developed over time. To be sure, a few personal anecdotes might be thrown in. It might spice one's narrative to include the tit-bit of information that 'Descartes liked women well enough to have a daughter by one'.[25] But such matters were thought quite irrelevant to an understanding of the nature of the great mathematician's intellectual accomplishments. Doubtless this *is* an irrelevant 'external' factor in this instance, but to take a more serious example: can we really ignore the social structure of eighteenth-century Sweden as one of the factors leading to the establishment of Linnaeus's theory? I think not. At the very least, it is a question that needs to be looked into.

Opinion now seems to be fairly settled that 'external' factors cannot be omitted if we wish to have a complete picture of science, or of the history of science. Consequently, the work of the historian of science is now considered to be very much more than reading through old books and journal articles and doing a scissors and paste job on them to present an historical account of the development of scientific theory.[26] This being so, it would seem necessary to achieve some kind of integration of 'internal' and 'external' historiography if we are to have a complete understanding of the history of science and an explanation of how science has reached its present state of development.[27]

But how is this integration to be achieved? We may note that the difficulty which we have discerned in relation to studies of the history of science has its parallels in studies of contemporary science, where people interested in understanding the contemporary scene are also seeking to achieve an integration of both 'internal' and 'external' factors. I would say this problem remains unresolved, or is, if you prefer, an active area of research, both in relation to studies in the history of science and contemporary sociology of science. Philosophical analyses of science having become tangled beyond all belief, and, having failed to give an account that meshes satisfactorily with either the current scientific practice or the history of science as it appears to historians, we find philosophers turning to the sociologist for aid and comfort, and so a whole new discipline is beginning to take shape, under the head, 'sociology of knowledge', which seeks to show how social factors act as determinants in the production of scientific knowledge,[28] and how the knowledge produced has social effects. If this program yields success, we may use our understanding of the present production of scientific knowledge as a lamp to guide us through the maze of the history of science. At this stage it is too early to say how studies in the sociology of knowledge will develop, and whether they will serve as a suitable guide to the history of science. One can say, however, that if the theory of the contemporary production of scientific knowledge is faulty we will undoubtedly end up with an unsatisfactory historiography of science, as did the scientist/historians who used an inductivist methodology in their historical researches.

So the question of the 'correct' method of writing the history of science remains unanswered and in my view no final answer can be given, or should be expected. Indeed, it would be naive to suppose that there can be any 'correct' and certain methods of procedure. There can be different ways of proceeding, according to the kinds of questions that are asked at any given time, and we cannot offer any firm guidance about the questions that may be asked in the future.

But for now, as I see it, the task of the historian remains that of discovering, by whatever means he can, the events that occurred in the past, piecing these together to form an intelligible account of what happened in the past. In the history of science the 'events' will often be intellectual – particular ideas occurring in people's minds at different times. These can only be determined indirectly, through traces left in the form of diaries, scientific journals, pieces of apparatus preserved in museums and the like. Also 'external' features will have to be taken into account when one seeks to determine the nature of the ideas that men have entertained in the past. Complete certainty in the historical account cannot be expected, and so the history of science, as with other branches of history, is constantly being rewritten. It may be that a well-founded theory of the production of scientific knowledge will be of inestimable value to the historian of science, but we must also expect – on past experience – that such a theory will not be found to be wholly satisfactory and will constantly be modified. So I do not expect to see the completion of any branch of the historiography of science, with or without the consideration of 'external' factors.

All this may leave the reader in a somewhat unsettled frame of mind. I have come up with no 'clear and distinct' prescriptions for the study of intellectual history or the history of science, for I do not believe that such rules can be laid down to satisfy all writers at all times and in all places.

However, it may help the reader to know some of the issues that underlie the present historiographical controversies – issues that should be known to him if he chooses to embark on his own historical investigation, and which should be borne in mind in reading this text.

NOTES APPENDIX

1   See A. Marwick, 'Introduction to the history of science', in A. Marwick, C. A. Russell & D. Goodman, *Science and Technology since 1800: The Historical Perspective*, Open University Press, Milton Keynes, 1973, pp.5-37 (p.8).

2   See A. C. Danto, 'Mere chronicle and history proper', *The Journal of Philosophy*, Vol. 50, 1953, pp.173-182.

3   It is noteworthy that while Darwin himself maintained that he worked on true Baconian principles, the geologist Adam Sedgwick, in reviewing *The Origin*, expressed his 'detestation of the theory' in part because it 'deserted the inductive track – the only track that leads to physical truth' ([A. Sedgwick,] 'Objections to Mr Darwin's theory of the origin of species', *The Spectator*, March 24, 1860, reprinted in D. L. Hull, *Darwin and his Critics*, Harvard University Press, Cambridge, Mass., 1973, pp.159-166 [at p.164]).

4   I use here a somewhat imperialistic metaphor, such as was favoured by some of the earlier scientist/historians. See, for example, A. Geikie, *The Founders of Geology*, 2nd edn, Macmillan, London, 1905, p.2. The Introduction to this work (reprinted 1962) gives an admirable statement of the historiographical presuppositions of an influential scientist/historian.

5   H. Butterfield, *The Whig Interpretation of History*, Penguin, Harmondsworth, 1973, p.9 (1st edn, London, 1931).

6   For a forthright critique of the historiography of the scientist/historians, see J. Agassi, 'Towards an historiography of science', *History and Theory*, Beiheft 2, 1963.

7   R. G. Collingwood, *The Idea of History*, O.U.P., Oxford, 1961, pp.282-283 (1st edn, 1946).

8   *Ibid.*, p.283.

9   See, for example, M. Krausz (ed.), *Critical Essays on the Philosophy of R. G. Collingwood*, Clarendon Press, Oxford, 1972.

10   This pronouncement appears on the cover of every issue of *The Journal of the History of Ideas*.

11   This book originated as a series of lectures delivered at Harvard University in 1933. It was first published in 1936 and was republished (New York) in 1960. See note 13, below.

12   See also A. O. Lovejoy, 'Reflections on the history of ideas', *The Journal of the History of Ideas*, Vol. 1, 1940, pp.3-23; P. P. Wiener, 'Some problems and methods in the history of ideas', *Journal of the History of Ideas*, Vol. 22, 1961, pp.531-548.

13   A. O. Lovejoy, *The Great Chain of Being*, Harper & Row, New York, 1960, p.7 (italics in original).

14   *Ibid.*, p.10.

15   *Ibid.*, p.11.

16   *Ibid.*, p.14.

17   *Ibid.*

18   *Ibid.*, p.19.

19   The historiographical solecisms frequently committed by historians of ideas have been brought into view in an important article by Quentin Skinner: 'Meaning and understanding in the history of ideas', *History and Theory*, Vol. 8, 1969, pp.3-53.

20   M. Foucault, 'Politics and the study of discourse', *Ideology and Consciousness*, Vol. 3, 1978, pp.7-26.

21   In his various psychoanalytical writings, Carl Jung (1875-1961) supposed, on the basis of common dream patterns and the common features of many traditional mythologies, that there is a 'universal collective unconscious', of which our own individual unconscious minds are but particular manifestations.

22   B. Hessen, 'The social and economic roots of Newton's 'Principia' ', in N. I. Bukharin *et al.*, *Science at the Cross Roads: Papers presented to the International Congress of the History of Science and Technology held in London from June 29th to July 3rd, 1931 by the delegates of the U.S.S.R.*, London, 1932, pp.1-62 (republished Cass, London, 1971).

23   J. D. Bernal, *The Social Function of Science*, Routledge, London, 1939.

24   See R. K. Merton, *Science, Technology and Society in Seventeenth Century England*, Fertig, New York, 1970 (1st published in *Osiris*, Vol. 4, 1938); N. W. Storer (ed.), *The Sociology of Science: Theoretical and Empirical Investigations*, Chicago University Press, Chicago, 1973.

25   See E. T. Bell, *Men of Mathematics*, 2nd paperback printing, Simon & Schuster, New York, 1962, p.42 (1st edn, 1937).

26   As P. B. Medawar has rightly pointed out, the published scientific paper usually says very little about the processes of discovery, so if one concentrates only on the published scientific literature one gains a very unbalanced picture of the history of science: 'Is the scientific paper a fraud?', *The Listener*, September 12, 1963.

27   For a recent review of the problem, see R. Johnston, 'Contextual knowledge: a model for the overthrow of the internal–external dichotomy in science', *The Australian and New Zealand Journal of Sociology*, Vol. 12, 1976, pp.193-203.

28   The following volumes are illustrative of this field: K. Mannheim, *Essays on the Sociology of Knowledge*, Routledge, London, 1952; B. Barnes, *Scientific Knowledge and Sociological Theory*, Routledge & Kegan Paul, London, 1972; and R. Whitley (ed.), *Social Processes of Scientific Development*, Routledge & Kegan Paul, London, 1974.

Suggestions for Further Reading

As will be clear from the main body of the text of this book, and the accompanying notes, the literature on our subject is very extensive. And one of the chief aims has been to try to reduce this wealth of material to manageable proportions. But for people with interests still not satisfied, the following notes may be useful as further signposts into the jungle of the secondary literature on Darwin, Darwinism, evolution and evolutionism. It should be noted that only books are referred to here, not the great number of journal articles of various kinds that are available.

For a general elementary history of biology, well illustrated, but not intending to be a profound historical contribution, the reader may consult Gordon Rattray Taylor's *The Science of Life* (Thames & Hudson, London, 1963). A much more detailed work is A. E. Nordenskiold's *The History of Biology* (A. A. Knopf, Inc., New York, 1928). Written by a Swedish author, this book gives perhaps undue favour to the work of Linnaeus, but it is a work of very considerable scholarship and authority, and even now offers one of the few attempts available in English to penetrate the jungle of German Nature Philosophy and the relations of this to biological thought. Another general history of biology that can be recommended is F. S. Bodenheimer, *The History of Biology: An Introduction* (Wm Dawson & Sons, London, 1958). General surveys for the eighteenth, nineteenth, and twentieth centuries respectively are: P. C. Ritterbush, *Overtures to Biology: The Speculations of Eighteenth-Century Naturalists* (Yale University Press, New Haven, 1964); W. Coleman, *Biology in the Nineteenth Century: Problems of Form, Function and Transformation* (John Wiley & Sons, Inc., New York, 1971*); G. E. Allen, *Life Science in the Twentieth Century* (John Wiley & Sons, Inc., New York, 1975*).

For general instructions to the theory of evolution one may turn to almost any modern elementary biological text. But an admirable, balanced discussion is to be found in J. M. Smith's *The Theory of Evolution* (Penguin Books, Harmondsworth, 1958*). A more recent survey that can be recommended is C. Patterson, *Evolution* (British Museum [Natural History]

---

*Items marked with asterisks are believed to be still in print at the time of writing. But publishers of the *first* English editions only are listed here.

& University of Queensland Press, London & St Lucia, 1978*).

For discussion of the Darwinian Revolution as a whole, I suggest Gertrude Himmelfarb's *Darwin and the Darwinian Revolution* (Chatto & Windus, London, 1959*). The author is a student of intellectual history with particular interests in the nineteenth century rather than a specialised historian of science or a practising biologist. The earlier reviews of the book tended to deprecate it and made much of the fact that it was not written by a person with specialised biological knowledge, and also, perhaps, because it dared to write critically of Darwin on occasions. But opinion now seems to be swinging in Ms Himmelfarb's favour, and her book is perhaps the best of the surveys of the general impact of Darwin's work on British thought and culture that are available. Also important as a general representation of the Darwinian Revolution (though chiefly concerned with the impact of Darwin's work on biology) is L. Eiseley, *Darwin's Century: Evolution and the Men who Discovered It* (Doubleday & Company, Inc., New York, 1958*). Eiseley's book is particularly informative for the history of anthropology, as is J. C. Greene's *The Death of Adam: Evolution and Its Impact on Western Thought* (Iowa State University Press, 1959*). Somewhat similar in character is G. Hardin's *Nature and Man's Fate* (Rinehart & Co., New York & Toronto, 1959*), although it should be noted that some of Hardin's interpretations have been questioned in certain areas, particularly on the influence of Fleeming Jenkin on Darwin's theories.

For a good book of readings from both primary and secondary sources on Darwin, with further bibliographical suggestions, I recommend P. Appleman (ed.), *Darwin: A Norton Critical Edition*, (W. W. Norton & Company, Inc., New York, 1970*); for a useful volume restricted to primary sources, emphasising particularly the relations between Darwinism and theology, see H. Y. Vanderpool (ed.), *Darwin and Darwinism: Revolutionary Insights Concerning Man, Nature, Religion, and Society* (D. Heath & Company, Lexington, 1973*). But probably the best treatment of Darwin and theology, setting out to *teach* the subject rather than merely display the texts, is J. H. Brooke *et al.*, *The Crisis of Evolution* (The Open University Press, Milton Keynes, 1974*). This book also has a very clear account of the biological background to Darwin's work.

No one has yet attempted a full-scale biography of Darwin, combined with a theoretical analysis of his work. In other words, he still awaits the definitive historical study. But there are, of course, excellent studies of restricted scope, and of these Sir Gavin de Beer's *Charles Darwin: Evolution by Natural Selection* (Thomas Nelson & Sons, London, 1963*) still stands at the head of the list, although his account of the discovery of the theory of evolution by natural selection has been superseded. Illustrated studies of Darwin's life and work that will be well received in school libraries are: J. S. Huxley & H. B. D. Kettlewell, *Charles Darwin and his World* (Thames & Hudson, London, 1965); A. Moorehead, *Darwin and the 'Beagle'* (Hamilton, London, 1969*). An interesting volume by M. T. Ghiselin *The Triumph of the Darwinian*

Method, (University of California Press, Berkeley & Los Angeles, 1969*) offers much information on Darwin's later works that is not readily available elsewhere, but the author's attempt to prove that all of Darwin's work is a perfect exemplification of Sir Karl Popper's falsificationist methodology of science becomes somewhat less than convincing at times. The standard work on Darwin's post-1859 period is now P. J. Vorzimmer's *Charles Darwin, The Years of Controversy: The Origin of Species and its Critics 1859-82* (University of London Press, London, 1972*). The critics' reception of Darwin can also be gauged from D. L. Hull, *Darwin and his Critics: The Reception of Darwin's Theory of Evolution by the Scientific Community* (Harvard University Press, Cambridge, Mass., 1974*). Another recent book that deals exhaustively with a particular aspect of Darwin's work is H. E. Gruber & P. H. Barrett, *Darwin on Man: A Psychological Study of Scientific Creativity,* (E. P. Dutton & Co. Inc. & Wildwood House, New York & London, 1974*). It should be noted here that Gruber described a very early version of Darwin's theory — based on a doctrine of 'monads' — which is to be found only in his notebooks and not in his published writings. I have not thought it necessary to include a discussion of this in the present introductory survey, but interested readers may consult Gruber and Barrett (pp. 129-149). Also of considerable importance in relation to Darwin's early thinking is: E. Manier, *The Young Darwin and his Cultural Circle: A study of Influences which Helped Shape the Language and Logic of the First Drafts of the Theory of Natural Selection* (D. Reidel Publishing Co., Dordrecht & Boston, Mass., 1978*).

Returning now to consider some of the aspects relating to the first section of the present book, it should be noted that for reasons of space I have chosen not to consider the aspects of the history of embryology that relate to the Darwinian Revolution although they are important. For those interested in this area, one may recommend E. B. Gasking, *Investigations into Generation: 1651-1828* (Hutchinson & Co. Ltd, London, 1967); J. M. Oppenheimer, *Essays in the History of Embryology and Biology* (MIT Press, Cambridge, Mass., 1967*) and S. J. Gould, *Ontogeny and Phylogeny* (The Belknap Press of Harvard University Press Cambridge [*Mass.*] *& London, 1977*).* Important discussions of pre-Darwinian thought are also contained in B. Glass, O. Temkin & W. L. Straus Jr (eds), *Forerunners of Darwin: 1745-1859* (The Johns Hopkins Press, Baltimore, 1959*).

Unfortunately I can recommend no general history of taxonomy, but there is a definitive study of the history of the concept of the Great Chain of Being in Western thought: A. O. Lovejoy, *The Great Chain of Being: A Study of the History of an Idea,* (Harvard University Press, Cambridge, Mass., 1936*). An authoritative study of Linnaeus is available in English: J. L. Larsen, *Reason and Experience: The Representation of Natural Order in the Work of Carl Von Linné* (University of California Press, Berkeley, 1971*). But the arguments here are somewhat difficult to follow and readers may prefer the more popular illustrated volume by W. Blunt: *The Compleat Naturalist: A Life of*

Linnaeus (Collins, London, 1971*). Buffon is considered in one of the essays contained in the Glass (*et al.*) volume, but a useful survey of his ideas by O. E. Fellows and S. F. Millikan probably offers a more suitable introduction to his thought: *Buffon*, (Twayne Publishers, Inc., New York, 1972*). Buffon's geological ideas (which have not been mentioned in our present study, although they are certainly of some importance in setting the scene for nineteenth-century evolutionism) are well described in F. C. Haber, *The Age of the World: Moses to Darwin* (The Johns Hopkins Press, Baltimore, 1959).

As stated in Chapter 3, the literature on Lamarck available in English is not very extensive and what is available is sometimes rather partisan in its approach. H. G. Cannon's *Lamarck and Modern Genetics* (Manchester University Press, Manchester, 1959) is celebrated for its attempt to vindicate Lamarck's reputation and show up deficiencies in the orthodox theory of evolution. The volume certainly makes interesting reading, although it is not generally considered that Cannon succeeded in establishing any concrete evidence for the Lamarckian principle of the inheritance of acquired characteristics. But see also Cannon's *Evolution of Living things* (Manchester University Press, Manchester, 1958). An attractive sketch of Lamarck's work is to be found in C. C. Gillispie's *The Edge of Objectivity* (Princeton University Press & London University Press, Princeton & London, 1960*) in Chapter 7, which also discusses the interaction of Lamarck and Cuvier. A recent study by R. W. Burkhardt provides the most authoritative account available in English: *The Spirit of System: Lamarck and Evolutionary Biology* (Yale University Press, New Haven & London, 1977*). See also the article on Lamarck in C. C. Gillispie (ed.), *Dictionary of Scientific Biography* (13 vols., Scribner, New York, 1970-1976*). There is a good treatment of Cuvier in W. Coleman, *Georges Cuvier, Zoologist: A Study in the History of Evolution Theory* (Harvard University Press, Cambridge, Mass., 1964). The account of Cuvier given in Chapter 3 of the present work is based on ideas found in the writings of the French philosopher/historian, Michel Foucault. But Foucault's ideas are extremely difficult to unravel without many readings of his texts. A much more approachable account which follows the interpretations mapped out by Foucault is to be found in F. Jacob, *The Logic of Living Systems: A History of Heredity* (Allen Lane, London, 1974* [1st French edn, Éditions Gallimard, Paris, 1970*]).

There has been much recent interest in Lyell, and a full-scale biography of him is being prepared by L. G. Wilson. The first volume (of three) is available as: *Charles Lyell: The Years to 1841: The Revolution in Geology* (Yale University Press, New Haven & London, 1971*). This study, when completed, will supersede E. Bailey, *Charles Lyell* (Thomas Nelson & Sons Ltd, London, 1962). Readers should also consult the facsimile edition of Lyell's *Principles* (Johnson Reprint Corporation, New York, 1969*), which has a valuable introduction by M. J. S. Rudwick. Rudwick has written several important articles on Lyell, including an essay on Lyell's ideas on the age of the Earth in C. J. Schneer (ed.), *Toward a History of Geology* (MIT Press,

Cambridge, Mass. & London, 1969*). Also important is the collection of papers to be found in *The British Journal for the History of Science* (Vol. 9, Part 2, 1976). One should mention here a recent study by P. J. Bowler, *Fossils and Progress: Palaeontology and the Idea of Progressive Evolution in the Nineteenth Century* (Science History Publications, New York, 1976*), which deals, *inter alia*, with Lyell and with Darwin's ideas on progressionism.

Turning to the problem of German Nature Philosophy, one finds that the literature available in English in this area is rather sparse and not easy to handle. There is a reasonable coverage in Nordenskiold's *History of Biology* (cited above) although reading this may lead one to have doubts as to the eanity of certain of the more outlandish exponents of the movement. The standard work on the relationship between natural science and German romanticism is A. G. F. Gode-Von Aesch, *Natural Science in German Romanticism* (Columbia University Press, New York, 1941); but this does not offer easy reading. Extremely helpful for the contrast that it presents between 'Enlightened' and 'Romantic' thought is M. H. Abrams, *The Mirror and the Lamp: Romantic Theory and the Critical Tradition* (Oxford University Press, New York, 1953). For a general overview of Romantic thought, see H. G. Schenk, *The Mind of the European Romantics* (Constable, London, 1966); also S. S. Prawer (ed.), *The Romantic Period in Germany* (Weidenfeld & Nicolson, London, 1970); and O. Walzel, *German Romanticism* (Frederick Unger Publishing Co., New York, 1965*). For a brief and clear account of Goethe's botanical and zoological theories, see R. Magnus, *Goethe as a Scientist* (Henry Schuman, New York, 1949). On Robert Chambers, the standard account is M. Millhauser, *Just Before Darwin: Robert Chambers and Vestiges* (Wesleyan University Press, Middletown, 1959). A facsimile of *Vestiges* is published by Leicester University Press and Humanities Press (Leicester & New York, 1969*).

An anthology of writings on deism has been edited by Peter Gay: *Deism: An Anthology* (Van Nostrand, Princeton, 1968*). And there is much interesting material on deism and natural theology in B. Willey, *The Eighteenth-Century Background* (Chatto & Windus, London, 1940*). A detailed discussion of the argument from design and its history appears in R. H. Hurlbut, *Newton, Hume and the Design Argument* (University of Nebraska Press, Lincoln, 1965). For a philosophical analysis, see T. McPherson, *The Argument From Design* (The Macmillan Press Ltd, London & Basingstoke, 1972*). A well-known study, containing an extensive discussion of Paley and his influence, is C. C. Gillispie, *Genesis and Geology: A Study in the Relations of Scientific Thought, Natural Theology, and Social Opinion in Great Britain, 1790-1850* (Harvard University Press, Cambridge Mass., 1951*). But Gillispie's work now appears somewhat 'Whiggish' in character. He does not treat some of the early nineteenth-century writers kindly! Paley's *Natural Theology* is available in facsimile from Gregg International Publishers Ltd (Farnborough, 1970*), and there is a good recent study of his philosophy by D. L. le Mahieu: *The Mind of William Paley:*

A Philosopher and his Age (University of Nebraska Press, Lincoln, Nebraska & London, 1976*).

The literature on Malthus is considerable. A convenient edition of the *Essay* is A. Flew (ed.), *Thomas Robert Malthus: An Essay on the Principle of Population* (Penguin Books Ltd., Harmondsworth, 1970*), which contains a useful analysis of Malthus's theory by Flew. The standard biography of Malthus is still J. Bonar, *Malthus and His Work* (G. Allen & Unwin, London, 1885). See also, for example, D. V. Glass (ed.), *Introduction to Malthus* (C. A. Watts, London, 1953); G. F. Macleary, *The Malthusian Population Theory* (G. Allen & Unwin, London, 1953); and G. Himmelfarb, *Victorian Minds* (Weidenfeld & Nicholson, London, 1968*). Those interested in contemporary problems of overpopulation must read P. R. & A. H. Ehrlich, *Population, Resources, Environment: Issues in Human Ecology* (W. H. Freeman & Co., San Francisco, 1970*).

As previously indicated, there is no shortage of biographical material on Darwin. Likewise, there are innumerable editions of *The Origin of Species*. The Penguin edition edited by J. W. Burrow is cheap and convenient (Penguin Books Ltd, Harmondsworth, 1968*). The 'variorum' edition edited by Morse Peckham lies securely within the domain of Darwin specialists: *The Origin of Species; A Variorum Text edited by Morse Peckham* (University of Pennsylvania Press, Philadelphia, 1959). Very helpful for all Darwin studies is R. B. Freeman, *The Works of Charles Darwin: An Annotated Bibliographical Handlist* (2nd edn, Wm Dawson & Sons Ltd & Archon Books, Folkeston & Hamden, 1977*). An outstanding account of natural selection in Darwin is C. Limoges, *La Selection Naturelle: Etude sur la Première Constitution d'un Concept [1837-1859]* (Presses Universitaires de France, Paris, 1970*). This book is not yet available in English.

There are two important modern studies of Wallace: W. B. George, *Biologist Philosopher: A Study of the Life and Writings of Alfred Russel Wallace* (Abelard-Schuman, London & New York, 1964); and H. L. McKinney, *Wallace and Natural Selection* (Yale University Press, New Haven, 1972*). The latter is interesting for the light it throws on the relationship between the work of Darwin and Wallace in the period leading up to the publication of *The Origin,* and an element of plagiarism on Darwin's part is hinted at. The question of simultaneous discoveries in science is discussed in a number of places in the writings of R. K. Merton. See, for example, *The Sociology of Science* (ed. N. W. Storer, Chicago University Press, Chicago, 1973*).

As stated above, Darwin's later work is discussed in detail by writers such as Gruber, Vorzimmer, Hull, Hardin, and Ghiselin. Several of Darwin's later works are again in print in various facsimile editions. An attractive account of his botanical investigations is to be found in M. Allen, *Darwin and his Flowers: the Key to Natural Selection* (Faber & Faber, London, 1977*). A more sophisticated, though less recent treatment is in R. P. Bell, *Darwin's Biological Work* (John Wiley & Sons, New York, 1964).

The standard biography of Mendel in English is still H. Iltis, *Life of Mendel* (G. Allen & Unwin, London, 1932). There is an excellent account of the precursors of Mendel in R. C. Olby, *Origins of Mendelism* (Constable, London, 1966*). And there are various histories of genetics that deal with Mendel's work, such as L. C. Dunn, *A Short History of Genetics* (McGraw-Hill Book Co., New York, 1965). Translations of Mendel's work appear in C. Stern & E. R. Sherwood (eds), *The Origin of Genetics: A Mendel Source Book* (W. H. Freeman & Co., San Francisco & London, 1966*). Philosophical problems relating to Mendelism and evolutionary theory in general are treated in M. Ruse, *The Philosophy of Biology* (Hutchinson University Library, London, 1973*), and D. L. Hull, *Philosophy of Biological Science* (Prentice-Hall, Inc., Englewood Cliffs, 1974*). For a *résumé* of the general doctrine of the synthetic theory of evolution, see de Beer's biography of Darwin, mentioned above, or consult the primary source, J. S. Huxley, *Evolution: The Modern Synthesis* (G. Allen & Unwin, London, 1942*).

There seems to be no general history of Neo-Lamarckism now available in English. But some of the arguments of a Neo-Lamarckian character that are still under discussion may be found in A. Hardy, *The Living Stream* (Collins, London, 1965). The Lysenko controversy is treated in detail by D. Joravsky in his *The Lysenko Affair* (Harvard University Press, Cambridge, Mass., 1970*); and in L. R. Graham, *Science and Philosophy in the Soviet Union* (Allen Lane, London, 1973*). We have a fascinating 'inside' account from a Russian biologist in Z. Medvedev, *The Rise and Fall of T. D. Lysenko* (Columbia Univeristy Press, New York, 1969*). A very interesting Marxist view, such as has not yet been much appreciated in the West, is to be found in H. & S. Rose (eds), *The Radicalisation of Science* (The Macmillan Press Ltd, London and Basingstoke, 1976*). See also: D. Lecourt, *Proletarian Science? The Case of Lysenko* (New Left Books, London, 1977*). The Nature/Nurture controversy still rages. For the 'Nature' point of view, see, for example, H. J. Eysenck, *The Inequality of Man* (Temple Smith, London, 1973*). For the 'Nurture' side of the argument, see, for example, P. R. Ehrlich & S. S. Feldman, *The Race Bomb: Skin Colour Prejudice and Intelligence* (Quadrangle/The New York Times Book Co., New York, 1977*). For a critical review of the methodologies of 'Nature' theorists in relation to I.Q. testing, see L. J. Kamin, *The Science and Politics of I.Q.* (Penguin Books, Harmondsworth, 1974*). A general review of the literature is provided by P. E. Vernon, *Intelligence: Heredity and Environment* (W. H. Freeman & Co., San Francisco, 1979*). Vernon, it may be noted, was a co-worker of Sir Cyril Burt, and in the text of his book he represents Burt's work in a generally favourable light. However, in a last-minute addendum to the book, dated Dec. 22, 1978, he acknowledges that Burt 'did perpetrate systematic fraud from about 1950 onwards'.

Accounts of the public reception of *The Origin* appear in many places. A useful, fairly chatty version is to be found in W. Irvine, *Apes, Angels and Victorians* (Weidenfeld & Nicolson, London, 1955), which also offers the reader plenty of information on the life and work of T. H. Huxley. The outstanding analysis of Darwin's impact on British thought, by means of a very thorough examination of the journal literature of the post-1859 period, is A. Ellegard, *Darwin and the General Reader: The Reception of Darwin's Theory of Evolution in the British Periodical Press, 1859-1872* (Göteborgs Universitets Arsskrift, Göthenburg, 1958). See also the Open University volume mentioned above on page 370. A convenient, compact account is given in an essay by R. M. Young, in A. Symondson (ed.), *The Victorian Crisis of Faith* (Society for Promoting Christian Knowledge, London, 1970). Readers interested in the reception of Darwin's ideas outside Britain should consult T. F. Glick (ed.), *The Comparative Reception of Darwinism* (The University of Texas Press, Austin, 1974*).

The standard authority on Herbert Spencer is now: J. D. Y. Peel, *Herbert Spencer: The Evolution of a Sociologist* (Heinemann, London, 1971). But an older work by W. H. Hudson *Herbert Spencer* (Constable & Co. Ltd, London, 1908) provides a much more accessible route to an understanding of Spencer's system. For selections of Spencer's writings see S. Andreski (ed.), *Herbert Spencer: Structure, Function and Evolution* (Thomas Nelson and Sons, Ltd, London, 1971*), or R. L. Carneiro (ed.), *The Evolution of Society* (Chicago University Press, Chicago, 1967). A useful essay on Spencer appears in P. B. Medawar, *The Art of the Soluble* (Methuen, London, 1967*). See also an article by J. C. Greene in M. Clagett (ed.), *Critical Problems in the History of Science* (The University of Wisconsin Press, Madison, 1959*).

The literature on Social Darwinism, particularly in relation to American thought, is extensive. See, for example, R. Hofstadter, *Social Darwinism in American Thought* (University of Pennsylvania Press, Philadelphia, 1944*); C. E. Russett, *Darwin in America: The Intellectual Response 1865-1912* (W. H. Freeman & Co., San Francisco, 1976*); S. Persons (ed.), *Evolutionary Thought in America* (Yale University Press, New Haven, 1950). Recently, J. K. Galbraith has prepared an interesting series of television programmes on the history of economic and social thought which discussed the phenomenon of Social Darwinism in an attractive manner. His material is now published as *The Age of Uncertainty*, (British Broadcasting Corporation & Andre Deutsch Ltd, London, 1977*). A useful series of readings on Social Darwinism is B. J. Loewenberg (ed.), *Darwinism: Reaction or Reform?* (Holt, Rinehart & Winston, New York, 1957). More advanced texts are: J. W. Burrow, *Evolution and Society: A Study in Victorian Social Theory* (Cambridge University Press, London, 1966*); M. P. Banton (ed.), *Darwinism and the Study of Society: A Centenary Symposium* (Tavistock Publications, London, 1961); S. Tax (ed.), *Evolution after Darwin: The Chicago Centennial* (Chicago University Press, Chicago, 1960). Articles by D. G. MacRae in S. A. Barnett (ed.), *A Century of Darwin* (Heinemann, London, 1958*), are also recommended.

I know of no up-to-date monograph especially devoted to a consideration of the influence of Darwinism on politics or political theory. But a nineteenth-century volume by D. G. Ritchie may be consulted with advantage: *Darwinism and Politics* (Swan Sonnenschein & Co., London, 1889). A chapter of Himmelfarb's volume (see above, page 370) does deal with the topic, and see the second half of John Bowle's *Politics and Opinion in the Nineteenth Century* (Jonathan Cape, London, 1954), entitled 'The political thought of the age of Darwin'. But chiefly the reader must work through primary sources and journal articles, some of which are to be found in the references to Chapter 17 of this book.

For an introduction to the relations between Darwin and theology, we are now well served by the Open University volume by J. H. Brooke *et al.* previously referred to. Very helpful also in this area is J. C. Greene, *Darwin and the Modern World View* (Louisiana State University Press, Baton Rouge, 1961*); and the Vanderpool and Appleman anthologies mentioned above (page 370). See also E. A. White, *Science and Religion in American Thought: The Impact of Naturalism,* (Stanford University Press, Stanford, 1952*); A. Richardson, *The Bible in the Age of Science,* Student Christian Movement Press, London, 1961; D. Bowen, *The Idea of the Victorian Church: A Study of the Church of England 1833-1889* (McGill University Press, Montreal, 1968*); O. Chadwick, *The Victorian Church* (2 vols., Black, London, 1966-1970*). The relationship between evolutionary theory and Protestant belief is discussed in detail in J. Dillenberger, *Protestant Thought and Natural Science* (Abingdon Press, New York, 1960). For a discussion of the relationship between religion and evolutionary biology, written by an eminent ornithologist, see D. Lack, *Evolutionary Theory and Christian Belief: The Unresolved Conflict* (Methuen & Co., London, 1957). See also E. Benz, *Evolution and Christian Hope: Man's Concept of the Future from the Early Fathers to Teilhard de Chardin* (Doubleday & Co., Inc., New York, 1966). For those who delight in the dust of intellectual battles, A. D. White's *A History of the Warfare of Science with Theology in Christendom* (2 vols, D. Appleton & Co. & Macmillan & Co., New York and London, 1896*) is still in print.

Some of the more important literature dealing with the relationship between Darwinism and philosophy is listed in the first footnote to Chapter 19 of this book. The articles by Fulton, Daiches Raphael and Passmore are particularly recommended.

The literature on Darwinism and psychology is very scattered, although most of the general histories of psychology treat the matter in passing. See, for example: G. Murphy, *An Historical Introduction to Modern Psychology* (Kegan Paul & Co., London, 1928*); or E. G. Boring, *A History of Experimental Psychology* (Century Co., New York and London, 1929*).

Early studies of the history of anthropology are: A. C. Haddon, *History of Anthropology* (Watts & Co., London, 1910); R. H. Lowie, *The History of Ethnological Theory* (Holt, Rinehart & Winston, New York, 1937); and T. K. Penniman, *A Hundred Years of Anthropology* (Duckworth, London, 1935). More up-to-date and more detailed is M. Harris, *The Rise of Anthropological*

Theory: A History of Theories of Culture (Thomas Y. Crowell Co. Inc., New York, 1968*), which gives considerable attention to the influence of evolutionism (both Spencerian and Darwinian) on studies of man. It should be noted that Harris writes from a Marxist standpoint, albeit a somewhat eccentric one in that it is avowedly anti-dialectical. As may be expected, his conclusions have been questioned in certain respects by non-Marxist writers. Papers relevant to our theme may be found in E. E. Evans-Pritchard, *Essays in Social Anthropology* (Faber & Faber, London, 1962); M. E. Spiro (ed.), *Context and Meaning in Cultural Anthropology* (Free Press & Collier-Macmillan, New York and London, 1965); and B. J. Meggers (ed.), *Evolution and Anthropology: A Centennial Appraisal* (The Anthropological Society of Washington, Washington, 1959). Two volumes by L. L. Snyder tell us something of the baneful influence of racism in Western society, and its relation to anthropological theory: *Race: A History of Modern Ethnic Theories* (Longman & Co., New York & Toronto, 1939); *The Idea of Racialism: Its Meaning and History* (Van Nostrand Reinhold Company & D. Van Nostrand Company (Canada), Ltd, New York and Toronto, 1962*). And an illuminating survey of our prejudices is to be found in the study of Jacques Barzun: *Race: A Study in Modern Superstition* (Harcourt Brace & Co., New York, 1937). Also recommended are: A. Montagu (ed.), *The Concept of Race* (Free Press, New York, 1964); L. Poliakov, *The Aryan Myth: A History of Racist and Nationalist Ideas in Europe* (Chatto-Heinemann [for Sussex University Press], London 1974*); J. S. Haller, *Outcasts from Evolution: Scientific Attitudes of Racial Inferiority, 1859-1900* (University of Illinois Press, Urbana, Chicago & London, 1971*); M. Banton, *The Idea of Race* (Tavistock Publications, London, 1977*).

Some references to the influence of Darwinism on literature have been given in the first footnote to Chapter 22. Here the interpretations of Lionel Stevenson are of fundamental importance. The volume by Leo Henkin, *Darwinism and the Novel*, provides an essential *entrée* to the subject, although the work is largely a *résumé* of the plots of the many relevant novels. Basil Willey has made a particular study of the relationship between Darwin and Samuel Butler which is of considerable interest: *Darwin and Butler: Two Versions of Evolution* (Chatto & Windus, London, 1960).

In considering the relationship between biological and social theories and music, one will naturally turn to J. Barzun, *Darwin, Marx, Wagner: Critique of a Heritage* (Little, Brown & Co., New York, 1941*). And for a history of musicology that emphasises the importance of evolutionism in the development of the subject, see W. D. Allen, *Philosophies of Music History: A Study of General Histories of Music 1600-1960* (Dover Publications, Inc., New York, 1962* [1st edn, American Book Co., New York, 1939]).

Finally, I should mention three invaluable sources of reference which may constantly be consulted with great benefit: P. Edward (ed.) *Encyclopedia of Philosophy* (8 vols, Macmillan & Co., New York 1967*); C. C. Gillispie (ed.), *Dictionary of Scientific Biography* (13 vols, Scribner, New York,

1970-1976*); P. P. Wiener (ed.), *Dictionary of the History of Ideas: Studies in Selected Pivotal Ideas* (5 vols, Scribner, New York 1973-1974*).

ADDENDA

Three books have come to hand recently, which are highly relevant to the themes of *Darwinian Impacts*, but which it was not possible to take into account in the preparation of this text. They are: H. Craven's *The Triumph of Evolution: American Scientists and the Heredity-Environment Controversy* (University of Pennsylvania Press, Philadelphia, 1978*); J. R. Moore, *The Post-Darwinian Controversies: A Study of the Protestant Struggle to Come to Terms with Darwin in Great Britain and America 1870-1900* (Cambridge University Press, Cambridge, 1979*); and M. Ruse, *The Darwinian Revolution* (University of Chicago Press, Chicago, 1979*).

Name Index

Subject Index